ذَٰلِكَ ٱلْكِتَٰبُ لَا رَيْبَ ۛ فِيهِ ۛ

MEANING OF THE
QUR'AN

THE FINAL REVELATION FROM
THE CREATOR

Translated by
Abdullah Yusuf Ali

SAEED INTERNATIONAL

MEANING OF THE QUR'AN

Translated by: **Abdullah Yusuf Ali**

ISBN : 978-81-905832-6-8

Edition: October **2011**

Published by:

SAEED INTERNATIONAL

G-26, IInd Floor,
Jangpura Extention,
New Delhi-110014
(INDIA)
Email: abs_pd@yahoo.com

Office: +91-11-42797671
Mobile: +91-9818492984

Printed in India

RELIABILITY AND VALIDITY OF THE QURAN

—DR. MAZHAR KAZI

The authenticity and truth of a document or information is usually determined by employing two scientific criteria; Reliability and Validity. Former is an external measure that evaluates the integrity of process and means through which a document or information is received. Latter is the internal measure that evaluates the factual nature and truth within the contents of a document.

We can clarify the concepts of "Reliability and "Validity" by using a simple example. Suppose a radio advertisement states that all items in a certain store are on sale for fifty percent off. Several people hear this news, and then mutually pass it to others. If the information that is passed from one person to the next is identical then the message will be considered as "Reliable". Furthermore, if people later find that all items in the store are on sale for fifty percent off, then this information will be considered as "Valid". Thus, while transmission of some information may be "Reliable" it is not necessary that the same information may be "Valid" as well, or vice versa. Nevertheless, the information will not be true unless it meets both of these criteria independently and simultaneously.

The Divine Revelation is the "Truth" in its own right. Human attempts for authentication and validation of this fact neither adds nor subtracts anything from its due rights and values. Even so, discussions in the following pages are meant to satisfy the needs of those who are generally unaware of the "Authenticity and "Divinity" of the Glorious Quran and would like to evaluate this "Divine Revelation" based on historical facts, human reasoning, common sense and logic.

RELIABILITY OR AUTHENTICITY OF THE QURAN

As discussed above, "Reliability" of the Quran can be determined by the integrity of its transmission from generation to generation. If evidence proves that no change has occurred in the transmission of the Quran and the text of the Quran today is exactly the same as it was revealed to Prophet Muhammad (PBUH), this will then establish the "Reliability" or authenticity of the Quran. In the following pages, readers will find abundant historical evidences that should more than suffice to establish the "Reliability" of the Quran beyond any shadow of a doubt.

Reliability of the Transmission of the Quran

It is a well known historical fact that two concomitant parallel channels were established to preserve and transmit the Quran from the very beginning of its revelation. The first channel consisted of preservation and transmission of the Quran by memorization and oral recitation by multiple persons as soon as a verse was revealed. The second channel consisted of rendition of each verse, immediately after its revelation, as a recorded document. Preservation of the Quran, therefore, is not dependent entirely upon paper record only. Memorization of Quran assures that even in the absence of any hard copy, each and every alphabet, word, sentence, punctuation, pronunciation and sequence of the verses in the Quran is eternally carved in the memory of countless believers. This is a continuous phenomenon by which the Quran has been preserved from the very beginning and is transmitted from generation to generation and place to place.

Preservation by memorization and oral transmission is a unique phenomenon which is specific only to the Quran, and no other book on the surface of earth can share this claim. This method of transmission also enjoys an absolute level of trust and serves as the golden standard against which all hard copies of the Quran are judged and evaluated for accuracy and authenticity.

Oral Transmission by Memorization

Prophet Muhammad (PBUH) was the first recipient and *"Hafiz"* (Memorizer) of the entire Quran. Moreover, throughout his life, he taught the Quran to all others by oral recitation. Recitation of at least some verses of the Quran is an integral part of the five obligatory daily prayers of every Muslim. Hence, to perform his daily prayers, each *Sahabi* (Prophet's companion) had to memorize at least some portion of Quran. Moreover, memorization of Quran was an ongoing obsession and passion of many *Sahaba*. As a result, a large number of *Sahaba* had memorized the entire Quran during the life of the Prophet (PBUH). In the annals of history, we can accurately identify the names of *Sahaba* who had memorized the entire Quran. This ensured the preservation of the Quran in the memory of the first generation of Muslims.

It is also a historical fact that the Prophet (PBUH) emphasized the virtues of learning and teaching the Quran. Following is a widely known *Hadith* (Prophet's saying).

> *The most superior among you are those who learn the*
> *Quran and teach it to others.*
> (Bukhari)

As a result of this and similar teachings, millions of Muslims have dedicated their entire live for accurate memorization and teaching of Quran. This has been a continuous phenomenon during the past fourteen centuries and there has never been a gap in this effort, Muslim generation for the last fourteen centuries had several *Huffaz* (plural of *Hafiz*) in every community. These persons orally transmitted the Quran to the next generation in their respective communities.

Taraweeh Salat is a special set of prayers offered during the month of *Ramadhan* (fasting). Usually a *Hafiz* leads these prayers in congregation, wherein he recites the entire Quran sequentially from his memory. He thus completes entire-recitation of the Quran by the end of the month. A number of other *Huffaz:* stand behind the leading *Hafiz.* They carefully listen to this recitation and provide spontaneous corrections for the slightest mistakes committed by the leading *Hafiz.* By this process all *Huffaz* in all Muslim communities through out the world, check, cross check, correct and reinforce the memorized text of the Quran, in a group setting, at least once a year. This has been a universal Muslim practice for the past fourteen centuries.

In the presence of such a system of ongoing cross checks for the accuracy of the transmission of memorized Quran on a global level, it is absolutely inconceivable that any deviation from the original could ever have interjected in the text of the Quran, or if such an attempt is made in the future, then it can survive scrutiny from countless *Huffaz* scattered all over the globe.

Written Transmission by Documentation

The Quran was revealed to the Blessed Prophet (PBUH) piacemeal over a period of 23 years. It is a documented fact that as soon as the Blessed Prophet (PBUH) received a revelation of the Quran, he used to dictate it to one of his scribes. At the same time he would also give special instructions regarding exact sequential order of the revealed verses and their precise place in the text of the Quran. Historians have preserved names of more than 40 persons who served as scribes of the Quran. Among this group, Zaid bin Thabit has been distinguished as the chief scribe.

Record of an incident which took place during the early years of revelations of the Quran in Makkah provides proof that the Quran was preserved in writing from the very beginning of its revelation. It relates to Umar ibn al-Khattab, the second Caliph, who at that time was an avowed enemy of Islam. One day he set out intending to kill the Prophet (PBUH). On his way, Umar met a person, who told him that before killing the Prophet (PBUH) he ought to set his household in order as his sister and bother in-law had already accepted Islam. Upon hearing this, Umar rushed back to her sister's home. When he reached her home, he heard voices of some recitation. Suspecting that she and her husband were reading the Quran, he attacked both of them in a violent manner. His sister was injured and started bleeding. Even so, she challenged him and said; even if he was to kill both of them, they will not give up Islam. The sight of his battered sister and her determination touched Umar's heart. He demanded to see the pages that they were reading. His sister refused to let him touch the Quran unless Umar purified himself physically. Umar complied, and then read the pages which consisted of a few verses from chapter 20 of the Quran. As he read the text, he was so struck by the truth of the message that he immediately rushed to the Prophet (PBUH) and embraced Islam. This incident shows that the Quran was documented in writing even during the earliest period of its revelation.

A number of Ahadith state that, during the time of Prophet (PBUH), written copies of the Quran were readily available in Madinah. According to one of these Ahadith, when a visitor came to Madinah, he was given a copy of the Quran so that he could learn about Islam by himself. In another report the Prophet (PBUH) has commanded:

> *Do not take (written) copies of Quran on a journey with*
> *you, lest it falls into hands of an enemy (who might*
> *desecrate it).*   (Muslim)

Details of the last pilgrimage of the Prophet (PBUH) and his famous "Farewell Address" to a gathering of 124,000 Muslims are recorded in books of Ahadith and history. In his address he said:

> *I am leaving behind with you two things; if you holdfast*
> *to them, you will never go astray; the book of Allah and*
> *the practice of His Prophet.*   (Muslim)

This reference to the "Book of Allah" is a clear indication that at that time the Quran was available as a written document.

Based on the above information, it is logical to conclude that the entire Quran was preserved in writing during the lifetime of Prophet Muhammad (PBUH).

Role of the first Caliph Abu Bakr: 10-13AH (632-635AD)

Abu Bakr became the first caliph (successor) when Prophet Muhammad (PBUH) passed away in 10AH (632 CE). During the first year of his caliphate (11 AH), seventy *Huffaz* were martyred in a battle. This alarming loss of *Huffaz* in the first generation of Muslims deeply distressed Umar ibn al-Khattab. He realized that memorization alone may not provide enough safeguard for preservation of the Quran. He asserted that complete text of the Quran must also be secured as a written document in a single volume. Umar approached Abu Bakr and persuaded him to undertake such a compilation.

The Quran was not compiled in a single bound book during the life of the Prophet (PBUH). One apparent reason for not doing so was that the Quran was being revealed continuously during the life of the Prophet (PBUH). He was not in a position to predict when next verses would be revealed and where they would be placed in the text of the Quran. Revelation of the entire Quran was completed with the demise of the Prophet (PBUH). Hence, it became possible to compile the entire text of the Quran in the form of a single book.

Abu Bakr entrusted this task to Zaid bin Thabit, the chief scribe of the Prophet (PBUH). In order to carry out his mission diligently, Zaid adopted some very stringent procedures. He made public announcements that all those who possessed any written portions of the Quran should bring these documents to him. Zaid had learnt and memorized the entire Quran from the Prophet (PBUH), but to guarantee the accuracy of the text, he did not rely on his memory alone. Therefore, he would compare all written documents against each other. He would then invite more than one person to recite the same portion from memory. General rule for acceptance of any written document was that a document would be considered authentic only if at least two reliable persons could recite the same passage from memory exactly in the same form. By these means Zaid was able to assure the reliability and authenticity of each and every word of the Quran. He then rewrote and sequentially compiled all verses of the Quran in the form of single a book.

This copy of the Quran was then entrusted to the safe keeping of Hafsa, one of the wives of Prophet (PBUH). This copy of the

Quran served as the official reference book against which all Quranic writings that existed at that time would be compared and authenticated.

Role of the third Caliph Uthman: 24-35 AH (644-655 CE)

By the time of the third Caliph Uthman, Islam had spread far and wide.

Muslims who belonged to distant and different places began to read the Quran in their specific local dialects. Serious differences then arose among Muslims of different places about the proper recitation of the Quran. Realizing the need, for bringing uniformity in the recitation of the Quran, Uthman once again commissioned Zaid bin Thabit along with three other scribes of the Prophet (PBUH) to rewrite the Quran in the dialect of Quraish, which was the dialect of Prophet Muhammad (PBUH). Zaid acquired the original-copy of the Quran from Hafsa. Based on this text, he scribed seven copies of the Quran in Quraish dialect. Later, Uthman sent one copy of this Quran to six different regional centers of the Muslim state and kept one copy in Madinah. Along with each copy of the Quran, he also sent a professional *"Qarr*(reciter) who was deputed to teach people to recite the Quran in Quraish dialect. This brought about complete uniformity in reading and scribing of the Quran for the entire Muslim world. Two of the seven copies of these Qurans are still available. One is at Tashkent in Central Asia and the other at Istanbul in Turkey. The fact that no change at all has occurred in the text of the Quran during the last fourteen centuries can be ascertained by comparing the present day copies of the Quran in any part of the world with these original references of the Quran.

Ibn Hazam, a well recognized Muslim scholar, has documented that at least 100,000 copies or portions of the Quran were documented during the period of Uthman)[1], and these were freely available in the Muslim world. A famous battle called "Siffin" took place in the year 36 AH (657 CK) during the Caliphate of Ali. This was a non-conclusive battle that raged on for several days. One party of the battle then put portions of the written Quran on their spears proclaiming that they seek settlement of issues by the Quran. This spectacle quickly brought the battle to an end. This incident is reported by Muslim as well as non-Muslim historians, and provides further evidence that numerous copies or portions of the written Quran were freely available to early Muslims.

Role of *Taba'ien*: Generation following Prophet's Companions

The Arabic script during the period of the Prophet (PBUH) and his companions consisted of basic alphabet symbols, which expressed the consonant sounds but did not facilitate proper pronunciation of specific words. Several Arabic alphabets were written by a single mark or line, such as Ba',

---

(1)   *The Quran A Gospels* by Dr. Layiah. published by EI-Falah Foundation. Houston. ("1998)

Ta', Tha' and Ya'. Only an experienced person could read this script correctly. Two important measures were introduced by *Taba'ien* scholars. Technically, these are known as *"Tashkeel"* and *"Nitqat"*. This further ensured uniform recitation of the Quran.

"Tashkeel" refers to diacritical sign of vowel sounds. Arabic names of these signs are *Fatha, Kasra* and *Dhamma*. In Urdu these signs are called *Zabar, Zaer* and *Paish*. *Taba'ien* added these signs to each and every alphabet in the text of the Quran prepared by Uthman.

This was a monumental task, which enabled even non-Arabs to correctly read each word of the Quran, e.g. application of the proper *"Tashkeel"* sound determines whether the letter Ba' should be pronounced as *ba, bi,* or *bu*.

"Nuqat" refers to the placing of dots which were added to indicate correct pronunciation of consonant sound, e.g. Ba' was given one dot, and Ya' given two dots at the bottom. Similarly, Ta' and Tha' were given two and three dots respectively at the top. In the earlier text these were represented by just one straight line. This remarkable work was done during 66-86 AH (685-705 CE). The addition of *"Tashkeel"* and *"Nuqat"* ensured absolute uniformity in the documentation and recitation of the Quran even by those whose mother tongue is not Arabic.

It is evident from these illustrations that the Quran was faithfully preserved and transmitted-by its believers by two different and independent channels i.e. oral and written. Whereas no change was needed in the oral transmission of the Quran, several improvements were made in the written transmission of the Quran. These improvements not only preserved the authenticity of the text but also brought an absolute and universal uniformity in the recitation of the Quran.

The text of any available copy of the Quran can now be verified simultaneously by two independent channels i.e. comparison with memorized text by countless *Huffaz* and comparison with two original preserved texts of the Quran. The Quran thus meets the criteria of its reliability beyond any shadow of doubt. It is thus the most authentic and pure book on the surface of the earth.

VALIDITY OF THE QURAN: Divine Nature of the Quran

Truth of a Divine act is not dependent upon any human acknowledgment or verification. The Quran is a Divine Book and a living miracle of Allah, the Exalted. Mankind does not have the mental capability, scientific tools or research techniques to understand and evaluate a Divine entity. As such, the discussion that follows should not be misconstrued as an attempt to prove and establish the Divine origin of the Quran. It is a humble human effort for gaining some understanding of the validity of the Quran as a Divine Revelation.

The word "miracle" in dictionaries is defined as a Divine Act. Thus by definition, only Allah, the Exalted, has the power and wisdom to cause and manifest any miracles. Thus, in a nascent, pristine sense, no human being can ever initiate or perform any miracle by his/her own will, power or capability. If we can establish that the language and the information in the Quran did not come from any human source, then, for our purposes, this fact would constitute a proof that the Quran is a miracle. This should then satisfy our quest for accepting the Quran as a Divine Revelation from Allah, the Exalted.

Most of the verses in the Quran are very clear and explicit. A few of them, on the other hand, describe concepts or use terms that are not fully understood by a certain generation of mankind. The Quran describes these passages as allegorical verses.

> *It is He Who has sent down the Book; in it are verses*
> *basic and fundamental; they are the foundation of the*
> *Book; others pre allegorical.*   (Al-e-Imran3: 7)

Each Muslim generation accepts such allegorical verses as Divine expression of mysteries and wisdom. As human knowledge advances to higher levels of understanding, each successive Muslim generation decodes a few allegorical verses to facts of science. The verses which were mysteries for previous generations become facts for their own generation. This has been the perpetual miracle of the Quran for the last fourteen centuries.

Human society comprises of numerous sectors. Moreover, individual members of the human race have varied interests and specialties. The Quran is a book of guidance for the entire mankind. Therefore, it provides specific miracles and challenges for all sectors of human society. At the same time, it also addresses the varied interests of individual members of the human race. Thus we find that the Quran provides miracles for those who excel in the intricacies of language and diction. It also provides miracles for those interested in specific domains of science such as chemistry, biology, astronomy, and embryology etc. At the same time, it provides miracles for those interested in past history, future prophecies, and the countless mysteries of nature. A fact that further adds to the miraculous nature of this Divine Revelation is the testimony that none of the discoveries of science, technology or history during the last fourteen centuries could find a single contradiction in the entire text of the Quran. This undisputed fact, in itself is sufficient proof for our assertion that the Quran is a miracle and Divine Revelation.

On the following pages I have listed examples of some recently discovered facts in science,, technology and history that corroborate the information in the Quran. For further details a reader can refer to two books that I have published earlier'[2].

Miracles in the Language of the Quran

1. Muslim and non-Muslim scholars readily acknowledge that Prophet Muhammad (PBUH) was an unlettered man. He never received any formal education, before or after the revelation of Quran. Therefore, he could not read, write or even sign his name. Yet, the Quran, in its entirety, is a unique monument of linguistic perfection which has never been matched by any one at any time. This fact stands out even more strikingly because the Quran has repeatedly challenged entire mankind to produce any passage which can match even the shortest passage in the Quran that consists of only three verses. This challenge is still open for all times and all persons. The fact is that this challenge has remained unmet during the past one thousand and four hundred years.

2. It is a common observation that every human language after a certain period of time undergoes a gradual change and assumes an entirely new shape or form. This is why the language of Bible is revised after every few years and every country has its own version of the language of Bible. Against all odds, the Quran is still read and understood in the entire world in the same language in which it was revealed more than 1,400 years ago. The fact that a book with such perfect, timeless language and a universal dialect was revealed through an unlettered Prophet is another living miracle of the Quran.

Miracles in the Challenges of the Quran

3. Find a contradiction in the Quran

> *Do they (unbelievers) not reflect upon the Quran; if it*
> *had been from (someone) other than Allah, they would*
> *surely have found therein many contradictions.*

> (Nisa 4:82)

---

(2)   Kazi. Mazhar: *130 Evident Miracles in the Quran,* Crescent Publishing House, Lefferts, New York. (1998)
        Kazi. Mazhar: *160 Miracles & Mysteries oj the Quran.* Al Minar Books, Philadelphia. Houston.

Readers Digest issue of December 1952 states: "Modern scholarship had uncovered nearly 6,000 errors in the New Testament alone".

4. Make a chapter like the one in the Quran

> *Do they say: He (Muhammad, PBUH) forged it? Say: Bring then a chapter like unto it, and call (to your aid) anyone besides Allah, if you speak the truth.* (Younus 10:37-38)

5. Produce ten verses like those in the Quran

> *Or they say: He (Muhammad, PBUH) forged it; Say: Bring you then (at least) ten verses like unto it, and call (to your aid) whomever you can besides Allah, if you speak the truth.*
> (Hud 11:13)

Miracles in Human History

6. Preservation of Pharaoh's body

> *We (Allah) will save your body, so that you may be a sign for Succeeding generations; though there are many who give no heed to Our signs.* (Younus 10: 92)

These verses refer to Pharaoh. The Bible states that Pharaoh had drowned but provides no information as to what happened to his body subsequently. The Quran affirms that Pharaoh was drowned and further states that his body was saved. It is now on display in a museum in Cairo. Egypt.

7. City of Iram

> *Have you not seen how your Lord dealt with 'Aad of Iram (who were very tall) like lofty pillars, the like of which no nation was created in the lands of the world.* (Fajr 89:6-8)

The National Geographic magazine, December 1978, gave a detailed account of the recent discovery of this city. No other religious or history book provides any description of people of Iram and their city, except the Quran.

Miracles in Astronomy

8. Beginning of the universe as a gaseous mass

> *He (Allah) comprehended in His design the heaven when it was (only) a smoke.* (Fussilat 41: 11)

9. Origin of the universe as one entity

> *Have they not, those who disbelieve, seen that the heavens and earth were joined together (as one piece), then We (Allah)*

> *parted them.*   (Anbiya 21:30)

10. Expansion of the universe

> *With power did We (Allah) construct the heavens. We are (continuously) expanding it.*   (Zariat 51:47)

11. Floating movement of planets in orbits

> *(Allah is the) One Who created the night and the day and the sun and the moon; all (celestial bodies), float along, each in its (own) orbit.*   (Anbiya 21:33)

12. Different nature for sun and moon

> *Allah is the One Who made the sun a shining object and the moon as a (reflected) light.*   (Younus 10:5)

> *By the sun and its light, and the moon when it reflects it.*
> (Shams 91:1-2)

The Bible refers to the sun and the moon with the word light. It adds to sun the word greater and to moon the word lesser. The Quran however uses two different words for sun and moon. It also acknowledges that sun is the source of light, and that the moon only reflects sun's light.

Miracles in Biology

13. Existence of opposite genders in all plants

> *And it is He (Allah) Who spread out the earth and set thereon mountains standing firm and (flowing) rivers and fruits of every kind He made in pairs, two and two.*   (Ra'ad 13:3)

Miracles in Human Beings

14. Presence of sensory nerves in skin

> *Those who reject Our signs, We (Allah) shall soon cast them into fire, as often as their skins are roasted through, We shall change it for them with fresh skins that they may taste the 'penalty (of Fire): For Allah is Exalted in Power, Wise.*
> (Nisa 4: 56)

Miracles in Chemistry

15. Presence of opposite radicals and ions

> *Glory be to Allah, Who created in pairs all things that the earth produces...*   (Yaseen 36: 36)

Miracles in Embryology

16. Origin of man by the sperm

> *Was he (man) not a mere sperm drop which is emitted.*
>
> (Qiyamah 75:37)

17. Covering of embryo by three layers

> *He (Allah) creates you in wombs of your mothers in stages*
> *one after the other in three veils of darkness; such is Allah,*
> *your Lord and Cherisher.*   (Zumur 39:6)

18. Development of embryo in stages

> *He (Allah) makes you in the womb of your mother in stages*
> *one after another ...*   (Zumur 39:6)

Miracles in Mysteries of Nature

19. Presence of ocean currents in sea water

> *He (Allah) has let loose the two oceans that they may meet*
> *together. Yet there stands between them a barrier which they*
> *do not transgress; So O assembly of Jinn and Men! Which*
> *manifestations of your Lord's Power will you deny?*
>
> (Rahman 55: 19-21)

20. Decrease of land due to melting of polar ice

> *See they not that We (Allah) gradually reduce the land from*
> *its outlying borders? When Allah commands something, there*
> *is none to put back His command.*   (Ra'ad 13:14)

Here it is appropriate to reemphasize that the Quran was revealed more than fourteen hundred years ago. At that time, there was no basis which could have enabled human mind to imagine any of the hidden mysteries of science and nature. Moreover, if Quran was a product of human scholarship or imagination then, at least, a few facts mentioned in the Quran should have been proven wrong by this time. On the contrary, we find that each additional human discovery serves only to prove that information provided in the Quran is the absolute truth. This being fact, we are left with no option but to accept that the Quran is a miracle and a Divine Revelation from the All-Knowing, All-Mighty Creator of the heavens and the earth.

A FEW UNPARALLAL FEATURES OF THE QURAN

In addition to above mentioned miracles, the Quran also has a few unique features which are not shared by previous Divine Books.

1. Original texts of all earlier Divine Books are lost and only translated versions of these books exist today. The Quran is the only book that exists in its original language.

2. Scholars of all other faiths admit that their respective Divine Books have been corrupted by man-made narrations. To illustrate this point, here is a quote from Herald Tribune International (Tuesday, December 23, 1993). "An Oregon State University scholar, Marcus Borg, whose study of Jesus set off a furor among fundamentalist Christians, got an endowed chair worth $3 million. Mr. Borg is the author of a book contending that 80% of the sayings attributed to Jesus in the Bible were added by later authors". On the contrary, no one has ever refuted or even challenged the authenticity of the Quran.

3. The existing manuscripts of all previous Divine Books can not be traced back directly to their respective Prophets. The evidences tracing the text of the Quran to Prophet Muhammad (PBUH) are so voluminous, and strong that even the harshest critics of Islam have been unable to deny this fact.

4. The Quran was revealed during a period of 23 years. Historians and commentators of the Quran have preserved details of time, place and events relating to revelation of each passage of the Quran. No such data is available for any other Divine Book.

5. All earlier Divine Books were revealed in languages that are now extinct or obsolete. The Quran was revealed in the Arabic language, which is still a living and vibrant language throughout the world.

6. All previously revealed Divine Books were sent as a guidance for selected groups of people, geographical area or specific era. The Quran addresses the entire humanity, present or future, and its commandments transcend all barriers of creed, time and space. The Quran is the only book that addresses its readers as "O Mankind!".

7. Words of Allah, the Exalted, are always pure and consist of highest principles of morality and ethics. Man has contaminated all former Divine Books to the extent that obscenities and even descriptions of incest have been added to the words of God. One can find such immoral stories and descriptions in all former Divine Books, e.g. the Bible states that Prophet Lot got drunk and had sex with two of his daughters (Genesis 19: 30-36). Allah, the Exalted, has kept the Quran free from contamination by any form of obscenity. Not a single verse of the Quran contains even a trace of immoral or obscene description.

8. One of the most unique features of the Quran is that it is the only Divine Book that can be and has been memorized by millions of men, women and children. It is noteworthy that such memorization includes not only the words of the Quran, but also the punctuation marks and diacritical signs associated with each and every word of the Quran. This fact stands out even more strikingly when we realize that Arabic is not a native language for 88% of the total Muslim population and yet, even those who do not understand the Arabic language memorize the Quran in its entirety. Furthermore, even blind persons, who can not see the written words with their diacritical sings, can memorize the Quran with all of these details. This fact defies all conventional human logic and reasoning and cannot be explained without invoking the concept of Divine intervention and Miracle.

When we consider all of above discussed unique and unparalleled features of the Quran, it should lead us, to a final conclusion; By all scales of human understanding, reason and logic, the Quran is indeed a Divine Revelation of Allah, the All-Wise and All-Knowing. Therefore, the prudent course; of action should be to honour and obey the Commandments of the Creator contained in this Divine Book.

Here I would like to reemphasize that the criteria of reliability and validity are human measures. A Divine entity cannot be judged by utilizing human scales. Moreover, the Quran is a Divine Book and as such does not need human evaluation. All of the above discussions are means only to educate the reader and not to evaluate the reliability and Validity of the Quran as a Divine Revelation. The fact is that the Quran is the absolute truth from the All-Mighty Creator of the worlds. Those who will "accept and follow this Divine Revelation shall achieve prosperity and those who will deny and reject this will be the losers.

TWO RECENT ACKNOWLEDGED MIRACLES IN QURAN

—Dr. Mazhar Kazi

Symmetry of Numerical Words

In recent years, scholars of linguistics have found numerous examples of surprising numerical correlation of words in the Quran. Composition of such numerical correlations during the whole text of the Quran that was revealed over a span of 23 years is beyond any human literary capability, dexterity or command. Literary persons often show their talents and command of language by composing prose and poetry in which choice of words and their numerical values refer to or convey a certain connotation. All such examples consist of only a single word, a single sentence or a short passage. These items have no relation to one another or share a common theme of a poem or passage. In contrast, numerical correlations of words in the Quran are not confined to a passage or chapter but run throughout the entire text of the Quran. Following are a few examples.

1. The Quran states that there are seven heavens. This description appears in only seven chapters.

2. The Quran states that the number of months prescribed by Allah is twelve. The Arabic word for month is *Shahr*. The word *Shahr* appears in the entire text of the Quran a total of 12 times.

3. Arabic word *Iman* means faith. It appears in the Quran 17 times. Arabic word *Kufr* means denial. This also appears in the Quran 17 times.

4. One of the derivatives of *Iman* is *Imanun*, and that of *Kufr* is *Kufrum*. Each of these words appears in the Quran only 8 times.

5. Arabic word *Malaika* means angels. It appears in the Quran 88 times. Arabic word *Shaitan* refers to devil. It also appears in the Quran 88 times.

6. Arabic word *Dunya* means world. It appears in the Quran 115 times. The word *Akhira* means the world hereafter. It also appears in the Quran 115 times.

7.   Arabic word *Teen* means clay and *Nutfa* refers to sperm. The Quran states that man is created from *Teen* and *Nutfa*. Each of these words is used in the Quran 112 times.

8.   *Rahman* and *Raheem* are two names of attributes of Allah. Former refers to Allah's mercy associated with justice and the latter refers to Allah's mercy associated with forgiveness. The word *Rahman* appears in the Quran a total of 57 times, but the word *Raheem* appears a total of 114 times, the exact double of 57. This relationship corresponds with the fundamental Islamic teachings that mercy of Allah overcomes his anger.

9.   The Arabic word *Rijal* means man, and the word *Nisa* means woman. Not surprisingly, each of these words is used exactly 24 times in the Quran.

10. The Arabic word for life is *Hay at* and the word for death is *Maul*. Both words appear in the Quran in exact same number, i.e. 145.

11. The Arabic word *Zakat* refers to Islamic poor-due and the word *Baraka* refers to blessings. Both appear in the Quran in exact same number, i.e. 32.

12. Description of darkness and light

> *He (Allah) brings them out of "Zulmat" (much darkness)*
> *into "Noor" (light).*   (Maida 5:16)

The word *"Zulmat"* means darkness. In the Quran it refers to different kinds of misguidance and ignorance, whose number may vary from person to person and place to place. Hence the Quran uses the word *"Zulmat"* both in singular and plural forms. In contrast, the Quran uses the word *"Noor"*. It means light and refers to the truth of Divine Guidance. There has always been one truth for every person and every place. Hence the Quran always uses the word *"Noor"* in the singular form. One should note that the Quran has a total of 84,630 words spread through 114 chapters. It is amazing to note that plural form of the word *"Noor"* does not appear even once throughout the entire text of the Quran.

13. Here is a very surprising correlation of a geological fact that needs a little decoding. The Arabic word for sea in the Quran appears 32 times and the word for land appears 13 times. Sum of these two figures is 45 that represents the total area of sea and land. Sea is mentioned in the Quran 32 times this is 71.1% of 45, which in turn represents the total of sea, and 13 out of 45 equals 28.8 which represents the total are of land. Modern science has now proved that water covers about 71% of

the earth, while the land covers about 28% of the earth.

The above examples are just a glimpse of numerical symmetry that the linguists are now discovering by using computer technology.

Mysteries of two different interjections in the Quran

The Quran gives a very detailed and microscopic description of the development of a human embryo. Dr. Keith Moore, a very prominent embryologist and a faculty member at University of Toronto, Canada stated that the terms to describe these stages in the Quran are so self descriptive and exhaustive that the embryologists should now replace their terms by those used by the Quran.

One of the mysteries of the description of embryonic development in Quran is the use of two different interjections; *Thumma* and *Fa.* While describing these stages the Quran alternatively uses *Thumma and Fa.* Arabic word *Thumma means,* "later" and refers to a delayed action, whereas the word *Fa* means "then", and refers to a change that takes place immediately. Where ever the Quran gives a description of the embryonic development, the word *Thumma* always appears three times, denoting that there are three distinct and well demarcated stages that follow each other with a little pause. The embryologists have recently discovered that the growth of the human embryo takes place in three distinct stages and that every successive stage is preceded by a little pause, needed for solidification of the previous stage. The Quran mentioned this fact centuries before scientists could discover it by using electron microscope.

While describing these embryonic changes, the Quran also uses the interjection *Fa.* It should be noted that the word *Fa* appears in varied numbers in between two *Thumma.* It thus refers that each stage in turn has a varied number of short-lived sub-stages that go on in quick succession without any delay or pause. Moreover, they may not be as distinct as to be classified as a distinct state. Hence, these sub-stages may differ in number. This in turn accounts for the use of a varied number *of Fas* by the Quran. The embryologists discovered this fact after fourteen centuries.

It should be noted that the numerical symmetry of words in the Quran has been discovered by using computer technology. The significance of this fact becomes all the more important when we realize that the Quran was revealed during a period of 23 years. It is impossible for a human mind to maintain a correct account of numerical relationships of a large number of varied words over a period of one quarter of a century.

Furthermore, details of developments of human embryo were discovered by modern scientists by using an electron microscope, discovered in 1940 CE. Yet, these details corroborate word by word with the text of the Quran, revealed more than fourteen centuries ago. This in turn add to the fact that the Quran is a miracle and a Divine Revelation from the All-Knowing Master and Creator of the universe.

TOWARDS UNDERSTANDING THE QURAN

Abridged from

"Towards Understanding the Quran" by A.A. Maudoodi[3]

Discussions on the following pages relate to two basic issues that are fundamental to understanding the Quran. The first deals with the specific features that are unique to the Quran. The second endeavors to answer a few questions that may arise in the novice student of the Quran. Unless the reader accepts these unique features of the Book, he or she will not get the desired benefit just by reading the Quran.

A Unique Book

All books authored by human beings deal with a certain domain of knowledge. The Quran, on the other hand, primarily deals with faith. Although, it also deals with human knowledge, but only as a reference to reinforce faith. Thus, the Quran, being a book of faith, has no valid comparison with any other human book of knowledge.

The common arrangement of human books presents information divided into distinct chapters, where each subject is sequentially arranged in the form of introduction, discussion and conclusion. Reader should realize that the Quran does not present its information, ideas, arguments, or message in a conventional style. It combines discussions of various seemingly unrelated topics in a very impressive, eloquently blended style. Thus, it gives moral instructions, lays down legal laws, invites mankind to monotheism, admonishes disbelievers and gives glad tidings to believers. Often we find the same subject repeated in more than one ways. Often a new topic is introduced right in the middle of another theme. From the perspective of faith, all of these seem to be blended in an amazingly cohesive way. *The* Quran presents historical events but not like as in a history book. Problems of philosophy and metaphysics are treated in a manner different from a text

---

(3)   A.A. Maudoodi: *Meaning and Message of the Quran,* Islamic Publications. Lahore. Pakistan. (1989)

book on the subject. Man and universe are mentioned in a language different from that of the text of natural science. Likewise, the Quran follows its unique approach for solving social, cultural and economic problems. Most of all, morality is taught in a way that has no parallel in human literature. These are a few basic themes that a reader will encounter while reading the Quran.

In order to receive the desired benefits from the Quran, the reader should accept the following facts. The Quran is the only book of its kind. Its literary style can not be compared to any other book. Its theme and address is unique in that it addresses the entire human race irrespective of the differences of time and space as well as those of race, sex, age, and education. It is with the acceptance of these facts that the blessings and benefits of the Guidance in every word and verse of the Quran will begin to seep into the conscious mind of the reader. Eventually, with the dawn of the absolute Truth, the reader is left awestruck by the magnificence of the Message therein.

Nature of the Book: A Divine Guidance

In order to benefit from the Quran, the reader should first consider the claim that is put forth by the Book and the person. Muhammad (PBUH) who served as the Messenger of this book. Both claim that the Quran is a Divine Revelation from Allah, the Exalted. Additionally, the reader must also acknowledge that mankind needs Divine Guidance to succeed in this world and the Hereafter. Unless, one acknowledges this fact, no Divine Book, especially the Quran can help him.

Adam (PBUH), the first man, and the first Messenger of Allah was given the first Divine Message. Allah then sent numerous Messengers after Adam (PBUH) to various groups of people at different times. As human society went through a process of gradual evolution, there was a need for a more comprehensive Divine Message. As such, every new Messenger was given a more detailed and comprehensive Message to meet the growing needs of his time and place. Prophet Muhammad (PBUH) was the last and final Messenger sent by Allah, the Exalted. As such the Guidance that was given to him is the culmination and conclusion of all previous Books. Thus, the Quran stands out as the final and eternal guidance from Allah, the Exalted. The Quran states this very clearly.

> *It was not (possible) for this Quran to be produced by someone other than Allah, for (it is) a confirmation of what was (revealed) before it, and it is a comprehensive description of (all former) Scriptures, about which there is no doubt, from the Lord of the Worlds.*   (Younus 10:37)

Central Theme

With the understanding that Quran is a Divine Revelation, we now turn to: The main subject, central theme and objective of this Divine Book. The main subject of this Book is mankind in general. The central theme of the Book is Divine Guidance that constantly invites mankind to follow the path of the Messenger. The objective of the Book is to inspire mankind to achieve peace and happiness in this world and eternal success and prosperity in the world hereafter.

The objective of the Quran is to guide mankind and not to teach specifics of the narrow domains of any branch of knowledge. Accordingly, the Quran invites mankind to Divine Guidance and skips all irrelevant details of science, history or philosophy. The Quran maintains its central theme by inspiring mankind to achieve higher levels of faith. The Quran makes its theme effective by utilizing all forms of style, rhetoric and address, yet maintaining a balance between human logic, and divine inspiration. At the same time, it reminds its reader of its ultimate objective by giving glad, tidings of happiness and success for those who would follow it, and warnings of severe punishment for those who would reject it. Once the reader develops an understanding that the Quran is a Divine Guidance for mankind with specific theme and objective, then the beautiful, concise, and magnificent style of the Quran becomes all too clearly understood and enjoyable. Various apparently unrelated verses and passages of the Quran then appear like pearls of the same necklace, where each pearl with different shape, texture and colour adds up to the beauty of the necklace. Thus, the whole of the Quran then becomes closely interconnected with its subject, theme, and objective.

Background of Revelations

Prophet Muhammad (PBUH) completed his mission during a period of twenty three years. He spent the first thirteen years at Makkah and the last ten years at Madinah. During this period, the Quran was revealed gradually, according to varying conditions of the Mission of the Prophet (PBUH) ana the emerging needs of Muslim community. In order to gain an in depth understanding and appreciation of all facets and meanings of specific verses, topics, and chapters of the Quran, it is necessary that the reader should be Well versed with the background of each specific revelation. Historians and scholars have painstakingly sifted through legends of these issues and have preserved the entire history, including the social and historical background associated with these revelations. The interested reader can find these detail, not in the text of the Quran, but in various commentaries of the Quran.

Chapters revealed in Makkah

In Makkah, the Prophet (PBUH) was surrounded by a prominent society of unbelievers and idol worshipers. Thus, the early revelations primarily addressed these persons and focused on three basic beliefs of Islam; unity of Allah, prophethood of Muhammad (PBUH), and accountability on the Day of Judgement. By and large, the entire Makkan verses revolve around these three basic themes. The early Makkah revelations also invited mankind to follow basic principles of morality, good conduct and respect of family relations.

Most of the early revelations are short and concise with a precise, incisive style which is more logical yet very poetic. These verses are very rhythmic, eloquent and forceful in a way that touches the heart and soul of the listener and reader alike. Universal truth in these verses is presented with a flavour, drawing upon familiar examples from their own environment, traditions and history. With the passage of time the local apposition to the Prophet (PBUH) became worse and sinister. Hence the tone of revelations during the later part of Makkah revelations changes from simple addresses to that of challenges and warnings. These revelations declare warnings of severe punishment for those who would reject this message and promises of boundless rewards for those who will accept this message. Hence, the later Makkan verses include detailed descriptions of Hell and Paradise.

As a result of the Prophet's mission, a few of the Makkans started accepting Islam. Thus there was a small but a growing Muslim community. Accordingly, a sizable section of Makkan verses address the needs of new Muslims. They reinforce their faith, give them hope, ana prepare them for future tests and challenges in life.

Chapters revealed in Madinah

The population of Madinah consisted of a complex of three major entities. First, there was an organized Muslim community with an emerging Muslim state. Second, there were established tribes of Christians and Jews. The third was a group of hypocrites, who were not true believers, but pretended to be Muslims because of the growing power of Islam. Hence, most of the verses revealed in Madinah address issues relating to these three sections of the society. These verses give several references to Old and New Testament and invite Christians and Jews to accept the new message in the Quran. They also give severe warnings to hypocrites for their conspiracies against Muslims. Most of these verses however, are addressed to Muslims and provide them necessary details of their personal and social conduct and responsibilities.

A major portion of the Madinah era Revelations deals with the legislative issues, social obligations and the personal responsibilities of the Believers. A great deal of emphasis however, is placed on the social obligations and duties of the Believers. At the same time they provide guidance during victory and defeat, adversity and prosperity, and war and peace.

There is also an ongoing dialogue with Christians and Jews with references to Old and New Testament, inviting them to accept the Message of the Final Messenger. They also contain stern warnings to hypocrites to mend their ways or suffer severe consequences.

As the revelations in Madinah dealt with more extensive subjects and civic issues, most of these chapters are longer than those reveled at Makkah. Moreover, in contract to verses revealed at Makkah, which carry a tone of sharp, matter of fact, decisive statements, warnings and challenges to non-Believers, the tone and style of revelations in Madinah is more conversational and exude with love and compassion for the Believers. The language of these verses is equally eloquent but not as poetic as the Makkan verses.

The Unique Style of the Quran

Gradual revelation of the Quran started a new Muslim Ummah (nation) amongst a hostile background of unbelievers. This continued for thirteen years in Makkah, leading to the establishment of an Islamic state in Madinah, where this Glorious revelation continued for ten years. Portions of the Quran repealed at Makkah focused mainly on three basic articles of Islamic faith and a few references to personal conduct of the Believers. In contrast, portions of the Quran revealed in Madinah focused on basic laws that govern the moral, social and legal obligations of the Believers. It is obvious that such a comprehensive and vibrant Book should not have the format, style and tone of a worldly book. Its tone and style should not be monotonous, but should change according to the background of its revelations. Hence, each and every section of the Quran has its specific style that reflects the background of the emerging Muslim Ummah.

It should also be noted that Quran was not revealed as a book, handout or pamphlets. Its verses were to be delivered by the Prophet (PBUH) as sermons and lectures. Each of these was related to a certain phase of Muslim Ummah or to a certain need of the Prophet's mission. The Prophet (PBUH) at the same time was entrusted with a comprehensive mission. He has to appeal both to human intellect and emotions. He had to educate and train them, imbue them with faith and courage. As a result he had to change their whole life, their minds, hearts, attitudes, priorities, as well as their daily conducts. The Quran was revealed to help the Prophet (PBUH) to achieve these comprehensive objectives. Therefore, the style, tone and the language of the Quran is not monotonous, but vibrant and keeps changing with the varying needs and objective of the mission of the Prophet (PBUH).

This in turn also explains the reason why the same theme in the Quran is often repeated over and over again. As long as there is a need to achieve a certain objective, the Quran keeps repeating the same message over and over again. It is, however, a miracle of the Quran that none of these repetitions reflect the monotony of style or language. Each repetition at it own place is equally impressive, elegant and unique.

Also, since the Quran is a Guidance for all humanity and for all ages to come, the same message is often presented with varying styles and tones so that each and every human mind with its specific intellect can comprehend its message. In addition, all chapters of the Quran contain repeated reference to its basic three articles of faith. At the same time, all of them inspire piety, fortitude, endurance, forgiveness, love and compassion. These basic moral values could not be neglected during any state of the Prophet's mission. These further accounts for the repeated descriptions of the same subject in the text of the Quran. The reader should accept these unique and specific features of the style and tone of the Quran. Only then he can appreciate its beauty and wisdom.

Universality of the Quran

A casual reader may misconstrue that the Quran being in Arabic language is primarily addressed to Arabs, who lived at the time of its revelation. No doubt, it often mentions those things which relate to Arab environment, culture and customs. However, nothing can be further from the truth. The Quran is the Guidance, for all mankind across all ages and spaces. Most of the examples and references to things that appear to be related to Arabs also apply to our environment and to those who lived before us.. Incidentally, groups of sizeable populations of the human race with pagan mentality', Christians, Jews and hypocrites have always lived and continue to live in an open nature milieu which is no different than the bygone Arab culture and environment.

A simple exercise will easily prove this point. I suggest the reader should take a pencil and underline those sections in the Quran which give an impression that they refer only to Arabs. He should then note down those moral principles, personal attributes, social obligations and legal codes that refer only to Arab culture. The reader will be amazed to note that the Quran takes a global approach that addresses mankind at large. In fact, the Quran is the only Divine Scripture wherein its verses repeatedly address the readers as "O Mankind!".

Another point in this respect is noteworthy. Every ideology, social system and religion must make references to specific cases and visible examples. None of them can teach only in abstract terms and capture human attention. It is impossible to build a model of life merely on abstract terms. The only proper method is to start a movement in a specific land and put its abstract ideas into a living model. If this model is visible and successful, it will catch the attention of others. Only then, other people will implement it in their own lands. It was for this reason that the first model Islamic State was established in the Arab peninsula. This model was so successful that today Islam is the religion of more than a billion people all over the globe. It should also be noted that the vast majority, i.e. 88% of the existing Muslim population today consists of non-Arabs.

What distinguishes a national system from an international system, and temporary system from a permanent system is evident from the teachings of the Quran. A national system aims to achieve benefits to its own constituents at the expense and interests of others. It preaches and follows theories, and laws which by their nature are not meant to benefit others. On the contrary, an international system protects the interests of all human beings, and is based on an ideology that benefits the entire human race. Also, the principles and theories of a temporary system keep on changing with time and space. Whereas, by definition no change ever occurs in the teachings of a permanent system. Considering all of these perspectives, the Quran distinguishes itself as a universal Book which is free from all barriers of time and space. It is one of these reasons that the Quran unlike other Divine Scriptures does not go through a revision after every few years. There has always existed only one copy of the Quran throughout all ages across all countries of the world.

All that has been presented before refers only to the domain of our knowledge, reason and intellect. We should however, remember that the Quran is basically a book of faith. While we can increase our knowledge by efforts and struggle, faith is truly a gift of God. He blesses this gift to those who seek it sincerely. The ultimate benefit of the Quran will come only to those who approach it with purity of mind and the sincerity of heart. The Quran demands an approach and attitude of love, respect and devotion that is due to a Divine Revelation. Along with this approach, the reader should also earnestly pray to Allah to open his heart, to show him the light and to give him the courage to accept and follow it. The more sincere and pure the reader will be in his intentions and efforts, the more he will receive the blessings from this Divine Guidance.

FROM THE PREFACE
TO THE FIRST EDITION

... It may be asked: Is there any need for a fresh English translation? To those who ask this question 1 commend a careful consideration of the facts which 1 have set out in my Note on Translation. After they have read it, 1 would invite them to take any particular passage, say 2:74 or 2:102, or 2:! 64 and compare it with any previous version they choose. If they find that I have helped them even the least bit further in understanding its meanings, or appreciating its beauty or catching something of the grandeur of the original, 1 would claim that my humble attempt is justified.

It is the duty of every Muslim, man, woman, or child, to read the Qur'an and understand it according to his own capacity. If any one of us attains some knowledge or understanding of it by study, contemplation, and the test of life, both outward and inward, it is his duty, according to his capacity, to instruct others, and share with them the joy and peace which result from contact with the spiritual world. The Qur'an — indeed every religious book — has to be read, not only with the tongue and voice and eyes, but with the best light that our intellect can supply, and even more, with the truest and purest light which our heart and conscience can give us. It is in this spirit that I would have my readers approach the Qur'an.

It was between the ages of four and five that I first learned to read its Arabic words, to revel in its rhythm and music, and wonder at its meaning. 1 have a dim recollection of the *Khatam* ceremony which closed that stage. It was called "completion"; it really just began a spiritual awakening that has gone on ever since my revered father taught me Arabic, but I must have imbibed from him into my innermost being something more, — something which told me that all the world's thoughts, all the world's most beautiful languages and literatures are but vehicles for that ineffable message which comes to the heart in rare moments of ecstasy. The soul of mysticism and ecstasy is in the Qur'an, as well as the plain guidance for the plain man which a world in a hurry affects to consider as sufficient. It is good to make this personal confession, to an age in which it is in the highest degree unfashionable to speak of religion or spiritual peace or consolation, an age in which words like these draw forth only derision, pity, or contempt.

I have explored Western lands, Western manners, and the depths of Western thought and Western learning, to an extent which has rarely fallen to the lot of an Eastern mortal. But I have never lost touch with Eastern heritage. Through all my successes and failures 1 have learned to rely more and more upon the one true thing in all life — the voice that speaks in a tongue above that of mortal man. For me the embodiment of that voice has been in the noble words of the Arabic Qur'~n, which I have tried to translate for myself and apply to my experience again and again. The service of the Qur'~n has been the pride and the privilege of many Muslims. I felt that with such life experience as has fallen to my lot, my service to the Qur'~n should be to present it in a fitting garb in English. That ambition I have cherished in my mind for more than forty years. I have collected books and materials for it. I have visited places, undertaken journeys, taken notes, sought the society of men, and tried to explore their thoughts and hearts, in order to equip myself for the task. Sometimes I have considered it too stupendous for me — the double task of understanding the original, and reproducing its nobility, its beauty, its poetry, its grandeur and its sweet practical reasonable application to everyday experience. Then I have blamed myself for lack of courage — the spiritual courage of men who dared all in the Cause which was so dear to them.

Two sets of apparently accidental circumstances at last decided me. A man's life is subject to inner storms far more devastating than those in the physical world around him. In such a storm, in the bitter anguish of a personal sorrow which nearly unseated my reason and made life seem meaningless, a new hope was born out of a systematic pursuit of my long cherished project. Watered by tears, my manuscript began to grow in depth and earnestness if not in bulk. I guarded it like a secret treasure. Wanderer that I am , I carried it about, thousands of miles, to all sorts of countries and among all sorts of people. At length, in the city of Lahore, I happened to mention the matter to some young people who held me in respect and affection. They showed an enthusiasm and an eagerness which surprised me. They almost took the matter out of my hands. They asked for immediate publication. 1 had various bits ready, but not even one *Sipara*. They made me promise to complete at least one *Sipara* before I left Lahore. As if by magic, a publisher, a *Katib* (calligraphist, to write the Arabic Text), an engraver of blocks for such text, and a printer were found, all equally anxious to push forward the scheme Blessed be youth, for its energy and determination! "Where others flinch, rash youth will dare!"

Gentle and discerning reader! what I wish to present to you is an English Interpretation. The English shall be, not a mere substitution of one word for another but the best expression I can give to the fullest meaning which 1 can understand from the Arabic Text. The rhythm, music, and exalted tone of the original should be reflected in the English Interpretation. It may be but a faint reflection, but such beauty and power as my pen can command shall be brought to its service. I want to make English itself an Islamic language, if such a person as I can do it, and I must give you all the accessory aid which I can...

The Text in English is printed... in parallel columns with the Arabic Text. Each *Sura* and the verse of each *Sura* is separately numbered, and the numbers are shown page by page.

... Every earnest and reverent student of the Quran, as he proceeds with his study, will find, with an inward joy difficult to describe, how this general meaning also enlarges as his own capacity for understanding increases It is like a traveller climbing a mountain; the higher he goes, the farther he sees. From a literary point of view the poet Keats has described his feeling when he discovered Chapman's Homer:

> The felt I like some watcher of the skies When a new planet swims into his ken, Or like stout Cortez when with eagle eyes. He started at the Pacific, —and all his men Looked at each other with a wild surmise,— Silent, upon a peak in Darien.

How much greater is the joy and sense of wonder and miracle when the Qur'an opens our spiritual eyes! The meaning which we thought we had grasped expands. New worlds are opened out. As we progress, still newer, and again newer worlds, "swim into our ken."

The miracle deepens and deepens, and almost completely absorbs us. And yet we know that the "face of Allah" — our final goal — has not yet been reached. We are in the *mulk* of Sulaiman (Q.2:102), which the evil ones denied, belied, and even turned into blasphemy. But we can ignore blasphemy, ridicule and contempt, for we are in the threshold of Realities and a little perfume from the garden of the Holy One has already gladdened our nostrils...

The Arabic Text I have had printed from photographic blocks, made for me by Master Muhammas Sharif, the calligraphy is from the pen of Pie 'Abdul Hamid, with whom I have been in touch and who has complied with my desire for a bold round hand, with the words clearly separated, the vowel points accurately placed over or under the letter to which they relate, and the verses duly numbered and placed in juxtaposition with their English equivalents. Calligraphy occupies an important place in Muslim Art, and it is my desire that my version should not in any way be deficient in this respect.

One final word to my readers. Read, study, and digest the Holy Book. Read slowly, and let it sink into your heart and soul. Such study will, like virtue, be its own reward. If you find anything in this volume to criticise, please let it not spoil your enjoyment of the rest. If you write to me, quoting chapter and verse, I shall be glad to consider your criticism, but let it not vex you if I exercise my own judgment in deciding for myself. Any corrections accepted will be gratefully acknowledged. On the other hand, if there is something that specially pleases you or help you. It will be a pleasure to know that my labour has not been in vain. If you address me care of my Publisher.

—ABDULLAH YUSUF ALI

Lahore 4th April, 1934
8th of the month
of Pilgrimage, 1352 H.

TRANSLITERATION OF ARABIC WORDS AND NAMES

Letter	Description	Sound		Letter	Description	Sound
ا	Consonantal sound	a		ط	....	t
ء				ظ	....	z
آ	Long vowel *	ā		ع	....	' (Inverted apostrophe)
ب	....	b		غ	....	gh
ت	....	t		ف	....	f
ث	....	th		ق	....	q
ج	....	j		ك	....	k
ح	....	h		ل	....	l
خ	....	kh		م	....	m
د	....	d		ن	....	n
ذ	....	z		ه	....	h
ر	....	r		و	consonant	w
ز	....	z		و	long vowel *	û
س	....	s		و	diphthong	au
ش	....	sh		ي	consonant	y
ص	....	s		ي	long vowel *	î
ض	....	dh		ي	diphthong	ai

Short vowels: ― (*fatha*)   a
               ― (*kasra*)   i
               ― (*dhamma*) u

1. For the *hamzat* ( ) I have used no distinctie sign. An apostrophe for it and an inverted apostrophe for the *'ain* ( ) or vice versa, is confusing to English readers. As a moved consonant, it is sufficiently shown in English by the long or short vowel which moves it. e.g., ab, Rauf. Where it is a hiatus preceded by a fatha. I have shown it by a second a; thus, Iqraa, the cuva of Hiraa. In other cases it has not been possible to show it without using a distinctive sign The name of the Holy Book is usually written Qur'an; but I prefer to write Qur'an. However a few words like *juz* have an apostrophe indicating *Hamza*.

---

1.   Where it is really pronounced long. Hence *khalaqna-kum* but *khalaqnal-insan*; *Abu Sufyan* but *Abul-Qasim; fin-nar* but *fi-hi.*

2. The final preceded by the short a is scarcely pronounced, and I have left it out. Hencem Sura, Fatiha, Hijra etc., where the Arabic spelling would require Surah, Fatihah, Hijrah etc.

3. In internationalised words and names I have used the spelling ordinarily current in English; e.g., Makkah, Madinah, Maulvi, Urdu, Islam, Israel, Abraham, Jacob. Here the boundary is thin and rather ill-defined, and possible my practice and that of my proof-readers have not been absolutely uniform. But inplace of Makkah and Madinah, the more accurate form of Makkah and Madinah is adopted.

Contents

SURAH—1

AL-FATIHA

(INTRODUCTION)

First comes that beautiful Surah, The Opening Chapter of Seven Verses, rightly called the Essence of the Book. It teacher us the perfect prayer. For if we can pray aright, It-means that we have some knowledge of Allah and His attributes, of His relations to us and His creation, which includes ourselves; that we glimpse the source from which we come, and that final goal which is our spiritual destiny under Allah's true judgement: then we offer ourselves to Allah and seek His light.

Prayer is the heart of Religion and Faith: but how shall we pray? What words shall convey the yearnings of our miserable, ignorant hearts to the knower of all? Is it worthy of Him or of our spiritual nature to ask for vanities, or even for such physical needs as our daily bread? The Inspired One taught us a Prayer that sums up our faith, our hope, and our aspiration in things that matter. We think in devotion of Allah's name and His Nature; we praise Him for His creation and His cherishing care; we call to mind the Realities, seen and unseen; we offer Him worship and ask for His guidance; and we know the straight form the crooked path by the light of His grace that illumines the righteous.

SURAH AL-FATIHAH (THE OPENING)

In the name of Allah, Most Gracious, Most Merciful

1. Praise be to Allah, the Cherisher and Sustainer of the Worlds:
2. Most Gracious, Most Merciful.
3. Master of the Day of Judgment.
4. You do we worship, and Your aid do we seek[1].
5. Show us the straight way.
6. The way of those on whom You have bestowed your Grace.
7. Those whose (portion) is not wrath[2], and who do not go astray.

---

1. The translator frequently uses some old forms of pronouns like 'thou', 'thine' etc. for ('you' 'yours') and other words like 'hath' 'showeth' 'knoweth' etc. (for 'has' 'shows', 'knows') which havebeen changed—**Publishers.**
2. Anger

SURAH—2
AL-BAQARAH
(INTRODUCTION)

As the Opening Surah sums up in seven beautiful verses the essence of the Quran, so this Surah sums up in 286 verses the whole teaching of the Quran It is a closely reasoned argument.

This is the longest Surah of the Quran and in it occurs the longest verse (2:282). The name of the Surah is from the Parable of the Heifer in 2: 67-71, which illustrates the insufficiency of carping obedience. When faith is lost, people put off obedience with various excuses; even when at last they obey iin the letter, they fail in the spirit, which means that they get fossilised, and their self-sufficiency prevents them from seeing that spiritually they are not alive but dead. For life is movement, activity, striving, fighting against baser things. And this is the burden of the Surah.

This is in the main an early Madinah Surah.

SURAH AL-BAQARAH (THE COW)
In the name of Allah, Most Gracious, Most Merciful

1.   A.L.M.

2.   This is the Book; in it is guidance sure, without doubt, to those who fear Allah;

3.   Who believe in the Unseen, are steadfast[3] in prayer, and spend out of what We have provided for them;

4.   And who believe in the Revelation sent to you, and sent before your time, and (in their hearts) have the assurance of the Hereafter.[4]

5.   They are on (true) guidance, from their Allah, and it is these who will prosper.

6.   As to those who reject Faith, it is the same to them whether you warn them or do not warn them; they will not believe.

7.   Allah has set a seal on their hearts and on their hearing. And

---

3.   Constant, firm   4. Life after death

on their eyes is a veil; great is the chastisement they (incur).

8. Of the people there are some who say: "We believe in Allah and the Last Day;" but they do not (really) believe.

9. Fain would they deceive Allah and those who believe, but they only deceive themselves, and realize (it) not!

10. In their hearts is a disease; and Allah has increased their disease: and grievous[5] is the chastisement[6] they (incur), because they are false (to themselves).

11. When it is said to them: "Make not mischief on the earth," they say: "Why, we only want to make peace!"

12. Of a surety, they are the ones who make mischief, but they realize (it) not.

13. When it is said to them: "Believe as the others believe:" They say: "Shall we believe as the fools believe?" Nay, of a surety they are the fools, but they do not know.

14. When they meet those who believe, they say: "We believe;" but when they are alone with their evil ones, they say: "We are really with you: we (were) only jesting."

15. Allah will throw back their mockery[7] on them, and give them rope in their trespasses; so they will wander like blind ones (to and fro).

16. These are they who have bartered[8] guidance for error: but their traffic[9] is profitless, and they have lost true direction.

17. Their similitude[10] is that of a man who kindled[11] a fire; when it lighted all around him, Allah took away their light and left them in utter[12] darkness, so they could not see.

18. Deaf, dumb, and blind, they will not return (to the path).

19. Or (another similitude) is that of a rain-laden cloud from the sky: In it are zones of darkness, and thunder and lightning:

---

5. Causing great harm and sorrow.
6. A punishment imposed for a violation of law.
7. Ridicule
8. Exchanged
9. Commerce or business
10. Likeness, parable
11. Lighted
12. Complete, total

they press their fingers in their ears to keep out the stunning[13] thunder-clap, the while they are in terror of death. But Allah is ever round the rejecters of Faith!

20. The lightning all but snatches away their sight; every time the light (helps) them, they walk therein, and when the darkness grows on them, they stand still. And if Allah willed, He could take away their faculty of hearing and seeing; for Allah has power over all things.

21. O you people! Adore[14] your Guardian-Allah, Who created you and those who came before you, that you my become righteous.

22. Who has made the earth your couch, and the heavens your canopy; and sent down rain from the heavens; and brought forth therewith fruits for your sustenance[15]; then do not set up rivals unto Allah when you know (the truth).

23. And if you are in doubt as to what We have revealed from time to time to Our servant, then produce a Sura like thereof; and call your witnesses or helpers (if there are any) besides Allah, if you are truthful-

24. But if you cannot- and of a surety you cannot- then fear the Fire whose fuel is men and stones,- which is prepared for those who reject Faith.

25. But give glad tidings[16] to those who believe and work righteousness, that their portion is Gardens beneath which rivers flow. Every time they are fed with fruits therefrom, they say: "Why, this is what we were fed with before," for they are given things in similitude; and they have therein spouses purified; and they abide[17] therein (for ever).

26. Allah disdains[18] not to use the similitude of things, lowest as well as highest. Those who believe know that it is Truth from their Allah; but those who reject Faith say: "What means Allah by this similitude?" By it He causes many to stray, and many

---

13. Startling
14. Worship and love
15. Means of livelihood
16. News
17. Dwell, live.
18. To consider unworthy of notice of response.

He leads into the right path; but He causes not to stray, except those who forsake (the path),-

27. Those who break Allah's Covenant[19] after it is ratified[20], and who sunder[21] what Allah has ordered to be joined, and do mischief on earth: these cause loss (only) to themselves.

28. How can you reject the Faith in Allah?- seeing that you were without life, and He gave you life; then will He cause you to die, and will again bring you to life; and again to Him will you return.

29. It is He Who has created for you all things that are on earth; moreover His design compre-hends the heavens, for He gave order and perfection to the seven firmaments[22]; and of all things He has perfect knowledge.

30. Behold, your Allah said to the angels: "I will create a vicegerent[23] on earth." They said: "Will You place therein one who will make mischief therein and shed blood?- while we do celebrate Your praises and glorify [24] Your holy (name)?" He said: "I know what you know not."

31. And He taught Adam the nature of all things; then He placed them before the angels, and said: "Tell Me the nature of these if you are right."

32. They said: "Glory to You, of knowledge we have none, save what You have taught us: in truth it is You Who are perfect in know-ledge and wisdom."

33. He said: "O Adam! tell them their natures." When he had told them, Allah said: "Did I not tell you that I know the secrets of heaven and earth, and I know what you reveal and what you conceal?"

34. And behold, We said to the angels: "Bow down to Adam" and they bowed down: not so Iblis: he refused and was haughty[25]: he was of those who reject Faith.

---

19. A Solemn pledge.
20. Confirmed, approved.
21. Divide, Separate
22. The arch or vault of Heaven, sky
23. A deputy
24. Adore, praise, extol.
25. Proud, arrogant

35.   We said: "O Adam! dwell you and your wife in the Garden; and eat of the bountiful[26] things therein as (where and when) you will; but approach not this tree, or you run into harm and transgression."[27]

36.   Then did Satan make them slip from the (Garden), and get them out of the state (of felicity[28]) in which they had been. We said: "Get you down, all (you people), with enmity between yourselves. On earth will be your dwelling-place and your means of livelihood for a time."

37.   Then learnt Adam from his Allah words of inspiration, and his Allah turned towards him; for He is Oft-Returning, Most Merciful.

38.   We said: "Get you down all from here; and if, as is sure, there comes to you Guidance from Me, whosoever follows My Guidance, on them shall be no fear, nor shall they grieve.

39.   "But those who reject Faith and belie[39] Our Signs, they shall be companions of the Fire; they shall abide therein."

40.   O Children of Israel! call to mind the (special) favour which I bestowed upon you, and fulfil your Covenant with Me as I fulfil My Covenant with you, and fear none but Me.

41.   And believe in what I reveal, confirming the revelation which is with you, and be not the first to reject Faith therein, nor sell My Signs for a small price; and fear Me, and Me alone.

42.   And cover not Truth with falsehood, nor conceal the Truth when you know (what it is).

43.   And be steadfast in prayer; practise regular charity; and bow down your heads with those who bow down (in worship).

44.   Do you enjoin[30] right conduct on the people, and forget (to practise it) yourselves, and yet you study the Scripture?[31] Will you not understand?

---

26.   Ample, abundant   27.   Offense, sin, violation
28.   Bliss, delight
29.   To be false to, to contradict, to misrepresent
30.   Direct, order   31.   Torah or Injil or both.

45. Nay, seek (Allah's) help with patient perseverance[32] and prayer: it is indeed hard, except to those who bring a lowly[33] spirit,-

46. Who bear in mind the certainty that they are to meet their Allah, and that they are to return to Him.

47. O Children of Israel! call to mind the (special) favour which I bestowed upon you, and that I preferred you to all others (for My Message).

48. Then guard yourselves against a day when one soul shall not avail another nor shall intercession[34] be accepted for her, nor shall compensation[35] be taken from her, nor shall anyone be helped (from outside).

49. And remember, We delivered[36] you from the people of Pharaoh[37]. They set you hard tasks and punishments, slaughtered your sons and let your women-folk live; therein was a tremendous[38] trial from your Allah.

50. And remember, We divided the sea for you and saved you and drowned Pharaoh's people within your very sight.

51. And remember We appoin-ted forty nights for Moses, and in his absence, you took the calf (for worship), and you did grievous wrong.

52. Even then We did forgive you; there was a chance for you to be grateful.

53. And remember We gave Moses the Scripture and the Criterion[39] (between right and wrong): there was a chance for you to be guided aright.

54. And remember, Moses said to his people: "O my people! you have indeed wronged yourselves by your worship of the calf: So turn (in repentance) to your Maker, and slay yourselves (the wrong-doers); that will be better for you in the sight of

---

32. Endurance, steadfastness   33. Humble
34. Pleading to Allah on behalf of another person.
35. Something given or received for a loss or injury—a payment to escape punishment for wrong done.
36. Freed, saved   37. Title of an old Egyptian king
38. Enomous, dreadful   39. Standard, yardstick

your Maker." Then He turned towards you (in forgiveness): for He is Oft- Returning, Most Merciful.

55. And remember, you said: "O Moses! we shall never believe in you until we see Allah manifestly," but you were dazed[40] with thunder and lightning even as you looked on.

56. Then We raised you up after your death: you had the chance to be grateful.

57. And We gave you the shade of clouds and sent down to you manna[41] and quails[42], saying: "Eat of the good things We have provided for you:" (But they rebelled); to Us they did no harm, but they harmed their own souls.

58. And remember, We said: "Enter this town, and eat of the plenty therein as you wish; but enter the gate with humility, in posture and in words, and We shall forgive you your faults and increase (the portion of) those who do good."

59. But the transgressors changed the word from that which had been given them; so We sent on the transgressors a plague from heaven, for that they infringed[43] (Our command) repeatedly.

60. And remember, Moses prayed for water for his people; We said: "Strike the rock with your staff." Then gushed[44] forth therefrom twelve springs. Each group knew its own place for water. So eat and drink of the sustenance[45] provided by Allah, and do no evil nor mischief on the (face of the) earth.

61. And remember, you said: "O Moses! we cannot endure one kind of food (always); so beseech your Allah for us to produce for us of what the earth grows, - its pot-herbs, and cucumbers, its garlic, lentils, and onions." He said: "Will you exchange the better for the worse? You go down to any town, and you

---

40. Stupefied, dazzled.
41. The food supplied by Allah miraculously to the Children of Israel in the wilderness,
42. A small bird of the pheasant family.   43.   Violated, trespassed.
44. Gush—A sudden copiesoutflow of water.
45. Means of livelihood.

shall find what you want!" They were covered with humiliation and misery; they drew on themselves the wrath of Allah. This because they went on rejecting the Signs of Allah and slaying His Messengers without just cause. This because they rebelled and went on transgressing.

62. Those who believe (in the Qur'an), and those who follow the Jewish (scriptures), and the Christians and the Sabians, - and who believe in Allah and the Last Day, and work righteousness, shall have their reward with their Allah; on them shall be no fear, nor shall they grieve.

63. And remember, We took your Covenant and We raised above you (the towering height) of Mount (Sinai): (saying): "Hold firmly to what We have given you and bring (ever) to remembrance what is therein: perchance[46] you may fear Allah."

64. But you turned back thereafter: had it not been for the Grace and Mercy of Allah to you, you had surely been among the lost.

65. And you knew well those amongst you who transgressed in the matter of the Sabbath: We said to them: "Be you apes, despised and rejected."

66. So We made it an example to their own time and to their posterity[47], and a lesson to those who fear Allah.

67. And remember, Moses said to his people: "Allah commands that you sacrifice a heifer".[48] They said: Do you wish to make a laughing-stock of us?" He said: "May Allah save me from being an ignorant (fool)!"

68. They said: "Beseech[49] on our behalf your Allah to make plain to us what (heifer) it is!" He said; "He says: the heifer should be neither too old nor too young, but of middling age: now do what you are commanded!"

69. They said: "Beseech on our behalf your Allah to make plain to us her colour." He said: "He says: A fawn-coloured[50] heifer,

---

46. Perhaps, maybe.
47. Their future generations.
48. A young cow.
49. Beg or request eagerly.
50. Light yellowish brown colour.

pure and rich in tone, the admiration of beholders!"

70. They said: "Beseech on our behalf your Allah to make plain to us what she is: to us all heifers are alike: we wish indeed for guidance, if Allah wills."

71. He said: "He says: a heifer not trained to till the soil or water the fields; sound and without blemish"[51]. They said: "Now you has brought the truth." Then they offered her in sacrifice, but not with good-will.

72. Remember, you slew a man and fell into a dispute among yourselves as to the crime: but Allah was to bring forth what you did hide.

73. So We said: "Strike the (body) with a piece of the (heifer)." Thus Allah brings the dead to life and shows you His Signs: perchance you may understand.

74. Thenceforth your hearts were hardened: they became like a rock and even worse in hardness. For among rocks there are some from which rivers gush forth; others there are which when split asunder send forth water; and others which sink for fear of Allah. And Allah is not unmindful of what you do.

75. Can you (O you men of Faith) entertain the hope that they will believe in you?- seeing that a party of them heard the Word of Allah, and perverted[52] it knowingly after they understood it.

76. Behold! when they meet the men of Faith, they say: "We believe": but when they meet each other in private, they say: "Shall you tell them what Allah has revealed to you, that they may engage you in argument about it before your Allah?"- do you not understand (their aim)?

77. Do they not know that Allah knows what they conceal and what they reveal?

78. And there are among them illiterates, who do not know the Book, but (see therein their own) desires, and they do nothing but conjecture.[53]

---

51. Flaw or defect.
52. Misinterpreted, distorted or misapplied.
53. For man opinion or theory without sufficient proof, guesswork.

79. Then woe to those who write the Book with their own hands, and then say:"This is from Allah," to traffic with it for a miserable price!- Woe to them for what their hands do write, and for the gain they make thereby.

80. And they say: "The Fire shall not touch us but for a few numbered days:" say: "Have you taken a promise from Allah, for He never breaks His promise? or is it that you say of Allah what you do not know?"

81. Nay, those who seek gain in evil, and are girt[54] round by their sins,- they are Companions of the Fire: therein shall they abide (for ever).

82. But those who have faith and work righteousness, they are Companions of the Garden: therein shall they abide (for ever).

83. And remember, We took a Covenant from the Children of Israel (to this effect): worship none but Allah; treat with kindness your parents and kindred, and orphans and those in need; speak fair to the people; be steadfast in prayer; and practise regular charity. Then you turned back, except a few among you, and you backslide[55] (even now).

84. And remember We took your Covenant (to this effect): shed no blood amongst you, nor turn out your own people from your homes: and this you solemnly ratified, and to this you can bear witness.

85. After this it is you, the same people, who slay among yourselves, and banish a party of you from their homes; assist (their enemies) against them, in guilt and rancour;[56] and if they come to you as captives, you ransom[57] them, though it was not lawful for you to banish them. Then is it only a part of the Book that you believe in, and do you reject the rest? But what is the reward for those among you who behave like this but disgrace in this life?- and on the Day of Judgment they shall be consigned[58] to the most grievous Chastisement. For Allah

---

54. Encircled.   55. Relapse into sinful behaviour.
56. Bitter resentment or ill will.
57. Rescue them from captivity by paying a demanded price.
58. Handedover, entrusted.

is not unmindful of what you do.

86.   These are the people who buy the life of this world at the price of the Hereafter: their Chastisement shall not be lightened nor shall they be helped.

87.   We gave Moses the Book and followed him up with a succession of Apostles[59]. We gave Jesus the son of Mary, clear (Signs) and strengthened him with the holy spirit. Is it that whenever there comes to you an Apostle with what you yourselves do not desire, you are puffed up with pride?-some you called impostors,[60] and others you slay!

88.   They say, "Our hearts are the wrappings[61] (which preserve Allah's Word: we need no more)." Nay, Allah's curse is on them for their blasphemy: little is it they believe.

89.   And when there comes to them a Book from Allah, confirming what is with them,- although from of old they had prayed for victory against those without Faith,- when there comes to them that which they (should) have recognized, they refuse to believe in it but the curse of Allah is on those without Faith.

90.   Miserable is the price for which they have sold their souls, in that they deny (the revelation) which Allah has sent down, in insolent envy that Allah of His Grace should send it to any of His servants He pleases: thus they have drawn on themselves Wrath upon Wrath. And humiliating is the punishment of those who reject Faith.

91.   When it is said to them, "Believe in what Allah has sent down," they say, "We believe in what was sent down to us:" yet they reject all besides, even if it be Truth confirming what is with them. Say: "Why then have you slain the prophets of Allah in times gone by, if you did indeed believe?"

92.   There came to you Moses with clear (Signs); yet you worshipped the Calf (even) after that, and you did behave

---

59.   Messengers   60.   Liars or deceivers.
61.   The covering in which something is wrapped.

wrongfully.

93. And remember, We took your Covenant and We raised above you (the towering height) of Mount (Sinai): (saying): "Hold firmly to what We have given you and hearken (to the Law)": they said: "We hear, and we disobey:"[62] and they had to drink into their hearts (of the taint) of the Calf because of their Faithlessness. Say: "Vile[63] indeed are the behests[64] of your Faith if you have any faith!"

94. Say: "If the last Home, with Allah, be for you specially, and not for anyone else, then you seek for death, if you are sincere."

95. But they will never seek for death, on account of the (sins) which their hands have sent on before them. And Allah is well-acquainted with the wrong-doers.

96. You will indeed find them, of all people, most greedy of life,- even more than the idolators: each one of them wishes he could be given a life of a thousand years: but the grant of such life will not save him from (due) punishment. For Allah sees well all that they do.

97. Say: Whoever is an enemy to Gabriel - for he brings down the (revelation) to your heart by Allah's will, a confirmation of what went before, and guidance and glad tidings for those who believe,

98. Whoever is an enemy to Allah and His Angels and Apostles, to Gabriel and Michael,- certainly Allah is an enemy to those who reject Faith.

99. We have sent down to you Manifest Signs (ayaat); and none reject them but those who are perverse.

100. Is it not (the case) that every time they make a Covenant, some party among them throw it aside?- Nay, most of them are faithless.

101. And when there came to them an Apostle from Allah, confirming what was with them, a party of the People of the

---

62. Evil trace of calf-worship.   63. Morally despicable

64. Commands, directives

Book threw away the Book of Allah behind their backs, as if (it had been something) they did not know!

102. They followed what the evil ones gave out (falsely) against the power of Solomon: the blasphemers were, not Solomon, but the evil ones, teaching men magic, and such things as came down at Babylon to the angels Harut and Marut. But neither of these taught anyone (such things) without saying: "We are only for trial; so do not blaspheme."[65] They learned from them the means to sow discord[66] between man and wife. But they could not thus harm anyone except by Allah's permission. And they learned what harmed them, not what profited them. And they knew that the buyers of (magic) would have no share in the happiness of the Hereafter. And vile was the price for which they did sell their souls, if they but knew!

103. If they had kept their Faith and guarded themselves from evil, far better had been the reward from their Allah, if they but knew!

104. O you who believe! say not (to the Apostle) words of ambiguous import[67], but words of respect; and hearken (to him): to those without Faith is a grievous punishment.

105. It is never the wish of those without Faith among the People of the Book, nor of the Pagans, that anything good should come down to you from your Allah. But Allah will choose for His special Mercy whom He will - for Allah is Allah of grace abounding.

106. None of Our revelations do We abrogate or cause to be forgotten, but We substitute something better or similar: don't you know that Allah has power over all things?

107. Don't you know that to Allah belongs the dominion of the heavens and the earth? And besides Him you have neither patron nor helper.

108. Would you question your Apostle as Moses was ques-tioned

---

65. To speak impiously of Allah or sacred things.
66. Disagreement, strife.
                                          67. Significance, meaning.

of old? But whoever changes from Faith to Unbelief, has strayed without doubt from the even way.

109. Quite a number of the People of the Book wish they could turn you (people) back to infidelity after you have believed, from selfish envy, after the Truth has become manifest unto them: but forgive and overlook, till Allah accomplish His purpose; for Allah has power over all things.

110. And be steadfast in prayer and regular in charity: and whatever good you send forth for your souls before you, you shall find it with Allah: for Allah sees well all that you do.

111. And they say: "None shall enter Paradise unless he be a Jew or a Christian." Those are their (vain) desires. Say: "Produce your proof if you are truthful."

112. Nay,- whoever submits his whole self to Allah and is a doer of good,- he will get his reward with his Allah; on such shall be no fear, nor shall they grieve.

113. The Jews say: "The Christians have nothing (to stand) upon"; and the Christians say: "The Jews have nothing (to stand) upon." Yet they (profess to) study the (same) Book. Like unto their word is what those say who do not know; but Allah will judge between them in their dispute on the Day of Judgment.

114. And who is more unjust than he who forbids that in places for the worship of Allah, Allah's name should be celebrated?-whose zeal is (in fact) to ruin them? It was not fitting that such should themselves enter them except in fear. For them there is nothing but disgrace in this world, and in the world to come, an exceeding torment.

115. To Allah belong the East and the West: whithersoever[68] you turn, there is the presence of Allah. For Allah is All-Pervading, All-Knowing.

116. They say: "Allah has begotten a son": glory be to Him.-Nay, to Him belongs all that is in the heavens and on earth: everything renders worship to Him.

---

68.   Whichever direction.

117. To Him is due the primal[69] origin of the heavens and the earth: when He decrees a matter, He says to it: "Be," and it is.

118. Those without knowledge say: "Why does not Allah speak to us? Or why does not a Sign come to us?" So said the people before them words of similar import. Their hearts are alike. We have indeed made clear the Signs for any people who hold firmly to Faith (in their hearts).

119. Surely We have sent you in truth as a bearer of glad tidings and a warner: but of you no question shall be asked of the Companions of the Blazing Fire.

120. Never will the Jews or the Christians be satisfied with you unless you follow their form of religion. Say: "The Guidance of Allah,- that is the (only) Guidance." If you were to follow their desires after the knowledge which has reached you, then you would find neither Protector nor Helper against Allah.

121. Those to whom We have sent the Book study it as it should be studied: they are the ones that believe therein: those who reject faith therein, - the loss is their own.

122. O Children of Israel! call to mind the special favour which I bestowed upon you, and that I preferred you to all others (for My Message).

123. Then guard yourselves against a Day when one soul shall not avail another, nor shall compensation be accepted from her nor shall intercession profit her nor shall anyone be helped (from outside).

124. And remember that Abraham was tried by his Allah with certain commands, which he fulfilled: He said: "I will make you an _Imam_[70] to the Nations." He pleaded: "And also (_Imams_) from my offspring!" He answered: "But My Promise is not within the reach of evil-doers."

125. And remember, We made the House a place of assembly for men and a place of safety; and you take the Station of Abraham as a place of prayer; and We covenanted with Abraham and

---

69. First, original

70. Leader

Isma'il, that they should sanctify My House for those who compass it round, or use it as a retreat, or bow, or prostrate themselves (therein in prayer).

126. And remember, Abraham said: "My Allah, make this a City of Peace, and feed its people with fruits,- such of them as believe in Allah and the Last Day." He said: "(Yes), and such as reject Faith,-for a while will I grant them their pleasure, but will soon drive them to the torment of Fire, - an evil destination (indeed)!"

127. And remember, Abraham and Isma'il raised the foundations of the House (with this prayer): "Our Allah! accept (this service) from us: for You are the All- Hearing, the All-Knowing.

128. "Our Allah! make of us Muslims, bowing to Your (Will), and of our progeny[71] a people Muslim, bowing to Your (Will); and show us our places for the celebration of (due) rites; and turn unto us (in Mercy); for You are the Oft-Returning, Most Merciful.

129. "Our Allah! send amongst them an Apostle of their own, who shall rehearse[72] Your Signs to them and instruct them in scripture[73] and Wisdom, and sanctify them: for You are the Exalted in Might, the Wise."

130. And who turns away from the religion of Abraham but such as debase their souls with folly? Him We chose and rendered pure in this world: and he will be in the Hereafter in the ranks of the Righteous.

131. Behold! his Allah said to him: "Bow (your will to Me):" he said: "I bow (my will) to the Allah and Cherisher of the Universe."

132. And this was the legacy[34] that Abraham left to his sons, and so did Jacob; "Oh my sons! Allah has chosen the Faith for you;then do not die except in the Faith of Islam."

133. Were you witnesses when Death appeared before Jacob? Behold, he said to his sons: "What will you worship after me?"

---

71. Offspring
73. The Book
72. Convey, repeat
74. Heritge, tradition

They said: "We shall worship your God (Allah) and the God (Allah) of your fathers, of Abraham, Isma'il and Isaac, - the One (True) God (Allah): to Him we bow (in Islam)."

134. That was a people who have passed away. They shall reap the fruit of what they did, and you of what you do! Of their merits there is no question in your case!

135. They say: "Become Jews or Christians if you would be guided (to salvation)." You say: "Nay! (I would rather) the Religion of Abraham the True, and he joined not gods with Allah."

136. You say: "We believe in Allah, and the revelation given to us, and to Abraham, Isma'il, Isaac, Jacob, and the Tribes, and that given to Moses and Jesus, and that given to (all) prophets from their Allah: we make no difference between one and another of them: and we bow to Allah (in Islam)."

137. So if they believe as you believe, they are indeed on the right path; but if they turn back, it is they who are in schism;[75] but Allah will suffice you as against them, and He is the All-Hearing, the All-Knowing.

138. (Our religion is) the Bap-tism of Allah: and who can baptize better than Allah? And it is He Whom we worship.

139. Say: Will you dispute with us about Allah, seeing that He is our Allah and your Allah; that we are responsible for our doings and you for yours; and that we are sincere (in our faith) in Him?

140. Or do you say that Abraham, Isma'il, Isaac, Jacob and the Tribes were Jews or Christians? Say: Do you know better than Allah? Ah! who is more unjust than those who conceal the testimony they have from Allah? But Allah is not unmindful of what you do!

141. That was a people who have passed away. They shall reap the fruit of what they did, and you of what you do! Of their merits there is no question in your case.

142. The fools among the people will say: "What has turned them

---

75.   Division or disunion into mutually opposed parties, hostility.

from the *Qibla*[76] to which they were used?" Say: To Allah belong both East and West: He guides whom He will to a Way that is straight.

143. Thus, have We made of you an Ummat justly balanced, that you might be witnesses over the nations, and the Apostle a witness over yourselves; and We appointed the *Qibla*[77] to which you were used, only to test those who followed the Apostle from those who would turn on their heels (from the Faith). Indeed it was (a change) momentous, except to those guided by Allah. And never would Allah make your faith of no effect. For Allah is to all people most surely full of kindness, Most Merciful.

144. We see the turning of your face (for guidance) to the hea-vens: now shall We turn you to a Qibla that shall please you. Turn then your face in the direction of the sacred Mosque: wherever you are, turn your faces in that direction. The people of the Book know well that that is the truth from their Allah. Nor is Allah unmindful of what they do.

145. Even if you were to bring to the people of the Book all the Signs (together), they would not follow your Qibla; nor are you going to follow their Qibla; nor indeed will they follow each other's Qibla. If you after the knowledge has reached you were to follow their (vain) desires,- then you were indeed (clearly) in the wrong.

146. The people of the Book know this as they know their own sons; but some of them conceal the truth which they themselves know.

147. The Truth is from your Allah; so be not at all in doubt.

148. To each is a goal to which Allah turns him; then strive together (as in a race) toward all that is good. Wheresoever you are, Allah will bring you together. For Allah has power over all things.

---

76. Direction faced in prayer.   77. Direction of Ka'bah (Makkah)

149.   From wheresoever you start forth, turn your face in the direction of the Sacred Mosque; that is indeed the truth from your Allah. And Allah is not unmind-ful of what you do.

150.   So from wheresoever you start forth, turn your face in the direction of the Sacred Mosque; and wheresoever you are, turn your face to it: that there be no ground of dispute against you among the people, except those of them that are bent on wickedness; so do not fear them, but fear Me; and that I may complete My favours on you, and you may (consent to) be guided;

151.   A similar (favour you have already received) in that We have sent among you an Apostle of your own, rehearsing to you Our Signs, and sanctifying you, and instructing you in Scripture and Wisdom, and in new Knowledge.

152.   Then you remember Me; I will remember you. Be grateful to Me, and do not reject Faith.

153.   O you who believe! seek help with patient perseverance and prayer; for Allah is with those who patiently persevere.[78]

154.   And do not say of those who are slain in the way of Allah: "They are dead." Nay, they are living, though you do not perceive (it).

155.   Be sure We shall test you with something of fear and hunger, some loss in goods or lives or the fruits (of your toil[79]), but give glad tidings to those who patiently persevere,

156.   Who say, when afflicted with calamity: "To Allah we belong, and to Him is our return":-

157.   They are those on whom (descend) blessings from Allah, and Mercy, and they are the ones that receive guidance.

158.   Behold! Safa and Marwa are among the Symbols of Allah. So if those who visit the House in the Season or at other times, should compass them round, it is no sin in them. And if any one obeys his own impulse to Good,- be sure that Allah is He Who recognises and knows.

---

78.   Endure   79.   Labour, work

159. Those who conceal the clear (Signs) We have sent down, and the Guidance, after We have made it clear for the People in the Book,- on them shall be Allah's curse, and the curse of those entitled to curse,-

160. Except those who repent and make amends and openly declare (the Truth): to them I turn; for I am Oft-Returning, Most Merciful.

161. Those who reject Faith, and die rejecting,- on them is Allah's curse, and the curse of angels, and of all mankind.

162. They will abide therein: their Chastisement will not be lightened, nor will respite be their (lot).

163. And your God (Allah) is One God (Allah): There is no god but He, Most Gracious, Most Merciful.

164. Behold! in the creation of the heavens and the earth; in the alternation of the night and the day; in the sailing of the ships through the ocean for the profit of mankind; in the rain which Allah sends down from the skies, and the life which He gives therewith to an earth that is dead; in the beasts of all kinds that He scatters through the earth; in the change of the winds, and the clouds which they trail like their slaves between the sky and the earth;- (here) indeed are Signs for a people that are wise.

165. Yet there are men who take (for worship) others besides Allah, as equal (with Allah): they love them as they should love Allah. But those of Faith are overflowing in their love for Allah. If only the unrighteous could see, behold, they would see the Chastisement: that to Allah belongs all power, and Allah will strongly enforce the Chastise-ment.

166. Then would those who are followed clear themselves of those who follow (them): they would see the Chastisement, and all relations between them would be cut off.

167. And those who followed would say: "If only we had one more chance, we would clear ourselves of them, as they have cleared themselves of us." Thus will Allah show them (the fruits of) their deeds as (nothing but) regrets. Nor will there be a way

for them out of the Fire.

168.   O you people! Eat of what is on earth, lawful and good; and do not follow the footsteps of the Satan, for he is to you an avowed enemy.

169.   For he commands you what is evil and shameful, and that you should say of Allah that of which you have no know-ledge.

170.   When it is said to them: "Follow what Allah has revea-led:" they say: "Nay! we shall follow the ways of our fathers." What! even though their fathers were void of wisdom and guidance?

171.   The parable of those who reject Faith is as if one were to shout like a goat- herd, to things that listen to nothing but calls and cries: deaf, dumb, and blind, they are void[80] of wisdom.

172.   O you who believe! Eat of the good things that We have provided for you and be grateful to Allah, if it is Him you worship.

173.   He has only forbidden you dead meat, and blood, and the flesh of swine, and that on which any other name has been invoked besides that of Allah. But if one is forced by necessity, without wilful disobedience, nor trans-gressing due limits,- then is he guiltless, for Allah is Oft-Forgiving, Most Merciful.

174.   Those who conceal Allah's revelations in the Book, and purchase for them a miserable profit,- they swallow into themselves nothing but Fire; Allah will not address them on the Day of Resurrection, nor purify them: grievous will be their Chastisement.

175.   They are the ones who buy Error in place of Guidance and Torment in place of Forgiveness. Ah! what boldness (they show) for the Fire!

176.   (Their doom is) because Allah sent down the Book in truth but those who seek causes of dispute in the Book are in a schism far (from the purpose).

177.   It is not righteousness that you turn your faces toward East or West; but it is righteousness - to believe in Allah and the Last

---

80.   Empty, lacking in

Day, and the Angels, and the Book, and the Messengers; to spend of your substance[81], out of love for Him, for your kin, for orphans, for the needy, for the wayfarer, for those who ask, and for the ransom of slaves; to be steadfast in prayer, and practice regular charity; to fulfil the contracts which you have made; and to be firm and patient, in pain (or suffering) and adversity, and throughout all periods of panic. Such are the people of truth, those who fear Allah.

178. O you who believe! The law of equality is prescribed to you in cases of murder: the free for the free, the slave for the slave, the woman for the woman. But if any remission[82] is made by the brother of the slain, then grant any reasonable demand, and compensate him with handsome gratitude. This is a concession and a Mercy from your Allah. After this whoever exceeds the limits shall be in grave Chastisement.

179. In the Law of Equality there is (saving of) Life to you, O you men of understanding; that you may restrain yourselves.

180. It is prescribed, when death approaches any of you, if he leave any goods that he make a bequest to parents and next of kin, according to reasonable usage; this is due from those who fear Allah.

181. If anyone changes the bequest after hearing it, the guilt shall be on those who make the change. For Allah hears and knows (all things).

182. But if anyone fears partiality or wrong-doing on the part of the testator, and makes peace between (the parties concerned), there is no wrong in him: for Allah is Oft-Forgiving, Most Merciful.

183. O you who believe! Fasting is prescribed[83] to you as it was prescribed to those before you, that you may (learn) self-restraint,-

184. (Fasting) for a fixed number of days; but if any of you is ill, or on a journey, the prescribed number (should be made up) from

---

81. Wealth or property	82. Decrease (in blood money)
83. Laid down, decreed	

days later. For those who can do it (with hardship), is a ransom, the feeding of one that is indigent.[84] But he that will give more, of his own free will,- it is better for him. And it is better for you that you fast, if you only knew.

185.   Ramadhan is the (month) in which was sent down the Qur'an, as a guide to mankind, also clear (Signs) for guidance and judgment (between right and wrong). So every one of you who is present (at his home) during that month should spend it in fasting, but if any one is ill, or on a journey, the prescribed period (should be made up) by days later. Allah intends every facility for you; He does not want to put you to difficulties. (He wants you) to complete the prescribed period, and to glorify Him in that He has guided you; and perchance you shall be grateful.

186.   When My servants ask you concerning Me, I am indeed close (to them): I listen to the prayer of every suppliant when he calls on Me: let them also, with a will, listen to My call, and believe in Me: that they may walk in the right way.

187.   Permitted to you, on the night of the fasts, is the approach to your wives. They are your garments and you are their garments. Allah knows what you used to do secretly among yourselves; but He turned to you and forgave you; so now associate with them, and seek what Allah has ordained for you, and eat and drink, until the white thread of dawn appear to you distinct from its black thread; then complete your fast till the night appears; but do not associate with your wives while you are in retreat in the mosques. Those are limits (set by) Allah: do not go near to those. Thus Allah makes clear His Signs to men: that they may learn self-restraint.

188.   And do not eat up your property among yourselves for vanities, nor use it as bait for the judges, with intent that you may eat up wrongfully and knowingly a little of (other) people's property.

189.   They ask you concerning the New Moons. Say: They are but

---

84.   Needy poor

signs to mark fixed periods of time in (the affairs of) men, and for Pilgrimage. It is no virtue if you enter your houses from the back: it is virtue if you fear Allah. Enter houses through the proper doors: and fear Allah: that you may achieve success.

190.   Fight in the cause of Allah those who fight you, but do not transgress limits; for Allah does not love transgressors.

191.   And slay them wherever you catch them, and turn them out from where they have turned you out; for tumult and oppression are worse than slaughter; but do not fight them at the Sacred Mosque, unless they (first) fight you there; but if they fight you, slay them. Such is the reward of those who suppress faith.

192.   But if they cease, Allah is Oft-Forgiving, Most Merciful.

193.   And fight them on until there is no more tumult or oppression, and there prevail justice and faith in Allah; but if they cease, let there be no hostility except to those who practise oppression.

194.   The prohibited month for the prohibited month,- and so for all things prohibited,- there is the law of equality. If then any one transgresses the prohibition against you, transgress you like-wise against him. But fear Allah, and know that Allah is with those who restrain themselves.

195.   And spend of your substance in the cause of Allah, and do not make your own hands contribute to (your) destruction; but do good; for Allah loves those who do good.

196.   And complete the Hajj or 'Umra in the service of Allah. But if you are prevented (from completing it), send an offering for sacrifice, such as you may find, and do not shave your heads until the offering reaches the place of sacrifice. And if any of you is ill, or has an ailment in his scalp, (necessitating shaving), (he should) in compensation either fast, or feed the poor, or offer sacrifice; and when you are in peaceful conditions (again), if any one wishes to continue the 'Umra or the Hajj, he must make an offering, such as he can afford, but if he cannot afford it, he should fast three days during the Hajj and seven days on his return, making ten days in all. This is for those whose household is not in (the precincts of) the Sacred Mosque. And

fear Allah, and know that Allah is strict in punishment.

197. For Hajj are the months well known. If any one undertakes that duty therein, let there be no obscenity, nor wickedness, nor wrangling in the Hajj. And whatever good you do, (be sure) Allah knows it. And take a provision (with you) for the journey, but the best of provisions is right conduct. So fear Me, O you that are wise.

198. It is no crime in you if you seek of the bounty of your Allah (during pilgrimage). Then when you pour down from (Mount) 'Arafat, celebrate the praises of Allah at the Sacred Monument, and celebrate His praises as He has directed you, even though, before this, you went astray.

199. Then pass on at a quick pace from the place whence it is usual for the multitude to do so, and ask for Allah's forgiveness. For Allah is Oft-Forgiving, Most Merciful.

200. So when you have accomplished your holy rites, celebrate the praises of Allah, as you used to celebrate the praises of your fathers,- yes, with far more heart and soul. There are men who say: "Our Allah! Give us (Your bounties) in this world!" but they will have no portion in the Hereafter.

201. And there are men who say: "Our Allah! Give us good in this world and good in the Hereafter, and save us from the torment of the Fire!"

202. To these will be allotted what they have earned; and Allah is quick in account.

203. Celebrate the praises of Allah during the Appointed Days. But if any one hastens to leave in two days, there is no blame on him, and if any one stays on, there is no blame on him, if his aim is to do right. Then fear Allah, and know that you will surely be gathered to Him.

204. There is the type of man whose speech about this world's life may dazzle you, and he calls Allah to witness about what is in his heart; yet he is the most contentious of enemies.

205. When he turns his back, his aim everywhere is to spread mischief through the earth and destroy crops and cattle. But

Allah does not love mischief.

206.   When it is said to him, "Fear Allah", he is led by arrogance to (more) crime. Enough for him is Hell; - an evil bed indeed (to lie on)!

207.   And there is the type of man who gives his life to earn the pleasure of Allah: and Allah is full of kindness to (His) devotees.

208.   O you who believe! Enter into Islam whole-heartedly; and do not follow the footsteps of the Satan; for he is to you an avowed enemy.

209.   If you backslide after the clear (Signs) have come to you, then know that Allah is Exalted in Power, Wise.

210.   Will they wait until Allah comes to them in canopies of clouds, with Angels (in His train) and the question is (thus) settled? but to Allah do all questions go back (for decision).

211.   Ask the Children of Israel how many Clear (Signs) We have sent them. But if any one, after Allah's favour has come to him, substitutes (something else), Allah is strict in punishment.

212.   The life of this world is alluring to those who reject faith, and they scoff at those who believe. But the righteous will be above them on the Day of Resurrection; for Allah bestows His abundance without measure on whom He will.

213.   Mankind was one single nation, and Allah sent Messengers with glad tidings and warnings; and with them He sent the Book in truth, to judge between people in matters wherein they differed; but the People of the Book, after the Clear Signs came to them, did not differ among themselves, except through selfish contumacy.[85] Allah by His Grace guided the Believers to the Truth, concerning that wherein they differed. For Allah guides whom He will to a path that is straight.

214.   Or do you think that you shall enter the Garden (of Bliss[86]) without such (trials) as came to those who passed away before you? They encountered suffe-ring and adversity, and were so shaken in spirit that even the Apostle and those of faith who

---

85.   Wilful disobedience to Allah   86.   Supreme joy, utter contentment

were with him cried: "When (will come) the help of Allah?" Ah! Verily, the help of Allah is (always) near!

215. They ask you what they should spend (in charity). Say: Whatever you spend that is good, is for parents and kindred and orphans and those in want and for wayfarers. And whatever you do that is good, - Allah knows it well.

216. Fighting is prescribed for you, and you dislike it. But it is possible that you dislike a thing which is good for you, and that you love a thing which is bad for you. But Allah knows, and you know not.

217. They ask you concerning fighting in the Prohibited Month. Say: "Fighting therein is a grave (offence); but graver is still in the sight of Allah to prevent access to the path of Allah, to deny Him, to prevent access to the Sacred Mosque, and drive out its members." Tumult and oppression are worse than slaughter. Nor will they cease fighting you until they turn you back from your faith if they can. And if any of you turn back from their faith and die in unbelief, their works will bear no fruit in this life and in the Hereafter; they will be companions of the Fire and will abide therein.

218. Those who believed and those who suffered exile and fought (and strove and struggled) in the path of Allah,- they have the hope of the Mercy of Allah: and Allah is Oft-Forgiving, Most Merciful.

219. They ask you concerning wine and gambling. Say: "In them is great sin, and some profit, for men; but the sin is greater than the profit." They ask you how much they are to spend; Say: "What is beyond your needs." Thus Allah makes clear to you His Signs: in order that you may consider-

220. (Their bearings) on this life and the Hereafter. They ask you concerning orphans. Say: "The best thing to do is what is for their good; if you mix their affairs with yours, they are your brethren; but Allah knows the man who means mischief from the man who means good. And if Allah had wished, He could have put you into difficulties: He is indeed Exalted in Power,

Wise."

221.   Do not marry unbelieving women (idolators), until they believe: a slave woman who believes is better than an unbelieving woman, even though she allure you. Nor marry (your girls) to unbelievers until they believe: a man slave who believes is better than an unbeliever, even though he allure you. Unbelievers do (but) beckon[87] you to the Fire. But Allah beckons by His Grace to the Garden (of Bliss) and forgiveness, and makes His Signs clear to mankind, so that they may celebrate His praise.

222.   They ask you concerning women's courses. Say: They are a hurt and a pollution: so keep away from women in their courses, and do not approach them until they are clean. But when they have purified themselves, you may approach them in any manner , time, or place ordained for you by Allah. For Allah loves those who turn to Him constantly and He loves those who keep themselves pure and clean.

223.   Your wives are a tilth[88] unto you; so approach your tilth when or how you will; but do some good act for your souls beforehand; and fear Allah. And know that you are to meet Him (in the Hereafter), and give (these) good tidings to those who believe.

224.   And make not Allah's (name) an excuse in your oaths against doing good, or acting rightly, or making peace between persons; for Allah is One Who hears and knows all things.

225.   Allah will not call you to account for thoughtlessness in your oaths, but for the intention in your hearts; and He is Oft-Forgiving, Most Forbearing.

226.   For those who take an oath for abstention from their wives, a waiting for four months is ordained; if then they return, Allah is Oft-Forgiving, Most Merciful.

227.   But if their intention is firm for divorce, Allah hears and knows all things.

---

87.   Lure to, summon on   88.   A cultivation, tillage

228.   Divorced women shall wait concerning themselves for three
        monthly periods. Nor is it lawful for them to hide what Allah
        has created in their wombs, if they have faith in Allah and the
        Last Day. And their husbands have the better right to take them
        back in that period, if they wish for reconciliation. And women
        shall have rights similar to the rights against them, according
        to what is equitable; but men have a degree (of advantage)
        over them. And Allah is Exalted in Power, Wise.

229.   A divorce is only permis-sible twice: after that, the parties
        should either hold together on equitable terms, or separate with
        kindness. It is not lawful for you, (men), to take back any of
        your gifts (from your wives), except when both parties fear
        that they would be unable to keep the limits ordained by Allah.
        If you (judges) do indeed fear that they would be unable to
        keep the limits ordained by Allah, there is no blame on either
        of them if she give something for her freedom. These are the
        limits ordained by Allah; so do not transgress them, if any do
        transgress the limits ordained by Allah, such persons wrong
        (themselves as well as others).

230.   So if a husband divorces his wife (irrevocably), he cannot,
        after that, re- marry her until after she has married another
        husband and he has divorced her. In that case there is no blame
        on either of them if they re-unite, provided they feel that they
        can keep the limits ordained by Allah. Such are the limits
        ordained[89] by Allah, which He makes plain to those who
        understand.

231.   When you divorce women, and they fulfil the term of their
        ('*Iddat*[90]), either take them back on equitable terms or set them
        free on equitable terms; but do not take them back to injure
        them, (or) to take undue advantage; if any one does that; he
        wrongs his own soul. Do not treat Allah's Signs as a jest, but

---

89.   Decreed, commanded or ordered
90.   The prescribed period of waiting during which a woman may not remarry
      after being widowed or divided.

solemnly rehearse Allah's favours on you, and the fact that He sent down to you the Book and Wisdom, for your instruction. And fear Allah, and know that Allah is well acquainted with all things.

232. When you divorce women, and they fulfil the term of their ('Iddat), do not prevent them from marrying their (former) husbands, if they mutually agree on equitable terms. This instruction is for all amongst you, who believe in Allah and the Last Day. That is (the course making for) most virtue and purity amongst you. And Allah knows, and you do not know.

233. The mothers shall give suck to their offspring for two whole years, if the father desires to complete the term. But he shall bear the cost of their food and clothing on equitable terms. No soul shall have a burden laid on it greater than it can bear. No mother shall be treated unfairly on account of her child. Nor father on account of his child, an heir shall be chargeable in the same way. If they both decide on weaning, by mutual consent, and after due consultation, there is no blame on them. If you decide on a foster-mother for your offspring, there is no blame on you, provided you pay (the mother) what you offered, on equitable terms. But fear Allah and know that Allah sees well what you do.

234. If any of you die and leave widows behind, they shall wait concerning themselves four months and ten days: when they have fulfilled their term, there is no blame on you if they dispose of themselves in a just and reasonable manner. And Allah is well acquainted with what you do.

235. There is no blame on you if you make an offer of betrothal[91] or hold it in your hearts. Allah knows that you cherish them in your hearts: but do not make a secret contract with them except in terms honourable, nor resolve on the tie of marriage till the term prescribed is fulfilled. And know that Allah knows what is in your hearts, and take heed of Him; and know that Allah is

---

91.   Engagement.

Oft-Forgiving, Most Forbearing.

236.   There is no blame on you if you divorce women before consummation or the fixation of their dower; but bestow on them (a suitable gift), the wealthy according to his means, and the poor according to his means;- a gift of a reasonable amount is due from those who wish to do the right thing.

237.   And if you divorce them before consummation, but after the fixation of a dower for them, then the half of the dower (is due to them), unless they remit it or (the man's half) is remitted by him in whose hands is the marriage tie; and the remission (of the man's half) is the nearest to righteousness. And do not forget liberality between yourselves. For Allah sees well all that you do.

238.   Guard strictly your (habit of) prayers, especially the Middle Prayer; and stand before Allah in a devout (frame of mind).

239.   If you fear (an enemy), pray on foot, or riding, (as may be most convenient), but when you are in security, celebrate Allah's praises in the manner He has taught you, which you knew not (before).

240.   Those of you who die and leave widows should bequeath for their widows a year's maintenance and residence; but if they leave (the residence), there is no blame on you for what they do with themselves, provided it is reasonable. And Allah is Exal-ted in Power, Wise.

241.   For divorced women maintenance (should be provi-ded) on a reasonable (scale). This is a duty on the righteous.

242.   Thus Allah Makes clear His Signs to you: in order that you may understand.

243.   Did you not turn your vision to those who abandoned their homes, though they were thousands (in number), for fear of death? Allah said to them: "Die"! Then He restored them to life. For Allah is full of bounty[92] to mankind, but most of them are ungrateful.

---

92.   Generosity, mercy or grace

244. Then fight in the cause of Allah, and know that Allah hears and knows all things.

245. Who is he that will loan to Allah a beautiful loan, which Allah will double unto his credit and multiply many times? It is Allah that gives (you) Want or Plenty, and to Him shall be your return.

246. Have you not turned your vision to the Chiefs of the Children of Israel after (the time of) Moses? They said to a Prophet (that was) among them: "Appoint for us a King, that we may fight in the cause of Allah." He said: "Is it not possible, if you were commanded to fight, that you will not fight?" They said: "How could we refuse to fight in the cause of Allah, seeing that we were turned out of our homes and our families?" But when they were commanded to fight, they turned back, except a small band among them. But Allah has full knowledge of those who do wrong.

247. Their Prophet said to them: "Allah has appointed Talut as king over you." They said: "How can he exercise authority over us when we are better fitted than he to exercise authority, and he is not even gifted, with wealth in abundance?" He said: "Allah has chosen him above you, and has gifted him abundantly with knowledge and bodily prowess[93]: Allah grants His authority to whom He pleases. Allah cares for all, and He knows all things."

248. And (further) their Prophet said to them: "A Sign of his authority is that there shall come to you the Ark of the Covenant, with (an assurance) therein of security from your Allah, and the relics[94] left by the family of Moses and the family of Aaron, carried by Angels. In this is a symbol for you if you indeed have faith."

249. When Talut set forth with the armies, he said: "Allah will test you at the stream: if any drinks of its water, he does not go with my army: only those who do not taste of it go with me: a mere sip out of the hand is excused." But they all drank of it,

---

93. Exceptional ability, skill or strength.
94. Surviving memorials.

except a few. When they crossed the river,- he and the faithful ones with him,- they said: "This day We cannot cope with Goliath and his forces." But those who were convinced that they must meet Allah, said: "How oft, by Allah's will, has a small force vanquished a big one? Allah is with those who steadfastly persevere."

250.   When they advanced to meet Goliath and his forces, they prayed: "Our Allah! Pour out constancy on us and make our steps firm: help us against those that reject faith."

251.   By Allah's will, they routed them; and David slew Goliath; and Allah gave him power and wisdom and taught him whatever (else) He willed. And did not Allah check one set of people by means of another, the earth would indeed be full of mischief: But Allah is full of bounty to all the worlds.

252.   These are the Signs of Allah: we rehearse them to you in truth: verily you are one of the Apostles.

253.   Those Messengers We endowed with gifts, some above others: to one of them Allah spoke; others He raised to degrees (of honour); to Jesus the son of Mary We gave Clear (Signs), and strengthened him with the holy spirit. If Allah had so willed, succeeding gene-rations would not have fought among each other, after Clear (Signs) had come to them, but they (chose) to wrangle, some believing and others rejecting. If Allah had so willed, they would not have fought each other; but Allah fulfills His plan.

254.   O you who believe! spend out of (the bounties) We have provided for you, before the Day comes when no bargaining (will avail), nor friendship nor intercession. Those who reject Faith- they are the wrong-doers.

255.   Allah! There is no god but He,-the Living, the Self-subsisting, Eternal. No slumber can seize Him nor sleep. His are all things in the heavens and on earth. Who is there can intercede in His presence except as He permits? He knows what (appears to His creatures as) Before or After or Behind them. Nor shall they compass of His knowledge except as He wills. His Throne

extends over the heavens and the earth, and He feels no fatigue in guarding and preserving them for He is the Most High, the Supreme (in glory).

256. Let there be no compul-sion in religion: Truth stands out clear from Error: whoever rejects Evil and believes in Allah has grasped the most trust-worthy hand-hold, that never breaks. And Allah hears and knows all things.

257. Allah is the Protector of those who have faith: from the depths of darkness He will lead them forth into light. Of those who reject faith the patrons are the Evil Ones: from light they will lead them forth into the depths of darkness. They will be companions of the fire, to dwell therein (for ever).

258. Have you not turned your vision to one who disputed with Abraham about his Allah, because Allah had granted him power? Abraham said: "My Allah is He Who gives life and death."He said: "I give life and death". Said Abraham: "But it is Allah that causes the sun to rise from the East: do you then cause it to rise from the West." Thus was he confounded who (in arrogance) rejected Faith. Nor does Allah give guidance to a people unjust.

259. Or (take) the similitude of one who passed by a hamlet[95], all in ruins to its roofs. He said: "Oh! how shall Allah bring it (ever) to life, after (this) its death?" but Allah caused him to die for a hundred years, then raised him up (again). He said: "How long did you tarry[96] (thus)?" He said: (Perhaps) a day or part of a day." He said: "Nay, you have tarried thus a hundred years; but look at your food and your drink; they show no signs of age; and look at your donkey: And that We may make of you a Sign for the people, Look further at the bones, how We bring them together and clothe them with flesh." When this was shown clearly to him, he said: "I know that Allah has power over all things."

260. Behold! Abraham said: "My Allah! Show me how You give

---

95. A small village   96. Stay

life to the dead." He said: "Do you not then believe?" He said: "Yes! but to satisfy my own understanding." He said: "Take four birds; tame them to turn to you; put a portion of them on every hill and call to them: they will come to you (flying) with speed. Then know that Allah is Exalted in Power, Wise."

261. The parable of those who spend their substance in the way of Allah is that of a grain of corn: it grows seven ears, and each ear has a hundred grains. Allah gives manifold increase to whom He pleases: and Allah cares for all and He knows all things.

262. Those who spend their substance in the cause of Allah, and do not follow up their gifts with reminders of their generosity or with injury,-for them their reward is with their Lord: on them shall be no fear, nor shall they grieve.

263. Kind words and the covering of faults are better than charity followed by injury. Allah is Free of all wants, and He is Most Forbearing.

264. O you who believe! waste not your charity by reminders of your generosity or by injury,- like those who spend their substance to be seen of men, but believe neither in Allah nor in the Last Day. They are in parable like a hard, barren rock, on which is a little soil: on it falls heavy rain, which leaves it (Just) a bare stone. They will be able to do nothing with anything they have earned. And Allah does not guide those who reject faith.

265. And the likeness of those who spend their substance, seeking to please Allah and to strengthen their souls, is as a garden, high and fertile: heavy rain falls on it but makes it yield a double increase of harvest, and if it does not receive heavy rain, light moisture suffices it. Allah sees well whatever you do.

266. Does any of you wish that he should have a garden with date-palms and vines and streams flowing underneath, and all kinds of fruit, while he is stricken with old age, and his children are not strong (enough to look after themselves)- that it should be caught in a whirlwind, with fire therein, and be burnt up? Thus does Allah make clear to you (His) Signs; that you may

consider.

267. O you who believe! Give of the good things which you have (honourably) earned, and of the fruits of the earth which We have produced for you, and do not even aim at getting anything which is bad, in order that out of it you may give away something, when you yourselves would not receive it except with closed eyes. And know that Allah is Free of all wants, and Worthy of all praise.

268. Satan threatens you with poverty and bids you to conduct unseemly. Allah promises you His forgiveness and bounties. And Allah cares for all and He knows all things.

269. He grants wisdom to whom He pleases; and he to whom wisdom is granted receives indeed a benefit overflowing; but none will grasp the Message but men of understanding.

270. And whatever you spend in charity or devotion, be sure Allah knows it all. But the wrong-doers have no helpers.

271. If you disclose (acts of) charity, even so it is well, but if you conceal them, and make them reach those (really) in need, that is best for you: It will remove from you some of your (stains of) evil. And Allah is well acquainted with what you do.

272. It is not required of you (O Apostle), to set them on the right path, but Allah sets on the right path whom He pleases. Whatever of good you give benefits your own souls, and you shall only do so seeking the "Face" of Allah. Whatever good you give, shall be rendered back to you, and you shall not be dealt with unjustly.

273. (Charity is) for those in need, who, in Allah's cause are restricted (from travel), and cannot move about in the land, seeking (for trade or work): the ignorant man thinks, because of their modesty, that they are free from want. You shall know them by their (unfailing) mark: they do not beg importunately[97] from all and sundry[98]. And whatever of good you give, be assured Allah knows it well.

---

97. Persistently   98. All individually and collectively

274.   Those who (in charity) spend of their goods by night and by day, in secret and in public, have their reward with their Lord: on them shall be no fear, nor shall they grieve.

275.   Those who devour interest[99] will not stand except as stands one whom the Satan One by his touch has driven to madness. That is because they say: "Trade is like interest," but Allah has permitted trade and forbidden interest. Those who after receiving direction from their Lord, desist, shall be pardoned for the past; their case is for Allah (to judge); but those who repeat (the offence) are com-panions of the Fire: they will abide therein (for ever).

276.   Allah will deprive interest of all blessing, but will give increase for deeds of charity: for He does not love ungrateful and wicked creatures.

277.   Those who believe, and do deeds of righteousness, and establish regular prayers and regular charity, will have their reward with their Lord: on them shall be no fear, nor shall they grieve.

278.   O you who believe! Fear Allah, and give up what remains of your demand for interest, if you are indeed believers.

279.   If you do it not, take notice of war from Allah and His Apostle: but if you turn back, you shall have your capital sums, deal not unjustly, and you shall not be dealt with unjustly.

280.   If the debtor is in a difficulty, grant him time till it is easy for him to repay. But if you remit it by way of charity, that is best for you if you only knew.

281.   And fear the Day when you shall be brought back to Allah. Then shall every soul be paid what it earned, and none shall be dealt with unjustly.

282.   O you who believe! When you deal with each other, in transactions involving future obligations in a fixed period of time, reduce them to writing. Let a scribe[100] write down faithfully as between the parties: let not the scribe refuse to

---

99.   Receiving in excess on money lent to others.
100. One who writes down.

write: as Allah has taught him, so let him write. Let him who incurs the liability dictate, but let him fear His Lord Allah, and not diminish anything of what he owes. If the party liable is mentally deficient, or weak, or unable himself to dictate, Let his guardian dictate faithfully. And get two witnesses, out of your own men, and if there are not two men, then a man and two women, such as you choose, for witnesses, so that if one of them errs, the other can remind her. The witnesses should not refuse when they are called on (for evidence). Disdain not to reduce to writing (your contract) for a future period, whether it be small or big: it is juster[101] in the sight of Allah, more suitable as evidence, and more convenient to prevent doubts among yourselves but if it be a transaction which you carry out on the spot among yourselves, there is no blame on you if you reduce it not to writing. But take witnesses whenever you make a commercial contract; and let neither scribe nor witness suffer harm. If you do (such harm), it would be wickedness in you. So fear Allah; for it is Allah that teaches you. And Allah is well acquainted with all things.

283.   If you are on a journey, and cannot find a scribe, a pledge[102] with possession (may serve the purpose). And if one of you deposits a thing on trust with another, Let the trustee (faithfully) discharge his trust, and let him fear his Lord. Conceal not evidence; for whoever conceals it,- his heart is tainted with sin. And Allah knows all that you do.

284.   To Allah belongs all that is in the heavens and on earth. Whether you show what is in your minds or conceal it, Allah calls you to account for it. He forgives whom He pleases, and punishes whom He pleases. For Allah has power over all things.

285.   The Apostle believes in what has been revealed to him from his Lord, as do the men of faith. Each one (of them) believes

---

101.   More Just
102.   Something given as security for the payment of a debt or fulfillment of a promise.

in Allah, His Angels, His Books, and His Apostles. "We make no distinction (they say) between one and another of His Apostles." And they say: "We hear, and we obey: (we seek) Your forgiveness, Our Lord, and to You is the end of all journeys."

286. On no soul Allah places a burden greater than it can bear. It gets every good that it earns, and it suffers every ill that it earns. (Pray:) "Our Lord! do not condemn us if we forget or fall into error; our Lord! do not lay on us a burden like that which You did lay on those before us; our Lord! do not lay on us a burden greater than we have strength to bear. Blot out our sins, and grant us forgiveness. Have mercy on us. You are our Protector; help us against those who stand against Faith

SURAH—3
AL-I-IMRAN
(INTRODUCTION)

This Surah is cognate to Surah 2, but the matter is here treated from a different point of view. The references to Badr (Ramadhan, H, 2) and Uhud (Shawwal, H. 3) give a clue to the dates of those passages.

Like Surah 2, it takes a general view of the religious history of mankind, with special reference to the People of the Book, proceeds to explain the birth of the new People of Islam and their ordinances, insists on the need of struggle and fighting in the cause of Truth, and exhorts those who have been blessed with Islam to remain constant in Faith, pray for guidance, and maintain their spiritual hope for the Future.

The new points of view developed are: (1) The emphasis is here laid on the duty of the Christians to accept the new light; the Christians are here specially appealed to as the jews were specially appealed to in the last Surah; (2) the lessons of the battles of Badr and Uhud are set out for the Muslim community; and (3) the responsibilities of that community are insisted on both internally and in their relations to those outside.

SURAH AL-'IMRAN (THE FAMILY OF 'IMRAN)

In the name of Allah, Most Gracious, Most Merciful

1. Alif-Lam-Mim

2. Allah! There is no god but He,-the Living, the Self-Subsisting[1], Eternal.

3. It is He Who sent down to you (step by step), in truth, the Book, confirming what went before it; and He sent down the Law (of Moses) and the Gospel (of Jesus).

4. Before this, as a guide to mankind, and He sent down the Criterion (of judgment between right and wrong). Then those who reject Faith in the Signs of Allah will suffer the severest chastisement, and Allah is Exalted in Might, Lord of Retribution.[2]

---

1. Existing by Himself and does not depend on anyone else.
2. Dispensing of reward and punishment.

5.   From Allah, verily nothing is hidden on earth or in the heavens.

6.   He it is Who shapes you in the wombs as He pleases. There is no god but He, the Exalted in Might, the Wise.

7.   He it is Who has sent down to you the Book: In it are verses basic or fundamental (of established meaning); they are the foundation of the Book: others are allegorical.[3] But those in whose hearts is perversity follow the part thereof that is allegorical, seeking discord, and searching for its hidden meanings, but no one knows its hidden meanings except Allah. And those who are firmly grounded in knowledge say: "We believe in the Book; the whole of it is from our Lord:" and none will grasp the Message except men of understanding.

8.   "Our Lord!" (they say), "Let not our hearts deviate now after You have guided us, but grant us mercy from Your Own Presence; for You are the Grantor of boun-ties without measure.

9.   "Our Lord! You are He that will gather mankind together against a Day about which there is no doubt; for Allah never fails in His promise."

10.   Those who reject Faith,- neither their possessions nor their (numerous) progeny will avail them nothing against Allah: they are themselves but fuel for the Fire.

11.   (Their plight will be) no better than that of the people of Pharaoh, and their pre-decessors: they denied our Signs, and Allah called them to account for their sins. For Allah is strict in punishment.

12.   Say to those who reject Faith: "Soon will you be vanquished[4] and gathered together to Hell,-an evil bed indeed (to lie on)!

13.   "There has already been for you a Sign in the two armies that met (in combat): one was fighting in the cause of Allah, the other resisting Allah; these saw with their own eyes twice their number. But Allah supports with His aid whom He pleases. In this is a warning for such as have eyes to see."

---

3.   Representing moral, spritual and abstract meanings figuratively or through symbols.   4.   Defeated

14. Fair in the eyes of men is the love of things they covet: Women and sons; heaped-up hoards of gold and silver; horses branded (for breed and excellence); and (wealth of) cattle and well-tilled land. Such are the possessions of this world's life; but in nearness to Allah is the best of the goals (to return to).

15. Say: Shall I give you glad tidings of things for better than those? For the righteous are Gardens in nearness to their Lord, with rivers flowing beneath; therein is their eternal home; with Companions pure (and holy); and the good pleasure of Allah. For in Allah's sight are (all) His servants.

16. (Namely), those who say: "Our Lord! we have indeed believed: forgive us, then, our sins, and save us from the agony of the Fire;"-

17. Those who show patience, firmness and self-control; who are true (in word and deed); who worship devoutly; who spend (in the way of Allah); and who pray for forgiveness in the early hours of the morning.

18. There is no god but He: that is the witness of Allah, His angels, and those endued with knowledge, standing firm on justice. There is no god but He, the Exalted in Power, the Wise.

19. The Religion before Allah is Islam (submission to His Will): nor did the People of the Book dissent therefrom except through envy of each other, after knowledge had come to them. But if any deny the Signs of Allah, Allah is swift in calling to account.

20. So if they dispute with you, say: "I have submitted my whole self to Allah and so have those who follow me." And say to the People of the Book and to those who are unlearned: "Do you (also) submit yourselves?" If they do, they are in right guidance, but if they turn back, your duty is to convey the Message; and in Allah's sight are (all) His servants.

21. As to those who deny the Signs of Allah, and in defiance of right, slay the prophets, and slay those who teach just dealing with mankind, announce to them a grievous chastisement.

22. They are those whose works will bear no fruit in this world and in the Hereafter, nor will they have anyone to help.

23. Have you not turned your vision to those who have been given a portion of the Book? They are invited to the Book of Allah, to settle their dispute, but a party of them turn back and decline (the arbitration).

24. This because they say: "The Fire shall not touch us but for a few numbered days": for their forgeries deceive them as to their own religion.

25. But how (will they fare) when We gather them together against a Day about which there is no doubt, and each soul will be paid out just what it has earned, without (favour or) injustice?

26. Say: "O Allah! Lord of Power (and Rule), You give power to whom You please, and You strip off power from whom You please: You endue with honour whom You please, and You bring low whom You please: In Your hand is all good. Verily, over all things You have power.

27. "You cause the Night to gain on the Day, and You cause the Day to gain on the Night; You bring the Living out of the Dead, and You bring the Dead out of the Living; and You give sustenance to whom You please, without measure ."

28. Let not the Believers take for friends or helpers Unbelievers rather than Believers: if any do that, in nothing will there be help from Allah: except by way of precaution, that you may guard yourselves from them. But Allah cautions you (to remember) Himself; for the final goal is to Allah.

29. Say: "Whether you hide what is in your hearts or reveal it, Allah knows it all: He knows what is in the heavens, and what is on earth. And Allah has power over all things.

30. "On the Day when every soul will be confronted with all the good it has done, and all the evil it has done, it will wish there were a great distance between it and its evil. But Allah cautions you (to remember) Himself. And Allah is full of kindness to those that serve Him."

31. Say: "If you do love Allah, follow me: Allah will love you and forgive you your sins: for Allah is Oft-Forgiving, Most Merciful."

32. Say: "Obey Allah and His Apostle": but if they turn back, Allah does not love those who reject Faith.

33. Allah chose Adam and Noah, the family of Abraham, and the family of 'Imran above all people,-

34. Offspring, one of the other: and Allah hears and knows all things.

35. Behold! a woman of 'Imran said: "O my Lord! I do dedicate unto You what is in my womb for Your special service: So accept this of me: for You hear and know all things."

36. When she delivered (the baby girl) she said: "O my Lord! Behold! I have delivered a female child!"- and Allah knew best what she brought forth- "And no wise is the male like the female. I have named her Mary, and I commend her and her offspring to Your protection from Satan, the Rejected."

37. Right graciously did her Lord accept her: He made her grow in purity and beauty: she was assigned to the care of Zakariya. Every time that he entered (Her) chamber to see her, He found her supplied with sustenance. He said: "O Mary! Wherefrom (comes) this to you?" She said: "From Allah: for Allah provides sustenance to whom He pleases without measure."

38. Zakariya prayed there to his Lord, saying: "O my Lord! Grant unto me from Your presence a progeny that is pure: for You are He Who hears prayer!

39. While he was standing in prayer in the chamber, the angels called unto him: "Allah gives you the glad tidings of Yahya, confirming the truth of a Word from Allah, and be (besides) noble, chaste, and a prophet,- of the (goodly) company of the righteous."

40. He said: "O my Lord! how shall I have a son, seeing I am very old, and my wife is barren?" "Thus," was the answer, "Allah accomplishes what He wills."

41. He said: "O my Lord! give me a Sign!" "Your Sign," was the answer, "shall be that you shall speak to no man for three days but with signals. Then celebrate the praises of your Lord again and again, and glorify Him in the evening and in the morning."

42.   Behold! the angels said: "O Mary! Allah has chosen you and purified you- chosen you above the women of all nations.

43   "O Mary! worship your Lord devoutly: Prostrate yourself and bow down (in prayer) with those who bow down."

44.   This is part of the tidings of the things unseen, which We reveal unto you (O Apostle!) by inspiration: you were not with them when they cast lots with arrows, as to which of them should be charged with the care of Mary: nor were you with them when they disputed (the point).

45.   Behold! the angels said: "O Mary! Allah gives you glad tidings of a Word from Him: his name will be Christ Jesus, the son of Mary, held in honour in this world and the Hereafter and of (the company of) those nearest to Allah;

46.   "He shall speak to the people in infancy and in maturity. And he shall be (of the company) of the righteous."

47.   She said: "O my Lord! how shall I have a son when no man has touched me?" He said: "Even so: Allah creates what He wills: When He has decreed a Plan, He but says to it, 'Be,' and it is!

48.   "And Allah will teach him the Book and Wisdom, the Torah and the Gospel,?

49.   "And (appoint him) an Apostle to the Children of Israel, (with this message): "'I have come to you, with a Sign from your Lord, in that I make for you out of clay, as it were, the figure of a bird, and breathe into it, and it becomes a bird by Allah's leave: and I heal those born blind, and the lepers, and I quicken[5] the dead, by Allah's leave; and I declare to you what you eat, and what you store in your houses. Surely therein is a Sign for you if you did believe;

50.   "'(I have come to you), to attest the Torah which was before me. And to make lawful to you part of what was (before) forbidden to you; I have come to you with a Sign from your Lord. So fear Allah, and obey me.

---

5.   To restore to life.

51. "'It is Allah Who is my Lord and your Lord; then worship Him. This is a Way that is straight.'"

52. When Jesus found unbelief on their part, he said: "Who will be my helpers to (the work of) Allah?" Said the disciples: "We are Allah's helpers: We believe in Allah, and you bear witness that we are Muslims.

53. "Our Lord! we believe in what You have revealed, and we follow the Apostle; then write us down among those who bear witness."

54. And (the unbelievers) plotted and planned, and Allah too planned, and the best of planners is Allah.

55. Behold! Allah said: "O Jesus! I will take you and raise you to Myself and clear you (of the falsehoods) of those who blaspheme; I will make those who follow you superior to those who reject faith, to the Day of Resurrection: then you shall all return to me, and I will judge between you of the matters wherein you dispute.

56. "As to those who reject faith, I will punish them with terrible agony in this world and in the Hereafter, nor will they have anyone to help."

57. "As to those who believe and work righteousness, Allah will pay them (in full) their reward; but Allah does not love those who do wrong."

58. "This is what We rehearse[6] to you of the Signs and the Message of Wisdom."

59. The similitude of Jesus before Allah is as that of Adam; He created him from dust, then said to him: "Be". And he was.

60. The Truth (comes) from Allah alone; so be not of those who doubt.

61. If any one disputes in this matter with you, now after (full) knowledge has come to you, say: "Come! let us gather together,- our sons and your sons, our women and your women, ourselves and yourselves: then let us earnestly pray, and invoke the curse

---

6.   Repeat

of Allah on those who lie!"

62. This is the true account: there is no god except Allah; and Allah-He is indeed the Exalted in Power, the Wise.

63. But if they turn back, Allah has full knowledge of those who do mischief.

64. Say: "O People of the Book! come to common terms as between us and you: that we worship none but Allah; that we associate no partners with Him; that we do not erect, from among ourselves, Lords and patrons other than Allah." If then they turn back, you say: "Bear witness that we (at least) are Muslims (bowing to Allah's Will).

65. You People of the Book! Why do you dispute about Abraham, when the Torah and the Gospel were not revealed till after him? Have you no understanding?

66. Ah! You are those who fell to disputing (even) in matters of which you had some knowledge! but why do you dispute in matters of which you have no knowledge? It is Allah Who knows, and you who do not know!

67. Abraham was not a Jew nor yet a Christian; but he was true in Faith, and bowed his will to Allah's (Which is Islam), and he did not join gods with Allah.

68. Without doubt, among men, the nearest of kin to Abraham, are those who follow him, as are also this Apostle and those who believe: And Allah is the Protector of those who have Faith.

69. It is the wish of a section of the People of the Book to lead you astray. But they shall lead astray (not you), but them-selves, and they do not perceive!

70. You People of the Book! Why do you reject the Signs of Allah, of which you are (yourselves) witnesses?

71. You People of the Book! Why do you clothe Truth with falsehood, and conceal the Truth, while you have knowledge?

72. A section of the People of the Book say: "Believe in the morning what is revealed to the Believers, but reject it at the end of the

---

7.   Injil

day; perchance they may (themselves) turn back;

73.   "And believe no one unless he follows your religion." Say: "True guidance is the guidance of Allah: (fear you) lest a revelation be sent to someone (else) like that which was sent to you? Or that those (receiving such revelation) should engage you in argument before your Lord?" Say: "All bounties are in the hand of Allah: He grants them to whom He pleases: and Allah cares for all, and He knows all things."

74.   For His Mercy He specially chooses whom He pleases; for Allah is the Lord of bounties unbounded.

75.   Among the People of the Book are some who, if entrusted with a hoard of gold, will (readily) pay it back; others, who, if entrusted with a single silver coin, will not repay it unless you constantly stood demanding, because, they say, "there is no call on us (to keep faith) with these ignorant (Pagans)." But they tell a lie against Allah, and (well) they know it.

76.   Nay, those that keep their plighted[8] faith and act aright, verily Allah loves those who act aright.

77.   As for those who sell the faith they owe to Allah and their own plighted word for a small price, they shall have no portion in the Hereafter: nor will Allah (deign[9]) to speak to them or look at them on the Day of Judgment, nor will He cleanse them (of sin): they shall have a grievous Chastise-ment.

78.   There is among them a section who distort the Book with their tongues: (as they read) you would think it is a part of the Book, but it is no part of the Book; and they say, "That is from Allah," but it is not from Allah: it is they who tell a lie against Allah, and (well) they know it!

79.   It is not (possible) that a man, to whom is given the Book, and Wisdom, and the Prophetic Office, should say to people: "You be my worshippers rather than Allah's": on the contrary (he would say) "You be worshippers of Him Who is truly the Cherisher of all: for you had taught the Book, and you have

---

8.   Pledge, bond or Covenant   9.   To think fit, to condescend to

studied it earnestly."

80.   Nor would he instruct you to take angels and prophets for Lords and Patrons. What! would he bid you to unbelief after you have bowed your will (to Allah in Islam)?

81.   Behold! Allah took the Covenant of the Prophets, saying: "I give you a Book and Wisdom; then comes to you an Apostle, confirming what is with you; you believe in him and render him help." Allah said: "Do you agree, and take this My Covenant as binding on you?" They said: "We agree." He said: "Then bear witness, and I am with you among the witnesses."

82.   If any turn back after this, they are perverted[10] trans-gressors.

83.   Do they seek for other than the Religion of Allah?- while all creatures in the heavens and on the earth have, willingly or unwillingly, bowed to His Will (accepted Islam), and to Him shall they all be brought back.

84.   Say: "We believe in Allah, and in what has been revealed to us and what was revealed to Abraham, Isma'il, Isaac, Jacob, and the Tribes, and in (the Books) given to Moses, Jesus, and the Prophets, from their Lord: we make no distinction between one and another among them, and to Allah do we bow our will (in Islam)."

85.   If anyone desires a religion other than Islam (submission to Allah), never will it be accepted of him; and in the Hereafter he will be in the ranks of those who have lost (all spiritual good).

86.   How shall Allah guide those who reject Faith after they accepted it and bore witness that the Apostle was true and that Clear Signs had come to them? But Allah does not guide a people unjust.

87.   Of such the reward is that on them (rests) the curse of Allah, of His angels, and of all mankind;-

88.   In that will they dwell; nor will their Chastisement be lightened, nor respite be their (lot);-

---

10.   Morally stray

89. Except for those that repent (even) after that, and make amends; for verily Allah is Oft-Forgiving, Most Merciful.

90. But those who reject Faith after they accepted it, and then go on adding to their defiance of Faith, - never will their repentance be accepted; for they are those who have (of set purpose) gone astray.

91. As to those who reject Faith, and die rejecting, - never would be accepted from any such as much gold as the earth contains, though they should offer it for ransom. For such is (in store) a Chastisement grievous, and they will find no helpers.

92. By no means shall you attain righteousness unless you give (freely) of that which you love; and whatever you give, of a truth Allah knows it well.

93. All food was lawful to the Children of Israel, except what Israel made unlawful for itself, before the Law (of Moses) was revealed. Say: " you bring the Law and study it, if you be men of truth."

94. If any, after this, invent a lie and attribute it to Allah, they are indeed unjust wrong-doers.

95. Say: "Allah speaks the Truth: follow the religion of Abraham, the sane in faith; he was not of the Pagans."

96. The first House (of worship) appointed for men was that at Bakka (Makkah); full of blessing and of guidance for all kinds of beings:

97. In it are Signs manifest; (for example), the Station of Abraham; whoever enters it attains security; pilgrimage thereto is a duty men owe to Allah,- those who can afford the journey; but if any deny faith, Allah does not stand in need of any of His creatures.

98. Say: "O People of the Book! Why do you reject the Signs of Allah, when Allah is Himself witness to all you do?"

99. Say: "O you People of the Book! Why do you obstruct those who believe, from the path of Allah, seeking to make it crooked, while you were yourselves witnesses (to Allah's Covenant)? But Allah is not unmindful of all that you do."

100. O you who believe! If you listen to a faction among the People of the Book, they would (indeed) render you apostates[11] after you have believed!

101. And how would you deny Faith while unto you are rehearsed the Signs of Allah, and among you lives the Apostle? Whoever holds firmly to Allah will be shown a Way that is straight.

102. O you who believe! Fear Allah as He should be feared, and do not die except in a state of Islam.

103. And hold fast, all together, by the Rope which Allah (stretches out for you), and be not divided among yourselves; and remember with gratitude Allah's favour on you; for you were enemies and He joined your hearts in love, so that by His Grace, you became brethren; and you were on the brink of the Pit of Fire, and He saved you from it. Thus Allah makes His Signs clear to you: that you may be guided.

104. Let there arise out of you a band of people inviting to all that is good, enjoining what is right, and forbidding what is wrong: they are the ones to attain felicity.[12]

105. Be not like those who are divided amongst themselves and fall into disputations[13] after receiving Clear Signs: for them is a dreadful Chastisement,-

106. On the Day when some faces will be (lit up with) white, and some faces will be (in the gloom of) black: to those whose faces will be black, (will be said): "Did you reject Faith after accepting it? Taste then the Chas-tisement for rejecting Faith."

107. But those whose faces will be (lit with) white,- they will be in (the light of) Allah's mercy: therein to dwell (for ever).

108. These are the Signs of Allah: We rehearse them to you in Truth: and Allah means no injustice to any of His creatures.

109. To Allah belongs all that is in the heavens and on earth: to Him do all questions go back (for decision).

---

11.   Those who abandon their religious faith.
12.   Bliss, supreme joy.
13.   Controversies, wrangling or bickerings.

110. You are the best of peoples, evolved for mankind, enjoining what is right, forbidding what is wrong, and believing in Allah. If only the People of the Book had faith, it were best for them: among them are some who have faith, but most of them are perverted transgressors.

111. They will do you no harm, barring a trifling annoyance;[14] if they come out to fight you, they will show you their backs, and no help shall they get.

112. Shame is pitched[15] over them (like a tent) wherever they are found, except when under a covenant (of protection) from Allah and from men; they draw on themselves wrath from Allah, and pitched over them is (the tent of) destitution. This because they rejected the Signs of Allah, and slew the Prophets in defiance[16] of right; this because they rebelled and transgressed beyond bounds.

113. Not all of them are alike: of the People of the Book are a portion that stand (for the right): they rehearse the Signs of Allah all night long, and they prostrate themselves in adoration.

114. They believe in Allah and the Last Day; they enjoin what is right, and forbid what is wrong; and they hasten (in emulation)[17] in (all) good works: they are in the ranks of the righteous.

115. Of the good that they do, nothing will be rejected of them; for Allah knows well those that do right.

116. Those who reject Faith,- neither their possessions nor their (numerous) progeny will avail them anything against Allah: they will be Companions of the Fire,- dwelling therein (for ever).

117. What they spend in the life of this (material) world may be likened to a wind which brings a nipping[18] frost: it strikes and destroys the harvest of men who have wronged their own souls:it is not Allah that has wronged them, but they wrong

---

14. A small nuisance
15. Set up, or hurled at them
16. Open disregard
17. In an effort to excel others.
18. Sharp and painful.

them-selves.

118.   O you who believe! take not into your intimacy those outside
your ranks: they will not fail to corrupt you. They only desire
your ruin: rank hatred[19] has already appeared from their mouths:
what their hearts conceal is far worse. We have made plain to
you the Signs, if you have wisdom.

119.   Ah! you are those who love them, but they do not love you,
though you believe in the whole of the Book. When they meet
you, they say, "We believe": but when they are alone, they bite
off the very tips of their fingers at you in their rage. Say: "Perish
in your rage; Allah knows well all the secrets of the heart."

120.   If anything that is good befalls you, it grieves them; but if
some misfortune overtakes you, they rejoice at it. But if you
are constant and do right, not the least harm will their cunning
do to you; for Allah compasses round about all that they do.

121.   Remember that morning you left your household (early) to
post the Faithful at their stations for battle: and Allah hears
and knows all things:

122.   Remember two of your parties meditated cowardice; but Allah
was their Protector, and in Allah the Faithful should (ever) put
their trust.

123.   Allah had helped you at Badr, when you were an insignificant
little force; then fear Allah; thus you may show your gratitude.

124.   Remember you said to the Faithful: "Is it not enough for you
that Allah should help you with three thousand angels
(specially) sent down?

125.   "Yes, - if you remain firm, and act aright, even if the enemy
should rush here on you in hot haste, your Lord would help
you with five thousand angels making a terrific onslaught.

126.   Allah made it but a message of hope for you, and an assurance
to your hearts: (in any case) there is no help except from Allah,
the Exalted, the Wise:

127.   That He might cut off a fringe of the Unbelievers or expose

---

19.   Bitter and virulent.

them to infamy, and they should then be turned back, frustrated of their purpose.

128. Not for you, (but for Allah), is the decision: whether He turn in mercy to them, or punish them; for they are indeed wrong-doers.

129. To Allah belonges all that is in the heavens and on earth. He forgives whom He pleases and punishes whom He pleases; but Allah is Oft-Forgiving, Most Merciful.

130. O you who believe! Devour not interest,[20] doubled and multiplied; but fear Allah; that you may (really) prosper.

131. Fear the Fire, which is pre-pared for those who reject Faith:

132. And obey Allah and the Apostle; that you may obtain mercy.

133. Be quick in the race for seeking forgiveness from your Lord, and for a Garden whose width is that (of the whole) of the heavens and of the earth, prepared for the righteous,-

134. Those who spend (freely), whether in prosperity, or in adversity; who restrain anger, and pardon (all) men; - for Allah loves those who do good,-

135. And those who, having done something to be ashamed of, or wronged their own souls, earnestly bring Allah to mind, and ask for forgiveness for their sins, - and who can forgive sins except Allah? - and are never obstinate in persisting knowingly in (the wrong) they have done.

136. For such the reward is forgiveness from their Lord, and Gardens with rivers flowing underneath,- an eternal dwelling: how excellent a recompense for those who work (and strive)!

137. Many were the Ways of Life that have passed away before you: travel through the earth, and see what was the end of those who rejected Truth.

138. Here is a plain statement to men, a guidance and instruction to those who fear Allah.

139. So lose not heart, nor fall into despair: for you must gain mastery if you are true in Faith.

---

20. Income received from lending money to others.

140. If a wound has touched you, be sure a similar wound has touched the others. Such days (of varying fortunes) We give to men and men by turns: that Allah may know those that believe, and that He may take to Himself from your ranks Martyr-witness- es (to Truth). And Allah does not love those that do wrong.

141. Allah's object also is to purge those that are true in Faith and to deprive of blessing those that resist Faith.

142. Did you think that you would enter Heaven without Allah testing those of you who fought hard (in His Cause) and remained steadfast?

143. You did indeed wish for death before you met him: now you have seen him with your own eyes, (and you flinch!)[21]

144. Muhammad is no more than an Apostle: many were the Apostles that passed away before him. If he died or were slain, will you then turn back on your heels? If any did turn back on his heels, not the least harm will he do to Allah; but Allah (on the other hand) will swiftly reward those who (serve Him) with gratitude.

145. Nor can a soul die except by Allah's leave, the term being fixed as by writing. If any do desire a reward in this life, We shall give it to him; and if any do desire a reward in the Hereafter, We shall give it to him. And swiftly shall We reward those that (serve Us with) gratitude.

146. How many of the prophets fought (in Allah's way), and with them (fought) large bands of godly men? But they never lost heart if they met with disaster in Allah's way, nor did they weaken (in will) nor give in. And Allah loves those who are firm and steadfast.

147. All that they said was: "Our Lord! forgive us our sins and anything we may have done that transgressed our duty: establish our feet firmly, and help us against those that resist Faith."

148. And Allah gave them a reward in this world, and the excellent

---

21.   Shrink or draw back

reward of the Hereafter. For Allah loves those who do good.

149. O you who believe! If you obey the Unbelievers, they will drive you back on your heels, and you will turn back (from Faith) to your own loss.

150. Nay, Allah is your protector, and He is the best of helpers.

151. Soon shall We cast terror into the hearts of the Unbelie-vers, for that they joined compa-nions with Allah, for which He had sent no authority: their abode will be the Fire: and evil is the home of the wrong-doers!

152. Allah did indeed fulfil His promise to you when you with His permission were about to annihilate your enemy, - until you flinched and fell to disputing about the order, and disobeyed it after He brought you in sight (of the booty) which you covet. Among you are some that hanker[22] after this world and some that desire the Hereafter. Then He diverted you from your foes in order to test you. But He forgave you: for Allah is full of grace to those who believe.

153. Behold! you were climbing up the high ground, without even casting a side glance at any one, and the Apostle in your rear was calling you back. There did Allah give you one distress after another by way of requital,[23] to teach you not to grieve for (the booty) that had escaped you and for (the ill) that had befallen you. For Allah is well aware of all that you do.

154. After (the excitement) of the distress, He sent down calm on a band of you overcome with slumber, while another band was stirred to anxiety by their own feelings, moved by wrong suspicions of Allah-suspicions due to ignorance. They said: "What affair is this of ours?" You say: "Indeed, this affair is wholly Allah's." They hide in their minds what they dare not reveal to you. They say (to themselves): "If we had had anything to do with this affair, We should not have been in the slaughter here ." Say: "Even if you had remained in your homes, those for whom death was decreed would certainly have gone forth

---

22. Greatly desire.   23. Retaliation or punishment.

to the place of their death"; but (all this was) that Allah might test what is in your breasts and purge what is in your hearts. For Allah knows well the secrets of your hearts.

155. Those of you who turned back on the day the two hosts met - it was Satan who caused them to fail, because of some (evil) they had done. But Allah has blotted out (their fault): for Allah is Oft-Forgiving, Most Forbea-ring.

156. O you who believe! Be not like the Unbelievers, who say of their brethren, when they are travelling through the earth or engaged in fighting: "If they had stayed with us, they would not have died, or been slain." This that Allah may make it a cause of sighs and regrets in their hearts. It is Allah that gives Life and Death, and Allah sees well all that you do.

157. And if you are slain, or die, in the way of Allah, forgiveness and mercy from Allah are far better than all they could amass.

158. And if you die, or are slain, lo! it is unto Allah that you are brought together.

159. It is part of the Mercy of Allah that you deal gently with them. If you were severe or harsh-hearted, they would have broken away from about you: so pass over (their faults), and ask for (Allah's) forgiveness for them; and consult them in affairs (of moment). Then, when you have taken a decision put your trust in Allah. For Allah loves those who put their trust (in Him).

160. If Allah helps you, none can overcome you: If He forsakes you, who is there, after that, that can help you? In Allah, then, let Believers put their trust.

161. No prophet could (ever) be false to his trust. If any person is so false, he shall, on the Day of Judgment, restore what he misappropriated;[24] then shall every soul receive its due, whatever it earned,-and none shall be dealt with unjustly.

162. Is the man who follows the good pleasure of Allah like the man who draws on himself the wrath of Allah, and whose abode is in Hell?- a woeful refuge!

---

24. To take something wrongfully or dishonestly.

163. They are in varying grades in the sight of Allah, and Allah sees well all that they do.

164. Allah conferred a great favour on the Believers when He sent among them an Apostle from among themselves, rehearsing unto them the Signs of Allah, sanctifying them, and instructing them in Scripture and Wisdom, while, before that, they had been in manifest error.

165. What! When a single disaster smites you, although you smote (your enemies) with one twice as great, do you say?- "Wherefrom is this?" Say (to them): "It is from yourselves: for Allah has power over all things."

166. What you suffered on the day the two armies met, was with the leave of Allah, in order that He might test the Believers,

167. And the Hypocrites also. These were told: "Come, fight in the way of Allah, or (at least) drive (the foe from your city)." They said: "Had we known how to fight, we should certainly have followed you." They were that day nearer to Unbelief than to Faith, saying with their lips what was not in their hearts. But Allah has full knowledge of all they conceal.

168. (They are) the ones that say, (of their slain brethren), while they themselves sit (at ease): "If only they had listened to us they would not have been slain." Say: "Avert death from your own selves, if you speak the truth."

169. Do not think of those who are slain in Allah's way as dead. Nay, they live, finding their sustenance in the presence of their Lord;

170. They rejoice in the Bounty provided by Allah: and with regard to those left behind, who have not yet joined them (in their bliss), the (Martyrs) glory in the fact that on them is no fear, nor have they (cause to) grieve.

171. They glory in the Grace and the Bounty from Allah, and in the fact that Allah lets not the reward of the Faithful to be lost (in the least).

172. Of those who answered the call of Allah and the Apostle, even after being wounded, those who do right and refrain from

wrong, have a great reward;-

173. Men said to them: "A great army is gathering against you": and frightened them: but it (only) increased their Faith: they said: "For us Allah is sufficient, and He is the best Disposer of affairs."

174. And they returned with Grace and Bounty from Allah: no harm ever touched them: for they followed the good pleasure of Allah: and Allah is the Lord of bounties unbounded.

175. It is only the Satan that suggests to you the fear of his votaries:[25] do not be afraid of them, but fear Me, if you have Faith.

176. Let not those grieve you who rush headlong into Unbelief: not the least harm will they do to Allah: Allah's plan is that He will give them no portion in the Hereafter, but a severe punishment.

177. Those who purchase Unbelief at the price of faith,- not the least harm will they do to Allah, but they will have a grievous punishment.

178. Let not the Unbelievers think that Our respite to them is good for themselves: We grant them respite that they may grow in their iniquity[26]: but they will have a shameful punishment.

179. Allah will not leave the Believers in the state in which you are now, until He separates what is evil from what is good. Nor will He disclose to you the secrets of the Unseen, but He chooses of His Apostles (for the purpose) whom He pleases. So believe in Allah and His Apostles: and if you believe and do right, you have a reward without measure.

180. And let not those who covetously withhold of the gifts which Allah has given them of His Grace, think that it is good for them: nay, it will be the worse for them: soon shall the things which they covetously withheld be tied to their necks like a twisted collar[27], on the Day of Judgment. To Allah belongs the heritage of the heavens and the earth; and Allah is well-acquainted with all that you do.

---

25. Devoted followers.   26. Unfairness, injustice.
27. A leather or metal band fastened around the neck of an animal.

181. Allah has heard the taunt[28] of those who say: "Truly, Allah is indigent[29] and we are rich!"-We shall certainly record their word and (their act) of slaying the Prophets in defiance of right, and We shall say: "You taste the Chastisement of the Scorching Fire!

182. "This is because of the (unrighteous deeds) which your hands sent on before you: for Allah never harms those who serve Him."

183. They (also) said: "Allah took our promise not to believe in an Apostle unless he showed us a sacrifice consumed by fire (from heaven)." Say: "There came to you Apostles before me, with Clear Signs and even with what you ask for: why then did you slay them, if you speak the truth?"

184. Then if they reject you, so were rejected Apostles before you, who came with Clear Signs, Books of dark prophe-cies, and the Book of Enlighten-ment.

185. Every soul shall have a taste of death: and only on the Day of Judgment shall you be paid your full recompense. Only he who is saved far from the Fire and admitted to the Garden will have attained the object (of Life): for the life of this world is but goods and chattels[30] of deception.

186. You shall certainly be tried and tested in your possessions and in your personal selves; and you shall certainly hear much that will grieve you, from those who received the Book before you and from those who worship many gods. But if you persevere patiently, and guard against evil,- then that will be a determining factor in all affairs.

187. And remember Allah took a Covenant from the People of the Book, to make it known and clear to mankind, and not to hide it; but they threw it away behind their backs, and purchased with it some miserable gain! and vile was the bargain they made!

---

28. A scornful reproach. 29. Destitute, poor.
30. Movable articles or personal property.

188.   Think not that those who exult in what they have brought about, and love to be praised for what they have not done,- think not that they can escape the Chastisement. For them is a Chastisement grievous indeed.

189.   To Allah belongs the dominion of the heavens and the earth; and Allah has power over all things.

190.   Behold! In the creation of the heavens and the earth, and the alternation of Night and Day,- there are indeed Signs for men of understanding,-

191.   Men who celebrate the praises of Allah, standing, sitting, and lying down on their sides, and contemplate the (wonders of) creation in the heavens and the earth, (with the thought): "Our Lord! You have created (all) this not for nothing! Glory to You! Give us salvation from the Chastisement of the Fire.

192.   "Our Lord! any whom You admit to the Fire, truly You have covered with shame, and never will wrong-doers find any helpers!

193.   "Our Lord! we have heard the call of one calling (us) to Faith, 'you believe in the Lord,' and we have believed. Our Lord! forgive us our sins, blot out from us our iniquities, and take to Yourself our souls in the company of the righteous.

194.   "Our Lord! Grant us what you promised to us through Your Apostles, and save us from shame on the Day of Judgment: for You never break Your promise."

195.   And their Lord has accep-ted of them, and answered them: "Never will I suffer to be lost the work of any of you, be he male or female: you are members, one of another: those who have left their homes, or been driven out therefrom, or suffered harm in My Cause, or fought or been slain,- verily, I will blot out from them their iniquities, and admit them into Gardens with rivers flowing beneath; - a reward from the Presence of Allah, and from His Presence is the best of rewards."

196.   Let not the strutting[31] about of the Unbelievers through the

---

31.   Walking with a vain, pompous bearing.

land deceive you:

197. Little is it for enjoyment: their ultimate abode is Hell: what an evil bed (to lie on)!

198. On the other hand, for those who fear their Lord, are Gardens, with rivers flowing beneath; therein are they to dwell (for ever),- a gift from the presence of Allah; and that which is in the Presence of Allah is the best (bliss) for the righteous.

199. And there are, certainly, among the People of the Book, those who believe in Allah, in the revelation to you, and in the revelation to them, bowing in humility to Allah: they will not sell the Signs of Allah for a miserable gain! for them is a reward with their Lord, and Allah is swift in account.

200. O you who believe! Persevere in patience and constancy; vie in such perseverance; strengthen each other; and fear Allah; that you may prosper.

SURAH—4
AL-NISAA
(INTRODUCTION)

This Surah is closely connected chronologically with Surah 3. Its subject-matter deals with the social problems which the Muslim community had to face immediately after Uhud. While the particular occasion made the necessity urgent, the principles laid down have permanently governed Muslim Law and social practice.

Broadly speaking, the Surah consists of two parts: (1) that dealing with women, orphans, inheritance, marriage and family rights generally, and (2) that dealing with the recalcitrants in the larger family, the community at Madinah, viz, the Hypocrites and their accomplices.

SURAH AN-NISA', (THE WOMEN)

In the name of Allah, Most Gracious, Most Merciful

1.   O mankind! reverence your Guardian-Lord, Who created you from a single Person, created, of like nature, his mate, and from them twain[1] scattered (like seeds) countless men and women;- reverence Allah, through Whom you demand your mutual (rights), and (reverence) the wombs (that bore you): for Allah ever watches over you.

2.   To orphans restore their property (when they reach their age), nor substitute (your) worthless things for (their) good ones; and do not devour their substance (by mixing it up) with your own. For this is indeed a great sin.

3.   If you fear that you shall not be able to deal justly with the orphans, marry women of your choice, two or three or four; but if you fear that you shall not be able to deal justly (with them), then only one, or (a captive) that your right hands possess, that will be more suitable, to prevent you from doing injustice.

4.   And give the women (on marriage) their dower as a free gift; but if they, of their own good pleasure, remit any part of it to

---

1.   From them two

you, take it and enjoy it with right good cheer.

5. To those weak of under-standing do not make over your property, which Allah has made a means of support for you, but feed and clothe them therewith, and speak to them words of kindness and justice.

6. Make trial of orphans until they reach the age of marriage; if then you find sound judgment in them, release their property to them but do not consume it wastefully, nor in haste against their growing up. If the guardian is well-off, let him claim no remuneration, but if he is poor, let him have for himself what is just and reasonable. When you release their property to them, take witnesses in their presence: but all-sufficient is Allah in taking account.

7. From what is left by parents and those nearest related there is a share for men and a share for women, whether the property be small or large,- a determinate[2] share.

8. But if at the time of division other relatives, or orphans, or poor, are present, feed them out of the (property), and speak to them words of kindness and justice.

9. Let those (disposing of an estate) have the same fear in their minds as they would have for their own if they had left a helpless family behind: let them fear Allah, and speak words of appropriate (comfort).

10. Those who unjustly eat up the property of orphans, eat up a Fire into their own bodies: they will soon be enduring a blazing Fire!

11. Allah (thus) directs you as regards your children's (inheritance): to the male, a portion equal to that of two females: if only daughters, two or more, their share is two-thirds of the inheritance; if only one, her share is a half. For parents, a sixth share of the inheritance to each, if the deceased left children; if no children, and the parents are the (only) heirs, the mother has a third; If the deceased left brothers (or sisters) the mother

---

2.   Definite or distinct

has a sixth. (The distribution in all cases is) after the payment of legacies and debts. You do not know whether your parents or your children are nearest to you in benefit. These are settled portions ordained by Allah; and Allah is All-knowing, All- wise.

12. In what your wives leave, your share is a half, if they leave no child; but if they leave a child, you get a fourth; after payment of legacies and debts. In what you leave, their share is a fourth, if you leave no child; but if you leave a child, they get one eighth; after payment of legacies and debts. If the man or woman whose inheritance is in question, has left neither ascendants[3] nor descendants, but has left a brother or a sister, each one of the two gets a sixth; but if more than two, they share in a third; after payment of legacies and debts; so that no loss is caused (to any one). Thus is it ordained by Allah; and Allah is All-knowing, Most Forbearing.

13. Those are limits set by Allah: those who obey Allah and His Apostle will be admitted to Gardens with rivers flowing beneath, to abide therein (for ever) and that will be the supreme achievement.

14. But those who disobey Allah and His Apostle and trans-gress His limits will be admitted to a Fire, to abide therein: and they shall have a humili-ating punishment.

15. If any of your women are guilty of lewdness[4], take the evidence of four (reliable) witnesses from amongst you against them; and if they testify, confine them to houses until death do claim them, or Allah ordain for them some (other) way.

16. If two men among you are guilty of lewdness, punish them both. If they repent and amend, leave them alone; for Allah is Oft-returning, Most Merciful.

17. Allah accepts the repen-tance of those who do evil in ignorance and repent soon afterwards; to them will Allah turn in mercy: for Allah is full of knowledge and wisdom.

18. Of no effect is the repentance of those who continue to do evil,

---

3.   Ancestors   4.   Inoecency, obscenity

until death faces one of them, and he says, "Now have I repented indeed;" nor of those who die rejecting Faith: for them We have prepared a punishment most grievous.

19. O you who believe! you are forbidden to inherit women against their will. Nor should you treat them with harshness, that you may take away part of the dower you have given them,- except where they have been guilty of open lewdness; on the contrary live with them on a footing of kindness and equity. If you take a dislike to them it may be that you dislike a thing, and Allah brings about through it a great deal of good.

20. But if you decide to take one wife in place of another, even if you had given the latter a whole treasure for dower, take not the least bit of it back: would you take it by slander and a manifest wrong?

21. And how could you take it when you have gone in to each other, and they have taken from you a solemn covenant?

22. And marry not women whom your fathers married,- except what is past: it was shameful and odious,- an abominable custom indeed.

23. Prohibited to you (for marriage) are:- your mothers, daughters, sisters; father's sisters, mother's sisters; brother's daughters, sister's daughters; foster-mothers (who gave you suck), foster-sisters; your wives' mothers; your step-daughters under your guardian-ship, born of your wives to whom you have gone in, - no prohibition if you have not gone in; - (those who have been) wives of your sons proceeding from your loins[5]; and two sisters in wedlock at one and the same time, except for what is past; for Allah is Oft-Forgiving, Most Merciful;-

24. Also (prohibited are) women already married, except those whom your right hands possess: thus has Allah ordained (prohibitions) against you: except for these, all others are lawful, provided you seek (them in marriage) with gifts from your property,- desiring chastity, not lust. Seeing that you derive

---

5. That is, your begotten offspring.

benefit from them, give them their dowers (at least) as prescribed; but if, after a dower is prescribed, you agree mutually (to vary it), there is no blame on you, and Allah is All-knowing, All-wise.

25. If any of you does not have the means wherewith to wed free believing women, they may wed believing girls from among those whom your right hands possess: and Allah has full knowledge about your Faith. You are one from another: wed them with the leave of their owners, and give them their dowers, according to what is reasonable: they should be chaste, not lustful, nor taking paramours[6]: when they are taken in wedlock, if they fall into shame, their punishment is half that for free women. This (permission) is for those among you who fear sin; but it is better for you that you practise self-restraint. And Allah is Oft-forgiving, Most Merciful.

26. Allah wishes to make clear to you and to show you the ordinances of those before you; and (He wishes to) turn to you (in Mercy): and Allah is All-knowing, All-wise.

27. Allah wishes to turn to you, but the wish of those who follow their lusts is that you should turn away (from Him),- far, far away.

28. Allah wishes to lighten your (difficulties): for man was created weak (in flesh).

29. O you who believe! do not eat up your property among yourselves in vanities: but let there be amongst you traffic and trade by mutual good-will: nor kill (or destroy) yourselves: for verily Allah has been to you Most Merciful!

30. If any do that in rancour and injustice,- soon shall We cast them into the Fire: and easy it is for Allah.

31. If you (but) eschew the most heinous of the things which you are forbidden to do, We shall expel out of you all the evil in you, and admit you to a gate of great honour.

32. And in no wise covet those things in which Allah has bestowed

---

6.   Illicit lovers

His gifts more freely on some of you than on others: to men is allotted what they earn, and to women what they earn: but ask Allah of His bounty. For Allah has full knowledge of all things.

33. To (benefit) every one, We have appointed shares and heirs to property left by parents and relatives. To those, also, to whom your right hand was pledged, give their due portion. For truly Allah is Witness to all things.

34. Men are the protectors and maintainers of women, because Allah has given the one more (strength) than the other, and because they support them from their means. Therefore, the righteous women are devoutly obedient, and guard in (the husband's) absence what Allah would have them guard. As to those women on whose part you fear disloyalty and ill-conduct, admonish them (first), (next), refuse to share their beds, (and last) beat them (lightly); but if they return to obedience, do not seek against them means (of annoyance): for Allah is Most High, Great (above you all).

35. If you fear a breach between them twain, appoint (two) arbiters, one from his family, and the other from hers; if they wish for peace, Allah will cause their reconciliation: for Allah has full knowledge, and is acquainted with all things.

36. Serve Allah, and join not any partners with Him; and do good - to parents, kinsfolk, orphans, those in need, neighbours who are near, neighbours who are strangers, the companion by your side, the way-farer (you meet), and what your right hands possess: for Allah does not love the arrogant, the vainglorious.[7]

37. (Nor) those who are niggardly or enjoin niggard-liness on others, or hide the bounties which Allah has bestowed on them; for We have prepared, for those who resist Faith, a Punishment that steeps them in contempt;-

38. Nor those who spend of their substance[8], to be seen of men, but have no faith in Allah and the Last Day: If any take the Satan for their intimate, what a dreadful intimate he is!

---

7.   Boastful, arrogant   8.   Wealth

39.   And what burden were it on them if they had faith in Allah and in the Last Day, and they spent out of what Allah has given them for sustenance? For Allah has full knowledge of them.

40.   Allah is never unjust in the least degree: if there is any good (done), He doubles it, and gives from His Own Presence a great reward.

41.   How then if We brought from each People a witness, and We brought you as a witness against these People!

42.   On that day those who reject Faith and disobey the Apostle will wish that the earth were made one with them: but never will they hide a single fact from Allah!

43.   O you who believe! do not approach prayers with a mind befogged, until you can understand all that you say,- nor in a state of ceremonial impurity (except when travelling on the road), until after washing your whole body. If you are ill, or on a journey, or one of you comes from offices of nature, or you have been in contact with women, and you find no water, then take for yourselves clean sand or earth, and rub there with your faces and hands. For Allah blots out sins and forgives again and again.

44.   Have you not turned your vision to those who were given a portion of the Book? They traffic⁹ in error, and wish that you should lose the right path.

45.   But Allah has full know-ledge of your enemies: Allah is enough for a Protector, and Allah is enough for a Helper.

46.   Of the Jews there are those who displace words from their (right) places, and say: "We hear and we disobey"; and "Hear what is not heard"; and "Ra'ina"¹⁰; with a twist of their tongues and a slander to Faith. If only they had said: "We hear and we obey"; and "Do hear"; and "Do look at us"; it would have

---

9.   Trade, bargain.
10.   *Ra ina* in Arabic means "Please attend to us." With a twist of their tongues, they suggested an insulting meaning, such as "O you that take us to pasture," or in Hebrew "Our bad one."

been better for them, and more proper; but Allah has cursed them for their Unbelief; and but few of them will believe.

47. O you People of the Book! believe in what We have (now) revealed, confirming what was (already) with you, before We change the face and fame of some (of you) beyond all recognition, and turn them hindwards, or curse them as We cursed the Sabbath-breakers, for the decision of Allah must be carried out.

48. Allah does not forgive that partners should be set up with Him; but He forgives anything else, to whom He pleases; to set up partners with Allah is to devise a sin most heinous[11] indeed.

49. Have you not turned your vision to those who claim sanc-tity for themselves? Nay- but Allah sanctifies whom He pleases. But never will they fail to receive justice in the least little thing.

50. See! how they invent a lie against Allah! but that by itself is a manifest sin!

51. Have you not turned your vision to those who were given a portion of the Book? They believe in sorcery[12] and evil, and say to the Unbelievers that they are better guided in the (right) way than the Believers!

52. They are (men) whom Allah has cursed: and those whom Allah has cursed, you will find, have no one to help.

53. Have they a share in dominion or power? Behold, they do not give a farthing to their fellow-men.

54. Or do they envy mankind for what Allah has given them of His bounty? But We had already given the people of Abraham the Book and wisdom, and conferred upon them a great kingdom.

55. Some of them believed, and some of them averted their faces from him: and enough is Hell for a burning fire.

56. Those who reject Our Signs, We shall soon cast (them) into the Fire: as often as their skins are roasted through, We shall change them for fresh skins, that they may taste the Chastisement: for Allah is Exalted in Power, Wise.

---

11. Monstrous, abominable   12. Magic

57.   But those who believe and do deeds of righteousness, We shall soon admit (them) to Gardens, with rivers flowing beneath, - their eternal home: therein shall they have Compa-nions pure and holy: We shall admit them to shades, cool and ever deepening.

58.   Allah commands you to render back your trusts to those to whom they are due; and when you judge between man and man, that you judge with justice: verily how excellent is the teaching which He gives you! for Allah is He Who hears and sees all things.

59.   O you who believe! obey Allah, and obey the Apostle, and those charged with authority among you. If you differ in anything among yourselves, refer it to Allah and His Apostle, if you do believe in Allah and the Last Day: that is best, and most suitable for final determination.

60.   Have you not turned your vision to those who declare that they believe in the revelations that have come to you and to those before you? Their (real) wish is to resort together for judgment (in their disputes) to the Satan, though they were ordered to reject him. But Satan's wish is to lead them astray far away (from the right).

61.   When it is said to them: "Come to what Allah has revealed, and to the Apostle": you see the Hypocrites avert their faces from you in disgust.

62.   How then, when they are seized by misfortune, because of the deeds which their hands have sent forth? Then they come to you, swearing by Allah: "We meant no more than good-will and conciliation!"

63.   Those men, Allah knows what is in their hearts; so keep clear of them, but admonish them, and speak to them a word to reach their very souls.

64.   We did not send an Apostle, but to be obeyed, in accordance with the Will of Allah. If they had only, when they were unjust to themselves, come to you and asked Allah's forgiveness, and the Apostle had asked forgiveness for them, they would have

found Allah indeed Oft-returning, Most Merciful.

65. But no, by your Lord, they can have no (real) Faith, until they make you judge in all disputes between them, and find in their souls no resistance against your decision, but accept them with the fullest conviction.

66. If We had ordered them to sacrifice their lives or to leave their homes, very few of them would have done it: but if they had done what they were (actually) told, it would have been best for them, and would have gone farthest to strengthen their (faith);

67. And We should then have given them from Our Presence a great reward;

68. And We should have shown them the Straight Way.

69. All who obey Allah and the Apostle are in the company of those on whom is the Grace of Allah, - of the Prophets (who teach), the Sincere (lovers of Truth), the Witnesses (who testify), and the Righteous (who do good): ah! what a beautiful Fellowship!

70. Such is the Bounty from Allah: and sufficient is it that Allah knows all.

71. O you who believe! take your precautions, and either go forth in parties or go forth all together.

72. There are certainly among you men who would tarry behind: if a misfortune befalls you, they say: "Allah favoured us in that we were not present among them."

73. But if good fortune comes to you from Allah, they would be sure to say - as if there had never been ties of affection between you and them - "Oh! I wish I had been with them; a fine thing should I then have made of it!"

74. Let those fight in the cause of Allah who sell the life of this world for the Hereafter. To him who fights in the cause of Allah,- whether he is slain or gets victory - soon shall We give him a reward of great (value).

75. And why should you not fight in the cause of Allah and of those who, being weak, are ill-treated (and oppressed)?- men,

women, and children, whose cry is: "Our Lord! Rescue us from this town, whose people are oppressors; and raise for us from You one who will protect; and raise for us from You one who will help!"

76.   Those who believe fight in the cause of Allah, and those who reject Faith fight in the cause of Evil: so you fight against the friends of Satan: feeble indeed is the cunning of Satan.

77.   Have you not turned your vision to those who were told to hold back their hands (from fight) but establish regular prayers and spend in regular charity? When (at length) the order for fighting was issued to them, behold! a section of them feared men as - or even more than - they should have feared Allah: they said: "Our Lord! Why have You ordered us to fight? Would You not grant us respite to our (natural) term, near (enough)?" Say: "Short is the enjoyment of this world: the Hereafter is the best for those who do right: never will you be dealt with unjustly in the very least!

78.   "Wherever you are, death will find you out, even if you are in towers built up strong and high!" If some good befalls them, they say, "This is from Allah"; but if evil, they say, "This is from you" (O Prophet). Say: "All things are from Allah." But what have come to these people, that they fail to understand a single fact?

79.   Whatever good, (O man!) happens to you, is from Allah; but whatever evil happens to you, is from your (own) soul. And We have sent you as an Apostle to (instruct) mankind. And enough is Allah for a Witness.

80.   He who obeys the Apostle, obeys Allah: but if any turn away, We have not sent you to watch over their (evil deeds).

81.   They have "Obedience" on their lips; but when they leave you, a section of them meditate all night on things very different from what you tell them. But Allah records their nightly (plots): so keep clear of them, and put your trust in Allah, and enough is Allah as a disposer of affairs.

82.   Do they not consider the Qur'an (with care)? Had it been from other than Allah, they would surely have found therein much discrepancy.

83.   When there comes to them some matter touching (public) safety or fear, they divulge[13] it. If they had only referred it to the Apostle, or to those charged with authority among them, the proper investigators would have tested it from them (direct). Were it not for the Grace and Mercy of Allah to you, all but a few of you would have fallen into the clutches of Satan.

84.   Then fight in Allah's cause - you are held responsible only for yourself - and motivate the Believers. It may be that Allah will restrain the fury of the Unbe-lievers; for Allah is the strongest in might and in punishment.

85.   Whoever recommends and helps a good cause becomes a partner therein: and whoever recommends and helps an evil cause, shares in its burden: and Allah has power over all things.

86.   When a (courteous) greeting is offered you, meet it with a greeting still more courteous, or (at least) of equal courtesy. Allah takes careful account of all things.

87.   Allah! There is no god but He: of a surety He will gather you together against the Day of Judgment, about which there is no doubt. And whose word can be truer than Allah's?

88.   Why should you be divided into two parties about the Hypocrites? Allah has upset them for their (evil) deeds. Would you guide those whom Allah has thrown out of the Way? For those whom Allah has thrown out of the Way, you will never find the Way.

89.   They but wish that you should reject Faith, as they do, and thus be on the same footing (as they): but do not take friends from their ranks until they flee in the way of Allah (from what is forbidden). But if they turn renegades[14], seize them and slay them wherever you find them; and (in any case) take no friends or helpers from their ranks;-

---

13.   Disclose   14.   Apostate

90.   Except those who join a group between whom and you there is
       a treaty (of peace), or those who approach you with hearts
       restraining them from fighting you as well as fighting their
       own people. If Allah had pleased, He could have given them
       power over you, and they would have fought you: therefore if
       they withdraw from you but do not fight you, and (instead)
       send you (guarantees) of peace, then Allah has opened no way
       for you (to war against them).

91.   Others you will find that wish to gain your confidence as well
       as that of their people: every time they are sent back to
       temptation, they succumb thereto: if they do not withdraw from
       you nor give you (guarantees) of peace besides restraining their
       hands, seize them and slay them wherever you get them: in
       their case We have provided you with a clear argument against
       them.

92.   Never should a Believer kill a Believer; but (if it so happens)
       by mistake, (compen-sation is due): if one (so) kills a Believer,
       it is ordained that he should free a believing slave, and pay
       compensation to the deceased's family, unless they remit it
       freely. If the deceased belonged to a people at war with you,
       and he was a Believer, the freeing of a believing slave (is
       enough). If he belonged to a people with whom you have treaty
       of mutual alliance, compensation should be paid to his family,
       and a believing slave be freed. For those who find this beyond
       their means, (is prescribed) a fast for two months running: by
       way of repentance to Allah: for Allah has all knowledge and
       all wisdom.

93.   If a man kills a Believer intentionally, his recompense is Hell,
       to abide therein (for ever): and the wrath and the curse of Allah
       are upon him, and a dreadful Chastisement is prepared for him.

94.   O you who believe! When you go abroad in the cause of Allah,
       investigate carefully, and do not say to any one who offers you
       a salutation: "you are not a Believer!" coveting the perishable
       goods of this life: with Allah are profits and spoils abundant.
       Even thus were you yourselves before, till Allah conferred on

you His favours: therefore carefully investigate. For Allah is well aware of all that you do.

95. Not equal are those Believers who sit (at home) and receive no hurt, and those who strive and fight in the cause of Allah with their goods and their persons. Allah has granted a grade higher to those who strive and fight with their goods and persons than to those who sit (at home). To all (in Faith) Allah has promised good: but those who strive and fight He has distinguished above those who sit (at home) by a special reward,-

96. Ranks specially bestowed by Him, and Forgiveness and Mercy. For Allah is Oft-forgiving, Most Merciful.

97. When angels take the souls of those who die in sin against their souls, they say: "In what (plight) were you?" They reply: "Weak and oppressed were we in the earth." They say: "Was not the earth of Allah spacious enough for you to move yourselves away (from evil)?" Such men will find their abode in Hell, - What an evil refuge! -

98. Except those who are (really) weak and oppressed - men, women, and children - who have no means in their power, nor (a guide-post) to direct their way.

99. For these, there is hope that Allah will forgive: for Allah blots out (sins) and forgives again and again.

100. He who forsakes his home in the cause of Allah, finds in the earth many a refuge, wide and spacious: should he die as a refugee from home for Allah and His Apostle, His reward becomes due and sure with Allah: And Allah is Oft-forgiving, Most Merciful.

101. When you travel through the earth, there is no blame on you if you shorten your prayers, for fear the Unbelievers may attack you: for the Unbelievers are open enemies to you.

102. When you (O Apostle) are with them, and stand to lead them in prayer, let one party of them stand up (in prayer) with you, taking their arms with them: when they finish their prostrations, let them take their position in the rear. And let the other party

come up which has not yet prayed - and let them pray with you, taking all precautions, and bearing arms: the Unbelievers wish, if you were negligent of your arms and your baggage, to assault you in a single rush. But there is no blame on you if you put away your arms because of the inconve-nience of rain or because you are ill; but take (every) precaution for yourselves. For the Unbelievers Allah has prepared a humiliating punishment.

103. When you pass (congre-gational) prayers, celebrate Allah's praises, standing, sitting down, or lying down on your sides; but when you are free from danger, set up regular Prayers: for such prayers are enjoined on Believers at stated times.

104. And do not slacken in following up the enemy: if you are suffering hardships, they are suffering similar hardships; but you have hope from Allah, while they have none. And Allah is full of knowledge and wisdom.

105. We have sent down to you the Book in truth, that you might judge between men, as guided by Allah: so be not (used) as an advocate by those who betray their trust;

106. But seek the forgiveness of Allah; for Allah is Oft-forgiving, Most Merciful.

107. Do not contend on behalf of such as betray their own souls; for Allah does not love one given to perfidy[15] and crime:

108. They may hide (their crimes) from men, but they cannot hide (them) from Allah, seeing that He is in their midst when they plot by night, in words that He cannot approve: and Allah compassess round all that they do.

109. Ah! these are the sort of men on whose behalf you may contend in this world; but who will contend with Allah on their behalf on the Day of Judgment, or who will carry their affairs through?

110. If any one does evil or wrongs his own soul but afterwards seeks Allah's forgiveness, he will find Allah Oft-forgiving, Most Merciful.

---

15.   Breach of faith, treachery

111. And if any one earns sin. he earns it against his own soul: for Allah is full of knowledge and wisdom.

112. But if any one earns a fault or a sin and throws it on to one that is innocent, he carries (on himself) (both) a falsehood and a flagrant sin.

113. But for the Grace of Allah to you and His Mercy, a party of them would certainly have plotted to lead you astray. But (in fact) they will only lead their own souls astray, and to you they can do no harm in the least. For Allah has sent down to you the Book and Wisdom and taught you what you did not know (before): and great is the Grace of Allah unto you.

114. In most of their secret talks there is no good: but if one exhorts to a deed of charity or justice or conciliation between men, (secrecy is permissible): to him who does this, seeking the good pleasure of Allah, We shall soon give a reward of the highest (value).

115. If anyone contends with the Apostle even after guidance has been plainly conve-yed to him, and follows a path other than that becoming to men of Faith, We shall leave him in the path he has chosen, and land him in Hell, - what an evil refuge!

116. Allah does not forgive (the sin of) joining other gods with Him; but He forgives whom He pleases other sins than this: one who joins other gods with Allah has strayed far, far away (from the Right).

117. (The Pagans), leaving Him, call but upon female deities: they call but upon Satan the persistent rebel!

118. Allah cursed him, but he said: "I will take of Your servants a portion marked off;

119. "I will mislead them, and I will create in them false desires; I will order them to slit the ears of cattle, and to deface the (fair) nature created by Allah." Whoever, forsaking Allah, takes Satan for a friend, of a surety has suffered a loss that is manifest.

120. Satan makes them promi-ses, and creates in them false desires; but Satan's promises are nothing but deception.

121. They (his dupes) will have their dwelling in Hell, and from it they will find no way of escape.

122. But those who believe and do deeds of righteousness, - We shall soon admit them to Gardens, with rivers flowing beneath, - to dwell therein for ever. Allah's promise is the truth, and whose word can be truer than Allah's?

123. Not your desires, nor those of the People of the Book (can prevail): whoever works evil, will be requited accor-dingly. Nor will he find, besides Allah any protector or helper.

124. If any do deeds of righteousness,- be they male or female - and have faith, they will enter Heaven, and not the least injustice will be done to them.

125. Who can be better in religion than one who submits his whole self to Allah, does good, and follows the way of Abraham the true in faith? For Allah took Abraham for a friend.

126. But to Allah belong all things in the heavens and on earth: and He it is that encompasses all things.

127. They ask your instruction concerning the Women. Say: Allah instructed you about them: and (remember) what has been rehearsed unto you in the Book, concerning the orphans of women to whom you do not give the portions prescribed, and yet whom you desire to marry, as also concerning the children who are weak and oppressed: that you stand firm for justice to orphans. There is not a good deed which you do, but Allah is well-acquainted therewith.

128. If a wife fears cruelty or desertion on her husband's part, there is no blame on them if they arrange an amicable settlement between themselves; and such settlement is best; even though men's souls are swayed by greed. But if you do good and practise self-restraint, Allah is well-acquainted with all that you do.

129. You are never able to be fair and just as between women, even if it is your ardent desire: but do not turn away (from a woman) altogether, so as to leave her (as it were) hanging (in the air). If you come to a friendly understanding, and practise self-

restraint, Allah is Oft-forgiving, Most Merciful.

130. But if they disagree (and must part), Allah will provide abundance for all from His all-reaching bounty: for Allah is He that cares for all and is Wise.

131. To Allah belong all things in the heavens and on earth. Verily We have directed the People of the Book before you, and you (O Muslims) to fear Allah. But if you deny Him, lo! to Allah belong all things in the heavens and on earth, and Allah is free of all wants, worthy of all praise.

132. Yes, to Allah belong all things in the heavens and on earth, and enough is Allah to carry through all affairs.

133. If it were His Will, He could destroy you, O mankind, and create another race; for Allah has power to do this.

134. If any one desires a reward in this life, in Allah's (gift) is the reward (both) of this life and of the hereafter: for Allah is He that hears and sees (all things).

135. O you who believe! stand out firmly for justice, as witnesses to Allah, even as against yourselves, or your parents, or your kin, and whether it be (against) rich or poor: for Allah can best protect both. Follow not the lusts (of your hearts), lest you swerve, and if you distort (justice) or decline to do justice, verily Allah is well-acquainted with all that you do.

136. O you who believe! Believe in Allah and His Apostle, and the scripture which He has sent to His Apostle and the scripture which He sent to those before (him). Any who denies Allah, His Angels, His Books, His Apostles, and the Day of Judgment, has gone far, far astray.

137. Those who believe, then reject Faith, then believe (again) and (again) reject Faith, and go on increasing in Unbelief, - Allah will not forgive them nor guide them on the Way.

138. To the Hypocrites give the glad tidings that there is for them (but) a grievous Chastise-ment.

139. Yes, to those who take for friends Unbelievers rather than Believers: is it honour they seek among them? Nay,- all honour is with Allah.

140.   Already He has sent you Word in the Book, that when you hear the Signs of Allah held in defiance and ridicule, you are not to sit with them unless they turn to a different theme: if you did, you would be like them. For Allah will collect the Hypocrites and those who defy Faith - all in Hell:-

141.   (These are) the ones who wait and watch about you: if you do gain a victory from Allah, they say: "Were we not with you?"- but if the Unbelievers gain a success, they say (to them): "Did we not gain an advantage over you, and did we not guard you from the Believers?" But Allah will judge between you on the Day of Judgment. And never will Allah grant to the Unbelievers a way (to triumph) over the Believers.

142.   The Hypocrites - they think they are over-reaching[16] Allah, but He will over- reach them: when they stand up to prayer, they stand without earnestness, to be seen of men, but little do they hold Allah in remembrance;

143.   (They are) distracted in mind even in the midst of it,- being (sincerely) for neither one group nor for another. Whom Allah leaves straying,- never will you find for him the Way.

144.   O you who believe! take not for friends Unbelievers rather than Believers: do you wish to offer Allah an open proof against yourselves?

145.   The Hypocrites will be in the lowest depths of the Fire: no helper will you find for them;-

146.   Except for those who repent, mend (their lives) hold fast to Allah, and purify their religion as in Allah's sight: if so they will be (numbered) with the Believers. And soon will Allah grant to the Believers a reward of immense value.

147.   What can Allah gain by your punishment, if you are grateful and you believe? Nay, it is Allah that recognises (all good), and knows all things.

148.   Allah does not love that evil should be noised abroad in public speech, except where injustice has been done; for Allah is He

---

16.   To get better of, especially by trick and deceit.

who hears and knows all things.

149. Whether you publish a good deed or conceal it or cover evil with pardon, verily Allah blots out (sins) and has power (in the judgment of values).

150. Those who deny Allah and His Apostles, and (those who) wish to separate Allah from His Apostles, saying: "We believe in some but reject others": and (those who) wish to take a course midway,-

151. They are in truth (equally) Unbelievers; and We have prepared for Unbelievers a humiliating punishment.

152. To those who believe in Allah and His Apostles and make no distinction between any of the Apostles, We shall soon give their (due) rewards: for Allah is Oft-forgiving, Most Merciful.

153. The people of the Book ask you to cause a book to descend to them from heaven: Indeed they asked Moses for an even greater (miracle), for they said: "Show us Allah in public," but they were dazed for their presumption, with thunder and lightning. Yet they worshipped the calf even after Clear Signs had come to them; even so We forgave them; and gave Moses manifest proofs of authority.

154. And for their Covenant We raised over them (the towering height) of Mount (Sinai); and (on another occasion) We said:"Enter the gate with humility"; and (once again) We commanded them: "do not transgress in the matter of the Sabbath." And We took from them a solemn Covenant.

155. (They have incurred divine displeasure): In that they broke their Covenant; that they rejected the Signs of Allah; that they slew the Messengers in defiance of right; that they said, "Our hearts are the wrappings (which preserve Allah's Word; We need no more)";- No, Allah has set the seal on their hearts for their blasphemy, and little is it they believe;-

156. That they rejected Faith; that they uttered against Mary a grave false charge;

157. That they said (in boast), "We killed Christ Jesus the son of Mary, the Apostle of Allah";- but they did not kill him, nor

crucified him, but so it was made to appear to them, and those who differ therein are full of doubts, with no (certain) knowledge, but only conjecture to follow, for of a surety they did not kill him :-

158. Nay, Allah raised him up unto Himself; and Allah is Exalted in Power, Wise;-

159. And there is none of the People of the Book but must believe in him before his death; and on the Day of Judgment he will be a witness against them;-

160. For the iniquity of the Jews We made unlawful for them certain (foods) good and whole-some which had been lawful for them;- in that they hindered many from Allah's Way;-

161. That they took interest, though they were forbidden; and that they devoured men's substance wrongfully;- We have prepared for those among them who reject Faith a grievous punishment.

162. But those among them who are well-grounded in knowledge, and the Believers, believe in what has been revealed to you and what was revealed before you: and (especially) those who establish regular prayer and practise regular charity and believe in Allah and in the Last Day: to them shall We soon give a great reward.

163. We have sent you inspi-ration, as We sent it to Noah and the Messengers after him: We sent inspiration to Abraham, Isma'il, Isaac, Jacob and the Tribes, to Jesus, Job, Jonah, Aaron, and Solomon, and to David We gave the Psalms.

164. Of some Apostles We have already told you the story; of others We have not;- and to Moses Allah spoke direct;-

165. Apostles who gave good news as well as warning, that mankind, after (the coming) of the Apostles, should have no plea against Allah: for Allah is Exalted in Power, Wise.

166. But Allah bears witness that what He has sent unto you He has sent from His (own) knowledge, and the Angels bear Witness: but enough is Allah for a Witness.

167. Those who reject Faith and keep off (men) from the way of Allah, have verily strayed far, far away from the Path.

168. Those who reject Faith and do wrong,- Allah will not forgive them nor guide them to any way-

169. Except the way of Hell, to dwell therein for ever. And this to Allah is easy.

170. O mankind! the Apostle has come to you in truth from Allah: believe in him: It is best for you. But if you reject Faith, to Allah belong all things in the heavens and on earth: And Allah is All-knowing, All-wise.

171. O People of the Book! commit no excesses in your religion: nor say of Allah anything but the truth. Christ Jesus the son of Mary was (no more than) an Apostle of Allah, and His Word, which He bestowed on Mary, and a spirit proceeding from Him: so believe in Allah and His Apostles. Do not say "Trinity" desist: it will be better for you: for Allah is One God: glory be to Him: (far Exalted is He) above having a son. To Him belong all things in the heavens and on earth. And enough is Allah as a Disposer of affairs.

172. Christ does not disdain to serve and worship Allah, nor do the angels, those nearest (to Allah): those who disdain His worship and are arrogant,-He will gather them all together unto Himself to (answer).

173. But to those who believe and do deeds of righteousness, He will give their (due) rewards,- and more, out of His bounty: but those who are disdainful and arrogant, He will punish with a grievous Chastisement; nor will they find, besides Allah, any to protect or help them.

174. O mankind! verily there has come to you a convincing proof from your Lord: for We have sent unto you a light (that is) manifest.

175. Then those who believe in Allah, and hold fast to Him,- soon will He admit them to Mercy and Grace from Himself, and guide them to Himself by a straight way.

176. They ask you for a legal decision. Say: Allah directs (thus) about those who leave no descendants or ascendants as heirs. If it is a man that dies, leaving a sister but no child, she shall

have half the inheritance: If (such a deceased was) a woman, who left no child, her brother takes her inheritance: If there are two sisters, they shall have two-thirds of the inheritance (between them): if there are brothers and sisters, (they share), the male having twice the share of the female. Thus does Allah make clear to you (His law), lest you err. And Allah has knowledge of all things.

SURAH—5
AL-MAIDAH
(INTRODUCTION)

This Surah deals, by way of recapitulation, with the backsliding of the Jews and Christians from their pure religions, to which the coping stone was placed by Islam. It refers particularly to the Christians, and to their solemn Sacrament of the Last Supper, to whose mystic meaning they are declared to have been false.

As a logical corollary to the corruption of the earlier religions of Allah, the practical precepts of Islam, about food, cleanliness, justice, and fidelity are recapitulated.

The third verse contains the memorable declaration: "This day have I perfected your religion for you", which was promulgated in 10 H., during the Apostle's last pilgrimage to Makkah. Chronologically it was the last verse to be revealed.

SURAH AL-MA'IDA (THE TABLE SPREAD)
In the name of Allah, Most Gracious, Most Merciful.

1. O you who believe! Fulfil (all) obligations. Lawful to you (for food) are all four-footed animals, with the exceptions named: But animals of the chase are forbidden while you are in the Sacred Precincts or in pilgrim garb: for Allah commands according to His Will and Plan.

2. O you who believe! violate not the sanctity of the Symbols of Allah, nor of the Sacred Month, nor of the animals brought for sacrifice, nor the Garlands that mark out such animals, nor the people resorting to the Sacred House, seeking of the bounty and good pleasure of their Lord. But when you are clear of the Sacred Precincts and of pilgrim garb, you may hunt and let not the hatred of some people in (once) shutting you out of the Sacred Mosque lead you to transgression (and hostility on your part). You help one another in righteousness and piety, but do not help one another in sin and rancour: fear Allah: for Allah is strict in punishment.

3.   Forbidden to you (for food) are: dead meat, blood, the flesh of
      swine, and that on which has been invoked the name of other
      than Allah; that which has been killed by strangling, or by a
      violent blow, or by a headlong fall, or by being gored[1] to death;
      that which has been (partly) eaten by a wild animal; unless you
      are able to slaughter it (in due form); that which is sacrificed
      on stone (altars); (forbidden) also is the division (of meat) by
      raffling with arrows: that is impiety. This day those who reject
      faith have given up all hopes of your religion: yet fear them
      not but fear Me. This day have I perfected your religion for
      you, completed My favour upon you, and have chosen for you
      Islam as your religion. But if any is forced by hunger, with no
      inclination to transgression, Allah is indeed Oft-forgiving, Most
      Merciful.

4.   They ask you what is lawful to them (as food). Say: lawful to
      you are (all) good and pure things: and what you have taught
      your trained hunting animals (to catch) in the manner directed
      to you by Allah: eat what they catch for you, but pronounce
      the name of Allah over it: and fear Allah; for Allah is swift in
      taking account.

5.   This day (all) good and pure things are made lawful to you.
      The food of the People of the Book is lawful to you and yours
      is lawful to them. (Law-ful to you in marriage) are (not only)
      chaste women who are Believers, but chaste women among
      the People of the Book, revealed before your time,- when you
      give them their due dowers, and desire chastity, not lewdness,
      nor secret intrigues. If any one rejects faith, fruitless is his
      work, and in the Hereafter he will be in the ranks of those who
      have lost (all spiritual good).

6.   O you who believe! when you prepare for prayer, wash your
      faces, and your hands (and arms) to the elbows; rub your heads
      (with water); and (wash) your feet to the ankles. If you are in a
      state of ceremonial impurity, bathe your whole body. But if

---

1.   Pierced with a horn or tusk

you are ill, or on a journey, or one of you comes from offices of nature, or you have been in contact with women, and you find no water, then take for yourselves clean sand or earth, and rub therewith your faces and hands. Allah does not wish to place you in a difficulty, but to make you clean, and to complete His favour to you, that you may be grateful.

7. And call in remembrance the favour of Allah to you, and His Covenant, which He ratified with you, when you said: "We hear and we obey": and fear Allah, for Allah knows well the secrets of your hearts.

8. O you who believe! stand out firmly for Allah, as witnesses to fair dealing, and let not the hatred of others to you make you swerve to wrong and depart from justice. Be just: that is next to piety: and fear Allah. For Allah is well-acquain-ted with all that you do.

9. To those who believe and do deeds of righteousness, Allah has promised forgiveness and a great reward.

10. Those who reject faith and deny Our Signs will be companions of Hell-fire.

11. O you who believe! call in remembrance the favour of Allah unto you when certain men formed the design to stretch out their hands against you, but (Allah) held back their hands from you: so fear Allah. And on Allah let Believers put (all) their trust.

12. Allah took (aforetime) a Covenant from the Children of Israel, and We appointed twelve captains among them. And Allah said: "I am with you: if you (but) establish regular prayers, practise regular charity, believe in My Apostles, honour and assist them, and loan to Allah a beautiful loan, verily I will wipe out from you your evils, and admit you to Gardens with rivers flowing beneath; but if any of you, after this, resists faith, he has truly wandered from the path of rectitude."[2]

13. But because of their breach of their Covenant, We cursed them,

---

2. Rightness, righteousness

and made their hearts grow hard; they change the words from their (right) places and forget a good part of the Message that was sent them, nor will you cease to find them- barring a few - ever bent on (new) deceits: but forgive them, and overlook (their misdeeds): for Allah loves those who are kind.

14. From those, too, who call themselves Christians, We did take a Covenant, but they forgot a good part of the message that was sent them: so We estranged them, with enmity and hatred between the one and the other, to the Day of judgment. And soon will Allah show them what it is they have done.

15. O people of the Book! there has come to you Our Apostle, revealing to you much that you used to hide in the Book, and passing over much (that is now unnecessary). There has come to you from Allah a (new) light and a perspicuous[3] Book,

16. Wherewith Allah guides all who seek His good pleasure to ways of peace and safety, and leads them out of darkness, by His Will, unto the light,- guides them to a Path that is Straight.

17. In blasphemy indeed are those that say that Allah is Christ the son of Mary. Say: "Who then has the least power against Allah, if His Will were to destroy Christ the son of Mary, his mother, and all - every one that is on the earth? For to Allah belongs the dominion of the heavens and the earth, and all that is between. He creates what He pleases. For Allah has power over all things."

18. (Both) the Jews and the Christians say: "We are sons of Allah, and His beloved." Say: "Why then does He punish you for your sins? Nay, you are but men,- of the men He has created: He forgives whom He pleases, and He punishes whom He pleases: and to Allah belongs the dominion of the heavens and the earth, and all that is between: and unto Him is the final goal (of all)".

19. O People of the Book! now has come to you, making (things) clear to you, Our Apostle, after the break in (the series of) Our

---

3.   Clearly expressed, easily understood

Apostles, lest you should say: "There came unto us no bringer of glad tidings and no warner (from evil)": But now has come to you a bringer of glad tidings and a warner (from evil). And Allah has power over all things.

20. Remember Moses said to his people: "O my people! call in remembrance the favour of Allah to you, when He produced prophets among you, made you kings, and gave you what He had not given to any other among the people.

21. "O my people! enter the holy land which Allah has assigned unto you, and do not turn back ignominiously[4], for then will you be overthrown, to your own ruin."

22. They said: "O Moses! In this land are a people of exceeding strength: never shall we enter it until they leave it: if (once) they leave, then we shall enter."

23. (But) among (their) Allah-fearing men were two on whom Allah had bestowed His grace: they said: "Assault them at the (proper) Gate: when once you are in, victory will be yours; But on Allah put your trust if you have faith."

24. They said: "O Moses! while they remain there, never shall we be able to enter, to the end of time. You go, and your Lord, and fight you two, while we sit here (and watch)."

25. He said: "O my Lord! I have power only over myself and my brother: so separate us from this rebellious people!"

26. Allah said: "Therefore the land will be out of their reach for forty years: In distraction they will wander through the land: but you do not grieve over these rebellious people.

27. Recite to them the truth of the story of the two sons of Adam. Behold! they each presented a sacrifice (to Allah): It was accepted from one, but not from the other. Said the latter: "Be sure I will slay you." "Surely," said the former, "Allah accepts of the sacrifice of those who are righteous.

28. "If you stretch your hand against me, to slay me, it is not for me to stretch my hand against you to slay you: for I do fear

---

4. In a humiliating manner

Allah, the Cherisher of the worlds.

29.   "For me, I intend to let you draw on yourself my sin as well as
       yours, for you will be among the companions of the Fire, and
       that is the reward of those who do wrong."

30.   The (selfish) soul of the other led him to the murder of his
       brother: he murdered him, and became (himself) one of the
       lost ones.

31.   Then Allah sent a raven, who scratched the ground, to show
       him how to hide the shame of his brother. "Woe is me!" said
       he; "Was I not even able to be as this raven, and to hide the
       shame of my brother?" then he became full of regrets-

32.   On that account: We ordained for the Children of Israel that if
       any one slew a person - unless it be for murder or for spreading
       mischief in the land - it would be as if he slew the whole people:
       and if any one saved a life, it would be as if he saved the life of
       the whole people. Then although there came to them Our
       Apostles with Clear Signs, yet, even after that, many of them
       continued to commit excesses in the land.

33.   The punishment of those who wage war against Allah and His
       Apostle, and strive with might and main[5] for mischief through
       the land is: execution, or crucifixion, or the cutting off of hands
       and feet from opposite sides, or exile from the land: that is
       their disgrace in this world, and a heavy punishment is theirs
       in the Hereafter;

34.   Except for those who repent before they fall into your power:
       in that case, know that Allah is Oft-forgiving, Most Merciful.

35.   O you who believe! do your duty to Allah, seek the means of
       approach unto Him, and strive with might and main in His
       cause: that you may prosper.

36.   As to those who reject Faith,- if they had everything on earth,
       and twice repeated, to give as ransom for the Chastisement of
       the Day of Judgment, it would never be accepted of them, theirs
       would be a grievous Chastisement.

---

5.   One's utmost power

37. Their wish will be to get out of the Fire, but never will they get out therefrom: their Chastisement will be one that endures.

38. As to the thief, male or female, cut off his or her hands: a punishment by way of example, from Allah, for their crime: and Allah is Exalted in power.

39. But if the thief repents after his crime, and amends his conduct, Allah turns to him in forgiveness; for Allah is Oft-forgiving, Most Merciful.

40. Do you not know that to Allah (alone) belongs the dominion of the heavens and the earth? He punishes whom He pleases, and He forgives whom He pleases: and Allah has power over all things.

41. O Apostle! let not those grieve you, who race each other into Unbelief: (whether it be) among those who say "We believe" with their lips but whose hearts have no faith; or it be among the Jews,- men who will listen to any lie,- will listen even to others who have never so much as come to you. They change the words from their (right) times and places: they say, "If you are given this, take it, but if not, beware!" If any one's trial is intended by Allah you have no authority in the least for him against Allah. For such - it is not Allah's will to purify their hearts. For them there is disgrace in this world, and in the Hereafter a heavy punishment.

42. (They are fond of) liste-ning to falsehood, of devouring anything forbidden. If they do come to you, either judge between them, or decline to interfere. If you decline, they cannot hurt you in the least. If you judge, judge in equity between them. For Allah loves those who judge in equity.

43. But why do they come to you for decision, when they have (their own) law before them?- therein is the (plain) Command of Allah; yet even after that, they would turn away. For they are not (really) People of Faith.

44. It was We Who revealed the Law (to Moses): therein was guidance and light. By its standard have been judged the Jews, by the prophets who bowed (as in Islam) to Allah's Will, by

the Rabbis and the Doctors of Law: for to them was entrusted the protection of Allah's Book, and they were witnesses there to: therefore fear not men, but fear Me, and sell not My Signs for a miserable price. If any do fail to judge by (the light of) what Allah has revealed, they are (no better than) Unbelievers.

45. We ordained therein for them: "Life for life, eye for eye, nose for nose, ear for ear, tooth for tooth, and wounds equal for equal." But if any one remits the retaliation by way of charity, it is an act of atonement for himself. And if any fail to judge by (the light of) what Allah has revealed, they are (no better than) wrong-doers.

46. And in their footsteps We sent Jesus the son of Mary, confirming the Law that had come before him: We sent him the Gospel: therein was guidance and light, and confirmation of the Law that had come before him: a guidance and an admonition to those who fear Allah.

47. Let the people of the Gospel judge by what Allah has revealed therein. If any do fail to judge by (the light of) what Allah has revealed, they are (no better than) those who rebel.

48. To you We sent the Scripture in truth, confirming the scripture that came before it, and guarding it in safety: so judge between them by what Allah has revealed, and do not follow their vain desires, diverging from the Truth that has come to you. To each among you We have prescribed a Law and an Open Way. If Allah had so willed, He would have made you a single people, but (His plan is) to test you in what He have given you: so strive as in a race in all virtues. The goal of you all is to Allah; it is He that will show you the truth of the matters in which you dispute;

49. And this (He commands): you Judge between them by what Allah has revealed, and follow not their vain desires, but beware of them lest they beguile you from any of that (teaching) which Allah has sent down to you. And if they turn away, be assured that for some of their crimes it is Allah's purpose to punish them. And truly most men are rebellious.

50. Do they then seek after a judgment of (the days of) ignorance? But who, for a people whose faith is assured, can give better judgment than Allah?

51. O you who believe! take not the Jews and the Christians for your friends and protectors: they are but friends and protectors to each other. And he amongst you that turns to them (for friendship) is of them. Verily Allah guides not a people unjust.

52. Those in whose hearts is a disease - you see how eagerly they run about amongst them, saying: "We do fear lest a change of fortune bring us disaster." Ah! perhaps Allah will give (you) victory, or a decision according to His Will. Then will they repent of the thoughts which they secretly harboured in their hearts.

53. And those who believe will say: "Are these the men who swore their strongest oaths by Allah, that they were with you?" All that they do will be in vain, and they will fall into (nothing but) ruin.

54. O you who believe! if any from among you turn back from his Faith, soon will Allah produce a people whom He will love as they will love Him,- lowly with the Believers, mighty against the Rejecters, fighting in the way of Allah, and never afraid of the reproaches of such as find fault. That is the Grace of Allah, which He will bestow on whom He pleases. And Allah encompasses all, and He knows all things.

55. Your (real) friends are (no less than) Allah, His Apostle, and the (fellowship of) Believers,- those who establish regular prayers and regular charity, and they bow down humbly (in worship).

56. As to those who turn (for friendship) to Allah, His Apostle, and the (Fellowship of) Belie-vers,- it is the Fellowship of Allah that must certainly triumph.

57. O you who believe! take not for friends and protectors those who take your religion for a mockery or sport,- whether among those who received the Scripture before you, or among those who reject Faith; but you should fear Allah, if you have Faith

(indeed).

58. When you proclaim your call to prayer, they take it (but) as mockery and sport; that is because they are a people without understanding.

59. Say: "O people of the Book! Do you disapprove of us for no other reason than that we believe in Allah, and the revelation that has come to us and that which came before (us), and (perhaps) that most of you are rebellious and disobedient?"

60. Say: "Shall I point out to you something much worse than this, (as judged) by the treatment it received from Allah? those who incurred the curse of Allah and His wrath, those of whom some He transformed into apes and swine, those who wor-shipped evil;- these are (many times) worse in rank, and far more astray from the even path!"

61. When they come to you, they say: "We believe": but in fact they enter with a mind against Faith, and they go out with the same. But Allah knows fully all that they hide.

62. You see many of them racing each other in sin and rancour, and their eating of things forbidden. Evil indeed are the things that they do.

63. Why do not the Rabbis and the Doctors of Law forbid them from their (habit of) uttering sinful words and eating things forbidden? Evil indeed are their works.

64. The Jews say: "Allah's hand is tied up." Be their hands tied up and be they accursed for the (blasphemy) they utter. Nay, both His hands are widely outstretched: He gives and spends (of His bounty) as He pleases. But the revelation that comes to you from Allah increases in most of them their obstinate rebellion and blasphemy. Amongst them we have placed enmity and hatred till the Day of Judgment. Every time they kindle the fire of war, Allah extinguishes it; but they (ever) strive to do mischief on earth. And Allah does not love those who do mischief.

65. If only the People of the Book had believed and been righteous, We should indeed have blotted out their iniquities and admitted

them to Gardens of Bliss.

66.   If only they had stood fast by the Law, the Gospel, and all the revelation that was sent to them from their Lord, they would have enjoyed happiness from every side. There is from among them a party on the right course: but many of them follow a course that is evil.

67.   O Apostle! proclaim the (Message) which has been sent to you from your Lord. If you did not, you would not have fulfilled and proclaimed His Mission. And Allah will defend you from men (who mean mischief). For Allah guides not those who reject Faith.

68.   Say: "O People of the Book! you have no ground to stand upon unless you stand fast by the Law, the Gospel, and all the revelation that has come to you from your Lord." It is the revelation that comes to you from your Lord, that increases in most of them their obstinate rebellion and blasphemy. But you do not grieve over (these) people without Faith.

69.   Those who believe (in the Qur'an), those who follow the Jewish (scriptures), and the Sabians and the Christians,- any who believe in Allah and the Last Day, and work righteous-ness,- on them shall be no fear, nor shall they grieve.

70.   We took the Covenant of the Children of Israel and sent them Apostles. Every time there came to them an Apostle with what they themselves did not desire, some (of these) they called impostors, and some they (go so far as to) slay.

71.   They thought there would be no trial (or punishment); so they became blind and deaf; yet Allah (in mercy) turned to them; yet again many of them became blind and deaf. But Allah sees well all that they do.

72.   They do blaspheme who say: "Allah is Christ the son of Mary." But Christ said: "O Children of Israel! worship Allah, my Lord and your Lord." Whoever joins other gods with Allah,- Allah will forbid him the Garden, and the Fire will be his abode. There will for the wrong-doers be no one to help.

73. They do blaspheme who say: Allah is one of three in a Trinity; for there is no god except One God. If they do not desist from their word (of blasphemy), verily a grievous Chastisement will befall the blasphemers among them.

74. Why do they not turn to Allah, and seek His forgive-ness? For Allah is Oft- forgiving, Most Merciful.

75. Christ the son of Mary was no more than an Apostle; many were the Apostles that passed away before him. His mother was a woman of truth. They had both to eat their (daily) food. See how Allah makes His Signs clear to them; yet see in what ways they are deluded away from the truth!

76. Say: "Will you worship, besides Allah, something which has no power either to harm or benefit you? But Allah,- He it is that hears and knows all things."

77. Say: "O people of the Book! exceed not in your religion the bounds (of what is proper), trespassing beyond the truth, nor follow the vain desires of people who went wrong in times gone by,- who misled many, and strayed (themselves) from the even way.

78. Curses were pronounced on those among the Children of Israel who rejected Faith, by the tongue of David and of Jesus the son of Mary: because they disobeyed and persisted in excesses.

79. Nor did they (usually) forbid one another the iniquities which they committed: evil indeed were the deeds which they did.

80. You see many of them tur-ning in friendship to the Unbe-lievers. Evil indeed are (the works) which their souls have sent forward before them (with the result), that Allah's wrath is on them, and in torment will they abide.

81. If only they had believed in Allah, in the Apostle, and in what has been revealed to him, never would they have taken them for friends and protectors, but most of them are rebellious wrong-doers.

82. Strongest among men in enmity to the Believers will you find the Jews and Pagans; and nearest among them in love to the Believers will you find those who say, "We are Christians":

because amongst these are men devoted to learning and men who have renounced the world, and they are not arrogant.

83.   And when they listen to the revelation received by the Apostle, you will see their eyes overflowing with tears, for they recognise the truth: they pray: "Our Lord! we believe; write us down among the witnesses.

84.   "What cause can we have not to believe in Allah and the truth which has come to us, seeing that we long for our Lord to admit us to the company of the righteous?"

85.   And for this their prayer Allah has rewarded them with Gardens, with rivers flowing underneath,- their eternal home. Such is the recompense of those who do good.

86.   But those who reject Faith and belie our Signs,-they shall be Companions of Hell-fire.

87.   O you who believe! Do not make unlawful the good things which Allah has made lawful for you, but commit no excess: for Allah does not love those given to excess.

88.   Eat of the things which Allah has provided for you, lawful and good; but fear Allah, in Whom you believe.

89.   Allah will not call you to account for what is futile in your oaths, but He will call you to account for your deliberate oaths: for expiation[6], feed ten indigent persons, on a scale of the average for the food of your families; or clothe them; or give a slave his freedom. If that is beyond your means, fast for three days. That is the expiation for the oaths you have sworn. But keep to your oaths. Thus Allah makes clear to you His Signs, that you may be grateful.

90.   O you who believe! Intoxicants and gambling, (dedi-cation of) stones, and (divination by) arrows, are an abomination,- of Satan's handiwork: eschew such (abomination), that you may prosper.

91.   Satan's plan is (but) to excite enmity and hatred between you, with intoxicants and gambling, and hinder you from the

---

6.   To make amends for

remembrance of Allah, and from prayer: will you not then abstain?

92. Obey Allah, and obey the Apostle, and beware (of evil): if you do turn back, you should know that it is Our Apostle's duty to proclaim (the Message) in the clearest manner.

93. On those who believe and do deeds of righteousness there is no blame for what they ate (in the past), when they guard themselves from evil, and believe, and do deeds of righteousness,- (or) again, guard themselves from evil and believe,- (or) again, guard themselves from evil and do good. For Allah loves those who do good.

94. O you who believe! Allah makes a trial of you in a little matter of game well within reach of your hands and your lances, that He may test who fears Him unseen: and who transgress thereafter, will have a grievous Chastisement.

95. O you who believe! do not kill game while in the Sacred Precincts or in pilgrim garb. If any of you does so intentionally, the compensation is an offering, brought to the Ka'ba, of a domestic animal equivalent to the one he killed, as adjudged by two just men among you; or by way of atonement, the feeding of the indigent; or its equivalent in fasts: that he may taste of the Chastisement of his deed. Allah forgives what is past: for repetition Allah will exact from him the Chastisement. For Allah is Exalted, and Lord of Retribution.

96. Lawful to you is the pursuit of water-game and its use for food,- for the benefit of your-selves and those who travel; but forbidden is the pursuit of land-game;- as long as you are in the Sacred Precincts or in pilgrim garb. And fear Allah, to Whom you shall be gathered back.

97. Allah made the Ka'ba, the Sacred House, an asylum of security for men, as also the Sacred Months, the animals for offerings, and the garlands that mark them: that you may know that Allah has knowledge of what is in the heavens and on earth and that Allah is well acquainted with all things.

98. You should know that Allah is strict in punishment and that Allah is Oft-forgiving, Most Merciful.

99. The Apostle's duty is but to proclaim (the Message). But Allah knows all that you reveal and all that you conceal.

100. Say: "Not equal are things that are bad and things that are good, even though the abun-dance of the bad may dazzle you; so fear Allah, O you that understand; that (so) you may prosper."

101. O you who believe! do not ask questions about things which, if made plain to you, may cause you trouble. But if you ask about things when the Qur'an is being revealed, they will be made plain to you, Allah will forgive those: for Allah is Oft-forgiving, Most Forbea-ring.

102. Some people before you did ask such questions, and on that account lost their faith.

103. It was not Allah Who instituted (superstitions like those of) a slit-ear she- camel, or a she-camel let loose for free pasture, or idol sacrifices for twin-births in animals, or stallion-camels freed from work: It is blasphemers who invent a lie against Allah; but most of them lack wisdom.

104. When it is said to them: "Come to what Allah has revealed; come to the Apostle": they say: "Enough for us are the ways we found our fathers following." what! even though their fathers were void of knowledge and guidance?

105. O you who believe! guard your own souls: If you follow (right) guidance, no hurt can come to you from those who stray. The goal of you all is to Allah: it is He that will show you the truth of all that you do.

106. O you who believe! When death approaches any of you, (take) witnesses among your-selves when making bequests,- two just men of your own (brotherhood) or others from outside if you are journeying through the earth, and the chance of death befalls you (thus). If you doubt (their truth), detain them both after prayer, and let them both swear by Allah: "We do not wish in this for any worldly gain, even though the (beneficiary) be our near relation: we shall not hide the evidence before Allah: if

we do, then behold! the sin be upon us!"

107. But if it gets known that these two were guilty of the sin (of perjury), let two others stand forth in their places,- nearest in kin from among those who claim a lawful right: let them swear by Allah: "We affirm that our witness is truer than that of those two, and that we have not trespassed (beyond the truth): if we did, behold! the wrong be upon us!"

108. That is most suitable: that they may give the evidence in its true nature and shape, or else they would fear that other oaths would be taken after their oaths. But fear Allah, and listen (to His counsel): for Allah does not guide a rebellious people:

109. One day Allah will gather the Apostles together, and ask: "What was the response you received (from men to your teaching)?" They will say: "We have no knowledge: it is You Who knows in full all that is hidden."

110. Then will Allah say: "O Jesus the son of Mary! recount My favour to you and to your mother. Behold! I strengthened you with the holy spirit, so that you did speak to the people in childhood and in maturity. Behold! I taught you the Book and Wisdom, the Law and the Gospel. And behold! you made out of clay, as it were, the figure of a bird, by My leave, and you breathed into it and it became a bird by My leave, and you healed those born blind, and the lepers, by My leave. And behold ! you brought forth the dead by My leave. And behold! I did restrain the Children of Israel from (violence to) you when you showed them the Clear Signs, and the Unbelievers among them said: 'This is nothing but evident magic.'

111. "And behold! I inspired the Disciples to have faith in Me and Mine Apostle: they said, 'We have faith, and you bear witness that we bow to Allah as Muslims'".

112. Behold! the Disciples said: "O Jesus the son of Mary! can your Lord send down to us a table set (with viands[7]) from heaven?" Jesus said: "Fear Allah, if you have faith."

7.   Articles of food

113.   They said: "We only wish to eat thereof and satisfy our hearts, and to know that you have indeed told us the truth; and that we ourselves may be witnesses to the miracle."

114.   Jesus the son of Mary said: "O Allah our Lord! send us from heaven a table set (with viands), that there may be for us - for the first and the last of us - a solemn festival and a Sign from You; and provide for our sustenance, for You are the best Sustainer (of our needs)."

115.   Allah said: "I will send it down to you: But if any of you after that resists faith, I will punish him with a Chastisement such as I have not inflicted on any one among all the peoples."

116.   And behold! Allah will say: "O Jesus the son of Mary! Did you say to men, worship me and my mother as gods in derogation of Allah'?" He will say: "Glory to You! never could I say what I had no right (to say). Had I said such a thing, You would indeed have known it. You know what is in my heart, though I do not know what is in Yours. For You know in full all that is hidden.

117.   "Never said I to them anything except what You commanded me to say, to wit[8], 'Worship Allah, my Lord and your Lord'; and I was a witness over them while I dwelt amongst them; when You took me up, You were the Watcher over them, and You are a Witness to all things.

118.   "If You punish them, they are Your servant: If You forgive them, You are the Exalted in power, the Wise."

119.   Allah will say: "This is a day on which the truthful will profit from their truth: theirs are Gardens, with rivers flowing beneath,- their eternal home: Allah well-pleased with them, and they with Allah: that is the great salvation, (the fulfilment of all desires).

120.   To Allah belongs the domi-nion of the heavens and the earth, and all that is therein, and it is He Who has power over all things.

---

8.   That is to say, namely

SURAH—6
AL-AN'AM
(INTRODUCTION)

This is a Surah of the late Makkan period. The greater part of it was revealed entire. Its place in the traditional order of arrangement is justified by logical considerations. We have already had the spiritual history of mankind, a discussion of the earlier revelations and how they were lost or' corrupted, the regulations for the outer life of the new Community and the points in which the Jews and Christians failed to maintain the central doctrine of Islam — the unity of Allah. The next step now taken is to expound this doctrine in relation to Pagan Arabia

---

SURAH AN'AM (THE CATTLE)
In the name of Allah, Most Gracious, Most Merciful

1. Praise be to Allah, Who created the heavens and the earth, and made the darkness and the light. Yet those who reject Faith hold (others) as equal, with their Guardian-Lord.

2. He it is Who created you from clay, and then decreed a stated term (for you). And there is in His presence another determined term; yet you doubt within yourselves!

3. And He is Allah in the heavens and on earth. He knows what you hide, and what you reveal, and He knows the (recompense) which you earn (by your deeds).

4. But never did a single one of the Signs of their Lord reach them, but they turned away therefrom.

5. And now they reject the truth when it reaches them: but soon shall they learn the reality of what they used to mock at.

6. Don't they see how many of those before them We destroyed?- generations We had established on the earth, in strength such as We have not given to you - for whom We poured out rain from the skies in abundance, and gave (fertile) streams flowing beneath their (feet): yet for their sins We destroyed them, and raised in their wake fresh generations (to succeed them).

7. If We had sent to you a written (message) on parchment[1], so that they could touch it with their hands, the Unbelie-vers would have been sure to say: "This is nothing but ob-vious magic!"

8. They say: "Why is not an angel sent down to him?" If We sent down an angel, the matter would be settled at once, and no respite would be granted them.

9. If We had made it an angel, We should have sent him as a man, and We should certainly have caused them confusion in a matter which they have already covered with confusion.

10. Mocked were (many) Apostles before you; but their scoffers[2] were hemmed[3] in by the thing that they mocked.

11. Say: "Travel through the earth and see what was the end of those who rejected Truth."

12. Say: "To whom belongs all that is in the heavens and on earth?" Say: "To Allah. He has inscribed[4] for Himself (the rule of) Mercy. That He will gather you together for the Day of Judgment, there is no doubt whatever. It is they who have lost their own souls, that will not believe.

13. To him belongs all that dwells (or lurks) in the Night and the Day. For He is the One Who hears and knows all things."

14. Say: "Shall I take for my protector any other than Allah, the Maker of the heavens and the earth? And He it is that feeds but is not fed." Say: "Nay! but I am commanded to be the first of those who bow to Allah (in Islam), and you be not of the company of those who join gods with Allah."

15. Say: "I would, if I disobeyed my Lord, indeed have fear of the Chastisement of a Mighty Day.

16. "On that day, if the Chas-tisement is averted from any, it is due to Allah's mercy; and that would be (Salvation), the obvious fulfilment of all desire.

17. "If Allah touch you with affliction, none can remove it but He;

---

1. Manuscript, scroll
2. Mockers, those who ridiculed it   3. Confined, enclosed
4. Decreed, decided

if He touch you with happiness, He has power over all things.

18. "He is the Irresistible, (wat-ching) from above over His wor-shippers; and He is the Wise, acquainted with all things."

19. Say: "What thing is most weighty in evidence?" Say: "Allah is Witness between me and you; this Qur'an has been revealed to me by inspiration, that I may warn you and all whom it reaches. Can you possibly bear witness that besides Allah there is another god?" Say: "Nay! I cannot bear witness!" Say: "But in truth He is the One God, and I truly am innocent of (your blasphemy of) joining others with Him."

20. Those to whom We have given the Book know this as they know their own sons. Those who have lost their own souls refuse therefore to believe.

21. Who does more wrong than he who invents a lie against Allah or rejects His Signs? But verily the wrong-doers shall never prosper.

22. One day We shall gather them all together: We shall say to those who ascribed partners (to Us): "Where are the partners whom you (invented and) talked about?"

23. There will then be (left) no subterfuge[5] for them but to say: "By Allah, our Lord, we were not those who joined gods with Allah."

24. Behold! how they lie against their own souls! But the (lie) which they invented will leave them in the lurch.[6]

25. Of them there are some who (pretend to) listen to you; but We have thrown veils on their hearts, So they do not understand it, and deafness in their ears; if they saw every one of the Signs, they will not believe in them; in so much that when they come to you, they (but) dispute with you; the Unbelievers say: "These are nothing but tales of the ancients."

26. Others they keep away from it, and themselves they keep away; but they only destroy their own souls, and they do not perceive it.

---

5.   Scheme or trick
6.   To desert an ally or friend in difficulties

27. If you could but see when they are confronted with the Fire! they will say: "Would that we were but sent back! then we would not reject the Signs of our Lord, but would be amongst those who believe!"

28. Yes, in their own (eyes) will become manifest what they concealed before. But if they were returned, they would certainly relapse to the things they were forbidden, for they are indeed liars.

29. And they (sometimes) say: "There is nothing except our life on this earth, and never shall we be raised up again."

30. If you could but see when they are confronted with their Lord! He will say: "Is not this the truth?" They will say: "Yes, by our Lord!" He will say: "You then test the Chastisement, because you rejected Faith."

31. Lost indeed are they who treat it as a falsehood that they must meet Allah,- until on a sudden the hour is on them, and they say: "Ah! woe unto us that we took no thought of it"; for they bear their burdens on their backs, and evil indeed are the burdens that they bear?

32. What is the life of this world but play and amusement? But best is the Home in the Hereafter, for those who are righteous. Will you not then understand?

33. We know indeed the grief which their words do cause you: It is not you they reject: it is the Signs of Allah, which the wicked contemn.[7]

34. Rejected were the Apos-tles before you: with patience and constancy they bore their rejection and their wrongs, until Our aid reached them: there is none that can alter the Words (and Decrees) of Allah. Already you have received some account of those Apostles.

35. If their spurning[8] is hard on your mind, yet if you were able to seek a tunnel in the ground or a ladder to the skies and bring

---

7. (Old English) Despise, treat with disregard
8. Rejection, disdain

them a Sign,- (what good?). If it were Allah's Will, He could gather them together to true guidance: so you be not amongst those who are swayed by ignorance (and impatience)!

36. Those who listen (in truth), be sure, will accept: as to the dead, Allah will raise them up; then will they be turned unto Him.

37. They say: "Why is not a Sign sent down to him from his Lord?" Say: "Allah has certainly power to send down a Sign: but most of them do not understand.

38. There is not an animal (that lives) on the earth, nor a being that flies on its wings, but (forms part of) communities like you. Nothing have we omitted from the Book, and they (all) shall be gathered to their Lord in the end.

39. Those who reject Our Signs are deaf and dumb,- in the midst of profound darkness: whom Allah wills, He leaves to wander: whom He wills, He places on the Way that is Straight.

40. Say: "You think to your-selves, if there come upon you the Wrath of Allah, or the Hour (that you dread), would you then call upon other than Allah?-(reply) if you are truthful!

41. "Nay,- On Him would you call, and if it be His Will, He would remove (the distress) which occasioned your call upon Him, and you would forget (the false gods) which you join with Him!"

42. Before you We sent (Apostles) to many nations, and We afflicted the nations with suffering and adversity, that they might learn humility.

43. When the suffering rea-ched them from Us, why then did they not learn humility? On the contrary their hearts became hardened, and Satan made their (sinful) acts seem alluring to them.

44. But when they forgot the warning they had received, We opened to them the gates of all (good) things, until, in the midst of their enjoyment of Our gifts, on a sudden, We called them to account, when lo! they were plunged in despair!

45. Of the wrong-doers the last remnant was cut off. Praise be to Allah, the Cherisher of the worlds.

46. Say: "Do you think, if Allah took away your hearing and your

sight, and sealed up your hearts, who - a god other than Allah - could restore them to you?" See how We explain the Signs by various (symbols); yet they turn aside.

47. Say: "Do you think, if the punishment of Allah comes to you, whether suddenly or openly, will any be destroyed except those who do wrong?

48. We send the Apostles only to give good news and to warn: so those who believe and mend (their lives),- upon them shall be no fear, nor shall they grieve.

49. But those who reject Our Signs,- punishment shall touch them, for that they did not cease from transgressing.

50. Say: "I tell you not that with me are the treasures of Allah, nor do I know what is hidden, nor do I tell you I am an angel. I but follow what is revealed to me." Say: "can the blind be held equal to the seeing?" Will you then not con-sider?

51. Give this warning to those in whose (hearts) is the fear that they will be brought (to judgment) before their Lord except for Him they will have no protector nor intercessor: that they may guard (against evil).

52. Do not send away those who call on their Lord morning and evening, seeking His Face. In nothing are you accountable for them, and in nothing are they accountable for you, that you should turn them away, and thus be (one) of the unjust.

53. Thus did We try some of them by comparison with others that they should say: "Is it these then that Allah has favoured from amongst us?" Does not Allah know best those who are grateful?

54. When those come to you who believe in Our Signs, say: "Peace be on you: Your Lord has inscribed for Himself (the rule of) Mercy: verily, if any of you did evil in ignorance, and thereafter repented, and amen-ded (his conduct), lo! He is Oft- forgiving, Most Merciful.

55. Thus do We explain the Signs in detail: so that the way of the sinners may be shown up.

56. Say: "I am forbidden to worship those - other than Allah - whom you call upon." Say: "I will not follow your vain desires:

If I did, I would stray from the path, and be not of the company of those who receive guidance."

57.   Say: "For me, I (work) on a clear Sign from my Lord, but you reject Him. What you would see hastened, is not in my power. The Command rests with none but Allah: He declares the Truth, and He is the best of judges."

58.   Say: "If what you would see hastened were in my power, the matter would be settled at once between you and me. But Allah knows best those who do wrong."

59.   With Him are the keys of the Unseen, the treasures that none knows but He. He knows whatever there is on the earth and in the sea. Not a leaf falls but with His knowledge: there is not a grain in the darkness (or depths) of the earth, nor anything fresh or dry (green or withered), but is (inscribed) in a Record clear (to those who can read).

60.   It is He Who takes your souls by night, and has knowledge of all that you have done by day: by day He raises you up again that a term appointed be fulfilled; In the end unto Him will be your return; then will He show you the truth of all that you did.

61.   He is the Irresistible, (watching) from above over His worshippers, and He sets guardians over you. At length, when death approaches one of you, Our angels take his soul, and they never fail in their duty.

62.   Then men are returned unto Allah, their Protector, the (only) Reality: Is not His the Command? and He is the Swiftest in taking account.

63.   Say: "Who is it that deliveres you from the dark recesses of land and sea, when you call upon Him in humility and silent terror: 'If He only delivers us from these (dangers), (we vow) we shall truly show our gratitude'.?"

64.   Say "It is Allah that delivers you from these and all (other) distresses: and yet you worship false gods!"

65.   Say: "He has power to send calamities on you, from above and below, or to cover you with confusion in party strife, giving you a taste of mutual vengeance - each from the other." See

how We explain the Signs by various (symbols); that they may understand.

66. But your people reject this, though it is the Truth. Say: "Not mine is the responsibility for arranging your affairs;

67. For every Message is a limit of time, and soon you shall know it."

68. When you see men engaged in vain discourse about Our Signs, turn away from them unless they turn to a different theme. If Satan ever makes you forget, then after recollection, do not sit in the company of those who do wrong.

69. On their account no responsibility falls on the righteous, but (their duty) is to remind them, that they may (learn to) fear Allah.

70. Leave alone those who take their religion to be mere play and amusement, and are deceived by the life of this world. But proclaim (to them) this (truth): that every soul delivers itself to ruin by its own acts: it will find for itself no protector or intercessor except Allah: if it offered every ransom, (or reparation), none will be accepted: such is (the end of) those who deliver themselves to ruin by their own acts: they will have for drink (only) boiling water, and for punishment, one most grievous for they persisted in rejecting Allah.

71. Say: "Shall we indeed call on others besides Allah,- things that can do us neither good nor harm,- and turn on our heels after receiving guidance from Allah? - like one whom the evil ones have made into a fool, wandering bewildered through the earth, his friends calling, 'Come to us', (vainly) guiding him to the path." Say: "Allah's guidance is the (only) guidance, and we have been directed to submit ourselves to the Lord of the worlds;-

72. "To establish regular prayers and to fear Allah for it is to Him that we shall be gathered together."

73. It is He Who created the heavens and the earth in true (proportions): the day He says, "Be," Behold! it is. His Word is the Truth. His will be the dominion the day the trumpet will

be blown. He knows the Unseen as well as that which is open.
For He is the Wise, well acquainted (with all things).

74.   Lo! Abraham said to his father Azar: "Do you take idols for
gods? For I see you and your people in manifest error."

75.   So also did We show Abraham the power and the laws of the
heavens and the earth, that he might (with understanding) have
certitude.

76.   When the night covered him over, he saw a star: He said: "This
is my Lord." But when it set, he said: "I do not love those that
set."

77.   When he saw the moon rising in splendour, he said: "This is
my Lord." But when the moon set, he said: "unless my Lord
guide me, I shall surely be among those who go astray."

78.   When he saw the sun rising in splendour, he said: "This is my
Lord; this is the greatest (of all)." But when the sun set, he
said: "O my people! I am indeed free from your (guilt) of giving
partners to Allah.

79.   "For me, I have set my face, firmly and truly, towards Him
Who created the heavens and the earth, and never shall I give
partners to Allah."

80.   His people disputed with him. He said: "Do you (come) to
dispute with me, about Allah, when He (Himself) has guided
me? I do not fear (the beings) you associate with Allah: unless
my Lord wills, (nothing can happen). My Lord comprehends
in His knowledge all things. Will you not (yourselves) be
admonished?

81.   "How should I fear (the beings) you associate with Allah, when
you do not fear to give partners to Allah without any warrant[9]
having been given to you? Which of (us) two parties has more
right to security? (Tell me) if you know.

82.   "It is those who believe and do not confuse their beliefs with
wrong - that are (truly) in security, for they are on (right)
guidance."

---

9.   Authority

83.　That was the reasoning about Us, which We gave to Abraham (to use) against his people: We raise whom We will, degree after degree: for your Lord is full of wisdom and knowledge.

84.　We gave him Isaac and Jacob: all (three) We guided: and before him, We guided Noah, and among his progeny[10], David, Solomon, Job, Joseph, Moses, and Aaron: thus We reward those who do good:

85.　And Zakariya and John, and Jesus and Elias all in the ranks of the Righteous:

86.　And Isma'il and Elisha, and Jonas, and Lot: and to all We gave favour above the nations:

87.　(To them) and to their fathers, and progeny and brethren: We chose them, and We guided them to a straight way.

88.　This is the guidance of Allah: He gives that guidance to whom He pleases, of His worshippers. If they were to join other gods with Him, all that they did would be vain for them.

89.　These were the men to whom We gave the Book, and Authority, and Prophethood: if these (their descendants) reject them, behold! We shall entrust their charge to a new people who do not reject them.

90.　Those were the (prophets) who received Allah's guidance: follow the guidance they received; Say: "No reward for this do I ask of you: this is no less than a Message for the nations."

91.　No just estimate of Allah do they make when they say: "Nothing does Allah send down to man (by way of revelation)" say: "Who then sent down the Book which Moses brought?- a light and guidance to man: but you make it into (separate) sheets for show, while you conceal much (of its contents): therein you were taught that which you did not know, neither you nor your fathers." Say: "Allah (sent it down)": then leave them to plunge in vain discourse and trifling.[11]

92.　And this is a Book which We have sent down, bringing blessings, and confirming (the revelations) which came before

---

10.　Descendants, offspring　　　　11.　Worthless

it: that you may warn the Mother of Cities[12] and all around her. Those who believe in the Hereafter believe in this (Book), and they are constant in guarding their prayers.

93.   Who can be more wicked than one who invents a lie against Allah, or says, "I have received inspiration," when he has received none, or (again) who says, "I can reveal the like of what Allah has revealed"? If you could but see how the wicked (do fare) in the flood of confusion at death! - the angels stretch forth their hands, (saying),"Yield up your souls: this day you shall receive your reward,- a Chastisement of shame, for that you used to tell lies against Allah, and scornfully to reject of His Signs!"

94.   "And behold! you come to Us bare and alone as We created you for the first time: you have left behind you all (the favours) which We bestowed on you: We do not see with you your intercessors whom you thought to be partners in your affairs: so now all relations between you have been cut off, and your (pet) fancies have left you in the lurch!"

95.   It is Allah Who causes the seed-grain and the date-stone to split and sprout. He causes the living to issue from the dead, and He is the One to cause the dead to issue from the living. That is Allah: then how are you deluded away from the truth?

96.   He it is that cleaves the day-break (from the dark): He makes the night for rest and tran-quillity, and the sun and moon for the reckoning (of time): Such is the judgment and ordering of (Him), the Exalted in Power, the Omniscient.

97.   It is He Who makes the stars (as beacons) for you, that you may guide yourselves, with their help, through the dark spaces of land and sea: We detail Our Signs for people who know.

98.   It is He Who has produced you from a single person: here is a place of sojourn and a place of departure: We detail Our Signs for people who understand.

99.   It is He Who sends down rain from the skies: with it We produce

12.   Makkah

vegetation of all kinds: from some We produce green (crops), out of which We pro-duce grain, heaped up (at har-vest); out of the date-palm and its sheaths (or spathes) (come) clusters of dates hanging low and near: and (then there are) gardens of grapes, and olives, and pomegranates, each similar (in kind) yet different (in variety): when they begin to bear fruit, feast your eyes with the fruit and the ripeness thereof. Behold! in these things there are Signs for people who believe.

100. Yet they make the Jinns equals with Allah, though Allah did create the Jinns; and they falsely, having no knowledge, attribute to Him sons and daughters. Praise and glory be to Him! (for He is) above what they attribute to Him!

101. To Him is due the primal origin of the heavens and the earth: how can He have a son when He has no consort? He created all things, and He has full knowledge of all things.

102. That is Allah, your Lord! there is no god but He, the Creator of all things: then worship Him and He has power to dispose of all affairs.

103. No vision can grasp Him, but His grasp is over all vision: He is above all comprehension, yet is acquainted with all things.

104. "Now have come to you, from your Lord, proofs (to open your eyes): if any will see, it will be for (the good of) his own soul; if any will be blind, it will be to his own (harm): I am not (here) to watch over your doings."

105. Thus do We explain the Signs by various (symbols): that they may say, "You have taught (us) diligently," and that We may make the matter clear to those who know.

106. Follow what you are taught by inspiration from your Lord: there is no god but He: and turn aside from those who join gods with Allah.

107. If it had been Allah's plan, they would not have taken false gods: but We made you not one to watch over their doings, nor are you set over them to dispose of their affairs.

108. You do not Revile[13] those whom they call upon besides Allah,

13.   Abuse, ridicule

lest they out of spite revile Allah in their ignorance. Thus have We made alluring to each people its own doings. In the end will they return to their Lord, and We shall then tell them the truth of all that they did.

109. They swear their strongest oaths by Allah, that if a (special) Sign came to them, by it they would believe. Say: "Certainly (all) Signs are in the power of Allah: but what will make you (Muslims) realize that (even) if (special) Signs came, they will not believe."?

110. We (too) shall turn to (confusion) their hearts and their eyes, even as they refused to believe in this in the first instance: We shall leave them in their trespasses, to wander in distraction.

111. Even if We sent angels to them, and the dead spoke to them, and We gathered together all things before their very eyes, they are not the ones to believe, unless it is in Allah's plan. But most of them ignore (the truth).

112. Likewise, We made for every Messenger an enemy, Satan among men and jinns, inspiring each other with flowery discourses by way of deception. If your Lord had so planned, they would not have done it: so leave them and their inventions alone.

113. To such (deceit) let the hearts of those incline, who have no faith in the Hereafter: let them delight in it, and let them earn from it what they may.

114. Say: "Shall I seek for judge other than Allah? - when He it is Who has sent to you the Book, explained in detail." They know full well, to whom We have given the Book, that it has been sent down from your Lord in truth. Never be then of those who doubt.

115. The Word of your Lord finds its fulfilment in truth and in justice: none can change His Words: for He is the One Who hears and knows all.

116. Were you to follow the common run of those on earth, they will lead you away from the Way of Allah. They follow nothing but conjecture: they do nothing but lie.

117. Your Lord knows best who strays from His Way: He knows best who they are that receive His guidance.

118. So eat of (meats) on which Allah's name has been pronounced, if you have faith in His Signs.

119. Why should you not eat of (meats) on which Allah's name has been pronounced, when He has explained to you in detail what is forbidden to you - except under compulsion of necessity? But many do mislead (men) by their appetites unchecked by knowledge. Your Lord knows best those who transgress.

120. Eschew[14] all sin, open or secret: those who earn sin will get due recompense for their "earnings."

121. Do not eat of (meats) on which Allah's name has not been pronounced: that would be impiety. But the evil ones ever inspire their friends to contend with you if you were to obey them, you would indeed be Pagans.

122. Can he who was dead, to whom We gave life, and a light whereby he can walk amongst men, be like him who is in the depths of darkness, from which he can never come out? Thus to those without Faith their own deeds seem pleasing.

123. Thus have We placed leaders in every town, its wicked men, to plot (and burrow[15]) therein: but they only plot against their own souls, and they do not perceive it.

124. When there comes to them a Sign (from Allah), they say: "We shall not believe until we receive one (exactly) like those received by Allah's Apostles." Allah knows best where (and how) to carry out His mission. Soon will the wicked be overtaken by humiliation before Allah, and a severe punishment, for all their plots.

125. Those whom Allah (in His Plan) wills to guide,- He opens their breast to Islam; those whom He wills to leave straying,- He makes their breast close and constricted,[16] as if they had to climb up to the skies: thus Allah (heaps) the Chastisement on

---

14. Avoid

15. Dig. hide (in a hole)

16. Shrunk, compressed

those who refuse to believe.

126.   This is the Way of your Lord, leading straight: We have detailed the Signs for those who receive admonition.

127.   For them will be a Home of peace in the presence of their Lord: He will be their friend, because they practised (righteousness).

128.   One day He will gather them all together, (and say): "O you assembly of Jinns! much (toll) did you take of men." Their friends amongst men will say: "Our Lord! we made profit from each other: but (alas!) we reached our term - which You appointed for us." He will say: "The Fire be your dwelling-place: you will dwell therein for ever, except as Allah wills." for your Lord is full of wisdom and knowledge.

129.   Thus We make the wrong-doers turn to each other, because of what they earn.

130.   "O you assembly of Jinns and men! did not the Messen-gers come to you from amongst you, setting forth unto you My Signs, and warning you of the meeting of this Day of yours?" They will say: "We bear witness against ourselves." It was the life of this world that deceived them. So they will bear witness against themselves that they rejected Faith.

131.   (The Apostles were sent) thus, for your Lord would not destroy men's habitations for their wrong-doing whilst their occupants were unwarned.

132.   To all are degrees (or ranks) according to their deeds: for your Lord is not unmindful of anything that they do.

133.   Your Lord is Self-sufficient, full of Mercy: if it were His Will, He could destroy you, and in your place appoint whom He will as your successors, even as He raised you up from the posterity[17] of other people.

134.   All that has been promised to you will come to pass: nor can you frustrate it (in the least bit).

135.   Say: "O my people! do whatever you can: I will do (my part):

---

17.   Offspring, discendants

soon will you know who it is whose end will be (best) in the Hereafter: certain it is that the wrong- doers will not prosper."

136. Out of what Allah has produced in abundance in tilth and in cattle, they assigned Him a share: they say, according to their fancies: "This is for Allah, and this" - for our "partners"! but the share of their "partners" does not reach Allah, whilst the share of Allah reaches their "partners" ! evil (and unjust) is their assignment!

137. Even so, in the eyes of most of the pagans, their "partners" made alluring the slaughter of their children, in order to lead them to their own destruction, and cause confusion in their religion. If Allah has willed, they would not have done so: but leave them and their inventions alone.

138. And they say that such and such cattle and crops are taboo, and none should eat of them except those whom - so they say - We wish; further, there are cattle forbidden to yoke or burden, and cattle on which, (at slaughter), the name of Allah is not pronounced; - inventions against Allah's name: soon will He requite[18] them for their inventions.

139. They say: "What is in the wombs of such and such cattle is specially reserved (for food) for our men, and forbidden to our women; but if it is still-born, then all have shares therein. For their (false) attribution (of superstitions to Allah), He will soon punish them: for He is full of wisdom and knowledge.

140. Lost are those who slay their children, from folly, without knowledge, and forbid food which Allah has provided for them, inventing (lies) against Allah. They have indeed gone astray and heeded no guidance.

141. It is He Who produces gardens, with trellises[19] and without, and dates, and tilth with produce of all kinds, and olives and pomegranates, similar (in kind) and different (in variety): eat of their fruit in their season, but render the dues that are proper

---

18. Repay (for one's good or bad deeds).
19. Lattice or grating of light wooden crossbars.

on the day that the harvest is gathered. But waste not by excess: for Allah does not love the wasters.

142.   Of the cattle are some for burden and some for meat: eat what Allah has provided for you, and follow not the footsteps of Satan: for he is to you an avowed enemy.

143.   (Take) eight (head of cattle) in (four) pairs: of sheep a pair, and of goats a pair; say, has He forbidden the two males, or the two females, or (the young) which the wombs of the two females enclose? Tell me with knowledge if you are truthful:

144.   Of camels a pair, and of oxen a pair; say, has He forbidden the two males, or the two females, or (the young) which the wombs of the two females enclose? - Were you present when Allah ordered you such a thing? But who does more wrong than one who invents a lie against Allah, to lead astray men without knowledge? For Allah does not guide people who do wrong.

145.   Say: "I do not find in the Message received by me by inspiration any (meat) forbid-den to be eaten by one who wishes to eat it, unless it be dead meat, or blood poured forth, or the flesh of swine,- for it is an abomination - or, what is impious, (meat) on which a name has been invoked, other than Allah's". But (even so), if a person is forced by necessity, without wilful disobedience, nor transgressing due limits,- your Lord is Oft-forgiving, Most Merciful.

146.   For those who followed the Jewish Law, We forbade every (animal) with undivided hoof, and We forbade them that fat of the ox and the sheep, except what adheres to their backs or their entrails, or is mixed up with a bone: this in recompense for their wilful disobedience: for We are true (in Our ordinances).

147.   If they accuse you of falsehood, say: "Your Lord is full of mercy all- embracing; but from people in guilt never will His wrath be turned back.

148.   Those who give partners (to Allah) will say: "If Allah had wished, we should not have given partners to Him nor would

our fathers; nor should we have had any taboos."[20] So did their ancestors argue falsely, until they tasted of Our wrath. Say: "Have you any (certain) knowledge? If so, produce it before us. You follow nothing but conjecture: you do nothing but lie."

149. Say: "With Allah is the argument that reaches home: if it had been His Will, He could indeed have guided you all."

150. Say: "Bring forward your witnesses to prove that Allah forbade you so and so." If they bring such witnesses, you should not be amongst them: nor you should follow the vain desires of such as treat Our Signs as falsehoods, and such as do not believe in the Hereafter: for they hold others as equal with their Guardian-Lord.

151. Say: "Come, I will rehearse[21] what Allah has (really) prohibited you from": Join not anything as equal with Him; be good to your parents; kill not your children on a plea of want;- We provide sustenance for you and for them;- do not come near to shameful deeds, whether open or secret; take not life, which Allah has made sacred, except by way of justice and law: thus does He command you, that you may learn wisdom.

152. And come not near to the orphan's property, except to improve it, until he attain the age of full strength; give measure and weight with (full) justice;- no burden do We place on any soul, but that which it can bear;- whenever you speak, speak justly, even if a near relative is concerned; and fulfil the Covenant of Allah: thus He commands you, that you may remember.

153. Verily, this is My Way, leading straight: follow it: do not follow (other) paths: they will scatter you about from His (great) path: thus He commands you that you may be righteous.

154. Moreover, We gave Moses the Book, completing (Our favour) to those who would do right, and explained all things in detail,- and a guide and a mercy, that they might believe in the meeting with their Lord.

---

20. Setting apart a person or thing as accursed or sacred, ban, prohibition.
21. Recite, recount

155.   And this is a Book which We have revealed as a blessing: so
        follow it and be righteous, that you may receive mercy:

156.   Lest you should say: "The Book was sent down to two Peoples
        before us, and for our part, we remained unacquainted with all
        that they learned by assiduous[22] study:"

157.   Or lest you should say: "If the Book had only been sent down
        to us, we should have followed its guidance better than they."
        Now then has come unto you a Clear (Sign) from your Lord,-
        and a guide and a mercy: then who could do more wrong than
        one who rejects Allah's Signs, and turns away therefrom? In
        good time shall We requite those who turn away from Our
        Signs, with a dreadful Chastisement, for their turning away.

158.   Are they waiting to see if the angels come to them, or your
        Lord (Himself), or certain of the Signs of your Lord! the day
        that certain of the Signs of your Lord do come, no good will it
        do to a soul to believe in them then, if it believed not before
        nor earned right-teousness through its Faith. Say: "You wait:
        we too are waiting."

159.   As for those who divide their religion and break up into sects,
        you have no part in them in the least: their affair is with Allah:
        He will in the end tell them the truth of all that they did.

160.   He that does good shall have ten times as much to his credit:
        he that does evil shall only be recompensed according to his
        evil: no wrong shall be done to (any of) them.

161.   Say: "Verily, my Lord has guided me to a way that is straight,-
        a religion of right,- the path (trod) by Abraham, the true in
        faith, and he (certainly) did not join gods with Allah."

162.   Say: "Truly, my prayer and my service of sacrifice, my life and
        my death, are (all) for Allah, the Cherisher of the Worlds:

163.   No partner has He: this I am commanded, and I am the first of
        those who bow to His Will.

164.   Say: "Shall I seek for (my) Cherisher other than Allah, when
        He is the Cherisher of all things (that exist)? Every soul draws

---

22.   Diligent

the meed[23] of its acts on none but itself: no bearer of burdens can bear the burden of another. Your goal in the end is towards Allah: He will tell you the truth of the things wherein you disputed."

165. It is He Who has made you (His) agents, inheritors of the earth: He has raised you in ranks, some above others: that He may try you in the gifts He has given you: for your Lord is quick in punishment: yet He is indeed Oft-forgiving, Most Merciful.

---

23. Reward

SURAH—7

AL-A'ARAF
(INTRODUCTION)

This Surah is closely connected, both chronologically and in respect of the argument, with the previous Surah. But it expounds the doctrine of revelation and man's spiritual history by illustrations from Adam onwards, through various Prophets, and the details of Moses' struggles, to the time of the Apostle Muhammad, in whom Allah's revelation is completed.

SURAH AL-A'ARAF (THE HEIGHTS)

In the name of Allah, Most Gracious, Most Merciful

1. Alif, Lam, Mim, Sad.

2. A Book revealed unto you,- So let your heart be oppressed no more by any difficulty on that account,- that with it you might warn (the erring) and teach the Believers.

3. Follow (O men!) the revelation given to you from your Lord, and follow not, as friends or protectors, other than Him. Little it is you remember of admonition.

4. How many towns have We destroyed (for their sins)? Our punishment took them on a sudden by night or while they slept for their afternoon rest.

5. When (thus) Our punish-ment took them, no cry did they utter but this: "Indeed we did wrong."

6. Then shall We question those to whom Our Message was sent and those by whom We sent it.

7. And verily, We shall recount their whole story with knowledge, for We were never absent (at any time or place).

8. The balance that day will be true (to a nicety): those whose scale (of good) will be heavy, will prosper:

9. Those whose scale will be light, will find their souls in perdition,[1] for that they wrong-fully treated Our Signs.

10. It is We Who have placed you with authority on earth, and provided you therein with means for the fulfilment of your

---

1.   Eternal death, damnation

life: small are the thanks that you give!

11. It is We Who created you and gave you shape; then We said the angels bow down to Adam, and they bowed down; not so Iblis; He refused to be of those who bow down.

12. (Allah) said: "What prevented you from bowing down when I commanded you?" He said: "I am better than he: you created me from fire, and him from clay."

13. (Allah) said: "Get you down from here: it is not for you to be arrogant here: get out, for you are of the meanest(of creatures)."

14. He said: "Give me respite till the day they are raised up."

15. (Allah) said: "Be you among those who have respite."

16. He said: "Because You have thrown me out of the way, I will lie in wait for them on Your Straight Way:

17. "Then I will assault them from before them and behind them, from their right and their left: nor will You find gratitude in most of them, (for Your mercies)."

18. (Allah) said: "Get out from this, disgraced and expelled. If any of them follow you,- I will fill Hell with you all.

19. "O Adam! You and your wife dwell in the Garden, and enjoy (its good things) as you wish: but do not approach this tree, or you run into harm and transgression."

20. Then began Satan to whis-per suggestions to them, in order to reveal to them their shame that was hidden from them (before): he said: "Your Lord only forbade you this tree, lest you should become angels or such beings as live for ever."

21. And he swore to them both, that he was their sincere adviser.

22. So by deceit he brought about their fall: when they tasted of the tree, their shame became manifest to them, and they began to sew together the leaves of the Garden over their bodies. And their Lord called to them: "Did I not forbid you that tree, and tell you that Satan was an avowed enemy to you?"

23. They said: "Our Lord! We have wronged our own souls: If You do not forgive us and do not bestow upon us Your Mercy, we shall certainly be lost."

24.   (Allah) said: "Get you down, with enmity between yourselves. On earth will be your dwelling-place and your means of livelihood,- for a time."

25.   He said: "Therein you shall live, and therein you shall die; but from it you shall be taken out (at last)."

26.   O you Children of Adam! We have bestowed raiment upon you to cover your shame, as well as to be an adornment to you. But the raiment of righteousness,- that is the best. Such are among the Signs of Allah, that they may receive admonition!

27.   O you Children of Adam! let not Satan seduce you, in the same manner as He got your parents out of the Garden, stripping them of their raiment, to expose their shame: for he and his tribe watch you from a position where you cannot see them: We made the Satan friends (only) to those without Faith.

28.   When they do anything that is shameful, they say: "We found our fathers doing so"; and "Allah commanded us thus": Say: "Nay, Allah never commands what is shameful: do you say of Allah what you do not know?"

29.   Say: "My Lord has com-manded justice; and that you set your whole selves (to Him) at every time and place of prayer, and call upon Him, making your devotion sincere as in His sight: such as He created you in the beginning, so shall you return."

30.   Some He has guided: others have (by their choice) deserved the loss of their way; in that they took the Satan, in preference to Allah, for their friends and protectors, and think that they receive guidance.

31.   O Children of Adam! wear your beautiful apparel at every time and place of prayer: eat and drink: but do not waste by excess, for Allah does not love the wasters.

32.   Say: Who has forbidden the beautiful (gifts) of Allah, which He has produced for His servants, and the things, clean and pure, which (He has provided) for sustenance? Say: They are, in the life of this world, for those who believe, (and) purely for them on the Day of Judgment. Thus do We explain the Signs

in detail for those who understand.

33.   Say: The things that my Lord has indeed forbidden are: shameful deeds, whether open or secret; sins and trespasses against truth or reason; assig-ning of partners to Allah, for which He has given no authority; and saying things about Allah of which you have no knowledge.

34.   To every people is a term appointed: when their term is reached, not an hour can they cause delay, nor (an hour) can they advance (it in anticipation).

35.   O you Children of Adam! whenever there come to you Apostles from amongst you, rehearsing My Signs to you,- those who are righteous and mend (their lives),- on them shall be no fear nor shall they grieve.

36.   But those who reject Our Signs and treat them with arrogance,- they are Compa-nions of the Fire, to dwell therein (for ever).

37.   Who is more unjust than one who invents a lie against Allah or rejects His Signs? For such, their portion appointed must reach them from the Book (of Decrees): until, when our messengers (of death) arrive and take their souls, they say: "Where are the things that you used to invoke besides Allah?" They will reply, "They have left us in the lurch," and they will bear witness against them-selves, that they had rejected Allah.

38.   He will say: "You enter in the company of the peoples who passed away before you - men and jinns, - into the Fire." Every time a new people enters, it curses its sister-people (that went before), until they follow each other, all into the Fire. Says the last about the first: "Our Lord! it is these that misled us: so give them a double Chastisement in the Fire." He will say: "Doubled for all" : but this you do not understand.

39.   Then the first will say to the last: "See then! You do not have any advantage over us; so you taste of the Chastisement for all that you did."

40.   To those who reject Our Signs and treat them with arrogance, no opening will there be of the gates of heaven, nor will they

enter the Garden, until the camel can pass through the eye of the needle: such is Our reward for those in sin.

41. For them there is Hell, as a couch (below) and folds of covering above: such is Our requital of those who do wrong.

42. But those who believe and work righteousness,- no burden do We place on any soul, but that which it can bear,-they will be Companions of the Garden, therein to dwell (for ever).

43. And We shall remove from their hearts any lurking sense of injury;- beneath them will be rivers flowing;- and they shall say: "Praise be to Allah, Who has guided us to this (felicity): never could we have found guidance, had it not been for the guidance of Allah: indeed it was the truth, that the Apostles of our Lord brought to us." And they shall hear the cry: "Behold! the Garden before you! you have been made its inheritors, for your deeds (of righteousness)."

44. The Companions of the Garden will call out to the Companions of the Fire: "We have indeed found the promises of our Lord to us true: have you also found Your Lord's promises true?" They shall say, "Yes"; But a a Crier shall proclaim between them: "The curse of Allah is on the wrong-doers;-

45. "Those who would hinder (men) from the path of Allah and would seek in it something crooked: they were those who denied the Hereafter."

46. Between them shall be a veil, and on the Heights will be men who would know every one by his marks: they will call out to the Companions of the Garden, "peace on you": they will not have entered, but will have an assurance (thereof).

47. When their eyes shall be turned towards the Companions of the Fire, they will say: "Our Lord! do not send us to the company of the wrong-doers."

48. The men on the Heights will call to certain men whom they will know from their marks, saying: "Of what profit to you were your hoards and your arrogant ways?

49. "Behold! are these not the men whom you swore that Allah

would never bless with His Mercy? you enter the Garden: no fear shall be on you, nor shall you grieve."

50. The Companions of the Fire will call to the Companions of the Garden: "Pour down to us water or anything that Allah provides for your sustenance." They will say: "Allah has forbidden both these things to those who rejected Him."

51. "Such as took their religion to be mere amusement and play, and were deceived by the life of the world." That day We shall forget them as they forgot the meeting of this day of theirs, and as they were wont to reject Our Signs.

52. For We had certainly sent to them a Book, based on knowledge, which We explained in detail,- a guide and a mercy to all who believe.

53. Do they just wait for the final fulfilment of the event? On the day the event is finally fulfilled, those who disregarded it before will say: "The Apostles of our Lord did indeed bring true (tidings). Have we no intercessors now to intercede on our behalf? Or could we be sent back? Then should we behave differently from our behaviour in the past." In fact they will have lost their souls, and the things they invented will leave them in the lurch.

54. Your Guardian-Lord is Allah, Who created the heavens and the earth in six Days, and is firmly established on the Throne (of authority): He draws the night as a veil over the day, each seeking the other in rapid succession: He created the sun, the moon, and the stars, (all) governed by laws under His Command. Is it not His to create and to govern? Blessed be Allah, the Cherisher and Sustainer of the Worlds.

55. Call on your Lord with humility and in private: for Allah does not love those who trespass beyond bounds.

56. Do no mischief on the earth, after it has been set in order, but call on Him with fear and longing (in your hearts): for the Mercy of Allah is (always) near to those who do good.

57. It is He Who sends the winds like heralds of glad tidings, going

before His mercy: when they have carried the heavy-laden clouds, We drive them to a land that is dead, make rain to descend thereon, and produce every kind of harvest therewith: thus shall We raise up the dead: perchance you may remember.

58.   From the land that is clean and good, by the Will of its Cherisher, springs up produce, (rich) after its kind: but from the land that is bad, springs up nothing but that which is niggardly: thus do We explain the Signs by various (symbols) to those who are grateful.

59.   We sent Noah to his people. He said: "O my people! worship Allah! you have no other god but Him. I fear for you the punishment of a dreadful Day!

60.   The leaders of his people said: "Ah! we see you evidently wandering (in mind)."

61.   He said: "O my people! no wandering is there in my (mind): on the contrary I am an Apostle from the Lord and Cherisher of the Worlds!

62.   "I but fulfil towards you the duties of my Lord's mission: sincere is my advice to you, and I know from Allah something that you do not know.

63.   "Do you wonder that there has come to you a message from your Lord, through a man of your own people, to warn you,- so that you may fear Allah and haply[2] receive His Mercy?"

64.   But they rejected him, and We delivered him, and those with him, in the Ark: but We overwhelmed in the Flood those who rejected Our Signs. They were indeed a blind people!

65.   To the 'Ad people, (We sent) Hud, one of their (own) brethren: he said: O my people! worship Allah! you have no other god but Him, will you not fear (Allah)?"

66.   The leaders of the Unbelievers among his people said: "Ah! we see you are an imbecile!" and "We think you are a liar!"

67.   He said: "O my people! I am no imbecile, but (I am) an Apostle from the Lord and Cherisher of the worlds!

---

2.   Perhaps, maybe

68. "I but fulfil towards you the duties of my Lord's mission: I am to you a sincere and trustworthy adviser.

69. "Do you wonder that there has come to you a message from your Lord through a man of your own people, to warn you? Call in remembrance that He made you inheritors after the people of Noah, and gave you a stature tall among the nations. Call in remembrance the benefits (you have received) from Allah: that so you may prosper."

70. They said: "Do you come to us that we may worship Allah alone, and give up the cult of our fathers? Bring us what you threaten us with, if so be that you tell the truth!"

71. He said: "Punishment and wrath have already come upon you from your Lord: do you dispute with me over names which you have devised - you and your fathers,- without authority from Allah? Then wait: I am amongst you, also waiting."

72. We saved him and those who adhered to him, by Our Mercy, and We cut off the roots of those who rejected Our Signs and did not believe.

73. To the Thamud people (We sent) Salih, one of their own brethren: He said: "O my people! worship Allah: you have no other god but Him. Now has come to you a clear (Sign) from your Lord! This she-camel of Allah is a Sign to you: so leave her to graze in Allah's earth, and let her come to no harm, or you shall be seized with a grievous punishment.

74. "And remember how He made you inheritors after the 'Ad people and gave you habitations in the land: you build for yourselves palaces and castles in (open) plains, and carve out homes in the mountains; so bring to remembrance the benefits (you have received) from Allah, and refrain from evil and mischief on the earth."

75. The leaders of the arrogant party among his people said to those who were reckoned powerless - those among them who believed: "Do you know indeed that Salih is an Apostle from his Lord?" They said: "We do indeed believe in the revelation

which has been sent through him."

76.   The arrogant party said: "For our part, we reject what you believe in."

77.   Then they hamstrung[3] the she-camel, and insolently defied the order of their Lord, saying: "O Salih! bring about your threats, if you are an Apostle (of Allah)!"

78.   So the earthquake took them unawares, and they lay prostrate in their homes in the morning!

79.   So Salih left them, saying: "O my people! I did indeed convey to you the message for which I was sent by my Lord: I gave you good counsel, but you do not love good counsellors!"

80.   We also (sent) Lut: he said to his people: "Do you commit lewdness[4] such as no people in creation (ever) committed before you?

81.   "For you practise your lusts on men in preference to women : you are indeed a people transgressing beyond bounds."

82.   And his people gave no answer but this: they said, "Drive them out of your city: these are indeed men who want to be clean and pure!"

83.   But We saved him and his family, except his wife: she was of those who lagged behind.

84.   And We rained down on them a shower (of brimstone): then see what was the end of those who indulged in sin and crime!

85.   To the Madyan people We sent Shu'aib, one of their own brethren: he said: "O my people! worship Allah; you have no other god but Him. Now has come unto you a clear (Sign) from your Lord! so give just measure and weight, nor withhold from the people the things that are their due; and do no mischief on the earth after it has been set in order: that will be best for you, if you have Faith.

86.   "And do not squat on every road, breathing threats, hindering from the path of Allah those who believe in Him, and seeking in it something crooked; but remember how you were small in

---

3.   To cripple by cutting the hamstrings (tendons at back of knee)
4.   Indecency, obscenity.

numbers, and He gave you increase. And hold in your mind's eye what was the end of those who did mischief.

87. "And if there is a party among you who believes in the Message with which I have been sent, and a party which does not believe, hold yourselves in patience until Allah decides between us: for He is the best to decide.

88. The leaders, the arrogant party among his people, said: "O Shu'aib! we shall certainly drive you out of our city - (you) and those who believe with you; or else you (and they) shall have to return to our ways and religion." He said: "What! even though we do detest (them)?

89. "We should indeed invent a lie against Allah, if we returned to your ways after Allah has rescued us therefrom; nor could we by any manner of means return thereto unless it be as in the will and plan of Allah, our Lord. Our Lord can reach out to the utmost recesses of things by His knowledge. In Allah is our trust. Our Lord! You decide between us and our people in truth, for You are the best to decide."

90. The leaders, the Unbelie-vers among his people, said: "If you follow Shu'aib, be sure then you are ruined!"

91. But the earthquake took them unawares, and they lay prostrate in their homes before the morning!

92. The men who rejected Shu'aib became as if they had never been in the homes where they had flourished: the men who rejected Shu'aib - it was they who were ruined!

93. So Shu'aib left them, saying: "O my people! I did indeed convey to you the Messages for which I was sent by my Lord: I gave you good counsel, but how shall I lament over a people who refuse to believe!"

94. Whenever We sent a prophet to a town, We took up its people in suffering and adversity, in order that they might learn humility.

95. Then We changed their suffering into prosperity, until they grew and multiplied, and began to say: "Our fathers (too) were

touched by suffering and affluence" ... Behold! We called them
to account of a sudden, while they did not realise (their peril).

96. If the people of the towns had but believed and feared Allah,
We should indeed have opened out to them (all kinds of)
blessings from heaven and earth; but they rejected (the truth),
and We brought them to book for their misdeeds.

97. Did the people of the towns feel secure against the coming of
Our wrath by night while they were asleep?

98. Or else did they feel secure against its coming in broad daylight
while they played about (care-free)?

99. Did they then feel secure against the Plan of Allah?- but no
one can feel secure from the Plan of Allah, except those
(doomed) to ruin!

100. To those who inherit the earth in succession to its (previous)
possessors, is it not a guiding, (lesson) that, if We so willed,
We could punish them (too) for their sins, and seal up their
hearts so that they could not hear?

101. Such were the towns whose story We (thus) relate unto you:
there came indeed to them their Apostles with clear (Signs):
But they would not believe what they had rejected before. Thus
does Allah seal up the hearts of those who reject Faith.

102. Most of the men We did not find (true) to their covenant: but
most of them We found rebellious and disobedient.

103. Then after them We sent Moses with Our Signs to Pharaoh
and his chiefs, but they wrongfully rejected them: So see what
was the end of those who made mischief.

104. Moses said: "O Pharaoh! I am an Apostle from the Lord of the
worlds,-

105. One for whom it is right to say nothing but truth about Allah.
Now I have come to you (people), from your Lord, with a
clear (Sign): So let the Children of Israel depart along with
me."

106. (Pharaoh) said: "If indeed you have come with a Sign, show it
forth,- if you are telling the truth."

107. Then (Moses) threw his rod, and behold! it was a serpent, plain (for all to see)!

108. And he drew out his hand, and behold! it was white to all beholders!

109. Said the Chiefs of the people of Pharaoh: "This is indeed a sorcerer[5] well- versed.

110. "His plan is to get you out of your land: then what is it you counsel?"

111. They said: "Keep him and his brother in suspense (for a while); and send to the cities men to collect-

112. And bring up to you all (our) sorcerers well-versed."

113. So there came the sorcerers to Pharaoh: they said, "of course we shall have a (suitable) reward if we win!"

114. He said: "Yes, (and more),- for you shall in that case be (raised to posts) nearest (to my person)."

115. They said: "O Moses! will you throw (first), or shall we have the (first) throw?"

116. Said Moses: "You throw (first)." So when they threw, they bewitched the eyes of the people, and struck terror into them: for they showed a great (feat of) magic.

117. We put it into Moses's mind by inspiration: "Throw (now) your rod":and behold! it swallows up straightway all the falsehoods which they fake!

118. Thus truth was confirmed, and all that they did was made of no effect.

119. So the (great ones) were vanquished there and then, and were made to look small.

120. But the sorcerers fell down prostrate in adoration.

121. Saying: "We believe in the Lord of the Worlds,-

122. "The Lord of Moses and Aaron."

123. Said Pharaoh: "Do you believe in Him before I give you permission? Surely this is a trick which you have planned in

---

5.   Magician

the city to drive out its people: but soon you shall know (the consequences).

124. "Be sure I will cut off your hands and your feet on opposite sides, and I will cause you all to die on the cross."

125. They said: "For us, we are but sent back to our Lord:

126. "But you wreak your ven-geance on us simply because we believed in the Signs of our Lord when they reached us! Our Lord! pour out on us patience and constancy, and take our souls unto You as Muslims (who bow to Your Will)!

127. Said the chiefs of Pharaoh's people:"Will you leave Moses and his people, to spread mis-chief in the land, and to abandon you and your gods?" He said: "We will slay their male child-ren; we will save alive (only) their females; and we have irresistible (power) over them."

128. Moses said to his people: "Pray for help from Allah, and (wait) in patience and constancy: for the earth is Allah's, to give as a heritage to such of His servants as He pleases; and the end is (best) for the righteous.

129. They said: "We have had (nothing but) trouble, both before and after you came to us." He said: "It may be that your Lord will destroy your enemy and make you inheritors in the earth; that so He may try you by your deeds."

130. We punished the people of Pharaoh with years (of drought) and shortness of crops; that they might receive admonition.

131. But when good (times) came, they said, "This is due to us;" when gripped by calamity, they ascribed it to evil omens connected with Moses and those with him! Behold! in truth the omens of evil are theirs in Allah's sight, but most of them do not understand!

132. They said (to Moses): "Whatever be the Signs you bring, to work therewith your sorcery on us, we shall never believe in you.

133. So We sent (plagues) on them: wholesale Death, Locusts, Lice, Frogs, and Blood: Signs openly self-explained: but they were

steeped in arrogance,- a people given to sin.

134. Every time the Chastise-ment fell on them, they said: "O Moses! on our behalf call on your Lord in virtue of His promise to you: If you will remove the Chas-tisement from us, we shall truly believe in you, and we shall send away the Children of Israel with you."

135. But every time We removed the plague from them according to a fixed term which they had to fulfil,- Behold! they broke their word!

136. So We exacted retribution from them: We drowned them in the sea, because they rejected Our Signs and failed to take warning from them.

137. And We made a people, considered weak (and of no account), inheritors of lands in both East and West, - lands whereon We sent down Our blessings. The fair promise of your Lord was fulfilled for the Children of Israel, because they had patience and constancy, and We levelled to the ground the great works and fine buildings which Pharaoh and his people erected (with such pride).

138. We took the Children of Israel (with safety) across the sea. They came upon a people devoted entirely to some idols they had. They said: "O Moses! fashion for us a god like the gods they have." He said: "Surely you are a people without knowledge.

139. "As to these folks,- the cult they are in is (but) a fragment of a ruin, and vain is the (worship) which they practise."

140. He said: "Shall I seek for you a god other than the (true) God, when it is Allah Who has endowed you with gifts above the nations?"

141. And remember We rescued you from Pharaoh's people, who afflicted you with the worst of penalties, Who slew your male children and saved alive your females: in that was a momentous[6] trial from your Lord.

6.   Important

142. We appointed for Moses thirty nights, and completed (the period) with ten (more): thus was completed the term (of communion) with his Lord, forty nights. And Moses had charged his brother Aaron (before he went up): "Act for me amongst my people: do right, and do not follow the way of those who do mischief."

143. When Moses came to the place appointed by Us, and his Lord addressed him, he said: "O my Lord! show (Yourself) to me, that I may look upon You." Allah said: "By no means can you see Me (direct); But look upon the Mount; if it abide in its place, then shall you see Me." When his Lord manifested His glory on the Mount, He made it as dust, and Moses fell down in a swoon. When he recovered his senses he said: "Glory be to You! To You I turn in repentance, and I am the first to believe."

144. (Allah) said: "O Moses! I have chosen you above (other) men, by the mission I (have given you) and the words I (have spoken to you): take then the (re-velation) which I give you, and be of those who give thanks."

145. And We ordained laws for him in the Tablets in all matters, both commanding and explaining all things, (and said): "Take and hold these with firmness, and enjoin your people to hold fast by the best in the precepts[7]: soon shall I show you the homes of the wicked,- (how they lie desolate)."

146. Those who behave arro-gantly on the earth in defiance of right - I will turn them away from My Signs: Even if they see all the Signs, they will not believe in them; and if they see the way of right conduct, they will not adopt it as the way; but if they see the way of error, that is the way they will adopt. For they have rejected Our Signs, and failed to take warning from them.

147. Those who reject Our Signs and the Meeting in the Hereafter,- vain are their deeds: can they expect to be rewarded except as they have wrought?[8]

---

7. Moral principles, rules, or teachings.   8. Worked or done.

148. The people of Moses made, in his absence, out of their ornaments, the image of a calf, (for worship) having lowing sound.[9] Did they not see that it could neither speak to them, nor show them the way? They took it for worship and they did wrong.

149. When they repented, and saw that they had erred, they said: "If our Lord have not mercy upon us and forgive us, we shall indeed be of those who perish."

150. When Moses came back to his people, angry and grieved, he said: "Evil it is that you have done in my place in my absence: did you make haste to bring on the judgment of your Lord?" He put down the Tablets, seized his brother by (the hair of) his head, and dragged him to him. Aaron said: "Son of my mother! The people did indeed reckon me as nothing, and went near to slaying me! Make not the enemies rejoice over my misfortune, nor count you me amongst the people of sin."

151. Moses prayed: "O my Lord! forgive me and my brother! Admit us to Your mercy! for You are the Most Merciful of those who show mercy!"

152. Those who took the calf (for worship) will indeed be overwhelmed with wrath from their Lord, and with shame in this life: thus do We recompense those who invent (falsehoods).

153. But those who do wrong but repent thereafter and (truly) believe,- verily your Lord is thereafter Oft-forgiving, Most Merciful.

154. When the anger of Moses was appeased, he took up the Tablets: in the writing thereon was Guidance and Mercy for such as fear their Lord.

155. And Moses chose seventy of his people for Our place of meeting: when they were seized with violent quaking,[10] he prayed: "O my Lord! if it had been Your Will You could have destroyed, long before, both them and me: would You destroy us for the deeds of the foolish ones among us? this is no more

---

9.   To moo (like a cow), a lowing sound.
10. Shaking

than Your trial: by it You cause whom You will to stray, and You lead whom You will into the right path. You are our Protector: so forgive us and give us Your Mercy; for You are the best of those who forgive.

156. "And ordain for us that which is good, in this life and in the Hereafter: for we have turned unto You." He said: "With My punishment I visit whom I will; but My Mercy extends to all things. That (Mercy) I shall ordain for those who do right, and pay Zakat, and those who believe in Our Signs;-

157. "Those who follow the Apostle, the unlettered Prophet, whom they find mentioned in their own (Scriptures),- in the Tourat[11] and the Gospel[12];- for he commands them what is just and forbids them what is evil; he allows them as lawful what is good (and pure) and prohibits them from what is bad (and impure); He releases them from their heavy burdens and from the yokes[13] that are upon them. So it is those who believe in him, honour him, help him, and follow the Light which is sent down with him,- it is they who will prosper."

158. Say: "O men! I am sent to you all, as the Apostle of Allah, to Whom belongs the dominion of the heavens and the earth: there is no god but He: it is He that gives both life and death. So believe in Allah and His Apostle, the unlettered Prophet, who believes in Allah and His Words: follow him that (so) you may be guided."

159. Of the people of Moses there is a section who guide and do justice in the light of truth.

160. We divided them into twelve tribes or nations. We directed Moses by inspiration, when his (thirsty) people asked him for water: "Strike the rock with your staff": out of it there gushed forth twelve springs: each group knew its own place for water. We gave them the shade of clouds, and sent down to them manna and quails,[14] (saying): "Eat of the good things We have

---

11. Torah
12. Injil
13. Servitude, or restrictions
14. See footnote on Al-Baqarat 2:57

provided for you": (but they rebelled); to Us they did no harm, but they harmed their own souls.

161. And remember it was said to them: "Dwell in this town and eat therein as you wish, but say the word of humility and enter the gate in a posture of humility: We shall forgive you your faults; We shall increase (the portion of) those who do good."

162. But the transgressors among them changed the word from that which had been given them so We sent on them a plague from heaven. For that they repeatedly transgressed.

163. Ask them concerning the town standing close by the sea. Behold! they transgressed in the matter of the Sabbath. For on the day of their Sabbath their fish did come to them, openly holding up their heads, but on the day they had no Sabbath, they did not come: thus did We make a trial of them, for they were given to transgression.

164. When some of them said: "Why do you preach to a people whom Allah will destroy or visit with a terrible punishment?"-said the preachers:" To discharge our duty to your Lord, and perchance they may fear Him."

165. When they disregarded the warnings that had been given them, We rescued those who forbade evil; but We visited the wrong-doers with a grievous punishment because they were given to transgre-ssion.

166. When in their insolence they transgressed (all) prohibi-tions, We said to them: "Be you apes, despised and rejected."

167. Behold! Your Lord did declare that He would send against them, to the Day of Judgment, those who would afflict them with grievous chastisement. Your Lord is quick in retribution, but He is also Oft-forgiving, Most Merciful.

168. We broke them up into sections on this earth. There are among them some that are the righteous, and some that are the opposite. We have tried them with both prosperity and adversity: in order that they might turn (to Us).

169. After them succeeded an (evil) generation: they inherited the

Book, but they chose (for themselves) the vanities of this world, saying (for excuse): "(Everything) will be forgiven us." (Even so), if similar vanities came their way, they would (again) seize them. Was not the Covenant of the Book taken from them, that they would not ascribe to Allah anything but the truth? And they study what is in the Book. But best for the righteous is the Home in the Hereafter. Will you not understand?

170. As to those who hold fast by the Book and establish regular prayer,- never shall We suffer the reward of the righteous to perish.

171. When We shook the Mount over them, as if it had been a canopy, and they thought it was going to fall on them (We said): "Hold firmly to what We have given you, and bring (ever) to remembrance what is therein; perchance you may fear Allah."

172. When your Lord drew forth from the Children of Adam- from their loins - their descendants, and made them testify concerning themselves, (saying): "Am I not your Lord (Who cherishes and sustains you)?"- they said: "Yes! We do testify!" (This), lest you should say on the Day of Judgment: "Of this we were never mindful":

173. Or lest you should say: "Our fathers before us may have taken false gods, but we are (their) descendants after them: will You then destroy us because of the deeds of men who were futile?"

174. Thus do We explain the Signs in detail; and perchance they may turn (to Us).

175. Relate to them the story of the man to whom We sent Our Signs, but he passed them by: so Satan followed him up, and he went astray.

176. If it had been Our Will, We should have elevated him with Our Signs; but he inclined to the earth, and followed his own vain desires. His similitude is that of a dog: if you attack him, he lolls out his tongue, or if you leave him alone, he (still) lolls out his tongue. That is the similitude of those who reject Our Signs; so relate the story; perchance they may reflect.

177. Evil as an example are people who reject Our Signs and wrong their own souls.

178. Whom Allah does guide,- he is on the right path: whom He rejects from His guidance,- such are the persons who perish.

179. Many are the Jinns and men We have made for Hell: they have hearts wherewith they do not understand, eyes where-with they do not see, and ears wherewith they do not hear. They are like cattle,- nay more misguided: for they are heedless (of warning).

180. The most beautiful names belong to Allah: so call on Him by them; but shun such men as use profanity[15] in His names: for what they do, they will soon be requited.

181. Of those We have created are people who direct (others) with truth. And dispense justice therewith.

182. Those who reject Our Signs, We shall gradually visit with punishment, in ways they perceive not;

183. Respite I will grant to them: for My scheme is strong (and unfailing).

184. Do they not reflect? Their companion is not seized with madness: he is but a perspicuous[16] warner.

185. Do they see nothing in the kingdom of the heavens and the earth and all that Allah has created? (Do they not see) that it may well be that their terms is near drawing to an end? In what Message after this will they then believe?

186. To such as Allah rejects from His guidance, there can be no guide: He will leave them in their trespasses, wandering in distraction.

187. They ask you about the (final) Hour - when will be its appointed time? Say: "The knowledge thereof is with my Lord (alone): none but He can reveal as to when it will occur. Heavy were its burden through the heavens and the earth. Only, all of a sudden will it come to you." They ask you as if you were eager in search thereof: say: "The knowledge thereof is with Allah (alone), but most men do not know."

---

15. Irreverence, blasphemy   16. Plain, easily understood

188. Say: "I have no power over any good or harm to myself except as Allah wills. If I had knowledge of the unseen, I should have multiplied all good, and no evil should have touched me: I am but a warner, and a bringer of glad tidings to those who have faith."

189. It is He Who created you from a single person, and made his mate of like nature, in order that he might dwell with her (in love). When they are united, she bears a light burden and carries it about (unnoticed). When she grows heavy, they both pray to Allah their Lord, (saying): "If you give us a goodly child, we vow we shall (ever) be grateful."

190. But when He gives them a goodly child, they ascribe to others a share in the gift they have received: but Allah is Exalted high above the partners they ascribe to Him.

191. Do they indeed ascribe to Him as partners things that can create nothing, but are them-selves created?

192. No aid can they give them, nor can they aid themselves!

193. If you call them to guidance, they will not obey: for you it is the same whether you call them or you hold your peace!

194. Verily those whom you call upon besides Allah are servants like you: call upon them, and let them listen to your prayer, if you are (indeed) truthful!

195. Have they feet to walk with? Or hands to lay hold with? Or eyes to see with? Or ears to hear with? Say: "Call your 'god-partners', scheme (your worst) against me, and give me no respite!

196. "For my Protector is Allah, Who revealed the Book (from time to time), and He will choose and befriend the righteous.

197. "But those you call upon besides Him, are unable to help you, and indeed to help themselves."

198. If you call them to guidance, they do not hear. You will see them looking at you, but they do not see.

199. Hold to forgiveness; command what is right; but turn away from the ignorant.

200. If a suggestion from Satan assails your (mind), seek refuge with Allah; for He hears and knows (all things).

201. Those who fear Allah, when a thought of evil from Satan assaults them, bring Allah to remembrance, when lo! they see (aright)!

202. But their brethren (the evil ones) plunge them deeper into error, and never relax (their efforts).

203. If you do not bring them a revelation, they say: "Why have you not got it together?" Say: "I but follow what is revealed to me from my Lord: this is (nothing but) Lights from your Lord, and Guidance, and Mercy, for any who have Faith."

204. When the Qur'an is read, listen to it with attention, and hold your peace: that you may receive Mercy.

205. And you (O reader!) bring your Lord to remembrance in your (very) soul, with humility and in reverence, without loudness in words, in the mornings and evenings; and you be not of those who are unheedful.

206. Those who are near to your Lord, do not disdain to do Him worship: they celebrate His praises, and bow down before Him.

———————

SURAH—8

AL-ANF'AL

(INTRODUCTION)

In the previous Introductions to the Surahs we have shown how each Surah is a step or gradation in the teaching of the Quran. The first seven Surahs, comprising a little less than one-third of the Quran, form a gradation, sketching the early spiritual history of man and leading up to the formation of the new *Ummah* or Community of the Holy Apostle. Now we begin another gradation, consolidating that *Ummah* and directing us as to various phases in our new collective life.

In this chapter we have the lessons of the Battle of Badr enforced in their larger aspects: (1) the question of war booty, (2) the true virtues necessary for fighting the good fight, (3) victory against odds; (4) clemency and consideration for one's own and for others in the hour of victory.

As regards booty taken in battle, the first point to note is that that should never be our aim in war. It is only an adventitious circumstance, a sort of windfall. Secondly, no soldier or troop has any inherent right to it. A righteous war is a community affair, and any accessions resulting from it belong to Allah, or the community or Cause. Thirdly, certain equitable principles of division should be laid down to check human greed and selfishness. A fifth share goes to the Commander, and he can use it at his discretion; for his own expenses, and for the relief of the poor and suffering, and the orphans and widows (8:41). The remainder was divided, according to the Prophet's practice, not only among those who were actually in the fight physically, but all who were in the enterprise, young and old, provided they loyally did some duty assigned to them. Fourthly, there should be no disputes, as they interfere, with internal discipline and harmony.

These principles are followed in the best modern practice of civilised nations. All acquisition of war belong absolutely to the Sovereign as representing the common wealth. In the distribution of booty not only the actual captors but also the "joint captors" and the "constructive captors" share see Sir R. Phillimore's *International Law* (1885), vol. 3, pp. 209-10, 221-4.

As regards the military virtues, which are the types of virtues throughout life, we are shown by an analysis of the incident of Badr how, against the greatest odds, Allah's help will give the victory if men are

fighting not for themselves but for the sacred Cause of Allah. And directions are given for the treatment of prisoners and for maintaining the solidarity of the Muslim community.

The date of this Surah is shortly after the battle of Badr which was fought on Friday, the 17th of Ramadhan in the second year of the Hijra.

SURAH AL-ANF'AL (THE SPOILS OF WAR)

In the name of Allah, Most Gracious, Most Merciful.

1. They ask you concerning (things taken as) spoils of war. Say: "(Such) spoils are at the disposal of Allah and the Apostle: so fear Allah, and keep straight the relations between yourselves: obey Allah and His Apostle, if you do believe."

2. For, Believers are those who, when Allah is mentioned, feel a tremor in their hearts, and when they hear His Signs rehearsed, find their faith strengthened, and put (all) their trust in their Lord;

3. Who establish regular prayers and spend (freely) out of the gifts We have given them for sustenance:

4. Such in truth are the Believers: they have grades of dignity with their Lord, and forgiveness, and generous sustenance:

5. Just as your Lord ordered you out of your house in truth, even though a party among the Believers disliked it.

6. Disputing with you concerning the truth after it was made manifest, as if they were being driven to death and they (actually) saw it.

7. Behold! Allah promised you one of the two (enemy) parties, that it should be yours: you wished that the one unarmed should be yours, but Allah willed to justify the Truth according to His words and to cut off the roots of the Unbelievers;-

8. That He might justify Truth and prove Falsehood false, distasteful though it be to those in guilt.

9. Remember you implored the assistance of your Lord, and He answered you: "I will assist you with a thousand of the angels, ranks on ranks."

10. Allah made it but a message of hope, and an assurance to your hearts: (in any case) there is no help except from Allah: and

Allah is Exalted in Power, Wise.

11. Remember He covered you with a sort of drowsiness, to give you calm as from Himself, and He caused rain to descend on you from heaven, to clean you therewith, to remove from you the stain of Satan, to strengthen your hearts, and to plant your feet firmly therewith.

12. Remember your Lord inspired the angels (with the message): "I am with you: give firmness to the Believers: I will instil terror into the hearts of the Unbelievers: you smite above their necks and smite all their finger-tips off them."

13. This because they conten-ded against Allah and His Apostle: if any contend against Allah and His Apostle, Allah is strict in punishment.

14. Thus (will it be said): "You taste then of the (punishment): for those who resist Allah, is the Chastisement of the Fire."

15. O you who believe! when you meet the Unbelievers in hostile array, never turn your backs to them.

16. If any do turn his back to them on such a day - unless it be in a stratagem[1] of war, or to retreat to a troop (of his own) - he draws on himself the wrath of Allah, and his abode is Hell,- an evil refuge (indeed)!

17. It is not you who slew them; it was Allah: when you threw (a handful of dust), it was not your act, but Allah's: in order that He might test the Believers by a gracious trial from Himself: for Allah is He Who hears and knows (all things).

18. That, and also because Allah is He Who makes feeble the plans and stratagems of the Unbelievers.

19. (O Unbelievers!) if you prayed for victory and judgment, now has the judgment come to you: if you desist (from wrong), it will be best for you: if you return (to the attack), so shall We. Not the least good will your forces be to you even if they were multiplied: for verily Allah is with those who believe!

20. O you who believe! Obey Allah and His Apostle, and do not

---

1. Plan, scheme

turn away from him when you hear (him speak).

21. Nor be like those who say, "We hear," but do not listen.

22. For the worst of beasts in the sight of Allah are the deaf and the dumb,- those who do not understand.

23. If Allah had found in them any good, He would indeed have made them listen: (as it is), if He had made them listen, they would but have turned back and declined (Faith).

24. O you who believe! give your response to Allah and His Apostle, when He calls you to that which will give you life; and know that Allah comes in between a man and his heart, and that it is He to Whom you shall (all) be gathered.

25. And fear tumult or oppression, which affects not in particular (only) those of you who do wrong: and know that Allah is strict in punishment.

26. Call to mind when you were a small (band), deemed weak through the land, and afraid that men might despoil[2] and kidnap you; but He provided a safe asylum for you, strengthened you with His aid, and gave you good things for sustenance: that you might be grateful.

27. O you that believe! do not betray the trust of Allah and the Apostle, nor misappropriate knowingly things entrusted to you.

28. And you should know that your possessions and your progeny are but a trial; and that it is Allah with Whom lies your highest reward.

29. O you who believe! if you fear Allah, He will grant you a Criterion (to judge between right and wrong), remove from you (all) evil (that may afflict) you, and forgive you: for Allah is the Lord of grace unbounded.

30. Remember how the Unbelievers plotted against you, to keep you in bonds[3], or slay you, or get you out (of your home). They plot and plan, and Allah too plans, but the best of planners is Allah.

---

2. Rob
3. "To keep in bonds," this is, to imprison, restraining one's physical freedom.

31.   When Our Signs are rehearsed to them, they say: "We have heard this (before): if we wished, we could say (words) like these: these are nothing but tales of the ancients."

32.   Remember how they said: "O Allah! if this is indeed the Truth from You, rain down on us a shower of stones from the sky, or send us a grievous Chastise-ment."

33.   But Allah was not going to send them a Chastisement whilst you were amongst them; nor was He going to send it whilst they could ask for pardon.

34.   But what plea have they that Allah should not punish them, when they keep out (men) from the Sacred Mosque - and they are not its guardians? No men can be its guardians except the righteous; but most of them do not understand.

35.   Their prayer at the House (of Allah) is nothing but whistling and clapping of hands: (its only answer can be), "You taste the Chastisement because you blasphemed."

36.   The Unbelievers spend their wealth to hinder (men) from the path of Allah, and so will they continue to spend; but in the end they will have (only) regrets and sighs; at length they will be overcome: and the Unbelievers will be gathered together to Hell;

37.   In order that Allah may separate the impure from the pure, put the impure, one on another, heap them together, and cast them into Hell. They will be the ones to have lost.

38.   Say to the Unbelievers, if (now) they desist (from Unbelief), their past would be forgiven them; but if they persist, the punishment of those before them is already (a matter of warning for them).

39.   And fight them on until there is no more tumult or oppression, and religion becomes Allah's in its entirety, but if they cease, surely Allah sees all that they do.

40.   If they refuse, be sure that Allah is your Protector - the Best to protect and the Best to help.

41.   And know that out of all the booty that you may acquire (in

war), a fifth share is assigned to Allah,- and to the Apostle, and to near relatives, orphans, the needy, and the wayfarer,- if you do believe in Allah and in the revelation We sent down to Our Servant on the Day of discrimination,- the Day of the meeting of the two forces. For Allah has power over all things.

42. Remember you were on the hither side of the valley, and they on the farther side, and the caravan on lower ground than you. Even if you had made a mutual appointment to meet, you would certainly have failed in the appointment: but (thus you met), that Allah might accomp-lish a matter already decided; that those who died might die after a Clear Sign (had been given), and those who lived might live after a Clear Sign (had been given). And verily Allah is He Who hears and knows (all things).

43. Remember in your dream Allah showed them to you as few: if He had shown them to you as many, you would surely have been discouraged, and you would surely have disputed in (your) decision; but Allah saved (you): for He knows well the (secrets) of (all) hearts.

44. And remember when you met, He showed them to you as few in your eyes, and He made you appear as contemptible[4] in their eyes: that Allah might accomplish a matter already decided. For to Allah do all questions go back (for decision).

45. O you who believe! When you meet a force, be firm, and call Allah in remembrance much (and often); that you may prosper:

46. And obey Allah and His Apostle; and fall into no disputes, lest you lose heart and your power depart; and be patient and persevering: for Allah is with those who patiently persevere:

47. And be not like those who started from their homes insolently and to be seen of men, and to hinder (men) from the path of Allah: for Allah compasses round about all that they do.

48. Remember Satan made their (sinful) acts seem alluring to them, and said: "No one among men can overcome you this day, while I am near to you": But when the two forces came in sight

---

4. Deserving Contempt (for being weak and small in number)

of each other, he turned on his heels, and said: "Lo! I am clear of you; Lo! I see what you do not see; Lo! I fear Allah: for Allah is strict in punishment."

49. Lo! the Hypocrites say, and those in whose hearts is a disease: "These people,- their religion has misled them." But if any trust in Allah, behold! Allah is Exalted in might, Wise.

50. If you could see, when the angels take the souls of the Unbelievers (at death), (how) they smite their faces and their backs, (saying): "Taste the Chastisement of the blazing Fire-

51. "Because of (the deeds) which your (own) hands sent forth; for Allah is never unjust to His servants:

52. "(Deeds) after the manner of the people of Pharaoh and of those before them: they rejected the Signs of Allah, and Allah punished them for their crimes: for Allah is Strong, and Strict in punishment:

53. "Because Allah will never change the Grace which He has bestowed on a people until they change what is in their (own) souls, and surely Allah is He Who hears and knows (all things)."

54. "(Deeds) after the manner of the people of Pharaoh and those before them": they treated as false the Signs of their Lord, so We destroyed them for their crimes, and We drowned the people of Pharaoh: for they were all oppressors and wrong-doers.

55. For the worst of beasts in the sight of Allah are those who reject Him: they will not believe.

56. They are those with whom you made a covenant, but they break their covenant every time, and they do not have the fear (of Allah).

57. If you encounter them in a battle deal severely with them so as to put terror in those who follow them, that they may remember.

58. If you fear treachery from any group, throw back (their covenant) to them, (so as to be) on equal terms: for Allah does not love the treacherous.

59. Let not the Unbelievers think that they can get the better (of the godly): they will never frustrate (them).

60.   Against them make ready your strength to the utmost of your power, including steeds of war, to strike terror into (the hearts of) the enemies, of Allah and your enemies, and others besides, whom you may not know, but whom Allah knows. Whatever you shall spend in the Cause of Allah, shall be repaid to you, and you shall not be treated unjustly.

61.   But if the enemy incline towards peace, you (also) incline towards peace, and trust in Allah: for He is the One that hears and knows (all things).

62.   Should they intend to deceive you,- verily Allah suffices you: He it is that has strengthened you with His aid and with (the company of) the Believers;

63.   And (moreover) He has put affection between their hearts: not if you had spent all that is in the earth, could you have produced that affection, but Allah has done it: for He is Exalted in might, Wise.

64.   O Apostle! sufficient to you is Allah,- (to you) and to those who follow you among the Believers.

65.   O Apostle! rouse the Believers to the fight. If there are twenty amongst you, patient and persevering, they will vanquish two hundred: if a hundred, they will vanquish a thousand of the Unbelievers: for these are a people without understanding.

66.   For the present, Allah has lightened your (task), for He knows that there is a weak spot in you: but (even so), if there are a hundred of you, patient and persevering, they will vanquish two hundred, and if a thousand, they will vanquish two thousand, with the leave of Allah: for Allah is with those who patiently persevere.

67.   It is not fitting for an Apostle that he should have prisoners of war until he has thoroughly subdued the land. You look for the temporal goods of this world; but Allah looks to the Hereafter: and Allah is Exalted in might, Wise.

68.   Had it not been for a previous ordainment[5] from Allah, a severe

---

5.   Decree, decision

penalty would have reached you for the (ransom) that you took.

69.   But (now) enjoy what you took in war, lawful and good: but fear Allah: for Allah is Oft-forgiving, Most Merciful.

70.   O Apostle! say to those who are captives in your hands: "If Allah finds any good in your hearts, He will give you something better than what has been taken from you, and He will forgive you: for Allah is Oft-forgiving, Most Merciful."

71.   But if they have treacherous designs against you,(O Apos-tle!), they have already been in treason against Allah, and so has He given (you) power over them. And Allah is He Who has (full) knowledge and wisdom.

72.   Those who believed, and adopted exile, and fought for the Faith, with their property and their persons, in the cause of Allah, as well as those who gave (them) asylum and aid,- these are (all) friends and protectors, one of another. As to those who believed but came not into exile, you owe no duty of protection to them until they come into exile; but if they seek your aid in religion, it is your duty to help them, except against a people with whom you have a treaty of mutual alliance. And (remem-ber) Allah sees all that you do.

73.   The Unbelievers are protectors, one of another: unless you do this, (protect each other), there would be tumult and oppression on earth, and great mischief.

74.   Those who believe, and adopt exile, and fight for the Faith, in the cause of Allah as well as those who give (them) asylum and aid,- these are (all) in very truth the Believers: for them is the forgiveness of sins and a provision most generous.

75.   And those who accept Faith subsequently, and adopt exile, and fight for the Faith in your company,- they are of you. But kindred by blood have prior rights against each other in the Book of Allah. Verily Allah is well-acquainted with all things.

SURAH—9
AT-TAUBA
(INTRODUCTION)

Logically this Surah follows up the argument of the last Surah (8), and indeed may be considered a part of it, although chronologically the two are separated by an interval of seven years.

We" saw that Surah 8 dealt with the large questions arising at the outset of the life of a new *Ummah* or organised nation: questions of defence under attack, distribution of war acquisitions after victory, the virtues needed for concerted action, and clemency and consideration for one's own and for enemies in the hour of victory We pass on in this Surah to deal with the question: What is to be done if the enemy breaks faith and is guilty of treachery? No nation can go on with a treaty if the other party violates it at will; but it is laid down that a period of four months should be allowed by way of notice after denunciation of the treaty; that due protection should be accorded in the intervening period; that there should always be open the door to repentance and reunion with the people of Allah; and that if all these fail, and war must be undertaken, it must be pushed with utmost vigour.

These are the general principles deducible from the Surah. The immediate occasion for their promulgation may be considered in connection with the chronological place of the Surah.

Chronologically, verses 1-29 were a notable declaration of State policy promulgated about the month of Shawwal, A.H. 9, and read out by Hadhrat 'Ali at the Pilgrimage two months later in order to give the policy the widest publicity possible. The remainder of the Surah verses 30-129, was revealed a little earlier, say, about the month of Ramadhan, A.H. 9, and sums up the lessons of the Apostle's Tabuk expedition in the summer of A.H. 9 (say October 630).

Tabuk is a place near the frontier of Arabia, quite close to what was then Byzantine territory in the Province of Syria (which included Palestine). It is about 350 miles northwest of Madinah, and 150 miles south of Ma'an. It had a fort and a spring of sweet water. In consequence of strong and persistent rumours that the Byzantines (Romans) were preparing to invade Arabia and that the Byzantine Emperor himself had arrived near the frontier for the purpose, the Apostle collected as large a force as he could, and marched to Tabuk. The Byzantine invasion did not come off. But the Apostle took the opportunity of consolidating the Muslim position in that direction and making treaties of alliance with certain Christian and Jewish tribes near the Gulf of

'Aqaba' On his return to Madinah he considered the situation. During his absence the Hypocrites had played, as always, a double game, and the policy hitherto followed, of free access to the sacred centre of Islam, to Muslims and Pagans alike, was now altered, as it had been abused by the enemies of Islam.

This is the only Surah to which the usual formula *of Bismillah* is not prefixed. It was among the last of the Surahs revealed, and though the Apostle had directed that it should follow Surah 8, it was not clear whether it was to form a separate Surah or only a part of Surah 8. It is now treated as a separate Surah, but the *Bismillah* is not prefixed to it, as there is not warrant for supposing that the Apostle used the *Bismillah* before it in his recitation of the Quran. The Surah is known under many names: the two most commonly used are (1) Tauba (Repentance), with reference to 9:104 and (2) Baraat (Immunity), the opening word of the Surah.

SURAH AL-TAUBA, OR BARA'AT
(REPENTANCE)

1. A (declaration) of immu-nity from Allah and His Apostle, to those of the Pagans with whom you have contracted mutual alliances:-

2. You go, then, for four months, backwards and forwards, (as you will), throughout the land, but know that you cannot frustrate Allah (by your falsehood) but that Allah will cover with shame those who reject Him.

3. And an announcement from Allah and His Apostle, to the people (assembled) on the day of the Great Pilgrimage,- that Allah and His Apostle dissolve (treaty) obligations with the Pagans. If then, you repent, it were best for you; but if you turn away, you (should) know that you cannot frustrate Allah. And proclaim a grievous Chastisement to those who reject Faith.

4. (But the treaties are) not dissolved with those Pagans with whom you have entered into alliance and who have not subsequently failed you in any thing, nor aided any one against you. So fulfil your agreements with them to the end of their term: for Allah loves the righteous.

5.   But when the forbidden months are past, then fight and slay the Pagans wherever you find them, and seize them, beleaguer[1] them, and lie in wait for them in every strategem (of war); but if they repent, and establish regular prayers and practise regular charity, then open the way for them: for Allah is Oft-forgiving, Most Merciful.

6.   If one amongst the Pagans ask you for asylum, grant it to him, so that he may hear the Word of Allah; and then escort him to where he can be secure. This is because they are men without knowledge.

7.   How can there be a league, before Allah and His Apostle, with the Pagans, except those with whom you made a treaty near the Sacred Mosque? As long as these stand true to you, you stand true to them: for Allah loves the righteous.

8.   How (can there be such a league), seeing that if they get an advantage over you, they do not respect in you the ties either of kinship or of covenant? With (fair words from) their mouths they please you, but their hearts are averse from you; and most of them are rebellious and wicked.

9.   They have sold the Signs of Allah for a miserable price, and (many) have they hindered from His Way: evil indeed are the deeds they have done.

10.   In a Believer they do not respect the ties either of kinship or of covenant! It is they who have transgressed all bounds.

11.   But (even so), if they repent, establish regular prayers, and practise regular charity,- then they are your brethren in Faith: (thus) do We explain the Signs in detail, for those who understand.

12.   But if they violate their oaths after their covenant, and taunt you for your Faith,- you fight the chiefs of Unfaith: for their oaths are nothing to them: that thus they may be restrained.

13.   Will you not fight people who violated their oaths, plotted to expel the Apostle, and took the aggressive by being the first

---

1.   Besiege

(to assault) you? Do you fear them? Nay, it is Allah Whom you should more justly fear, if you believe!

14. Fight them, and Allah will punish them by your hands, cover them with shame, help you (to victory) over them, heal the breasts of Believers,

15. And still[2] the indignation of their hearts. For Allah will turn (in mercy) to whom He will; and Allah is All-Knowing, All-Wise.

16. Or do you think that you shall be abandoned, as though Allah did not know those among you who strive with might and main, and take none for friends and protectors except Allah, His Apostle, and the (community of) Believers? But Allah is well-acquainted with (all) that you do.

17. It is not for such as join gods with Allah, to visit or maintain the mosques of Allah while they witness against their own souls to infidelity. The works of such bear no fruit: In Fire shall they dwell.

18. The mosques of Allah shall be visited and maintained by such as believe in Allah and the Last Day, establish regular prayers, and practise regular charity, and fear none (at all) except Allah. It is they who are expected to be on true guidance.

19. Do you make the giving of drink to pilgrims, or the maintenance of the Sacred Mosque, equal to (the pious service of) those who believe in Allah and the Last Day, and strive with might and main[3] in the cause of Allah? They are not comparable in the sight of Allah: and Allah does not guide those who do wrong.

20. Those who believe, and suffer exile and strive with might and main, in Allah's cause, with their goods and their persons, have the highest rank in the sight of Allah: they are the people who will achieve (salvation).

21. Their Lord gives them glad tidings of a Mercy from Himself, of His good pleasure, and of Gardens for them, wherein are delights that endure:

22. They will dwell therein for ever. Verily in Allah's presence is a

---

2. Soothe, pacify.   3. With all one's power

reward, the greatest (of all).

23. O you who believe! Do not take for protectors your fathers and your brothers if they love infidelity above Faith: if any of you do so, they do wrong.

24. Say: If it be that your fathers, your sons, your brothers, your mates, or your kindred; the wealth that you have gained; the commerce in which you fear a decline: or the dwellings in which you delight - are dearer to you than Allah, or His Apostle, or the striving in His cause;- then wait until Allah brings about His Decision: and Allah does not guide the rebellious.

25. Assuredly Allah did help you in many battle-fields and on the day of Hunain: behold! your great numbers elated[4] you, but they availed you nothing: the land, for all that it is wide, did constrain[5] you, and you turned back in retreat.

26. But Allah poured His calm on the Apostle and on the Believers, and sent down forces which you did not see: He punished the Unbelievers; thus does He reward those without Faith.

27. Again will Allah, after this, turn (in mercy) to whom He will: for Allah is Oft- forgiving, Most Merciful.

28. O you who believe! Truly the Pagans are unclean; so let them not, after this year of theirs, approach the Sacred Mosque. And if you fear poverty, soon will Allah enrich you, if He wills, out of His bounty, for Allah is All-Knowing, All-Wise.

29. Fight those who do not believe in Allah nor the Last Day, nor hold that forbidden which has been forbidden by Allah and His Apostle, nor acknowledge the Religion of Truth, (even if they are) of the People of the Book, until they pay the *Jizya*[6] with willing submission, and feel themselves subdued.

30. The Jews call 'Uzair a son of Allah, and the Christians call Christ the son of Allah. That is a saying from their mouth;(in this) they but imitate what the Unbelievers of old used to say. Allah's curse be on them: how they are deluded away from

---

4. To make proud.
5. Confine forcibly, become narrow and difficul.
6. Poll-tax.

the Truth!

31.   They take their priests and their anchorites[7] to be their lords besides Allah (in derogation[8] of Allah) Allah (they take as their Lord) Christ the son of Mary; yet they were comman-ded to worship but One God (Allah): there is no god but He. Praise and glory to Him: (far is He) from having the partners they associate (with Him).

32.   Fain would they extin-guish Allah's light with their mouths, but Allah will not allow but that His Light should be perfected, even though the Unbelievers may detest (it).

33.   It is He Who has sent His Apostle with Guidance and the Religion of Truth, to proclaim it over all religion, even though the Pagans may detest (it).

34.   O you who believe! there are indeed many among the priests and anchorites, who in falsehood devour the[9] substance of men and hinder (them) from the Way of Allah. And there are those who bury gold and silver and do not spend it in the Way of Allah: announce to them a most grievous Chastisement-

35.   On the Day when heat will be produced out of that (wealth) in the fire of Hell, and with it will be branded their foreheads, their flanks[10], and their backs- "This is the (treasure) which you buried for yourselves: you then taste the (treasures) you buried!"

36.   The number of months in the sight of Allah is twelve (in a year)- so ordained by Him the day He created the heavens and the earth; of them four are sacred: that is the straight usage. So do not wrong yourselves therein, and fight the Pagans all together as they fight you all together. But know that Allah is with those who restrain themselves.

37.   Verily the transposing[11] (of a prohibited month) is an addition to Unbelief: the Unbelievers are led to wrong thereby: for they

---

7.   Hermits
8.   Discredit, belittling (His authority, position or majesty)
9.   Property, wealth   10.   Sides
11.   Transfering, interchanging

make it lawful one year, and forbidden another year, in order to adjust the number of months forbidden by Allah and make such forbidden ones lawful. The evil of their course seems pleasing to them. But Allah does not guide those who reject Faith.

38. O you who believe! what is the matter with you, that, when you are asked to go forth in the Cause of Allah, you cling heavily to the earth? Do you prefer the life of this world to the Hereafter? But little is the comfort of this life, as compared with the Hereafter.

39. Unless you go forth, He will punish you with a grievous Chastisement, and put others in your place; but Him you would not harm in the least. For Allah has power over all things.

40. If you help not (your leader), (it is no matter): for Allah did indeed help him, when the Unbelievers drove him out: he had no more than one companion; they two were in the Cave, and he said to his companion, "Have no fear, for Allah is with us": then Allah sent down His peace upon him, and strengthened him with forces which you did not see, and humbled to the depths the word of the Unbelievers. But the word of Allah is exalted to the heights: for Allah is Exalted in might, Wise.

41. You go forth, (whether equipped) lightly or heavily, and strive and struggle, with your goods and your persons, in the Cause of Allah. That is best for you, if you (but) knew.

42. If there had been imme-diate gain (in sight), and the journey easy, they would (all) without doubt have followed you, but the distance was long, (and weighed) on them. They would indeed swear by Allah, "If we only could, we should certainly have come out with you": they would destroy their own souls; for Allah knows that they are certainly lying.

43. Allah gave you grace! Why did you grant them exemption until those who told the truth were seen by you in a clear light, and you had proved the liars?

44. Those who believe in Allah and the Last Day ask you for no

exemption from fighting with their goods and persons. And Allah knows well those who do their duty.

45.   Only those ask you for exemption who do not believe in Allah and the Last Day, and whose hearts are in doubt, so that they are tossed in their doubts to and fro.

46.   If they had intended to come out, they would certainly have made some preparation therefor; but Allah was averse to their being sent forth; so He made them lag behind, and they were told, "You sit among those who sit (inactive)."

47.   If they had come out with you, they would not have added to your (strength) but only (made for) disorder, hurrying here and there in your midst and sowing sedition[12] among you, and there would have been some among you who would have listened to them. But Allah knows well those who do wrong.

48.   Indeed they had plotted sedition before, and upset matters for you, until, the Truth arrived, and the Decree of Allah became manifest, much to their disgust.

49.   Among them is (many) a man who says: "Grant me ex-emption and do not draw me into trial." Have they not fallen into trial already? and indeed Hell surrounds the Unbelievers (on all sides).

50.   If good befalls you, it grieves them; but if a misfortune befalls you, they say, "We took indeed our precautions beforehand," and they turn away rejoicing.

51.   Say: "Nothing will happen to us except what Allah has decreed for us: He is our Protector": and on Allah let the Believers put their trust.

52.   Say: "Can you expect for us (any fate) other than one of two glorious things- (martyr-dom or victory)? But we can expect for you either that Allah will send His punishment from Himself, or by our hands. So wait (expectant); we too will wait with you."

---

12.   Rebellion, treason

53. Say: "Spend (for the Cause) willingly or unwillingly: from you it will not be accepted: for you are indeed a people rebellious and wicked."

54. The only reasons why their contributions are not accepted are: that they reject Allah and His Apostle; that they come to prayer without earnestness; and that they offer contributions unwillingly.

55. Let not their wealth nor their (following in) sons dazzle you: in reality Allah's plan is to punish them with these things in this life, and that their souls may perish in their (very) denial of Allah.

56. They swear by Allah that they are indeed of you; but they are not of you: yet they are afraid (to appear in their true colours).

57. If they could find a place to flee to, or caves, or a place of concealment, they would turn straightway thereto, with an obstinate rush.

58. And among them are men who slander you in the matter of (the distribution of) the alms: if they are given part thereof, they are pleased, but if not, behold! they are indignant!

59. If only they had been content with what Allah and His Apostle gave them, and had said, "Sufficient unto us is Allah! Allah and His Apostle will soon give us of His bounty: to Allah do we turn our hopes!" (that would have been the right course).

60. Alms are for the poor and the needy, and those employed to administer the (funds); for those whose hearts have been (recently) reconciled (to Truth); for those in bondage and in debt; in the cause of Allah; and for the wayfarer: (thus is it) ordained by Allah, and Allah is full of knowledge and wisdom.

61. Among them are men who slander the Prophet and say, "He is (all) ear." Say, "He listens to what is best for you: he believes in Allah, has faith in the Believers, and is a Mercy to those of you who believe." But those who slander the Apostle will have a grievous Chastise-ment.

62. To you they swear by Allah, In order to please you: But it is

more fitting that they should please Allah and His Apostle, if they are Believers.

63. Do they not know that for those who oppose Allah and His Apostle, is the Fire of Hell?- wherein they shall dwell. That is the supreme disgrace.

64. The Hypocrites are afraid lest a Sura should be sent down about them, showing them what is (really passing) in their hearts. Say: "Mock you! But verily Allah will bring to light all that you fear (should be revealed).

65. If you question them, they declare (with emphasis): "We were only talking idly and in play." Say: "Was it at Allah, and His Signs, and His Apostle, that you were mocking?"

66. You do not make any excuses: you have rejected Faith after you had accepted it. If We pardon some of you, We will punish others amongst you, for that they are in sin.

67. The Hypocrites, men and women, (have an understan-ding) with each other: They enjoin evil, and forbid what is just, and are close with their hands. They have for-gotten Allah; so He has forgot-ten them. Verily the Hypocrites are rebellious and perverse.

68. Allah has promised the Hypocrites men and women, and the rejecters, of Faith, the fire of Hell: therein shall they dwell: sufficient is it for them: for them is the curse of Allah, and an enduring punishment,-

69. As in the case of those before you: they were mightier than you in power, and more flourishing in wealth and children. They had their enjoyment of their portion: and you have of yours, as did those before you; and you indulge in idle talk as they did. They!- their works are fruitless in this world and in the Hereafter, and they will lose (all spiritual good).

70. Has not the story reached them of those before them?- the People of Noah, and 'Ad, and Thamud; the People of Abraham, the men of Midian, and the cities overthrown. To them came their Apostles with Clear Signs. It is not Allah Who wrongs

them, but they wrong their own souls.

71. The Believers, men and women, are protectors, one of another: they enjoin what is just, and forbid what is evil: they observe regular prayers, practise regular charity, and obey Allah and His Apostle. On them will Allah pour His mercy: for Allah is Exalted in power, Wise.

72. Allah has promised to Believers, men and women, Gardens under which rivers flow, to dwell therein, and beautiful mansions in Gardens of everlasting bliss. But the greatest bliss is the Good pleasure of Allah: that is the supreme felicity.[13]

73. O Prophet! strive hard against the Unbelievers and the Hypocrites, and be firm against them, their abode is Hell,- an evil refuge indeed.

74. They swear by Allah that they said nothing (evil), but indeed they uttered blasphemy, and they did it after accepting Islam; and they meditated a plot which they were unable to carry out: this revenge of theirs was (their) only return for the bounty with which Allah and His Apostle had enriched them! If they repent, it will be best for them; but if they turn back (to their evil ways), Allah will punish them with a grievous Chastisement in this life and in the Hereafter: they shall have none on earth to protect or help them.

75. Amongst them are men who made a Covenant with Allah, that if He bestowed on them of His bounty, they would give (largely) in charity, and be truly amongst those who are righteous.

76. But when He did bestow of His bounty, they became covetous,[14] and turned back (from their Covenant), averse (from its fulfilment).

77. So He has put as a conse-quence Hypocrisy into their hearts, (to last) till the Day, whereon they shall meet Him: because they broke their Covenant with Allah, and be-cause they lied (again and again).

78. Do they not know that Allah knows their secret (thoughts) and

---

13. Bliss, delight

14. Jealous, eagerly desirous

their secret counsels, and that Allah knows well all things unseen?

79. Those who slander such of the Believers as give themselves freely to (deeds of) charity, as well as such as can find nothing to give except the fruits of their labour,- and throw ridicule on them,- Allah will throw back their ridicule on them: and they shall have a grievous Chastise-ment.

80. Whether you ask for their forgiveness, or not, (their sin is unforgivable): if you ask seventy times for their forgive-ness, Allah will not forgive them: because they have rejected Allah and His Apostle: and Allah does not guide those who are perversely rebellious.

81. Those who were left behind (in the Tabuk expedition) rejoiced in their inaction behind the back of the Apostle of Allah: they hated to strive and fight, with their goods and their persons, in the Cause of Allah: they said, "Do not go forth in the heat." Say, "The fire of Hell is fiercer in heat." If only they could understand!

82. Let them laugh a little: much will they weep: a recom-pense for the (evil) that they do.

83. If, then, Allah bring you back to any of them, and they ask your permission to come out (with you), say: "Never shall you come out with me, nor fight an enemy with me: for you preferred to sit inactive on the first occasion: then you sit (now) with those who lag behind."

84. Nor do you ever pray for any of them that dies, nor stand at his grave; for they rejected Allah and His Apostle, and died in a state of perverse rebellion.

85. Nor let their wealth nor their children dazzle you: Allah's plan is to punish them with these things in this world, and that their souls may perish in their (very) denial of Allah.

86. When a Sura comes down, enjoining them to believe in Allah and to strive and fight along with His Apostle, those with wealth and influence among them ask you for exemption, and say:

"Leave us (behind): we would be with those who sit (at home)."

87. They prefer to be with (the women), who remain behind (at home): their hearts are sealed and so they do not understand.

88. But the Apostle, and those who believe with him, strive and fight with their wealth and their persons: for them are (all) good things: and it is they who will prosper.

89. Allah has prepared for them Gardens under which rivers flow, to dwell therein: that is the supreme felicity.

90. And there were, among the desert Arabs (also), men who made excuses and came to claim exemption; and those who were false to Allah and His Apostle (merely) sat inactive. Soon will a grievous Chastisement seize the Unbelievers among them.

91. There is no blame on those who are infirm, or ill, or who find no resources to spend (on the Cause), if they are sincere (in duty) to Allah and His Apostle: no ground (of complaint) can there be against such as do right: and Allah is Oft-forgiving, Most Merciful.

92. Nor (is there blame) on those who came to you to be provided with mounts, and when you said, "I can not find any mounts for you," they turned back, their eyes strea-ming with tears of grief that they had no resources wherewith to provide the expenses.

93. The ground (of complaint) is against such as claim exemption while they are rich. They prefer to stay with the (women) who remain behind: Allah has sealed their hearts; so they do not know (what they miss).

94. They will present their excuses to you when you return to them. You say: "Present no excuses: we shall not believe you: Allah has already informed us of the true state of matters concerning you: It is your actions that Allah and His Apostle will observe: in the end you will be brought back to Him Who knows what is hidden and what is open: then He will show you the truth of all that you did."

95. They will swear to you by Allah, when you return to them, that

you may leave them alone. So leave them alone: for they are an abomination, and Hell is their dwelling-place,-a fitting recompense for the (evil) that they did.

96.   They will swear unto you, that you may be pleased with them, but if you are pleased with them, Allah is not pleased with those who disobey.

97   The Arabs of the desert are the worst in unbelief and hypocrisy, and most fitted to be in ignorance of the command which Allah has sent down to His Apostle: But Allah is All-knowing, All-Wise.

98.   Some of the desert Arabs look upon their payments as a fine, and watch for disasters for you: on them be the disaster of evil: for Allah is He that hears and knows (all things).

99.   But some of the desert Arabs believe in Allah and the Last Day, and look on their payments as pious gifts bringing them nearer to Allah and obtaining the prayers of the Apostle. Yes, indeed they bring them nearer (to Him): soon will Allah admit them to His Mercy: for Allah is Oft-forgiving, Most Merciful.

100. The vanguard (of Islam)- the first of those who forsook (their homes) and of those who gave them aid, and (also) those who follow them in (all) good deeds,- well- pleased is Allah with them, as are they with Him: for them He has prepared Gardens under which rivers flow, to dwell therein for ever: that is the supreme felicity.

101. Certain of the desert Arabs round about you are Hypocrites, as well as (desert Arabs) among the Medina folk: they are obstinate in hypocrisy: you do not know them: We know them: twice shall We punish them: and in addition they shall be sent to a grievous Chastisement.

102. Others (there are who) have acknowledged their wrong-doings: they have mixed an act that was good with another that was evil. Perhaps Allah will turn to them (in Mercy): for Allah is Oft-forgiving, Most Merciful.

103. Of their goods, take alms, that so you might purify and sanctify

them; and pray on their behalf. Verily, your prayers are a source of security for them: and Allah is One Who hears and knows.

104. Do they not know that Allah accepts repentance from His votaries[15] and receives their gifts of charity, and that Allah is verily He, the Oft-Returning, Most Merciful.

105. And say: "Work (righ-teousness): soon will Allah observe your work, and His Apostle, and the Believers: soon will you be brought back to the Knower of what is hidden and what is open: then will He show you the truth of all that you did."

106. There are (yet) others, held in suspense for the command of Allah, whether He will punish them, or turn in mercy to them: and Allah is All-Knowing, Wise.

107. And there are those who put up a mosque by way of mischief and infidelity - to disunite the Believers - and in preparation for one who warred against Allah and His Apostle aforetime. They will indeed swear that their intention is nothing but good; but Allah declares that they are certainly liars.

108. You never stand forth therein. There is a mosque whose foundation was laid from the first day on piety; it is more worthy of your standing forth (for prayer) therein. In it are men who love to be purified; and Allah loves those who make themselves pure.

109. Which then is best? - he that lays his foundation on piety to Allah and His Good Pleasure? - or he that lays his foundation on an undermined sand-cliff ready to crumble to pieces? And it crumbles to pieces with him, into the fire of Hell. And Allah does not guide people that do wrong.

110. The foundation of those who so build is never free from suspicion and shakiness in their hearts, until their hearts are cut to pieces. And Allah is All-Knowing, Wise.

111. Allah has purchased of the Believers their persons and their goods; for theirs (in return) is the Garden (of Paradise): they fight in His Cause, and slay and are slain: a promise binding

---

15. Devoted servants

on Him in Truth, through the Torah, the Gospel, and the Qur'an: and who is more faithful to his Covenant than Allah? Then rejoice in the bargain which you have concluded: that is the supreme achievement.

112.   Those that turn (to Allah) in repentance; that serve Him, and praise Him; that wander in devotion to the Cause of Allah,: that bow down and prostrate themselves in prayer; that enjoin good and forbid evil; and observe the limits set by Allah;- (these do rejoice). So proclaim the glad tidings to the Believers.

113.   It is not fitting, for the Prophet and those who believe, that they should pray for forgiveness for Pagans, even though they be of kin, after it is clear to them that they are companions of the Fire.

114.   And Abraham prayed for his father's forgiveness only because of a promise he had made to him. But when it became clear to him that he was an enemy to Allah, he dissocia-ted himself from him: for Abraham was most tender-hearted, forbearing.

115.   And Allah will not mislead a people after He has guided them, in order that He may make clear to them what to fear (and avoid)- for Allah has knowledge of all things.

116.   To Allah belongs the dominion of the heavens and the earth. He gives life and He takes it. Except for Him you have no protector nor helper.

117.   Allah turned with favour to the Prophet, the Muhajirs, and the Ansar,- who followed him in a time of distress, after that the hearts of a part of them had nearly swerved (from duty); but He turned to them (also): for He is to them Most Kind, Most Merciful.

118.   (He turned in mercy also) to the three who were left behind; (they felt guilty) to such a degree that the earth seemed constrained to them, for all its spaciousness, and their (very) souls seemed straitened to them,- and they perceived that there is no fleeing from Allah (and no refuge) but to Himself. Then

---

16.   Displeasure and anger

He turned to them, that they might repent: for Allah is Oft-Returning, Most Merciful.

119.   O you who believe! Fear Allah and be with those who are true (in word and deed).

120.   It was not fitting for the people of Medina and the Bedouin Arabs of the neighbour-hood, to refuse to follow Allah's Apostle, nor to prefer their own lives to his: because nothing could they suffer or do, but was reckoned to their credit as a deed of righteousness, whether they suffered thirst, or fatigue, or hunger, in the Cause of Allah, or trod paths to raise the ire of the Unbelievers, or received any injury whatever from an enemy: for Allah does not suffer the reward to be lost of those who do good;-

121.   Nor could they spend anything (for the Cause) - small or great-nor cut across a valley, but the deed is inscribed to their credit: that Allah may requite their deed with the best (possible reward).

122.   Nor should the Believers all go forth together: if a contingent[17] from every expe-dition remained behind, they could devote themselves to studies in religion, and admo-nish the people when they return to them,- that thus they (may learn) to guard themselves (against evil).

123.   O you who believe! Fight the Unbelievers who gird[18] you about, and let them find firmness in you: and know that Allah is with those who fear Him.

124.   Whenever there comes down a Sura, some of them say: "Which of you has had his faith increased by it?" Yes, those who believe,- their faith is increased and they do rejoice.

125.   But those in whose hearts is a disease,- it will add doubt to their doubt, and they will die in a state of Unbelief.

126.   Don't they see that they are tried every year once or twice? Yet they do not turn in repentance, and they take no heed.

127.   Whenever there comes down a Sura, they look at each other,

---

17.   A group   18   Encircle

(saying), "Does anyone see you?" Then they turn aside: Allah has turned their hearts (from the light); for they are a people that do not understand.

128. Now has come to you an Apostle from amongst your-selves: it grieves him that you should perish: he is ardently an-xious over you: to the Believers he is most kind and merciful.

129. But if they turn away, say: "Allah is sufficient for me: there is no god but He: on Him is my trust,- He the Lord of the Throne (of Glory) Supreme!"

SURAH YUNUS
(INTRODUCTION)

Chronologically this Surah and the five that follow (Surah 11. 12, 13, 14, and 15) are closely connected, and were revealed in the late Makkan period, as the great event of the *Hijrat* was gradually approaching down the stream of Time. But their chronology has no particular significance.

On the other hand their arrangement in the gradation of Quranic teaching fits in with the subject-matter. S. 8 and S. 9 were mainly concerned with the first questions that arose on the formation of the new and organised Community of Islam in its conflict with those who wished to suppress or destroy it or use force to prevent its growth and the consolidation of its ideals. See introductions to those Surahs. The present group leads us to the questions that face us when external hostility has been met, and our relations to Allah have to be considered from a higher standpoint than that of self-preservation. How does revelation work? What is the meaning of divine grace and its withdraw!? How do the Messengers of Allah deliver their Message? How should we receive it?

All these questions revolve round the revelation of the Quran and each Surah of this group, except the 13 has, the Abbreviated Letters A.L.R. attached to it. S. 13 has the latters A.L.M.R., and we shall discuss this variation when we come to S. 13.

The Abbreviated Letters are mystic symbols, about whose meaning there is no authoritative explanation. If the present group A.L.R. is cognate to the group A.L.M., we have to consider and form some idea in our minds as to the probable meaning of the variation. We think A.L.M. to be a symbol of those Surahs that del with the beginning, the middle, and the end of man's spiritual history,-the origin, the present position, and the things to come in the Last Days (eschatology, to use a theological term). A.L. stand as symbols of the first two, and M. of the last. In the present group of Surahs we can understand the absence of M., the symbol standing for such matter. In its place comes R., which is phonetically allied to L.L. is produced by the impact of the tongue to but front of the plate, and R. to the middle of the plate. In many languages the letters L. and R. are interchangeable; e.g. in Arabic, al-Rahman becomes ar-Rahman, and R. in imperfect enunciation becomes L., as in Chines lallations. If L. is a symbol of present-day things looking to the future, we may take R. as a symbol of present-day things looking within, i.e. into the interior of the organisation of the *Ummah*. And this symbolism fits in with the subject-matter of the Surahs in question. But no one should be dogmatic in speculation about mystic Symbols.

Let us now consider Surah 10 alone, the central theme is that Allah's wonderful creation must not be viewed bus us as a creation of material things only, once made and finished with. Most wonderful of all is how He reveals Himself to men by men, and the Message disbelieved until it is too late for repentance; and how, as in the case of Yunus (Jonah) and his people, even the rejection (when repentance supervenes) does not prevent Allah's grace and mercy from working, and how far that working is beyond man's comprehension.

SURAH YUNUS (JONAH)

In the name of Allah, Most Gracious, Most Merciful.

1.   Alif-Lam-Raa. These are the Ayats of the Book of Wisdom.

2.   Is it a matter of wonder-ment to men that We have sent Our inspiration to a man from among themselves?- that he should warn mankind (of their danger), and give the good news to the Believers that they have before their Lord, the lofty rank of Truth. (But) the Unbelievers say: "This is indeed an evident sorcerer!"

3 .   Verily your Lord is Allah, Who created the heavens and the earth in six days, and is firmly established on the throne (of authority), regulating and gover-ning all things. No intercessor (can plead with Him) except after His leave (has been obtai-ned). This is Allah your Lord; you therefore serve Him: will you not receive admonition?

4 .   To Him will be your return- of all of you. The promise of Allah is true and sure. It is He Who begins the process of crea-tion, and repeats it, that He may reward with justice those who believe and work righteousness; but those who reject Him will have draughts[1] of boiling fluids, and a Chastisement grievous, because they did reject Him.

5.   It is He Who made the sun to be a shining glory and the moon

---

1.   A dose of liquid etc., single act of drinking.

to be a light (of beauty), and measured out stages for it, that you might know the number of years and the count (of time). Nowise did Allah create this but in truth and righteousness. (Thus) He explains His Signs in detail, for those who understand.

6. Verily, in the alternation of the night and the day, and in all that Allah has created, in the heavens and the earth, are Signs for those who fear Him.

7. Those who do not rest their hope on their meeting with Us, but are pleased and satisfied with the life of the present, and those who do not heed Our Signs,-

8. Their abode is the Fire, because of the (evil) they earned.

9. Those who believe, and work righteousness,- their Lord will guide them because of their faith: beneath them will flow rivers in Gardens of Bliss.

10. (This will be) their cry therein: "Glory to You, O Allah!" And "Peace" will be their greeting therein! and the close of their cry will be: "Praise be to Allah, the Cherisher and Sustainer of the Worlds!"

11. If Allah were to hasten for men the ill (they have earned) as they would fain hasten on the good,- then would their respite be settled at once. But We leave those who do not rest their hope on their meeting with Us, in their trespasses, wandering in distraction to and fro.

12. When trouble touches a man, He cries unto Us (in all postures)- lying down on his side, or sitting, or standing. But when We have solved his trouble, he passes on his way as if he had never cried to us for a trouble that touched him! Thus do the deeds of transgressors seem fair in their eyes!

13. We destroyed generations before you when they did wrong: their Apostles came to them with Clear Signs, but they would not believe! Thus do We requite those who sin!

14. Then We made you heirs in the land after them, to see how you would behave!

15. But when Our Clear Signs are rehearsed to them, those who do not rest their hope on their meeting with Us, say: "Bring us a Qur'an other than this, or change this," say: "It is not for me, of my own accord, to change it: I follow nothing but what is revealed to me: if I were to disobey my Lord, I should myself fear the Chastisement of a Great Day (to come)."

16. Say: "If Allah had so willed, I should not have rehearsed it to you, nor would He have made it known to you. A whole lifetime before this I have tarried amongst you: will you not then understand?"

17. Who does more wrong than such as forge a lie against Allah, or deny His Signs? But never will prosper those who sin.

18. They serve, besides Allah, things that do not hurt them nor profit them, and they say: "These are our intercessors with Allah." Say: "Do you indeed inform Allah of something He knows not, in the heavens or on earth?- Glory to Him! and far is He above the partners they ascribe (to Him)!"

19. Mankind was but one nation, but differed (later). Had it not been for a Word that went forth before from your Lord, their differences would have been settled between them.

20. They say: "Why is not a Sign sent down to him from his Lord?" Say: "The Unseen is only for Allah (to know). Then you wait: I too will wait with you."

21. When We make mankind taste of some mercy after adversity has touched them, behold! they take to plotting against Our Signs! Say: "Swifter to plan is Allah!" Verily, Our angels record all the plots that you make.

22. He it is Who enables you to traverse through land and sea; so that you even board ships;- they sail with them with a favourable wind, and they rejoice thereat; then comes a stormy wind and the waves come to them from all sides, and they think they are being overwhelmed: they cry to Allah, sincerely offering (their) duty to Him saying, "If You deliver us from this, we shall truly show our gratitude!"

23.   But when He delivers them, behold! they transgress insolently through the earth in defiance of right! O mankind! your insolence is against your own souls,- an enjoyment of the life of the present: in the end, to Us is your return, and We shall show you the truth of all that you did.

24.   The likeness of the life of the Present is as the rain which We send down from the skies: by its mingling arises the produce of the earth- which provides food for men and animals: (It grows) till the earth is clad with its golden ornaments and is decked[2] out (in beauty): the people to whom it belongs think they have all powers of disposal over it: there reaches it Our command by night or by day, and We make it like a har-vest clean-mown, as if it had not flourished only the day before! Thus do We explain the Signs in detail for those who reflect.

25.   But Allah calls to the Home of Peace: He guides whom He pleases to a Way that is straight.

26.   To those who do right is a goodly (reward)- Yes, more (than in measure)! No darkness nor shame shall cover their faces! They are companions of the Garden; they will abide therein (for ever).

27.   But those who have earned evil will have a reward of like evil: ignominy[3] will cover their (faces): no defender will they have from (the wrath of) Allah: their faces will be covered, as it were, with pieces from the depths of the darkness of Night : they are Companions of the Fire: they will abide therein (for ever)!

28.   One Day We shall gather them all together. Then We shall say to those who joined gods (with Us): "To your place! you and those you joined as 'partners' We shall separate them, and their "Partners" shall say: "It was not us that you worshipped!

29.   "Enough is Allah for a witness between us and you: we certainly knew nothing of your worship of us!"

30.   There will every soul prove (the fruits of) the deeds it sent before: they will be brought back to Allah, their rightful Lord,

---

2.   Decorated, adorned, beautified   3.   Disgrace

and their invented falsehoods will leave them in the lurch.

31.   Say: "Who is it that sus-tains you (in life) from the sky and from the earth? Or who is it that has power over hearing and sight? And who is it that brings out the living from the dead and the dead from the living? And who is it that rules and regulates all affairs?" They will soon say, "Allah". Say, "Will you not then show piety (to Him)?"

32.   Such is Allah, your real Cherisher and Sustainer; apart from Truth, what (remains) but error? How then are you turned away?

33.   Thus is the Word of your Lord proved true against those who rebel: verily they will not believe.

34.   Say: "Of your 'partners', can any originate creation and repeat it?" Say: "It is Allah Who originates creation and repeats it: then how are you deluded away (from the truth)?"

35.   Say: "Of your 'partners' is there any that can give any guidance towards Truth?" Say: "It is Allah Who gives guidance towards Truth. Is then He Who gives guidance to truth more worthy to be followed, or he who finds not guidance (himself) unless he is guided? what then is the matter with you? How do you judge.

36.   But most of them follow nothing but conjecture: truly conjecture can be of no avail against Truth. Verily Allah is well aware of all that they do.

37.   This Qur'an is not such as can be produced by other than Allah; on the contrary it is a confirmation of (revelations) that went before it, and a fuller explanation of the Book - wherein there is no doubt - from the Lord of the Worlds.

38.   Or do they say, "He forged it"? Say: "Bring then a Sura like it, and call (to your aid) anyone you can, besides Allah, if it be you speak the truth!"

39.   Nay, they charge with false-hood that whose knowledge they cannot compass,[4] even before the elucidation[5] thereof has reached them: thus did those before them make charges of falsehood: but see what was the end of those who did wrong!

---

4.   Grasp or understand mentally   5.   Clarification or explanation

40. Of them there are some who believe therein, and some who do not: and your Lord knows best those who are out for mischief.

41. If they charge you with falsehood, say: "My work to me, and yours to you! you are free from responsibility for what I do, and I for what you do!"

42. Among them are some who (pretend to) listen to you: but can you make the deaf to hear,- even though they are without understanding?

43. And among them are some who look at you: but can you guide the blind,- even though they will not see?

44. Verily Allah will not deal unjustly with man in anything: It is man that wrongs his own soul.

45. One day He will gather them together: (It will be) as if they had tarried but an hour of a day: they will recognise each other: assuredly those will be lost who denied the meeting with Allah and refused to receive true guidance.

46. Whether We show you (realized in your life-time) some part of what We promise them,- or We take your soul (to Our Mercy) (before that),- in any case, to Us is their return: ultimately Allah is Witness to all that they do.

47. To every people (was sent) an Apostle: when their Apostle comes (before them), the matter will be judged between them with justice, and they will not be wronged.

48. They say: "When will this promise come to pass,- if you speak the truth?"

49. Say: "I have no power over any harm or profit to myself except as Allah wills. To every people is a term appoin-ted: when their term is reached, not an hour can they cause delay, nor (an hour) can they advance (it in anticipation)."[6]

50. Say: "Do you see,- if His punishment should come to you by night or by day,- what portion of it would the Sinners wish to hasten?

---

6.   Expectation

51.   "Would you then believe in it at last, when it actually comes to pass? (It will then be said): 'Ah! now? and you wan-ted (aforetime) to hasten it on!'

52.   "At length will be said to the wrong-doers: 'you taste the enduring punishment! You get the recompense of what you earned!'"

53.   They seek to be informed by you: "Is that true?" Say: "Yes, by my Lord! it is the very truth and you cannot frustrate it!"

54.   Every soul that has sinned, if it possessed all that is on earth, would fain give it in ransom: they would declare (their) repentance when they see the Chastisement: but the judgment between them will be with justice, and no wrong will be done to them.

55.   Is it not (the case) that to Allah belongs whatever is in the heavens and on earth? Is it not (the case) that Allah's promise is assuredly true? Yet most of them do not understand.

56.   It is He Who gives life and who takes it, and to Him shall you all be brought back.

57.   O mankind! there has come to you a direction from your Lord and a healing for the (diseases) in your hearts,- and for those who believe, a Gui-dance and a Mercy.

58.   Say: "In the Bounty of Allah, and in His Mercy,- in that let them rejoice": that is better than the (wealth) they hoard.

59.   Say: "Do you see what things Allah has sent down to you for sustenance? Yet you hold forbidden some things thereof and (some things) lawful." Say: "Has Allah indeed permitted you, or do you invent (things) to attribute to Allah?"

60.   And what do those think who invent lies against Allah, of the Day of Judgment? Verily Allah is full of Bounty to mankind, but most of them are ungrateful.

61.   In whatever business you may be, and whatever portion you may be reciting from the Qur'an,- and whatever deed you (mankind) may be doing,- We are Witnesses thereof when you are deeply engrossed therein. Nor is hidden from your Lord

(so much as) the weight of an atom on the earth or in heaven. And not the least and not the greatest of these things but are recorded in a clear Record.

62. Behold! verily on the friends of Allah there is no fear, nor shall they grieve;

63. Those who believe and (constantly) guard against evil;-

64. For them are Glad Tidings, in the life of the Present and in the Hereafter; no change can there be in the Words of Allah. This is indeed the supreme felicity.

65. Let not their speech grieve you: for all power and honour belong to Allah: It is He Who hears and knows (all things).

66. Behold! verily to Allah belong all creatures, in the heavens and on earth. What do they follow who worship as His "partners" other than Allah? They follow nothing but fancy, and they do nothing but lie.

67. He it is that has made for you the Night that you may rest therein, and the Day to make things visible (to you). Verily in this are Signs for those who listen (to His Message).

68. They say: "God (Alalh) has begotten a son!" - Glory be to Him! He is Self-Sufficient! His are all things in the heavens and on earth! No warrant[7] have you for this! Do you say about Allah what you do not know?

69. Say: "Those who invent a lie against Allah will never prosper."

70. A little enjoyment in this world!- and then, to Us will be their return, then shall We make them taste the severest Chastisement for their blasphemies.

71. Relate to them the story of Noah. Behold! he said to his people: "O my people, if it be hard on your (mind) that I should stay (with you) and comme-morate the Signs of Allah,- yet I put my trust in Allah. You then get an agreement about your plan and among your partners, so your plan be not to you dark and dubious.[8] Then pass your sentence on me, and give me no respite.

---

7.   Authority   8.   Uncertain, ambiguous

72.   "But if you turn back, (consider): no reward have I asked of
        you: my reward is only due from Allah, and I have been
        commanded to be of those who submit to Allah's Will (in
        Islam)."

73.   They rejected him, but We delivered him, and those with him,
        in the Ark, and We made them inherit (the earth), while We
        overwhelmed in the flood those who rejected Our Signs. Then
        see what was the end of those who were warned (but heeded
        not)!

74.   Then after him We sent (many) Apostles to their peoples: they
        brought them Clear Signs, but they would not believe what
        they had already rejected beforehand. Thus do We seal the
        hearts of the trans-gressors.

75.   Then after them We sent Moses and Aaron to Pharaoh and his
        chiefs with Our Signs. But they were arrogant: they were a
        people in sin.

76.   When the Truth did come to them from Us, they said: "This is
        indeed evident sorcery!"

77.   Moses said: "Do you say (this) about the Truth when it has
        (actually) reached you? Is sorcery (like) this? But sorce-rers
        will not prosper."

78.   They said: "Have you come to us to turn us away from the
        ways we found our fathers following,- in order that you and
        your brother may have greatness in the land? But we shall not
        believe in you!"

79.   Pharaoh said: "Bring me every sorcerer well versed."

80.   When the sorcerers came, Moses said to them: "You throw
        what you (wish) to throw!"

81.   When they had had their throw, Moses said: "What you have
        brought is sorcery: Allah will surely make it of no effect: for
        Allah does not prosper the work of those who make mischief.

82.   "And Allah by His Words proves and establishes His Truth,
        however much the Sinners may hate it!"

83.   But none believed in Moses except some children of his people,

because of the fear of Pharaoh and his chiefs, lest they should persecute them; and certainly Pharaoh was mighty on the earth and one who transgressed all bounds.

84. Moses said: "O my people! If you do (really) believe in Allah, then in Him put your trust if you submit (your will to His)."

85. They said: "In Allah do we put our trust. Our Lord! do not make us a trial for those who practise oppression;

86. "And deliver us by Your Mercy from those who reject (You)."

87. We inspired Moses and his brother with this Message: "Provide dwellings for your people in Egypt, make your dwellings into places of worship, and establish regular prayers: and give Glad Tidings to those who believe!"

88. Moses prayed: "Our Lord! You have indeed bestowed on Pharaoh and his Chiefs splen-dour and wealth in the life of the Present, and so, our Lord, they mislead (men) from Your Path. Our Lord, deface the features of their wealth, and send hardness to their hearts, so they will not believe until they see the grievous Chastisement."

89. Allah said: "Accepted is your prayer (O Moses and Aaron)! So you stand straight, and do not follow the path of those who do not know."

90. We took the Children of Israel across the sea: Pharaoh and his hosts followed them in insolence and spite.[9] At length, when overwhelmed with the flood, he said: "I believe that there is no god except Him Whom the Children of Israel believe in: I am of those who submit (to Allah in Islam)."

91. (It was said to him): "Ah now!- But a little while before, you were in rebellion!- and you did mischief (and violence)!

92. "This day shall We save you in your body, that you may be a Sign to those who come after you! but verily, many among mankind are heedless of Our Signs!"

93. We settled the Children of Israel in a beautiful dwelling-place, and provided for them sustenance of the best: it was after

9.   Malice, hatred

knowledge had been granted to them, that they fell into schisms.[10] Verily Allah will judge between them as to the schisms amongst them, on the Day of Judgment.

94. If you were in doubt as to what We have revealed to you, then ask those who have been reading the Book before you: the Truth has indeed come to you from your Lord: so be in no wise of those in doubt.

95. Nor be of those who reject the Signs of Allah, or you shall be of those who perish.

96. Those against whom the Word of your Lord has been verified would not believe-

97. Even if every Sign was brought to them,- until they see (for themselves) the Chastise-ment grievous .

98. Why was there not a single township (among those We warned), which believed,- so its faith should have profited it,- except the people of Jonah? When they believed, We remo-ved from them the Chastisement of ignominy[11] in the life of the present, and permitted them to enjoy (their life) for a while.

99. If it had been your Lord's Will, they would all have believed,- all who are on earth! Will you then compel mankind, against their will, to believe!

100. No soul can believe, except by the Will of Allah, and He will place Doubt (or obscu-rity) on those who will not understand.

101. Say: "Behold all that is in the heavens and on earth"; but neither Signs nor Warners profit those who do not believe.

102. Do they then expect (any thing) but (what happened in) the days of the men who passed away before them? Say: "You wait then: for I, too, will wait with you."

103. In the end We deliver Our Apostles and those who believe: thus is it fitting on Our part that We should deliver those who believe!

104. Say: "O you men! If you are in doubt as to my religion, (behold!)

---

10. To be divided into mutually opposing parties.
11. Disgrace

I do not worship what you worship, other than Allah! But I worship Allah - Who will take your souls (at death): I am commanded to be (in the ranks) of the Believers,

105. "And further (thus): 'set your face towards Religion with true piety, and never in any wise be of the Unbelievers;

106. "'Nor call on any, other than Allah;- Such will neither profit you nor hurt you: if you do so, behold! you shall certainly be of those who do wrong.'"

107. If Allah touches you with hurt, there is none can remove it but He: if He designs some benefit for you, there is none can keep back His favour: He causes it to reach whomsoever of His servants He pleases. And He is the Oft-Forgiving, Most Merciful.

108. Say: "O you men! Now   Truth has reached you from your Lord! those who receive guidance, do so for the good of their own souls; those who stray, do so to their own loss: and I am not (set) over you to arrange your affairs."

109. You follow the inspiration sent to you, and be patient and constant, till Allah do decide: for He is the Best to decide.

SURAH—11
SURAH HUD
(INTRODUCTION)

For the chronological place of this Surah and the general arguments of Surahs 10 to 15, see introduction to S. 10.

In subject— matter this Surah supplements the preceding one. In the last Surah stress was laid on that side of Allah's dealings with man which leads to Mercy: here stress is laid on the side which deals with justice and the punishment of Sin when all Grace is resisted.

SURAH HUD (THE PROPHET HUD)

In the name of Allah, Most Gracious, Most Merciful.

1. Alif - Lam - Raa (This is) a Book, with verses basic or fundamental (of established meaning), further explained in detail,- from One Who is Wise and Well-Acquainted (with all things):

2. (It teaches) that you should worship none but Allah. (Say): "Verily I am (sent) to you from Him to warn and to bring glad tidings:

3. "(And to preach thus), 'You seek the forgiveness of your Lord, and turn to Him in repentance; that He may grant you enjoyment, good (and true), for a term appointed, and bestow His abounding grace on all who abound in merit! But if you turn away , then I fear for you the Chastisement of a Great Day:

4. 'To Allah is your return, and He has power over all things."

5. Behold! they fold up their hearts, that they may lie hid from Him! Ah! even when they cover themselves with their garments, He knows what they conceal, and what they reveal: for He knows well the (inmost secrets) of the hearts.

6. There is no moving crea-ture on earth but its sustenance depends on Allah: He knows the time and place of its definite abode and its temporary deposit: all is in a clear Record.

7. He it is Who created the heavens and the earth in six Days - and His Throne was over the waters - that He might try you,

which of you is best in conduct. But if you were to say to them, "You shall indeed be raised up after death", the Unbelievers would be sure to say, "This is nothing but obvious sorcery!"

8. If We delay the Chastise-ment for them for a definite term, they are sure to say, "What keeps it back?" Ah! On the day it (actually) reaches them, nothing will turn it away from them, and they will be comp-letely encircled by that which they used to mock at!

9. If We give man a taste of Mercy from Ourselves, and then withdraw it from him, behold! he is in despair and (falls into) blasphemy.

10. But if We give him a taste of (Our) favours after adversity has touched him, he is sure to say, "All evil has departed from me:" behold! he falls into exultation[1] and pride.

11. Not so do those who show patience and constancy, and work righteousness; for them is forgiveness (of sins) and a great reward.

12. Perchance you may (feel the inclination) to give up a part of what is revealed to you, and your heart feels straitened lest they say, "Why is not a treasure sent down to him, or why does not an angel come down with him?" But you are there only to warn! It is Allah that arranges all affairs!

13. Or they may say, "He forged it," Say, "You then bring ten Suras forged, like unto it, and call (to your aid) whom-soever you can, other than Allah!- If you speak the truth!

14. "If then they (your false gods) do not answer your (call), you (should) know that this Revelation is sent down (replete[2]) with the knowledge of Allah, and that there is no god but He! Will you even then submit (to Islam)?"

15. Those who desire the life of the present and its glitter,- to them We shall pay (the price of) their deeds therein,- without diminution.[3]

---

1. Rejoice, revel   2. Satiated, full
3. Decrease

16. They are those for whom there is nothing in the Hereafter but the Fire: vain are the designs they frame therein, and of no effect are the deeds that they do!

17. Can they be (like) those who accept a Clear (Sign) from their Lord, and whom a witness from Himself teaches, as did the Book of Moses before it,- a guide and a mercy? They believe therein; but those of the Sects that reject it,- the Fire will be their promised meeting-place. Be not then in doubt thereon: for it is the Truth from your Lord: yet many among men do not believe!

18. Who does more wrong than those who invent a lie against Allah? They will be turned back to the presence of their Lord, and the witnesses will say, "These are the ones who lied against their Lord! Behold! the Curse of Allah is on those who do wrong!-

19. "Those who would hinder (men) from the path of Allah and would seek in it something crooked: these were they who denied the Hereafter!"

20. They will in no wise frustrate (His design) on earth, nor have they protectors besides Allah! Their Chastisement will be doubled! They lost the power to hear and they did not see!

21. They are the ones who have lost their own souls: and the (fancies) they invented have left them in the lurch!

22. Without a doubt, these are the very ones who will lose most in the Hereafter!

23. But those who believe and work righteousness, and humble themselves before their Lord,- they will be Companions of the Garden, to dwell therein for ever!

24. These two kinds (of men) may be compared to the blind and deaf, and those who can see and hear well. Are they equal when compared? Will you not then take heed?

25. We sent Noah to his people (with a mission): "I have come to you with a Clear Warning:

26. "That you serve none but Allah: Verily I do fear for you the

Chastisement of a Grievous Day."

27. But the chiefs of the Unbelievers among his people said: "We see (in) you nothing but a man like ourselves: nor do we see that any follow you but the meanest among us, in judgment immature: nor do we see in you (all) any merit above us: in fact we think you are liars!"

28. He said: "O my people! do you see if (it be that) I have a Clear Sign from my Lord, and that He has sent Mercy to me from His Own Presence, but that the Mercy has been obscured from your sight? Shall we compel you to accept it when you are averse to it?

29. "And O my people! I ask you for no wealth in return: my reward is from none but Allah: but I will not drive away (in contempt) those who believe: for verily they are to meet their Lord, and you, I see are the ignorant ones!

30. "And O my people! who would help me against Allah if I drove them away? Will you not then take heed?

31. "I do not tell you that with me are the Treasures of Allah, nor do I know what is hidden, nor I claim to be an angel. Nor yet do I say, of those whom your eyes do despise that Allah will not grant them (all) that is good: Allah knows best what is in their souls: I should, if I did, indeed be a wrong-doer."

32. They said: "O Noah! You have disputed with us, and much have you prolonged the dispute with us: now bring upon us what you threaten us with, if you speak the truth!?"

33. He said: "Truly, Allah will bring it on you if He wills,- and then, you will not be able to frustrate it!

34. "Of no profit will be my counsel to you, much as I desire to give you (good) counsel, if it be that Allah wills to leave you astray: He is your Lord! and to Him will you return!"

35. Or do they say, "He has forged it"? Say: "If I had forged it, on me were my sin! and I am free of the sins of which you are guilty!

36. It was revealed to Noah: "None of your people will believe except those who have believed already! So grieve no longer

over their (evil) deeds.

37.   "But construct an Ark under Our eyes and Our inspi-ration, and address Me no (fur-ther) on behalf of those who are in sin: for they are about to be overwhelmed (in the Flood)."

38.   Forthwith he (starts) constructing the Ark: every time that the Chiefs of his people passed by him, they threw ridicule on him. He said: "If you ridicule us now, we (in our turn) can look down on you with ridicule likewise!

39.   "But soon you will know who it is on whom will descend a Chastisement that will cover them with shame,- on whom will be unloosed a lasting Chastisement:"

40.   At length, behold! there came Our Command, and the fountains of the earth gushed forth! We said: "Embark therein, of each kind two, male and female, and your family - except those against whom the Word has already gone forth,- and the Believers." But only a few believed with him.

41.   So he said: "You embark on the Ark, In the name of Allah, whether it move or be at rest! For my Lord is, be sure, Oft-Forgiving, Most Merciful!"

42.   So the Ark floated with them on the waves (towering) like mountains, and Noah called out to his son, who had separated himself (from the rest): "O my son! embark with us, and be not with the Unbelievers!"

43.   The son replied: "I will betake myself to some moun-tain: it will save me from the water." Noah said: "This day nothing can save, from the Command of Allah, any but those on whom He has mercy! "And the waves came between them, and the son was among those overwhelmed in the Flood.

44.   Then the word went forth: "O earth! swallow up your water, and O sky! withhold (your rain)!" And the water abated, and the matter was ended. The Ark rested on Mount Judi, and the word went forth: "Away with those who do wrong!"

45.   And Noah called upon his Lord, and said: "O my Lord! surely my son is of my family! And Your promise is true, and You are

the Justest of Judges!"

46. He said: "O Noah! He is not of your family: for his conduct is unrighteous. So do not ask of Me that of which you have no knowledge! I give you counsel, lest you act like the ignorant!"

47. Noah said: "O my Lord! I do seek refuge with You, lest I ask You for that of which I have no knowledge. And unless You forgive me and have Mercy on me, I should indeed be lost!"

48. The word came: "O Noah! come down (from the Ark) with peace from Us, and Blessing on you and on some of the peoples (who will spring) from those with you: but (there will be other) peoples to whom We shall grant their pleasures (for a time), but in the end a grievous Chastisement will reach them from Us."

49. Such are some of the stories of the Unseen, which We have revealed to you: before this, neither you nor your people knew them. So persevere patiently: for the End is for those who are righteous.

50. To the 'Ad People (We sent) Hud, one of their own brethren. He said: "O my people! worship Allah! you have no other god but Him. (Your other gods) you do nothing but invent!

51. "O my people! I ask of you no reward for this (Message). My reward is from none but Him Who created me: will you not then understand?

52. "And O my people! Ask forgiveness of your Lord, and turn to Him (in repentance): He will send you the skies pouring abundant rain, and add strength to your strength: so you do not turn back in sin!"

53. They said: "O Hud! You have brought us no Clear (Sign), and we are not the ones to desert our gods on your word! Nor shall we believe in you!

54. "We say nothing but that (perhaps) some of our gods may have seized you with imbeci-lity." He said: "I call Allah to witness, and you do bear witness, that I am free from the sin of ascribing, to Him,

55. "Other gods as partners! So scheme (your worst) against me, all of you, and give me no respite.

56. "I put my trust in Allah, my Lord and your Lord! There is not a moving creature, but He has grasp of its fore-lock. Verily, it is my Lord that is on a straight Path.

57. "If you turn away,- I (at least) have conveyed the Message with which I was sent to you. My Lord will make another people to succeed you, and you will not harm Him in the least. For my Lord has care and watch over all things."

58. So when Our decree issued, We saved Hud and those who believed with him, by (special) Grace from Ourselves: We saved them from a severe Chastisement.

59. Such were the 'Ad People: they rejected the Signs of their Lord and Cherisher; disobeyed His Apostles; and followed the command of every powerful, obstinate transgressor.

60. And they were pursued by a Curse in this life,- and on the Day of Judgment. Ah! Behold! For the 'Ad rejected their Lord and Cherisher! Ah! Behold! Removed (from sight) were 'Ad, the people of Hud!

61. To the Thamud People (We sent) Salih, one of their own brethren. He said: "O my people! Worship Allah: you have no other god but Him. It is He Who has produced you from the earth and settled you therein: then ask forgiveness of Him, and turn to Him (in repentance): for my Lord is (always) near, ready to answer."

62. They said: "O Salih! you have been of us!- a centre of our hopes hitherto! Do you (now) forbid us the worship of what our fathers worshipped? But we are really in suspicious (disquie-ting) doubt as to that to which you invite us."

63. He said: "O my people! Do you see? if I have a Clear (Sign) from my Lord and He has sent Mercy to me from Himself,- who then can help me against Allah if I were to disobey Him? What then would you add to my (portion) but perdition?[4]

---

4.   Damnation

64. "And O my people! this she-camel of Allah is a symbol to you: leave her to feed on Allah's (free) earth, and inflict no harm on her, or a swift Chastisement will seize you!"

65. But they hamstrung her. So he said: "Enjoy yourselves in your homes for three days: (then will be your ruin): (behold) there is a promise not to be belied!"

66. When Our Decree issued, We saved Salih and those who believed with him, by (special) Grace from Ourselves - and from the Ignominy of that Day. For your Lord - He is the Strong One, and Able to enforce His Will.

67. The (mighty) Blast over-took the wrong-doers, and they lay prostrate in their homes before the morning,-

68. As if they had never dwelt and flourished there. Ah! Behold! For the Thamud rejec-ted their Lord and Cherisher! Ah! Behold! Removed (from sight) were the Thamud!

69. There came Our Messen-gers to Abraham with glad tidings. They said, "Peace!" He answered, "Peace!" and haste-ned to entertain them with a roasted calf.

70. But when he saw their hands did not go towards the (meal), he felt some mistrust of them, and conceived a fear of them. They said: "Fear not: we have been sent against the people of Lut."

71. And his wife was standing (there), and she laughed: but We gave her glad tidings of Isaac, and after him, of Jacob.

72. She said: "Alas for me! shall I bear a child, seeing I am an old woman, and my husband here is an old man? That would indeed be a wonderful thing!"

73. They said: "Do you won-der at Allah's decree? The Grace of Allah and His blessings on you, O you people of the house! for He is indeed worthy of all praise, full of all glory!"

74. When fear had passed from (the mind of) Abraham and the glad tidings had reached him, he began to plead with Us for Lut's people.

75. For Abraham was, without doubt, forbearing (of faults), compassionate, and given to look to Allah.

76.   O Abraham! Do not seek this. The decree of your Lord has gone forth: for them there comes a Chastisement that cannot be turned back!

77.   When Our Messengers came to Lut, he was grieved on their account and felt himself powerless (to protect) them. He said: "This is a distressful day."

78.   And his people came rushing towards him, and they had been long in the habit of practising abominations. He said: "O my people! Here are my daughters: they are purer for you (if you marry)! Now fear Allah, and do not cover me with shame about my guests! Isn't there among you a single right-minded man?"

79.   They said: "You know well we have no need of your daughters: indeed you know quite well what we want!"

80.   He said: "Would that I had power to suppress you or that I could betake myself to some powerful support."

81.   (The Messengers) said: "O Lut! We are Messengers from your Lord! By no means they shall reach you! Now travel with your family while yet a part of the night remains, and let not any of you look back: but your wife (will remain behind): to her will happen what happens to the people. Morning is their appointed time: is not the morning near?"

82.   When Our decree issued, We turned (the cities) upside down, and rained down on them brimstones hard as baked clay, spread, layer on layer,-

83.   Marked as from your Lord: nor are they ever far from those who do wrong!

84.   To the Madyan People (We sent) Shu'aib, one of their own brethren: he said: "O my people! worship Allah: you have no other god but Him. And do not give short measure or weight: I see you in prosperity, but I fear for you the Chastise-ment of a Day that will compass (you) all round.

85.   "And O my people! give just measure and weight, nor withhold from the people the things that are their due: do not commit evil in the land with intent to do mischief.

86. "That which is left you by Allah is best for you, if you (but) believed! but I am not set over you to keep watch!"

87. They said: "O Shu'aib! Does your (religion of) prayer command you that we leave off the worship which our fathers practised, or that we leave off doing what we like with our property? truly, you are the one that forbears with faults and is right-minded!"

88. He said: "O my people! Do you see whether I have a Clear (Sign) from my Lord, and He has given me sustenance (pure and) good as from Him-self? I do not wish, in opposition to you, to do that which I forbid you to do. I only desire (your) betterment to the best of my power; and my success (in my task) can only come from Allah. In Him I trust, and to Him I turn.

89. "And O my people! let not my dissent (from you) cause you to sin, lest you suffer a fate similar to that of the people of Noah or of Hud or of Salih, nor are the people of Lut far off from you!

90. "But ask forgiveness of your Lord, and turn to Him (in repentance): for my Lord is indeed full of mercy and loving-kindness."

91. They said: "O Shu'aib! much of what you say we do not understand! In fact among us we see that you have no strength! Were it not for your family, we should certainly have stoned you! For you have among us no great position!"

92. He said: "O my people! is then my family of more consideration with you than Allah? For you cast Him away behind your backs (with contempt). But verily my Lord encompasses on all sides all that you do!

93. "And O my people! do whatever you can: I will do (my part): soon will you know who it is on whom descends the Chastisement of ignominy; and who is a liar! and you watch! for I too am watching with you!"

94. When Our decree issued, We saved Shu'aib and those who

believed with him, by (special) Mercy from Our selves: but the (mighty) Blast seized the wrong-doers, and they lay prostrate in their homes by the morning,-

95.   As if they had never dwelt and flourished there! Ah! Behold! How the Madyan were removed (from sight) as were removed the Thamud.

96.   And We sent Moses, With Our Clear (Signs) and an authority manifest,

97.   Unto Pharaoh and his Chiefs: but they followed the command of Pharaoh and the command of Pharaoh was no right (guide).

98.   He will go before his people on the Day of Judgment, and lead them into the Fire (as cattle are led to water): but woeful indeed will be the place to which they are led!

99.   And they are followed by a curse in this (life) and on the Day of Judgment: and woeful is the gift which shall be given (to them)!

100. These are some of the stories of communities which We relate to you: of them some are standing, and some have been mown down (by the sickle of time).

101. It was not We that wronged them: they wronged their own souls: the deities, other than Allah, whom they invoked, profited them no whit[5] when there issued the decree of your Lord: nor did they add anything (to their lot) but perdition!

102. Such is the chastisement of your Lord when He chastises communities in the midst of their wrong: grievous, indeed, and severe is His chastisement.

103. In that is a Sign for those who fear the Chastisement of the Hereafter: that is a Day for which mankind will be gathered together: that will be a Day of Testimony.

104. Nor shall We delay it but for a term appointed.

105. The day it arrives, no soul shall speak except by His leave: of those (gathered) some will be wretched and some will be blessed.

---

5.   Not in the least

106. Those who are wretched shall be in the Fire: there will be for them therein (nothing but) the heaving of sighs and sobs:

107. They will dwell therein for all the time that the heavens and the earth endure, except as your Lord wills: for your Lord is the (sure) Accomp-lisher of what He plans.

108. And those who are blessed shall be in the Garden: they will dwell therein for all the time that the heavens and the earth endure, except as your Lord wills: a gift without break.

109. Be not then in doubt as to what these men worship. They worship nothing but what their fathers worshipped before (them): but verily We shall pay them back (in full) their portion without (the least) abatement.[6]

110. We certainly gave the Book to Moses, but differences arose therein: had it not been that a Word had gone forth before from your Lord, the matter would have been decided between them, but they are in suspicious doubt concerning it.

111. And, of a surety, to all will your Lord pay back (in full the recompense) of their deeds: for He knows well all that they do.

112. Therefore stand firm (in the straight Path) as you are commanded,- you and those who with you turn (unto Allah); and do not transgress (from the Path): for He sees well all that you do.

113. And incline not to those who do wrong, or the Fire will seize you; and you have no protectors other than Allah, nor shall you be helped.

114. And establish regular prayers at the two ends of the day and at the approaches of the night: for those things, that are good remove those that are evil: be that the word of rememb-rance to those who remember (their Lord):

115. And be steadfast in patience; for verily Allah will not suffer the reward of the righteous to perish.

116. Why were there not, among the generations before you, persons

---

6. Decrease

possessed of balanced good sense, prohi-biting (men) from mischief in the earth - except a few among them whom We saved (from harm)? But the wrong-doers pursued the enjoyment of the good things of life which were given them, and persisted in sin.

117. Nor would your Lord be the One to destroy communities for a single wrong- doing, if its members were likely to mend.

118. If your Lord had so willed, He could have made mankind one people: but they will not cease to dispute.

119. Except those on whom your Lord has bestowed His Mercy: and for this He created them: and the Word of your Lord shall be fulfilled: "I will fill Hell with (disobedient) jinns and men all together."

120. All that We relate to you of the stories of the Apostles,- with it We make firm your heart: in them there comes to you the Truth, as well as an exhortation and a message of remembrance to those who believe.

121. Say to those who do not believe: "Do whatever you can: we shall do our part;

122. "And you wait! we too shall wait."

123. To Allah do belong the unseen (secrets) of the heavens and the earth, and to Him goes back every affair (for decision): then worship Him, and put your trust in Him: and your Lord is not unmindful of anything that you do.

SURAH —12
SURAH YUSUF
(INTRODUCTION)

For the chronological place of this Surah and the general argument of Surahs 10 to 15 see Introduction to Surah 10.

In subject-matter this Surah is entirely taken up with the story (recapitulated rather than told) of Joseph, the youngest (but one) of the twelve sons of the patriarch Jocob. the story is called the most beautiful of stories (12:3) for many reasons: (1) it is the most details of any in the Quran; (2) it is full of human vicissitudes, and has therefore deservedly appealed to men and women of all classes; (3) it paints in vivid colours, with their spiritual implications, the most varied aspects of life-the patriarch's old age and the confidence between him and his little best-beloved son, the elder brother's jealousy of this little son, their plot and their father's grief, the sale of the father's darling into slavery for a miserable little price, carnal love contrasted with purity and chastity, false charges, prison the interpretation of dreams, low life and high life, Innocence raised to honour; the sweet "revenge" of Forgiveness and Benevolence, high matters of State and administration, humility in exaltation, filial love, and the beauty of Piety and Truth.

The story is similar to but not identical with the Biblical story; but the atmosphere is wholly deferent. The Biblical story is like a folk-tate in which morality has no place. Its tendency is to exalt the clever and financially-minded Jew against the Egyptian, and to explain certain ethnic and tribal peculiarities in later Jewish history. Joseph is shown as buying up all the cattle and the land of the poor Egyptians for the State under the stress of famine conditions, and making the Israelites "rulers" over Pharaoh's cattle. The Quranic story , on the other hand, is less a narrative than a highly spiritual sermon of allegory explaining the seeming contradictions in life, the enduring nature of virtue in a world full of flux and change, and the marvellous working of Allah's eternal purpose in His Plan as unfolded to us on the wide canvas of history. This aspect of the matter has been a favourite with Muslim poets and Sufi exegetists.

SURAH YUSUF OR JOSEPH

In the name of Allah, Most Gracious, Most Merciful.

1. Alif - Lam - Raa. These are the Symbols (or Verses) of the Perspicuous Book.

2. We have sent it down as an Arabic Qur'an, in order that you may learn wisdom.

3. We do relate to you the most beautiful of stories, in that We reveal to you this (portion of the) Qur'an: before this, you too were among those who did not know it.

4. Behold! Joseph said to his father: "O my father! I saw eleven stars and the sun and the moon: I saw them prostrate themselves to me!"

5. Said (the father): "My (dear) little son! do not relate your vision to your brothers, lest they concoct¹ a plot against you: for Satan is to man an avowed enemy!

6. "Thus will your Lord choose you and teach you the interpretation of stories (and events) and perfect His favour to you and to the posterity of Jacob - even as He perfected it to your fathers Abraham and Isaac aforetime! for Allah is full of knowledge and wisdom."

7. Verily in Joseph and his brethren are Signs (or Symbols) for Seekers (after Truth).

8. They said: "Truly Joseph and his brother are loved more by our father than we: but we are a goodly body! really our father is obviously wandering (in his mind)!

9. "You slay Joseph or cast him out to some (unknown) land, that so the favour of your father may be given to you alone: (there will be time enough) for you to be righteous after that!"

10. Said one of them: "do not slay Joseph, but if you must do something, throw him down to the bottom of the well: he will be picked up by some caravan of travellers."

11. They said: "O our father! why do you not trust us with Joseph,- seeing we are indeed his sincere well-wishers?

---

1. Invent, devise

12.   "Send him with us tomorrow to enjoy himself and play, and we shall take every care of him."

13.   (Jacob) said: "Really it saddens me that you should take him away: I fear lest the wolf should devour him while you do not attend to him."

14.   They said: "If the wolf were to devour him while we are (so large) a party, then should we indeed (first) have perished ourselves!"

15.   So they took him away, and they all agreed to throw him down to the bottom of the well: and We put into his heart (this Message): 'Of a surety you shall (one day) tell them the truth of this their affair while they do not know (you)'

16.   Then they came to their father in the early part of the night, weeping.

17.   They said: "O our father! We went racing with one another, and left Joseph with our things; and the wolf devoured him. But you will never believe us even though we tell the truth."

18.   They stained his shirt with false blood. He said: "Nay, but your minds have made up a tale (that may pass) with you. (For me) patience is most fitting: against that which you assert, it is Allah (alone) Whose help can be sought"..

19.   Then there came a caravan of travellers: they sent their water-carrier (for water), and he let down his bucket (into the well)...He said: "Ah there! Good news! Here is a (fine) young man!" So they concealed him as a treasure! But Allah knows well all that they do!

20.   The (Brethren) sold him for a miserable price, for a few dirhams counted out: in such low estimation did they hold him!

21.   The man in Egypt who bought him, said to his wife: "Make his stay (among us) honourable: may be he will bring us much good, or we shall adopt him as a son." Thus We established Joseph in the land, that We might teach him the interpretation of stories (and events). And Allah has full power and control over His affairs; but most among man-kind do not know it.

22.	When Joseph attained his full manhood, We gave him power and knowledge: thus do We reward those who do right.

23.	But she in whose house he was, sought to seduce him from his (true) self: she fastened the doors, and said: "Now come, you (dear one)!" He said: "Allah forbid! truly (your husband) is my lord! he made my sojourn agreeable! truly to no good come those who do wrong!"

24.	And (with passion) she desired him, and he would have desired her, but that he saw the evidence of his Lord: thus (did We order) that We might turn away from him (all) evil and shameful deeds: for he was one of Our servants, sincere and purified.

25.	So they both raced each other to the door, and she tore his shirt from the back: they both found her lord near the door. She said: "What is the (fitting) punishment for one who formed an evil design against your wife, but prison or a grievous chastisement?"

26.	He said: "It was she that sought to seduce me - from my (true) self." And one of her household saw (this) and bore witness, (thus):- "If it be that his shirt is torn from the front, then her tale is true, and he is a liar!

27.	"But if it be that his shirt is torn from the back, then is she the liar, and he is telling the truth!"

28.	So when he saw his shirt,- that it was torn at the back,- (her husband) said: "Behold! It is a snare[2] of you women! truly, mighty is your snare!

29.	"O Joseph, pass this over! (O wife), ask forgiveness for your sin, for truly you have been at fault!"

30.	Ladies said in the City: "The wife of the (great) 'Aziz is seeking to seduce her slave from his (true) self: Truly he has inspired her with violent love: we see she is evidently going astray."

31.	When she heard of their malicious talk, she sent for them and prepared a banquet for them: she gave each of them a knife: and she said (to Joseph), "Come out before them." When they

---

2.	Trap

saw him, they extolled him, and (in their amazement) cut their hands: they said, "Allah preserve us! no mortal is this! this is none other than a noble angel!"

32. She said: "There before you is the man about whom you blamed me! I sought to seduce him from his (true) self but he firmly saved himself guiltless!....And now, if he does not my bidding, he shall certainly be cast into prison, and (what is more) be of the company of the vilest!"[3]

33. He said: "O my Lord! the prison is more to my liking than that to which they invite me: unless You turn away their snare from me, I should (in my youth-ful folly) feel inclined toward them and join the ranks of the ignorant."

34. So his Lord hearkened to him (in his prayer), and turned away from him their snare: verily He hears and knows (all things).

35. Then it occurred to the men, after they had seen the Signs, (that it was best) to imprison him for a time.

36. Now with him there came into the prison two young men, said one of them: "I see myself (in a dream) pressing wine." Said the other: "I see myself (in a dream) carrying bread on my head, and birds are eating thereof." "Tell us" (they said) "the truth and meaning thereof: for we see you are one that does good (to all)."

37. He said: "Before any food comes (in due course) to feed either of you, I will surely reveal to you the truth and meaning of this ere it befall you: that is part of the (duty) which my Lord has taught me. I have (I assure you) abandoned the ways of a people that do not believe in Allah and that (even) deny the Hereafter.

38. "And I follow the ways of my fathers,- Abraham, Isaac, and Jacob; and never could we attribute any partners whatever to Allah: that (comes) of the grace of Allah to us and to mankind: yet most men are not grateful.

39. "O my two companions of the prison! (I ask you): are many lords differing among them-selves better, or the One God

---

3. Meanest people

(Allah), Supreme and Irresistible?

40.	"If not Him, you worship nothing but names which you have named,- you and your fathers,- for which Allah has sent down no authority: the Command is for none but Allah: He has commanded that you worship none but Him: that is the right religion, but most men do not understand.

41.	"O my two companions of the prison! As to one of you, he will pour out the wine for his lord to drink: as for the other, he will hang from the cross, and the birds will eat from off his head. (So) has been decreed that matter whereof you twain[4] do enquire"...

42.	And of the two, to that one whom he considered about to be saved, he said: "Mention me to your lord." But Satan made him forget to mention him to his lord: and (Joseph) lingered in prison a few (more) years.

43.	The king (of Egypt) said: "I do see (in a vision) seven fat kine,[5] whom seven lean ones devour,- and seven green ears of corn, and seven (others) withered. O you chiefs! Expound to me my vision if it be that you can interpret visions."

44.	They said: "A confused medley[6] of dreams: and we are not skilled in the interpretation of dreams."

45.	But the man who had been released, one of the two (who had been in prison) and who now remembered him after (so long) a space of time, said: "I will tell you the truth of its interpretation: you send me (therefore)."

46.	"O Joseph!" (he said) "O man of truth! Expound to us (the dream) of seven fat kine whom seven lean ones devour, and of seven green ears of corn and (seven) others withered: that I may return to the people, and that they may understand."

47.	(Joseph) said: "For seven years you shall diligently sow as is your wont[7]: and the harvests that you reap, you shall leave them in the ear,- except a little, of which you shall eat.

4.	Two	5.	Cows
6.	Mixture	7.	Custom

48. "Then will come after that (period) seven dreadful (years), which will devour what you shall have laid by in advance for them,- (all) except a little which you shall have (specially) guarded.

49. "Then will come after that (period) a year in which the people will have abundant water, and in which they will press (wine and oil)."

50. So the king said: "You bring him to me." But when the messenger came to him, (Joseph) said: "You go back to your lord, and ask him, 'What is the state of mind of the ladies who cut their hands'? For my Lord is certainly well aware of their snare."

51. (The king) said (to the ladies): "What was your affair when you sought to seduce Joseph from his (true) self?" The ladies said: "Allah preserve us! We do not know any evil against him!" Said the 'Aziz's wife: "Now is the truth manifest (to all): it was I who sought to seduce him from his (true) self: he is indeed of those who are (ever) true (and virtuous).

52. "This (I say), in order that he may know that I have never been false to him in his absence, and that Allah will never guide the snare of the false ones.

53. "Nor do I absolve my own self (of blame): the (human) soul is certainly prone to evil, unless my Lord bestows His Mercy: but surely my Lord is Oft- Forgiving, Most Merciful."

54. So the king said: "Bring him to me; I will take him specially to serve about my own person." Therefore when he had spoken to him, he said: "Be assured this day, you are, before our own presence, with rank firmly established, and fidelity fully proved!"

55. (Joseph) said: "Set me over the store-houses of the land: I will indeed guard them, as one that knows (their importance)."

56. Thus We gave established power to Joseph in the land, to take possession therein as, when, or where he pleased. We bestow of Our Mercy on whom We please, and We suffer not, to be

lost, the reward of those who do good.

57. But verily the reward of the Hereafter is the best, for those who believe, and are constant in righteousness.

58. Then came Joseph's breth-ren: they entered his presence, and he knew them, but they did not know him.

59. And when he had furni-shed them forth with provisions (suitable) for them, he said: "Bring to me a brother you have, of the same father as your-selves, (but a different mother): do you not see that I pay out full measure, and that I do provide the best hospitality?

60. "Now if you do not bring him to me, you shall have no measure (of corn) from me, nor you shall (even) come near me."

61. They said: "We shall cer-tainly seek to get our wish about him from his father: indeed we shall do it."

62. And (Joseph) told his ser-vants to put their stock-in-trade (with which they had bartered) into their saddle-bags, so they should know it only when they returned to their people, in order that they might come back.

63. Now when they returned to their father, they said: "O our father! No more measure of grain shall we get (unless we take our brother): so send our brother with us, that we may get our measure; and we will indeed take every care of him."

64. He said: "Shall I trust you with him with any result other than when I trusted you with his brother aforetime? But Allah is the best to take care (of him), and He is the Most Merciful of those who show mercy!"

65. Then when they opened their baggage, they found their stock-in-trade had been returned to them. They said: "O our father! What (more) can we desire? this our stock-in-trade has been returned to us: we shall get (more) food for our family; we shall take care of our brother; and add (at the same time) a full camel's load (of grain to our provisions). This is but a small quantity.

66. (Jacob) said: "Never will I send him with you until you swear a solemn oath to me, in Allah's name, that you will be sure to

bring him back to me unless you are yourselves hemmed[8] in (and made power-less). And when they had sworn their solemn oath, he said: "Over all that we say, be Allah the Witness and Guardian!"

67.   Further he said: "O my sons! enter not all by one gate: you enter by different gates. Not that I can profit you anything against Allah (with my advice): none can command except Allah: on Him do I put my trust: and let all that trust put their trust on Him."

68.   And when they entered in the manner their father had enjoined, it did not profit them in the least against (the plan of) Allah: it was but a necessity of Jacob's soul, which he dis-charged. For he was, by Our instruction, full of knowledge (and experience): but most men do not know.

69.   Now when they came into Joseph's presence, he received his (full) brother to stay with him. He said (to him): "Behold! I am your (own) brother; so do not grieve at anything of their doings."

70.   At length when he had furnished them forth with provisions (suitable) for them, he put the drinking cup into his brother's saddle-bag. Then shouted out a Crier:"O you (in) the caravan! behold! you are thieves, without doubt!"

71.   They said, turning toward them: "What is it that you miss?"

72.   They said: "We miss the great beaker[9] of the King; for him who produces it, is (the reward of) a camel load; I will be bound by it."

73.   (The brothers) said: "By Allah! you know well that we did not come to make mischief in the land, and we are no thieves!"

74.   (The Egyptians) said: "What then shall be the penalty of this, if you are (proved) to have lied?"

75.   They said: "The penalty should be that he in whose saddle-bag it is found, should be held (as bondman[10]) to atone for the

---

8.   Surrounded   9.   A drinking vessel, tumbler
10.   Captive, slave

(crime). Thus it is we punish the wrong- doers!"

76.   So he began (the search) with their baggage, before (he came to) the baggage of his brother: at length he brought it out of his brother's baggage. Thus did We plan for Joseph. He could not take his brother by the law of the king except that Allah willed it (so). We raise to degrees (of wisdom) whom We please: but over all endued with know-ledge is One, the All-Knowing.

77.   They said: "If he steals, there was a brother of his who stole before (him)." But these things Joseph kept locked in his heart, revealing not the secrets to them. He (simply) said (to himself): "You are the worse situated; and Allah knows best the truth of what you assert!"

78.   They said: "O exalted one! Behold! he has a father, aged and venerable[11], (who will grieve for him); so take one of us in his place; for we see that you are (gracious) in doing good."

79.   He said: "Allah forbid that we take other than him with whom we found our property: indeed (if we did so), we should be acting wrongfully.

80.   Now when they saw no hope of his (yielding), they held a conference in private. The leader among them said: "Don't you know that your father took an oath from you in Allah's name, and how, before this, you failed in your duty with Joseph? Therefore I will not leave this land until my father permits me, or Allah commands me; and He is the best to command.

81.   "You turn back to your father, and say, 'O our father! Behold! your son committed theft! we bear witness only to what we know, and we could not well guard against the unseen!

82.   "'Ask at the town where we have been and the caravan in which we returned, and (you will find) we are indeed telling the truth.'"

83.   Jacob said: "Nay, but you have yourselves contrived a story (good enough) for you. So patience is most fitting (for me). May be Allah will bring them (back) all to me (in the end). For He is indeed full of knowledge and wisdom."

---

11.   Honourable, respected, revered

84.   And he turned away from them, and said: "How great is my grief for Joseph!" And his eyes became white with sorrow, and he fell into silent melancholy.[12]

85.   They said: "By Allah! (Never) will you cease to remember Joseph until you reach the last extremity of illness, or until you die!"

86.   He said: "I only complain of my distraction and anguish to Allah, and I know from Allah that which you do not know.

87.   "O my sons! you go and enquire about Joseph and his brother, and never give up hope of Allah's soothing Mercy: truly no one despairs of Allah's soothing Mercy, except those who have no faith."

88.   Then, when they came (back) into (Joseph's) presence they said: "O exalted one! distress has seized us and our family: we have (now) brought but scanty capital: so pay us full measure, (we pray you), and treat it as charity to us: for Allah rewards the charitable."

89.   He said: "Do you know how you dealt with Joseph and his brother, not knowing (what you were doing)?"

90. They said: "Are you indeed Joseph?" He said, "I am Joseph, and this is my brother: Allah has indeed been gracious to us (all): behold, he that is righteous and patient,- never will Allah suffer the reward to be lost, of those who do right."

91.   They said: "By Allah! indeed Allah has preferred you above us, and we certainly have been guilty of sin!"

92.   He said: "This day let no reproach be (cast) on you: Allah will forgive you, and He is the Most Merciful of those who show mercy!

93.   "Go with this my shirt, and cast it over the face of my father: he will come to see (clearly). Then you come (here) to me together with all your family."

94.   When the Caravan left (Egypt), their father said: "I do indeed scent the presence of Joseph: nay, think me not a dotard."[13]

---

12.   Depression and gloom   13.   Feeble-minded from age

95.   They said: "By Allah! truly you are in your old wandering mind."

96.   Then when the bearer of the good news came, he cast (the shirt) over his face, and he forthwith regained clear sight. He said: "Did I not say to you, 'I know from Allah that which you do not know?'"

97.   They said: "O our father! ask for us forgiveness for our sins, for we were truly at fault."

98.   He said: "Soon will I ask my Lord for forgiveness for you: for He is indeed Oft-Forgiving, Most Merciful."

99.   Then when they entered the presence of Joseph, he provided a home for his parents with himself, and said: "you enter Egypt (all) in safety if it please Allah."

100.   And he raised his parents high on the throne (of dignity), and they fell down in prostration, (all) before him. He said: "O my father! this is the fulfilment of my vision of old! Allah has made it come true! He was indeed good to me when He took me out of prison and brought you (all here) out of the desert, (even) after Satan had sown enmity between me and my brothers. Verily my Lord understands best the mysteries of all that He plans to do. For verily He is full of knowledge and wisdom.

101.   "O my Lord! You have indeed bestowed on me some power, and taught me something of the interpretation of dreams and events,- O You Creator of the heavens and the earth! You are my Protector in this world and in the Hereafter. You take my soul (at death) as one submitting to Your Will (as a Muslim), and unite me with the righteous."

102.   Such is one of the stories of what happened unseen, which We reveal by inspiration unto you; nor were you (present) with them when they concerted their plans together in the process of weaving their plots.

103.   Yet no faith will the greater part of mankind have, however ardently you do desire it.

104.   And no reward do you ask of them for this: it is no less than a message for all creatures.

105.   And how many Signs in the heavens and the earth do they pass by? Yet they turn (their faces) away from them!

106.   And most of them do not believe in Allah without associ-ating (others as partners) with Him!

107.   Do they then feel secure from the coming against them of the covering veil of the wrath of Allah,- or of the coming against them of the (final) Hour all of a sudden while they perceive not?

108.   You say: "This is my way: I do invite to Allah,- on evi-dence clear as the seeing with one's eyes,- I and whoever follows me. Glory to Allah! and never will I join gods with Allah!"

109.   Nor did We send before you (as Messengers) any but men, whom We inspired,- (men) living in human habitations. Do they not travel through the earth, and see what was the end of those before them? But the home of the Hereafter is best, for those who do right. Will you not then understand?

110.   (Respite will be granted) until, when the Messengers give up hope (of their people) and (come to) think that they were treated as liars, there reaches them Our help, and those whom We will are delivered into safety. But never will be warded off Our punishment from those who are in sin.

111.   There is, in their stories, instruction for men endued with understanding. It is not a tale invented, but a confirmation of what went before it,- a detailed exposition of all things, and a Guide and a Mercy to any such as believe.

SURAH—13

SURAH Al-R'AD

(INTRODUCTION)

The chronological place of this Surah and the general argument of Surahs 10 to 15 has been described in the Introduction to S. 10.

The special argument of this Surah deals with that aspect of Allah's revelation of Himself to man and His dealings with him, which is concerned with certain contrasts which are here pointed out. There is the revelation to the Prophets, which comes in spoken words adapted to the language of the various men and groups of men to whom it comes; and there is the parallel revelation or Sighs in the constant laws of external nature, on this earth and in the visible heavens. There is the contrast between recurring life and death already in the external world: why should men disbelieve in the life after death? They mock at the idea of punishment because it is deferred: but can they not see Allah's power and glory in thunder and the forces of nature? All creation praises Him: it is the good that endures and the evil that is swept away like froth or scum. Not only in miracles but in the normal working of the world, are shown Allah's power and mercy. What is punishment in this world, compared to that in the life of come? Even here "there are Signs of the working of His law: plot or plan as men will, it is Allah's will that must prevail. This is illustrated in Joseph's story in the preceding Surah.

SURAH AL-R'AD (THUNDER)

In the name of Allah, Most Gracious, Most Merciful.

1.   Alif-Lam-Mim-Raa. These are the Signs (or Verses) of the Book: that which has been revealed to you from your Lord is the Truth; but most men do not believe.

2.   Allah is He Who raised the heavens without any pillars that you can see; is firmly established on the Throne (of Authority); He has subjected the sun and the moon (to His Law)! Each one runs (its course) for a term appointed. He regulates all affairs, explaining the Signs in detail, that you may believe with certainty in the meeting with your Lord.

3.   And it is He Who spread out the earth, and set thereon mountains standing firm and (flowing) rivers: and fruit of every

kind He made in pairs, two and two: He draws the night as a veil over the day. Behold, verily in these things there are Signs for those who consider!

4. And in the earth are tracts (diverse though) neighboring, and gardens of vines and fields sown with corn, and palm-trees growing out of single roots or otherwise: watered with the same water, yet some of them We make more excellent than others to eat. Behold, verily in these things there are Signs for those who understand!

5. If you do marvel (at their want of faith), strange is their saying: "When we are (actually) dust, shall we indeed then be in a renewed creation?" They are those who deny their Lord! They are those round whose necks will be yokes (of servi-tude): they will be Companions of the Fire, to dwell therein (for ever)!

6. They ask you to hasten on the evil in preference to the good: yet before them, have come to pass, (many) exemplary punish-ments! But verily your Lord is full of forgiveness for mankind for their wrong-doing. And verily your Lord is (also) strict in punishment.

7. And the Unbelievers say: "Why is not a Sign sent down to him from his Lord?" But you are truly a warner, and to every people a guide.

8. Allah knows what every female (womb) bears, by how much the wombs fall short (of their time or number) or do exceed. Every single thing is before His sight, in (due) proportion.

9. He knows the unseen and that which is open: He is the Great, the Most High.

10. It is the same (to Him) whether any of you conceal his speech or declare it openly; whether he lie hid by night or walk forth freely by day.

11. For each (such person) there are (angels) in succession, before and behind him: they guard him by command of Allah. Verily never will Allah change the condition of a people until they change it themselves (with their own souls). But when (once)

Allah wills a people's punishment, there can be no turning it back, nor will they find, besides Him, any to protect.

12. It is He Who shows you the lightning, by way both of fear and of hope: it is He Who raises up the clouds, heavy with (fertilising) rain!

13. Nay, thunder repeats His praises, and so do the angels, with awe: He flings the loud-voiced thunder-bolts, and therewith He strikes whom-soever He will..Yet these (are the men) who (dare to) dispute about Allah, with the strength of His power (supreme)!

14. For Him (alone) is prayer in Truth: any others that they call upon besides Him hear them no more than if they were to stretch forth their hands for water to reach their mouths but it reaches them not: for the prayer of those without Faith is nothing but (futile) wandering (in the mind).

15. Whatever beings there are in the heavens and the earth do prostrate themselves to Allah (acknowledging subjection),- with good-will or in spite of themselves: so do their shadows in the mornings and evenings.

16. Say: "Who is the Lord and Sustainer of the heavens and the earth?" Say: "(It is) Allah." Say: "Do you then take (for worship) protectors other than Him, such as have no power either for good or for harm to themselves?" Say: "Are the blind equal with those who see? Or the depths of darkness equal with light?" Or do they assign to Allah partners who have created (anything) as He has created, so that the creation seemed to them similar? Say: "Allah is the Creator of all things: He is the One, the Supreme and Irresistible."

17. He sends down water from the skies, and the channels flow, each according to its measure: but the torrent bears away the foam that mounts up to the surface. Even so, from that (ore[1]) which they heat in the fire, to make ornaments or utensils

---

1.   Naturally occuring mineral, metal, especially gold

therewith, there is a scum[2] likewise. Thus Allah (by parables) shows forth Truth and Vanity. For the scum disappears like forth cast out; while that which is for the good of mankind remains on the earth. Thus Allah sets forth parables.

18. For those who respond to their Lord, are (all) good things. But those who do not respond to Him,- even if they had all that is in the heavens and on earth, and as much more, (in vain) would they offer it for ransom. For them will the reckoning be terrible: their abode will be Hell,- what a bed of misery!

19. Is then one who knows that that which has been revealed to you from your Lord is the Truth, like one who is blind? It is those who are endued with understan-ding that receive admonition;-

20. Those who fulfil the Covenant of Allah and do not fail in their plighted word;

21. Those who join together those things which Allah has commanded to be joined, hold their Lord in awe, and fear the terrible reckoning;

22. Those who patiently perse-vere, seeking the countenance of their Lord; establish regular prayers; spend out of (the gifts) We have bestowed for their sustenance, secretly and openly; and turn off Evil with good: for such there is the final attainment of the (Eternal) Home,-

23. Gardens of perpetual bliss: they shall enter there, as well as the righteous among their fathers, their spouses, and their offspring: and angels shall enter unto them from every gate (with the salutation):

24. "Peace unto you for that you persevered in patience! Now how excellent is the final Home!"

25. But those who break the Covenant of Allah, after having plighted their word thereto, and cut asunder those things which Allah has commanded to be joined, and work mischief in the land;- on them is the Curse; for them is the terrible Home!

---

2. Impurities that rise to surface of liquid especially in boiling, floating film, refuse.

26.   Allah enlarges, or grants by (strict) measure, the sustenance (which He gives) to whomso He pleases. (The worldly) rejoice in the life of this world: but the life of this world is but little comfort in the Hereafter.

27.   The Unbelievers say: "Why is not a Sign sent down to him from his Lord?" Say: "Truly Allah leaves to stray, whom He will; But He guides to Himself those who turn to Him in penitence;[3]

28.   "Those who believe, and whose hearts find satisfaction in the remembrance of Allah: for without doubt in the remembrance of Allah do hearts find satisfaction.

29.   "For those who believe and work righteousness, is (every) blessedness, and a beautiful place of (final) return."

30.   Thus We have sent you amongst a People before whom (long since) have (other) Peoples (gone and) passed away; in order that you might rehearse unto them what We send down to you by inspiration; yet they reject (Him), the Most Gracious! Say: "He is my Lord! There is no god but He! On Him is my trust, and to Him do I turn!"

31.   If there were a Qur'an with which mountains were moved, or the earth were cloven asunder, or the dead were made to speak, (this would be the one!) but, truly, the Command is with Allah in all things! Do not the Believers know, that, had Allah (so) willed, He could have guided all mankind (to the right)? But the Unbelievers,- never will disaster cease to seize them for their (ill) deeds, or to settle close to their homes, until the promise of Allah come to pass, for, verily, Allah will not fail in His promise.

32.   Mocked were (many) Messengers before you: but I granted respite to the Unbe-lievers, and finally I punished them: then how (terrible) was My requital!

33.   Is then He Who stands over every soul (and knows) all that it does, (like any others)? And yet they ascribe partners to Allah.

---

3.   Repentance

Say: "But name them! Is it that you will inform Him of something He does not know on earth, or is it (just) a show of words?" Nay! to those who believe not, their pretence seems pleasing, but they are kept back (thereby) from the Path. And those whom Allah leaves to stray, no one can guide.

34. For them is a Panalty in the life of this world, but harder, truly, is the Penalty of the Hereafter: and they do not have any defender against Allah.

35. The parable of the Garden which the righteous are pro-mised!- beneath it flow rivers: perpetual is the enjoyment thereof and the shade therein: such is the End of the Righteous; and the End of Unbelievers is the Fire.

36. Those to whom We have given the Book rejoice at what has been revealed unto you: but there are among the clans those who reject a part thereof. Say: "I am commanded to worship Allah, and not to join partners with Him. To Him I call, and to Him is my return."

37. Thus We have revealed it to be a judgment of authority in Arabic. Were you to follow their (vain) desires after the knowledge which has reached you, then you would find neither protector nor defender against Allah.

38. We sent Messengers before you, and appointed for them wives and children: and it was never the part of a Messenger to bring a Sign except as Allah permitted (or commanded). For each period is a Book (revealed).

39. Allah blots out or confirms what He pleases: with Him is the Mother of the Book.

40. Whether We shall show you (within your life-time) part of what We promised them or take to Ourselves your soul (before it is all accomplished),- your duty is to make (the Message) reach them: it is Our part to call them to account.

41. Don't they see that We gradually reduce the land (in their control) from its outlying borders? (Where) Allah commands, there is none to put back His command: and He is Swift in calling to account.

42. Those before them (also) devised plots; but in all things the master- planning is Allah's. He knows the doings of every soul: and soon will the Unbelie-vers know who gets home in the End.

43. The Unbelievers say: "No Messenger are you." Say: "Enough for a witness between me and you is Allah, and such as have knowledge of the Book."

SURAH —14
SURAH IBRAHIM
(INTRODUCTION)

For the chronology and the general argument of this Surah in the series Surahs 10 to 15, see Introduction to S. 10.

The special subject-matter of this Surah, is a continuation of the concluding portion of the last Surah, which explained how Allah's revelation gains ground in spite of selfish men's oppositions, Here illustrations are given from the story of Moses and Abraham, and Abraham's Prayer for Makkah forms the core of the Surah.

SURAH IBRAHIM (ABRAHAM)

In the name of Allah, Most Gracious, Most Merciful.

1. *Alif - Lam - Raa.* A Book which We have revealed to you, in order that you might lead mankind out of the depths of darkness into light - by the leave of their Lord - to the Way of (Him) the Exalted in Power, worthy of all Praise!-

2. Of Allah, to Whom do belong all things in the heavens and on earth! But alas for the Unbelievers for a terrible Penalty (their Unfaith will bring them)!-

3. Those who love the life of this world more than the Hereafter, who hinder (men) from the Path of Allah and seek therein something crooked: they are astray by a long distance.

4. We did not send a Messen-ger except (to teach) in the language of his (own) people, in order to make (things) clear to them. Now Allah leaves stray-ing those whom He pleases and guides whom He pleases: and He is Exalted in Power, full of Wisdom.

5. We sent Moses with Our Signs (and the command). "Bring out your people from the depths of darkness into light, and teach them to remember the Days of Allah." Verily in this there are Signs for such as are firmly patient and constant,- grateful and appreciative.

6. Remember! Moses said to his people: "Call to mind the favour of Allah to you when He delivered you from the people of Pharaoh: they set you hard tasks and punishments, slaugh-tered

your sons, and let your women-folk live: therein was a tremendous trial from your Lord."

7.   And remember! your Lord caused to be declared (public-ly): "If you are grateful, I will add more (favours) to you; But if you show ingratitude, truly My punishment is terrible indeed."

8.   And Moses said: "If you show ingratitude, you and all on earth together, yet is Allah free of all wants, worthy of all praise.

9.   Has not the story reached you, (O people!), of those who (went) before you? - of the people of Noah, and 'Ad, and Thamud? - and of those who (came) after them? None knows them but Allah. To them came Messengers with Clear (Signs); but they put their hands up to their mouths, and said: "We do deny (the mission) on which you have been sent, and we are really in suspicious (disquie-ting) doubt as to that to which you invite us."

10. Their Messengers said: "Is there a doubt about Allah, the Creator of the heavens and the earth? It is He Who invites you, in order that He may forgive you your sins and give you respite for a term appointed!" They said: "Ah! you are no more than human, like ourselves! You wish to turn us away from the (gods) our fathers used to worship: then bring us some clear authority."

11. Their Messengers said to them: "True, we are human like yourselves, but Allah grants His grace to such of His servants as He pleases. It is not for us to bring you an authority except as Allah permits. And on Allah let all men of faith put their trust.

12. "We do not have any reason why we should not put our trust on Allah. Indeed He has guided us to the Ways we (follow). We shall certainly bear with patience all the hurt you may cause us. For those who put their trust should put their trust on Allah."

13. And the Unbelievers said to their Messengers: "Be sure we shall drive you out of our land, or you shall return to our religion." But their Lord ins-pired (this Message) to them: "Verily We shall cause the wrong-doers to perish!

14. "And verily We shall cause you to abide in the land, and succeed them. This for such as fear the Time when they shall stand before My tribunal,[1] such as fear the punishment denounced."

15. But they sought victory and decision (there and then), and frustration was the lot of every powerful obstinate transgressor.

16. In front of such a one is Hell, and he is given, for drink, boiling fetid[2] water.

17. In gulps[3] will he sip it, but never will he be near swal-lowing it down his throat: death will come to him from every quarter, yet he will not die: and in front of him will be a chastisement unrelenting.

18. The parable of those who reject their Lord is that their works are as ashes, on which the wind blows furiously on a tem-pestuous day: no power have they over anything that they have earned: that is the straying far, far (from the goal).

19. Don't you see that Allah created the heavens and the earth in Truth? If He so will, He can remove you and put (in your place) a new Creation?

20. Nor is that for Allah any great matter.

21. They will all be marshalled[4] before Allah together: then will the weak say to those who were arrogant, "For us, we but followed you; can you then avail us at all against the Wrath of Allah?" They will reply, "If we had received the Guidance of Allah, we should have given it to you: to us it makes no difference (now) whether we rage, or bear (these torments) with patience: for ourselves there is no way of escape."

22. And Satan will say when the matter is decided: "It was Allah Who gave you a promise of Truth: I too promised, but I failed in my promise to you. I had no authority over you except to call you, but you listened to me: then reproach not me, but reproach your own souls. I cannot listen to your cries, nor can you listen to mine. I reject your former act in associating me

---

1. Judgment-seat
2. Stinking
3. Large mouthful of a drink
4. Gathered

with Allah. For wrong-doers there must be a grievous Penalty."

23.   But those who believe and work righteousness will be admitted to Gardens beneath which rivers flow,- to dwell therein for ever with the leave of their Lord. Their greeting therein will be: "Peace!"

24.   Do you not see how Allah sets forth a parable? - a goodly Word like a goodly tree, whose root is firmly fixed, and its branches (reach) to the heavens.

25.   It brings forth its fruit at all times, by the leave of its Lord. So Allah sets forth parables for men, in order that they may receive admonition.

26.   And the parable of an evil Word is that of an evil tree: It is torn up by the root from the surface of the earth: it has no stability.

27.   Allah will establish in strength those who believe, with the Word that stands firm, in this world and in the Hereafter; but Allah will leave, to stray, those who do wrong: Allah does what He wills.

28.   Have you not turned your vision to those who have exchanged the favour of Allah into blasphemy and caused their People to descend to the House of Perdition?-

29.   Into Hell? They will burn therein,- an evil place to stay in!

30.   And they set up (idols) as equal to Allah, to mislead (men) from the Path! Say: "Enjoy (your brief power)! But verily you are making straightway for Hell!"

31.   Speak to My servants who have believed, that they may establish regular prayers, and spend (in charity) out of the Sustenance We have given them, secretly and openly, before the coming of a Day in which there will be neither mutual bargai-ning nor befriending.

32.   It is Allah Who has created the heavens and the earth and sends down rain from the skies, and with it brings out fruits wherewith to feed you; it is He Who have made the ships subject to you, that they may sail through the sea by His Command; and He has made the rivers (also) subject to you.

33.   And He has made subject to you the sun and the moon, both diligently pursuing their courses; and He has (also) made the Night and the Day subject to you.

34.   And He gives you of all that you ask for. But if you count the favours of Allah, never will you be able to number them. Verily, man is given up to injustice and ingratitude.

35.   Remember Abraham said: "O my Lord! make this city one of peace and security: and preserve me and my sons from worshipping idols.

36.   "O my Lord! they have indeed led astray many among mankind; he then who follows my (ways) is of me, and he that disobeys me,- but You are indeed Oft-Forgiving, Most Merciful.

37.   "O our Lord! I have made some of my offspring to dwell in a valley without cultivation, by Your Sacred House; in order, O our Lord, that they may establish regular Prayer: so fill the hearts of some among men with love toward them, and feed them with fruits: so that they may give thanks.

38.   "O our Lord! truly You do know what we conceal and what we reveal: for nothing whatever is hidden from Allah, whether on earth or in heaven.

39.   "Praise be to Allah, Who has granted to me in old age Isma'il and Isaac: for truly my Lord is He, the Hearer of Prayer!

40.   O my Lord! make me one who establishes regular Prayer, and also (raise such) among my offspring O our Lord! and You accept my Prayer.

41.   "O our Lord! cover (us) with Your Forgiveness - me, my parents, and (all) Believers, on the Day that the Reckoning will be established!

42.   Think not that Allah does not heed the deeds of those who do wrong. He but gives them respite against a Day when the eyes will fixedly stare in horror,-

43.   They running forward with necks outstretched, their heads uplifted, their gaze returning not toward them, and their hearts a (gaping) void!

44.   So warn mankind of the Day when the Wrath will reach them: then will the wrong-doers say: "Our Lord! respite us (if only) for a short Term: we will answer Your Call, and follow the Messengers!" "What! were you not wont to swear aforetime that you should suffer no decline?

45.   "And you dwelt in the dwellings of men who wronged their own souls; you were clearly shown how We dealt with them; and We put forth (many) Parables in your behoof!"

46.   Mighty indeed were the plots which they made, but their plots were (well) within the sight of Allah, even though they were such as to shake the hills!

47.   Never think that Allah would fail His Messengers in His promise: for Allah is Exalted in Power, - the Lord of Retribution.

48.   One day the Earth will be changed to a different Earth, and so will be the Heavens, and (men) will be marshalled forth, before Allah, the One, the Irresistible;

49.   And you will see the Sinners that day bound together in fetters;-

50.   Their garments of liquid pitch[5], and their faces covered with Fire.

51.   That Allah may requite each soul according to its deserts; and verily Allah is Swift in calling to account.

52.   Here is a Message for mankind: let them take war-ning therefrom, and let them know that He is (no other than) One God (Allah): let men of understanding take heed.

---

5.   Thick dark inflammable liquid.

SURAH—15
SURAH AL-HIJR
(INTRODUCTION)

This is the last of the six Surahs of the A.L.M. series (10 to 15). Its place in chronology is the late Makkan period, probably somewhere near the middle of that period. See Introduction to S. 10 where will be found also an indication of the general subject-matter of the whole series in the gradation of Quranic teaching.

The special subject-matter of this Surah is the protection of Allah's Revelation and Allah's Truth. Evil arose from Pride and the warping of man's will, but Allah's Mercy is the antidote, as was proved in the case of Abraham arid Lot, and might have been proved by the people of the Aika and the Hijr if they had only attended to Allah's "Signs". The Quran, beginning with the Seven Oft-repeated Verses, is the precious vehicle for the praises of Allah.

SURAH AL-HIJR (THE ROCKY TRACT)
In the name of Allah, Most Gracious, Most Merciful.

1. Alif - Lam- Ra. These are the Ayats of Revelation,- of a Qur'an that makes things clear.

2. Again and again will those who disbelieve, wish that they had bowed (to Allah's Will) in Islam.

3. Leave them alone, to enjoy (the good things of this life) and to please themselves: let (false) hope amuse them: soon will knowledge (undeceive them).

4. We never destroyed a population that had not a term decreed and assigned before-hand.

5. Neither can a people anticipate its Term, nor delay it.

6. They say: "O you to whom the Message is being revealed! truly you are mad (or posse-ssed)!

7. "Why don't you bring the angels to us if it be that you have the Truth?"

8. We do not send the angels down except for just cause: if they came (to the ungodly), behold! no respite would they have!

9. We have, without doubt, sent down the Message; and We will assuredly guard it (from corruption).

10.   We sent Messengers before you amongst the religious sects of old:

11.   But never came a Messen-ger to them but they mocked him.

12.   Even so do We let it creep into the hearts of the sinners.

13.   That they should not believe in the (Message); but the ways of the ancients have passed away.

14.   Even if We opened out to them a gate from heaven, and they were to continue (all day) ascending therein,

15.   They would only say: "Our eyes have been intoxicated: nay, we have been bewitched by sorcery."

16.   It is We Who have set out the zodiacal signs[1] in the heavens, and made them fair-seeming to (all) beholders;

17.   And (moreover) We have guarded them from every evil spirit accursed:

18.   But any that gains a hearing by stealth, is pursued by a flaming fire, bright (to see).

19.   And We have spread out the earth (like a carpet); set thereon mountains firm and immovable; and produced therein all kinds of things in due balance.

20.   And We have provided therein means of subsistence,- for you and for those for whose sustenance you are not respon-sible.

21.   And there is not a thing but its (sources and) treasures (inexhaustible) are with Us; but We only send down thereof in due and ascertainable measures.

22.   And We send the fecundating[2] winds, then cause the rain to descend from the sky, therewith providing you with water (in abundance), though you are not the guardians of its stores.

23.   And verily, it is We Who give life, and Who give death: it is We Who remain inheritors (after all else passes away).

24.   To Us are known those of you who hasten forward, and those who lag behind.

---

1.   Names of groups of fixed stars (or constellations) in the belt of heavens that is divided into 12 equal parts.

2.   Fertilizing

25. Assuredly it is your Lord Who will gather them together: for He is perfect in Wisdom and Knowledge.

26. We created man from sounding[3] clay, from mud moulded into shape;

27. And the Jinn race, We had created before, from the fire of a scorching wind.

28. Behold! your Lord said to the angels: "I am about to create man, from sounding clay from mud moulded into shape;

29. "When I have fashioned him (in due proportion) and breathed into him of My spirit, you fall down in obeisance[4] unto him."

30. So the angels prostrated themselves, all of them together:

31. Not so Iblis: he refused to be among those who prostrated themselves.

32. (Allah) said: "O Iblis! what is your reason for not being among those who prostrated themselves?"

33. (Iblis) said: "I am not one to prostrate myself to man, whom You created from sounding clay, from mud moulded into shape."

34. (Allah) said: "Then get out from here; for you are rejected, accursed.

35. "And the curse shall be on you till the day of Judgment."

36. (Iblis) said: "O my Lord! give me then respite till the Day the (dead) are raised."

37. (Allah) said: "Respite is granted to you,

38. "Till the Day of the Time Appointed."

39. (Iblis) said: "O my Lord! because You have put me in the wrong, I will make (wrong) fair-seeming to them on the earth, and I will put them all in the wrong,-

40. "Except Your servants among them, sincere and purified (by Your Grace)."

41. (Allah) said: "This (Way of My sincere servants) is indeed a Way that leads straight to Me.

---

3. Giving forth sound
4. Gesture, especially prostration, expressing submission, respect or salutation.

42. "For over My servants no authority shall you have, except such as put themselves in the wrong and follow you."

43. And verily, Hell is the promised abode for them all!

44. To it are seven Gates: for each of those Gates is a (special) class (of sinners) assigned.

45. The righteous (will be) amid Gardens and fountains (of clear-flowing water).

46. (Their greeting will be): "You enter here in peace and security."

47. And We shall remove from their hearts any lurking sense of injury: (they will be) brothers (joyfully) facing each other on thrones (of dignity).

48. There no sense of fatigue shall touch them, nor shall they (ever) be asked to leave.

49. Tell My servants that I am indeed the Oft-Forgiving, Most Merciful;

50. And that My Penalty will be indeed the most grievous Penalty.

51. Tell them about the guests of Abraham.

52. When they entered his presence and said, "Peace!" he said, "We feel afraid of you!"

53. They said: "Fear not! We give you glad tidings of a son endowed with wisdom."

54. He said: "Do you give me glad tidings that old age has seized me? Of what, then, is your good news?"

55. They said: "We give you glad tidings in truth: be not then in despair!"

56. He said: "And who des-pairs of the mercy of his Lord, but such as go astray?"

57. Abraham said: "What then is the business on which you (have come), O you messengers (of Allah)?"

58. They said: "We have been sent to a people (deep) in sin,

59. "Excepting the adherents of Lut: we are certainly (charged) to save them (from harm),- all -

60. "Except his wife, who, We have ascertained, will be among those who will lag behind."

61. At length when the messen-gers arrived among the adherents of Lut,

62. He said: "You appear to be uncommon folk."

63. They said: "Yes, we have come to you to accomplish that of which they doubt.

64. "We have brought to you that which is inevitably due, and assuredly we tell the truth.

65. "Then travel by night with your household, when a portion of the night (yet remains), and you bring up the rear: let no one amongst you look back, but pass on whither you are ordered."

66. And We made known this decree to him, that the last remnants of those (sinners) should be cut off by the morning.

67. The inhabitants of the city came in (mad) joy (at news of the young men).

68. Lut said: "These are my guests: do not disgrace me:

69. "But fear Allah, and shame me not."

70. They said: "Did we not forbid you (to speak) for all and sundry?"[5]

71. He said: "There are my daughters (to marry), if you must act (so)."

72. Verily, by your life (O Prophet), in their wild intoxi-cation, they wander in distrac-tion, to and fro.

73. But the (mighty) Blast overtook them before morning,

74. And We turned (the cities) upside down, and rained down on them brimstones hard as baked clay.

75. Behold! in this are Signs for those who by tokens do understand.

76. And the (cities were) right on the high-road.

77. Behold! in this is a Sign for those who believe!

78. And the Companions of the Wood were also wrong-doers;

79. So We exacted retribution[6] from them. They were both on an open highway, plain to see.

---

5. Everyone, collectively and individually
6. Punished them

80. The Companions of the Rocky Tract also rejected the Messengers:

81. We sent them Our Sings, but they persisted in turning away from them.

82. Out of the mountains did they hew[7] (their) edifices[8], (feeling themselves) secure.

83. But the (mighty) Blast seized them of a morning,

84. And of no avail to them was all that they did (with such art and care)!

85. We did not create the hea-vens, the earth, and all between them, but for just ends. And the Hour is surely coming (when this will be manifest). So overlook (any human faults) with gracious forgiveness.

86. For verily it is your Lord Who is the Master-Creator, knowing all things.

87. And We have bestowed upon you the Seven Oft-repeated (verses) and the Grand Qur'an.

88. Do not strain your eyes (wistfully[9]) at what We have bestowed on certain classes of them, nor grieve over them: but lower your wing (in gentleness) to the Believers.

89. And say: "I am indeed he that warns openly and without ambiguity,"-

90. (Of just such wrath) as We sent down on those who divided (Scripture into arbitrary[10] parts),-

91. (So also on such) as have made Qur'an into shreds[11] (as they please).

92. Therefore, by the Lord, We will, of a surety, call them to account.

93. For all their deeds.

94. Therefore expound[12] open-ly what you are commanded, and turn away from those who join false gods with Allah.

---

7.   Cut-carve   8.   Buildings
9.   Longingly
10. Based on mere opinion or random choice
11. Bits and pieces   12. Explain

95. For sufficient are We to you against those who scoff,[95]

96. Those who adopt, with Allah, another god: but soon will they come to know.

97. We do indeed know how your heart is distressed at what they say.

98. But celebrate the praises of your Lord, and be of those who prostrate themselves in adoration.[14]

99. And serve your Lord until there come to you the Hour that is Certain.

---

13. Ridicule, make fun of   14. Worship

SURAH AN-NAHL
(INTRODUCTION)

Chronologically this Surahs, like the six which preceded it, belongs to the late Makkan period, except perhaps verse 110 and some of the verses that follow, but the chronology has no significance. In subject-matter it sums up, from a new point of view, the arguments on the great questions of Allah's dealings with man, His Self-revelation to man and how the Messengers and the Message are writ large in every phase of Allah's Creation and the life of Man. The new point of view is that Nature points to Nature's Allah.

SURAH AN-NAHL (THE BEE)

In the name of Allah, Most Gracious, Most Merciful.

1. (Inevitable) comes (to pass) the Command of Allah: do not then seek to hasten it: glory to Him, and far is He above having the partners they ascribe to Him!

2. He sends down His angels with inspiration of His Command, to such of His servants as He pleases, (saying): "Warn (Man) that there is no god but I: so do your duty to Me."

3. He has created the heave-ns and the earth for just ends: far is He above having the partners they ascribe to Him!

4. He has created man from a sperm-drop; and behold this same (man) becomes an open disputer!

5. And He has created cattle for you (men): from them you derive warmth, and numerous benefits, and of their (meat) you eat.

6. And you have a sense of pride and beauty in them as you drive them home in the evening, and as you lead them forth to pasture in the morning.

7. And they carry your heavy loads to lands that you could not (otherwise) reach except with souls distressed: for your Lord is indeed Most Kind, Most Merciful,

8. And (He has created) horses, mules, and donkeys, for you to ride and use for show; and He has created (other) things of which you have no knowledge.

9. And to Allah leads straight the Way, but there are ways that turn aside: if Allah had willed, He could have guided all of you.

10. It is He Who sends down rain from the sky: from it you drink, and out of it (grows) the vegetation on which you feed your cattle.

11. With it He produces for you corn, olives, date-palms, grapes and every kind of fruit: verily in this is a Sign for those who give thought.

12. He has made subject to you the Night and the Day; the Sun and the Moon; and the Stars are in subjection by His Command: verily in this are Signs for men who are wise.

13. And the things on this earth which He has multiplied in varying colours (and qualities): verily in this is a Sign for men who celebrate the praises of Allah (in gratitude).

14. It is He Who has made the sea subject, that you may eat thereof flesh that is fresh and tender, and that you may extract therefrom ornaments to wear; and you see the ships therein that plough the waves, that you may seek (thus) of the bounty of Allah and that you may be grateful.

15. And He has set up on the earth mountains standing firm, lest it should shake with you; and rivers and roads; that you may guide yourselves;

16. And marks and sign-posts; and by the stars (men) guide themselves.

17. Is then He Who creates like one that creates not? Will you not receive admonition?[1]

18. If you would count up the favours of Allah, never would you be able to number them: for Allah is Oft-Forgiving, Most Merciful.

19. And Allah knows what you conceal, and what you reveal.

20. Those whom they invoke[2] besides Allah create nothing and are themselves created.

---

1. Warning, counsel 2. Summon, to call on

21. (They are things) dead, lifeless: nor do they know when they will be raised up.

22. Your God (Allah) is One God (Allah): as to those who do not believe in the Hereafter, their hearts refuse to know, and they are arrogant.

23. Undoubtedly Allah knows what they conceal, and what they reveal: verily He does not love the arrogant.

24. When it is said to them, "What is it that your Lord has revealed?" they say, "Tales of the ancients!"

25. Let them bear, on the Day of Judgment, their own burdens in full, and also (something) of the burdens of those without knowledge, whom they misled. Alas, how grievous the burdens they will bear!

26. Those before them also plotted (against Allah's Way): but Allah took their structures from their foundations, and the roof fell down on them from above; and the Wrath seized them from directions they did not perceive.

27. Then, on the Day of Judgment, He will cover them with shame, and say: "Where are My 'partners' concerning whom you used to dispute (with the godly)?" Those endued with knowledge will say: "This Day, indeed, are the Unbelievers covered with Shame and Misery,-

28. "(Namely) those whose lives the angels take in a state of wrong-doing to their own souls." Then would they offer submi-ssion (with the pretence[3]), "We did no evil (knowingly)." (The angels will reply), "Nay, but verily Allah knows all that you did;

29. "So enter the gates of Hell, to dwell therein. Thus evil indeed is the abode[4] of the arrogant."

30. To the righteous (when) it is said, "What is it that your Lord has revealed?" they say, "All that is good." To those who do good, there is good in this world, and the Home of the Hereafter is even better and excellent indeed is the Home of the righteous,-

---

3.   False claim   4.   Home of house

31. Gardens of Eternity which they will enter: beneath them flow (pleasant) rivers: they will have therein all that they wish: thus Allah rewards the righteous,-

32. (Namely) those whose lives the angels take in a state of purity, saying (to them), "Peace be on you; you enter the Garden, because of (the good) which you did (in the world)."

33. Do the (ungodly) wait until the angels come to them, or there comes the Command of your Lord (for their doom[5])? So did those who went before them. But Allah did not wrong them: nay, they wronged their own souls.

34. But the evil results of their deeds overtook them, and that very (Wrath) at which they had scoffed[6] hemmed them in.[7]

35. The worshippers of false gods say: "If Allah had so willed, we should not have worshipped anything but Him - neither we nor our fathers,- nor should we have prescribed prohibitions other than His." So did those who went before them. But what is the mission of Messengers but to preach the Clear Message?

36. For We assuredly sent amongst every People a Messenger, (with the Com-mand), "Serve Allah, and eschew[8] Evil": of the People were some whom Allah guided, and some on whom error became inevitably (estab-lished). So travel through the earth, and see what was the end of those who denied (the Truth).

37. If you are anxious for their guidance, yet Allah does not guide (any) such as He leaves to stray, and there is none to help them.

38. They swear their strongest oaths by Allah, that Allah will not raise up those who die: nay, but it is a promise (binding) on Him in truth: but most among mankind do not realize it.

39. (They must be raised up), in order that He may manifest to them the truth of that wherein they differ, and that the rejecters of Truth may realize that they had indeed (surrendered to) Falsehood.

40. For to anything which We have willed, We but say the Word,

---

5. Ruin, condemnation
6. Made fun of
7. Encircled them
8. Avoid

"Be", and it is.

41.   To those who leave their homes in the cause of Allah, after suffering oppression,- We will assuredly give a goodly home in this world; but truly the reward of the Hereafter will be greater. If they only realized (this)!

42.   (They are) those who persevere[9] in patience, and put their trust on their Lord.

43.   And before you also the Messengers We sent were but men, to whom We granted inspi-ration: if you do not realize this, ask of those who possess the Message.

44.   (We sent them) with Clear Signs and Books of dark pro-phesies; and We have sent down to you (also) the Message; that you may explain clearly to men what is sent for them, and that they may give thought.

45.   Do then those who devise evil (plots) feel secure that Allah will not cause the earth to swallow them up, or that the Wrath will not seize them from directions they little perceive?-

46.   Or that He may not call them to account in the midst of their goings to and fro, without a chance of their frustrating Him?

47.   Or that He may not call them to account by a process of slow wastage - for your Lord is indeed full of kindness and mercy.

48.   Do they not look at Allah's creation, (even) among (inani-mate) things,- how their (very) shadows turn round, from the right and the left, prostrating themselves to Allah, and that in the humblest manner?

49.   And to Allah does obeisance[10] all that is in the heavens and on earth, whether moving (living) creatures or the angels: for none are arrogant (before their Lord).

50.   They all revere[11] their Lord, high above them, and they do all that they are commanded.

51.   Allah has said: "Do not take (for worship) two gods: for He is just One God (Allah): then fear Me (and Me alone)."

---

9.   Persist, remain steadfast   10.   Adore, worship, honour
11.   Bow

52. To Him belongs whatever is in the heavens and on earth, and to Him is duty due always: then will you fear other than Allah?

53. And you have no good thing but is from Allah: and moreover, when you are touched by distress, to Him you cry with groans;

54. Yet, when He removes the distress from you, behold! some of you turn to other gods to join with their Lord-

55. (As if) to show their ingratitude for the favours We have bestowed on them! then enjoy (your brief day): but soon will you know (your folly)!

56. And they (even) assign, to things they do not know, a portion out of that which We have bestowed for their suste-nance! By Allah, you shall certainly be called to account for your false inventions.

57. And they assign daughters for Allah! - Glory be to Him! - and for themselves (sons,- the issue) they desire!

58. When news is brought to one of them, of (the birth of) a female (child), his face darkens, and he is filled with inward grief!

59. With shame he hides himself from his people, because of the bad news he has had! Shall he retain it on (sufferance[12] and) contempt, or bury it in the dust? Ah! what an evil (choice) they decide on?

60. To those who believe not in the Hereafter, applies the similitude of evil: to Allah applies the highest similitude: for He is the Exalted in Power, full of Wisdom.

61. If Allah were to punish men for their wrong-doing, He would not leave, on the (earth), a single living creature: but He gives them respite[13] for a stated Term: when their Term expires, they would not be able to delay (the punishment) for a single hour, just as they would not be able to advance[14] it (for a single hour).

62. They attribute to Allah what they hate (for themselves), and

---

12. Toleration or permission
13. Delay, interval (of rest or relief), reprieve
14. To cause to happen before its due time.

their tongues assert the falsehood that all good things are for themselves: without doubt for them is the Fire, and they will be the first to be hastened on into it!

63. By Allah, We (also) sent (Our Messengers) to Peoples before you but Satan made, (to the wicked), their own acts seem alluring[15]: he is also their patron today, but they shall have a most grievous Penalty.

64. And We sent down the Book to you for the express purpose, that you should make clear to them those things in which they differ, and that it should be a guide and a mercy to those who believe.

65. And Allah sends down rain from the skies, and gives therewith life to the earth after its death: verily in this is a Sign for those who listen.

66. And verily in cattle (too) will you find an instructive[16] Sign. From what is within their bodies, between excretions[17] and blood, We produce, for your drink, milk, pure and agreeable to those who drink it.

67. And from the fruit of the date-palm and the vine[18], you get out wholesome[19] drink and food; behold, in this also is a Sign for those who are wise.

68. And your Lord taught the Bee to build its cells in hills, on trees, and in (men's) habitations;[20]

69. Then to eat of all the produce (of the earth), and find with skill the spacious paths of its Lord: there issues from within their bodies a drink of varying colours, wherein is healing for men: verily in this is a Sign for those who give thought .

70. It is Allah Who creates you and takes your souls at death; and of you there are some who are sent back to a feeble age, so that they know nothing after having known (much): for Allah is All-Knowing, All-Powerful.

---

15. Charming   16. Enlightening
17. Waste discharged from body especially faeces and urine.
18. Plant whose fruit is the grape   19. Healthful
20. Dwelling places

71. Allah has bestowed His gifts of sustenance more freely on some of you than on others: those more favoured are not going to throw back their gifts to those whom their right hands possess, so as to be equal in that respect. Will they then deny the favours of Allah?

72. And Allah has made for you mates (and companions) of your own nature, and made for you, out of them, sons and daughters and grandchildren, and provided for you sustenance of the best: will they then believe in vain things, and be ungrateful for Allah's favours?-

73. And worship others than Allah,- such as have no power of providing them, for sustenance, with anything in heavens or earth, and cannot possibly have such power?

74. Do not invent similitudes for Allah: for Allah knows, and you do not know.

75. Allah sets forth the Parable (of two men: one) a slave under the dominion[21] of another; he has no power of any sort; and (the other) a man on whom We have bestowed goodly favours from Ourselves, and he spends thereof (freely), privately and publicly: are the two equal? (By no means;) praise be to Allah. But most of them do not understand.

76. Allah sets forth (another) Parable of two men: one of them dumb, with no power of any sort; a wearisome burden is he to his master; whichever way he directs him, he brings no good: is such a man equal with one who commands Justice, and is on a Straight Way?

77. To Allah belongs the Mystery of the heavens and the earth. And the Decision of the Hour (of Judgment) is as the twinkling of an eye, or even quicker: for Allah has power over all things.

78. It is He Who brought you forth from the wombs of your mothers when you knew nothing; and He gave you hearing and sight and intelli-gence and affections: that you may give thanks (to

---

21. Control, authority

Allah).

79. Do they not look at the birds, held poised[22] in the midst of (the air and) the sky? Nothing holds them up but (the power of) Allah. Verily in this are Signs for those who believe.

80. It is Allah Who made your habitations homes of rest and quiet for you; and made for you, out of the skins of animals, (tents for) dwellings, which you find so light (and handy) when you travel and when you stop (in your travels); and out of their wool, and their soft fibres (between wool and hair),and their hair, rich stuff and articles of convenience (to serve you) for a time.

81. It is Allah Who made. Out of the things He created, some things to give you shade; of the hills He made some for your shelter; He made you garments to protect you from heat, and coats of mail to protect you from your (mutual) violence. Thus He completes His favours on you, that you may bow to His Will (in Islam).

82. But if they turn away, your duty is only to preach the Clear Message.

83. They recognise the favours of Allah; then they deny them; and most of them are (creatures) ungrateful.

84. One Day We shall raise from all Peoples a Witness: then will no excuse be accepted from Unbelievers, nor will they receive any favours.

85. When the wrong-doers (actually) see the Penalty, then it will in no way be mitigated[23], nor will they then receive respite.

86. When those who gave partners to Allah will see their "partners", they will say: "Our Lord! these are our 'partners,' those whom we used to invoke besides You." But they will throw back their word at them (and say): "Indeed you are liars!"

87. That day they shall (openly) show (their) submission to Allah; and all their inventions shall leave them in the lurch.[24]

---

22. Held in suspended or supported position, balanced
23. Abandon them in difficulty and time of need
24. Blood relations

88.   Those who reject Allah and hinder (men) from the Path of Allah - for them We will add Penalty to Penalty; for that they used to spread mischief.

89.   One day We shall raise from all Peoples a witness against them, from amongst themselves: and We shall bring you as a witness against these (your people): and We have sent down to you the Book explai-ning all things, a Guide, a Mercy, and Glad Tidings to Muslims.

90.   Allah commands justice, the doing of good, and liberality to kith and kin[25], and He forbids all shameful deeds, and injustice and rebellion: He instructs you, that you may receive admonition.

91.   Fulfil the Covenant of Allah when you have entered into it, and do not break your oaths after you have confirmed them; indeed you have made Allah your surety; for Allah knows all that you do.

92.   And be not like a woman who breaks into untwisted strands[26] the yarn[27] which she has spun, after it has become strong. Nor take your oaths to practise deception between yourselves, lest one party should be more numerous than another: for Allah will test you by this; and on the Day of Judgment He will certainly make clear to you (the truth of) that wherein you disagree.

93.   If Allah so willed, He could make you all one People: but He leaves straying whom He pleases, and He guides whom He pleases: but you shall cer-tainly be called to account for all your actions.

94.   And do not take your oaths, to practise deception between yourselves, with the result that someone's foot may slip after it was firmly planted, and you may have to taste the evil (consequen-ces) of having hindered (men) from the Path of Allah, and a mighty Wrath descend on you.

---

25.   Blood relations   26.   Fibers

27.   Thread

95.   Nor sell the Covenant of Allah for a miserable price: for with
       Allah is (a prize) far better for you, if you only knew.

96.   What is with you must vanish: what is with Allah will endure.
       And We will certainly bestow, on those who patiently persevere,
       their reward accor-ding to the best of their actions.

97.   Whoever works right-eousness, man or woman, and has Faith,
       verily, to him We will give a new Life, a life that is good and
       pure and We will bestow on such their reward according to the
       best of their actions.

98.   When you read the Qur'an, seek Allah's protection from Satan
       the Rejected One.

99.   He does not have any authority over those who believe and
       put their trust in their Lord.

100.   His authority is over those only, who take him as a patron and
       who join partners with Allah.

101.   When We substitute one revelation for another,- and Allah
       knows best what He reveals (in stages),- they say, "You are but
       a forger": but most of them do not understand.

102.   Say, the Holy Spirit has brought the revelation from your Lord
       in Truth, in order to strengthen those who believe, and as a
       Guide and Glad Tidings to Muslims.

103.   We know indeed that they say, "It is a man that teaches him."
       The tongue of him they wickedly point to is notably foreign,
       while this is Arabic, pure and clear.

104.   Those who do not believe in the Signs of Allah,- Allah will not
       guide them, and theirs will be a grievous Penalty.

105.   It is those who do not believe in the Signs of Allah, that forge
       falsehood: it is they who lie!

106.   Any one who, after accepting faith in Allah, utters Unbelief,-
       except under com-pulsion, his heart remaining firm in Faith -
       but such as open their breast to Unbelief, on them is Wrath
       from Allah, and for them will be a dreadful Penalty.

107.   This because they love the life of this world better than the
       Hereafter: and Allah will not guide those who reject Faith.

108. Those are they whose hearts, ears, and eyes Allah has sealed up, and they take no heed.

109. Without doubt, in the Hereafter they will perish.

110. But verily your Lord,- to those who leave their homes after trials and persecutions,- and who thereafter strive and fight for the faith and patiently persevere,- your Lord, after all this is Oft-Forgiving, Most Merciful.

111. One Day every soul will come up struggling for itself, and every soul will be recom-pensed (fully) for all its actions, and none will be unjustly dealt with.

112. Allah sets forth a Parable: a city enjoying security and quiet, abundantly supplied with sustenance from every place: yet was it ungrateful for the favours of Allah: so Allah made it taste of hunger and terror (in extremes) (closing in on it) like a garment (from every side), because of the (evil) which (its people) wrought.

113. And there came to them a Messenger from among them-selves, but they falsely rejected him; so the Wrath seized them even in the midst of their iniquities.[113]

114. So eat of the sustenance which Allah has provided for you, lawful and good; and be grateful for the favours of Allah, if it is He Whom you serve.

115. He has only forbidden you dead meat, and blood, and the flesh of swine, and any (food) over which the name of other than Allah has been invoked. But if one is forced by necessity, without wilful disobedience, nor transgressing due limits,- then Allah is Oft-Forgiving, Most Merciful.

116. But say not - for any false thing that your tongues may put forth,- "This is lawful, and this is forbidden," so as to ascribe false things to Allah. For those who ascribe false things to Allah, will never prosper.

117. (In such falsehood) is but a paltry profit; but they will have a most grievous Penalty.

---

113. Wickedness, gross injustice

118. To the Jews We prohibited such things as We have mentioned to you before: We did them no wrong, but they were used to doing wrong to themselves.

119. But verily your Lord,- to those who do wrong in ignorance, but who thereafter repent and make amends,- your Lord, after all this, is Oft-Forgiving, Most Merciful.

120. Abraham was indeed a model, devoutly obedient to Allah, (and) true in Faith, and he did not join gods with Allah:

121. He showed his gratitude for the favours of Allah, Who chose him, and guided him to a Straight Way.

122. And We gave him Good in this world, and he will be, in the Hereafter, in the ranks of the Righteous.

123. So We have taught you the inspired (message), "Follow the ways of Abraham, the True in Faith, and he did not join gods with Allah."

124. The Sabbath was only made (strict) for those who disagreed (as to its observance); but Allah will judge between them on the Day of Judgment, as to their differences.

125. Invite (all) to the Way of your Lord with wisdom and beautiful preaching; and argue with them in ways that are best and most gracious: for your Lord knows best, who have strayed from His Path, and who receive guidance.

126. And if you do catch them out, catch them out no worse than they catch you out: but if you show patience, that is indeed the best (course) for those who are patient.

127. And you be patient, for your patience is but from Allah; nor grieve over them: and do not distress yourself because of their plots.

128. For Allah is with those who restrain themselves, and those who do good.

SURAH —17

SURAH AL-ISRAA

(INTRODUCTION)

In the gradation of spiritual teaching (see Introduction to Surah 7), we saw that the first seven Surahs sketched the early spiritual history of man, and led up to the formation of the new *Ummah* of Islam. Surahs 8 to 16 formed another series dealing with the formation of the new *Ummah* and its consolidation, and Allah's dealing with man taken as an *Ummah* and considered in his social relation in organised communities (see Introduction to Surahs 8,10, and 16). We now come to a fresh series, (Surahs 17-29), which may be considered in three parts. Surahs 17-21 begin with an allusion to the *Miraj* (of which more later), and proceed to spiritual history as touching individuals rather than nations. The old prophets and stories of the past are now referred to from this point of view. Surahs 22-25 refer to Hajj (Pilgrimage), worship and prayer, chastity, privacy, etc., as related to a man's individual spiritual growth. Surahs 26-29 go back to the old prophets and stories of the past, as illustrating the growth of the individual soul in the reactions against the lives of the communities, and the reaction of the communities to the lives of its great individual souls.

Let us now consider S. 17 itself, it opens with the mystic Vision of the Ascension of the Holy Prophet: he was transported from the Sacred Mosque (of Makkah) to the Farthest Mosque (of Jerusalem) in a night and shown some of the Signs of Allah. The majority of Commentators take this Night Journey literally, but allow that there were other occasions on which a spiritual Journey or Vision occurred. Even on the supposition of a miraculous bodily Journey, it is conceded that the body was almost transformed into a spiritual fineness, the Hadith literature gives details of this Journey and its study helps to elucidate its mystic meaning. The Holy Prophet was first transported to the seat of the earlier revelations in Jerusalem, and then taken through the seven heavens, even to the Sublime Throne, and initiated into the spiritual mysteries of the human soul struggling in Space and Time, the Spaniard, Miguel Asin, Arabic Professor in the University of Madrid, has shown that this *Miraj* literature had a great influence on the Mediaeval literature of Europe, and especially on the great Italian poem, the *Divine Comedy* (or Drama) of Dante, which towers like a landmark in mediaeval European literature.

The reference to this great mystic story of the *Miraj* is a fitting prelude to the journey of the human soul in its spiritual growth in life. The first step in such growth must be through moral conduct-the reciprocal rights of parents and children, kindness to our fellowmen, courage and firmness in the hour of danger, a sense of personal responsibility, and a sense of Allah's Presence through prayer and praise.

The *Miraj* is usually dated to the 27th night of the month of Rajab (though other dates, e.g. 27th of Rabi' 1, are also given) in the year before the Hijra. This fixes the date of the opening verses of the Surah, though portions of the Surah may have been a little earlier.

SURAH AL-ISRAA (THE CHILDREN OF ISRAEL)
In the name of Allah, Most Gracious, Most Merciful.

1. Glory to (Allah) Who took His Servant for a Journey by night from the Sacred Mosque to the Farthest Mosque, whose precincts[1] We did bless,- in order that We might show him some of Our Signs: for He is the One Who hears and sees (all things).

2. We gave Moses the Book, and made it a Guide to the Children of Israel, (commanding): "Do not take other than Me as Disposer of (your) affairs."

3. O you that are sprung from those whom We carried (in the Ark) with Noah! Verily he was a devotee[3] most grateful.

4. And We gave (clear) warning to the Children of Israel in the Book, that twice would they do mischief on the earth and be elated with mighty arrogance (and twice would they be punished)!

5. When the first of the warnings came to pass, We sent against you Our servants given to terrible warfare: they entered the very inmost parts of your homes; and it was a warning (completely) fulfilled.

6. Then We granted you the Return as against them: We gave you increase in resources and sons, and made you the more

---

1. Surroundings, enclosed space
2. One devoted most zealously to service of Allah
3. Jubilant

numerous in man-power.

7.   If you did well, you did well for yourselves; if you did evil, (you did it) against yourselves. So when the second of the warnings came to pass, (We permitted your enemies) to disfigure[4] your faces, and to enter your Temple as they had entered it before, and to visit with destruction all that fell into their power.

8.   It may be that your Lord may (yet) show Mercy to you; but if you revert (to your sins), We shall revert (to Our punishments): and We have made Hell a prison for those who reject (all Faith).

9.   Verily this Qur'an guides to that which is most right (or stable), and gives the glad tidings to the Believers who work deeds of righteousness, that they shall have a magnificent reward;

10.   And to those who do not believe in the Hereafter, (it announces) that We have prepared for them a Penalty Grievous (indeed).

11.   The prayer that man should make for good, he makes for evil; for man is given to hasty (deeds).

12.   We have made the Night and the Day as two (of Our) Signs: the Sign of the Night We have obscured, while the Sign of the Day We have made to enlighten you; that you may seek bounty from your Lord, and that you may know the number and count of the years: We have explained all things in detail.

13.   Every man's fate We have fastened on his own neck: on the Day of Judgment We shall bring out for him a scroll,[5] which he will see spread open.

14.   (It will be said to him:) "Read your (own) record: suffi-cient is your soul this day to make out an account against you."

15.   Who receives guidance, receives it for his own benefit: who goes astray does so to his own loss: no bearer of burdens can bear the burden of another: nor would We visit with Our Wrath until We had sent a Messenger (to give warning).

16.   When We decide to dest-roy a population, We (first) send a definite order to those among them who are given the good

---

4.   Distort, mar   5.   A roll of paper or parchment

things of this life and yet transgress; so that the word is proved true against them: then (it is) We destroy them utterly.

17. How many generations have We destroyed after Noah? And enough is your Lord to note and see the sins of His servants.

18. If any do wish for the transitory[6] things (of this life), We readily[7] grant them - such things as We will, to such persons as We will: in the end We have provided Hell for them: they will burn therein, disgraced and rejected.

19. Those who do wish for the (things of) the Hereafter, and strive therefor with all due striving, and have Faith,- they are the ones whose striving is acceptable (to Allah).

20. Of the bounties of your Lord We bestow freely on all- these as well as those: the bounties of your Lord are not closed (to anyone).

21. See how We have besto-wed more on some than on others; but verily the Hereafter is more in rank and gradation and more in excellence.

22. Take not with Allah another object of worship; or you (O man!) will sit in disgrace and destitution.[8]

23. Your Lord has decreed that you worship none but Him, and that you be kind to parents. Whether one or both of them attain old age in your life, say not to them a word of contempt, nor repel them, but address them in terms of honour.

24. And, out of kindness, lower to them the wing of humility, and say: "My Lord! bestow on them Your Mercy even as they cherished me in childhood."

25. Your Lord knows best what is in your hearts: If you do deeds of righteousness, verily He is Most Forgiving to those who turn to Him again and again (in true penitence).[9]

26. And render to the kindred[10] their due rights, as (also) to those in want, and to the wayfarer: but squander not (your wealth) in the manner of a spendthrift.[11]

6.	Temporary	7.	Freely, quickly
8.	Indigence, privation	9.	Repentance
10.	Relatives	11.	Extravagant

27. Verily spendthrifts are brothers of the Evil Ones; and the Evil One is to his Lord (Himself) ungrateful.

28. And even if you have to turn away from them in pursuit of the Mercy from your Lord which you do expect, yet speak to them a word of easy kindness.

29. Make not your hand tied (like a miser's) to your neck, nor stretch it forth to its utmost reach, so that you become blameworthy and destitute.

30. Verily your Lord provides sustenance in abundance for whom He pleases, and He provides in a just measure. For He knows and regards all His servants.

31. Do not kill your children for fear of want: We shall provide sustenance for them as well as for you. Verily the killing of them is a great sin.

32. Nor come near to adultery: for it is a shameful (deed) and an evil, opening the road (to other evils).

33. Nor take life - which Allah has made sacred - except for just cause. And if anyone is slain wrongfully, We have given his heir authority (to demand Qisas or to forgive): but let him not exceed bounds in the matter of taking life; for he is helped (by the Law).

34. Come not near to the orphan's property except to improve it, until he attains the age of full strength; and fulfil (every) engagement, for (every) engagement will be enquired into (on the Day of Reckoning).

35. Give full measure when you measure, and weigh with a balance that is straight: that is the most fitting and the most advantageous in the final determination.

36. And do not pursue that of which you have no knowledge; for every act of hearing, or of seeing or of (feeling in) the heart will be enquired into (on the Day of Reckoning).

37. Nor walk on the earth with insolence: for you can not rend the earth asunder, nor reach the mountains in height.

38. Of all such things the evil is hateful in the sight of your Lord.

39. These are among the (precepts[12] of) wisdom, which your Lord has revealed to you. Do not take, with Allah, another object of worship, lest you should be thrown into Hell, blameworthy and rejected.

40. Has then your Lord (O Pagans!) preferred for you sons, and taken for Himself daughters among the angels? Truly you utter a most dreadful saying!

41. We have explained (things) in various (ways) in this Qur'an, in order that they may receive admonition, but it only increases their flight (from the Truth)!

42. Say: If there had been (other) gods with Him, as they say,- behold, they would certainly have sought out a way to the Lord of the Throne!

43. Glory to Him! He is high above all that they say!- Exalted and Great (beyond measure)!

44. The seven heavens and the earth, and all beings therein, declare His glory: there is not a thing but celebrates His praise; and yet you do not understand how they declare His glory! Verily He is Oft-Forbearing, Most Forgiving!

45. When you recite the Qur'an, We put between you and those who do not believe in the Hereafter, an invisible veil:

46. And We put coverings over their hearts (and minds) lest they should understand the Qur'an, and deafness into their ears: when you commemorate[13] your Lord and Him alone in the Qur'an, they turn on their backs, fleeing (from the Truth).

47. We know best why it is they listen, when they listen to you: and when they meet in private conference, behold, the wicked say, "You follow none other than a man bewitched!"

48. See what similes they strike for you: but they have gone astray, and never can they find a way.

49. They say: "What! when we are reduced to bones and dust, should we really be raised up (to be) a new creation?"

50. Say: "(Nay!) be you stones or iron.

---

12.   Principles   13.   Glorify

51. "Or any created matter which, in your minds, is hardest (to be raised up),- (yet you shall be raised up)!" Then they will say: "Who will cause us to return?" Say: "He Who created you first!" Then they will wag[14] their heads toward you, and say, "When will that be?" Say, "May be it will be quite soon!

52. "It will be on a Day when He will call you, and you will answer (His call) with (words of) His praise, and you will think that you tarried but a little while!"

53. Say to My servants that they should (only) say those things that are best: for Satan sows dissensions[15] among them: for Satan is to man an avowed enemy.

54. It is your Lord that knows you best: If He please, He grants you mercy, or if He please, punishment: We have not sent you to be a disposer of their affairs for them.

55. And it is your Lord that knows best all beings that are in the heavens and on earth: We bestowed on some prophets more (and other) gifts than on others: and We gave to David (the gift of) the Psalms.

56. Say: "Call on those - besides Him - whom you fancy: they have neither the power to remove your troubles from you nor to change them."

57. Those whom they call upon do desire (for themselves) means of access to their Lord, - even those who are nearest: they hope for His Mercy and fear His Wrath: for the Wrath of your Lord is something to take heed of.

58. There is not a population but We shall destroy it before the Day of Judgment or punish it with a dreadful Penalty: that is written in the (eternal) Record.

59. And We refrain from sending the Signs, only because the men of former generations treated them as false: We sent the she-camel to the Thamud to open their eyes, but they treated her wrongfully: We only send the Signs by way of terror (and warning from evil).

---

14. Shake   15. Conflict, strife

60.   Behold! We told you that your Lord encompasses man-kind
        round about: We granted the vision which We showed you, but
        as a trial for men,- as also the Cursed Tree (mentioned) in the
        Qur'an: We put terror (and warning) into them, but it only
        increases their inordinate[16] transgression!

61.   Behold! We said to the angels: "Bow down to Adam": They
        bowed down except Iblis: he said, "Shall I bow down to one
        whom You created from clay?"

62.   He said: "Do You see? this is the one whom You have honoured
        above me! If You will but respite me to the Day of Judgment,
        I will surely bring his descendants under my sway - all but a
        few!"

63.   (Allah) said: "Go you away; if any of them follow you, verily
        Hell will be the recom-pense of you (all)- an ample
        recompense.[17]

64.   "Lead to destruction those whom you can among them, with
        your (seductive) voice; make assaults on them with your cavalry
        and your infantry; mutually share with them wealth and
        children; and make promises to them." But Satan promises
        them nothing but deceit.

65.   "As for My servants, no authority you shall have over them:"
        enough is your Lord for a Disposer of affairs.

66.   Your Lord is He that makes the ship go smoothly for you
        through the sea, in order that you may seek of His Bounty. For
        He is to you most Merciful.

67.   When distress seizes you at sea, those that you call upon -
        besides Himself - leave you in the lurch! but when He brings
        you back safe to land, you turn away (from Him). Most
        ungrateful is man!

68.   Do you then feel secure that He will not cause you to be
        swallowed up beneath the earth when you are on land, or that
        He will not send against you a violent tornado (with showers
        of stones) so that you shall find no protector?

---

16.   Excessive, extreme   17.   Reward

69.   Or do you feel secure that He will not send you back a second time to sea and send against you a heavy gale[18] to drown you because of your ingratitude, so that you find no helper therein against Us?

70.   We have honoured the sons of Adam; provided them with transport on land and sea; given them for sustenance things good and pure; and conferred on them special favours, above a great part of Our Creation.

71.   One day We shall call to-gether all human beings with their (respective) *Imams*[19]: those who are given their record in their right hand will read it (with pleasure), and they will not be dealt with unjustly in the least.

72.   But those who were blind in this world, will be blind in the Hereafter, and most astray from the Path.

73.   And their purpose was to tempt you away from that which We had revealed to you, to substitute in Our name some-thing quite different; (in that case), behold! they would cer-tainly have made you (their) friend!

74.   And had We not given you strength, you would nearly have inclined to them a little.

75.   In that case, We should have made you taste a double portion (of punishment) in this life, and a double portion after death: and moreover you would have found none to help you against Us!

76.   Their purpose was to scare you off the land, in order to expel you; but in that case they would not have stayed (therein) after you, except for a little while.

77.   (This was Our) way with the Messengers We sent before you: you will find no change in Our ways.

78.   Establish regular prayers at the sun's decline till the dark-ness of the night, and the recital of the Qur'an in morning prayer, for the recital in the morning carry (angels') testimony.

---

18.   Storm
19.   The Arabic word *Imam* here may mean a leader, revelation or revealed Book, or record of deeds.

79. And as for the night[20] keep awake a part of it as an additional prayer for you, soon will your Lord raise you to a Station of Praise and Glory!

80. Say: "O my Lord! Let my entry be by the Gate of Truth and Honour, and likewise my exit by the Gate of Truth and Honour; and grant me from Your Presence an authority to aid (me)."

81. And say: "Truth has (now) arrived, and Falsehood peri-shed: for Falsehood is (by its nature) bound to perish."

82. We send down (stage by stage) in the Qur'an that which is a healing and a mercy to those who believe: to the unjust it causes nothing but loss after loss.

83. Yet when We bestow Our favours on man, he turns away and becomes remote on his side (instead of coming to Us), and when evil seizes him he gives himself up to despair.

84. Say: "Everyone acts accor-ding to his own disposition: but your Lord knows best who it is that is best guided on the Way."

85. They ask you concerning the Spirit (of inspiration). Say: "The Spirit (comes) by com-mand of my Lord: of knowledge it is only a little that is commu-nicated to you, (O men!)"

86. If it were Our Will, We could take away that which We have sent you by inspiration: then would you find none to plead your affair in that matter as against Us,-

87. Except for Mercy from your Lord: for His Bounty is to you (indeed) great.

88. Say: "If the whole of man-kind and Jinns were to gather together to produce the like of this Qur'an, they could not produce the like thereof, even if they backed up each other with help and support.

89. And We have explained to man, in this Qur'an, every kind of similitude: yet the greater part of men refuse (to receive it) except with ingratitude!

90. They say: "We shall not believe in you, until you cause a spring to gush forth for us from the earth,

---

20.   Early hours of dawn

91. "Or (until) you have a garden of date trees and vines, and cause rivers to gush forth in their midst, carrying abundant water;

92. "Or you cause the sky to fall in pieces, as you say (will happen), against us; or you bring Allah and the angels before (us) face to face:

93. "Or you have a house adorned with gold, or you mount a ladder right into the skies. No, we shall not even believe in your mounting until you send down to us a book that we could read." Say: "Glory to my Lord! Am I not but a man,- a Messenger?"

94. What kept men back from belief when Guidance came to them, was nothing but this: they said, "Has Allah sent a man (like us) to be (His) Messenger?"

95. Say, "If there were settled, on earth, angels walking about in peace and quiet, We should certainly have sent them down from the heavens an angel for a Messenger."

96. Say: "Enough is Allah for a Witness between me and you: for He is well acquainted with His servants, and He sees (all things).

97. It is he whom Allah guides, that is on true guidance; but he whom He leaves astray - for such you will find no protector besides Him. On the Day of Judgment We shall gather them together, prone[21] on their faces, blind, dumb, and deaf: their abode will be Hell: every time it shows abatement[22], We shall increase for them the fierceness of the Fire.

98. That is their recompense, because they rejected Our Signs, and said, "When we are reduced to bones and broken dust, should we really be raised up (to be) a new Creation?"

99. Don't they see that Allah, Who created the heavens and the earth, has power to create the like of them (anew)? Only He has decreed a term appointed, of which there is no doubt. But the unjust refuse (to receive it) except with ingratitude.

100. Say: "If you had control of the Treasures of the Mercy of my Lord, behold, you would keep them back, for fear of spending them: for man is (ever) miserly!"

---

21. Prostrate, with face downwards   22. Decrease in intensity

101. To Moses We gave Nine Clear Signs: ask the Children of Israel: when he came to them, Pharaoh said to him: "O Moses! I consider you, indeed, to have been worked upon by sorcery!

102. Moses said, "You know well that these things have been sent down by none but the Lord of the heavens and the earth as eye-opening evidence: and I consider you indeed, O Pharaoh, to be one doomed to destruction!"

103. So he resolved to remove them from the face of the earth: but We drowned him and all who were with him.

104. And We said thereafter to the Children of Israel, "Dwell securely in the land (of pro-mise)": but when the second of the warnings came to pass, We gathered you together in a mingled crowd.

105. We sent down the (Qur'ān) in Truth, and in Truth has it descended: and We sent you but to give Glad Tidings and to warn (sinners).

106. (It is) a Qur'ān which We have divided (into parts from time to time), in order that you might recite it to men at intervals: We have revealed it by stages.

107. Say: "Whether you believe in it or not, it is true that those who were given knowledge beforehand, when it is recited to them, fall down on their faces in humble prostration,

108. "And they say: 'Glory to our Lord! Truly has the promise of our Lord been fulfilled!'"

109. They fall down on their faces in tears, and it increases their (earnest) humility.

110. Say: "Call upon Allah, or call upon Rahman: by whatever name you call upon Him, (it is well): for to Him belong the Most Beautiful Names. Neither speak your Prayer aloud, nor speak it in a low tone, but seek a middle course between."

111. Say: "Praise be to Allah, Who begets no son, and has no partner in (His) dominion: nor (needs) He any to protect Him from humiliation: yes, magnify Him for His greatness and glory!

---

22. *Rahman* (Arabic), means the Beneficent, the Gracious One. It is one of the 99 Most Beautiful names of Allah.   24.   Kingdom power.

SURAH—18

SURAH AL-KAHF
(INTRODUCTION)

It has been explained in the Introduction to S. 17 how the five Surahs 17 to 21 develop the theme of the individual soul's spiritual history, and how they fit into the general scheme of exposition.

This particular Makkan Surah may be called a lesson on the brevity and mystery of Life. First there is the story of the Companions of the Cave who slept therein for a long period, and yet thought they had been there only a day or less. Then there is the story of the mysterious Teacher who shows Moses how Life itself is a parable. And further there is the story of Zul-qarnain, the two horned one, the powerful ruler of west and east, who made an iron wall to protect the weak against the strong. The parables refer to the brevity, uncertainly, and vanity of this life; to the many paradoxes in it, which can only be understood by patience and the fullness of knowledge; and to the need of guarding our spiritual gains against the incursions of evil.

SURAH AL-KAHF (OR THE CAVE)

In the name of Allah, Most Gracious, Most Merciful.

1. Praise be to Allah, Who has sent to His Servant the Book, and has allowed therein no crookedness:

2. (He has made it) Straight (and Clear) in order that He may warn (the godless) of a terrible Punishment from Him, and that He may give Glad Tidings to the Believers who work righteous Deeds, that they shall have a goodly Reward,

3. Wherein they shall remain for ever:

4. Further, that He may warn those (also) who say, "Allah has begotten a son":

5. They do not have any knowledge of such a thing, nor had their fathers. It is a grievous thing that issues from their mouths as a saying. What they say is nothing but falsehood!

6. You would only, per-chance, fret[1] yourself to death, following after them, in grief, if they do not believe in this Message.

---

1. Torment or distress yourself with grief

7.   That which is on earth We have made but as a glittering show
       for the earth, in order that We may test them - as to which of
       them are best in conduct.

8.   Verily what is on earth We shall make but as dust and dry soil
       (without growth or herbage).

9.   Or do you reflect that the Companions of the Cave and of the
       Inscription were wonders among Our Signs?

10.   Behold, the youths betook themselves to the Cave: they said,
       "Our Lord! bestow on us Mercy from Yourself, and dispose of
       our affair for us in the right way!"

11.   Then We drew (a veil) over their ears, for a number of years,
       in the Cave, (so that they did not hear):

12.   Then We roused them, in order to test which of the two parties
       was best at calculating the term of years they had tarried!

13.   We relate to you their story in truth: they were youths who
       believed in their Lord, and We advanced them in guidance:

14.   We gave strength to their hearts: behold, they stood up and
       said: "Our Lord is the Lord of the heavens and of the earth:
       never shall we call upon any god other than Him: if we did, we
       should indeed have uttered an enormity!²

15.   "These our people have taken for worship gods other than Him:
       why do they not bring forward an authority clear (and
       convincing) for what they do? Who does more wrong than
       such as invent a falsehood against Allah?

16.   "When you turn away from them and the things they worship
       other than Allah, betake yourselves to the Cave: your Lord
       will shower His mercies on you and dispose of your affair
       towards comfort and ease."

17.   You would have seen the sun, when it rose, declining to the
       right from their Cave, and when it set, turning away from them
       to the left, while they lay in the open space in the midst of the
       Cave. Such are among the Signs of Allah: He whom Allah
       guides is rightly guided; but he whom Allah leaves to stray,-

---

2.   A dreadful crime, monstrous wickedness

for him you will find no protector to lead him to the Right Way.

18. You would have deemed them awake, whilst they were asleep, and We turned them on their right and on their left sides: their dog stretching forth his two fore-legs on the threshold: if you had come up on to them, you would have certainly turned back from them in flight, and would certainly have been filled with terror of them.

19. Such (being their state), We raised them up (from sleep), that they might question each other. Said one of them, "How long have you stayed (here)?" They said, "We have stayed (perhaps) a day, or part of a day." (At length) they (all) said, "Allah (alone) knows best how long you have stayed here.... Now you send one of you with this money of yours to the town: let him find out which is the best food (to be had) and bring some to you, that (you may) satisfy your hunger there-with: and let him behave with care and courtesy, and let him not inform anyone about you.

20. "For if they should come upon you, they would stone you or force you to return to their cult[3], and in that case you would never attain prosperity."

21. Thus We made their case known to the people, that they might know that the promise of Allah is true, and that there can be no doubt about the Hour of Judgment. Behold, they dispute among themselves as to their affair. (Some) said, "Construct a building over them": Their Lord knows best about them: those who prevailed over their affair said, "Let us surely build a place of worship over them."

22. (Some) say they were three, the dog being the fourth among them; (others) say they were five, the dog being the sixth,- doubtfully guessing at the unknown; (yet others) say they were seven, the dog being the eighth. You say: "My Lord knows best their number; it is but few that know their (real case)." Do

---

3. System of religious worship, devotion or homage to a person or thing.

not enter, therefore, into controversies concerning them, except on a matter that is clear, nor consult any of them about (the affair of) the Sleepers.

23.   Nor say of anything, "I shall be sure to do so and so tomorrow"-

24.   Without adding, "If Allah so wills" and call your Lord to mind when you forget, and say, "I hope that my Lord will guide me ever closer (even) than this to the right road."

25.   So they stayed in their Cave three hundred years, and (some) add nine (more).

26.   Say: "Allah knows best how long they stayed: with Him is (the knowledge of) the secrets of the heavens and the earth: how clearly He sees, how finely He hears (everything)! They have no protector other than Him; nor does He share His Command with any person whatsoever.

27.   And recite (and teach) what has been revealed to you of the Book of your Lord: none can change His Words, and none will you find as a refuge other than Him.

28.   And keep your soul content with those who call on their Lord morning and eve-ning, seeking His Face; and let not your eyes pass beyond them, seeking the pomp and glitter of this Life; nor obey any whose heart We have permitted to neglect the remembrance of Us, one who follows his own desires, whose case has gone beyond all bounds.

29.   Say, "The Truth is from your Lord": let him who will believe, and let him who will reject (it): for the wrong-doers We have prepared a Fire whose (smoke and flames), like the walls and roof of a tent, will hem them in: if they implore relief they will be granted water like melted brass, that will scald[4] their faces. How dreadful the drink! How uncomfortable a couch to recline on!

30.   As to those who believe and work righteousness, verily We shall not suffer to perish the reward of any who do a (single) righteous deed.

---

4.   Injure or burn (skin, etc.) with hot liquid or vapor.

31. For them will be Gardens of Eternity; beneath them rivers will flow; they will be adorned therein with bracelets of gold, and they will wear green garments of fine silk and heavy brocade:[5] they will recline therein on raised thrones. How good the recompense! How beautiful a couch to recline on!

32. Set forth to them the parable of two men: for one of them We provided two gardens of grapevines[5] and surrounded them with date palms; in between the two We placed corn-fields.

33. Each of those gardens brought forth its produce, and did not fail in the least therein: in the midst of them We caused a river to flow.

34. (Abundant) was the pro-duce this man had : he said to his companion, in the course of a mutual argument: "I have more wealth than you, and more honour and power in (my following of) men."

35. He went into his garden in a state (of mind) unjust to his soul: he said, "I deem not that this will ever perish,

36. "Nor do I deem that the Hour (of Judgment) will (ever) come: even if I am brought back to my Lord, I shall surely find (there) something better in exchange."

37. His companion said to him, in the course of the argu-ment with him: "Do you deny Him Who created you out of dust, then out of a sperm-drop, then fashioned you into a man?

38. "But (I think) for my part that He is Allah, my Lord, and none shall I associate with my Lord.

39. "Why did you not, as you went into your garden, say: 'Allah's Will (be done)! There is no power but with Allah!' If you see me less than you in wealth and sons,

40. "It may be that my Lord will give me something better than your garden, and that He will send on your garden thunderbolts (by way of reckoning) from heaven, making it (but) slippery sand!

---

5. Fabric woven with raised patterns of threads of gold or other metal.
6. Grape plants

41. "Or the water of the garden will run off underground so that you will never be able to find it."

42. So his fruits (and enjoy-ment) were encompassed (with ruin), and he remained twisting and turning his hands over what he had spent on his property, which had (now) tumbled to pieces to its very foundations, and he could only say, "Woe is me! Would I had never ascribed partners to my Lord and Cherisher!"

43. Nor had he numbers to help him against Allah, nor was he able to deliver himself.

44. There, the (only) protec-tion comes from Allah, the True One. He is the Best to reward, and the Best to give success.

45. Set forth to them the similitude of the life of this world: It is like the rain which We send down from the skies: the earth's vegetation absorbs it, but soon it becomes dry stubble, which the winds do scatter: it is (only) Allah Who prevails over all things.

46. Wealth and sons are allurements of the life of this world: but the things that endure, Good Deeds, are best in the sight of your Lord, as rewards, and best as (the foundation for) hopes.

47. One Day We shall remove the mountains, and you will see the earth as a level stretch, and We shall gather them, all together, nor shall We leave out any one of them.

48. And they will be marshalled[8] before your Lord in ranks, (with the announcement), "Now you have come to Us (bare) as We created you first: yes, you thought We shall not fulfil the appointment made to you to meet (Us)!":

49. And the Book (of Deeds) will be placed (before you); and you will see the sinful in great terror because of what is (recorded) therein; they will say, "Ah! woe to us! what a Book is this! It leaves out nothing small or great, but takes account thereof!" They will find all that they did, placed before them: and not one will your Lord treat with injustice.

---

7. Cut stalks of cereal plants left sticking up after harvest.
8. Assembled

50. Behold! We said to the angels, "Bow down to Adam": they bowed down except Iblis. He was one of the Jinns, and he broke the Command of his Lord. Will you then take him and his progeny[9] as protectors rather than Me? And they are enemies to you! Evil would be the exchange for the wrong-doers!

51. I called them not to witness the creation of the heavens and the earth, nor (even) their own creation: nor is it for Me to take as helpers such as lead (men) astray!

52. One Day He will say, "Call on those whom you thought to be My partners," and they will call on them, but they will not listen to them; and We shall make for them a place of common perdition.[10]

53. And the Sinful shall see the fire and apprehend[11] that they have to fall therein: no means will they find to turn away therefrom.

54. We have explained in detail in this Qur'an, for the benefit of mankind, every kind of similitude: but man is, in most things, contentious.[12]

55. And what is there to keep back men from believing, now that guidance has come to them, nor from praying for forgive-ness from their Lord, but that (they ask that) the ways of the ancients be repeated with them, or the Wrath be brought to them face to face?

56. We only send the Messengers to give glad tidings and to give warning but the Unbelievers dispute with vain argument, in order therewith to weaken the Truth, and they treat My Signs as a jest as also the fact that they are warned.

57. And who does more wrong than one who is reminded of the Signs of his Lord, but turns away from them, forgetting the (deeds) which his hands have sent forth? Verily We have set veils over their hearts lest they should understand this, and over their ears, deafness. If you call them to guidance, even then they will never accept guidance.

---

9. Offspring
10. Eternal death, damnation
11. Perceive
12. Quarrelsome

58. But your Lord is Most forgiving, full of Mercy. If He were to call them (at once) to account for what they have earned, then surely He would have hastened their punish-ment: but they have their appointed time, beyond which they will find no refuge.

59. Such were the populations We destroyed when they committed iniquities;[13] but We fixed an appointed time for their destruction.

60. Behold, Moses said to his attendant, "I will not give up until I reach the junction of the two seas or (until) I spend years and years in travel."

61. But when they reached the Junction, they forgot (about) their Fish, which took its course through the sea (straight) as in a tunnel.

62. When they had passed on (some distance), Moses said to his attendant: "Bring us our early meal; truly we have suffered much fatigue at this (stage of) our journey."

63. He replied: "Did you see (what happened) when we betook ourselves to the rock? I indeed forgot (about) the Fish: none but Satan made me forget to tell (you) about it: it took its course through the sea in a marvellous way!"

64. Moses said: "That was what we were seeking after:" so they went back on their footsteps, following (the path they had come).

65. So they found one of Our servants, on whom We had bestowed Mercy from Our-selves and whom We had taught knowledge from Our Own Presence.

66. Moses said to him: "May I follow you, on the footing[14] that you teach me something of the (Higher) Truth which you have been taught?"

67. (The other) said: "Verily you will not be able to have patience with me!"

68. "And how can you have patience about things about which your understanding is not complete?"

---

13. Gross injustice   14. Position, conditions

69. Moses said: "You will find me, if Allah so will, (truly) patient: nor shall I disobey you in any matter."

70. The other said: "If then you would follow me, ask me no questions about anything until I myself speak to you concerning it."

71. So they both proceeded: until, when they were in the boat, he scuttled[15] it. Said Moses: "Have you scuttled it in order to drown those in it? Truly a strange thing you have done!"

72. He answered: "Did I not tell you that you can have no patience with me?"

73. Moses said: "Do not rebuke me for forgetting, nor grieve me by raising difficulties in my case."

74. Then they proceeded: until, when they met a young man, he slew him. Moses said: "Have you slain an innocent person who had slain none? Truly a foul (unheard-of) thing you have done!"

75. He answered: "Did I not tell you that you can have no patience with me?"

76. (Moses) said: "If ever I ask you about anything after this, do not keep me in your company: then you would have received (full) excuse from my side."

77. Then they proceeded: until, when they came to the inhabitants of a town, they asked them for food, but they refused them hospitality. They found there a wall on the point of falling down, but he set it up straight. (Moses) said: "If you had wished, surely you could have exacted some recompense for it!"

78. He answered: "This is the parting between me and you: now will I tell you the interpretation of (those things) over which you were unable to hold patience.

79. "As for the boat, it belonged to certain men in dire[16] want: they plied[17] on the water: I but wished to render it unserviceable, for there was after them a certain king who seized on every boat by force.

---

15. Made a hole
16. Urgent
17. Worked

80. "As for the youth, his parents were people of Faith, and we feared that he would grieve them by obstinate rebel-lion and ingratitude (to Allah).

81. "So we desired that their Lord would give them in ex-change (a son) better in purity (of conduct) and closer in affection.

82. "As for the wall, it belon-ged to two youths, orphans, in the Town; there was, beneath it, a buried treasure, to which they were entitled: their father had been a righteous man: so your Lord desired that they should attain their age of full strength and get out their treasure - a mercy (and favour) from your Lord. I did it not of my own accord. Such is the interpreta-tion of (those things) over which you were unable to hold patience."

83. They ask you concerning Zul-qarnain. Say, "I will rehear-se to you something of his story."

84. Verily We established his power on earth, and We gave him the ways and the means to all ends.

85. One (such) way he followed,

86. Until, when he reached the setting of the sun, he found it set in a spring of murky water: near it he found a People: We said: "O Zul-qarnain! (you have authority,) either to punish them, or to treat them with kindness."

87. He said: "Whoever does wrong, we shall punish him; then he shall be sent back to his Lord; and He will punish him with a punishment unheard-of (before).

88. "But whoever believes, and works righteousness,-he shall have a goodly reward, and his task will be easy as We order it by our command."

89. Then he followed (an-other) way,

90. Until, when he came to the rising of the sun, he found it rising on a people for whom We had provided no covering protection against the sun.

91. (He left them) as they were: We completely under-stood what was before him.

92. Then he followed (an-other) way,

93. Until, when he reached (a tract) between two mountains, he found, beneath them, a people who scarcely understood a word.

94. They said: "O Zul-qarnain! the Gog and Magog (People) do great mischief on earth: shall we then render you tribute in order that you might erect a barrier between us and them?

95. He said: "(The power) in which my Lord has established me is better (than tribute): help me therefore with strength (and labor): I will erect a strong barrier between you and them:

96. "Bring me blocks of iron." At length, when he had filled up the space between the two steep mountain-sides, he said, "Blow (with your bellows)" then, when he had made it (red) as fire, he said: "Bring me, that I may pour over it, molten lead."

97. Thus they were made powerless to scale it or to dig through it.

98. He said: "This is a mercy from my Lord: but when the promise of my Lord comes to pass, He will make it into dust; and the promise of my Lord is true."

99. On that day We shall leave them to surge like waves on one another: the trumpet will be blown, and We shall collect them all together.

100. And We shall present Hell that day for Unbelievers to see, all spread out,-

101. (Unbelievers) whose eyes had been under a veil from remembrance of Me, and who had been unable even to hear.

102. Do the Unbelievers think that they can take My servants as protectors besides Me? Verily We have prepared Hell for the Unbelievers for (their) enter-tainment.

103. Say: "Shall we tell you of those who lose most in respect of their deeds?-

104. "Those whose efforts have been wasted in this life, while they thought that they were acquiring good by their works?"

105. They are those who deny the Signs of their Lord and the fact of their having to meet Him (in the Hereafter): vain will be their works, nor shall We, on the Day of Judgment, give them any weight.

106. That is their reward, Hell, because they rejected Faith, and took My Signs and My Messengers by way of jest.

107. As to those who believe and work righteous deeds, they have, for their entertainment, the Gardens of Paradise,

108. Wherein they shall dwell (for ever), no change will they wish for from them.

109. Say: "If the ocean were ink (wherewith to write out) the words of my Lord, sooner would the ocean be exhausted than would the words of my Lord, even if we added another ocean like it, for its aid."

110. Say: "I am but a man like yourselves, (but) the inspiration has come to me, that your God is One God: whoever expects to meet his Lord, let him work righteousness, and, in the worship of his Lord, admit no one as partner.

————————

SURAH—19
SURAH MARYAM
(INTRODUCTION)

The spiritual growth of man as an individual soul having been explained in S. 17 as beginning with the first principles of moral conduct and in S. 18 as being dependent upon out realisation of the brevity and mystery of this life and the true use of power as in the story of Zul-qarnain, we now pass on to the story of individual Messengers of Allah in their personal relations with their environment, —Yahya with his father Zakariya, Jesus with his mother Mary, Abraham with his unbelieving father, Moses with his brother Aaron, Ismail with his family, and Idris in the high station to which he was called. Seeing how these great ones fitted into the scheme of life, man is condemned for his want of faith, or for regarding his faith to superstition, and warned of the Hereafter.

In chronology, it was revealed before the first resort of the batch of Muslims to Abyssinia, say seven years before the Hijrat.

SURAH MARYAM (MARY)

In the name of Allah, Most Gracious, Most Merciful.

1. Kaf. Ha. Ya. 'Ain. Sad.
2. (This is) a recital[1] of the Mercy of your Lord to His servant Zakariya.
3. Behold! he cried to his Lord in secret,
4. Praying: "O my Lord! infirm indeed are my bones, and the hair of my head glistens with grey: but never am I unblest, O my Lord, in my prayer to You!
5. "Now I fear (what) my relatives (and colleagues) (will do) after me: but my wife is barren: so give me an heir as from Yourself,-
6. "(One that) will (truly) represent me, and represent the posterity[2] of Jacob; and make him, O my Lord! one with whom You are well-pleased!"
7. (His prayer was answered): "O Zakariya! We give you good news of a son: his name shall be Yahya: on none by that name

---

1. Report, recount
2. Offspring

have We conferred distinction before."

8. He said: "O my Lord! How shall I have a son, when my wife is barren and I have grown quite decrepit—3 from old age?"

9. He said: "So (it will be) your Lord says, 'That is easy for Me: I indeed created you before, when you had been nothing!'"

10. (Zakariya) said: "O my Lord! give me a Sign." "your Sign," was the answer, "shall be that you shall speak to no man for three nights, although you are not dumb."

11. So Zakariya came out to his people from his chamber: he told them by signs to celebrate Allah's praises in the morning and in the evening.

12. (To his son came the com-mand): "O Yahya! take hold of the Book with might," and We gave him Wisdom even as a youth,

13. And piety (for all crea-tures) as from Us, and purity: he was devout,

14. And kind to his parents, and he was not overbearing⁴ or rebellious.

15. So Peace on him the day he was born, the day that he dies, and the day that he will be raised up to life (again)!

16. Relate in the Book (the story of) Mary, when she withdrew from her family to a place in the East.

17. She placed a screen (to screen herself) from them; then We sent to her Our angel, and he appeared before her as a man in all respects.

18. She said: "I seek refuge from you to (Allah) Most Gracious: (come not near) if you fear Allah."

19. He said: "Nay, I am only a messenger from your Lord, (to announce) to you the gift of a holy son.

20. She said: "How shall I have a son, seeing that no man has touched me, and I am not unchaste?"

21. He said: "So (it will be): your Lord says 'That is easy for Me: and (We wish) to appoint him as a Sign unto men and a Mercy

---

3. Weak, infirm   4. Bossy, domineering

from Us':It is a matter (so) decreed."

22. So she conceived him, and she retired with him to a remote place.

23. And the pains of childbirth drove her to the trunk of a palm-tree: She cried (in her anguish): "Ah! would that I had died before this! would that I had been a thing forgotten and out of sight!"

24. But (a voice) cried to her from beneath the (palm-tree): "Do not grieve! for your Lord has provided a rivulet beneath you;

25. "And shake toward yourself the trunk of the palm-tree: it will let fall fresh ripe dates upon you.

26. "So eat and drink and cool (your) eye. And if you see any man, say, 'I have vowed a fast to (Allah) Most Gracious, and this day I will not enter into talk with any human being"

27. At length she brought the (babe) to her people, carrying him (in her arms). They said: "O Mary! truly an amazing thing you have brought!

28. "O sister of Aaron! your father was not a man of evil, nor your mother an unchaste woman !"

29. But she pointed to the babe. They said: "How can we talk to one who is a child in the cradle?"

30. He said: "I am indeed a servant of Allah: He has given me Revelation and made me a prophet;

31. "And He has made me blessed wheresoever I be, and has enjoined on me Prayer and Charity as long as I live;

32. "(He) has made me kind to my mother, and not overbearing or miserable;

33. "So peace is on me the day I was born, the day that I die, and the day that I shall be raised up to life (again)"!

34. Such (was) Jesus the son of Mary: (it is) a statement of truth, about which they (vainly) dispute.

35. It is not befitting to (the majesty of) Allah that He should beget a son. Glory be to Him! when He determines a matter, He only says to it, "Be", and it is.

36.   Verily Allah is my Lord and your Lord: you, therefore serve Him: this is a Way that is straight.

37.   But the sects differ among themselves: and woe to the Unbelievers because of the (coming) Judgment of a momentous[5] Day!

38.   How plainly will they see and hear, the Day that they will appear before Us! but the unjust today are in manifest error!

39.   But warn them of the Day of Distress, when the matter will be determined: for (behold,) they are negligent and they do not believe!

40.   It is We Who will inherit the earth, and all beings thereon: to Us will they all be returned.

41.   (Also) mention in the Book (the story of) Abraham: He was a man of Truth, a prophet.

42.   Behold, he said to his father: "O my father! why worship that which does not hear and does not see, and can profit you nothing?

43.   "O my father! to me has come knowledge which has not reached you: so follow me: I will guide you to a Way that is even and straight.

44.   "O my father! do not serve Satan: for Satan is a rebel against (Allah) Most Gracious.

45.   "O my father! I fear lest a Penalty afflict you from (Allah) Most Gracious, so that you become a friend to Satan."

46.   (The father) replied: "Do you hate my gods, O Abraham? If you do not forbear[6], I will indeed stone you: now get away from me for a good long while!"

47.   Abraham said: "Peace be on you: I will pray to my Lord for your forgiveness: for He is to me Most Gracious.

48.   "And I will turn away from you (all) and from those whom you invoke besides Allah: I will call on my Lord: perhaps, by my prayer to my Lord, I shall be not unblest."

49.   When he had turned away from them and from those whom

---

5.   Very important   6.   Abstain

they worshipped besides Allah, We bestowed on him Isaac and Jacob, and each one of them We made a prophet.

50. And We bestowed of Our Mercy on them, and We granted them lofty honour on the tongue of truth.

51. Also mention in the Book (the story of) Moses: for he was specially chosen, and he was a Messenger (and) a prophet.

52. And We called him from the right side of Mount (Sinai), and made him draw near to Us, for mystic (converse).

53. And, out of Our Mercy, We gave him his brother Aaron, (also) a prophet.

54. Also mention in the Book (the story of) Isma'il: he was (strictly) true to what he pro-mised, and he was a Messenger (and) a prophet.

55. He used to enjoin on his people Prayer and Charity, and he was most accep-table in the sight of his Lord.

56. Also mention in the Book the case of Idris: he was a man of truth (and sincerity), (and) a prophet:

57. And We raised him to a lofty station.

58. Those were some of the prophets on whom Allah bestowed His Grace,- of the posterity of Adam, and of those whom We carried (in the Ark) with Noah, and of the posterity of Abraham and Israel of those whom We guided and chose. Whenever the Signs of (Allah) Most Gracious were rehearsed to them, they would fall down in prostrate adoration and in tears.

59. But after them there followed a posterity who missed prayers and followed after lusts soon, then, they will face Destruction,-

60. Except those who repent and believe, and work right-eousness: for these will enter the Garden and will not be wronged in the least,-

61. Gardens of Eternity, those which (Allah) Most Gracious has promised to His servants in the Unseen: for His promise must (necessarily) come to pass.

62. They will not hear any vain discourse there, but only salutations of Peace: and therein they will have their sustenance, morning

and evening.

63.   Such is the Garden which We give as an inheritance to those of Our servants who guard against evil.

64.   (The angels say:) "We do not descend but by command of your Lord: to Him belongs what is before us and what is behind us, and what is between: and your Lord never forgets,-

65.   "Lord of the heavens and of the earth, and of all that is between them; so worship Him, and be constant and patient in His worship: do you know of any who is worthy of the same Name as He?"

66.   Man says: "What! When I am dead, shall I then be raised up alive?"

67.   But does not man call to mind that We created him before, out of nothing?

68.   So, by your Lord, without doubt, We shall gather them together, and (also) the Evil Ones (with them); then We shall bring them forth on their knees round about Hell:

69.   Then We shall certainly drag out from every sect all those who were worst in obsti-nate rebellion against (Allah) Most Gracious.

70.   And certainly We know best those who are most worthy of being burned therein.

71.   Not one of you but will pass over it: this is, with your Lord, a Decree which must be accomplished.

72.   But We shall save those who guarded against evil, and We shall leave the wrong-doers therein, (humbled) to their knees.

73.   When Our Clear Signs are rehearsed to them, the Unbe-lievers say to those who believe, "Which of the two sides is best in point of position? which makes the best show in Council?"

74.   But how many (countless) generations before them We have destroyed, who were even better in equipment and in glitter to the eye?

75.   Say: "If any men go astray, (Allah) Most Gracious extends (the rope) to them, until, when they see the warning of Allah

(being fulfilled) - either in punishment or in (the approach of) the Hour,- they will at length realise who is worst in position, and (who) weakest in forces!

76. "And Allah advances those in guidance who seek guidance: and the things that endure, Good Deeds, are best in the sight of your Lord, as rewards, and best in respect of (their) eventual returns."

77. Have you then seen the (sort of) man who rejects Our Signs, yet says: "I shall certainly be given wealth and children?"

78. Has he penetrated to the Unseen, or has he taken a contract with (Allah) Most Gracious?

79. Nay! We shall record what he says, and We shall add and add to his punishment.

80. To Us shall return all that he talks of, and he shall appear before Us bare and alone.

81. And they have taken (for worship) gods other than Allah, to give them power and glory!

82. Instead, they shall reject their worship, and become adversaries against them.

83. Don't you see that We have set the Evil Ones on against the unbelievers, to incite them with fury?

84. So make no haste against them, for We but count out to them a (limited) number (of days).

85. The day We shall gather the righteous to (Allah) Most Gracious, like a band presented before a king for honours,

86. And We shall drive the sinners to Hell, like thirsty cattle driven down to water,-

87. None shall have the power of intercession[7], but such a one as has received permission (or promise) from (Allah) Most Gracious.

88. They say: "(Allah) Most Gracious has begotten a son!"

89. Indeed you have put forth a thing most monstrous!

90. At it the skies are ready to burst, the earth to split asunder, and

---

7. Intervention

the mountains to fall down in utter ruin,

91.   That they should invoke a son for (Allah) Most Gracious.

92.   For it is not consonant[8] with the majesty of (Allah) Most Gracious that He should beget a son.

93.   Not one of the beings in the heavens and the earth but must come to (Allah) Most Gracious as a servant.

94.   He takes an account of them (all), and has numbered them (all) exactly.

95.   And everyone of them will come to Him singly on the Day of Judgment.

96.   On those who believe and work deeds of righteousness, (Allah) Most Gracious will bestow Love.

97.   So We have made the (Qur'an) easy in your own tongue, that with it you may give glad tidings to the righteous, and warnings to people given to contention.[9]

98.   But how many (countless) generations before them We have destroyed? Can you find a single one of them (now) or hear (so much as) a whisper of them?

---

8.   Consistent with   9.   Strife

SURAH—20
SURAH TA-HA
(INTRODUCTION)

The chronology of this Surah has some significance: it has some relation to the spiritual lessons which it teaches.

It was used with great effect in that remarkable scene which resulted in Hadhrat 'Umar's conversion, and which took place about her husband, but they bore the attack with exemplary patience, and declared their faith. 'Umar was so struck with their sincerity and fortitude that he asked to see the leaf from which they had been reading. It was given to him: his soul was touched, arid he not only came into the Faith but became one of its strongest supporters and champions.

The leaf contained some portion of this Surah, perhaps the introductory portion. The mystic letters *Ta-Ha* are prefixed to this Surah. What do they mean? The earliest tradition is that they denote a dialectical interjection meaning "O man!" If so, the title is particularly appropriate in two ways: (1) It was a direct and personal address to a man in a high state of excitement tempted by his temper to do grievous wrong, but called by Allah's Grace, as by a personal appeal, to face the realities, for Allah knew his inmost secret thought (20:7): the revelation was sent by Allah Most Gracious, out of His Grace and Mercy (20:5). (2) It takes up the story from the last Surah, of man as a spiritual being and illustrates in further details. It tells the story of Moses in the crisis of his life when he received Allah's Commission and in his personal relations with his mother, and how he came to be brought up in the Pharaoh's house, to learn all the wisdom of the Egyptians, for use in Allah's service, and in his personal relations with Pharaoh, whom we take to be his adoptive father (28:9). If further tells the story of a fallen soul who misled the Israelites into idolatry, and recalls how man's Arch-enemy Satan caused his fall. Prayer and praise are necessary to man to cure his spiritual blindness and enable him to appreciate Allah's revelation.

SURAH TA-HA (MYSTIC LETTERS, T.H.)
In the name of Allah, Most Gracious, Most Merciful.

1.   Ta-Ha.
2.   We have not sent down the Qur'an to you to be (an occasion) for your distress,

3.   But only as an admonition to those who fear (Allah),-

4.   A revelation from Him Who created the earth and the heavens on high.

5.   (Allah) Most Gracious is firmly established on the throne (of authority).

6.   To Him belongs what is in the heavens and on earth, and all between them, and all beneath the soil.

7.   If you pronounce the word aloud, (it is no matter): for verily He knows what is secret and what is yet more hidden.

8.   Allah! there is no god but He! To Him belong the most Beautiful Names.

9.   Has the story of Moses reached you?

10.   Behold, he saw a fire: so he said to his family, "You tarry[1]; I perceive a fire; perhaps I can bring you some burning brand therefrom, or find some gui-dance at the fire."

11.   But when he came to the fire, a voice was heard: "O Moses!

12.   "Verily I am your Lord! Therefore (in My presence) put off your shoes: you are in the sacred valley Tuwa.

13.   "I have chosen you: listen, then, to the inspiration (sent to you).

14.   "Verily, I am Allah: There is no god but I: so you serve Me (only), and establish regular prayer for celebrating My praise.

15.   "Verily the Hour is coming—I have[2] kept it hidden — for every soul to receive its reward by the measure of its Endeavor.

16.   "Therefore let not such as do not believe therein but follow their own lusts, divert you therefrom, lest you perish!".

17.   "And what is that in your right hand, O Moses?"

18.   He said, "It is my rod: on it I lean; with it I beat down fodder for my flocks; and in it I find other uses."

19.   (Allah) said, "Throw it, O Moses!"

20.   He threw it, and behold! it was a snake, active in motion.

21.   (Allah) said, "Seize it, and fear not: We shall return it at once to its former condition"..

22.   "Now draw your hand close to your side: it shall come forth

---

1.   Stay   2.   Plan

white (and shining), without harm (or stain),- as another Sign,-

23. "In order that We may show you (two) of our Greater Signs.

24. " You go to Pharaoh, for he has indeed transgressed all bounds."

25. (Moses) said: "O my Lord! expand me my breast;

26. "Ease my task for me;

27. "And remove the impediment[3] from my speech,

28. "So they may understand what I say:

29. "And give me a Minister from my family,

30. "Aaron, my brother;

31. "Add to my strength through him,

32. "And make him share my task:

33. "That we may celebrate Your praise without stint,[4]

34. "And remember You without stint:

35. "For You are He that (ever) regards us."

36. (Allah) said: "Granted is your prayer, O Moses!"

37. "And indeed We confe-rred a favour on you another time (before).

38. "Behold! We sent to your mother, by inspiration, the message:

39. "'Throw (the child) into the chest[5], and throw (the chest) into the river: the river will cast him up on the bank, and he will be taken up by one who is an enemy to Me and an enemy to him': but I cast (the garment of) love over you from Me: and (this) in order that you may be reared under Mine eye.

40. "Behold! your sister goes forth and says, 'shall I show you one who will nurse and rear the (child)?' So We brought you back to your mother, that her eye might be cooled and she should not grieve. Then you slew a man, but We saved you from trouble, and We tried you in various ways. Then you tarried a number of years with the people of Midian. Then you came hither as ordained[6], O Moses!

41. "And I have prepared you for Myself (for service")..

42. "Go, you and your brother, with My Signs, and slacken[7] not,

---

3.	Handicap	4.	Without any limitation, unlimited
5.	A cabinet, a strong box	6.	Decreed
7.	Relax		

either of you, in keeping Me in remembrance.

43. "Go, both of you, to Pharaoh, for he has indeed transgressed all bounds;

44. "But speak to him mildly; perchance he may take warning or fear (Allah)."

45. They (Moses and Aaron) said: "Our Lord! We fear lest he hasten with insolence against us, or lest he transgress all bounds."

46. He said: "Do not fear: for I am with you: I hear and see (everything).

47. "So you both go to him, and say, 'Verily we are Messen-gers sent by your Lord: send forth, therefore, the Children of Israel with us, and afflict them not: with a Sign, indeed, we have come from your Lord! and peace to all who follow guidance!

48. "'Verily it has been revealed to us that the Chastise-ment (awaits) those who reject and turn away.'"

49. (When this message was delivered), (Pharaoh) said: "Who, then, O Moses, is the Lord of you two?"

50. He said: "Our Lord is He Who gave to each (created) thing its form and nature, and further, gave (it) guidance."

51. (Pharaoh) said: "What then is the condition of previous generations?"

52. He replied: "The know-ledge of that is with my Lord, duly recorded: my Lord never errs, nor forgets,-

53. "He Who has made for you the earth like a carpet spread out; has enabled you to go about therein by roads (and channels); and has sent down water from the sky." With it have We produced diverse pairs of plants each separate from the others.

54. Eat (for yourselves) and pasture your cattle: verily, in this are Signs for men endued with understanding.

55. From the (earth) We created you, and into it We shall return you, and from it We shall bring you out once again.

56. And We showed Pharaoh all Our Signs, but he rejected and refused.

57. He said: "Have you come to drive us out of our land with your magic, O Moses?

58. "But we can surely produce magic to match yours! So make a tryst[8] between us and you, which we shall not fail to keep - neither we nor you - in a place where both shall have even chances."

59. Moses said: "Your tryst is the Day of the Festival, and let the people be assembled when the sun is well up."

60. So Pharaoh withdrew: he concerted[9] his plan, and then came (back).

61. Moses said to him: Woe to you! You do not forge a lie against Allah, lest He destroy you (at once) utterly by chastise-ment: the forger must suffer frustration!"

62. So they disputed, one with another, over their affair, but they kept their talk secret.

63. They said: "These two are certainly (expert) magicians: their object is to drive you out from your land with their magic, and to do away with your most cherished institutions.

64. "Therefore concert your plan, and then assemble in (serried[10]) ranks: he wins (all along) today who gains the upper hand."

65. They said: "O Moses! whether will you that you throw (first) or that we be the first to throw?"

66. He said, "Nay, you throw first!" Then behold their ropes and their rods-so it seemed to him on account of their magic - began to be in lively motion!

67. So Moses conceived in his mind a (sort of) fear.

68. We said: "Do not fear! for you have indeed the upper hand:

69. "Throw that which is in your right hand: quickly it will swallow up that which they have faked[11]; what they have faked is but a magician's trick: and the magician does not thrive, (no matter) where he goes."

70. So the magicians were thrown down to prostration: they said, "We believe in the Lord of Aaron and Moses".

---

8.   Appointment
9.   Arranged (by cooperation and agreement with his party)
10.   (Rows of soldiers, etc.) Pressed together, close, without gaps
11.   Forged

71. (Pharaoh) said: "Do you believe in Him before I give you permission? Surely this must be your leader, who has taught you magic! Be sure I will cut off your hands and feet on opposite sides, and I will have you crucified on trunks of palm-trees: so you shall know for certain, which of us can give the more severe and the more lasting punishment!"

72. They said: "Never shall we regard you as more than the Clear Sings that have come to us, or than Him Who created us! so decree whatever you desire to decree: for you can only decree (touching) the life of this world.

73. "For us, we have believed in our Lord: may He forgive us our faults, and the magic to which you compelled us: for Allah is Best and Most Abiding."

74. Verily he who comes to his Lord as a sinner (at Judgment),- for him is Hell: therein shall he neither die nor live.

75. But such as come to Him as Believers who have worked righteous deeds,-for them are ranks exalted,-

76. Gardens of Eternity, beneath which flow rivers: they will dwell therein for ever: such is the reward of those who purify themselves (from evil).

77. We sent an inspiration to Moses: "Travel by night with My servants, and strike a dry path for them through the sea, without fear of being overtaken (by Pharaoh) and without (any other) fear."

78. Then Pharaoh pursued them with his forces, but the waters completely overwhelmed them and covered them up.

79. Pharaoh led his people astray instead of leading them aright.

80. O you Children of Israel! We delivered you from your enemy, and We made a Covenant with you on the right side of Mount (Sinai), and We sent down to you Manna[12] and quails:

81. (Saying): "Eat of the good things We have provided for your sustenance, but commit no excess therein, lest My Wrath should justly descend on you: and those on whom descends My Wrath,

---

12. See Qur'an 2:57 & 7:160

do perish indeed!

82. "But, without doubt, I am (also) He that forgives again and again, to those who repent, belie-ve, and do right,- who, in fine, are ready to receive true guidance."

83. (When Moses was up on the Mount, Allah said:) "What made you hasten in advance of your people, O Moses?"

84. He replied: "Behold, they are close on my footsteps: I hastened to You, O my Lord, to please You."

85. (Allah) said: "We have tested your people in your absence: the Samiri has led them astray."

86. So Moses returned to his people in a state of indignation and sorrow. He said: "O my people! did not your Lord make a handsome promise to you? Did then the promise seem to you long (in coming)? Or did you desire that Wrath should descend from your Lord on you, and so you broke your promise to me?"

87. They said: "We did not break the promise to you, as far as lay in our power: but we were made to carry the weight of the ornaments of the (whole) people, and we threw them (into the fire), and that was what the Samiri suggested.

88. "Then he brought out (of the fire) before the (people) the image of a calf: it seemed to low:[13] so they said: This is your god, and the god of Moses, but (Moses) has forgotten!"

89. Could they not see that it could not return them a word (for answer), and that it had no power either to harm them or to do them good?

90. Aaron had already, before this said to them: "O my people! you are being tested in this: for verily your Lord is (Allah) Most Gracious; so follow me and obey my command."

91. They had said: "We will not cease to worship it, but we will devote ourselves to it until Moses returns to us."

92. (Moses) said: "O Aaron! what kept you back, when you saw them going wrong,

---

13. To moo like a cow

93.   "From following me? Did you then disobey my order?"

94.   (Aaron) replied: "O son of my mother! Do not seize (me) by my beard nor by (the hair of) my head! Truly I feared lest you should say, 'you have caused a division among the children of Israel, and you did not respect my word!'"

95.   (Moses) said: "What then is your case, O Samiri?"

96.   He replied: "I saw what they did not see: so I took a handful (of dust) from the footprint of the Messenger, and threw it (into the calf): thus did my soul suggest to me."

97.   (Moses) said: "Get you gone! But your (punishment) in this life will be that you will say, 'Touch me not'; and moreover (for a future Penalty) you have a promise that will not fail: now look at your god, of whom you have become a devoted wor-shipper: we will certainly (melt) it in a blazing fire and scatter it broadcast[14] in the sea!"

98.   But the God of you all is the One God (Allah): there is no god but He: all things He comprehends[15] in His knowledge.

99.   Thus do We relate to you some stories of what happened before: for We have sent you a Message from Our Own Presence.

100. If any do turn away therefrom, verily they will bear a burden on the Day of judgment;

101. They will abide in this (state): and grievous will be the burden to them on that Day,-

102. The Day when the Trumpet will be sounded: that Day, We shall gather the sinful, blear-eyed[16] (with terror).

103. In whispers will they consult each other: "You tarried not longer than ten (Days);"

104. We know best what they will say, when their leader most eminent in conduct will say: "You did not tarry longer than a day!"

105. They ask you concerning the Mountains: say, "My Lord will

---

14.   Scatter widely   15.   Include, covers

16.   (Eyes) dim-sighted, dull

uproot them and scatter them as dust;

106. "He will leave them as plains smooth and level;

107. "Nothing crooked or cur-ved will you see in their place."

108. On that Day they will follow the Caller (straight): no crookedness (can they show) him: all sounds shall humble them-selves in the Presence of (Allah) Most Gracious: nothing shall you hear but the tramp of their feet (as they march).

109. On that Day no intercession shall avail except for those for whom permission has been gran-ted by (Allah) Most Gracious and whose word is acceptable to Him.

110. He knows what (appears to His creatures as) before or after or behind them: but they shall not compass it with their knowledge.

111. (All) faces shall be humbled before (Him) - the Living, the Self-subsisting, Eternal: hopeless indeed will be the man that carries iniquity[17] (on his back).

112. But he who works deeds of righteousness, and has faith, will have no fear of harm nor of any curtailment[18] (of what is his due).

113. Thus have We sent this down - an Arabic Qur'an - and explained therein in detail some of the warnings, in order that they may fear Allah, or that it may cause their remembrance (of Him).

114. High above all is Allah, the King, the Truth! Be not in haste with the Qur'an before its revelation to you is completed, but say, "O my Lord! advance me in knowledge."

115. We had already, before-hand, taken the covenant of Adam, but he forgot: and We found on his part no firm resolve[20].

116. When We said to the angels, "Prostrate yourselves to Adam", they prostrated themselves, but not Iblis: he refused.

117. Then We said: "O Adam! verily, this is an enemy to you and your wife: so let him not get you both out of the Garden, so that you are landed in misery.

---

17. Gross injustice   18.   Reduction
19. Determination
20. Place of frequent resort, dwelling place.

118.   "There is therein (enough provision) for you not to go hungry nor to go naked,

119.   "Nor to suffer from thirst, nor from the sun's heat."

120.   But Satan whispered evil to him: he said, "O Adam! shall I lead you to the Tree of Eternity and to a kingdom that never decays?"

121.   In the result, they both ate of the tree, and so their nakedness appeared to them: they began to sew together, for their covering, leaves from the Garden: thus Adam disobeyed his Lord, and allowed himself to be seduced.

122.   But his Lord chose him (for His Grace): He turned to him, and gave him guidance.

123.   He said: "Get you down, both of you,- all together, from the Garden, with enmity one to another: but if, as is sure, there comes to you guidance from Me, whosoever follows My guidance, will not lose his way, nor fall into misery.

124.   "But whosoever turns away from My Message, verily for him is a life narrowed down, and We shall raise him up blind on the Day of Judgment."

125.   He will say: "O my Lord! why have you raised me up blind, while I had sight (before)?"

126.   (Allah) will say: "Thus did you, when Our Signs came unto you, disregard them: so will you, this day, be disregarded."

127.   And thus do We recom-pense him who transgresses beyond bounds and does not believe in the Sings of his Lord: and the Chastisement of the Hereafter is far more grievous and more enduring.

128.   Is it not a warning to such men (to call to mind) how many generations before them We destroyed, in whose haunts they (now) move? Verily, in this are Signs for men endued with understanding.

129.   Had it not been for a Word that went forth before from your Lord, (their punishment) must necessarily have come; but there is a term appointed (for respite).

130. Therefore be patient with what they say, and celebrate (constantly) the praises of your Lord, before the rising of the sun, and before its setting; yes, celebrate them for part of the hours of the night, and at the sides of the day: that you may have (spiritual) joy.

131. Nor strain your eyes in longing for the things We have given for enjoyment to parties of them, the splendor of the life of this world, through which We test them: but the provision of your Lord is better and more enduring.

132. Enjoin prayer on your people, and be constant therein. We ask you not to provide sustenance: We provide it for you. But the (fruit of) the Hereafter is for righteousness.

133. They say: "Why does he not bring us a Sign from his Lord?" Has not a Clear Sign come to them of all that was in the former Books of revelation?

134. And if We had inflicted on them a penalty before this, they would have said: "Our Lord! If only You had sent us a Messenger, we should certainly have followed Your Signs before we were humbled and put to shame."

135. Say: "Each one (of us) is waiting: you wait, therefore, and soon you shall know who it is that is on the straight and even way, and who it is that has received guidance."

SURAH—21

SURAH AL-ANBIYAA
(INTRODUCTION)

The Last Surah dealt with the individual story (spiritual) of Moses and Aaron, and contrasted it with the growth of evil in individuals like Pharaoh and the Samiri, and ended with a warning against Evil, and an exhortation to the purification of the soul with prayer and praise. This Surah begins with the external obstacles placed by Evil against such purification, and gives the assurance of Allah's power to defend men, illustrating this with reference to Abraham's fight against idolatry, Lot's flight against unnatural wickedness, Noah's against unbelief, that of David and Solomon against injustice and failure to proclaim Allah's glory by making full use of man's Allah-given faculties and power, that of Job against impatience and want of self-confidence, that of Ismail, Idris and Zul-Kifl against want of steady perseverance, that of Zunnun against hasty anger, that of Zakariya against spiritual isolation, and that of Mary against the lusts of this world. In each illusion there is a special point about the soul's purification. The common point is that the Prophets were not, as the vulgar suppose, just irresistible men. They had to win their ground inch by inch against all kinds of resistance from evil.

The chronology of this Surah has no significance. It probably dates from the middle of the Makkan period of inspiration.

───────────

SURAH AMBIYYA (THE PROPHETS)

In the name of Allah, Most Gracious, Most Merciful.

1. Closer and closer to mankind comes their Recko-ning: yet they do not heed and they turn away.

2. Never comes (anything) to them of a renewed Message from their Lord, but they listen to it as in jest,-

3. Their hearts toying as with trifles. The wrong-doers conceal their private counsels, (saying), "Is this (one) more than a man like yourselves? Will you go to witchcraft with your eyes open?"

4. Say: "My Lord knows (every) word (spoken) in the heavens and on earth: He is the One that hears and knows (all things)."

5.   "Nay," they say, "(these are) medleys[1] of dreams! - Nay, he forged it! - Nay, he is (but) a poet! Let him then bring us a Sign like the ones that were sent to (Prophets) of old!"

6.   (As to those) before them, not one of the populations which We destroyed believed: will these believe?

7.   Before you, also, the Messengers We sent were but men, to whom We granted inspi-ration: if you do not realise this, ask of those who possess the Message.

8.   Nor did We give them bodies that ate no food, nor were they exempt from death.

9.   In the end We fulfilled to them Our Promise, and We saved them and those whom We pleased, but We destroyed those who transgressed beyond bounds.

10.   We have revealed for you (O men!) a book in which is a Message for you: will you not then understand?

11.   How many were the populations We utterly dest-royed because of their iniqui-ties, setting up in their places other peoples?

12.   Yet, when they felt Our Punishment (coming), behold, they (tried to) flee from it.

13.   Flee not, but return to the good things of this life which were given you, and to your homes, in order that you may be called to account.

14.   They said: "Ah! woe to us! We were indeed wrong-doers!"

15.   And that cry of theirs did not cease, till We made them as a field that is mown, as ashes silent and quenched.

16.   Not for (idle) sport did We create the heavens and the earth and all that is between!

17.   If it had been Our wish to take (just) a pastime[2], We should surely have taken it from the things nearest to Us, if We would do (such a thing)!

18.   Nay, We hurl the Truth against falsehood, and it knocks out its brain, and behold, falsehood perishes! Ah! woe be to you for the (false) things you ascribe (to Us).

---

1.   Mixture   2.   Amusement, hobby

19. To Him belong all (creatures) in the heavens and on earth: even those who are in His (very) Presence are not too proud to serve Him, nor are they (ever) weary (of His service):

20. They celebrate His praises night and day, nor do they ever flag[3] or intermit[4].

21. Or have they taken (for worship) gods from the earth who can raise (the dead)?

22. If there were, in the heavens and the earth, other gods besides Allah, there would have been confusion in both! But glory to Allah, the Lord of the Throne: (high is He) above what they attribute to Him!

23. He cannot be questioned for His acts, but they will be questioned (for theirs).

24. Or have they taken for worship (other) gods besides Him? Say, "Bring your convin-cing proof: this is the Message of those with me and the Message of those before me." But most of them do not know the Truth, and so turn away.

25. Not a Messenger did We send before you without this inspiration sent by Us to him: that there is no god but I; therefore worship and serve Me.

26. And they say: "(Allah) Most Gracious has begotten offspring." Glory to Him! They are (but) servants raised to honour.

27. They do not speak before He speaks, and they act (in all things) by His Command.

28. He knows what is before them, and what is behind them, and they offer no intercession except for those who are accep-table, and they stand in awe and reverence of His (glory).

29. If any of them should say, "I am a god besides Him", such a one We should reward with Hell: thus do We reward those who do wrong.

30. Do not the Unbelievers see that the heavens and the earth were joined together (as one unit of Creation), before We clove[3]

---

1. Weaken, lose vigor, lag   2. Discontinue, stop
3. Spilit

them asunder? We made from water every living thing. Will they not then believe?

31. And We have set on the earth mountains standing firm, lest it should shake with them, and We have made therein broad highways (between mountains) for them to pass through: that they may receive guidance.

32. And We have made the heavens as a canopy well guarded: yet do they turn away from the Signs which these things (point to)!

33. It is He Who created the Night and the Day, and the sun and the moon: all (the celestial[6] bodies) swim along, each in its rounded course.

34. We did not grant to any man before you permanent life (here): if then you should die, would they live permanently?

35. Every soul shall have a taste of death: and We test you by evil and by good by way of trial. To Us must you return.

36. When the Unbelievers see you, they do not treat you except with ridicule. "Is this," (they say), "the one who talks of your gods?" and they blaspheme[7] at the mention of (Allah) Most Gracious!

37. Man is a creature of haste: soon (enough) will I show you My Signs; then you will not ask Me to hasten them!

38. They say: "When will this promise come to pass, if you are telling the truth?"

39. If only the Unbelievers knew (the time) when they will not be able to ward off the fire from their faces, nor yet from their backs, and (when) no help can reach them!

40. Nay, it may come to them all of a sudden and confound[8] them: no power will they have then to avert it, nor will they (then) get respite.

41. Mocked were (many) Messengers before you; but their scoffers were hemmed in by the thing that they mocked.

---

6.   Astronomical
8.   Baffle, daze

7.   Profane, mention with disrespect, sesecrate

42.   Say: "Who can keep you safe by night and by day from (the Wrath of) Allah Most Gracious?" Yet they turn away from the mention of their Lord.

43.   Or have they gods that can guard them from Us? They have no power to aid themselves, nor can they be defended from Us.

44.   Nay, We gave the good things of this life to these men and their fathers until the period grew long for them; do not they see that We gradually reduce the land (in their control) from its outlying borders? Is it then they who will win?

45.   Say, "I do but warn you according to revelation": but the deaf will not hear the call, (even) when they are warned!

46.   If but a breath of the Wrath of your Lord do touch them, they will then say, "Woe to us! we did wrong indeed!"

47.   We shall set up scales of justice for the Day of Judgment, so that not a soul will be dealt with unjustly in the least, and if there be (no more than) the weight of a mustard seed, We will bring it (to account): and enough are We to take account.

48.   In the past We granted to Moses and Aaron the Criterion⁹ (for judgment), and a Light and a Message for those who would do right,-

49.   Those who fear their Lord in their most secret thoughts, and who hold the Hour (of Judgment) in awe.

50.   And this is a blessed Message which We have sent down: will you then reject it?

51.   We bestowed aforetime on Abraham his rectitude¹⁰ of conduct, and We were well acquainted with him.

52.   Behold! he said to his father and his people, "What are these images, to which you are (so assiduously¹¹) devoted?"

53.   They said, "We found our fathers worshipping them."

54.   He said, "Indeed you have been in manifest error - you and your fathers."

55.   They said, "Have you brought us the Truth, or are you one of those who jest?"

---

9.   Standard (to distinguish between good and evil)
10.   Moral correctness   11.   Persistently and diligently

56. He said, "Nay, your Lord is the Lord of the heavens and the earth, He Who created them (from nothing): and I am a witness to this (truth).

57. "And by Allah, I have a plan for your idols - after you go away and turn your backs".

58. So he broke them to pieces, (all) but the biggest of them, that they might turn (and address themselves) to it.

59. They said, "Who has done this to our gods? He must indeed be some man of impiety!"

60. They said, "We heard a youth talk of them: he is called Abraham."

61. They said, "Then bring him before the eyes of the people, that they may bear witness."

62. They said, "Are you the one that did this with our gods, O Abraham?"

63. He said: "Nay, this was done by - this is their biggest one! ask them, if they can speak intelligently!"

64. So they turned to themselves and said, "Surely you are the ones in the wrong!"

65. Then they were confoun-ded with shame: (they said), "you know full well that these (idols) do not speak!"

66. (Abraham) said, "Do you then worship, besides Allah, things that can neither be of any good to you nor do you harm?

67. "Fie upon you, and upon the things that you worship besides Allah! Have you no sense?".

68. They said, "Burn him and protect your gods, if you do (anything at all)!"

69. We said, "O Fire! you be cool, and (a means of) safety for Abraham!"

70. Then they planned[12] against him, but We made them the ones that lost most!

71. But We delivered him and (his nephew) Lut (and directed them) to the land which We have blessed for the nations.

---

12. Plotted

72. And We bestowed on him Isaac and, as an additional gift, (a grandson), Jacob, and We made righteous men of every one (of them).

73. And We made them leaders, guiding (men) by Our Command, and We sent them inspiration to do good deeds, to establish regular prayers, and to practise regular charity; and they constantly served Us (and Us only).

74. And to Lut, too, We gave Judgment and Knowledge, and We saved him from the town which practised abominations[13]: truly they were a people given to Evil, a rebellious people.

75. And We admitted him to Our Mercy: for he was one of the Righteous.

76. (Remember) Noah, when he cried (to Us) aforetime: We listened to his (prayer) and delivered him and his family from great distress.

77. We helped him against people who rejected Our Signs: truly they were a people given to Evil: so We drowned them (in the Flood) all together.

78. And remember David and Solomon, when they gave judgment in the matter of the field into which the sheep of certain people had strayed by night: We witnessed their judgment.

79. To Solomon We inspired the (right) understanding of the matter: to each (of them) We gave Judgment and Knowledge; it was Our power that made the hills and the birds celebrate Our praises, with David: it was We Who did (all these things).

80. It was We Who taught him the making of coats of mail[14] for your benefit, to guard you from each other's violence: will you then be grateful?

81. (It was Our power that made) the violent (unruly) wind flow (tamely) for Solomon, to his order, to the land which We had blessed: for We do know all things.

82. And of the evil ones, were some who dived for him, and did other work besides; and it was We Who guarded them.

---

13. Evil, obscenities   14. Defensive armour for the body

83.   And (remember) Job, when He cried to his Lord, "Truly distress has seized me, but you are the Most Merciful of those that are merciful."

84.   So We listened to him: We removed the distress that was on him, and We restored his people to him, and doubled their number,- as a Grace from Our-selves, and a thing for commemoration[15], for all who serve Us.

85.   And (remember) Isma'il, Idris, and Zul-kifl, all (men) of constancy and patience;

86.   We admitted them to Our Mercy: for they were of the righteous ones.

87.   And remember Zun-nun, when he departed in wrath: he imagined that We had no power over him! but he cried through the depths of darkness, "There is no god but You: glory to You: I was indeed wrong!"

88.   So We listened to him: and delivered him from distress: and thus do We deliver those who have faith.

89.   And (remember) Zakariya, when he cried to his Lord: "O my Lord! do not leave me without offspring, though You are the best of inheritors."

90.   So We listened to him: and We granted him Yahya: We cured his wife's (Barrenness) for him. These (three) were ever quick in emulation[16] in good works; they used to call on Us with love and reverence, and humble themselves before Us.

91.   And (remember) her who guarded her chastity: We breathed into her of Our spirit, and We made her and her son a Sign for all peoples.

92.   Verily, this brotherhood of yours is a single brotherhood, and I am your Lord and Cherisher: therefore serve Me (and no other).

93.   But (later generations) cut off their affair (of unity), one from another: (yet) they will all return to Us.

94.   Whoever works any act of righteousness and has faith,- his endeavour will not be rejected: We shall record it in his favour.

---

15.   A celebration in memory of   16.   Trying to excel others

95. But there is a ban on any population which We have destroyed: that they shall not return,

96. Until the Gog and Magog (people) are let through (their barrier), and they swiftly swarm from every hill.

97. Then will the True Promise draw near (of fulfilment): then behold! the eyes of the Unbelievers will fixedly stare in horror: "Ah! woe to us! we were indeed heedless of this; nay, we truly did wrong!"

98. Verily you, (Unbelievers), and the (false) gods that you worship besides Allah, are (but) fuel for Hell! To it will you (surely) come!

99. If these had been gods, they would not have got there! but each one will abide therein.

100. There, sobbing will be their lot, nor will they there hear (anything else.)

101. Those for whom the Good (record) from Us has gone before, will be removed far therefrom.

102. Not the slightest sound will they hear of Hell: what their souls desired, in that they will dwell.

103. The Great Terror will bring them no grief: but the angels will meet them (with mutual greetings): "This is your Day,- (the Day) that you were promised."

104. The Day that We roll up the heavens like a scroll[17] rolled up for books (completed),- even as We produced the first creation, so shall We produce a new one: a promise We have undertaken: truly shall We fulfil it.

105. Before this We wrote in the Psalms, after the Message (given to Moses): My servants, the righteous, shall inherit the earth."

106. Verily in this (Qur'an) is a Message for people who would (truly) worship Allah.

107. We sent you not, but as a Mercy for all creatures.

108. Say: "What has come to me by inspiration is that your God is One God: will you therefore bow to His Will (in Islam)?"

---

17.   A roll of paper or parchment

109. But if they turn back, say: "I have proclaimed the Message to you all alike and in truth; but I do not know whether that which you are promised is near or far.

110. "It is He Who knows what is open in speech and what you hide (in your hearts).

111. "I do not know but that it may be a trial for you, and a grant of (worldly) livelihood (to you) for a time."

112. Say: "O my Lord! You judge in truth!" "Our Lord Most Gracious is the One Whose assistance should be sought against the blasphemies you utter!

SURAH—22
SURAH AL-HAJJ
(INTRODUCTION)

We now come to a new series of four Surahs, dealing with the environments and methods contributing to our spiritual progress, as the last five Surahs dealt with the Messengers who came in various ways to proclaim the Truth and conquer evil. See Introduction to S. 17.

The subject-matter of this particular Surah is concerned mainly with the spiritual implications of the Sacred House, the Pilgrimage, the Sacrifices, Striving and Fighting in defence of Truth when attacked, and other acts that make for Unselfishness and uproot Falsehood.

On the chronology of this Surah, opinion is divided. Some parts were probably revealed in the later Makkan period, and some in Madinah. But the chronological question has no significance here.

SURAH HAJJ (THE PILGRIMAGE)

In the name of Allah, Most Gracious, Most Merciful.

1.   O mankind! fear your Lord! for the convulsion[1] of the Hour (of Judgment) will be a thing terrible!

2.   The Day you shall see it, every mother giving suck shall forget her suckling-babe, and every pregnant female shall drop her load (unformed): you shall see mankind as in a drunken riot, yet not drunk: but dreadful will be the Chastise-ment of Allah.

3.   And yet among men there are such as dispute about Allah, without knowledge, and follow every evil one obstinate in rebellion!

4.   About the (Evil One) it is decreed that whoever turns to him for friendship, he will lead him astray, and he will guide him to the Penalty of the Fire.

5.   O mankind! if you have a doubt about the Resurrection, (consider) that We created you out of dust, then out of sperm, then out of a leech-like clot, then out of a morsel of flesh, partly formed and partly unformed, in order that We may

---

1.   Violent natural disturbance, esp. earthquake

manifest (Our power) to you; and We cause whom We will to rest in the wombs for an appointed term, then do We bring you out as babes, then (foster you) that you may reach your age of full strength; and some of you are called to die, and some are sent back to the feeblest old age, so that they know nothing after having known (much), and (further), you see the earth barren and lifeless, but when We pour down rain on it, it is stirred (to life), it swells, and it puts forth every kind of beautiful growth (in pairs).

6.   This is so, because Allah is the Reality: it is He Who gives life to the dead, and it is He Who has power over all things.

7.   And verily the Hour will come: there can be no doubt about it, or about (the fact) that Allah will raise up all who are in the graves.

8.   Yet there is among men such a one as disputes about Allah, without knowledge, without guidance, and without a Book of Enlightenment,-

9.   (Disdainfully[2]) bending his side, in order to lead (men) astray from the Path of Allah: for him there is disgrace in this life, and on the Day of Judgment We shall make him taste the Penalty of burning (Fire).

10.   (It will be said): "This is because of the deeds which your hands sent forth, for verily Allah is not unjust to His servants.

11.   There are among men some who serve Allah, as it were, on the verge: if good befalls them, they are, there-with, well content; but if a trial comes to them, they turn on their faces: they lose both this world and the Hereafter: that is loss for all to see!

12.   They call on such deities, besides Allah, as can neither hurt nor profit them: that is straying far indeed (from the Way)!

13.   (Perhaps) they call on one whose hurt is nearer than his profit: evil, indeed, is the patron, and evil the companion (for help)!

14.   Verily Allah will admit those who believe and work righteous deeds, to Gardens, beneath which rivers flow: for Allah carries

---

2.   Scornfully, contemptuously

out all that He plans.

15.   If any think that Allah will not help him (His Messenger) in this world and the Hereafter, let him stretch out a rope to the ceiling and cut (himself) off: then let him see whether his plan will remove that which enrages (him)!

16.   Thus We have sent down Clear Sings; and verily Allah guides whom He will!

17.   Those who believe (in the Qur'an), those who follow the Jewish (scriptures), and the Sabians, Christians, Magians, and Polytheists,- Allah will judge between them on the Day of Judgment: for Allah is Witness of all things.

18.   Do you not see that to Allah bow down in worship all things that are in the heavens and on earth,- the sun, the moon, the stars; the hills, the trees, the animals; and a great number among mankind? But a great number are (also) such as are fit for Punishment: and such as Allah shall disgrace,- none can raise to honour: for Allah carries out all that He wills.

19.   These two antagonists[3] dispute with each other about their Lord: but those who deny (their Lord),- for them will be cut out a garment of Fire: over their heads will be poured out boiling water.

20.   With it will be scalded[4] what is within their bodies, as well as (their) skins.

21.   In addition there will be maces[5] of iron (to punish) them.

22.   Every time they wish to get away therefrom, from anguish, they will be forced back therein, and (it will be said), "You taste the Penalty of Burning!"

23.   Allah will admit those who believe and work righteous deeds, to Gardens beneath which rivers flow: they shall be adorned therein with bracelets of gold and pearls; and their garments there will be of silk.

24.   For they have been guided (in this life) to the purest of speeches; they have been guided to the Path of Him Who is Worthy of

---

3.   Adversaries   4.   Burn with hot liquid
5.   Heavy metal-headed and spiked clubs or sticks.

(all) Praise.

25. As to those who have rejected (Allah), and would keep back (men) from the Way of Allah, and from the Sacred Mosque, which We have made (open) to (all) men - equal is the dweller there and the visitor from the country - and any whose purpose therein is profanity or wrong-doing - them will We cause to taste of a most grievous Penalty.

26. Behold! We gave the site, to Abraham, of the (Sacred) House, (saying): "Do not asso-ciate anything (in worship) with Me; and sanctify My House for those who compass it round, or stand up, or bow, or prostrate themselves (therein in prayer).

27. "And proclaim the Pilgri-mage among men: they will come to you on foot and (mounted) on every kind of camel, lean on account of jour-neys through deep and distant mountain highways;

28. "That they may witness the benefits (provided) for them, and celebrate the name of Allah, through the Days appointed, over the cattle which He has provided for them (for sacrifice): then you eat thereof and feed the distressed ones in want.

29. "Then let them complete the rites prescribed for them, perform their vows, and (again) circumambulate[6] the Ancient House."

30. Such (is the Pilgrimage): whoever honours the sacred rites of Allah, for him it is good in the sight of his Lord. Lawful to you (for food in Pilgrimage) are cattle, except those mentioned to you (as exceptions): but shun the abomination of idols, and shun the word that is false,-

31. Being true in faith to Allah, and never assigning partners to Him: if anyone assigns partners to Allah, he is as if he had fallen from heaven and been snatched up by birds, or the wind had swooped (like a bird on its prey) and thrown him into a far- distant place.

32. Such (is his state): and who-ever holds in honour the symbols of Allah, (in the sacrifice of animals), such (honour) should

---

6. Go around, make *tawaf*.

come truly from piety of heart.

33. In them you have benefits for a term appointed: in the end their place of sacrifice is near the Ancient House.

34. To every people We appointed rites (of sacrifice), that they might celebrate the name of Allah over the sustenance He gave them from animals (fit for food). But your God is One God (Allah): submit then your wills to Him (in Islam): and you give the good news to those who humble themselves,-

35. To those whose hearts, when Allah is mentioned, are filled with fear, who show patient perseverance over their afflictions[8], keep up regular prayer, and spend (in charity) out of what We have bestowed upon them.

36. The sacrificial camels We have made for you as among the Symbols from Allah: in them is (much) good for you: then pronounce the name of Allah over them as they line up (for sacrifice): when they are down on their sides (after slaughter), you eat thereof, and feed such as (beg not but) live in contentment, and such as beg with due humility: thus have We made animals subject to you, that you may be grateful.

37. It is not their meat nor their blood, that reaches Allah: it is your piety that reaches Him: He has thus made them subject to you, that you may glorify Allah for His guidance to you and proclaim the good news to all who do right.

38. Verily Allah will defend (from ill) those who believe: verily, Allah does not love any that is a traitor to faith, or show ingratitude.

39. To those against whom war is made, permission is given (to fight), because they are wronged;- and verily, Allah is most powerful for their aid;-

40. (They are) those who have been expelled from their homes in defiance[9] of right,- (for no cause) except that they say, "Our Lord is Allah". Did not Allah check one set of people by means of another, there would surely have been pulled down

---

7.   Steadfastness, patience   8.   Hardships, distress
9.   Open resistance

monasteries, churches, synagogues, and mosques, in which the name of Allah is commemorated in abundant measure. Allah will certainly aid those who aid His (cause);- for verily Allah is full of Strength, Exalted in Might, (able to enforce His Will).

41. (They are) those who, if We establish them in the land, establish regular prayer and give regular charity, enjoin the right and forbid wrong: with Allah rests the end (and decision) of (all) affairs.

42. If they treat your (mission) as false, so did the peoples before them (with their prophets),- the People of Noah, and 'Ad and Thamud;

43. Those of Abraham and Lut;

44. And the Companions of the Madyan People; and Moses was rejected (in the same way). But I granted respite to the Un-believers, and (only) after that did I punish them: but how (terrible) was My rejection (of them)!

45. How many populations have We destroyed, which were given to wrong-doing? They tumbled down on their roofs. And how many wells are lying idle and neglected, and castles lofty and well-built?

46. Do they not travel through the land, so that their hearts (and minds) may thus learn wisdom and their ears may thus learn to hear? Truly it is not their eyes that are blind, but their hearts which are in their breasts.

47. Yet they ask you to hasten on the Punishment! But Allah will not fail in His Promise. Verily a Day in the sight of your Lord is like a thousand years of your reckoning.[10]

48. And to how many popula-tions did I give respite, which were given to wrong-doing? In the end I punished them. To Me is the destination (of all).

49. Say: "O men! I am (sent) to you only to give a Clear Warning:

50. "Those who believe and work righteousness, for them is forgiveness and a sustenance most generous.

---

10. Calculation

51. "But those who strive against Our Signs, to frustrate them,- they will be Companions of the Fire."

52. Never did We send a Messenger or a prophet before you, but, when he framed a desire, Satan threw some (vanity) into his desire: but Allah will cancel anything (vain) that Satan throws in, and Allah will confirm (and establish) His Signs: for Allah is full of Knowledge and Wisdom:

53. That He may make the suggestions thrown in by Satan, but a trial for those in whose hearts is a disease and who are hardened of heart: verily the wrong-doers are in a schism[11] far (from the Truth):

54. And that those on whom knowledge has been bestowed may learn that the (Qur'an) is the Truth from your Lord, and that they may believe therein, and their hearts may be made humbly (open) to it: for verily Allah is the Guide of those who believe, to the Straight Way.

55. Those who reject Faith will not cease to be in doubt concerning (Revelation) until the Hour (of Judgment) comes suddenly upon them, or there comes to them the Penalty of a Day of Disaster.

56. On that Day the Dominion[12] will be that of Allah: He will judge between them: so those who believe and work righteous deeds will be in Gardens of Delight.

57. And for those who reject Faith and deny Our Signs, there will be a humiliating Punishment.

58. Those who leave their homes in the cause of Allah, and are then slain or die,- on them Allah will bestow verily a goodly Provision: truly Allah is He Who bestows the best Provision.

59. Verily He will admit them to a place with which they shall be well pleased: for Allah is All-Knowing, Most Forbearing.

60. That (is so). And if one has retaliated to no greater extent than the injury he received, and is again set upon inordinately[13], Allah will help him: for Allah is One that blots out (sins) and forgives (again and again).

---

11. Division of a group into opposing parties.
12. Authority, sovereignty.   13. Aggressively, immoderately

61. That is because Allah merges night into day, and He merges day into night, and verily it is Allah Who hears and sees (all things).

62. That is because Allah - He is the Reality; and those besides Him whom they invoke[14],- they are but vain Falsehood: verily Allah is He, Most High, Most Great.

63. Don't you see that Allah sends down rain from the sky, and forthwith the earth becomes clothed with green? for Allah is He Who understands the finest mysteries, and is well-acquainted (with them).

64. To Him belongs all that is in the heavens and on earth: for verily Allah,- He is free of all wants, Worthy of all Praise.

65. Don't you see that Allah has made subject to you (men) all that is on the earth, and the ships that sail through the sea by His Command? He withholds the sky (rain) from failing on the earth except by His leave: for Allah is Most Kind and Most Merciful to man.

66. It is He Who gave you life, will cause you to die, and will again give you life: truly man is a most ungrateful creature!

67. To every people We have appointed rites and ceremonies which they must follow: let them not then dispute with you on the matter, but you do invite (them) to your Lord: for you are assuredly on the Right Way.

68. If they do wrangle[15] with you, say, "Allah knows best what it is you are doing."

69. "Allah will judge between you on the Day of Judgment concerning the matters in which you differ."

70. Don't you know that Allah knows all that is in heaven and on earth? Indeed it is all in a Record, and that is easy for Allah.

71. Yet they worship besides Allah, things for which no authority has been sent down to them, and of which they have (really) no knowledge: for those that do wrong there is no helper.

72. When Our Clear Signs are rehearsed[16] to them, you will notice

14. Call upon   15. Dispute, argue
16. Recited, repeated

a denial on the faces of the Unbelievers! they nearly attack with violence those who rehearse Our Signs to them. Say, "Shall I tell you of something (far) worse than these Signs? It is the Fire (of Hell)! Allah has promised it to the Unbelievers! and evil is that destination!"

73. O men! Here is a parable set forth! listen to it! Those on whom, besides Allah, you call, cannot create (even) a fly, if they all met together for the purpose! And if the fly should snatch away anything from them, they would have no power to release it from the fly. Feeble are those who petition and those whom they petition!

74. No just estimate have they made of Allah: for Allah is He Who is strong and able to carry out His Will.

75. Allah chooses Messen-gers from angels and from men, for Allah is He Who hears and sees (all things).

76. He knows what is before them and what is behind them: and to Allah go back all questions (for decision).

77. O you who believe! Bow down, prostrate yourselves, and adore your Lord; and do good; that you may prosper.

78. And strive in His cause as you ought to strive, (with sincerity and under discipline). He has chosen you, and has imposed no difficulties on you in religion; it is the cult[17] of your father Abraham. It is He Who has named you Muslims, both before and in this (Revelation); that the Messenger may be a witness for you, and you be witnesses for mankind! So establish regular Prayer, give regular Charity, and hold fast to Allah! He is your Protector - the Best to protect and the Best to help!

---

17.   Way

SURAH AL-MUMINUN
(INTRODUCTION)

This Surah deals with the virtues which are the seed-bed of Faith, especially in an environment in which Truth is denied and its votaries insulted and persecuted. But Truth is One and must prevail. Those who do wrong will be filled with vain regrets when it is too late for repentance.

It belongs to the late Makkan period.

SURAH MU-MINUN (OR THE BELIEVERS)

In the name of Allah, Most Gracious, Most Merciful.

1. The Believers must (eventually) win through,
2. Those who humble themselves in their prayers;
3. Who avoid vain talk;
4. Who are active in deeds of charity;
5. Who abstain from sex,
6. Except with those joined to them in the marriage bond, or (the captives) whom their right hands possess,- for (in their case) they are free from blame,
7. But those whose desires exceed those limits are trans-gressors;-
8. Those who faithfully observe their trusts and their covenants;
9. And who (strictly) guard their prayers;-
10. These will be the heirs,
11. Who will inherit Paradise: they will dwell therein (for ever).
12. We created man from a quintessence[1] (of clay);
13. Then We placed him as (a drop of) sperm in a place of rest, firmly fixed;
14. Then We made the sperm into a clot of congealed[2] blood; then of that clot We made a (foetus) lump; then We made out of that lump bones and clothed the bones with flesh; then We developed out of it another creature. So blessed be Allah, the Best to create!
15. After that, at length you will die.

---

1. Refined extract
2. Solidified

16.   Again, on the Day of Judgment, you will be raised up.

17.   And We have made, above you, seven tracts; and We are never unmindful of (Our) Creation.

18.   And We send down water from the sky according to (due) measure, and We cause it to soak in the soil; and We certainly are able to drain it off (with ease).

19.   With it We grow for you gardens of date-palms and vines: in them you have abundant fruits: and of them you eat (and have enjoyment),-

20.   Also a tree springing out of Mount Sinai, which produces oil, and relish for those who use it for food.

21.   And in cattle (too) you have an instructive example: from within their bodies We produce (milk) for you to drink; there are, in them, (besides), numerous (other) benefits for you; and of their (meat) you eat;

22.   And on them, as well as in ships, you ride.

23.   We sent Noah to his people: he said, "O my people; worship Allah, you have no other god but Him. Will you not fear (Him)?"

24.   The chiefs of the Unbe-lievers among his people said: "He is no more than a man like yourselves: his wish is to assert his superiority over you. If Allah had wished (to send Messengers), He could have sent down angels; never did we hear such a thing (as he says), among our ancestors of old."

25.   (And some said): "He is only a man possessed; wait (and have patience) with him for a time."

26.   (Noah) said: "O my Lord! help me: for that they accuse me of falsehood!"

27.   So We inspired him (with this message): "Construct the Ark within Our sight and under Our guidance: then when comes Our command, and the fountains of the earth gush forth, you take on board pairs of every species, male and female, and your family- except those of them against whom the Word has already gone forth: and do not address Me in favour of the

wrong-doers; for they shall be drowned (in the Flood).

28. And when you have embarked on the Ark - you and those with you,- say: "Praise be to Allah, Who has saved us from the people who do wrong."

29. And say: "O my Lord! enable me to disembark with Your blessing: for You are the Best to enable (us) to disem-bark."

30. Verily in this there are Signs (for men to understand); (thus) do We try (men).

31. Then We raised after them another generation.

32. And We sent to them a Messenger from among them-selves, (saying), "Worship Allah! you have no other god but Him. Will you not fear (Him)?"

33. And the chiefs of his people, who disbelieved and denied the Meeting in the Hereafter, and on whom We had bestowed the good things of this life, said: "He is no more than a man like yourselves: he eats of that of which you eat, and drinks of what you drink.

34. "If you obey a man like yourselves, behold, it is certain you will be lost.

35. "Does he promise that when you die and become dust and bones, you shall be brought forth (again)?

36. "Far, very far is that which you are promised!

37. "There is nothing but our life in this world! We shall die and we live! But we shall never be raised up again!

38. "He is only a man who invents a lie against Allah, but we are not the ones to believe in him!"

39. (The prophet) said: "O my Lord! help me: for that they accuse me of falsehood."

40. (Alalh) said: "In but a little while, they are sure to be sorry!"

41. Then the Blast overtook them with justice, and We made them as rubbish of dead leaves (floating on the stream of Time)! So away with the people who do wrong!

42. Then We raised after them other generations.

43. No people can hasten their term, nor can they delay (it).

44.   Then We sent Our Mess-engers in succession: every time there came to a people their Messenger, they accused him of falsehood: so We made them follow each other (in punish-ment): We made them as a tale (that is told): so away with a people that will not believe!

45.   Then We sent Moses and his brother Aaron, with Our Signs and authority manifest,

46.   To Pharaoh and his Chiefs: but these behaved insolently: they were an arrogant people.

47.   They said: "Shall we believe in two men like our-selves? And their people are subject to us!"

48.   So they (rejected) and accused them of falsehood, and they became of those who were destroyed.

49.   And We gave Moses the Book, in order that they might receive guidance.

50.   And We made the son of Mary and his mother as a Sign: We gave them both shelter on high ground, affording rest and security and furnished with springs.

51.   O you Messengers! enjoy (all) things good and pure, and work righteousness: for I am well-acquainted with (all) that you do.

52.   And verily this Brother-hood of yours is a single Brotherhood, and I am your Lord and Cherisher: therefore fear Me (and no other).

53.   But people have cut off their affair (of unity), between them, into sects: each party re-joices in that which is with itself

54.   But leave them in their confused ignorance for a time.

55.   Do they think that because We have granted them abun-dance of wealth and sons,

56.   We would hasten them on in every good? Nay, they do not understand.

57.   Verily those who live in awe for fear of their Lord;

58.   Those who believe in the Signs of their Lord;

59.   Those who do not join (in worship) partners with their Lord;

60.   And those who dispense their charity with their hearts full of

fear, because they will return to their Lord;-

61. It is these who hasten in every good work, and these who are foremost in them.

62. On no soul do We place a burden greater than it can bear: before Us is a record which clearly speaks the truth: they will never be wronged.

63. But their hearts are in confused ignorance of this; and there are, besides that, deeds of theirs, which they will (continue) to do,-

64. Until, when We seize in Punishment those of them who received the good things of this world, behold, they will groan in supplication!

65. (It will be said): "Do not groan in supplication this day: for you shall certainly not be helped by Us.

66. "My Signs used to be rehearsed to you, but you used to turn back on your heels-

67. "In arrogance: talking nonsense about the (Qur'an), like one telling fables by night."

68. Do they not ponder over the Word (of Allah), or has anything (new) come to them that did not come to their fathers of old?

69. Or do they not recognise their Messenger, that they deny him?

70. Or do they say, "He is possessed"? Nay, he has brought them the Truth, but most of them hate the Truth.

71. If the Truth had been in accord with their desires, truly the heavens and the earth, and all beings therein would have been in confusion and corruption! Nay, We have sent them their admonition, but they turn away from their admonition.

72. Or is it that you ask them for some recompense[3]? But the recompense of your Lord is best: He is the Best of those who give sustenance.

73. But verily you call them to the Straight Way;

74. And verily those who do not believe in the Hereafter are deviating from that Way.

---

3. Reward

75.   If We had mercy on them and removed the distress which is on them, they would obstinately persist in their transgression, wandering in distraction to and fro.

76.   We inflicted Punishment on them, but they did not humble themselves to their Lord, nor do they submissively entreat (Him)!-

77.   Until We open on them a gate leading to a severe Punish-ment: then lo! they will be plunged in despair therein!

78.   It is He Who has created for you (the faculties of) hearing, sight, feeling and understanding: but little thanks it is you give!

79.   And He has multiplied you through the earth, and to Him you shall be gathered back.

80.   It is He Who gives life and death, and to Him (is due) the alternation of Night and Day: will you not then understand?

81.   On the contrary they say things similar to what the ancients said.

82.   They say: "What! when we die and become dust and bones, could we really be raised up again?

83.   "Such things have been promised to us and to our fathers before! they are nothing but tales of the ancients!"

84.   Say: "To whom belong the earth and all beings therein? (say) if you know!"

85.   They will say, "To Allah!" say: "Yet will you not receive admonition?"

86.   Say: "Who is the Lord of the seven heavens, and the Lord of the Throne (of Glory) Supreme?"

87.   They will say, "(They belong) to Allah." Say: "Will you not then fear?"

88.   Say: "Who is it in whose hands is the governance of all things,- who protects (all), but is not protected (of any)? (say) if you know."

89.   They will say, "(It belongs) to Allah." Say: "Then how are you deluded?"

90.   We have sent them the Truth: but they indeed practise

Falsehood!

91. No son did Allah beget, nor is there any god along with Him: (if there were many gods), behold, each god would have taken away what he had created, and some would have lorded it over others! Glory to Allah! (He is free) from the (sort of) things they attribute to Him!

92. He knows what is hidden and what is open: too high is He for the partners they attribute to Him!

93. Say: "O my Lord! if You will show me (in my lifetime) that which they are warned against,-

94. "Then, O my Lord! put me not amongst the people who do wrong!"

95. And We are certainly able to show you (in fulfilment) that against which they are warned.

96. Repel evil with that which is best: We are well acquainted with the things they say.

97. And say "O my Lord! I seek refuge with You from the suggestions of the Evil Ones.

98. "And I seek refuge with You O my Lord! lest they should come near me."

99. (In Falsehood will they be) until, when death comes to one of them, he says: "O my Lord! send me back (to life),-

100. "In order that I may work righteousness in the things I neglected." - "By no means! It is but a word he says."- Before them is a Partition till the Day they are raised up.

101. Then when the Trumpet is blown, there will be no more relationships between them that Day, nor will one ask after another!

102. Then those whose balance (of good deeds) is heavy,- they will attain salvation:

103. But those whose balance is light, will be those who have lost their souls, in Hell will they abide.

104. The Fire will burn their faces, and they will therein grin, with their lips displaced.

105. "Were not My Signs rehearsed to you, and you but treated them as falsehoods?"

106. They will say: "Our Lord! our misfortune overwhelmed us, and we became a people astray!

107. "Our Lord! bring us out of this: if ever we return (to evil), then shall we be wrong-doers indeed!"

108. He will say: "Be you driven into it (with ignominy[4])! and do not speak to Me!

109. "A part of My servants there was, who used to pray, Our Lord! we believe; then You forgive us, and have mercy upon us: for You are the Best of those who show mercy!"

110. "But you treated them with ridicule, so much so that (ridicule of) them made you forget My Message while you were laughing at them!

111. "I have rewarded them this day for their patience and constancy: they are indeed the ones that have achieved bliss..."

112. He will say: "What number of years did you stay on earth?"

113. They will say: "We stayed a day or part of a day: but ask those who keep account."

114. He will say: "You stayed not but a little,- if you had only known!

115. "Did you then think that We had created you in jest, and that you would not be brought back to Us (for account)?"

116. Therefore exalted be Allah, the King, the Reality: there is no god but He, the Lord of the Throne of Honour!

117. If anyone invokes, besides Allah, any other god, he has no authority therefor; and his reckoning[5] will be only with his Lord! and verily the Unbelievers shall not prosper!

118. So say: "O my Lord! Grant us forgiveness and mercy! for You are the Best of those who show mercy!"

---

4. Disgrace   5. Account

SURAH—24
SURAH AN-NUR
(INTRODUCTION)

The environmental and social influences which most frequently wreck our spiritual ideals have to do with sex, and especially with its misuse, whether in the form of unregulated behavior, of false charges or scandals, or breach of the refined conventions of personal or domestic privacy. Our complete conquest of all pitfalls in such matters enables us to rise to the higher regions of Light and of Allah-created Nature, about which a mystic doctrine is suggested. This subject is continued in the next Surah.

As the reprobation of false slanders about women (24:11 -20) is connected with an incident that happened to Hadhrat Aa'isha in milieu of Pagan Makkah was testing the Makkans in their most arrogant mood.

SURHA NUR (THE LIGHT)

In the name of Allah, Most Gracious, Most Merciful.

1. A Surah which We have sent down and which We have ordained: in it We have sent down Clear Signs, in order that you may receive admonition.

2. The woman and the man guilty of adultery or forni-cation,- flog each of them with a hundred stripes: let not com-passion move you in their case, in a matter prescribed by Allah, if you believe in Allah and the Last Day: and let a party of the Believers witness their punish-ment.

3. Let no man guilty of adultery or fornication marry any but a woman similarly guilty, or an Unbeliever: nor let any but such a man or an Unbeliever marry such a woman: to the Believers such a thing is forbidden.

4. And those who launch a charge against chaste women, and produce not four witnesses (to support their allegations[1]),- flog them with eighty stripes; and reject their evidence ever after: for such men are wicked transgressors;-

5. Unless they repent thereafter and mend (their conduct); for Allah is Oft-Forgiving, Most Merciful.

---

1. Claim, charge

6.   And for those who launch a charge against their spouses, and
        have (in support) no evidence but their own,- their solitary
        evidence (can be received) if they bear witness four times (with
        an oath) by Allah that they are solemnly telling the truth;

7.   And the fifth (oath) (should be) that they solemnly invoke the
        curse of Allah on themselves if they tell a lie.

8.   But it would avert the punishment from the wife, if she bears
        witness four times (with an oath) by Allah, that (her husband)
        is telling a lie;

9.   And the fifth (oath) should be that she solemnly invokes the
        wrath of Allah on herself if (her accuser) is telling the truth.

10.   If it were not for Allah's grace and mercy on you, and that
        Allah is Oft- Returning, full of Wisdom,- (you would be ruined
        indeed).

11.   Those who brought forward the lie are a body among
        yourselves: think it not to be an evil to you; on the contrary it
        is good for you: to every man among them (will come the
        punishment) of the sin that he earned, and to him who took on
        himself the lead among them, will be a Penalty grie-vous.

12.   Why did not the Believers - men and women - when you heard
        of the affair,- thought well of their people and say, "This
        (charge) is an obvious lie" ?

13.   Why did they not bring four witnesses to prove it? When they
        have not brought the witnesses, such men, in the sight of Allah,
        (stand forth) them-selves as liars!

14.   Were it not for the grace and mercy of Allah on you, in this
        world and the Hereafter, a grievous Penalty would have seized
        you in that you rushed glibly[2] into this affair.

15.   Behold, you received it on your tongues, and said out of your
        mouths things of which you had no knowledge; and you thought
        it to be a light matter, while it was most serious in the sight of
        Allah.

16.   And why did you not, when you heard it, say? - "It is not right

---

2.   Carelessly, rashly

of us to speak of this: Glory to Allah! this is a most serious slander!"[3]

17. Allah admonishes you, that you may never repeat such (conduct), if you are (true) Believers.

18. And Allah makes the Signs plain to you: for Allah is full of knowledge and wisdom.

19. Those who love (to see) scandal published broadcast among the Believers, will have a grievous Penalty in this life and in the Hereafter: Allah knows, and you do not know.

20. Were it not for the grace and mercy of Allah on you, and that Allah is full of kindness and mercy, (you would be ruined indeed).

21. O you who believe! Do not follow Satan's footsteps: if any will follow the footsteps of Satan, he will (but) command what is shameful and wrong: and were it not for the grace and mercy of Allah on you, not one of you would ever have been pure: but Allah purifies whom He pleases: And Allah is One Who hears and knows (all things).

22. Let not those among you who are endued with grace and amplitude[4] of means resolve by oath against helping their kinsmen, those in want, and those who have left their homes in Allah's cause: let them forgive and overlook, do you not wish that Allah should forgive you? For Allah is Oft-Forgiving, Most Merciful.

23. Those who slander chaste women, indiscreet[5] but believing, are cursed in this life and in the Hereafter: for them is a grievous Penalty,-

24. On the Day when their tongues, their hands, and their feet will bear witness against them as to their actions.

25. On that Day Allah will pay them back (all) their just dues, and they will realise that Allah is the (very) Truth, that makes all things manifest.

26. Women impure are for men impure, and men impure for women

---

3. Defamation, libel   4. Abundance
5. Tactless

impure and women of purity are for men of purity, and men of purity are for women of purity: these are not affected by what people say: for them there is forgiveness, and a provision honourable.

27. O you who believe! Do not enter houses other than your own, until you have asked permission and saluted those in them: that is best for you, in order that you may heed (what is seemly).

28. If you find no one in the house, do not enter until permi-ssion is given to you: if you are asked to go back, go back: that makes for greater purity for yourselves: and Allah knows well all that you do.

29. It is no fault on your part to enter houses not used for living in, which serve some (other) use for you: And Allah has know-ledge of what you reveal and what you conceal.

30. Say to the believing men that they should lower their gaze and guard their modesty: that will make for greater purity for them: and Allah is well acquainted with all that they do.

31. And say to the believing women that they should lower their gaze and guard their modesty; that they should not display their beauty and ornaments except what (must ordinarily) appear thereof; that they should draw their veils over their bosoms and not display their beauty except to their husbands, their fathers, their husband's fathers, their sons, their husbands' sons, their brothers or their brothers' sons, or their sisters' sons, or their women, or the slaves whom their right hands possess, or male servants free of sexual urge, or small children who have no sense of the shame of sex; and that they should not strike their feet in order to draw attention to their hidden orna-ments. And O you Believers! You turn all together towards Allah, that you may attain Bliss.

32. Marry those among you who are single, or the virtuous ones among your slaves, male or female: if they are in poverty, Allah will give them means out of His grace: for Allah encom-passes all, and He knows all things.

33. Let those who find not the wherewithal[6] for marriage keep themselves chaste, until Allah gives them means out of His grace. And if any of your slaves ask for a deed in writing (to enable them to earn their freedom for a certain sum), give them such a deed if you know any good in them: yes, give them something yourselves out of the means which Allah has given to you. But do not force your maids to prostitution when they desire chastity, in order that you may make a gain in the goods of this life. But if anyone compels them, yet, after such compulsion, is Allah, Oft-Forgiving, Most Merciful (to them),

34. We have already sent down to you verses making things clear, an illustration from (the story of) people who passed away before you, and an admonition for those who fear (Allah).

35. Allah is the Light of the heavens and the earth. The parable of His Light is as if there were a Niche and within it a Lamp: the Lamp enclosed in Glass: the glass as it were a brilliant star: lit from a blessed Tree, an Olive, neither of the East nor of the West, whose Oil is well-nigh Luminous, though fire scarce touched it: Light upon Light! Allah guides whom He will to His Light: Allah sets forth Parables for men: and Allah knows all things.

36. (Lit is such a Light) in houses, which Allah has per-mitted to be raised to honour; for the celebration, in them, of His name: in them is He glorified in the mornings and in the evenings, (again and again),-

37. By men whom neither traffic[7] nor merchandise[8] can divert from the remembrance of Allah, nor from regular Prayer, nor from paying Zakat; their (only) fear is for the Day when hearts and eyes will be turned about,-

38. That Allah may reward them according to the best of their deeds, and add even more for them out of His Grace: for Allah provides for those whom He will, without measure.

---

6. Money or means 　　　　7. Business, Commerce
8. Goods for sale

39.   But the Unbelievers,- their deeds are like a mirage in sandy deserts, which the man parched[9] with thirst mistakes for water; until when he comes up to it, he finds it to be nothing: but he finds Allah (ever) with him, and Allah will pay him his account: and Allah is swift in taking account.

40.   Or (the Unbelievers' state) is like the depths of darkness in a vast deep ocean, overwhelmed with billow[10] topped by billow, topped by (dark) clouds: depths of darkness, one above another: if a man stretches out his hand, he can hardly see it! for any to whom Allah does not give light, there is no light!

41.   Do not you see that it is Allah Whose praises all beings in the heavens and on earth do celebrate, and the birds (of the air) with wings outspread? Each one knows its own (mode of) prayer and praise. And Allah knows well all that they do.

42.   Yes, to Allah belongs the dominion of the heavens and the earth; and to Allah is the final goal (of all).

43.   Don't you see that Allah makes the clouds move gently, then joins them together, then makes them into a heap? - then you will see rain issue forth from their midst. And He sends down from the sky mountain masses (of clouds) wherein is hail: He strikes therewith whom He pleases and He turns it away from whom He pleases. The vivid flash of His lightning well-nigh blinds the sight.

44.   It is Allah Who alternates the Night and the Day: verily in these things is an instructive example for those who have vision!

45.   And Allah has created every animal from water: of them there are some that creep on their bellies; some that walk on two legs; and some that walk on four. Allah creates what He wills; for verily Allah has power over all things.

46.   We have indeed sent down signs that make things manifest: and Allah guides whom He wills to a way that is straight.

47.   They say, "We believe in Allah and in the Messenger, and we obey": but even after that, some of them turn away: they are

---

9.   Hot and dry   10.   Waves

not (really) Believers.

48.   When they are summoned to Allah and His Messenger, in order that He may judge between them, behold, some of them decline (to come).

49.   But if the right is on their side, they come to him with all submission.

50.   Is it that there is a disease in their hearts? or do they doubt, or are they in fear, that Allah and His Messenger will deal unjustly with them? Nay, it is they themselves who do wrong.

51.   The answer of the Belie-vers, when summoned to Allah and His Messenger, in order that he may judge between them, is no other than this: they say, "We hear and we obey": it is such as these that will attain felicity.

52.   It is such as obey Allah and His Messenger, and fear Allah and do right, that will win (in the end).

53.   They swear their strongest oaths by Allah that, if only you would command them, they would leave (their homes). Say: "Do not swear, obedience is (more) reasonable; verily, Allah is well acquainted with all that you do."

54.   Say: "Obey Allah, and obey the Messenger: but if you turn away, he is only responsible for the duty placed on him and you for that placed on you. If you obey him, you shall be on right guidance. The Messen-ger's duty is only to preach the clear (Message) .

55.   Allah has promised, to those among you who believe and work righteous deeds, that He will, of a surety, grant them in the land, inheritance (of power), as He granted it to those before them; that He will establish in authority their religion - the one which He has chosen for them; and that He will change (their state), after the fear in which they (lived), to one of security and peace: 'They will worship Me (alone) and not associate any one with Me. 'If any do reject Faith after this, they are rebellious and wicked.

56.   So establish regular Prayer and give regular Charity; and obey the Messenger; that you may receive mercy.

57.   You should never think that the Unbelievers are going to frustrate (Allah's Plan) on earth: their abode is the Fire,- and it is indeed an evil refuge!

58.   O you who believe! Let those whom your right hands possess, and the (children) among you who have not come of age ask your permission (before they come to your presence), on three occasions: before morning prayer; the while you doff[11] your clothes for the noonday heat; and after the late-night prayer: these are your three times of undress[12]: outside those times it is not wrong for you or for them to move about attending to each other: Thus Allah makes clear the Signs to you: for Allah is full of knowledge and wisdom.

59.   But when the children among you come of age, let them (also) ask for permission, as do those senior to them (in age): thus Allah makes clear His Signs to you: for Allah is full of knowledge and wisdom.

60.   Such elderly women as are past the prospect of marriage,- there is no blame on them if they lay aside their (outer) garments, provided they make not a wanton[13] display of their beauty: but it is best for them to be modest: and Allah is One Who sees and knows all things.

61.   It is no fault in the blind nor in one born lame, nor in one afflicted with illness, nor in yourselves, that you should eat in your own houses, or those of your fathers, or your mothers, or your brothers, or your sisters, or your father's brothers or your father's sisters, or your mohter's brothers, or your mother's sisters, or in houses of which the keys are in your possession, or in the house of a sincere friend of yours: there is no blame on you, whether you eat in company or separately. But if you enter houses, salute each other - a greeting of blessing and purity as from Allah. Thus Allah makes clear the Signs to you: that you may understand.

---

11.   Remove, take off   12.   Privacy
13.   Irresponsible, unchaste

62. Only those are Believers, who believe in Allah and His Messenger: when they are with him on a matter requiring collective action, they do not depart until they have asked for his leave; those who ask for your leave are those who believe in Allah and His Messenger; so when they ask for your leave, for some business of theirs, give leave to those of them whom you will, and ask Allah for their forgiveness: for Allah is Oft-Forgiving, Most Merciful.

63. Deem not the summons of the Messenger among your-selves like the summons of one of you to another: Allah knows those of you who slip away under shelter of some excuse: then let those beware who withstand the Messenger's order, lest some trial befall them, or a grievous Penalty be inflicted on them.

64. Be quite sure that to Allah belongs whatever is in the heavens and on earth. Well does He know what you are intent upon: and one day they will be brought back to Him, and He will tell them the truth of what they did: for Allah knows all things.

SURAH—25
SURAH AL-FURQAN
(INTRODUCTION)

This Surah further develops the contrast between Light and Darkness, as symbolical of knowledge and ignorance, righteousness and sin, spiritual progress and degradation. It closes with a definition of the deeds by which the righteous are known in the environment of this world.

It is mainly an early Makkan Surah, but its date has no significance.

———————

SURAH FURQAN (THE CRITERION)
In the name of Allah, Most Gracious, Most Merciful.

1.   Blessed is He Who sent down the Criterion[1] to His servant, that it may be an admonition to all creatures;-

2.   He to Whom belongs the dominion of the heavens and the earth: no son has He begotten, nor has He a partner in His dominion: it is He who created all things, and ordered them in due proportions.

3.   Yet have they taken, besides Him, gods that can create nothing but are them-selves created; that have no control of hurt or good to themselves; nor can they control death nor life nor resurrection.

4.   But the Misbelievers say: "Nothing is this but a lie which he has forged, and others have helped him at it." In truth it is they who have put forward an iniquity and a falsehood.

5.   And they say: "Tales of the ancients, which he has caused to be written: and they are dictated before him morning and evening."

6.   Say: "The (Qur'an) was sent down by Him Who knows the mystery (that is) in the heavens and the earth: verily He is Oft-Forgiving, Most Merciful."

7.   And they say: "What sort of a Messenger is this, who eats food, and walks through the streets? Why has not an angel been sent down to him to give admonition with him?

———————
1.   A standard to judge between good and evil.

8.	"Or (Why) has not a treasure been bestowed on him, or why has he (not) a garden for enjoyment?" The wicked say: "You follow none other than a man bewitched."

9.	See what kinds of comparisons they make for you! But they have gone astray, and never a way will they be able to find!

10.	Blessed is He Who, if that were His Will, could give you better (things) than those,- Gardens beneath which rivers flow; and He could give you palaces (secure to dwell in).

11.	Nay, they deny the Hour (of the judgment to come): but We have prepared a blazing fire for such as deny the Hour:

12.	When it sees them from a place far off, they will hear its fury[12] and its raging sigh.

13.	And when they are cast, bound together into a constricted[13] place therein, they will plead for destruction there and then!

14.	"This day do not plead for a single destruction: plead for destruction oft- repeated!"

15.	Say: "Is that best, or the eternal Garden, promised to the righteous? for them, that is a reward as well as a goal (of attainment).

16.	"For them there will be therein all that they wish for: they will dwell (there) for ever: a promise binding upon your Lord."

17.	The day He will gather them together as well as those whom they worship besides Allah, He will ask: "Was it you who let these My servants astray, or did they stray from the Path themselves?"

18.	They will say: "Glory to You! Not meet[4] was it for us that we should take for protectors others besides You: but You bestowed on them and their fathers, good things (in life), until they forgot the Message: for they were a people (worth-less and) lost."

19.	(Allah will say): "Now have they proved you liars in what you say: so you cannot avert (your penalty) nor (get) help." And whoever among you does wrong, him shall We cause to taste

---

2.	Anger 3.	Narrow
4.	Suitable, proper, fit

of a grievous Penalty.

20.   And the Messengers whom We sent before you were all (men)
       who ate food and walked through the streets: We have made
       some of you as a trial for others: will you have patience? for
       Allah is One Who sees (all things).

21.   Such as do not fear the meeting with Us (for Judgment) say:
       "Why are not the angels sent down to us, or (why) do we not
       see our Lord?" Indeed they have an arrogant conceit[5] of
       themselves, and mighty is the insolence of their impiety!

22.   The Day they see the an-gels,- no joy will there be to the sinners
       that Day: the (angels) will say: "There is a barrier forbidden
       (to you) altogether!"

23.   And We shall turn to what-ever deeds they did (in this life),
       and We shall make such deeds as floating dust scattered about.

24.   The Companions of the Garden will be well, that Day, in their
       abode, and have the fairest of places for repose.[6]

25.   The Day the heaven shall be rent asunder with clouds, and
       angels shall be sent down, descending (in ranks),-

26.   That Day, the dominion as of right and truth, shall be (wholly)
       for (Allah) Most Mer-ciful: it will be a Day of dire[7] difficulty
       for the Misbelievers.

27.   The Day that the wrong-doer will bite at his hands, he will say,
       "Oh! would that I had taken a (straight) path with the
       Messenger!

28.   "Ah! woe is me! Would that I had never taken such a one for a
       friend!

29.   "He did lead me astray from the Message (of Allah) after it
       had come to me! Ah! the Evil One is but a traitor to man!"

30.   Then the Messenger will say: "O my Lord! Truly my people
       took this Qur'an for just foolish nonsense."

31.   Thus have We made for every prophet an enemy among the
       sinners: but enough is your Lord to guide and to help.

---

5.   Personal vanity   6.   Rest
7.   Dreadful

32. Those who reject Faith say: "Why is not the Qur'an revealed to him all at once? Thus (is it revealed), that We may strengthen your heart thereby, and We have rehearsed[8] it to you in slow, well-arranged stages, gradually.

33. And no question do they bring to you but We reveal to you the truth and the best explanation (thereof).

34. Those who will be gathered to Hell (prone[9]) on their faces,- they will be in an evil plight, and, as to Path, most astray.

35. (Before this,) We sent Moses the Book, and appointed his brother Aaron with him as Minister;[10]

36. And We commanded: "You both go, to the people who have rejected Our Signs:" and those (people) We destroyed with utter destruction.

37. And the people of Noah,- when they rejected the Messen-gers, We drowned them, and We made them as a Sign for mankind; and We have prepared for (all) wrong-doers a grievous Penalty;-

38. As also 'Ad and Thamud, and the Companions of the Rass, and many a generation between them.

39. To each one We set forth parables and examples; and each one We broke to utter annihilation (for their sins).

40. And the (Unbelievers) must indeed have passed by the town on which was rained a shower of evil: did they not then see it (with their own eyes)? But they do not fear the Resurrection.

41. When they see you, they treat you no otherwise than in mockery: "Is this the one whom Allah has sent as a Messenger?"

42. "He indeed would well- nigh have misled us from our gods, had it not been that we were constant to them!" - Soon will they know, when they see the Penalty, who it is that is most misled in Path!

43. Do you see such a one as takes for his god his own passion (or impulse)? Could you be a disposer of affairs for him?

44. Or do you think that most of them listen or understand? They are only like cattle;- nay, they are worse astray in Path.

8. Recited, repeated   9. Lying with face downwards
10. Helper

45. Have you not turned your vision to your Lord?- How does He prolong the shadow! If He willed, He could make it stationary! then do We make the sun its guide;

46. Then We draw it in towards Ourselves,- a contraction by easy stages.

47. And He it is Who makes the Night as a robe[11] for you, and Sleep as Repose, and makes the Day (as it were) a Resurrection.

48. And He it is Who sends the winds as heralds[12] of glad tidings, going before His mercy, and We send down pure water from the sky,-

49. That with it We may give life to a dead land, and slake[13] the thirst of things We have created,- cattle and men in great numbers.

50. And We have distributed the (water) amongst them, in order that they may celebrate (Our) praises, but most men are averse (to anything) but (rank[14]) ingratitude.

51. Had it been Our Will, We could have sent a warner to every centre of population.

52. Therefore do not listen to the Unbelievers, but strive against them with the utmost strenuousness[15], with the (Qur'ān).

53. It is He Who has let free the two bodies of flowing water: One palatable[16] and sweet, and the other salt and bitter; yet He has made a barrier between them, a parti-tion that is forbidden to be passed.

54. It is He Who has created man from water: then He has established relationships of lineage[17] and marriage: for your Lord has power (over all things).

55. Yet do they worship, besides Allah, things that can neither profit them nor harm them: and the Misbeliever is a helper (of Evil), against his own Lord!

56. But We sent you only to give glad tidings and admonition.

---

11. Covering, dress
13. Satisfy, quench
15. Vigor and force
17. Ancestry, parentage
12. Couriers, Messengers
14. Gross, virulent, offensive
16. Appetizing

57.   Say: "No reward do I ask of you for it but this: that each one who will may take a (straight) Path to his Lord."

58.   And put your trust in Him Who lives and dies not; and celebrate His praise; and enough is He to be acquainted with the faults of His servants;-

59.   He Who created the heavens and the earth and all that is between, in six days, and is firmly established on the Throne (of Authority): Allah Most Gracious: you ask then, about Him of any acquainted (with such things).

60.   When it is said to them, "You Adore[18] (Allah) Most Gracious!", they say, "And what is (Allah) Most Gracious? Shall we adore that which you command us?" And it increases their flight (from the Truth).

61.   Blessed is He Who made constellations[19] in the skies, and placed therein a Lamp and a Moon giving light;

62.   And it is He Who made the Night and the Day to follow each other: for such as desire to be mindful or to show their gratitude.

63.   And the servants of (Allah) Most Gracious are those who walk on the earth in humility, and when the ignorant address them, they say, "Peace!";

64.   Those who spend the night in adoration of their Lord prostrate and standing;

65.   Those who say, "Our Lord! avert from us the Wrath of Hell, for its Wrath is indeed an affliction grievous,-

66.   "Evil indeed is it as an abode, and as a place to rest in";

67.   Those who, when they spend, are not extravagant and not niggardly, but hold a just (balan-ce) between those (extremes).

68.   Those who do not invoke, with Allah, any other god, nor slay such life as Allah has made sacred except for just cause, nor commit fornication; - and any that does this (not only) meets punishment.

69.   (But) the Penalty on the Day of Judgment will be doubled to him, and he will dwell therein in ignominy[20],-

---

18.   Worship and love   19.   Groups of stars

20.   Disgrace

70. Unless he repents, believes, and works righteous deeds, for Allah will change the evil of such persons into good, and Allah is Oft-Forgiving, Most Merciful,

71. And whoever repents and does good has truly turned to Allah with an (acceptable) conversion;-

72. Those who witness no falsehood, and, if they pass by futility[21], they pass by it with honourable (avoidance);

73. Those who, when they are admonished with the Signs of their Lord, droop not down at them as if they were deaf or blind;

74. And those who pray, "Our Lord! Grant unto us wives and offspring who will be the comfort of our eyes, and give us (the grace) to lead the righteous."

75. Those are the ones who will be rewarded with the highest place in heaven, be-cause of their patient cons-tancy: therein shall they be met with salutations and peace,

76. Dwelling therein;- how beau-tiful an abode and place of rest!

77. Say (to the Rejecters): "My Lord is not uneasy because of you if you do not call on Him: but you have indeed rejected (Him), and soon will come the inevitable (punishment)!"

---

21. Vain or useless thing or work

SURAH—26

SURAH ASH-SHUARAA

(INTRODUCTION)

This Surah begins a new series of four Surahs (26-29), which illustrate the contrast between the spirit of Prophecy and spiritual Light and the reaction to it in the communities among whom it appeared, by going back to old Prophets and the stories of the Past, as explained in the introduction to S. 17.

In this particular Surah we have the stroy of Moses in his fight with Pharaoh and of Pharaoh's discomfiture. Other Prophets mentioned are Abraham, Noah, Hud, Salih, Lut and Shuaib. The lesson is drawn that the Quran is a continuation and fulfillment of previous Revelations, and is pure Truth, unlike the poetry of vain poets.

Chronologically, the Surah belongs to the middle Makkan period, when the contact of the Light of Prophecy with the milieu of Pagan Makkah was testing the Makkans in their most arrogant mood.

SURAH SHU'ARAA (THE POETS)

In the name of Allah, Most Gracious, Most Merciful.

1. Ta. Sin. Mim.
2. These are Verses of the Book that makes (things) clear.
3. It may be you will kill yourself with grief, that they do not become Believers.
4. If (such) were Our Will, We could send down to them from the sky a Sign, to which they would bend their necks in humility.
5. But there doesn't come to them a newly-revealed Message from (Allah) Most Gracious, but they turn away therefrom.
6. They have indeed rejected (the Message): so they will know soon (enough) the truth of what they mocked at!
7. Do they not look at the earth,- how many noble things of all kinds We have produced therein?
8. Verily, in this is a Sign: but most of them do not believe.
9. And verily, your Lord is He, the Exalted in Might, Most Merciful.

10.   Behold, your Lord called Moses: "Go to the people of iniquity,-

11.   "The people of Pharaoh: will they not fear Allah?"

12.   He said: "O my Lord! I do fear that they will charge me with falsehood:

13.   "My breast will be straitened[1]. And my speech may not go (smoothly): so send unto Aaron.

14.   "And (further), they have a charge of crime against me; and I fear they may slay me."

15.   Allah said: "By no means! proceed then, both of you, with Our Signs; We are with you, and will listen (to your call).

16.   "So go forth, both of you, to Pharaoh, and say: 'We have been sent by the Lord and Cherisher of the worlds;

17.   "'You send with us the Children of Israel.'"

18.   (Pharaoh) said: "Did we not cherish you as a child among us, and did you not stay in our midst many years of your life?

19.   "And you did a deed of yours which (you know) you did, and you are an ungrateful (wretch)!"

20.   Moses said: "I did it then, when I was in error.

21.   "So I fled from you (all) when I feared you; but my Lord has (since) invested me with judgment (and wisdom) and appointed me as one of the Messengers.

22.   "And this is the favour with which you do reproach me,- that you have enslaved the Children of Israel!"

23.   Pharaoh said: "And what is the 'Lord and Cherisher of the worlds'?"

24.   (Moses) said: "The Lord and Cherisher of the heavens and the earth, and all between,- if you want to be quite sure."

25.   (Pharaoh) said to those around: "Did you not listen (to what he says)?"

26.   (Moses) said: "Your Lord and the Lord of your fathers from the beginning!"

27.   (Pharaoh) said: "Truly your Messenger who has been sent to you is a veritable[2] madman!"

---

1.   Become narrow   2.   Truly, absolutely

28. (Moses) said: "Lord of the East and the West, and all between! if you only had sense!"

29. (Pharaoh) said: "If you do put forward any god other than me, I will certainly put you in prison!"

30. (Moses) said: "Even if I showed you something clear (and) convincing?"

31. (Pharaoh) said: "Show it then, if you tell the truth!"

32. So (Moses) threw his rod, and behold, it was a serpent, plain (for all to see)!

33. And he drew out his hand, and behold, it was white to all beholders!

34. (Pharaoh) said to the Chiefs around him: "This is indeed a sorcerer[3] well-versed:

35. "His plan is to get you out of your land by his sorcery; then what is it you counsel?"

36. They said: "Keep him and his brother in suspense (for a while), and dispatch to the Cities heralds[4] to collect-

37. "And bring up to you all (our) sorcerers well-versed."

38. So the sorcerers were got together for the appointment of a day well-known,

39. And the people were told: "Are you (now) assembled?-

40. "That we may follow the sorcerers (in religion) if they win?"

41. So when the sorcerers arrived, they said to Pharaoh: "Of course - shall we have a (suitable) reward if we win?

42. He said: "Yes, (and more),- for you shall in that case be (raised to posts) nearest (to my person)."

43. Moses said to them: You "throw that which you are about to throw!"

44. So they threw their ropes and their rods, and said: "By the might of Pharaoh, it is we who will certainly win!"

45. Then Moses threw his rod, when, behold, it straightway swallows up all the falsehoods which they fake.[5]

46. Then did the sorcerers fall down, prostrate in adoration,

---

3. Magician   4. Messengers

5. Forge

47.   Saying: "We believe in the Lord of the Worlds,

48.   "The Lord of Moses and Aaron."

49.   Said (Pharaoh): "You believe in Him before I give you permission? Surely he is your leader, who has taught you sorcery! but soon you shall know! "Be sure I will cut off your hands and your feet on opposite sides, and I will cause you all to die on the cross!"

50.   They said: "No matter! for us, we shall but return to our Lord!

51.   "Only, our desire is that our Lord will forgive us our faults, that we may become foremost among the Believers!"

52.   By inspiration We told Moses: "Travel by night with My servants; for surely you shall be pursued."

53.   Then Pharaoh sent heralds to (all) the Cities,

54.   (Saying): "These (Israeli-tes) are but a small band,

55.   "And they are raging furiously against us;

56.   "But we are a multitude amply fore-warned."

57.   So We expelled them from gardens, springs,

58.   Treasures, and every kind of honourable position;

59.   Thus it was, but We made the Children of Israel inheritors of such things.

60.   So they pursued them at sunrise.

61.   And when the two bodies saw each other, the people of Moses said: "We are sure to be overtaken."

62.   (Moses) said: "By no means! My Lord is with me! soon will He guide me!"

63.   Then We told Moses by inspiration: "Strike the sea with your rod." So it divided, and each separate part became like the huge, firm mass of a mountain.

64.   And We made the other party approach there.

65.   We delivered Moses and all who were with him;

66.   But We drowned the others.

67.   Verily in this is a Sign: but most of them do not believe.

68.   And verily your Lord is He, the Exalted in Might, Most Merciful.

69.   And rehearse to them (some-thing of) Abraham's story.

70.   Behold, he said to his father and his people: "What do you worship?"

71.   They said: "We worship idols, and we remain constantly in attendance on them."

72.   He said: "Do they listen to you when you call (on them),

73.   Or they do you good or harm?"

74.   They said: "Nay, but we found our fathers doing thus (what we do)."

75.   He said: "Do you then see whom you have been worship-ping,-

76.   "You and your fathers before you?-

77.   "For they are enemies to me; not so the Lord and Cherisher of the Worlds;

78.   "Who created me, and it is He Who guides me;

79.   "Who gives me food and drink,

80.   "And when I am ill, it is He Who cures me;

81.   "Who will cause me to die, and then to live (again);

82.   "And who, I hope, will forgive me my faults on the day of Judgment.

83.   "O my Lord! bestow wisdom on me, and join me with the righteous;

84.   "Grant me honourable mention on the tongue of truth among the latest (generations);

85.   "Make me one of the inheri-tors of the Garden of Bliss;

86.   "Forgive my father, for that he is among those astray;

87.   "And let me not be in disgrace on the Day when (men) will be raised up;-

88.   "The Day whereon neither wealth nor sons will avail,

89.   "But only he (will prosper) that brings to Allah a sound heart;

90.   "To the righteous, the Garden will be brought near,

91.   "And to those straying in Evil, the Fire will be placed in full view;

92.   "And it shall be said to them: 'Where are the (gods) you worshipped-

93.   "'Besides Allah? Can they help you or help themselves?'

94.   "Then they will be thrown headlong into the (Fire),- they and

those straying in Evil,

95. "And the whole hosts of Iblis together.

96. "They will say there in their mutual bickerings[6]:

97. "'By Allah, we were truly in an error manifest,-

98. "'When we held you as equals with the Lord of the Worlds;

99. "'And our seducers[7] were only those who were steeped in guilt.

100. "Now, then, we have none to intercede (for us),

101. "Nor a single friend to feel (for us).

102. "Now if we only had a chance of return, we shall truly be of those who believe!"

103. Verily in this is a Sign but most of them do not believe.

104. And verily your Lord is He, the Exalted in Might, Most Merciful.

105. The people of Noah rejected the Messengers.

106. Behold, their brother Noah said to them: "Will you not fear (Allah)?

107. "I am to you a Messenger worthy of all trust:

108. "So fear Allah, and obey me.

109. "No reward do I ask of you for it: my reward is only from the Lord of the Worlds:

110. "So fear Allah, and obey me."

111. They said: "Shall we believe in you when it is the meanest[11] that follow you?"

112. He said: "And what do I know as to what they do?

113. "Their account is only with my Lord, if you could (but) understand.

114. "I am not one to drive away those who believe.

115. "I am sent only to warn plainly in public."

116. They said: "If you desist not, O Noah! you shall be stoned (to death)."

117. He said: "O my Lord! truly my people have rejected me.

118. "You judge, then, between me and them openly, and deliver me and those of the Believers who are with me."

---

6. Quarter, wranglings   7.   Tempters
8. People of low classes

119.   So We delivered him and those with him, in the Ark filled (with all creatures).

120.   Thereafter We drowned those who remained behind.

121.   Verily in this is a Sign: but most of them do not believe.

122.   And verily your Lord is He, the Exalted in Might, Most Merciful.

123.   The 'Ad (people) rejected the Messengers.

124.   Behold, their brother Hud said to them: "Will you not fear (Allah)?

125.   "I am to you a Messenger worthy of all trust:

126.   "So fear Allah and obey me.

127.   "No reward do I ask of you for it: my reward is only from the Lord of the Worlds.

128.   "Do you build a landmark on every high place to amuse yourselves?

129.   "And do you get for yourselves fine buildings in the hope of living therein (for ever)?

130.   "And when you strike, you strike like tyrants.

131.   "Now fear Allah, and obey me.

132.   "Yes, fear Him Who has bestowed on you freely all that you know.

133.   "Freely has He bestowed on you cattle and sons,-

134.   "And Gardens and Springs.

135.   "Truly I fear for you the Penalty of a Great Day."

136.   They said: "It is the same to us whether you admonish[9] us or be not among (our) admo-nishers!

137.   "This is no other than a customary device of the ancients,

138.   "And we are not the ones to receive Pains and Penalties!"

139.   So they rejected him, and We destroyed them. Verily in this is a Sign: but most of them do not believe.

140.   And verily your Lord is He, the Exalted in Might, Most Merciful.

141.   The Thamud (people) rejected the Messengers.

---

9.   Warn

142.   Behold, their brother Salih said to them: "Will you not fear (Allah)?

143.   "I am to you a Messenger worthy of all trust.

144.   "So fear Allah, and obey me.

145.   "No reward do I ask of you for it: my reward is only from the Lord of the Worlds.

146.   "Will you be left secure, in (the enjoyment of) all that you have here?-

147.   "Gardens and Springs,

148.   "And corn-fields and date-palms with spathes[10] near breaking (with the weight of fruit)?

149.   "And you carve houses out of (rocky) mountains with great skill.

150.   "But fear Allah and obey me;

151.   "And do not follow the bidding of those who are extra-vagant,-

152.   "Who make mischief in the land, and do not mend (their ways)."

153.   They said: "You are only one of those bewitched!

154.   "You are no more than a mortal like us: then bring us a Sign, if you tell the truth!"

155.   He said: "Here is a she-camel: she has a right of watering, and you have a right of watering, (severally) on a day appointed.

156.   "Do not touch her with harm, lest the Penalty of a Great Day seize you."

157.   But they hamstrung[11] her: then they became full of regrets.

158.   But the Penalty seized them. Verily in this is a Sign: but most of them do not believe.

159.   And verily your Lord is He, the Exalted in Might, Most Merciful.

160.   The people of Lut rejected the Messengers.

161.   Behold, their brother Lut said to them: "Will you not fear (Allah)?

162.   "I am to you a Messenger worthy of all trust.

163.   "So fear Allah and obey me.

---

10.   Clusters   11.   Companions

164. "No reward do I ask of you for it: my reward is only from the Lord of the Worlds.
165. "Of all the creatures in the world, will you approach males,
166. "And leave those whom Allah has created for you to be your mates? Nay, you are a people transgressing (all limits)!"
167. They said: "If you do not desist, O Lut! you will assuredly be cast out!"
168. He said: "I do detest your doings."
169. "O my Lord! deliver me and my family from such things as they do!"
170. So We delivered him and his family,- all
171. Except an old woman who lingered[12] behind.
172. But the rest We destroyed utterly.
173. We rained down on them a shower (of brimstone): and evil was the shower on those who were admonished (but heeded not)!
174. Verily in this is a Sign: but most of them do not believe.
175. And verily your Lord is He, the Exalted in Might, Most Merciful.
176. The Companions of the Wood rejected the Messengers.
177. Behold, Shu'aib said to them: "Will you not fear (Allah)?
178. "I am to you a Messenger worthy of all trust.
179. "So fear Allah and obey me.
180. "No reward do I ask of you for it: my reward is only from the Lord of the Worlds.
181. "Give just measure, and cause no loss (to others by fraud).
182. "And weigh with scales true and upright.
183. "And do not withhold things justly due to men, nor do evil in the land, working mis-chief.
184. "And fear Him Who created you and (Who created) the generations before (you)"
185. They said: "You are only one of those bewitched!
186. "You are no more than a mortal like us, and indeed we think

---

12. Remained

you are a liar!

187. "Now cause a piece of the sky to fall on us, if you are truthful!"

188. He said: "My Lord knows best what you do."

189. But they rejected him. Then the punishment of a day of overshadowing gloom seized them, and that was the Penalty of a Great Day.

190. Verily in that is a Sign: but most of them do not believe.

191. And verily your Lord is He, the Exalted in Might, Most Merciful.

192. Verily this is a Revelation from the Lord of the Worlds:

193. With it came down the spirit of Faith and Truth-

194. To your heart and mind, that you may admonish.

195. In the perspicuous[13] Arabic tongue.

196. Without doubt it is (announced) in the mystic Books of former peoples.

197. Is it not a Sign to them that the Learned of the Children of Israel knew it (as true)?

198. Had We revealed it to any of the non-Arabs,

199. And had he recited it to them, they would not have believed in it.

200. Thus have We caused it to enter the hearts of the sinners.

201. They will not believe in it until they see the grievous Penalty;

202. But the (Penalty) will come to them of a sudden, while they perceive it not;

203. Then they will say: "Shall we be respited?"

204. Do they then ask for Our Penalty to be hastened on?

205. Do you see? If We do let them enjoy (this life) for a few years,

206. Yet there comes to them at length the (Punishment) which they were promised!

207. It will not profit them that they enjoyed (this life)!

208. Never did We destroy a town, but had its warners–

209. By way of reminder; and We are never unjust.

210. No evil ones have brought down this (Revelation):

---

13.   Clear, plain, easily understood

211. It would neither suit them nor would they be able (to produce it).

212. Indeed they have been removed far from even (a chance of) hearing it.

213. So do not call on any other god with Allah, or you will be among those under the Penalty.

214. And admonish your nearest kinsmen,

215. And lower your wing to the Believers who follow you.

216. Then if they disobey you, say: "I am free (of responsi-bility) for what you do!"

217. And put your trust on the Exalted in Might, the Merciful,

218. Who sees you standing forth (in prayer),

219. And your movements among those who prostrate themselves,

220. For it is He Who hears and knows all things.

221. Shall I inform you, (O people!), on whom it is that the evil ones descend?

222. They descend on every lying, wicked person,

223. (Into whose ears) they pour hearsay[14] vanities[15], and most of them are liars.

224. And the Poets,- it is those straying in Evil, who follow them:

225. Don't you see that they wan-der distracted in every valley?-

226. And that they say what they do not practise?-

227. Except those who believe, work righteousness, engage much in the remembrance of Allah, and defend themselves only after they are unjustly attacked. And soon will the unjust assailants know what vicissitudes[16] their affairs will take!

---

14. Gossip   15. Useless things

16. Change of circumstances

SURAH—27

SURAH AN-NAML
(INTRODUCTION)

This Surah is cognate in subject to the one preceding it and the two following it. Its chronological place is also in the same group of four.

Here there is much mystic symbolism. Wonders in the physical world are types of greater wonders in the spiritual world. The Fire, the White Hand and the Rod, in the story of Moses; the speech of birds, the crowds of Jinns and men pitted against a humble ant, and the Hoopoe and the Queen of Sheba, in Solomon's story; the defeat of the plot of the nine wicked men in the story of Salih, and the crime of sin with open eyes in the story of Lot;— lead up to the lessons of true and false worship and the miracles of Allah's grace and revelation.

SURAH AL-NAML (THE ANTS)

In the name of Allah, Most Gracious, Most Merciful.

1.   Ta. Seen. These are verses of the Qur'an,-a Book that makes (things) clear;

2.   A Guide and Glad Tidings for the Believers,-

3.   Those who establish regular prayers and give in regular charity, and also have (full) assurance of the Hereafter.

4.   As to those who do not believe in the Hereafter, We have made their deeds pleasing in their eyes; and so they wander about in distraction.

5.   Such are they for whom a grievous Penalty is (waiting); and in the Hereafter theirs will be the greatest loss.

6.   As to you, the Qur'an is bestowed upon you from the presence of One Who is Wise and All-knowing.

7.   Behold! Moses said to his family: "I perceive a fire; soon will I bring you from there some information, or I will bring you a burning brand to light our fuel, that you may warm yourselves.

8.   But when he came to the (fire), a voice was heard: "Blessed are those in the fire and those around: and Glory to Allah, the Lord of the worlds.

9.   "O Moses! Verily, I am Allah, the Exalted in Might, the Wise!.

10. "Now you throw your rod!" But when he saw it moving (of its own accord)as if it had been a snake, he turned back in retreat, and retraced not his steps: "O Moses!" (it was said), "Fear not: truly, in My presence, those called as Messengers have no fear,-

11. "But if any have done wrong and have thereafter substituted good to take the place of evil, truly, I am Oft-Forgiving, Most Merciful.

12. "Now put your hand into your bosom, and it will come forth white without stain (or harm): (these are) among the nine Signs (you will take) to Pharaoh and his people: for they are a people rebellious in trans-gression."

13. But when Our Signs came to them, that should have opened their eyes, they said: "This is sorcery manifest!"

14. And they rejected those Signs in iniquity and arrogance, though their souls were convinced thereof: so see what was the end of those who acted corruptly!

15. We gave (in the past) knowledge to David and Solomon: and they both said: "Praise be to Allah, Who has favoured us above many of His servants who believe!"

16. And Solomon was David's heir. He said: "O you people! we have been taught the speech of birds, and on us has been bestowed (a little) of all things: this is indeed Grace manifest (from Allah.)"

17. And before Solomon were marshalled[1] his hosts[2],- of Jinns and men and birds, and they were all kept in order and ranks.

18. At length, when they came to a (lowly) valley of ants, one of the ants said: "O you ants, get into your habitations, lest Solomon and his hosts crush you (under foot) without knowing it."

19. So he smiled, amused at her speech; and he said: "O my Lord! so order me that I may be grateful for Your favours, which You have bestowed on me and on my parents, and that I may work the righteousness that will please You: and admit me, by Your

---

1. Gathered   2. Armies

Grace, to the ranks of Your Righteous Servants."

20.   And he took a muster[3] of the Birds; and he said: "Why is it I do not see the Hoopoe? Or is he among the absentees?

21.   "I will certainly punish him with a severe penalty, or execute him, unless he brings me a clear reason (for absence)."

22.   But the Hoopoe did not tarry far: he (came up and) said: "I have compassed (territory) which you have not compassed, and I have come to you from Saba with true tidings[4] true.

23.   "I found (there) a woman ruling over them and provided with every requisite[5]; and she has a magnificent throne.

24.   "I found her and her people worshipping the sun besides Allah: Satan has made their deeds seem pleasing in their eyes, and has kept them away from the Path,- so they receive no guidance,-

25.   "(Kept them away from the Path), that they should not worship Allah, Who brings to light what is hidden in the heavens and the earth, and knows what you hide and what you reveal.

26.   "Allah!- there is no god but He!- Lord of the Throne Supreme!"

27.   (Solomon) said: "Soon shall we see whether you have told the truth or lied!

28.   "You go, with this letter of mine, and deliver it to them: then draw back from them, and (wait to) see what answer they return".

29.   (The queen) said: "You chiefs! here is delivered to me - a letter worthy of respect.

30.   "It is from Solomon, and is (as follows): 'In the name of Allah, Most Gracious, Most Merciful:

31.   "'You be not arrogant against me, but come to me in sub-mission (to the true Religion).'

32.   She said: "You chiefs! Advise me in (this) my affair: no affair have I decided except in your presence."

33.   They said: "We are endued[6] with strength, and given to

---

3.   Inspection, to check numbers   4.   News
5.   thing needed for success   6.   Possess

vehement[7] war: but the command is with you; so consider what you will command."

34. She said: "Kings, when they enter a country, despoil[8] it, and make the noblest of its people its meanest, thus do they behave.

35. "But I am going to send him a present, and (wait) to see with what (answer) (my) ambassadors return."

36. Now when (the embassy) came to Solomon, he said: "Will you give me abundance in wealth? But that which Allah has given me is better than that which He has given you! Nay it is you who rejoice in your gift!

37. "Go back to them, and be sure we shall come to them with such hosts as they will never be able to meet: we shall expel them from there in disgrace, and they will feel humbled (indeed)."

38. He said (to his own men): "You Chiefs! which of you can bring me her throne before they come to me in submission?"

39. An 'Ifrit[9], of the Jinns said: "I will bring it to you before you rise from your Council: indeed I have full strength for the purpose, and may be trusted."

40. Said one who had know-ledge of the Book: "I will bring it to you within the twinkling of an eye!" Then when (Solomon) saw it placed firmly before him, he said: "This is by the Grace of my Lord!- to test me whether I am grateful or ungrateful! and if any is grateful, truly his gratitude is (a gain) for his own soul; but if any is ungrateful, truly my Lord is Free of all Needs, Supreme in Honour !"

41. He said: "Transform her throne out of all recognition by her; let us see whether she is guided (to the truth) or is one of those who receive no guidance."

42. So when she arrived, she was asked, "Is this your throne?" She said, "It was just like this; and knowledge was bestowed on us in advance of this, and we have submitted to Allah (in Islam)."

---

7. Fierce
8. Plinder
9. A huge, powerful jinn

43.   And he diverted her from the worship of others besides Allah:
       for she was (sprung) of a people that had no faith.

44.   She was asked to enter the lofty Palace: but when she saw it,
       she thought it was a lake of water, and she (tucked up her skirts),
       uncovering her legs. He said: "This is but a palace paved
       smooth with slabs of glass." She said: "O my Lord! I have
       indeed wronged my soul: I do (now) submit (in Islam), with
       Solomon, to the Lord of the Worlds."

45.   We sent (aforetime), to the Thamud, their brother Salih, saying,
       "Serve Allah": But behold, they became two factions
       quarrelling with each other.

46.   He said: "O my people! why do you ask to hasten on the evil in
       preference to the good? If only you ask Allah for forgiveness,
       you may hope to receive mercy.

47.   They said: "Ill omen[11] do we augur[12] from you and those that
       are with you". He said: "Your ill omen is with Allah; yes, you
       are a people under trial."

48.   There were in the city nine men of a family, who made mischief
       in the land, and would not reform.

49.   They said: "Swear a mutual oath by Allah that we shall make a
       secret night attack on him and his people, and that we shall
       then say to his heir (when he seeks vengeance): "We were not
       present at the slaughter of his people, and we are positively
       telling the truth."'

50.   They plotted and planned, but We too planned, even while
       they perceived it not.

51.   Then see what was the end of their plot!- this, that We destroyed
       them and their people, all (of them).

52.   Now such were their houses, - in utter ruin, - because they
       practised wrong-doing. Verily in this is a Sign for people of
       knowledge.

53.   And We saved those who believed and practised righteousness.

---

10.   Groups   11.   Sign, forewarning
12.   Predict, foretell

54. (We also sent) Lut (as a Messenger): behold, he said to his people, "Do you do what is shameful though you see (its iniquity[13])?

55. Would you really app-roach men in your lusts rather than women? Nay, you are a people (grossly) ignorant!

56. But his people gave no other answer but this: they said, "Drive out the followers of Lut from your city: these are indeed men who want to be clean and pure!"

57. But We saved him and his family, except his wife; her We destined[14] to be of those who lagged behind.

58. And We rained down on them a shower (of brimstone): and evil was the shower on those who were admonished (but heeded not)!

59. Say: Praise be to Allah, and Peace on His servants whom He has chosen (for His Message). (Who) is better?- Allah or the false gods they associate (with Him)?

60. Or, who has created the heavens and the earth, and who sends you down rain from the sky? Yes, with it We cause to grow well-planted orchards[15] full of beauty and delight: it is not in your power to cause the growth of the trees in them. (Can there be another) god besides Allah? Nay, they are a people who swerve from justice.

61. Or, who has made the earth firm to live in; made rivers in its midst; set thereon mountains immovable; and made a separating bar between the two bodies of flowing water? (can there be another) god besides Allah? Nay, most of them do not know.

62. Or, who listens to the (soul) distressed when it calls on Him, and Who relieves its suffering, and makes you (mankind) inheritors of the earth? (Can there be another) god besides Allah? Little it is that you heed.

63. Or, who guides you through the depths of darkness on land and sea, and who sends the winds as heralds of glad tidings,

---

13. Wickedness
14. Decree, fated
15. Enclosure with fruit trees

going before His Mercy? (Can there be another) god besides Allah?- High is Allah above what they associate with Him!

64. Or, who originates Creation, then repeats it, and who gives you sustenance from heaven and earth? (Can there be another) god besides Allah? Say, "Bring forth your argument, if you are telling the truth!"

65. Say: None in the heavens or on earth, except Allah, knows what is hidden: nor can they perceive when they shall be raised up (for Judgment).

66. Still less can their knowledge comprehend[16] the Hereafter; nay, they are in doubt and uncertainty thereanent;[17] nay, they are blind thereto[18].

67. The Unbelievers say: "What! when we become dust,- we and our fathers,- shall we really be raised (from the dead)?

68. "It is true we were pro-mised this,- we and our fathers before (us): these are nothing but tales of the ancients."

69. Say: "You go through the earth and see what has been the end of those guilty (of sin)."

70. But grieve not over them, nor distress yourself because of their plots.

71. They also say: "When will this promise (come to pass)? (Say) if you are truthful."

72. Say: "It may be that some of the events which you wish to hasten on may be (close) in your pursuit!"

73. But verily your Lord is full of grace to mankind: yet most of them are ungrateful.

74. And verily your Lord knows all that their hearts hide, as well as all that they reveal.

75. Nor is there anything of the Unseen, in heaven or earth, but is (recorded) in a clear record.

76. Verily this Qur'an ex-plains to the Children of Israel most of the matters in which they disagree.

77. And it certainly is a Guide and a Mercy to those who believe.

---

16. Grasp   17. About that matter
18. To it.

78. Verily your Lord will decide between them by His Decree: and He is Exalted in Might, All-Knowing.

79. So put your trust in Allah: for you are on (the path of) manifest Truth.

80. Truly you can not cause the dead to listen, nor can you cause the deaf to hear the call, (especially) when they turn back in retreat.

81. Nor can you be a guide to the Blind, (to prevent them) from straying: only those will you get to listen who believe in Our Signs, and they will bow in Islam.

82. And when the Word is fulfilled against them (the unjust), We shall produce from the earth a Beast to (face) them: he will speak to them, for that mankind did not believe with assurance in Our Signs.

83. One Day We shall gather together from every people a troop of those who reject Our Signs, and they shall be kept in ranks,-

84. Until, when they come (before the Judgment-seat), (Allah) will say: "Did you reject My Signs, though you did not comprehend them in knowledge, or what was it you did?"

85. And the Word will be fulfilled against them, because of their wrong-doing, and they will be unable to speak (in plea[19]).

86. Do they not see that We have made the Night for them to rest in and the Day to give them light? Verily in this are Signs for any people that believe!

87. And the Day that the Trumpet will be sounded - then will be smitten[20] with terror those who are in the heavens, and those who are on earth, except such as Allah will please (to exempt): and all shall come to His (Presence) as beings conscious of their lowliness.

88. You see the mountains and think them firmly fixed: but they shall pass away as the clouds pass away: (such is) the artistry of Allah, Who disposes of all things in perfect order: for He is well acquainted with all that you do.

---

19. In defence   20. Stricken

89.   If any do good, good will (accrue) to them therefrom; and they
       will be secure from terror that Day.

90.   And if any do evil, their faces will be thrown headlong[21] into
       the Fire: "Do you receive a reward other than that which you
       have earned by your deeds?"

91.   For me, I have been commanded to serve the Lord of this City,
       Him Who has sanctified[22] it and to Whom (belong) all things:
       and I am commanded to be of those who bow in Islam to Allah's
       Will,-

92.   And to rehearse[23] the Qur'an: and if any accept guidance, they
       do it for the good of their own souls, and if any stray, say: "I
       am only a Warner".

93.   And say: "Praise be to Allah, Who will soon show you His
       Signs, so that you shall know them"; and your Lord is not
       unmindful of all that you do.

---

21.   Head foremost   22.   Blessed
23.   Recite

SURAH—28

SURAH AL-QASAS
(INTRODUCTION)

This Surah continues the subject of Revelation and its reception by those to whom it is sent. But it emphasises new points: how the recipient of inspiration is prepared for his high destiny, even in the growth of his ordinary life, and how the rejection of Allah's Message by groups of men or by individuals is caused by overweening arrogance or avarice. The plight of those who reject the Truth is contrasted with the rewards of the righteous.

With the possible exception of a few verses, it belongs to the late Makkan period, just preceding the Hijrat.

SURAH QASAS (THE NARRATION)

In the name of Allah, Most Gracious, Most Merciful.

1. Ta. Sin. Mim.

2. These are Verses of the Book that makes (things) clear.

3. We rehearse[1] to you some of the story of Moses and Pharaoh in Truth, for people who believe.

4. Truly Pharaoh elated[2] himself in the land and broke up its people into sections, depressing[3] a small group among them: their sons he slew, but he kept alive their females: for he was indeed a maker of mischief.

5. And We wished to be gracious to those who were being depressed in the land, to make them leaders (in Faith) and make them heirs,

6. To establish a firm place for them in the land, and to show Pharaoh, Haman, and their hosts, at their hands, the very things against which they were taking precautions.

7. So We sent this inspiration to the mother of Moses: "Suckle (your child), but when you have fears about him, cast him into the river, but fear not nor grieve: for We shall restore him to you, and We shall make him one of Our Messengers."

8. Then the people of Pharaoh picked him up (from the river): (it

---

1. Recount, relate   2.   Jubilant and arrogant
3. Oppressing

was intended) that (Moses) should be to them an adversary and a cause of sorrow: for Pharaoh and Haman and (all) their hosts were men of sin.

9. The wife of Pharaoh said: "(Here is) a joy of the eye, for me and for you: do not slay him. It may be that he will be of use to us, or we may adopt him as a son." And they did not perceive (what they were doing)!

10. But there came to be a void in the heart of the mother of Moses: she was going almost to disclose his (case), had We not strengthened her heart (with faith), so that she might remain a (firm) believer.

11. And she said to the sister of (Moses), "Follow him". So she (the sister) watched him in the character of a stranger. And they did not know.

12. And We ordained that he refused suck at first, until (his sister came up and) said: "Shall I point out to you the people of a house that will nourish and bring him up for you and be sincerely attached to him?"...

13. Thus We restored him to his mother, that her eye might be comforted, that she might not grieve, and that she might know that the promise of Allah is true: but most of them do not understand.

14. When he reached full age, and was firmly established (in life), We bestowed on him wis-dom and knowledge: for thus do We reward those who do good.

15. And he entered the City at a time when its people were not watching: and he found there two men fighting,- one of his own religion, and the other, of his foes. Now the man of his own religion appealed to him against his foe, and Moses struck him with his fist and made an end of him. He said: "This is a work of Evil (Satan): for he is an enemy that manifestly misleads!"

16. He prayed: "O my Lord! I have indeed wronged my soul! You then forgive me!" So (Allah) forgave him: for He is the Oft-Forgiving, Most Merciful.

17.   He said: "O my Lord! For that You have bestowed Your Grace
      on me, never shall I be a help to those who sin!"

18.   So he saw the morning in the City, looking about in a state of
      fear, when behold, the man who had, the day before, sought
      his help called aloud for his help (again). Moses said to him:"
      You are truly, it is clear, a quarrelsome fellow!"

19.   Then, when he decided to lay hold of the man who was an
      enemy to both of them, who was an enemy to both of them,
      that man said: "O Moses! is it your intention to slay me as you
      slew a man yesterday? Your intention is none other than to
      become a powerful violent man in the land, and not to be one
      who sets things right!"

20.   And there came a man, running, from the furthest end of the
      City. He said: "O Moses! the Chiefs are taking counsel together
      about you, to slay you: so you get away, for I do give you
      sincere advice."

21.   He therefore got away therefrom, looking about, in a state of
      fear. He prayed "O my Lord! save me from people given to
      wrong-doing."

22.   Then, when he turned his face towards (the land of) Madyan,
      he said: "I do hope that my Lord will show me the smooth and
      straight Path."

23.   And when he arrived at the watering (place) in Madyan, he
      found there a group of men watering (their flocks), and besides
      them he found two women who were keeping back (their
      flocks). He said: "What is the matter with you?" They said:
      "We can not water (our flocks) until the shepherds take back
      (their flocks): and our father is a very old man."

24.   So he watered (their flocks) for them; then he turned back to
      the shade, and said:"O my Lord! truly I am in (desperate) need
      of any good that You do send me!"

25.   Afterwards one of the (damsels[4]) came (back) to him, walking
      bashfully[5]. She said: "My father invites you that he may reward

---

4.   Young women   5.   Modestly, shyly

you for having watered (our flocks) for us." So when he came to him and narrated the story, he said: "you do not fear: (well) have you escaped from unjust people."

26. Said one of the (damsels): "O my (dear) father! engage him on wages: truly the best of men for you to employ is the (man) who is strong and trustworthy."

27. He said: "I intend to wed one of these my daughters to you, on condition that you serve me for eight years; but if you complete ten years, it will be (grace[6]) from you. But I intend not to place you under a difficulty: you will find me, indeed, if Allah wills, one of the righteous."

28. He said: "Be that (the agreement) between me and you: whichever of the two terms I fulfil, let there be no ill-will to me. Be Allah a Witness to what we say."

29. Now when Moses had fulfilled the term, and was travelling with his family, he perceived a fire in the direction of Mount Tur. He said to his family: "You tarry; I perceive a fire; I hope to bring you from there some information, or a burning firebrand[7], that you may warm yourselves."

30. But when he came to the (Fire), a voice was heard from the right bank of the valley, from a tree in hallowed[8] ground: "O Moses! Verily I am Allah, the Lord of the Worlds....

31. "Now you throw your rod!" but when he saw it moving (of its own accord) as if it had been a snake, he turned back in retreat, and did not retrace his steps: O Moses!" (It was said), "Draw near, and do not fear: for you are of those who are secure.

32. "Move your hand into your bosom, and it will come forth white without stain (or harm), and draw your hand close to your side (to guard) against fear. Those are the two credentials[9] from your Lord to Pharaoh and his Chiefs: for truly they are a people rebellious and wicked."

33. He said: "O my Lord! I have slain a man among them, and I fear lest they slay me.

---

6.   Favour   7.   Piece of burning wood
8.   Sacred   9.   Evidence or a clear proof

34. "And my brother Aaron - he is more eloquent in speech than I: so send him with me as a helper, to confirm (and streng-then) me: for I fear that they may accuse of falsehood."

35. He said: "We will cer-tainly strengthen your arm through your brother, and invest you both with authority, so they shall not be able to touch you: with Our Signs you shall triumph,- you two as well as those who follow you."

36. When Moses came to them with Our Clear Signs, they said: "This is nothing but sorcery faked[10] up: never did we hear the like among our fathers of old!"

37. Moses said: "My Lord knows best who it is that comes with guidance from Him and whose End will be best in the Hereafter: certain it is that the wrong-doers will not prosper."

38. Pharaoh said: "O Chiefs! no god do I know for you but myself: therefore, O Haman! light me a (klin[11] to bake bricks) out of clay, and build me a lofty palace, that I may mount up to the god of Moses: but as far as I am concerned, I think he (Moses) is a liar!"

39. And he was arrogant and insolent in the land, beyond reason,- he and his hosts: they thought that they would not have to return to Us!

40. So We seized him and his hosts, and We flung them into the sea: now behold what was the End of those who did wrong!

41. And We made them (but) leaders inviting to the Fire; and on the Day of Judgment no help shall they find.

42. In this world We made a curse to follow them and on the Day of Judgment they will be among the loathed (and despised).

43. We revealed to Moses the Book after We had destroyed the earlier generations, (to give) Insight to men, and Guidance and Mercy, that they might receive admonition.

44. You were not on the Western side when We decreed the Commission[12] to Moses, nor were you a witness (of those events).

---

10. Forged, artificial
11. Furnance or oven
12. Appointment as a Messenger

45. But We raised up (new) generations, and long were the ages that passed over them; but you were not a dweller among the people of Madyan, rehearsing Our Signs to them; but it is We Who send Messengers (with inspiration).

46. Nor were you at the side of (the Mountain of) Tur when We called (to Moses). Yet (you are sent) as a Mercy from your Lord, to give warning to a people to whom no warner had come before you: in order that they may receive admonition.

47. If (We had) not (sent you to the Quraish),- in case a calamity should seize them for (the deeds) that their hands have sent forth, they might say: "Our Lord! why did You not sent us a Messenger? We should then have followed Your Signs and been amongst those who believe!"

48. But (now), when the Truth has come to them from Ourse-lves, they say, "Why are not (Signs) sent to him, like those which were sent to Moses?" Do they not then reject (the Signs) which were formerly sent to Moses? They say: "Two kinds of sorcery, each assisting the other!" And they say: "For us, we reject all (such things)!"

49. Say: "Then you bring a Book from Allah, which is a better guide than either of them, that I may follow it! (do), if you are truthful!"

50. But if they hearken[13] not to you, know that they only follow their own lusts: and who is more astray than one who follow his own lusts, devoid of guidance from Allah? for Allah does not guide people given to wrong-doing.

51. Now We have caused the Word to reach them themselves, in order that they may receive admonition.

52. Those to whom We sent the Book before this,- they do believe in this (Revelation):

53. And when it is recited to them, they say: "We believe therein, for it is the Truth from our Lord: indeed we have been Muslims (bowing to Allah's Will) from before this.

---

13. Respond, listen

54. Twice will they be given their reward, for that they have persevered[14], that they avert Evil with Good, and that they spend (in charity) out of what We have given them.

55. And when they hear vain talk, they turn away therefrom and say: "To us our deeds, and to you yours; Peace be on you: we do not seek the ignorant."

56. It is true you will not be able to guide everyone whom you love; but Allah guides those whom He will and He knows best those who receive guidance.

57. They say: "If we were to follow the guidance with you, we should be snatched away from our land." Have We not established for them a secure sanctuary[15], to which are brought as tribute fruits of all kinds,- a provision from Ourselves? but most of them do not understand.

58. And how many popu-lations We destroyed, which exulted[16] in their life (of ease and plenty)! now those habitations of theirs, after them, are deserted,- all but a (miserable) few! and We are their heirs!

59. Nor was your Lord the one to destroy a population until He had sent to its centre a Messen-ger, rehearsing to them Our Signs; nor are We going to destroy a population except when its members practise iniquity[17].

60. The (material) things which you are given are but the conveniences[18] of this life and the glitter thereof; but that which is with Allah is better and more enduring: will you not then be wise?

61. Are (these two) alike?- one to whom We have made a goodly promise, and who is going to reach its (fulfilment), and one to whom We have given the good things of this life, but who, on the Day of Judgment,is to be among those brought up (for punishment)?

62. That Day (Allah) will call to them, and say "Where are My

---

14. Remained constant, steadfast
15. Haven, refuge
16. Behaved arrogantly
17. Wickedness, wrong
18. Comforts

'partners'?- whom you imagined (to be such)?"

63.   Those against whom the charge will be proved, will say: "Our Lord! These are the ones whom we led astray: we led them astray, as we were astray ourselves: we free ourselves (from them) in Your presence: it was not us they worshipped."

64.   It will be said (to them): "Call upon your 'partners' (for help)" :they will call upon them, but they will not listen to them; and they will see the Penalty (before them); (how they will wish) 'if only they had been open to guidance!'

65.   That Day (Allah) will call to them, and say: "What was the answer you gave to the Messen-gers?"

66.   Then the (whole) story that Day will seem obscure[19] to them (like light to the blind) and they will not be able (even) to question each other.

67.   But any that (in this life) had repented, believed, and worked righteousness, haply he shall be one of the successful.

68.   Your Lord creates and chooses as He pleases: no choice have they (in the matter): Glory to Allah! and far is He above the partners they ascribe[20] (to Him)!

69.   And your Lord knows all that their hearts conceal and all that they reveal.

70.   And He is Allah: there is no god but He. To Him be praise, at the first and at the last: for Him is the Command, and to Him you shall (all) be brought back.

71.   Say, do you see? If Allah were to make the night perpetual[21] over you to the Day of Judgment, what god is there other than Allah, Who can give you light[22]? Will you not then hearken?

72.   Say, do you see? If Allah were to make the Day perpetual over you to the Day of Judgment, what god is there other than Allah, Who can give you a Night in which you can rest? Will you not then see?

73.   It is out of His Mercy that He has made for you Night and Day,- that you may rest therein, and that you may seek of His

---

19.   Dim, unfamiliar   20.   Assign
21.   Eternal, constant   22.   Information and knowledge

Grace;- and in order that you may be grateful.

74. The Day that He will call on them, He will say: "Where are My 'partners'?- whom you imagined (to be such)?"

75. And from each people We shall draw a witness, and We shall say: "Produce your Proof": then they shall know that the Truth is in Allah (alone), and the (lies) which they invented will leave them in lurch[23].

76. Qarun was doubtless, of the people of Moses; but he acted insolently[24] towards them: such were the treasures We had bestowed on him that their very keys would have been a burden to a body of strong men. Behold, his people said to him: "Do not exult[25], for Allah does not love those who exult (in riches).

77. "But seek, with the (wealth) which Allah has bestowed on you, the Home of the Hereafter, nor forget your portion in this world: but you do good, as Allah has been good to you, and do not seek (occasions for) mischief in the land: for Allah does not love those who do mischief."

78. He said: "This has been given to me because of a certain knowledge which I have." Did he not know that Allah had destroyed, before him, (whole) generations,- which were superior to him in strength and greater in the amount (of riches) they had collected? but the wicked are not called (imme-diately) to account for their sins.

79. So he went forth among his people in the (pride of his worldly) glitter. Said those whose aim is the Life of this World: "Oh! that we had the like of what Qarun has got! For he is truly a lord of mighty good fortune!"

80. But those who had been granted (true) knowledge said: "Alas for you! The reward of Allah (in the Hereafter) is best for those who believe and work righteousness: but this none shall attain, save those who steadfastly persevere (in good)."

81. Then We caused the earth to swallow up him and his house;

---

23. A most difficult position   24. Rudely, arrogantly

25. Be not proud

and he had not (the least little) party to help him against Allah,
nor could he defend himself.

82.   And those who had envied his position the day before began
to say on the morrow: "Ah! it is indeed Allah Who enlarges
the provision or restricts it, to any of His servants He pleases!
Had it not been that Allah was gracious to us, He could have
caused the earth to swallow us up! Ah! those who reject Allah
will assuredly never prosper."

83.   That Home of the Here-after We shall give to those who do
not intend high-handedness or mischief on earth: and the end
is (best) for the righteous.

84.   If any does good, the reward to him is better than his deed; but
if any does evil, the doers of evil are only punished (to the
extent) of their deeds.

85.   Verily He Who ordained the Qur'an for you, will bring you
back to the Place of Return. Say: "My Lord knows best who it
is that brings true guidance, and who is in manifest error."

86.   And you had not expected that the Book would be sent to you
except as a Mercy from your Lord: therefore you do not lend
support in any way to those who reject (Allah's Message).

87.   And let nothing keep you back from the Signs of Allah after
they have been revealed to you: and invite (men) to your Lord,
and be not of the company of those who join gods with Allah.

88.   And do not call, besides Allah, on another god. There is no
god but He. Everything (that exists) will perish except His Own
Face. To Him belongs the Command, and to Him will you (all)
be brought back.

SURAH—29

SURAH AL-ANKABUT

(INTRODUCTION)

This Surah is the last of the series begun with S. 17 in which the growth of the spiritual man as an individual is considered, especially illustrated by the way in which the great Apostles were prepared for their work and received their mission, and the nature of Revelation in relation to the environments in which it was promulgated. (See Introduction to S. 17). It also closes the sub-series beginning with S. 26 which is concerned with the spiritual Light, and the reactions to it at certain periods of spiritual history. (See Introduction S. 26).

The last Surah closed with a reference to the doctrine of the *Ma'ad*, or final Return of man to Allah. This theme is further developed here, and as it is continued in the subsequent three Surahs all bearing the Abbreviated Letters A.L.M., it forms a connecting link between the present series and those three Surahs.

In particular, emphasis is laid here on the necessity of linking actual conduct with the reception of Allah's revelation, and reference is again made to the stories of Noah, Abraham, and Lot among the Apostles, and the stories of Midian, Ad, Thamud, and Pharaoh among the rejecters of Allah's Message. This world's life is contrasted with the real Life of the Hereafter.

Chronologically, the main Surah belongs to the late Middle Makkan period, but the chronology has no significance except as showing how clearly the vision of the Future was revealed long before the Hijrat, to the struggling Brotherhood of Islam.

SURAH ANKABUT (THE SPIDER)

In the name of Allah, Most Gracious, Most Merciful.

1. Alif- Lam- Mim.
2. Do men think that they will be left alone on saying, "We believe", and that they will not be tested?
3. We tested those before them, and Allah will certainly know those who are true from those who are false.
4. Do those who practise evil think that they will get the better of Us? Evil is their judgment!

5.   For those whose hopes are in the meeting with Allah (in the Hereafter, let them strive); for the term (appointed) by Allah is surely coming and He hears and knows (all things).

6.   And if any strive (with might and main), they do so for their own souls: for Allah is free of all needs from all creation.

7.   Those who believe and work righteous deeds,- from them We shall blot out all evil (that may be) in them, and We shall reward them according to the best of their deeds.

8.   We have enjoined on man kindness to parents: but if they (either of them) strive (to force) you to join with Me (in worship) anything of which you have no knowledge, do not obey them. You have (all) to return to Me, and I will tell you (the truth) of all that you did.

9.   And those who believe and work righteous deeds,- them We shall admit to the company of the Righteous.

10. Then there are among men such as say, "We believe in Allah"; but when they suffer affliction[1] in (the cause of) Allah, they treat men's oppression as if it were the Wrath of Allah! And if help comes (to you) from your Lord, they are sure to say, "We have (always) been with you!" Does not Allah know best all that is in the hearts of all creation?

11. And Allah most certainly knows those who believe, and as certainly those who are Hypocrites.

12. And the Unbelievers say to those who believe: "Follow our path, and we will bear (the consequences) of your faults." Never in the least will they bear their faults: in fact they are liars!

13. They will bear their own burdens, and (other) burdens along with their own, and on the Day of Judgment they will be called to account for their falsehoods.

14. We (once) sent Noah to his people, and he tarried[2] among them a thousand years less fifty: but the Deluge[3] overwhelmed[4] them while they (persisted in) sin.

---

1.   Hardship, injury   2.   Lived
3.   Flood   4.   Drowned

15. But We saved him and the companions of the Ark, and We made the (Ark) a Sign for all peoples!

16. And (We also saved) Abraham: behold, he said to his people, "Serve Allah and fear Him: that will be best for you- If you understand!

17. "For you worship idols besides Allah, and you invent falsehood. The things that you worship besides Allah have no power to give you sustenance: then you seek sustenance from Allah, serve Him, and be grateful to Him: to Him will be your return.

18. "And if you reject (the Message), so did generations before you: and the duty of the Messenger is only to preach publicly (and clearly)."

19. Don't they see how Allah originates creation, then repeats it: truly that is easy for Allah.

20. Say: "Travel through the earth and see how Allah originated creation; so will Allah produce a later creation: for Allah has power over all things.

21. "He punishes whom He pleases, and He grants Mercy to whom He pleases, and towards Him are you turned.

22. "Not on earth nor in heaven will you be able (fleeing) to frustrate (His Plan), nor have you, besides Allah, any protector or helper."

23. Those who reject the Signs of Allah and the Meeting with Him (in the Hereafter),- it is they who shall despair of My Mercy: it is they who will (suffer) a most grievous Penalty.

24. So nothing was the answer of (Abraham's) people except that they said: "Slay him or burn him." But Allah saved him from the Fire. Verily in this are Signs for people who believe.

25. And he said: "For you, you have taken (for worship) idols besides Allah, out of mutual love and regard between yourselves in this life; but on the Day of Judgment you shall disown each other and curse each other: and your abode will be the Fire, and you shall have none to help."

26. But Lut had faith in Him: he said: "I will leave home for the sake of my Lord: for He is Exalted in Might, and Wise."

27.   And We gave (Abraham) Isaac and Jacob, and ordained among his progeny[5] Prophethood and Revelation, and We granted him his reward in this life; and he will be in the Hereafter (of the company) of the Righteous.

28.   And (remember) Lut: behold, he said to his people: "You commit lewdness[6], such as no people in Creation (ever) committed before you.

29.   "Do you indeed approach men, and cut off the highway?- and practise wickedness (even) in your councils?" But his people gave no answer but this: they said: "Bring us the Wrath of Allah if you tell the truth."

30.   He said: "O my Lord! You help me against people who do mischief!"

31.   When Our Messengers came to Abraham with the good news, they said: "We are indeed going to destroy the people of this township: for truly they are (addicted to) crime."

32.   He said: "But there is Lut there." They said: "Well do we know who is there : we will certainly save him and his following, except his wife: she is of those who lag behind!"

33.   And when Our Messen-gers came to Lut, he was grieved on their account, and felt himself powerless (to protect) them: but they said: "Do not fear, nor grieve: we are (here) to save you and your following, except your wife: she is of those who lag behind.

34.   "For we are going to bring down on the people of this township a Punishment from heaven, because they have been wickedly rebellious."

35.   And We have left thereof an evident Sign, for any people who (care to) understand.

36.   To the Madyan (people) (We sent) their brother Shu'aib. Then he said: "O my people! serve Allah, and fear the Last Day: nor commit evil on the earth, with intent to do mischief."

37.   But they rejected him: then the mighty Blast seized them, and

---

5.   Offspring   6.   Indecency, obscenity

they lay prostrate in their homes by the morning.

38.	(Remember also) the 'Ad and the Thamud (people): clearly will appear to you from (the traces) of their buildings (their fate): the Evil One made their deeds alluring to them, and kept them back from the Path, though they were gifted with Intelligence and Skill.

39.	(Remember also) Qarun, Pharaoh, and Haman: there came to them Moses with Clear Signs, but they behaved with insolence on the earth; yet they could not overreach[7] (Us).

40.	Each one of them We seized for his crime: of them, against some We sent a violent tornado (with showers of stones); some were caught by a (mighty) Blast; some We caused the earth to swallow up; and some We drowned (in the waters): It was not Allah Who injured (or oppressed) them: they injured (and oppressed) their own souls.

41.	The parable of those who take protectors other than Allah is that of the Spider, who builds (to itself) a house; but truly the flimsiest[8] of houses is the Spider's house;- if they but knew.

42.	Verily Allah knows of (every thing) whatever that they call upon besides Him: and He is Exalted (in power), Wise.

43.	And such are the Parables We set forth for mankind, but only those understand them who have knowledge.

44.	Allah created the heavens and the earth in true (propor-tions): verily in that is a Sign for those who believe.

45.	Recite what is sent of the Book by inspiration to you,and establish regular Prayer: for Prayer restrains from shameful and unjust deeds; and remem-brance of Allah is the greatest (thing in life) without doubt. And Allah knows the (deeds) that you do.

46.	And you do not dispute with the People of the Book, except with means better (than mere disputation), unless it be with those of them who inflict wrong (and injury): but say, "We believe in the Revelation which has come down to us and in

---

7.	Outwit, outstrip			8.	Weakest

that which came down to you; our God and your God is One; and it is to Him we bow (in Islam)."

47. And thus (it is) that We have sent down the Book to you. So the People of the Book believe therein, as also do some of these (pagan Arabs): and none but Unbelie-vers reject Our Signs.

48. And you were not (able) to recite a Book before this (Book came), nor are you (able) to transcribe[9] it with your right hand: in that case, indeed, would the talkers of vanities[10] have doubted.

49. Nay, here are Signs self-evident in the hearts of those endowed with knowledge: and none but the unjust reject Our Signs.

50. Yet they say: "Why are not Signs sent down to him from his Lord?" Say: "The Signs are in-deed with Allah: and I am indeed a clear Warner."

51. And is it not enough for them that We have sent down to you the Book which is rehearsed to them? Verily, in it is Mercy and a Reminder to those who believe.

52. Say: "Enough is Allah for a Witness between me and you: He knows what is in the heavens and on earth. And it is those who believe in vanities and reject Allah, that will perish (in the end).

53. They ask you to hasten on the Punishment (for them): had it not been for a term (of respite) appointed, the Punishment would certainly have come to them: and it will certainly reach them,- of a sudden, while they perceive not!

54. They ask you to hasten on the Punishment: but, of a surety, Hell will encompass the Rejec-ters of Faith!-

55. On the Day that the Punishment shall cover them from above them and from below them, and (a Voice) shall say: "You taste (the fruits) of your deeds!"

56. O My servants who be-lieve! Truly, spacious is My Earth: therefore you serve Me - (and Me alone)!

57. Every soul shall have a taste of death: in the end to Us you

---

9.   Write down   10.   Unrealities, futilities

shall be brought back.

58. But those who believe and work deeds of righteousness - to them We shall give a Home in Heaven,-lofty mansions beneath which flow rivers,- to dwell therein for ever;- an excellent reward for those who do (good)!-

59. Those who persevere in patience, and put their trust in their Lord and Cherisher.

60. How many are the crea-tures that do not carry their own sustenance? It is Allah Who feeds (both) them and you: for He hears and knows (all things).

61. If indeed you ask them who has created the heavens and the earth and subjected the sun and the moon (to His Law), they will certainly reply, "Allah". How are they then deluded away (from the truth)?

62. Allah enlarges the suste-nance (which He gives) to whichever of His servants He pleases; and He (similarly) grants by (strict) measure, (as He pleases): for Allah has full knowledge of all things.

63. And if indeed you ask them Who it is that sends down rain from the sky, and gives life therewith to the earth after its death, they will certainly reply, "Allah!" Say, "Praise be to Allah!" But most of them do not understand.

64. What is the life of this world but amusement and play? But verily the Home in the Hereafter,- that is life indeed, if they but knew.

65. Now, if they embark on a boat, they call on Allah, making their devotion sincerely (and exclusively) to Him; but when He has delivered them safely to (dry) land, behold, they give a share (of their worship to others)!-

66. Disdaining[11] ungratefully Our gifts, and giving them-selves up to (worldly) enjoyment! But soon will they know.

67. Do they not then see that We have made a sanctuary[12] secure, and that men are being snatched away from all around them?

---

11. Rejecting contemptuously   12. A sacred place, place of refuge

Then, do they believe in that which is vain, and reject the Grace of Allah?

68.   And who does more wrong than he who invents a lie against Allah or rejects the Truth when it reaches him? Is there not a home in Hell for those who reject Faith?

69.   And those who strive in Our (Cause),- We will certainly guide them to Our Paths: for verily Allah is with those who do right.

SURAH—30
SURAH AR-RUM
(INTRODUCTION)

This Surah, as remarked in the Introduction to the last Surah, deals with the question of Ma'ad or the Final End of Things, from venous points of view. In the last Surah, we saw that Revelation was linked up with Life and Conduct, and Time (looking backwards and forwards) figured forth the frailty of this Life. In (his Surah the Time theme and its mystery are brought into relation with human history in the foreground and the evolution of the world in all its aspects in the background. The corruption introduced by man is cleared away by Allah, Whose Universal Plan points to the Hereafter. We shall se that the next two Surahs (31 and 32) present the theme in other aspects. All four are introduced with the Abbreviated Letters A.L.M. which (without being dogmatic) I have suggested as symbolical of the Past, Present and Future.

The choronology of this Surah is significant. It was revealed about the 7th or the 6th year before the Hijrat, corresponding to 615-16 of the Christian era, when the tide of Persian conquest over the Roman Empire was running strong. The Christian Empire of Rome had lost Jerusalem to the Persians, and Christianity had been humbled in the dust. At that time it seemed outside the bounds of human possibility, even to one intimately acquainted with the inner resources and conditions of the Persian and Roman armies and empires, that the tables would be turned and the position reversed within the space of eight or nine years. The pro-Persian Pagan Quraish rejoiced exceedingly, and redoubled their taunts and prosecution against the Holy Prophet, whose Message was a renewal of the Message of Christ preached in Jerusalem. Then was this passage 30: l-6 revealed, clearly foreshadowing the final defeat of Persia as a prelude to the destruction of the Persian Empire. There is no doubt about the prohecy and its fulfilment. For the exculting Pagans of Makkah laid a heavy wager against the fulfilment of the prohecy with Hazrat Abu Bakr, and they lost it on its fulfilment.

But the rise and fall even of such mighty empires as the Persian and Roman Empires were but small events on the chequer-board of Time, compared to a mightier movement that was taking birth in the promulgation of Islam. In the seventh or sixth year *before* the Hijrat, and for a year or two after the Hijrat, Islam was struggling in the world like the still small voice in the conscience of humanity. It was scarcely heeded, and when it sought to insist upon its divine claim, it was insulted, assaulted, persecuted, boycotted, and (as it seemed) suppressed. The agony of Ta-if (two years before the Hijrat) and the murder-plot on the eve of the Hijrat were yet to come. But the purpose of Allah is not to be thwarted. Badr (A.H. 2=A.D. 624), rightly called the critical Day of decision, began to redress the balance of outward events in early Islam, in the same year in which Issues began to redress the balance of outward events in Persio-Roman relations. Mightier events were yet to come. A new inner World was being created through Islam. This spiritual Revolution was of infinitely greater moment in world-history. The toppling down of priest-craft and false worship, the restoration of simplicity in faith and life, the rehabilitation of this life as the first step to the understanding of the Hereafter, the displacement of superstition and hairsplitting theology by a spirit of rational inquiry and knowledge, and the recognition of the divine as covering not merely an isolated thing called "Religion" but he whole way of Life, Thought, and Feeling,— this was and is the true Message of Islam and its mission. Its struggle-its fight-continues, but it is not without effect, as may be seen in the march of centuries in world-history.

SURAH RUM (THE ROMAN EMPIRE)

In the name of Allah, Most Gracious, Most Merciful.

1. Alif - Lam - Mim.

2. The Roman Empire has been defeated-

3. In a land close by; but they, (even) after (this) defeat of theirs, will soon be victorious-

4. Within a few years. With Allah is the Command, in the Past and in the Future: on that Day shall the Believers rejoice-

5. With the help of Allah. He helps whom He will, and He is Exalted in Might, Most Merciful.

6. (It is) the promise of Allah. Never does Allah depart from His promise: but most men do not understand.

7. They know but the outer (things) in the life of this world: but they are heedless of the Hereafter.

8. Do they not reflect in their own minds? Not but for just ends and for a term appointed, did Allah create the heavens and the earth, and all between them: yet there are truly many among men who deny the meeting with their Lord (at the Resurrection)!

9. Do they not travel through the Earth, and see what was the End of those before them? They were superior to them in strength: they tilled the soil and populated it in greater numbers than these have done: there came to them their Messengers with Clear (Signs). (which they rejected, to their own destruction): it was not Allah Who wronged them, but they wronged their own souls.

10. In the long run evil in the extreme will be the End of those who do evil; for that they rejected the Signs of Allah, and held them up to ridicule.

11. It is Allah Who begins (the process of) creation; then repeats it; then you shall be brought back to Him.

12. On the Day that the Hour will be established, the guilty will be struck dumb with despair.

13. No intercessor will they have among their "Partners" and they will (themselves) reject their "Partners".

14. On the Day that the Hour will be established,- that Day shall (all men) be sorted out.

15. Then those who have believed and worked righteous deeds, shall be made happy in a Mead[1] of Delight.

16. And those who have rejected Faith and falsely denied Our Signs and the meeting of the Hereafter,- such shall be brought forth to Punishment.

17. So (give) glory to Allah, when you reach eventide[2] and when you rise in the morning;

18. Yes, to Him be praise, in the heavens and on earth; and in the late afternoon and when the day begins to decline.

19. It is He Who brings out the living from the dead, and brings out the dead from the living, and Who gives life to the earth after it is dead: and thus you shall be brought out (from the dead).

20. Among His Signs is this, that He created you from dust; and then,- behold, you are men scattered (far and wide)!

---

1. Meadow

2. Evening time

21.   And among His Signs is this, that He created for you mates[3] from among yourselves, that you may dwell in tranquillity[4] with them, and He has put love and mercy between your (hearts): verily in that are Signs for those who reflect.

22.   And among His Signs is the creation of the heavens and the earth, and the variations in your languages and your colours: verily in that are Signs for those who know.

23.   And among His Signs is the sleep that you take by night and by day, and the quest[5] that you (make for livelihood) out of His Bounty[6]: verily in that are Signs for those who hearken.

24.   And among His Signs, He shows you the lightning, by way both of fear and of hope, and He sends down rain from the sky and with it gives life to the earth after it is dead: verily in that are Signs for those who are wise.

25.   And among His Signs is this, that heaven and earth stand by His Command: then when He calls you, by a single call, from the earth, behold, you (straightway) come forth.

26.   To Him belongs every being that is in the heavens and on earth: all are devoutly[7] obedient to Him.

27.   It is He Who begins (the process of) creation; then repeats it; and for Him it is most easy. To Him belongs the loftiest similitude (we can think of) in the heavens and the earth: for He is Exalted in Might, full of Wisdom.

28.   He propounds[8] to you a similitude from your own (experience): do you have partners among those whom your right hands possess, to share as equals in the wealth We have bestowed on you? Do you fear them as you fear each other? Thus do We explain the Signs in detail to a people that understand.

29.   Nay, the wrong-doers (merely) follow their own lusts, being devoid of knowledge. But who will guide those whom Allah leaves astray? To them there will be no helpers.

---

3.   Spouses, companions   4.   Peace and calm
5.   Search   6.   Grace, blessings
7.   Earnestly   8.   Propose for consideration

30. So you set your face stea-dily and truly to the Faith: (establish) Allah's handiwork according to the pattern on which He has made mankind: no change (let there be) in the work (wrought[9]) by Allah: that is the standard Religion: but most among mankind do not under-stand.

31. You turn back in repentance to Him, and fear Him: establish regular prayers, and you be not among those who join gods with Allah,-

32. Those who split up their Religion, and become (mere) Sects,- each party rejoicing in that which is with itself!

33. When trouble touches men, they cry to their Lord, turning back to Him in repen-tance: but when He gives them a taste of Mercy as from Himself, behold, some of them pay part-worship to other gods besides their Lord,-

34. (As if) to show their ingra-titude for the (favours) We have bestowed on them! Then enjoy (your brief day); but soon will you know (your folly)

35. Or have We sent down authority to them, which points out to them the things to which they pay part-worship?

36. When We give men a taste of Mercy, they exult[10] thereat: and when some evil afflicts them because of what their (own) hands have sent forth, behold, they are in despair!

37. Do not they see that Allah enlarges the provision and restricts it, to whomsoever He pleases? Verily in that are Signs for those who believe.

38. So give what is due to kindred[11], the needy, and the wayfarer[12]. That is best for those who seek the Countenance of Allah, and it is they who will prosper.

39. That which you lay out for increase through the property of (other) people, will have no increase with Allah: but that which you lay out for charity, seeking the Countenance of Allah, (will increase): it is these who will get a recompense multiplied.

---

9. Done
10. Glorify,become proud
11. Relatives
12. Traveller

40. It is Allah Who has created you: further, He has provided for your sustenance; then He will cause you to die; and again He will give you life. Are there any of your (false) "Partners" who can do any single one of these things? Glory to Him! and High is He above the partners they attribute (to Him)!

41. Mischief has appeared on land and sea because of (the meed[13]) that the hands of men have earned, that (Allah) may give them a taste of some of their deeds: in order that they may turn back (from Evil).

42. Say: "Travel through the earth and see what was the end of those before (you): most of them worshipped others besides Allah."

43. But you set your face to the right Religion, before there come from Allah the Day which there is no chance of averting: on that Day men shall be divided (in two).

44. Those who reject Faith will suffer from that rejection: and those who work righteous-ness will make provision for themselves (in heaven):

45. That He may reward those who believe and work righteous deeds, out of His Bounty. For He does not love those who reject Faith.

46. Among His Signs is this, that He sends the Winds, as heralds[14] of Glad Tidings, giving you a taste of His (Grace and) Mercy,- that the ships may sail (majestically) by His Command and that you may seek of His Bounty: in order that you may be grateful.

47. We sent indeed, before you, Messengers to their (respective) peoples, and they came to them with Clear Signs: then, to those who transgressed, We meted[15] out Retribution[16]: and it was due from Us to aid those who believed.

48. It is Allah Who sends the Winds, and they raise the Clouds: then He spreads them in the sky as He wills, and breaks them

---

13. Reward	14. Messengers
15. Apportion, allot	16. Punishment

into fragments, until you see rain-drops issue from the midst thereof: then when He has made them reach such of His servants as He wills, behold, they do rejoice!-

49. Even though, before they received (the rain) - just before this - they were dumb with despair!

50. Then contemplate[17] (O man!) the memorials of Allah's Mercy!- how He gives life to the earth after its death: verily the same will give life to the men who are dead: for He has power over all things.

51. And if We (but) send a Wind from which they see (their tilth[18]) turn yellow,- behold, they become, thereafter, Ungrateful (Unbelievers)!

52. So verily you can not make the dead to hear, nor can you make the deaf to hear the call, when they show their backs and turn away.

53. Nor can you lead back the blind from their straying: only those you will make to hear, who believe in Our Signs and submit (their wills in Islam).

54. It is Allah Who created you in a state of (helpless) weakness, then gave (you) strength after weakness, then, after strength, gave (you) weakness and a hoary[19] head: He creates as He wills, and it is He Who has all knowledge and power.

55. On the Day that the Hour (of Reckoning) will be estab-lished, the transgressors will swear that they did not tarry but an hour: thus were they used to being deluded!

56. But those endued with knowledge and faith will say: "Indeed you tarried within Allah's Decree, to the Day of Resurrection, and this is the Day of Resurrection: but you-you were not aware!"

57. So on that Day no excuse of theirs will avail the Trans-gressors, nor will they be invited (then) to seek grace (by repentance).

---

17. Consider
18. Cultivation
19. Gray

58. Verily We have propoun-ded for men, in this Qur'an every kind of Parable: but if you bring to them any Sign, the Un-believers are sure to say, "You do nothing but talk vanities."[20]

59. Thus Allah seals up the hearts of those who do not understand.

60. So patiently persevere: for verily the promise of Allah is true: nor let those shake your firmness, who have (them-selves) no certainty of faith.

---

20.   Vain things

SURAH—31

SURAH LUQMAN
(INTRODUCTION)

The argument of the Final End of Things is here continued from another point of view. What is Wisdom? Where shall she be found? Will she solve the mysteries of Time and Nature, and that world higher than physical Nature, which brings us nearer to Allah? "Yes," is the answer: "If, as in the advice of Luqman the Wise, human wisdom looks to Allah in true worship, ennobles every act of life with true kindness, but avoids the false indulgence that infringes the divine law, and in short follows the golden mean of virtue". And this is indicated by every Sign in Nature. The chronology of the Surah has no significance. In the main, it belongs to the late Makkan period.

SURAH LUQMAN (THE WISE)

In the name of Allah, Most Gracious, Most Merciful.

1. Alif- Lam-Mim.
2. These are Verses of the Wise Book,-
3. A Guide and a Mercy to the Doers of Good,-
4. Those who establish regu-lar Prayer, and give regular Charity, and have (in their hearts) the assurance of the Hereafter.
5. These are on (true) gui-dance from their Lord: and these are the ones who will prosper.
6. But there are, among men, those who purchase idle tales, without knowledge (or mea-ning), to mislead (men) from the Path of Allah and throw ridicule (on the Path): for such there will be a Humiliating Penalty.
7. When Our Signs are re-hearsed to such a one, he turns away in arrogance, as if he did not hear them, as if there were deafness in both his ears: announce to him a grievous Penalty.
8. For those who believe and work righteous deeds, there will be Gardens of Bliss,-
9. To dwell therein. The promise of Allah is true: and He is Exalted in Power, Wise.
10. He created the heavens without any pillars that you can see; He set on the earth mountains standing firm, lest it should shake

with you; and He scat-tered through it beasts of all kinds. We send down rain from the sky, and produce on the earth every kind of noble creature, in pairs.

11. Such is the Creation of Allah: now show Me what is there that others besides Him have created: nay, but the Trans-gressors are in manifest error.

12. We bestowed (in the past) Wisdom on Luqman: "Show (your) gratitude to Allah." and who is (so) grateful does so to the profit of his own soul: but if any is ungrateful, verily Allah is free of all wants, Worthy of all praise.

13. Behold, Luqman said to his son by way of instruction: "O my son! do not join in worship (others) with Allah: for false worship is indeed the highest wrong-doing."

14. And We have enjoined on man (to be good) to his parents: in travail¹ upon travail his mother bore him, and in two years was his weaning²: (hear the command), "Show gratitude to Me and to your parents: to Me is (your final) Goal.

15. "But if they strive to make you join in worship with Me things of which you have no knowledge, do not obey them; yet bear them company in this life with justice (and consi-deration), and follow the way of those who turn to Me (in love): in the end the return of you all is to Me, and I will tell you the truth (and meaning) of all that you did."

16. "O my son!" (said Luq-man), "If there be (but) the weight of a mustard-seed and it were (hidden) in a rock, or (any-where) in the heavens or on earth, Allah will bring it forth: for Allah is Subtle and Aware.

17. "O my son! establish regular prayer, enjoin what is just, and forbid what is wrong: and bear with patient constancy whatever betide you; for this is firmness (of purpose) in (the conduct of) affairs.

18. "And do not swell your cheek (for pride) at men, nor walk in

---

1. Distress, hardship
2. To accustom infant to food other than milk.

insolence[3] through the earth; for Allah does not love any arrogant boaster.

19. "And be moderate in your pace[4], and lower your voice;for the harshest of sounds without doubt is the braying of the ass."

20. Do you not see that Allah has subjected to your (use) all things in the heavens and on earth, and has made His bounties flow to you in excee-ding measure, (both) seen and unseen? Yet there are among men those who dispute about Allah, without knowledge and without guidance, and without a Book to enlighten them!

21. When they are told to follow the (Revelation) that Allah has sent down, they say: "Nay, we shall follow the ways that we found our fathers (following). "What! even if it is Satan beckoning[5] them to the Penalty of the (Blazing) Fire?

22. Whoever submits his whole self to Allah, and is a doer of good, has grasped indeed the most trustworthy hand-hold: and with Allah rests the End and Decision of (all) affairs.

23. But if any reject Faith, let not his rejection grieve you: to Us is their return, and We shall tell them the truth of their deeds: for Allah knows well all that is in (men's) hearts.

24. We grant them their plea-sure for a little while: in the end We shall drive them to an unrelenting[6] chastisement[7].

25. If you ask them, who it is that created the heavens and the earth. They will certainly say, "Allah". Say: "Praise be to Allah!" But most of them do not understand.

26. To Allah belong all things in heaven and earth: verily Allah is He (that is) free of all wants, worthy of all praise.

27. And if all the trees on earth were pens and the ocean (were ink), with seven oceans behind it to add to its (supply), yet the Words of Allah would not be exhausted (in the writing): for Allah is Exalted in Power, full of Wisdom.

---

3. Impertinence, arrogane
4. Manner of walking, gaint
5. Inviting them
6. Punishment
7. Incesant

28.   And your creation or your resurrection is in no wise but as an individual soul: for Allah is He Who hears and sees (all things).

29.   Don't you see that Allah merges Night into Day and he merges Day into Night; that He has subjected the sun, and the moon (to His Law), each run-ning its course for a term appointed; and that Allah is well-acquainted with all that you do?

30.   That is because Allah is the (only) Reality, and because whatever else they invoke besides Him is Falsehood; and because Allah,- He is the Most High, Most Great.

31.   Don't you see that the ships sail through the ocean by the Grace of Allah?- that He may show you of His Signs? Verily in this are Signs for all who constantly persevere and give thanks.

32.   When a wave covers them like the canopy (of clouds), they call to Allah, offering Him sincere devotion. But when He has delivered them safely to land, there are among them those that halt between (right and wrong). But none reject Our Signs except only a perfidious[8] ungrateful (wretch[9])!

33.   O mankind! do your duty to your Lord, and fear (the coming of) a Day when no father can avail anything for his son, nor a son avail anything for his father. Verily, the promise of Allah is true: let not then this present life deceive you, nor let the Chief Deceiver deceive you about Allah.

34.   Verily the knowledge of the Hour is with Allah (alone). It is He Who sends down rain, and He Who knows what is in the wombs. Nor does any one know what it is that he will earn on the morrow: nor does any one know in what land he is to die. Verily with Allah is full knowledge and He is acquainted (with all things).

---

8.   Treacherous, disloyal   9.   Miserable person

SURAH—32
SURAH AS-SAJDAH
(INTRODUCTION)

This short Surah closes the series of the four A.L.M. Surahs, which began with the 29th Its theme is the mystery of Creation, the mystery of Time and the mystery of the Ma'ad (the Final End) as viewed through the light of Allah's revelation. The contemplation of these mysteries should lead to Faith and the adoration of Allah. In chronology it belongs to the middle Makkan period and is therefore a little earlier than the last, but its chronology has no significance.

SURAH SAJDA (ADORATION)

In the name of Allah, Most Gracious, Most Merciful.

1. Alif- Lam-Mim.

2. (This is) the revelation of the Book in which there is no doubt,- from the Lord of the Worlds.

3. Or do they say, "He has forged it"? Nay, it is the Truth from your Lord, that you may admonish a people to whom no warner has come before you: in order that they may receive guidance.

4. It is Allah Who has created the heavens and the earth, and all between them, in six Days, and is firmly established on the Throne (of authority): you have none, besides Him, to protect or intercede (for you): will you not then receive admonition?

5. He rules (all) affairs from the heavens to the earth: in the end (all affairs) will go up to Him, on a Day, the space[1] whereof will be (as) a thousand years of your reckoning.

6. Such is He, the Knower of all things, hidden and open, the Exalted (in power), the Merciful;-

7. He Who has made every-thing which He has created most good: He began the creation of man with (nothing more than) clay,

8. And made his progeny[2] from a quintessence[3] of the nature of a fluid despised:

---

1. Length, range	2. Descendants, offspring
3. Finest extract	

9.   But He fashioned him in due proportion, and breathed into him something of His spirit. And He gave you (the faculties of) hearing and sight and feeling (and understanding): little thanks do you give!

10. And they say: "What! when we lie, hidden and lost, in the earth, shall we indeed be in a Creation renewed? Nay, they deny the Meeting with their Lord.

11. Say: "The Angel of Death, put in charge of you, will (duly) take your souls: then you shall be brought back to your Lord."

12. If only you could see when the guilty ones will bend low their heads before their Lord, (saying:) "Our Lord! We have seen and we have heard: now then send us back (to the world): we will work righteousness: for we do indeed (now) believe."

13. If We had so willed, We could certainly have brought every soul its true guidance: but the Word from Me will come true, "I will fill Hell with Jinns and men all together."

14. "Then you taste - for you forgot the Meeting of this Day of yours, and We too will forget you - you taste the Penalty of Eternity for your (evil) deeds!"

15. Only those believe in Our Signs, who, when these are recited to them, fall down in adoration[4], and celebrate the praises of their Lord, nor are they (ever) puffed[5] up with pride.

16. Their limbs do forsake[6] their beds of sleep, the while they call on their Lord, in Fear and Hope: and they spend (in charity) out of the sustenance which We have bestowed on them.

17. Now no person knows what delights of the eye are kept hidden (in reserve) for them - as a reward for their (good) deeds.

18. Is then the man who belie-ves no better than the man who is rebellious and wicked? Not equal are they.

19. For those who believe and do righteous deeds are Gardens as hospitable homes, for their (good) deeds.

20. As to those who are rebellious and wicked, their abode will be

---

4.   Worship   5.   Swollen
6.   Leave

the Fire: every time they wish to get away therefrom, they will be forced back thereinto, and it will be said to them: "You taste the Penalty of the Fire, the which you were wont to reject as false."

21. And indeed We will make them taste of the Penalty of this (life) prior[7] to the supreme Penalty, in order that they may (repent and) return.

22. And who does more wrong than one to whom are recited the Signs of his Lord, and who then turns away therefrom? Verily from those who transgress We shall exact[8] (due) Retribution[9].

23. We did indeed before this give the Book to Moses: be not then in doubt of its reaching (you): and We made it a guide to the Children of Israel.

24. And We appointed from among them, leaders, giving guidance under Our command, so long as they persevered with patience and continued to have faith in Our Signs.

25. Verily your Lord will judge between them on the Day of Judgment, in the matters wherein they differ (among themselves).

26. Does it not teach them a lesson, how many generations We destroyed before them, in whose dwellings they (now) go to and fro? Verily in that are Signs: do they not then listen?

27. And do they not see that We do drive rain to parched[10] soil (bare of herbage[11]), and produce therewith crops, providing food for their cattle and themselves? Have they not the vision?[12]

28. They say: "When will this Decision be, if you are telling the truth?"

29. Say: "On the Day of Decision, no profit will it be to Unbelievers if they (then) believe! nor will they be granted a respite[13]."

30. So turn away from them, and wait: they too are waiting.

---

7. Before
8. Claim, demand
9. Punishment
10. Dry and hot
11. Plants or growth
12. Insight
13. Delay

SURAH 33

SURAH AL-AHZAB

(INTRODUCTION)

The series of mystic Surahs beginning with S. 26 having been closed with the last Surah, we now come back to the hard facts of this life. Two questions are mainly considered here, viz, (1) the attempt by violence and brute force to crush the truth, and (2) the attempt, by slander or unseemly conduct, to poison the relations of women with men.

As regards the first, the story of the Ahzab or Confederates, who tried to surround and annihilate the Muslim community in Madinah, is full of underhand intrigues on the part of such diverse enemies as the Pagan Quraish, the Jews (Banu Nadhir) who had been already expelled from Madinah for their treachery, the Ghatafan tribe of Bedouin Arabs from the interior, and the Jewish tribe Banu Quraiza in Madinah. This was the unholy Confederacy against Islam. But though they caused a great deal of anxiety and suffering to the beleaguered Muslims, Islam came triumphantly out of the trial and got more firmly established than ever.

The Quraish in Makkah had tried all sorts of persecution, boycott, insult, and bodily injuries to the Muslims, leading to their partial *Hijrat* to Abyssinia and their *Hijrat* as a body to Madinah. The first armed conflict between them and the Muslims took place at Badr in Ramadhan A.H. 2, when the Quraish were signally defeated. Next year (Shawwal A.H. 3) they came to take revenge on Madinah. The battle was fought at Uhud, and though the Muslims suffered severely, Madinah was saved and the Makkans had to return to Makkah with their object frustrated. Then they began to make a network of intrigues and alliances, and besieged Madinah with a force of 10,000 men in Shawwal and Zul-qa'd A.H. 5. This is the siege of the Confederates referred to in 33: 9-27, which lasted over two weeks: some accounts give 27 days. It caused much suffering, from hunger, cold, an unceasing shower of arrows, and constant general or concentrated assaults. But it ended in the discomfiture of the Confederates, and established Islam firmer than ever. It was a well organised and formidable attack, but the Muslims had made preparations to meet it. One of the preparations, which took the enemy by surprise, was the Trench *(Khandaq)* dug round Madinah by the Prophet's order and under the supervision of Salman the Persian. The siege and battle are therefore known as the Battle of the Trench or the Battle of the Confederates.

As regards the position and dignity of the ladies of the Prophet's Household and the Muslim women generally, salutary principles are laid down to safeguard their honour and protect them from slander and insult. The ladies of the Household interested themselves in social work and work of instruction for the Muslim women, and Muslim women were being trained more and more in community service. Two of them (the two Zainabs) devoted themselves to the poor. The nursing of the wounded on or by the battlefield was specially necessary in those days of warfare. The Prophet's daughter, Fatima, then aged about 19 to 20, lovingly nursed her father's wounds at Uhud (A.H. 3); Rufaida nursed S'ad Ibn Mu'az's wounds at the Khaibar expedition (A.H. 7) Muslim women went out from Madinah for nursing service.

A portion of this Surah sums up the lessons of the Battle of the Trench and must have been revealed sometime after that Battle (Shawwal A.H. 5). The marriage with Zainab referred to in verse 37 also took place in the same year. Some portions (e.g. verse 27) were probably revealed in A.H. 7 after the Khaibar settlement.

SURAH AHZAB (THE CONFEDERATES)

In the name of Allah, Most Gracious, Most Merciful.

1. O Prophet! Fear Allah, and do not hearken[1] to the Unbelievers and the Hypocrites: verily Allah is full of Knowledge and Wisdom.

2. But follow that which comes to you by inspiration from your Lord: for Allah is well acquainted with (all) that you do.

3. And put your trust in Allah, and enough is Allah as a Disposer of affairs.

4. Allah has not made for any man two hearts in his (one) body: nor has He made your wives whom you divorce by *Zihar*[2] your mothers: nor has He made your adopted sons your sons. Such is (only) your (manner of) speech by your mouths. But Allah tells (you) the Truth, and He shows the (right) Way.

5. Call them by (the names of) their fathers: that is juster in the sight of Allah. But if you do not know their father's (names,

---

1. Listen
2. *Ziher*: An evil Arab custom. A husband would pronounce words implying that his wife was like his mother. After that she could not demand her rights as wife, nor could she contract another marriage.

call them) your Brothers in faith, or your *Maulas*[3]. But there is no blame on you if you make a mistake therein: (what counts is) the intention of your hearts: and Allah is Oft-Returning, Most Merciful.

6. The Prophet is closer to the Believers than their own selves, and his wives are their mothers. Blood-relations among each other have closer personal ties, in the Decree of Allah than (the Brotherhood of) Believers and *Muhajirs*: never-theless you do what is just to your closest friends: such is the writing in the Decree (of Allah).

7. And remember We took from the prophets their Covenant: as (We did) from you: from Noah, Abraham, Moses, and Jesus the son of Mary: We took from them a solemn Covenant:[4]

8. So that (Allah) may question the (custodians) of Truth concerning the Truth they (were charged with): and He has prepared for the Unbelievers a grievous Penalty.

9. O you who believe! Re-member the Grace of Allah, (bestowed) on you, when there came down on you hosts (to overwhelm you): but We sent against them a hurricane[9] and forces that you did not see: but Allah sees (clearly) all that you do.

10. Behold! They came on you from above you and from below you, and behold, the eyes became dim and the hearts gaped up to the throats, and you imagined various (vain) thou-ghts about Allah!

11. In that situation were the Believers tried: they were sha-ken as by a tremendous[6] shaking.

12. And behold! The Hypo-crites and those in whose hearts is a disease (even) say: "Allah and His Messenger promised us nothing but delusions."[7]

13. Behold! A party among them said: "You men of Yathrib! you cannot stand (the attack)! therefore go back!" And a band of them ask for leave of the Prophet, saying, "Truly our houses

---

3.   *Maulas*: Freed men   4.   Pledge, vow
5.   Storm   6.   Huge, dreadful
7.   Illusion

are bare and exposed," though they were not exposed: they intended nothing but to run away.

14. And if an entry had been effected to them from the sides of the (City), and they had been incited to sedition[8], they would certainly have brought it to pass, with none but a brief delay!

15. And yet they had already covenanted with Allah not to turn their backs, and a covenant with Allah must (surely) be answered for.

16. Say: "Running away will not profit you if you are running away from death or slaughter[9]; and even if (you do escape), no more than a brief (respite) will you be allowed to enjoy!"

17. Say: "Who is it that can screen you from Allah if it be His wish to give you punishment or to give you Mercy?" Nor will they find for themselves, besides Allah, any protector or helper.

18. Verily Allah knows those among you who keep back (men) and those who say to their brethren, "Come along to us", but come not to the fight except for just a little while.

19. Covetous over you. Then when fear comes, you will see them looking to you, their eyes revolving, like (those of) one over whom death hovers[10]: but when the fear is past, they will smite[11] you with sharp tongues, covetous of goods. Such men have no faith, and so Allah has made their deeds of none effect: and that is easy for Allah.

20. They think that the Confederates[12] have not withdrawn; and if the Confederates should come (again), they would wish they were in the deserts (wandering) among the Bedouins, and seeking news about you (from a safe distance); and if they were in your midst, they would fight but little.

21. You have indeed in the Messenger of Allah a beautiful pattern (of conduct) for any one whose hope is in Allah and the Final Day, and who engages much in the Praise of Allah.

---

8. Rebellion
9. Massacre
10. Hangs around
11. Strike
12. Allies

22.   When the Believers saw the Confederate forces, they said: "This is what Allah and His Messenger had promised us, and Allah and His Messenger told us what was true." And it only added to their faith and their zeal in obedience.

23.   Among the Believers are men who have been true to their covenant with Allah: of them some have completed their vow (to the extreme), and some (still) wait: but they have never changed (their determination) in the least:

24.   That Allah may reward the men of Truth for their Truth, and punish the Hypocrites if that be His Will, or turn to them in Mercy: for Allah is Oft-Forgi-ving, Most Merciful.

25.   And Allah turned back the Unbelievers for (all) their fury[13], no advantage did they gain; and enough is Allah for the Believers in their fight. And Allah is full of Strength, Able to enforce His Will.

26.   And those of the People of the Book who aided them- Allah took them down from their strongholds[14] and cast terror into their hearts, (so that) some you slew, and some you made prisoners.

27.   And He made you heirs of their lands, their houses, and their goods, and of a land which you had not frequented (before). And Allah has power over all things.

28.   O Prophet! Say to your Consorts[15]:"If it be that you desire the life of this World, and its glitter,- then come! I will provide for your enjoyment and set you free in a handsome manner.

29.   But if you seek Allah and His Apostle, and the Home of the Hereafter, verily Allah has prepared for the well-doers amongst you a great reward.

30.   O Consorts of the Prophet! If any of you were guilty of evident unseemly conduct, the Punishment would be doubled to her, and that is easy for Allah.

31.   But any of you that is devout in the service of Allah and His

---

13.   Anger, fierceness   14.   Fortresses
15.   Wives

Apostle, and works righteousness,- to her shall We grant her reward twice: and We have prepared for her a generous Sustenance.

32. O Consorts of the Prophet! You are not like any of the (other) women: if you do fear (Allah), be not too complaisant[16] of speech, lest one in whose heart is a disease should be moved with desire: but you speak a speech (that is) just.

33. And stay quietly in your houses, and make not a dazzling[17] display, like that of the former Times of Ignorance; and establish regular Prayer, and give regular Charity; and obey Allah and His Apostle. And Allah only wishes to remove all abomination[18] from you, you members of the Family, and to make you pure and spotless.

34. And recite what is rehearsed to you in your homes, of the Signs of Allah and His Wisdom: for Allah understands the finest mysteries and is well-acquainted (with them).

35. For Muslim men and women, - for believing men and women, for devout men and women, for true men and women, for men and women who are patient and constant, for men and women who humble themselves, for men and women who give in Charity, for men and women who fast (and deny themselves), for men and women who guard their chastity, and for men and women who engage much in Allah's praise, - for them Allah has prepared forgiveness and great reward.

36. It is not fitting for a Believer, man or woman, when a matter has been decided by Allah and His Apostle, to have any option about their decision: if any one disobeys Allah and His Apostle, he is indeed on a clearly wrong Path.

37. Behold! You said to one who had received the grace of Allah and your favour: "You retain (in wedlock) your wife, and fear Allah." But you hid in your heart that which Allah was about to make manifest: you feared the people, but it is more fitting

---

16. Polite, soft-spoken   17.   Bright, confusing
18. Evil

that you should fear Allah. Then when Zaid had dissolved (his marriage) with her, with the necessary (formality), We joined her in marriage to you: in order that (in future) there may be no difficulty to the Believers in (the matter of) marriage with the wives of their adopted sons, when the latter have dissolved with the necessary (formality) (their marriage) with them. And Allah's command must be fulfilled.

38.   There can be no difficulty to the Prophet in what Allah has indicated to him as a duty. It was the practice (approved) of Allah amongst those of old that have passed away. And the command of Allah is a decree determined.

39.   (It is the practice of those) who preach the Messages of Allah, and fear Him, and fear none but Allah. And enough is Allah to call (men) to account.

40.   Muhammad is not the father of any of your men, but (he is) the Apostle of Allah, and the Seal of the Prophets: and Allah has full knowledge of all things.

41.   O you who believe! Celebrate the praises of Allah, and do this often;

42.   And glorify Him morning and evening.

43.   He it is Who sends bles-sings on you, as do His angels, that He may bring you out from the depths of Darkness into Light: and He is Full of Mercy to the Believers.

44.   Their salutation on the Day they meet Him will be "Peace!"; and He has prepared for them a generous Reward.

45.   O Prophet! Truly We have sent you as a Witness, a Bearer of Glad Tidings, and a Warner,-

46.   And as one who invites to Allah's (Grace) by His leave, and as a Lamp spreading Light.

47.   Then give the glad tidings to the Believers, that they shall have from Allah a very great Bounty.

48.   And do not obey (the behests[19]) of the Unbelievers and the Hypocrites, and do not heed their annoyances[20], but put your

---

19.   Commands   20.   Provocations

trust in Allah. For enough is Allah as a Disposer of affairs.

49. O you who believe! When you marry believing women, and then divorce them before you have touched them, no period of 'Iddat have you to count in respect of them: so give them a present, and set them free in a handsome manner.

50. O Prophet! We have made lawful to you your wives to whom you have paid their dowers; and those whom your right hand possesses out of the prisoners of war whom Allah has assigned to you; and daughters of your paternal uncles and aunts, and daughters of your maternal uncles and aunts, who migrated (from Makkah) with you; and any believing woman who dedicates her soul to the Prophet if the Prophet wishes to wed her;- this only for you, and not for the Believers (at large); We know what We have appointed for them as to their wives and the captives whom their right hands possess;- in order that there should be no difficulty for you. And Allah is Oft-Forgiving, Most Merciful.

51. You may defer (the turn of) any of them that you please, and you may receive any you please: and there is no blame on you if you invite one whose (turn) you had set aside. This were closer[21] to the cooling of their eyes, the prevention of their grief, and their satisfaction - that of all of them - with that which you have to give them: and Allah knows (all) that is in your hearts: and Allah is All- Knowing, Most Forbearing.

52. It is not lawful for you (to marry more) women after this, nor to change them for (other) wives, even though their beauty attract you, except any your right hand should possess (as handmaidens): and Allah watches over all things.

53. O you who believe! Do not enter the Prophet's houses,- until leave is given you,- for a meal, (and then) not (so early as) to wait for its preparation: but when you are invited, enter; and when you have taken your meal, disperse, without seeking familiar talk. Such (behaviour) annoys the Prophet: he is

---

21. Here it means most proper or suitable

ashamed to dismiss you, but Allah is not ashamed (to tell you) the truth. And when you ask (his ladies) for anything you want, ask them from before a screen: that makes for greater purity for your hearts and for theirs. Nor is it right for you that you should annoy Allah's Apostle, or that you should marry his widows after him at any time. Truly such a thing is in Allah's sight an enormity.[22]

54.   Whether you reveal any-thing or conceal it, verily Allah has full knowledge of all things.

55.   There is no blame (on these ladies if they appear) before their fathers or their sons, their brothers, or their brother's sons, or their sisters' sons, or their women, or the (slaves) whom their right hands possess. And (ladies), fear Allah; for Allah is Witness to all things.

56.   Allah and His angels send blessings on the Prophet: O you that believe! you send blessings on him, and salute him with all respect.

57.   Those who annoy[23] Allah and His Apostle - Allah has cursed them in this World and in the Hereafter, and has prepared for them a humiliating Punish-ment.

58.   And those who annoy believing men and women undeser-vedly[24], bear (on themselves) a calumny[25] and a glaring sin.

59.   O Prophet! Tell your wives and daughters, and the believing women, that they should cast their outer garments over their persons (when out doors[26]): that is most convenient, that they should be known (as such) and not molested[27]. And Allah is Oft-Forgiving, Most Merciful.

60.   Truly, if the Hypocrites, and those in whose hearts is a disease, and those who stir up sedition in the City, desist not, We shall certainly stir you up against them: then will they not be able to stay in it as your neighbours for any length of time:

61.   They shall have a curse on them: wherever they are found,

---

22.   Dreadful sin or crime   23.   Vex, cause pain
24.   Without just cause or reason   25.   Slander
26.   Outside their houses   27.   Harassed

they shall be seized and slain (without mercy).

62. (Such was) the practice (approved) of Allah among those who lived aforetime: no change you will find in the practice (approved) of Allah.

63. Men ask you concerning the Hour: say, "The knowledge thereof is with Allah (alone)": and what will make you understand?- perchance the Hour is near!

64. Verily Allah has cursed the Unbelievers and prepared for them a Blazing Fire.

65. To dwell therein for ever: no protector will they find, nor helper.

66. The Day that their faces will be turned upside down in the Fire, they will say: "Woe to us! would that we had obeyed Allah and obeyed the Apostle!"

67. And they would say: "Our Lord! We obeyed our chiefs and our great ones, and they misled us as to the (right) Path.

68. "Our Lord! Give them double Chastisement and curse them with a very great Curse!"

69. O you who believe! You do not be like those who vexed and insulted Moses, but Allah cleared him of the (calumnies) they had uttered: and he was honourable in Allah's sight.

70. O you who believe! Fear Allah, and (always) say a word directed to the Right:

71. That He may make your conduct whole and sound and forgive you your sins: he that obeys Allah and His Apostle, has already attained the highest Achievement.

72. We did indeed offer the Trust to the Heavens and the Earth and the Mountains; but they refused to undertake it, being afraid thereof: but man undertook it;- he was indeed unjust and foolish;

73. (With the result) that Allah has to punish the Hypocrites, men and women, and the Unbelievers, men and women, and Allah turns in Mercy to the Believers, men and women: for Allah is Oft-Forgiving, Most Merciful.

SURAH—34

SURAH SABA

(INTRODUCTION)

Now we begin a series of Surahs, S. 34 to S. 39, which recapitulate some of the features of the spiritual world This Surah leads off with emphasis on Allah's Mercy and Power and Truth. Then (in S. 35) we are told how angels manifest the Power of Allah, and how different is Good from Evil and Truth from Falsehood. S. 34 is devoted to the Holy Prophet and the Quran that came through him. In S. 37 the emphasis is on the snares of the Evil One; in S. 38, on the conquest of evil by wisdom and power as in the case of David and Soloman, and by Patience and Constancy as in the case of Job: and in S. 39 on the Final Judgment, which will sort out Faith from Unfaith and give to each its due.

The chronology has here no significance, this Surah belongs to the early Makkan period.

SURAH SABA (THE CITY OF SABA)

In the name of Allah, Most Gracious, Most Merciful.

1. Praise be to Allah, to Whom belong all things in the heavens and on earth: to Him be Praise in the Hereafter: and He is Full of Wisdom, acquainted with all things.

2. He knows all that goes into the earth, and all that comes out thereof; and all that comes down from the sky and all that ascends thereto and He is the Most Merciful, the Oft-Forgiving.

3. The Unbelievers say, "Ne-ver to us will come the Hour": Say, "Nay! but most surely, by my Lord, it will come upon you;- by Him Who knows the unseen,- from Whom is not hidden the least little atom in the heavens or on earth: nor is there anything less than that, or greater, but is in the Record Perspicuous.[1]

4. That He may reward those who believe and work deeds of righteousness: for such is For-giveness and a Sustenance Most Generous."

5. But those who strive aga-inst Our Signs, to frustrate[2] them,- for such will be a Chastisement,- a Punishment most humiliating.

---

1.   Easily understood and expressed   2.   To thwart, baffle

6.   And those to whom knowledge has come see that the (Revelation) sent down to you from your Lord - that is the Truth, and that it guides to the Path of the Exalted (in Might), Worthy of all praise.

7.   The Unbelievers say (in ridicule[3]): "Shall we point out to you a man that will tell you, when you are all scattered to pieces in disintegration[4], that you shall (then be raised) in a New Creation?

8.   "Has he invented a false-hood against Allah, or has a spirit (seized) him?"- nay, it is those who do not believe in the Hereafter, that are in (real) Chas-tisement, and in farthest error.

9.   See they not what is before them and behind them, of the sky and the earth? If We wished, We could cause the earth to swallow them up, or cause a piece of the sky to fall upon them. Verily in this is a Sign for every devotee[5] that turns to Allah (in repentance).

10.   We bestowed Grace afore-time on David from ourselves: "O you Mountains! You sing back the Praises of Allah with him! and you birds (also)! And We made the iron soft for him;-

11.   (Commanding), "You make coats of mail, balancing well the rings of chain armour, and you work righteousness; for be sure I see (clearly) all that you do."

12.   And to Solomon (We made) the Wind (obedient): its early morning (stride) was a month's (journey), and its evening (stri-de) was a month's (journey); and We made a font[6] of molten brass to flow for him; and there were Jinns that worked in front of him, by the leave of his Lord, and if any of them turned aside from Our command, We made him taste of the Chastisement of the Blazing Fire.

13.   They worked for him as he desired, (making) Arches, Images, Basins as large as Reservoirs, and (cooking) cauldrons[7] fixed (in their places): "You work, sons of David, with thanks! but few of My servants are grateful!"

---

3. In jest   4. Crumbled to dust
5. Worshipper   6. Fountain
7. Large boiling vessel.

14.   Then, when We decreed (Solomon's) death, nothing showed them his death except a little worm of the earth, which kept (slowly) gnawing[8] away at his staff: so when he fell down, the Jinns saw plainly that if they had known the unseen, they would not have tarried[9] in the humiliating Chastisement (of their task).

15.   There was, for Saba, aforetime, a Sign in their home-land - two Gardens to the right and to the left. "Eat of the Sustenance (provided) by your Lord, and be grateful to Him: a territory fair and happy, and a Lord Oft-Forgiving!

16.   But they turned away (from Allah), and We sent against them the flood (released) from the Dams, and We converted their two garden (rows) into " gardens" producing bitter fruit, and tamarisks[10], and some few (stunted[11]) Lotetrees.

17.   That was the requital[12] We gave them because they un-gratefully rejected Faith: and never do We give (such) requital except to such as are ungrateful rejecters.

18.   Between them and the Cities on which We had poured Our blessings, We had placed Cities in prominent positions, and between them We had appointed stages of journey in due proportion: "Travel therein, secure, by night and by day."

19.   But they said: "Our Lord! Place longer distances between our journey-stages": but they wronged themselves (therein). At length We made them as a tale (that is told), and We dispersed them all in scattered frag-ments. Verily in this are Signs for every (soul that is) patiently constant and grateful.

20.   And on them Satan proved true his idea, and they followed him, all but a party that believed.

21.   But he had no authority over them,- except that We might test the man who believes in the Hereafter from him who is in doubt concerning it: and your Lord watches over all things.

22.   Say: "Call upon other (gods) whom you fancy[13], besides Allah: they have no power,- not the weight of an atom,- in the heavens

---

8.   Eating way   9.   Remained
10. A kind of ever green shurb   11. Retarded
12. Punishment   13. Imagine

or on earth: no (sort of) share have they therein, nor is any of them a helper to Allah.

23. "No intercession can avail in His Presence, except for those for whom He has granted permission. So far (is this the case) that, when terror is removed from their hearts (at the Day of Judgment, then) they will say, 'What is it that your Lord commanded?' They will say, 'That which is true and just; and He is the Most High, Most Great'."

24. Say: "Who gives you sustenance, from the heavens and the earth?" Say: "It is Allah; and certain it is that either we or you are on right guidance or in manifest error!"

25. Say: "You shall not be questioned as to our sins, nor shall we be questioned as to what you do."

26. Say: "Our Lord will gather us together and will in the end decide the matter between us (and you) in truth and justice: and He is the One to decide, the One Who knows all."

27. Say: "Show me those whom you have joined with Him as partners: by no means (can you). Nay, He is Allah, the Exalted in Power, the Wise."

28. We have not sent you but as a universal (Messenger) to men, giving them glad tidings, and warning them (against sin), but most men do not understand.

29. They say: "When will this promise (come to pass) if you are telling the truth?"

30. Say: "The appointment to you is for a Day, which you cannot put back for an hour nor put forward."

31. The Unbelievers say: "We shall neither believe in this scripture nor in (any) that (came) before it." Could you but see when the wrong-doers will be made to stand before their Lord, throwing back the word (of blame) on one another! Those who were deemed weak[14] will say to the arrogant ones: "Had it not been for you, we should certainly have been believers!"

32. The arrogant ones will say to those who had been despised:

---

14. Considered weak and looked down upon

"Was it we who kept you back from Guidance after it reached you? Nay, rather, it was you who transgressed.

33.   Those who had been despised will say to the arrogant ones: "Nay! it was a plot (of yours) by day and by night: behold! you (constantly) ordered us to be ungrateful to Allah and to attribute equals to Him!" They will declare (their) repentance when they see the Chastisement: We shall put yokes on the necks of the Unbelievers: it would only be a requital for their (ill) Deeds.

34.   Never did We send a War-ner to a population, but the wealthy ones among them said: "We do not believe in the (Mes-sage) with which you have been sent."

35.   They said: "We have more in wealth and in sons, and we cannot be punished."

36.   Say: "Verily my Lord enlarges and restricts the Provision to whom He pleases, but most men do not under-stand."

37.   It is not your wealth nor your sons, that will bring you nearer to Us in degree: but only those who believe and work righteousness - these are the ones for whom there is a multi-plied Reward for their deeds, while secure they (reside) in the dwellings on high!

38.   Those who strive against Our Signs, to frustrate them, will be given over into Punish-ment.

39.   Say: "Verily my Lord en-larges and restricts the Suste-nance to such of His servants as He pleases: and nothing do you spend in the least (in His Cause) but He replaces it: for He is the Best of those who grant Suste-nance.

40.   One Day He will gather them all together, and say to the angels, "Were it you that these men used to worship?"

41.   They will say, "Glory to You! our (tie) is with You - as Protector - not with them. Nay, but they worshipped the Jinns: most of them believed in them."

42.   So on that Day no power shall they have over each other, for profit or harm: and We shall say to the wrong-doers, "You taste the Chastisement of the Fire,- the which you were wont

to deny!"

43. When Our Clear Signs are rehearsed to them, they say, "This is only a man who wishes to hinder you from the (wor-ship) which your fathers practised." And they say, "This is only a falsehood invented!" And the Unbelievers say of the Truth when it comes to them, "This is nothing but evident magic!"

44. But We had not given them Books which they could study, nor sent Apostles to them before you as Warners.

45. And their predecessors rejected (the Truth); these have not received a tenth of what We had granted to those: yet when they rejected My Apostles, how (terrible) was My rejection (of them)!

46. Say: "I do admonish you on one point: that you do stand up before Allah,- (It may be) in pairs, or (it may be) singly,- and reflect (within yourselves): your Companion is not possessed: he is no less than a Warner to you, in face of a terrible Chastise-ment."

47. Say: "No reward do I ask of you: it is (all) in your interest: my reward is only due from Allah: and He is Witness to all things."

48. Say: "Verily my Lord casts the (mantle[15] of) Truth (over His servants),- He that has full know-ledge of (all) that is hidden."

49. Say: "The Truth has arrived, and Falsehood neither creates anything new, nor restores anything."

50. Say: "If I am astray, I only stray to the loss of my own soul: but if I receive guidance, it is because of the inspiration of my Lord to me: it is He Who hears all things, and is (ever) near."

51. If you could but see when they will quake[16] with terror; but then there will be no escape (for them), and they will be seized from a position (quite) near.

52. And they will say, "We do believe (now) in the (Truth)"; but how could they receive (Faith) from a position (so) far off,-

53. Seeing that they did reject Faith (entirely) before, and that they

---

15. Cloak, covering
16. Tremble
17. Utter or circulate false reports about

(continually) cast (slanders[17]) on the Unseen from a position far off?

54. And between them and their desires, is placed a barrier, as was done in the past with their partisans: for they were indeed in suspicious (disquieting) doubt.

SURAH—35
SURAH FATIR
(INTRODUCTION)

See Introduction to the last Surah.

This Surah deals with the mystery of Creation and its maintenance, with various forces typified by the wings of Angels. Whether See Introduction to S. 34. This particular Surah is devoted to the Holy Prophet and the Revelation which he brought. The Abbreviated Letters *Ya-Sin* are usually construed as a title of the Holy Prophet. But it is not permissible to be dogmatic about the meaning of Abbreviated Letters. This Surah is considered to be "the heart of the Quran," as it concerns the central figure in the teaching of Islam and central doctrine of Revelation and the Hereafter. As referring to the Hereafter, it is appropriately read in solemn ceremonies after death.

In chronology it belongs to the middle or early Makkan period.

In S. 37: 130 (a cognate Surah) occurs the word *Il-ya-sin.*

SURAH FATIR (THE ORIGINATOR OF CREATION)

In the name of Allah, Most Gracious, Most Merciful.

1. Praise be to Allah, Who created (out of nothing) the heavens and the earth, Who made the angels messengers with wings,- two, or three, or four (pairs): He adds to Creation as He pleases: for Allah has power over all things.

2. What Allah out of His Mercy bestows on mankind there is none can withhold: what He withholds, there is none can grant, apart from Him: and He is the Exalted in Power, full of Wisdom.

3. O men! Call to mind the grace of Allah unto you! Is there a creator, other than Allah, to give you sustenance from heaven or earth? There is no god but He: how then are you deluded away from the Truth?

4. And if they reject you, so were Apostles rejected before you: to Allah go back for decision all affairs.

5. O men! Certainly the promise of Allah is true. Let not then this present life deceive you, nor let the Chief Deceiver deceive you about Allah.

6. Verily Satan is an enemy to you: so treat him as an enemy. He only invites his adherents, that they may become com-panions

of the Blazing Fire.

7.   For those who reject Allah, is a terrible Chastise-ment: but for those who believe and work righteous deeds, is Forgiveness, and a magnificent Reward.

8.   Is he, then, to whom the evil of his conduct is made alluring[1], so that he looks upon it as good, (equal to one who is rightly guided)? For Allah leaves to stray whom He wills, and guides whom He wills. So let not your soul go out in (vainly) sighing after them: for Allah knows well all that they do!

9.   It is Allah Who sends forth the Winds, so that they raise up the Clouds, and We drive them to a land that is dead, and revive the earth therewith after its death: even so (will be) the Resurrection!

10.   If any do seek for glory and power,- to Allah belong all glory and power. To Him mount up (all) Words of Purity: it is He Who exalts each Deed of Righ-teousness. Those that lay Plots of Evil,- for them is a terrible penalty; and the plotting of such will be void[2] (of result).

11.   And Allah created you from dust; then from a sperm-drop; then He made you in pairs. And no female conceives, or lays down (her load), but with His knowledge. Nor is a man long-lived granted length of days, nor is a part cut off from his life, but is in a Decree (orda-ined). All this is easy to Allah.

12.   Nor are the two bodies of flowing water alike,- the one palatable, sweet, and pleasant to drink, and the other, salt and bitter. Yet from each (kind of water) you eat flesh fresh and tender, and you extract orna-ments to wear; and you see the ships therein that plough the waves, that you may seek (thus) of the Bounty of Allah that you may be grateful.

13.   He merges Night into Day, and He merges Day into Night, and He has subjected the sun and the moon (to His Law): each one runs its course for a term appointed. Such is Allah your Lord: to Him belongs all Dominion[3]. And those whom you invoke

---

1.   Appealing   2.   Null, invalid.
3.   Sovereignty, power

besides Him have not the least power.

14. If you invoke them, they will not listen to your call, and if they were to listen, they cannot answer your (prayer). On the Day of Judgment they will reject your "Partnership". And none, (O man!) can tell you (the Truth) like the One Who is acquainted with all things.

15. O you men! It is you that have need of Allah: but Allah is the One Free of all wants, Worthy of all praise.

16. If He so pleased, He could blot you out and bring in a New Creation.

17. Nor is that (at all) difficult for Allah.

18. Nor can a bearer of burdens bear another's burden. If one heavily laden should call another to (bear) his load, not the least portion of it can be carried (by the other), even though he be nearly related. You can but admonish such as fear their Lord unseen and establish regular Prayer. And whoever purifies himself does so for the benefit of his own soul; and the destination (of all) is to Allah.

19. The blind and the seeing are not alike;

20. Nor are the depths of Darkness and the Light;

21. Nor are the (chilly) shade and the (genial[4]) heat of the sun:

22. Nor are alike those that are living and those that are dead. Allah can make any that He wills to hear; but you cannot make those to hear who are (buried) in graves.

23. You are no other than a warner.

24. Verily We have sent you in truth, as a bearer of glad tidings, and as a warner: and there never was a people, without a warner having lived among them (in the past).

25. And if they reject you, so did their predecessors[5], to whom came their Apostles with Clear Signs, Books of dark prophecies, and the Book of Enlightenment.

26. In the end I punished those who rejected Faith: and how

---

4. Pleasant
5. Forefathers, those who lived before them

(terrible) was My rejection (of them)!

27. Do you not see that Allah sends down rain from the sky? With it We then bring out pro-duce of various colours. And in the mountains are tracts white and red, of various shades of colour, and black intense in hue.[6]

28. And so amongst men and crawling creatures and cattle, they are of various colours. Those truly fear Allah, among His servants, who have know-ledge: for Allah is Exalted in Might, Oft-Forgiving.

29. Those who rehearse[7] the Book of Allah, establish regular Prayer, and spend (in charity) out of what We have provided for them, secretly and openly, hope for a commerce[8] that will never fail:

30. For He will pay them their meed[9], nay, He will give them (even) more out of His Bounty: for He is Oft-Forgiving, Most Ready to appreciate (service).

31. That which We have revealed to you of the Book is the Truth,- confirming what was (revealed) before it: for Allah is assuredly- with respect to His servants - well acquain-ted and fully Observant.

32. Then We have given the Book for inheritance to such of Our Servants as We have chosen: but there are among them some who wrong their own souls; some who follow a middle course; and some who are, by Allah's leave, foremost in good deeds; that is the highest Grace.

33. Gardens of Eternity will they enter: therein they will be adorned[10] with bracelets of gold and pearls; and their garments there will be of silk.

34. And they will say: "Praise be to Allah, Who has removed from us (all) sorrow: for our Lord is indeed Oft-Forgiving ready to appreciate (service):

35. "Who has, out of His Bounty, settled us in a Home that will

---

6. Colour
7. Study, recite
8. Trade
9. Merited reward they rightly deserve
10. Decorated

last: no toil[11] nor sense of weariness[12] shall touch us therein."

36. But those who reject (Allah) — for them will be the Fire of Hell: no term shall be determined for them, so they should die, nor shall its Chastisement be lightened for them. Thus do We reward every ungrateful one!

37. Therein they will cry aloud (for assistance): "Our Lord! Bring us out: we shall work right-teousness, not the (deeds) we used to do!" "Did We not give you long enough life so that he that would should receive admonition? And (moreover) the warner came to you. So you taste (the fruits of your deeds): for the wrong-doers there is no helper."

38. Verily Allah knows (all) the hidden things of the heavens and the earth: verily He has full knowledge of all that is in (men's) hearts.

39. He it is that has made you inheritors in the earth: if, then, any do reject (Allah), their rejection (works) against them-selves: their rejection but adds to the odium[13] for the Unbelievers in the sight of their Lord: their rejection but adds to (their own) undoing.

40. Say: "Have you seen (these) 'Partners' of yours whom you call upon besides Allah? Show me what it is they have created in the (wide) earth. Or have they a share in the heavens? Or have We given them a Book from which they (can derive) clear (evidence)?- Nay, the wrong-doers promise each other nothing but delusions[14].

41. It is Allah Who sustains the heavens and the earth, lest they cease (to function): and if they should fail, there is none - not one - can sustain them thereafter: Verily He is Most Forbearing, Oft-Forgiving.

42. They swore their strongest oaths by Allah that if a warner came to them, they would follow his guidance better than any (other) of the Peoples: but when a warner came to them, it has only

---

11. Hard labour	12. Boredom, fatigue
13. Widespread dislike oir hatred	14. Deceptions

increased their flight (from righteousness),-

43. On account of their arrogance in the land and their plotting of Evil. But the plotting of Evil will hem in[15] only the authors thereof. Now are they but looking for the way the ancients were dealt with? But no change will you find in Allah's way (of dealing): no turning off will you find in Allah's way (of dealing).

44. Do they not travel through the earth, and see what was the End of those before them,- though they were superior to them in strength? Nor is Allah to be frustrated[16] by anything whatever in the heavens or on earth: for He is All-Knowing, All-Powerful.

45. If Allah were to punish men according to what they deserve, He would not leave on the back of the (earth) a single living creature: but He gives them respite for a stated Term: when their Term expires, verily Allah has in His sight all His servants.

---

15. Encircle   16. Thwarted, upset, baffled.

SURAH—36

SURAH YASIN
(INTRODUCTION)

See Introduction to S. 34. This particular Surah is devoted to the Holy Prophet and the Revelation which he brought. The Abbreviated Letters *Ya-Sin* are usually construed as a title of the Holy Prophet. But it is not permissible to be dogmatic about the meaning of Abbreviated Letters. This Surah is considered to be "the heart of the Quran," as it concerns the central figure in the teaching of Islam and central doctrine of Revelation and the Hereafter As referring to the Hereafter, it is appropriately read in solemn ceremonies after death.

In chronology it belongs to the middle or early Makkan period.

In S, 37: 130 (a cognate Surah) occurs the word *ll-ya-sin.*

SURAH YA-SIN

In the name of Allah, Most Gracious, Most Merciful.

1. Ya-Sin.
2. By the Qur'an, full of Wisdom,-
3. You are indeed one of the Apostles,
4. On a Straight Way.
5. It is a Revelation sent down by (Him), the Exalted in Might, Most Merciful.
6. In order that you may ad-monish a people, whose fathers had received no admonition, and who therefore remain heed-less (of the Signs of Allah).
7. The Word is proved true against the greater part of them: for they do not believe.
8. We have put yokes[1] round their necks right up to their chins, so that their heads are forced up (and they cannot see).
9. And We have put a bar[2] in front of them and a bar behind them, and further, We have covered them up; so that they cannot see.
10. The same is it to them whether you admonish them or you do

---

1. Yoke: A device usually consisting of a crosspiece and fitting an animals' neck.
2. An immaterial barrier or obstacle.

not admonish them: they will not believe.

11. You can but admonish such a one as follows the Message and fears the (Lord) Most Gracious, unseen: give such a one, therefore, good tidings of Forgiveness and a Reward most generous.

12. Verily We shall give life to the dead, and We record that which they send before and that which they leave behind, and of all things have We taken account in a clear Book (of evidence).

13. Set forth to them, by way of a parable, the (story of) the Companions of the City. Be-hold! there came Apostles to it.

14. When We (first) sent to them two Apostles, they rejec-ted them: but We strengthened them with a third: they said, "Truly, we have been sent on a mission to you."

15. The (people) said: "You are only men like ourselves; and (Allah) Most Gracious sends no sort of revelation: you do nothing but lie."

16. They said: "Our Lord knows that we have been sent on a mission to you:

17. "And our duty is only to proclaim the clear Message."

18. The (people) said: "For us, we augur[3] an evil omen[4] from you: if you do not desist, we will certainly stone you. And a grievous punishment indeed will be inflicted on you by us."

19. They said: "Your evil omens are with yourselves: (you deem[5] this an evil omen), if you are admonished: Nay, but you are a people transgressing[6] all bounds!"

20. Then there came running from the farthest part of the City, a man, saying, "O my people! Obey the Apostles:

21. "Obey those who ask no reward of you (for themselves), and who have themselves received Guidance.

22. "It would not be reasonable in me if I did not serve Him Who created me, and to Whom you shall (all) be brought back.

23. "Shall I take (other) gods besides Him? If (Allah) Most

---

3. Predict, foretell 4. An event suggesting something good or evil
5. Consider
6 Violating bounds or laws or reason, morality, or decency

Gracious should intend some adversity[7] for me, of no use whatever will be their intercession for me, nor can they deliver me.

24. "I would indeed, if I were to do so, be in manifest Error.

25. "For me, I have faith in the Lord of you (all): listen, then, to me!"

26. It was said: "You enter the Garden." He said: "Ah me! Would that my People knew (what I know)!-

27. "For that my Lord has granted me Forgiveness and has enrolled[8] me among those held in honour!"

28. And We did not send down against his People, after him, any hosts[9] from heaven, nor was it needful for Us so to do.

29. It was no more than a single mighty Blast[10], and behold! they were (like ashes) quenched[11] and silent.

30. Ah! Alas for (My) ser-vants! There comes not an Apostle to them but they mock[12] him!

31. Don't they see how many generations before them We destroyed? Not to them will they return:

32. But each one of them all - will be brought before Us (for judgment).

33. A Sign for them is the earth that is dead: We do give it life, and produce grain therefrom, of which you do eat.

34. And We produce therein orchards with date-palms and vines, and We cause springs to gush forth therein:

35. That they may enjoy the fruits of this (artistry): it was not their hands that made this: will they not then give thanks?

36. Glory to Allah, Who created in pairs all things that the earth produces, as well as their own (human) kind and (other) things of which they have no knowledge.

37. And a Sign for them is the Night: We withdraw therefrom the Day, and behold they are plunged in darkness;

38. And the Sun runs his course for a period determined for him: that is the decree of (Him), the Exalted in Might, the All-

8. Enlishted, included
9. Armies
10. A loud thunder, explosion, burst
11. Extinguished, dead
12. Make fun of.

Knowing.

39. And the Moon,- We have measured for her mansions[13] (to traverse[14]) till she returns like the old (and withered) lower part of a date-stalk.[15]

40. It is not permitted to the Sun to catch up the Moon, nor can the Night outstrip[16] the Day: each (just) swims along in (its own) orbit[17] (according to Law).

41. And a Sign for them is that We bore their race (through the Flood) in the loaded Ark[18];

42. And We have created for them similar (vessels[19]) on which they ride.

43. If it were Our Will, We could drown them: then would there be no helper (to hear their cry), nor could they be delivered,

44. Except by way of Mercy from Us, and by way of (worldly) convenience (to serve them) for a time.

45. When they are told, "You fear that which is before you and that which will be after you, in order that you may receive Mercy," (they turn back).

46. Not a Sign comes to them from among the Signs of their Lord, but they turn away therefrom.

47. And when they are told, "You spend of (the bounties[20]) with which Allah has provided you," the Unbelievers say to those who believe: "Shall we then feed those whom, if Allah had so willed, He would have fed, (Himself)?- you are in nothing but manifest error."

48. Further, they say, "When will this promise (come to pass), if what you say is true?"

---

13. Twenty-eight divisions of the sky occupied by the moon in successive days of a month.
14. To travel.
15. Main stem of palm tree, or a slender attachment of it.
16. Surpass   17. Circuit, course
18. Boat, or the ship in which Prophet Noah (P.B.U.H.) and his followers were saved.
19. Ships   20. Blessings.

49.	They will not (have to) wait for anything but a single Blast: it will seize them while they are yet disputing among themselves!

50.	No (chance) will they then have, by will, to dispose (of their affairs), nor to return to their own people!

51.	The trumpet shall be sounded, when behold! from the sepulchres[21] (men) will rush forth to their Lord!

52.	They will say: "Ah! woe unto us! Who has raised us up from our beds of repose?[22]"... (A voice will say:) "This is what (Allah) Most Gracious had promised. And true was the word of the Apostles!"

53.	It will be no more than a single Blast, when lo! they will all be brought up before Us!

54.	Then, on that Day, not a soul will be wronged in the least, and you shall but be repaid the meeds[23] of your past Deeds.

55.	Verily the Companions of the Garden shall that Day have joy in all that they do;

56.	They and their associates will be in groves of (cool) shade, reclining on Thrones (of dignity);

57.	(Every) fruit (enjoyment) will be there for them; they shall have whatever they call for;

58.	"Peace!"-a Word (of saluta-tion) from a Lord, Most Merciful!

59.	"And O you in sin! You get apart this Day!

60.	"Did I not enjoin on you, O you children of Adam, that you should not worship Satan; for that he was to you an enemy avowed[24]?-

61.	"And that you should worship Me, (for that) this was the Straight Way?

62.	"But he did lead astray a great multitude[25] of you. Did you not, then, understand?

63.	"This is the Hell of which you were (repeatedly) warned!

64.	"You embrace the (fire) this Day, for that you (persistently) rejected (Truth)."

21.	Tombs, especially cut in rock or built of sotne or brick

22.	Rest	23.	The merited reward

24.	Self-proclaimed	25.	Crowd, a great many people

65.   That Day We shall set a seal on their mouths. But their hands will speak to Us, and their feet bear witness, to all that they did.

66.   If it had been Our Will, We could surely have blotted out[26] their eyes; then should they have run about groping for the Path, but how could they have seen?

67.   And if it had been Our Will, We could have transformed[27] them (to remain) in their places; then they should have been unable to move about, nor could they have returned (after error).

68.   If We grant long life to any, We cause him to be reversed in nature: will they not then under-stand?

69.   We have not instructed the (Prophet) in Poetry, nor is it meet[28] for him: this is no less than a Message and a Qur'an making things clear:

70.   That it may give admoni-tion to any (who are) alive, and that the Word[29] may be proved against those who reject (Truth).

71.   Don't they see that it is We Who have created for them - among the things which Our hands have fashioned - cattle, which are under their dominion?-

72.   And that We have subjected them to their (use)? of them some do carry them and some they eat:

73.   And they have (other) profits from them (besides), and they get (milk) to drink. Will they not then be grateful?

74.   Yet they take (for worship) gods other than Allah, (hoping) that they might be helped!

75.   They have not the power to help them: but they will be brought up (before Our Judgment-seat) as a troop[30] (to be condemned[31]).

76.   Let not their speech, then, grieve you. Verily We know what they hide as well as what they disclose.

77.   Does not man see that it is We Who created him from sperm?

---

26.   Destroyed
27.   Change them utterly in their form, outward appearance, character, disposition.
28.   Suitable, fit, proper   29.   Accusation, indictment
30.   A band, group of people   31.   Sentenced

Yet behold! he (stands forth) as an open adversary![32]

78.   And he makes comparisons for Us, and forgets his own (origin and) Creation: he says, "Who can give life to (dry) bones and decomposed[33] ones (at that)?"

79.   Say, "He will give them life Who created them for the first time! for He is Well-versed in every kind of creation!-

80.   "The same Who produces for you fire out of the green tree, when behold! you kindle[34] therewith (your own fires)!

81.   "Is not He Who created the heavens and the earth able to create the like thereof?" - yes, indeed! for He is the Creator Supreme, of skill and knowledge (infinite)!

82.   Verily, when He intends a thing, His Command is, "Be", and it is!

83.   So glory to Him in Whose hands is the dominion of all things: and to Him will you be all brought back.

---

32.   Rival, antagonist, disputant.   33.   Rotten
31.   To light.

SURAH—37

SURAH AS-SAFFAT
(INTRODUCTION)

As explained in the Introduction to S. 34. This is the fourth of a series of Surahs in which the mysteries of the spiritual world are manifested in different ways, tending to the defeat and final extirpation of Evil. The defeat of Evil is throughout connected with Revelation, and here the ranged fight is illustrated by a reference to the angels in heaven and to the earlier Prophets in our earthly history, from Noah to Jonah. In chronology this Surah belongs to the early middle Makkan period.

SURAH SAFFAT (THOSE RANGED IN RANKS)

In the name of Allah, Most Gracious, Most Merciful.

1.   By those who range themselves in ranks,

2.   And so are strong in repelling (evil),

3.   And thus proclaim the Message (of Allah)!

4.   Verily, verily, your God (Allah) is One!-

5.   Lord of the heavens and of the earth and all between them, and Lord of every point at the rising of the sun!

6.   We have indeed decked[1] the lower heaven with beauty (in) the stars,-

7.   (For beauty) and for guard against all obstinate rebellious evil spirits,

8.   (So) they should not strain their ears in the direction of the Exalted Assembly but be cast away from every side,

9.   Repulsed, for they are under a perpetual[2] Chastisement,

10.   Except such as snatch away something by stealth, and they are pursued by a flaming Fire, of piercing brightness.

11.   Just ask their opinion: are they the more difficult to create, or the (other) beings We have created? We have created them out of a sticky clay!

12.   Truly you marvel[3], while they ridicule,-

---

1.   Beautiful   2.   Eternal, lasting
3.   To be amazed

13. And, when they are admonished, pay no heed,-

14. And, when they see a Sign, turn it to mockery,-[4]

15. And say, "This is nothing but evident sorcery![5]

16. "What! when we die, and become dust and bones, shall we (then) be raised up (again)

17. "And also our fathers of old?"

18. You say: "Yes, and you shall then be humiliated (on account of your evil)."

19. Then it will be a single (compelling) cry; and behold, they will begin to see!

20. They will say, "Ah! woe to us! this is the Day of Judgment!"

21. (A voice will say,) "This is the Day of Sorting Out, whose Truth you (once) denied!"

22. "Bring you up", it shall be said, "The wrong-doers and their wives, and the things they worshipped-

23. "Besides Allah, and lead them to the Way to the (fierce) Fire.

24. "But stop them, for they must be asked:

25. "'What is the matter with you that you do not help each other?'"

26. Nay, but that day they shall submit (to Judgment);

27. And they will turn to one another, and question one another.

28. They will say: "It was you who used to come to us from the right hand (of power and autho-rity)!"

29. They will reply: "Nay, you yourselves had no Faith!

30. "Nor had we any authority over you. Nay, it was you who were a people in obstinate rebellion!

31. "So now has been proved true, against us, the Word of our Lord that we shall indeed (have to) taste (the punishment of our sins).

32. "We led you astray: for truly we were ourselves astray."

33. Truly, that Day, they will (all) share in the Chastisement.

34. Verily that is how We shall deal with sinners.

35. For they, when they were told that there is no god except Allah, would puff[6] themselves up with pride,

---

4. Joke, ridicule   5. Magic
6. To be swollen (with pride)

36. And say: "What! shall we give up our gods for the sake of a Poet possessed[7]?"

37. Nay! he has come with the (very) Truth, and he confirms (the Message of) the Apostles (before him).

38. You shall indeed taste of the grievous Chastisement;-

39. But it will be no more than the retribution[8] of (the Evil) that you have wrought[9];-

40. But the sincere (and devoted) Servants of Allah,-

41. For them is a Sustenance determined,

42. Fruits (Delights); and they (shall enjoy) honour and dignity,

43. In Gardens of Felicity,[10]

44. Facing each other on Thrones (of dignity):

45. Round will be passed to them a cup from a clear-flowing fountain,

46. Crystal-white, of a taste deli-cious to those who drink (thereof),

47. Free from headiness[11]; nor will they suffer intoxication therefrom.

48. And besides them will be chaste women, restraining their glances, with big eyes (of wonder and beauty).

49. As if they were (delicate) eggs closely guarded.

50. Then they will turn to one another and question one another.

51. One of them will start the talk and say: "I had an intimate companion (on the earth),

52. Who used to say, "What! are you among those who bear witness to the truth (of the Message)?"

53. "'When we die and become dust and bones, shall we indeed receive rewards and punish-ments?'

54. (A voice) said: "Would you like to look down?"

55. He looked down and saw him in the midst of the Fire.

56. He said: "By Allah! you were little short of bringing me to perdition![12]

---

7.   Mad, possessed (of madness)   8.   Punishment
9.   Worked, practiced or did   10. Bliss, happiness
11. Violence or recklessness (caused by liquor)

57. "Had it not been for the Grace of my Lord, I should certainly have been among those brought (there)!

58. "Is it (the case) that we shall not die,

59. "Except our first death, and that we shall not be punished?"

60. Verily this is the supreme achievement!

61. For the like of this let all strive, who wish to strive.

62. Is that the better entertain-ment or the Tree of Zaqqum?[13]

63. For We have truly made it (as) a trial for the wrong-doers.

64. For it is a tree that springs out of the bottom of Hell-fire:

65. The shoots of its fruit-stalks are like the heads of devils:

66. Truly they will eat thereof and fill their bellies therewith.

67. Then on top of that they will be given a mixture made of boiling water.

68. Then their return shall be to the (Blazing) Fire.

69. Truly they found their fathers on the wrong Path;

70. So they (too) were rushed down on their footsteps!

71. And truly before them, many of the ancients went astray;

72. But We sent aforetime, among them, (Apostles) to admonish them;-

73. Then see what was the end of those who were admonished (but heeded not),-

74. Except the sincere (and devoted) Servants of Allah.

75. (In the days of old), Noah cried to Us, and We are the best to hear prayer.

76. And We delivered him and his people from the Great Calamity,

77. And made his progeny[14] to endure (on the earth)

78. And We left (this blessing) for him among generations to come in later times:

79. "Peace and salutation to Noah among the nations!"

80. Thus indeed do We reward those who do right.

81. For he was one of Our believing Servants.

---

12. Eternal damnation
13. Compare this bitter tree of Hell with the one mentioned in 17:60
14. Offspring

82.   Then the rest We over-whelmed[15] in the Flood.

83.   Verily among those who followed his Way was Abraham.

84.   Behold! he approached his Lord with a sound heart.

85.   Behold! he said to his father and to his people, "What is that which you worship?

86.   "Is it a falsehood - gods other than Allah- that you desire?

87.   "Then what is your idea about the Lord of the Worlds?"

88.   Then did he cast a glance at the Stars.

89.   And he said, "I am indeed sick (at heart)!"

90.   So they turned away from him, and departed.

91.   Then he turned to their gods and said, "Will you not eat (of the offerings before you)?...

92.   "What is the matter with you that you speak not (intelligently)?"

93.   Then he turned upon them, striking (them) with the right hand.

94.   Then came (the worship-pers) with hurried steps, and faced (him).

95.   He said: "Do you worship that which you have (yourselves) carved[16]?

96.   "But Allah has created you and your handiwork!"

97.   They said, "Build him a furnace, and throw him into the blazing fire!"

98.   (This failing), they then sought a strategem against him, but We made them the ones most humiliated!

99.   He said: "I will go to my Lord! He will surely guide me!

100.   "O my Lord! Grant me a righteous (son)!"

101.   So We gave him the good news of a boy ready to suffer and forbear.

102.   Then, when (the son) reached (the age of) (serious) work with him, he said: "O my son! I see in vision that I offer you in sacrifice: now see what is your view!" (The son) said: "O my father! Do as you are commanded: you will find me, if Allah

---

15.   Engulfed, drowned
16.   Produced by a process of cutting (stone or wood etc.)

so wills, one practising patience and constancy!"

103. So when they had both submitted their wills (to Allah), and he had laid him prostrate on his forehead (for sacrifice),

104. We called out to him "O Abraham!

105. "You have already fulfilled the vision!" - thus indeed do We reward those who do right.

106. For this was obviously a trial,-

107. And We ransomed[17] him with a momentous[18] sacrifice:

108. And We left (this blessing) for him among generations (to come) in later times:

109. "Peace and salutation to Abraham!"

110. Thus indeed do We reward those who do right.

111. For he was one of Our believing Servants.

112. And We gave him the good news of Isaac - a prophet,- one of the Righteous.

113. We blessed him and Isaac: but of their progeny are (some) that do right, and (some) that obviously do wrong, to their own souls.

114. Again (of old) We bestowed Our favour on Moses and Aaron,

115. And We delivered them and their people from (their) Great Calamity;

116. And We helped them, so they overcame (their troubles);

117. And We gave them the Book which helps to make things clear;

118. And We guided them to the Straight Way.

119. And We left (this blessing) for them among generations (to come) in later times:

120. "Peace and salutation to Moses and Aaron!"

121. Thus indeed do We reward those who do right.

122. For they were two of Our believing Servants.

123. So also was Elias among those sent (by Us).

124. Behold, he said to his people, "Will you not fear (Allah)?

125. "Will you call upon Baal and forsake the Best of Creators,

126. "Allah, your Lord and Cherisher and the Lord and Cherisher

---

17. Redeem, deliver and replace   18. Most significant

of your fathers of old?"

127. But they rejected him, and they will certainly be called up (for punishment),-

128. Except the sincere and devoted Servants of Allah (among them).

129. And We left (this blessing) for him among generations (to come) in later times:

130. "Peace and salutation to such as Elias!"

131. Thus indeed do We reward those who do right.

132. For he was one of Our believing Servants.

133. So also was Lut among those sent (by Us).

134. Behold, We delivered him and his adherents, all;

135. Except an old woman who   was among those who lagged behind:

136. Then We destroyed the rest.

137. Verily, you pass by their (sites), by day-

138. And by night: will you not understand?

139. So also was Jonah among those sent (by Us).

140. When he ran away (like a slave from captivity) to the ship (fully) laden,

141. He (agreed to) cast lots, and he was condemned:

142. Then the big fish swallowed him, and he had done acts worthy of blame.

143. Had it not been that he (repented and) glorified Allah,

144. He would certainly have remained inside the fish till the Day of Resurrection.

145. But We cast him forth on the naked shore in a state of sickness,

146. And We caused to grow, over him, a spreading plant of the gourd kind.

147. And We sent him (on a mission) to a hundred thousand (men) or more.

148. And they believe; so We permitted them to enjoy (their life) for a while.

149. Now ask them their opinion: is it that your Lord has (only) daughters, and they have sons?-

150. Or that We created the angels female, and they are witnesses

(thereto)?

151. Is it not, that they say, from their own invention,

152. "Allah has begotten children"? But they are liars!

153. Did He (then) choose daughters rather than sons?

154. What is the matter with you? How do you judge?

155. Will you not then receive admonition.

156. Or do you have an authority manifest?

157. Then you bring your Book (of authority) if you be truthful!

158. And they have invented a blood-relationship between Him and the Jinns: but the Jinns know (quite well) that they have indeed to appear (before His Judgment-seat)!

159. Glory to Allah! (He is free) from the things they ascribe (to Him)!

160. Not (so do) the Servants of Allah, sincere and devoted.

161. For, verily, neither you nor those you worship-

162. Can lead (any) into temp-tation concerning Allah,

163. Except such as are (themselves) going to the blazing Fire!

164. (Those ranged in ranks say): "Not one of us but has a place appointed;

165. "And we are verily ranged in ranks (for service);

166. "And we are verily those who declare (Allah's) glory!"

167. And there were those who said,

168. "If only we had had before us a Message from those of old,

169. "We should certainly have been Servants of Allah, sincere (and devoted)!"

170. But (now that the Qur'an has come), they reject it: but soon will they know!

171. Already has Our Word been passed before (this) to Our Servants sent (by Us),

172. That they would certainly be assisted,

173. And that Our forces,- they surely must conquer.

174. So you turn away from them for a little while,

175. And watch them (how they fare), and they soon shall see (how you fare)!

176. Do they wish (indeed) to hurry on our Punishment?

177. But when it descends into the open space before them, evil will be the morning for those who were warned (and heeded not)!

178. So you turn away from them for a little while,

179. And watch (how they fare) and they soon shall see (how you fare)!

180. Glory to your Lord, the Lord of Honor and Power! (He is free) from what they ascribe (to Him)!

181. And Peace on the Apostles!

182. And praise to Allah, the Lord and Cherisher of the Worlds!

SURAH—38
SURAH SAD
(INTRODUCTION)

For the place of this Surah in the series of six, dealing with some of the mysteries of the spiritual world, see Introduction to S. 34.

This Surah, both in chronology and subject-matter, is cognate to S. 37, and carries forward the same argument. But here the emphasis is laid on the working of earthly power when combined with spiritual power, and it is pointed out how much more significant (and real) spiritual power is. For this reason the illustrative stories are mainly those of David and Solomon who were kings as well as prophets, and a parallel is suggested with the unfolding public life of our Holy Prophet.

SURAH SAAD

In the name of Allah, Most Gracious, Most Merciful.

1. Saad: By the Qur'an, full of Admonition: (this is the Truth).

2. But the Unbelievers (are steeped) in Self-glory and Separatism.

3. How many generations before them did We destroy? In the end they cried (for mercy)- when there was no longer time for being saved!

4. So they wonder that a Warner has come to them from among themselves! and the Unbelievers say, "This is a sorcerer telling lies!

5. "Has he made the gods (all) into one God (Allah)? Truly this is a wonderful thing!"

6. And the leaders among them go away (impatiently), (saying), "You walk away, and remain constant to your gods! For this is truly a thing designed (against you)!

7. "We never heard (the like) of this among the people of these latter days: this is nothing but a made-up tale!"

8. "What! Has the Message been sent to him - (of all persons) among us?"...But they are in doubt concerning My (Own) Message! Nay, they have not yet tasted My Punishment!

9. Or have they the Treasures of the Mercy of your Lord,- the Exalted in Power, the Grantor of Bounties without measure?

10. Or have they the dominion of the heavens and the earth and all between? If so, let them mount up with the ropes and means (to reach that end)!

11. They are but a host of confederates[1] and they will be put to flight.

12. Before them (were many who) rejected Apostles,- the People of Noah, and 'Ad, and Pharaoh, the Lord of Stakes,[2]

13. And Thamud, and the people of Lut, and the Companions of the Wood; - such were the Confederates.

14. Not one (of them) but rejected the Apostles, but My Punishment came justly and inevitably[3] (on them).

15. These (today) only wait for a single mighty Blast, which (when it comes) will brook[4] no delay.

16. They say: "Our Lord! hasten to us our sentence (even) before the Day of Account!"

17. Have patience at what they say, and remember Our Servant David, the man of strength: for he ever turned (to Allah).

18. It was We that made the hills declare, in unison[5] with him, Our praises, at eventide[6] and at break of day,

19. And the birds gathered (in assemblies): all with him turned (to Allah).

20. We strengthened his kingdom, and gave him wisdom and sound judgment in speech and decision.

21. Has the story of the Disputants reached you? Behold, they climbed over the wall of the private chamber;

22. When they entered the presence of David, and he was terrified of them, they said: "Fear not: we are two disputants, one of whom has wronged the other: decide now between us with truth, and treat us not with injustice, but guide us to the even Path.

---

1. Allies
2. Pegs, poles (with which armies pitched their tents), hence lord of many armies.
3. Certainly, unavoidable   4.   Tolerate, give no respite.
5. Agreement, coinciding (in pitch), concora
6. Evening

23. "This man is my brother: he has nine and ninety ewes[7], and I have (but) one: yet he says, 'Commit her to my care,' and is (more-over) harsh to me in speech."

24. (David) said: "He has undoubtedly wronged you in demanding your (single) ewe to be added to his (flock of) ewes: truly many are the partners (in business) who wrong each other: not so do those who believe and work deeds of righteousness, and how few are they?"...and David gathered that We had tried him: he asked for-giveness of his Lord, fell down, bowing (in prostration), and turned (to Allah in repentance).

25. So We forgave him this (lapse[8]): he enjoyed, indeed, a Near Approach to Us, and a beautiful Place of (Final) Return.

26. O David! We did indeed make you a vicegerent on earth: so you judge between men in truth (and justice): nor do you follow the lusts (of your heart), for they will mislead you from the Path of Allah: for those who wander astray from the Path of Allah, is a Chastisement Grievous, for that they forget the Day of Account.

27. Not without purpose did We create heaven and earth and all between! that were the thought of Unbelievers! but woe to the Unbelievers because of the Fire (of Hell)!

28. Shall We treat those who believe and work deeds of righteousness, the same as those who do mischief on earth? Shall We treat those who guard against evil, the same as those who turn aside from the right?

29. (Here is) a Book which We have sent down unto you, full of blessings, that they may meditate[9] on its Signs, and that men of under-standing may receive admonition.

30. To David We gave Solo-mon (for a son),- how excellent in Our service! ever did he turn (to Us).

31. Behold, there were brought before him, at eventide, coursers[10] of the highest breeding, and swift of foot;

---

7. Female sheep
8. Oversight, omission
9. Think, study
10. Swift horses

32. And he said, "Truly do I love the love of Good, with a view to the glory of my Lord," until (the sun) was hidden in the veil (of Night):

33. "Bring them back to me." Then he began to pass his hand over (their) legs and their necks.

34. And We did try Solomon: We placed on his throne a body (without life); but he turned (to Us in true devotion):

35. He said, "O my Lord! Forgive me, and grant me a kingdom which, (it may be), does not suit another after me: for You are the Grantor of Bounties (without measure)."

36. Then We subjected the wind to his power, to flow gently to his order, whithersoever[11] he willed,-

37. As also the evil ones, (including) every kind of builder and diver,-

38. As also others bound together in fetters.

39. "Such are Our Bounties: whether you bestow them (on others) or withhold them, no account will be asked."

40. And he enjoyed, indeed, a Near Approach to Us, and a beautiful Place of (Final) Return.

41. Commemorate Our Servant Job. Behold! he cried to his Lord: "The Evil One has afflicted me with distress and suffering!"

42. (The command was given:) "Strike with your foot: here is (water) wherein to wash, cool and refreshing, and (water) to drink."

43. And We gave him (back) his people, and doubled their number,- as a Grace from Ourselves, and a thing for commemoration[13], for all who have Understanding.

44. "And take in your hand a little grass, and strike therewith: and do not break (your oath)." Truly We found him full of patience and constancy. How excellent in Our service! ever did he turn (to Us)!

45. And commemorate Our Servants Abraham, Isaac, and Jacob, possessors of Power and Vision.

---

11. Wherever   12. Celebrating the memory

46. Verily We chose them for a special (purpose)- proclaiming the Message of the Hereafter.

47. They were, in Our sight, truly, of the company of the Elect and the Good.

48. And commemorate Ismail, Elisha, and Zul-Kifl: each of them was of the company of the Good.

49. This is a Message (of admo-nition): and verily, for the Righteous, is a beautiful place of (final) Return,-

50. Gardens of Eternity, whose doors will (ever) be open to them;

51. Therein will they recline (at ease): therein can they call (at pleasure) for fruit in abundance, and (delicious) drink;

52. And beside them will be chaste women restraining their glances, (companions) of equal age.

53. Such is the Promise made to you for the Day of Account!

54. Truly such will be Our Bounty (to you); it will never fail;-

55. Yes, such! but - for the wrong-doers will be an evil place of (final) Return!-

56. Hell!- They will burn therein,- an evil bed (indeed, to lie on)!-

57. Yes, such!- Then shall they taste it, - a boiling fluid, and a fluid dark murky[13], intensely cold!-

58. And other penalties of a similar kind, to match them!

59. Here is a troop[14] rushing headlong with you! No welcome for them! truly, they shall burn in the Fire!

60. (Then followers shall cry to the misleaders:) "Nay, you (too)! No welcome for you! It is you who have brought this upon us! Now evil is (this) place to stay in!"

61. They will say: "Our Lord! Whoever brought this upon us,- add to him a double Chas-tisement in the Fire!"

62. And they will say: "What has happened to us that we do not see men whom we used to number among the bad ones?

63. "Did we treat them (as such) in ridicule, or have (our) eyes failed to perceive them?"

64. Truly that is just and fitting,-the mutual recriminations[15] of

---

13. Thick, dirty   14. A band, group

15 Retort, Accusation, countercharge

the People of the Fire!

65. Say: "Truly I am a Warner: no god is there but the One God (Allah), Supreme and Irresis-tible,-

66. The Lord of the heavens and the earth, and all between,- Exalted in Might, able to enforce His Will, forgiving again and again."

67. Say: "That is a Message Supreme (above all)-

68. "From which you do turn away!

69. "No knowledge have I of the chiefs on high, when they discuss (matters) among themselves.

70. 'Only this has been revealed to me: that I am to give warning plainly and publicly."

71. Behold, your Lord said to the angels: "I am about to create man from clay:

72. "When I have fashioned him (in due proportion) and breathed into him of My spirit, you fall down in prostration[16] before him."

73. So the angels prostrated themselves, all of them together.

74. Not so Iblis: he was haughty, and became one of those who reject Faith.

75. (Allah) said: "O Iblis! What prevents you from prostrating yourself to one whom I have created with My hands? Are you haughty? Or are you one of the high (and mighty) ones?"

76. (Iblis) said: "I am better than he: You created me from fire, and him You created from clay."

77. (Allah) said: "Then you get out from here: for you are rejected, accursed.

78. "And My Curse shall be on you till the Day of Judgment."

79. (Iblis) said: "O my Lord! Give me then respite[17] till the Day the (dead) are raised."

80. (Allah) said: "Respite then is granted to you-

81. "Till the Day of the Time Appointed."

82. (Iblis) said: "Then, by Your Power, I will put them all in the

---

16.   Gesture especially a bow or curtsy, expressing submission, respect or salutation.
17.   Delay

wrong,-

83. "Except Your Servants amongst them, sincere and purified (by Your grace).

84. (Allah) said: "Then it is just and fitting - and I say what is just and fitting-

85. "That I will certainly fill Hell with you and those that follow you,- every one."

86. Say: "No reward do I ask of you for this (Qur'an), nor I am a pretender.

87. "This is no less than a Message to (all) the Worlds.

88. "And you shall certainly know the truth of it (all) after a while."

SURAH—39

SURAH AZ-ZUMAR

(INTRODUCTION)

This is the last of the series of six Surahs beginning with S. 34, which deal with the mysteries of the spiritual world, as leading up to the *Ma'ad*, or the Hereafter. See Introduction to S. 34.

Its subject-matter is how Creation in its great variety is yet sorted out in Groups or Classes, all governed by one Plan, and created and sustained by One Allah, Who will separate Good from Evil at the last Day. The word *zumar* occurs in verses 71 and 73.

Its chronology has no significance. Its belongs to the late Makkan period.

SURAH ZUMAR (THE CROWDS)

In the name of Allah, Most Gracious, Most Merciful.

1. The revelation of this Book is from Allah, the Exalted in Power, full of Wisdom.

2. Verily it is We Who have revealed the Book to you in Truth: so serve Allah, offering Him sincere devotion.

3. Is it not to Allah that sincere devotion is due? But those who take for protectors others than Allah (say): "We only serve them in order that they may bring us nearer to Allah." Truly Allah will judge between them in that wherein they differ. But Allah does not guide such as are false and ungrateful.

4. Had Allah wished to take to Himself a son, He could have chosen whom He pleased out of those whom He creates: but Glory be to Him! (He is above such things.) He is Allah, the One, the Irresistible.

5. He created the heavens and the earth in true (proportions): He makes the Night overlap the Day, and the Day overlap the Night: He has subjected the sun and the moon (to His law): each one follows a course for a time appointed. Is not He the Exalted in Power - He Who forgives again and again?

6. He created you (all) from a single person: then created, of like nature, his mate; and He sent down for you eight head of cattle in pairs: He makes you, in the wombs of your mothers, in stages,

one after another, in three veils of darkness. Such is Allah, your Lord and Cherisher: to Him belongs (all) dominion. There is no god but He: then how are you turned away (from your true Centre)?

7. If you reject (Allah), truly Allah has no need of you; but He does not like ingratitude from His servants: if you are grateful, He is pleased with you. No bearer of burdens can bear the burden of another. In the end, to your Lord is your Return, when He will tell you the truth of all that you did (in this life). For He knows well all that is in (men's) hearts.

8. When some trouble tou-ches man, he cries to his Lord, turning to Him in repentance: but when He bestows a favour upon him as from Himself, (man) forgets what he cried and prayed for before, and he sets up rivals to Allah, thus misleading others from Allah's Path. Say, "Enjoy your blasphemy for a little while: verily you are (one) of the Companions of the Fire!"

9. Is one who worships devoutly during the hours of the night prostrating himself or standing (in adoration[1]), who takes heed of the Hereafter, and who places his hope in the Mercy of his Lord - (like one who does not)? Say: "Are those equal, those who know and those who do not know? It is those who are endued[2] with understanding that receive admonition.

10. Say: "O you My servants who believe! Fear your Lord, good is (the reward) for those who do good in this world. Spacious is Allah's earth! those who patiently persevere will truly receive a reward without measure!"

11. Say: "Verily, I am commanded to serve Allah with sincere devotion;

12. "And I am commanded to be the first of those who bow to Allah in Islam."

13. Say: "I would, if I disobe-yed my Lord, indeed have fear of the Penalty of a Mighty Day."

14. Say: "It is Allah I serve, with my sincere (and exclusive) devotion:

---

1. Worship 2. Furnished with, given

15. "You serve what you will besides Him." Say: "Truly, those in loss are those who lose their own souls and their People on the Day of Judgment: Ah! that is indeed the (real and) evident Loss!

16. They shall have Layers of Fire above them, and Layers (of Fire) below them: with this Allah warns off His servants: "O My servants! then you fear Me!"

17. Those who eschew[3] Evil,- and do not fall into its worship,- and turn to Allah (in repen-tance),- for them is Good News: so announce the Good News to My servants,-

18. Those who listen to the Word, and follow the best (meaning) in it: those are the ones whom Allah has guided, and those are the ones endued with understanding.

19. Is, then, one against whom the decree of Punishment is justly due (equal to one who eschews Evil)? Would you, then, deliver one (who is) in the Fire?

20. But it is for those who fear their Lord. That lofty mansions, one above another, have been built: beneath them flow rivers (of delight): (such is) the Promise of Allah: never does Allah fail in (His) promise.

21. Do not you see that Allah sends down rain from the sky, and leads it through springs in the earth? Then He causes to grow, therewith, produce of various colours: then it withers; you will see it grow yellow; then He makes it dry up and crumble away. Truly, in this, is a Message of remembrance to men of understanding.

22. Is one whose heart Allah has opened to Islam, so that he has received Enlightenment from Allah, (no better than one hard-hearted)? Woe to those whose hearts are hardened against celebrating the praises of Allah! they are manifestly wandering (in error)

23. Allah has revealed (from time to time) the most beautiful Message in the form of a Book, consistent with itself, (yet)

---

3.   Avoid

repeating (its teaching in various aspects): the skins of those who fear their Lord tremble threat; then their skins and their hearts do soften to the celebration of Allah's praises. Such is the guidance of Allah: He guides herewith whom He pleases, but such as Allah leaves to stray, can have none to guide.

24. Is, then, one who has to fear the brunt[4] of the Chastisement on the Day of Judgment (and receive it) on his face, (like one guarded therefrom)? It will be said to the wrong-doers: "You taste (the fruits of) what you earned!"

25. Those before them (also) rejected (revelation), and so the Punishment came to them from directions they did not perceive.

26. So Allah gave them a taste of humiliation in the present life, but greater is the punishment of the Hereafter, if they only knew!

27. We have put forth for men, in this Qur'an every kind of Parable, in order that they may receive admonition.

28. (It is) a Qur'an in Arabic, without any crookedness (therein): in order that they may guard against Evil.

29. Allah puts forth a Parable -a man belonging to many partners at variance[5] with each other, and a man belonging entirely to one master: are those two equal in comparison? Praise be to Allah! but most of them have no knowledge.

30. Truly you will die (one day), and truly they (too) will die (one day).

31. In the end you will (all), on the Day of Judgment, settle your disputes in the presence of your Lord.

32. Who, then, does more wrong than one who utters a lie concerning Allah, and rejects the Truth when it comes to him; is there not in Hell an abode for blasphemers?

33. And he who brings the Truth and he who confirms (and supports) it - such are the men who do right.

34. They shall have all that they wish for, in the presence of their Lord: such is the reward of those who do good:

35. So that Allah will turn off from them (even) the worst in their

---

4. Chief stress or force of   5. In disagreement

deeds and give them their reward according to the best of what they have done.

36. Is not Allah enough for his servant? But they try to frighten you with other (gods) besides Him! for such as Allah leaves to stray, there can be no guide.

37. And such as Allah guides there can be none to lead astray. Is not Allah Exalted in Power, (Able to enforce His Will), Lord of Retribution?[6]

38. If indeed you ask them who it is that created the heavens and the earth, they would be sure to say, "Allah". Say: "Do you see then? the things that you invoke besides Allah,- can they, if Allah wills some Penalty for me, remove His Penalty?- Or if He wills some Grace for me, can they keep back His Grace?" Say: "Sufficient is Allah for me! In Him trust those who put their trust."

39. Say: "O my People! Do whatever you can: I will do (my part): but soon you will know-

40. "Who it is to whom comes a Chastisement of ignominy[7], and on whom descends a Penalty that abides[8]."

41. Verily We have revealed the Book to you in Truth, for (instructing) mankind. He, then, that receives guidance benefits his own soul: but he that strays injures his own soul. Nor you are set over them to dispose of their affairs.

42. It is Allah that takes the souls (of men) at death; and those that die not (He takes) during their sleep: those on whom He has passed the decree of death, He keeps back (from returning to life), but the rest He sends (to their bodies) for a term appointed. Verily in this are Signs for those who reflect.

43. What! Do they take for intercessors others besides Allah? Say: "Even if they have no power whatever and no intelligence?"

44. Say: "To Allah belongs exclusively (the right to grant) intercession: to Him belongs the dominion of the heavens and the earth: In the End, it is to Him that you shall be brought back."

---

6. Punishment   7. Disgrace
8. Lasts, endures

45. When Allah, the One and Only, is mentioned, the hearts of those who do not believe in the Hereafter are filled with disgust and horror; but when (gods) other than He are mentioned, behold, they are filled with joy!

46. Say: "O Allah! Creator of the heavens and the earth! Knower of all that is hidden and open! it is You that will judge between Your servants in those matters about which they have differed."

47. Even if the wrong-doers had all that there is on earth, and as much more, (in vain) would they offer it for ransom[9] from the pain of the Chastisement on the Day of Judgment: but something will confront them from Allah, which they could never have counted upon!

48. For the evils of their deeds will confront them, and they will be (completely) encircled by that which they used to mock[10] at!

49. Now, when trouble touches man, he cries to Us: but when We bestow a favour upon him as from Ourselves, he says, "This has been given to me because of a certain knowledge (I have)!" Nay, but this is but a trial, but most of them do not understand!

50. Thus did the (generations) before them say! But all that they did was of no profit to them.

51. Nay, the evil results of their deeds overtook them. And the wrong-doers of this (generation)-the evil results of their deeds will soon overtake them (too), and they shall never escape.

52. Do they not know that Allah enlarges the provision or restricts it, for any He pleases? Verily, in this are Signs for those who believe!

53. Say: "O My servants who have transgressed against their souls! do not despair of the Mercy of Allah: for Allah forgives all sins: for He is Oft-Forgiving, Most Merciful.

54. "You turn to your Lord (in repentance) and bow to His (Will), before the Chastisement comes on you: after that you shall not be helped.

55. "And follow the best of (the courses) revealed to you from

---

9.   In exchange   10.   Make fun of

your Lord, before the Chastisement comes on you - of a sudden, while you do not perceive!-

56. "Lest the soul should (then) say: 'Ah! woe is me!- In that I neglected (my duty) towards Allah, and was but among those who mocked!'-

57. "Or (lest) it should say: 'If only Allah had guided me, I should certainly have been among the righteous!'

58. "Or (lest) it should say when it (actually) sees the Chastisement: 'If only I had another chance, I should certainly be among those who do good!'

59. "(The reply will be:) 'Nay, but there came to you My Signs, and you rejected them: you were haughty, and became one of those who reject faith!'

60. On the Day of Judgment you will see those who told lies against Allah;- their faces will be turned black; Is there not in Hell an abode for the haughty?[11]

61. But Allah will deliver the righteous to their place of salvation: no evil shall touch them, nor shall they grieve.

62. Allah is the Creator of all things, and He is the Guardian and Disposer of all affairs.

63. To Him belong the keys of the heavens and the earth: and those who reject the Signs of Allah,- it is they who will be in loss.

64. Say: "Is it someone other than Allah that you order me to worship, O you ignorant ones?"

65. But it has already been revealed to you,- as it was to those before you,- "If you were to join (gods with Allah), truly fruitless will be your work (in life), and you will surely be in the ranks of those who lose (all spritualy good)".

66. Nay, but worship Allah, and be of those who give thanks.

67. Nay just estimate have they made of Allah, such as is due to Him: on the Day of Judgment the whole of the earth will be but His handful, and the heavens will be rolled up in His right hand: glory to Him! High is He above the Partners they attribute

---

11. Proud, arrogant

to Him!

68. The Trumpet will (just) be sounded, when all that are in the heavens and on earth will swoon[12], except such as it will please Allah (to exempt). Then will a second one be sounded, when, behold, they will be standing and looking on!

69. And the Earth will shine with the glory of its Lord: the Record (of deeds) will be placed (open); the prophets and the witnesses will be brought for-ward and a just decision pronoun-ced between them; and they will not be wronged (in the least).

70. And to every soul will be paid in full (the fruit) of its deeds; and (Allah) knows best all that they do.

71. The Unbelievers will be led to Hell in crowd: until, when they arrive there, its gates will be opened. And its keepers will say, "Did not Apostles come to you from among yourselves, rehearsing[13] to you the Signs of your Lord, and warning you of the Meeting of This Day of yours?" The answer will be: "True: but the Decree of Punish-ment has been proved true against the Unbelievers!"

72. (To them) will be said: "You enter the gates of Hell, to dwell therein: and evil is (this) abode of the arrogant!"

73. And those who feared their Lord will be led to the Garden in crowds: until behold, they arrive there; its gates will be opened; and its Keepers will say: "Peace be upon you! you have done well you enter here, to dwell therein."

74. They will say: "Praise be to Allah, Who has truly fulfilled His Promise to us, and has given us (this) land in heritage: we can dwell in the Garden as we will: how excellent a reward for those who work (righteousness)!"

75. And you will see the angels surrounding the Throne (Divine) on all sides, singing Glory and Praise to their Lord. The Decision between them (at Judgment) will be in (perfect) justice, and the cry (on all sides) will be, "Praise be to Allah, the Lord of the Worlds!"

---

12. Faint, collapse   13. Reciting

SURAH—40
SURAH AL-MU-MIN
(INTRODUCTION)

This Surah is called "The Believer" *(Mu-mim)* from the story of the individual Believer among the people of Pharaoh, who declares his faith and looks to the Future (verses 28-45). It is also called *Ghafir* (He who forgives, see verse 3). In S. 23, called *The Believers (Mu-minun),* the argument was about the collective force of Faith and Virtue. Here it is about the Individual's witness to Faith and Virtue, and his triumph in the End.

We now begin a series of seven Surahs (40-46) to which are affixed the abbreviated Letters *Ha-Min.* Chronologically they all belong to the same period, the later Makkan Period, and they immediately follow the last Surah in time. As to the precise meaning of *Ha-Mim* no authoritative explanation is available. If *Min.* here has a signification similar to *Mim* in A.L.M. it means the End of things, the Last Day, and all these Surahs direct our special attention to that. *Ha,* the emphatic guttural, in contrast with the softer breathing of *Alif,* may be meant to suggest that the Beginning is only for the End, the Present for the Future, and to emphasise the eschatological element in Faith. But this is mere conjecture, and should be taken for no more than it is worth.

The general theme of the whole series is the relation of Faith to Unfaith, Revelation to Rejection, Goodness to Evil, Truth to Falsehood. It is shown that the first in each of these pairs is the real friend, helper, and protector of man, while the second is his enemy. The very word *Hamim* in that sense is used in Surahs 40 and 41 (40: 18 and 41: 34), while in the other Surahs we have words of equivalent import, e.g. *wali* or *nasir* (42: 8 and 31); *qarin* (43:36,38); *Maula* (44:41); *auliya ar nasirin* (45:19,34); and *auliyaa* (46:32). Is it permissible to connect the Abbreviated Letters *Ha-Mim* with these ideas as expressed in the word *Hamim?*

To S. 40. To prevent confusion with other Surahs of the *Ha-Mim* series, the word *Sajdah* is sometimes added to the title, making it *Ha-Mim as-Sajdah,* the double title being necessary as there is another Surah called *Sajdah* (S. 32). To avoid the double title it is sometimes called *Fussilat,* from the occurrence of the word in verse 3.

The meaning *of Ha-Mim* has been explained in the Introduction to S. 40, where will also be found a note on the chronology and general theme of the seven *Ha-Mim* Surahs.

For this particular Surah the theme is that the basis of Faith and Revelation is Allah's Power and Goodness, and the fruit of both is man's righteousness and healing.

SURAH MUMIN (THE BELIEVER)

In the name of Allah, Most Gracious, Most Merciful.

1. Ha-Mim

2. The revelation of this Book is from Allah, Exalted in Power, full of Knowledge,-

3. Who forgives sin, accepts repentance, is Strict in pu-nishment, and has a long reach (in all things). There is no god but He: to Him is the final goal.

4. None can dispute about the Signs of Allah but the Unbe-lievers. Let not, then, their strutting[1] about through the land deceive you!

5. But (there were people) before them, who denied (the Signs),- the People of Noah, and the Confederates (of Evil) after them; and every People plotted against their prophet, to seize him, and disputed by means of vanities, therewith to condemn the Truth; but it was I that seized them! and how (terrible) was My Requital![2]

6. Thus was the Decree of your Lord proved true against the Unbelievers; that truly they are Companions of the Fire!

7. Those who sustain the Throne (of Allah) and those around it sing Glory and Praise to their Lord; believe in Him; and implore Forgiveness for those who believe: "Our Lord! Your Reach is over all things, in Mercy and Knowledge. Forgive, then, those who turn in Repen-tance, and follow Your Path; and preserve them from the Chastisement of the Blazing Fire!

8. "And grant, our Lord! that they enter the Gardens of Eternity, which You have promised to them, and to the righteous among their fathers, their wives, and their posterity[3]! For You are (He), the Exalted in Might, full of Wisdom.

9. "And preserve them from (all) ills; and any whom You preserve

---

1. Walking with pompous of affected stiff erect gait
2. Punishment   3. Offsprint

from ills that Day,- on them You will have bestowed Mercy indeed: and that will be truly (for them) the highest Achievement".

10. The Unbelievers will be addressed: "Greater was the aversion[4] of Allah to you than (is) your aversion to yourselves, seeing that you were called to the Faith and you used to refuse."

11. They will say: "Our Lord! Twice have You made us without life, and twice have You given us Life! Now we have recognised our sins: Is there any way out (of this)?"

12. (The answer will be:) "This is because, when Allah was invoked[5] as the Only (object of worship), you rejected Faith, but when partners were joined to Him, you believed! the Command is with Allah, Most High, Most Great!"

13. He it is Who shows you His Signs, and sends down sustenance for you from the sky: but only those receive admoni-tion who turn (to Allah).

14. You call, then, upon Allah with sincere devotion to Him, even though the Unbelievers may detest it.

15. Raised high above ranks (or degrees), (He is) the Lord of the Throne (of Authority): by His Command He sends the Spirit (of inspiration) to any of His servants He pleases, that it may warn (men) of the Day of Mutual Meeting,-

16. The Day whereon they will (all) come forth: not a single thing concerning them is hidden from Allah. Whose will be the dominion[6] that Day?" That of Allah, the One, the Irresistible!

17. That Day will every soul be requited[7] for what it earned; no injustice will there be that Day, for Allah is Swift in taking account.

18. Warn them of the Day that is (ever) drawing near, when the hearts will (come) right up to the throats to choke (them); no intimate friend nor intercessor will the wrong-doers have, who could be listened to.

---

4. Repugnance, disgust   5. Called upon
6. Authority, sovereignty   7. Rewarded or punished

19. (Allah) knows of (the tricks) that deceive with the eyes, and all that the hearts (of men) conceal.

20. And Allah will judge with (justice and) Truth: but those whom (men) invoke besides Him, will not (be in a position) to judge at all. Verily it is Allah (alone) Who hears and sees (all things).

21. Do they not travel through the earth and see what was the End of those before them? They were even superior to them in strength, and in the traces[8] (they have left) in the land: but Allah called them to account for their sins, and none had they to defend them against Allah.

22. That was because there came to them their Apostles with Clear (Signs), but they rejected them: so Allah called them to account: for He is full of Strength, Strict in Punishment.

23. Of old We sent Moses, with Our Signs and an Authority manifest,

24. To Pharaoh, Haman, and Qarun; but they called (him)" a sorcerer[9] telling lies!"...

25. Now, when he came to them in Truth, from Us, they said, "Slay the sons of those who believe with him, and keep alive their females," but the plots of Unbelievers (end) in nothing but errors (and delusions)!...

26. Said Pharaoh: "Leave me to slay Moses; and let him call on his Lord! What I fear is lest he should change your religion, or lest he should cause mischief to appear in the land!"

27. Moses said: "I have indeed called upon my Lord and your Lord (for protection) from every arrogant one who does not believe in the Day of Account!"

28. A believer, a man from among the people of Pharaoh, who had concealed his faith, said: "Will you slay a man because he says, 'My Lord is Allah'?- when he has indeed come to you with Clear (Signs) from your Lord? and if he be a liar, on him is (the sin of) his lie: but, if he is telling the Truth, then will fall on you something of the (calamity[10]) of which he warns you:

---

8. Remains, relics
9. Magician
10. Catastrophe, disaster

truly Allah does not guide one who transgresses and lies!

29. "O my People! Yours is the dominion this day: you have the upper hand in the land: but who will help us from the Punishment of Allah, should it befall us?" Pharaoh said: "I but point out to you that which I see (myself); nor do I guide you but to the Path of Right!"

30. Then said the man who believed: "O my people! Truly I do fear for you something like the Day (of disaster) of the Confederates (in sin)!-

31. "Something like the fate of the People of Noah, the 'Ad, and the Thamud, and those who came after them: but Allah never wishes injustice to His servants.

32. "And O my people! I fear for you a Day when there will be mutual calling (and wailing),-

33. "A Day when you shall turn your backs and flee: no defender shall you have from Allah: any whom Allah leaves to stray, there is none to guide.

34. "And to you there came Joseph in times gone by, with Clear Signs, but you did not cease to doubt of the (mission) for which he had come: at length, when he died, you said: Allah will not send any Messenger after him. Thus Allah leaves to stray such as transgress and live in doubt,-

35. "(Such) as dispute about the Signs of Allah, without any authority that has reached them, grievous and odious[11] (is such conduct) in the sight of Allah and of the Believers. Thus Allah seals up every heart of arrogant and obstinate transgressors."

36. Pharaoh said: "O Haman! build me a lofty palace, that I may attain the ways and means,-

37. "The ways and means of (reaching) the heavens, and that I may mount up to the God of Moses: But as far as I am concerned, I think (Moses) is a liar!" Thus was made alluring[12], in Pharaoh's eyes, the evil of his deeds, and he was hindered from the Path; and the plot of Pharaoh led to nothing but perdition[13]

---

11. Detestable, loathsome   12. Attractive, appealing
13. Eternal death, damnation

(for him).

38. The man who believed said further: "O my people! follow me: I will lead you to the Path of Right.

39. "O my people! This life of the present is nothing but (temporary) convenience: It is the Hereafter that is the Home that will last.

40. "He that works evil will not be requited but by the like thereof: and he that works a righteous deed - whether man or woman - and is a Believer- such will enter the Garden (of Bliss):therein will they have abundance without measure.

41. "And O my people! How (strange) it is for me to call you to Salvation while you call me to the Fire!

42. "You do call upon me to blaspheme[14] against Allah, and to join with Him partners of whom I have no knowledge; and I call you to the Exalted in Power, Who forgives again and again!"

43. "Without doubt you do call me to one who is not fit to be called to, whether in this world, or in the Hereafter; our return will be to Allah; and the transgressors will be Companions of the Fire!

44. "Soon will you remember what I say to you (now)-My (own) affair I commit to Allah: for Allah (ever) watches over His servants."

45. Then Allah saved him from (every) ill that they plotted (against him), but the burnt[15] of the Penalty encompassed[16] on all sides the People of Pharaoh.

46. In front of the Fire will they be brought, morning and evening: and (the sentence will be) on the Day that Judgment will be established: "You cast the People of Pharaoh into the severest Chastisement!"

47. Behold, they will dispute with each other in the Fire! The weak ones (who followed) will say to those who had been arrogant, "We but followed you: can you then take (on your-selves) from us some share of the Fire?

48. Those who had been arrogant will say: "We are all in this (Fire)!

---

14. To speak profanely, curse or swear   15. Force or impact
16. Encircled

Truly, Allah has judged between (His) servants!"

49. Those in the Fire will say to the Keepers of Hell: "Pray to your Lord to lighten us the Penalty for a day (at least)!"

50. They will say: "Did there not come to you your Apostles with Clear Signs?" They will say, "Yes". They will reply, "Then pray (as you like)! But the prayer of those without Faith is nothing but (futile[17] wandering) in (mazes[18] of) error!"

51. We will, without doubt, help Our Apostles and those who believe, (both) in this world's life and on the Day when the Wit-nesses will stand forth,-

52. The Day when no profit will it be to Wrong-doers to present their excuses, but they will (only) have the Curse and the Home of Misery.

53. We did aforetime give Moses the (Book of) Guidance, and We gave the Book in inheri-tance to the Children of Israel,-

54. A Guide and a Message to men of Understanding.

55. Patiently, then, persevere: for the Promise of Allah is true: and ask forgiveness for your fault, and celebrate the Praises of your Lord in the evening and in the morning.

56. Those who dispute about the Signs of Allah without any authority bestowed on them,-there is nothing in their breasts but (the quest of) greatness, which they shall never attain to: seek refuge, then, in Allah: It is He Who hears and sees (all things).

57. Assuredly the creation of the heavens and the earth is a greater (matter) than the creation of men: yet most men do not understand.

58. Not equal are the blind and those who (clearly) see: nor are (equal) those who believe and work deeds of righteousness, and those who do evil. Little do you learn by admonition!

59. The Hour will certainly come: therein is no doubt: yet most men do not believe.

60. And your Lord says: "Call on Me; I will answer your (Prayer):

---

17.   Vain, useless   18.   Web, network

but those who are too arrogant to serve Me will surely find themselves in Hell - in humiliation!"

61. It is Allah Who has made the Night for you, that you may rest therein, and the Day as that which helps (you) to see. Verily Allah is full of Grace and Bounty to men: yet most men give no thanks.

62. Such is Allah, your Lord, the Creator of all things, there is no god but He: then how you are deluded away from the Truth!

63. Thus are deluded those who are wont[19] to reject the Signs of Allah.

64. It is Allah Who has made for you the earth as a resting place, and the sky as a canopy[20], and has given you shape- and made your shapes beautiful,- and has provided for you Sustenance, of things pure and good;- such is Allah your Lord. So Glory to Allah, the Lord of the Worlds!

65. He is the Living (One): there is no god but He: call upon Him, giving Him sincere devotion. Praise be to Allah, Lord of the Worlds!

66. Say: "I have been forbid-den to invoke those whom you invoke besides Allah,- seeing that the Clear Sings have come to me from my Lord; and I have been commanded to submit (in Islam) to the Lord of the Worlds."

67. It is He Who has created you from dust, then from a sperm-drop, then from a leech-like clot; then He gets you out (into the light) as a child: then lets you (grow and) reach your age of full strength; then lets you become old,- though of you there are some who die before;- and lets you reach a term appointed; in order that you may learn wisdom.

68. It is He Who gives Life and Death; and when He decides upon an affair, He says to it, "Be", and it is.

69. Don't you see those that dispute concerning the Sings of Allah? How are they turned away (from Reality)?-

70. Those who reject the Book and the (revelations) with which

---

19. Accustomed to   20. Covering, an overhanging shelter

We sent Our Apostles: but soon shall they know,-

71.   When the yokes (shall be) round their necks, and the chains; they shall be dragged along-

72.   In the boiling fetid[21] fluid: then in the Fire they shall be burned;

73.   Then shall it be said to them: "Where are the (deities) to which you gave part- worship-

74.   "Besides Allah?" They will reply: "They have left us in the lurch: nay, we did not invoke of old, anything (that had real existence)." Thus does Allah leave the Unbelievers to stray.

75.   "That was because you were wont to rejoice on the earth in things other than the Truth, and that you were wont to be insolent.

76.   "You enter the gates of Hell, to dwell therein: and evil is (this) abode of the arrogant!"

77.   So persevere in patience; for the Promise of Allah is true: and whether We show you (in this life) some part of what We promise them,- or We take your soul (to Our Mercy) (before that),-(in any case) it is to Us that they shall (all) return.

78.   We did aforetime send Apostles before you: of them there are some whose story We have related to you, and some whose story We have not related to you. It was not (possible) for any Apostle to bring a Sign except by the leave of Allah: but when the Command of Allah issued, the matter was decided in truth and justice, and there perished, there and then those who stood on Falsehoods.

79.   It is Allah Who made cattle for you, that you may use some for riding and some for food;

80.   And there are (other) advantages in them for you (besides); that you may through them attain to any need (there may be) in your hearts; and on them and on ships you are carried.

81.   And He shows you (always) His Signs: then which of the Signs of Allah will you deny?

82.   Do they not travel through the earth and see what was the End

---

21.   Stinking

of those before them? They were more numerous than these and superior in strength and in the traces (they have left) in the land: yet all that they accomp-lished was of no profit to them.

83. For when their Apostles came to them with Clear Signs, they exulted[22] in such knowledge (and skill) as they had; but that very (wrath) at which they were wont to scoff[23] hemmed[24] them in.

84. But when they saw Our Punishment, they said: "We believe in Allah,- the One Allah - and we reject the partners we used to join with Him."

85. But their professing the Faith when they (actually) saw Our Punishment, was not going to profit them. (Such has been) Allah's Way of dealing with His servants (from the most ancient times). And even thus did the Rejecters of Allah perish (utterly)!

---

22. Were proud of
24. Encircled them

23. Make fun of

SURAH—41
SURAH FUSSILAT
(INTRODUCTION)

This is the second of the series of seven Surahs bearing the Abbreviated Letters *Ha-Mim,* as explained in the Introduction to S. 40. To prevent confusion with other Surahs of the *Ha-Mim* series, the word *Sajdah* is sometimes added to the title, making it *Ha-Mim as-Sajdah,* the double title being necessary as there is another Surah called *Sajdah* (S. 32). To avoid the double title it is sometimes called *Fussilat,* from the occurrence of the word in verse 3.

The meaning *of Ha-Mim* has been explained in the Introduction to S. 40, where will also be found a note on the chronology and general theme of the seven *Ha-Mim* Surahs.

For this particular Surah the theme is that the basis of Faith and Revelation is Allah's Power and Goodness, and the fruit of both is man's righteousness and healing.

SURAH HA-MIM SAJDA (FUSSILAT)

In the name of Allah, Most Gracious, Most Merciful.

1. Ha -Mim:

2. A Revelation from (Allah), Most Gracious, Most Merciful;-

3. A Book, whereof the verses are explained in detail;- a Qur'an in Arabic, for people who understand;-

4. Giving good news and admonition: yet most of them turn away, and so they do not hear.

5. They say: "Our hearts are under veils, (concealed) from that to which you invite us, and in our ears is a deafness, and between us and you is a screen: so you do (what you will); for us, we shall do (what we will!)"

6. You say : "I am but a man like you: It is revealed to me by Inspiration, that your God is One God: so stand true to Him, and ask for His Forgiveness." And woe to those who join gods with Allah,-

7. Those who do not practise regular Charity, and who even deny the Hereafter.

8. For those who believe and work deeds of righteousness is a reward that will never fail.

9. Say: Is it that you deny Him Who created the earth in two Days? And do you join equals with Him? He is the Lord of (all) the Worlds.

10. He set on the (earth), mountains standing firm, high above it, and bestowed blessings on the earth, and measured therein its sustenance in four Days, alike for (all) who ask.

11. Moreover He compre-hended in His design the sky, and it had been (as) smoke: He said to it and to the earth: "You come together, willingly or un-willingly." They said: "We do come (together), in willing obedience."

12. So He completed them as seven firmaments[1] in two Days, and He assigned[2] to each heaven its duty and command. And We adorned the lower heaven with lights, and (provided it) with guard. Such is the Decree of (Him) the Exalted in Might, Full of Knowledge.

13. But if they turn away, you say: "I have warned you of a stunning Punishment (as of thunder and lightning) like that which (overtook) the 'Ad and the Thamud!"

14. Behold, the Apostles came to them, from before them and behind them, (preaching): "Serve none but Allah." They said, "If our Lord had so pleased, He would certainly have sent down angels (to preach). Now we reject your mission (altogether)."

15. Now the 'Ad behaved arrogantly through the land, against (all) truth and reason, and said: "Who is superior to us in strength?" What! did they not see that Allah, Who created them, was superior to them in strength? But they continued to reject Our Signs!

16. So We sent against them a furious wind through days of disaster, that We might give them a taste of a Chastisement of humiliation in this life; but the Chastisement of the Hereafter will be more humilia-ting still: and they will find no help.

17. As to the Thamud, We gave them Guidance, but they preferred

---

1. Groups of stars   2. Allotted

blindness (of heart) to Guidance: so the stunning Punishment of humiliation seized them, because of what they had earned.

18. But We delivered those who believed and practised righteousness.

19. On the Day that the enemies of Allah will be gathered together to the Fire, they will be marched in ranks.

20. At length, when they reach the (Fire), their hearing, their sight, and their skins will bear witness against them, as to (all) their deeds.

21. They will say to their skins: "Why do you bear witness against us?" They will say: "Allah has given us speech,- (He) Who gives speech to everything: He created you for the first time, and unto Him were you to return.

22. "You did not seek to hide yourselves, lest your hearing, your sight, and your skins should bear witness against you! But you thought that Allah did not know many of the things that you used to do!

23. "But this thought of yours which you entertained concer-ning your Lord, has brought you to destruction, and (now) you have become of those utterly lost!"

24. If, then, they have patience, the Fire will be a home for them! and if they beg to be received into favour, into favour will they not (then) be received.

25. And We have destined[3] for them intimate companions (of like nature), who made alluring to them what was before them and behind them; and the sentence among the previous generations of Jinns and men, who have passed away, is proved against them; for they are utterly lost.

26. The Unbelievers say: "Do not listen to this Qur'an, but talk at random in the midst of its (reading), that you may gain the upper hand!"

27. But We will certainly give the Unbelievers a taste of a severe Chastisement, and We will requite them for the worst of their deeds.

---

3.   Appointed, decreed

28. Such is the requital of the enemies of Allah,- the Fire: therein will be for them the Eternal Home: a (fit) requital, for that they were wont[4] to reject Our Signs.

29. And the Unbelievers will say: "Our Lord! Show us those, among Jinns and men, who misled us: We shall crush them beneath our feet, so that they become the vilest[5] (before all)."

30. In the case of those who say, "Our Lord is Allah", and, further, stand straight and steadfast, the angels descend on them (from time to time): "Fear you not!" (they suggest), "Nor grieve! but receive the Glad Tidings of the Garden (of Bliss), the which you were promised!

31. "We are your protectors in this life and in the Hereafter: therein you shall have all that your souls shall desire; therein you shall have all that you ask for!-

32. "A hospitable[6] gift from One Oft-Forgiving, Most Merciful!"

33. Who is better in speech than one who calls (men) to Allah, works righteousness, and says, "I am of those who bow in Islam"?

34. Nor can Goodness and Evil be equal. Repel (Evil) with what is better: then will he between whom and you was hatred, become as it were your friend and intimate!

35. And no one will be granted such goodness except those who exercise patience and self-restraint,- none but persons of the greatest good fortune.

36. And if (at any time) an incitement to discord[7] is made to you by the Evil One, seek refuge in Allah. He is the One Who hears and knows all things.

37. Among His Signs are the Night and the Day, and the Sun and the Moon. Do not adore[8] the sun and the moon, but adore Allah, Who created them, if it is Him you wish to serve.

38. But if the (Unbelievers) are arrogant, (no matter): for in the presence of your Lord are those who celebrate His praises by

---

4. Accustomed to   5. Lowest
6. Generous   7. Strife, lack of harmony
8. Worship

night and by day. And they never flag[9] (nor feel themselves above it).

39. And among His Signs is this: that you see the earth barren and desolate; but when We send down rain to it, it is stirred to life and yields increase. Truly, He Who gives life to the (dead) earth can surely give life to (men) who are dead. For He has power over all things.

40. Those who pervert[10] the Truth in Our Signs are not hidden from Us. Which is better?- he that is cast into the Fire, or he that comes safe through, on the Day of Judgment? Do what you will: verily He sees (clearly) all that you do.

41. Those who reject the Mes-sage when it comes to them (are not hidden from Us). And indeed it is a Book of exalted power.

42. No falsehood can app-roach it from before or behind it: It is sent down by One full of Wisdom, Worthy of all Praise.

43. Nothing is said to you that was not said to the Apostles before you: that your Lord has at His Command (all) forgiveness as well as a most Grievous Chastisement.

44. Had We sent this as a Qur'an (in a language) other than Arabic, they would have said: "Why are not its verses explained in detail? What! (a Book) not in Arabic and (a Messenger) an Arab?" Say: "It is a Guide and a Healing to those who believe ; and for those who do not believe, there is a deafness in their ears, and it is blindness in their (eyes): they are (as it were) being called from a place far distant!"

45. We certainly gave Moses the Book aforetime: but disputes arose therein. Had it not been for a Word that went forth before from your Lord, (their differences) would have been settled between them: but they remained in suspicious disquieting[11] doubt thereon.

46. Whoever works righteousness benefits his own soul; whoever works evil, it is against his own soul: nor is your Lord ever unjust (in the least) to His servants.

---

9.   Slack   10.   Corrupt, distort
11. Upsetting, distressing

47.   To Him is referred the Knowledge of the Hour (of Judgment: He knows all): No date-fruit comes out of its sheath, nor does a female conceive (within her womb) nor bring forth (young), but by His knowledge. The Day that (Allah) will propound[12] to them the (question), "Where are the partners (you attributed) to Me?" They will say, "We do assure You not one of us can bear witness!"

48.   The (deities) they used to invoke aforetime will leave them in the lurch[13], and they will perceive that they have no way of escape.

49.   Man does not weary of asking for good (things), but if ill touches him, he gives up all hope (and) is lost in despair.

50.   When We give him a taste of some Mercy from Ourselves, after some adversity has touched him, he is sure to say, "This is due to my (merit): I do not think that the Hour (of Judgment) will (ever) be established; but if I am brought back to my Lord, I have (much) good (stored) in His sight!" But We will show the Unbelievers the truth of all that they did, and We shall give them the taste of a severe Chastise-ment.

51.   When We bestow favours on man, he turns away, and gets himself remote on his side (instead of coming to Us); and when evil seizes him, (he comes) full of prolonged prayer!

52.   Say: "Do you see if the (Revelation) is (really) from Allah, and yet do you reject it? Who is more astray than one who is in a schism[14] far (from any purpose)?"

53.   Soon will We show them Our Signs in the (furthest) regions (of the earth), and in their own souls, until it becomes manifest to them that this is the Truth. Is it not enough that your Lord Witnessess all things?

54.   Ah indeed! Are they in doubt concerning the Meeting with their Lord? Ah indeed! It is He that encompasses all things!

---

12.   Propose, offer for consideration
13.   Most different time
14.   Division of a group into mutually opposing parties.

SURAH—42

SURAH ASH-SHURA

(INTRODUCTION)

This is the third Surah of the *Ha-Mim* series of seven Surahs, for which see the Introduction to S. 40.

The theme is how evil and blasphemy can be cured by the Mercy and Guidance of Allah, which come through His Revelation. Men are asked to settle their differences in patience by mutual Consultation (42: 38), which explains the title of the Surah.

SURAH SHURA (CONSULTATION)

In the name of Allah, Most Gracious, Most Merciful.

1.   Ha-Mim

2.   Ain. Sin. Qaf.

3.   Thus (He) sends inspiration to you as (He did) to those before you,- Allah, Exalted in Power, full of Wisdom.

4.   To Him belongs all that is in the heavens and on earth: and He is Most High, Most Great.

5.   The heavens are almost rent asunder from above them (by His Glory): and the angels celebrate the Praises of their Lord, and pray for forgiveness for (all) beings on earth: behold! Verily Allah is He, the Oft-Forgiving, Most Merciful.

6.   And those who take as protectors others besides Him,- Allah watches over them; and you are not the disposer of their affairs.

7.   Thus We have sent by inspiration to you an Arabic Qur'an: that you may warn the Mother of Cities[1] and all around her,- and warn (them) of the Day of Assembly, of which there is no doubt: (when) some will be in the Garden, and some in the Blazing Fire.

8.   If Allah had so willed, He could have made them a single people; but He admits whom He will to His Mercy; and the wrong-doers will have no protector nor helper.

9.   What! Have they taken (for worship) protectors besides Him? But it is Allah,- He is the Protector, and it is He Who gives life

---

1.   Makkah

to the dead: It is He Who has power over all things.

10. Whatever it be wherein you differ, the decision thereof is with Allah: such is Allah my Lord: In Him I trust, and to Him I turn.

11. (He is) the Creator of the heavens and the earth: He has made for you pairs from among yourselves, and pairs among cattle: by this means does He multiply you: there is nothing whatever like unto Him, and He is the One that hears and sees (all things).

12. To Him belong the keys of the heavens and the earth: He enlarges and restricts the sustenance to whom He will: for He knows full well all things.

13. The same Religion He has established for you as that which He enjoined[2] on Noah - the which We have sent by inspiration to you - and that which We enjoined on Abraham, Moses, and Jesus: namely, that you should remain steadfast in Religion, and make no divisions therein: to those who worship other things than Allah, hard is the (way) to which you call them. Allah chooses to Himself those whom He pleases, and guides to Himself those who turn (to Him).

14. And they became divided only after Knowledge reached them,- through selfish envy as between themselves. Had it not been for a Word that went forth before from your Lord, (tending[3]) to a term appointed, the matter would have been settled between them: but truly those who have inherited the Book after them are in suspicious (disquieting) doubt concerning it.

15. Now then, for that (reason), call (them to the Faith), and stand steadfast as you are commanded, nor you follow their vain desires; but say: "I believe in the Book which Allah has sent down; and I am commanded to judge justly between you. Allah is our Lord and your Lord: for us (is the responsibility for) our deeds, and for you for your deeds. There is no contention[4] between us and you. Allah will bring us together, and to Him is (our) Final Goal.

16. But those who dispute concerning Allah after He has been

2. Commanded, prescribed
3. To be moving or directed to
4. Strife, controversy

accepted,- futile[5] is their dispute in the Sight of their Lord: on them is wrath, and for them will be a Chastisement terrible.

17. It is Allah Who has sent down the Book in Truth, and the Balance (by which to weigh conduct). And what will make you realise that perhaps the Hour is close at hand?

18. Only those wish to hasten it who do not believe in it: those who believe hold it in awe, and know that it is the Truth. Behold, verily those that dispute concerning the Hour are far astray.

19. Gracious is Allah to His servants: He gives sustenance to whom He pleases: and He is Strong, the Mighty.

20. To any that desires the tilth[6] of the Hereafter, We give increase in his tilth, and to any that desires the tilth of this world, We grant somewhat thereof, but he has no share or lot in the Hereafter.

21. What! have they partners (in godhead), who have establi-shed for them some religion without the permission of Allah? Had it not been for the Decree of Judgment, the matter would have been decided between them (at once). But verily the Wrong-doers will have a grievous Chastisement.

22. You will see the Wrong-doers in fear on account of what they have earned, and (the burden of) that must (necessarily) fall on them. But those who believe and work righteous deeds will be in the luxuriant[7] meads[8] of the Gardens: they shall have, before their Lord, all that they wish for. That will indeed be the magni-ficent Bounty (of Allah).

23. That is (the Bounty) whereof Allah gives Glad Tidings to His Servants who believe and do righteous deeds. Say: "No reward do I ask of you for this except the love of those near of kin." And if any one earns any good, We shall give him an increase of good in respect thereof: for Allah is Oft-Forgiving, Most Ready to appreciate (service).

24. What! Do they say, "He has forged[9] a falsehood against Allah"?

---

5.   Vain, useless   6.   Cultivation, Reward
7.   Lush and profuse   8.   Meado, a well-watered grassy land
9.   Fabricated

But if Allah willed, He could seal up your heart. And Allah blots out Vanity, and proves the Truth by His Words. For He knows well the secrets of all hearts.

25. He is the One that accepts repentance from His servants and forgives sins: and He knows all that you do.

26. And He listens to those who believe and do deeds of righteousness, and gives them increase of His Bounty: but for the Unbelievers their is a terrible Chastisement.

27. If Allah were to enlarge the provision for His servants, they would indeed transgress beyond all bounds through the earth; but He sends (it) down in due measure as He pleases. For He is with His servants Well-acquainted, Watchful.

28. He is the One that sends down rain (even) after (men) have given up all hope, and scatters His Mercy (far and wide). And He is the Protector, Worthy of all Praise.

29. And among His Signs is the creation of the heavens and the earth, and the living creatures that He has scattered through them: and He has power to gather them together when He wills.

30. Whatever misfortune happens to you, is because of the things your hands have wrought[10], and for many (of them) He grants forgiveness.

31. Nor can you escape[11] (anything), (fleeing) through the earth; nor have you, besides Allah, any one to protect or to help.

32. And among His Signs are the ships, smooth-running through the ocean, (tall) as mountains.

33. If it be His Will, He can still the Wind: then would they become motionless on the back of the (ocean). Verily in this are Signs for everyone who patiently perseveres and is grateful.

34. Or He can cause them to perish because of the (evil) which (the men) have earned; but much does He forgive.

35. But let those know, who dispute about Our Signs, that there is for them no way of escape.

36. Whatever you are given (here) is (but) a convenience of this life: but that which is with Allah is better and more lasting: (it

---

10. Done   11. Frustrate, baffle

is) for those who believe and put their trust in their Lord.

37. Those who avoid the greater crimes and shameful deeds, and, when they are angry even then forgive;

38. Those who hearken to their Lord, and establish regular Prayer; who (conduct) their affairs by mutual consultation; who spend out of what We bestow on them for Sustenance;

39. And those who, when an oppressive wrong is inflicted on them, (are not cowed[12] but) help and defend themselves.

40. The recompense[13] for an injury is an injury equal thereto (in degree): but if a person forgives and makes reconciliation[14], his reward is due from Allah: for (Allah) does not love those who do wrong.

41. But indeed if any do help and defend themselves after a wrong (done) to them, against such there is no cause of blame.

42. The blame is only against those who oppress men with wrong-doing and insolently transgress beyond bounds through the land, defying right and justice: for such there will be a Chastisement grievous.

43. But indeed if any show patience and forgive, that would truly be an affair of great resolution.

44. For any whom Allah lea-ves astray, there is no protector thereafter. And you will see the Wrong-doers, when in sight of the Penalty, say: "Is there any way (to effect) a return?"

45. And you will see them brought forward to the (Chastisement), in a humble frame of mind because of (their) disgrace, (and) looking with a stealthy glance. And the Believers will say: "Those are indeed in loss, who have given to perdition their own selves and those belonging to them on the Day of Judgment. Behold! Truly the Wrong-doers are in a lasting Chastisement!"

46. And no protectors have they to help them, other than Allah. And for any whom Allah leaves to stray, there is no way (to the Goal).

---

12. Intimidated, to subdue the spirit
13. Compensation, amends
14. Heal and settle, make friendly (after estragement)

47. You hearken to your Lord, before there come a Day which there will be no putting back, because of (the ordainment of) Allah! that Day there will be for you no place of refuge nor will there be for you any room for denial (of your sins)!

48. If then they turn away, We have not sent you as a guard over them. Your duty is but to convey (the Message). And truly, when We give man a taste of a Mercy from Ourselves, he exults[15] thereat[16], but when some ill happens to him, on account of the deeds which his hands have sent forth, truly then man is ungrateful!

49. To Allah belongs the dominion of the heavens and the earth. He creates what He wills (and plans). He bestows[17] (children) male or female according to His Will (and Plan),

50. Or He bestows both males and females, and He leaves barren whom He will: for He is full of Knowledge and Power.

51. It is not fitting for a man that Allah should speak to him except by inspiration, or from behind a veil, or by the sending of a Messenger to reveal, with Allah's permis-sion, what Allah wills: for He is Most High, Most Wise.

52. And thus We have, by Our Command, sent inspiration to you: you did not know (before) what was Revelation, and what was Faith; but We have made the (Qur'an) a Light, wherewith We guide such of Our servants as We will; and verily you do guide (men) to the Straight Way,-

53. The Way of Allah, to Whom belongs whatever is in the heavens and whatever is on earth. Behold (how) all affairs tend towards Allah!

---

15. Becomes happy and proud
16. On that a account, because of it
17. Grants

SURAH—43
SURAH AZ-ZUKHRUF
(INTRODUCTION)

This is the fourth Surah of the *Ha-Mim* series of seven Surahs. For their chronology and general theme see the Introduction to S. 40.

This Surah deals with the contrasts between the real glory of Truth and Revelation and the false glitter of what people like to believe and worship. It cites that examples of Abraham, Moses, and Jesus, as exposing the False holding up the Truth. The keyword *Zukhruf* (GoLd Adornments) occurs in verse 38, but the idea occurs all through the Surah.

SURAH ZUKHRUF (GOLD ADORNMENTS)

In the name of Allah, Most Gracious, Most Merciful.

1. Ha-Mim

2. By the Book that makes things clear,-

3. We have made it a Qur'an in Arabic, that you may be able to understand (and learn wisdom).

4. And verily, it is in the Mother of the Book, in Our Presence, high (in dignity), full of wisdom.

5. Shall We then take away the Message from you and repel (you) for that you are a people transgressing[1] beyond bounds?

6. But how many were the prophets We sent amongst the peoples of old?

7. And never came there a prophet to them but they mocked[2] him.

8. So We destroyed (them)- stronger in power than these;- and (thus) has passed on the Parable of the peoples of old.

9. If you were to question them, 'Who created the heavens and the earth?' They would be sure to reply, 'they were created by (Him), the Exalted in Power, full of Knowledge';-

10. (Yes, the same that) has made for you the earth (like a carpet) spread out, and has made for you roads (and channels) therein, in order that you may find guidance (on the way);

11. Who sends down (from time to time) rain from the sky in due

---

1. Trespassing   2. Made fun of him

measure;- and We raise to life therewith a land that is dead; even so will you be raised (from the dead);-

12. That has created pairs in all things, and has made for you ships and cattle on which you ride,

13. In order that you may sit firm and square on their backs, and when so seated, you may celebrate the (kind) favour of your Lord, and say, "Glory to Him Who has subjected these to our (use), for we could never have accomplished this (by ourselves),

14. "And to our Lord, surely, must we turn back!"

15. Yet they attribute to some of His servants a share with Him (in His godhead)! truly is man a blasphemous ingrate[3] avowed[4]!

16. What! Has He taken daughters out of what He Himself creates, and granted to you sons for choice?

17. When news is brought to one of them of (the birth of) what he sets up as a likeness to (Allah) Most Gracious, his face darkens, and he is filled with inward grief!

18. Is then one brought up among trinkets[5], and unable to give a clear account in a dispute (to be associated with Allah)?

19. And they make into females angels who themselves serve Allah. Did they witness their creation? Their evidence will be recorded, and they will be called to account!

20. ("Ah!") they say, "If it had been the Will of (Allah) Most Gracious, we should not have worshipped such (deities)!" Of that they have no knowledge! they do nothing but lie!

21. What! have We given them a Book before this, to which they are holding fast?

22. Nay! they say: "We found our fathers following a certain religion, and we do guide ourselves by their footsteps."

23. Just in the same way, whenever We sent a Warner before you to any people, the wealthy ones among them said: "We found our fathers following a certain religion, and we will certainly follow in their foot-steps."

24. He said: "What! Even if I brought you better guidance than that

---

3. Ungrateful   4. Confessed, admitted
5. Trifling ornaments, small fancy articles.

which you found your fathers following?" They said: "For us, we deny that you (prophets) are sent (on a mission at all)."

25.   So We exacted[6] retribution[7] from them: now see what was the end of those who rejected (Truth)!

26.   Behold! Abraham said to his father and his people: "I do indeed clear myself of what you worship:

27.   "(I worship) only Him Who made me, and He will certainly guide me."

28.   And he left it as a Word to endure among those who came after him, that they may turn back (to Allah).

29.   Yes, I have given the good things of this life to these (men) and their fathers, until the Truth has come to them, and an Apostle making things clear.

30.   But when the Truth came to them, they said: "This is sorcery[8], and we do reject it."

31.   Also, they say: "Why is not this Qur'an sent down to some leading man in either of the two (chief) cities?"

32.   Is it they who would portion out the Mercy of your Lord? It is We Who portion out between them their livelihood in the life of this world: and We raise some of them above others in ranks, so that some may command work from others. But the Mercy of your Lord is better than the (wealth) which they amass[9].

33.   And were it not that (all) men might become of one community, We would provide, for everyone that blasphemes against (Allah) Most Gracious, silver roofs for their houses and (silver) stairways on which to go up,

34.   And (silver) doors to their houses, and thrones (of silver) on which they could recline,

35.   And also adornments[10] of gold. But all this were nothing but enjoyment[11] of the present life: The Hereafter, in the sight of your Lord is for the Righteous.

36.   If anyone withdraws himself from remembrance of (Allah) Most

---

6.   Inflicted   7.   Punishment

8.   Magic   9.   Collect, hoard

10. Ornaments, decorations   11. Things or articles for daily use

Gracious, We appoint for him an evil one, to be an intimate companion to him.

37. Such (evil ones) really hinder them from the Path, but they think that they are being guided aright!

38. At length, when (such a one) comes to Us, he says (to his evil companion): "Would that between me and you were the distance of East and West!" Ah! evil is the companion (indeed)!

39. When you have done wrong, it will avail you nothing, that Day, that you shall be partners in Punishment!

40. Can you then make the deaf to hear, or give direction to the blind or to such as (wander) in manifest error?

41. Even if We take you away, We shall be sure to exact retribution from them,

42. Or We shall show you that (accomplished) which We have promised them: for verily We shall prevail over them.

43. So you hold fast to the Revelation sent down to you; verily you are on a Straight Way.

44. The (Qur'an) is indeed the message, for you and for your people; and soon shall you (all) be brought to account.

45. And you question our Apostles whom We sent before you; did We appoint any deities other than (Allah) Most Gra-cious, to be worshipped?

46. We sent Moses afore time, with Our Signs, to Pharaoh and his Chiefs: he said, "I am an Apostle of the Lord of the Worlds."

47. But when he came to them with Our Signs, behold they ridiculed them.

48. We showed them Sign after Sign, each greater than its fellow, and We seized them with Punishment, in order that they might turn (to Us).

49. And they said, "O you sorcerer! Invoke your Lord for us according to His covenant[12] with you; for we shall truly accept guidance."

50. But when We removed the Penalty from them, behold, they broke their word.

---

12. A solemn promise

51.   And Pharaoh proclaimed among his people, saying: O my people! Does not the dominion of Egypt belong to me, (witness) these streams flowing underneath my (palace)? Do you not see then?

52.   "Am I not better than this (Moses), who is a contemptible[13] wretch[14] and can scarcely express himself clearly?

53.   "Then why are not gold bracelets bestowed on him, or (why) come (not) with him angels accompanying him in procession?"

54.   Thus he made fools of his people, and they obeyed him: truly they were a rebellious people (against Allah).

55.   When at length they provoked Us, We exacted retribution from them, and We drowned them all.

56.   And We made them (a people) of the Past and an Example to later ages.

57.   When (Jesus) the son of Mary is held up as an example, behold, your people raise a clamour[15] threat (in ridicule)!

58.   And they say, "Are our gods best, or he?" This they set forth to you, only by way of disputation[16]: yes, they are a contentious[17] people.

59.   He was no more than a servant: We granted Our favour to him, and We made him an example to the Children of Israel.

60.   And if it were Our Will, We could make angels from amongst you, succeeding each other on the earth.

61.   And (Jesus) shall be a Sign (for the coming of) the Hour (of Judgment): therefore have no doubt about the (Hour), but you follow Me: this is a Straight Way.

62.   Let not the Evil One hinder you: for he is to you an avowed enemy.

63.   When Jesus came with Clear Signs, he said: "Now I have come to you with Wisdom, and in order to make clear to you some of the (points) on which you dispute: therefore fear Allah and obey me.

---

13.   Insignificant   14.   Unfortunate, miserable person
15.   Uproar   16.   Debate, discussion
17.   Quarrelsome

64. "For Allah, He is my Lord and your Lord: so you worship Him: this is a Straight Way."

65. But sects from among themselves fell into disagree-ment: then woe to the wrong-doers, from the Chastisement of a Grievous Day!

66. Do they only wait for the Hour - that it should come on them all of a sudden, while they do not perceive?

67. Friends on that day will be foes, one to another,- except the Righteous.

68. My devotees[18]! no fear shall be on you that Day, nor shall you grieve,-

69. (Being) those who have believed in Our Signs and bowed (their wills to Ours) in Islam.

70. You enter the Garden, you and your wives, in (beauty and) rejoicing.

71. To them will be passed round, dishes and goblets[19] of gold: there will be there all that the souls could desire, all that the eyes could delight in: and you shall abide therein (for ever).

72. Such will be the Garden of which you are made heirs for your (good) deeds (in life).

73. You shall have therein abundance of fruit, from which you shall have satisfaction.

74. The sinners will be in the Punishment of Hell, to dwell therein (for ever):

75. Nowise[20] will the (punishment) be lightened for them, and in despair will they be there overwhelmed[21].

76. Nowise shall We be unjust to them: but it is they who have been unjust themselves.

77. They will cry: "O Malik[22]! would that your Lord put an end to us!" He will say, "Nay, but you shall abide!"

78. Verily We have brought the Truth to you: but most of you have a hatred for Truth.

---

18. Decoted servants
19. Drinking cups
20. In no way, by no means
21. Engulfed, drowned
22. Malik: The angel in charge in Hell.

79.   What! have they settled some plan (among themselves)? But it is We Who settle things.

80.   Or do they think that We do not hear their secrets and their private counsels? Indeed (We do), and Our Messengers are by them, to record.

81.   Say: "If (Allah) Most Gracious had a son, I would be the first to worship."

82.   Glory to the Lord of the heavens and the earth, the Lord of the Throne (of Authority)! (He is free) from the things they attribute (to Him)!

83.   So leave them to babble[23] and play (with vanities) until they meet that Day of theirs, which they have been promised.

84.   It is He Who is Allah in heaven and Allah on earth; and He is full of Wisdom and Know-ledge.

85.   And blessed is He to Whom belongs the dominion of the heavens and the earth, and all between them: with Him is the Knowledge of the Hour (of Judgment): and to Him shall you be brought back.

86.   And those whom they invoke besides Allah have no power of intercession;- only he who bears witness to the Truth, and they know (him).

87.   If you ask them, Who created them, they will certainly say, Allah: how then are they deluded away (from the Truth)?

88.   (Allah has knowledge) of the (Prophet's) cry, "O my Lord! Truly these are a people who will not believe!"

89.   But turn away from them, and say "Peace!" But soon shall they know!

---

23.   Chatter, to talk nonsense

SURAH—44

SURAH AD-DUKHAN

(INTRODUCTION)

For the chronology and the general theme of the Surahs of the *Ha-Mim* series, of which this is the fifth, see the Introduction to S. 40.

The theme of this particular Surah is how worldly pride and power are humbled in the dust if they resist spiritual forces, and how Evil and Good find their true setting in the Hereafter.

The title-word *Dukhan* occurs in verse 10. It means smoke or mist, and may refer to a drought or famine.

SURAH DUKHAN (SMOKE OR MIST)

In the name of Allah, Most Gracious, Most Merciful.

1. Ha-Mim.
2. By the Book that makes things clear;-
3. We sent it down during a Blessed Night: for We (ever) wish to warn (against Evil).
4. In that (Night) is made distinct every affair of wisdom,
5. By command, from Our Presence. For We (ever) send (revelations),
6. As a Mercy from your Lord: for He hears and knows (all things);
7. The Lord of the heavens and the earth and all between them, if you (but) have an assured faith.
8. There is no god but He: It is He Who gives life and gives death,- the Lord and Cherisher to you and your earliest ancestors.
9. Yet they play about in doubt.
10. Then you watch for the Day that the sky will bring forth a kind of smoke (or mist) plainly visible,
11. Enveloping the people: this will be a Grievous Chastisement.
12. (They will say:) "Our Lord! remove the Chastisement from us, for we do really believe!"
13. How shall the Message be (effectual) for them, seeing that an Apostle explaining things clearly has (already) come to them,-
14. Yet they turn away from him and say: "Tutored (by others), a

man possessed![1]"

15.   We shall indeed remove the Chastisement for a while, (but) truly you will revert (to your ways).

16.   One day We shall seize you with a mighty onslaught[2]: We will indeed (then) exact Retribution[3]!

17.   We tried, before them, the people of Pharaoh: there came to them an Apostle most honourable,

18.   Saying: "Restore to me the servants of Allah: I am to you an Apostle worthy of all trust;

19.   "And be not arrogant as against Allah: for I come to you with authority manifest[4].

20.   "For me, I have sought safety with my Lord and your Lord, against your injuring me.

21.   And if you do not believe me, at least keep yourselves away from me.".

22.   (But they were aggres-sive:) then he cried to his Lord: "These are indeed a people given to sin."

23.   (The reply came:) "March forth with My servants by night: for you are sure to be pursued.

24.   "And leave the sea as a furrow[5] (divided): for they are a host (destined) to be drowned."

25.   How many were the gardens and springs they left behind,

26.   And corn-fields and noble buildings,

27.   And wealth (and conve-niences of lief), wherein they had taken such delight!

28.   Thus (was their end)! And We made other people inherit (those things)!

29.   And neither heaven nor earth shed a tear over them: nor were they given a respite[6] (again).

30.   We delivered aforetime the Children of Israel from humiliating Punishment,

---

1.	Mad	2.	Raid, fierce attack
3.	Punishment	4.	Obvious, clear
5.	A trench, hollow between ridges, channel		
6.	Delay (or opportunity)		

31. Inflicted by Pharaoh, for he was arrogant (even) among inordinate[7] transgressors[8].

32. And We chose them aforetime above the nations, knowingly,

33. And granted them Signs in which there was a manifest trial.

34. As to these (Quraish), they say forsooth[9]:

35. "There is nothing beyond our first death, and we shall not be raised again.

36. "Then bring (back) our forefathers, if what you say is true!"

37. What! Are they better than the people of Tubba[10] and those who were before them? We destroyed them because they were guilty of sin.

38. We did not create the hea-vens, the earth, and all between them, merely in (idle) sport:

39. We did not create them except for just ends: but most of them do not understand.

40. Verily the Day of sorting out is the time appointed for all of them,-

41. The Day when no protec-tor can avail his client in any thing, and no help can they receive,

42. Except such as receive Allah's Mercy: for He is Exalted in Might, Most Merciful.

43. Verily the tree of Zaqqum,-

44. Will be the food of the Sinful,-

45. Like molten brass; it will boil in their insides.

46. Like the boiling of scalding[11] water.

47. (A voice will cry): "You seize him and drag him into the midst of the Blazing Fire!

48. "Then pour over his head the Chastisement of Boiling Water,

49. You "taste (this)! Truly you were mighty, full of honour!

50. "Truly this is what you used to doubt!"

---

7. Immoderate, excessive
8. Those who violate and go beyond bounds of law, decency, etc.,
9. (Used ironically or in a derogatory sense) Truly, n doubt
10. Family name of ancient Himyar kings of Yemen.
11. Boiling

51.   As to the Righteous (they will be) in a position of security,

52.   Among Gardens and Springs;

53.   Dressed in fine silk and in rich brocade[12], they will face each
       other;

54.   So; and We shall join them to Companions with beautiful, big
       and lustrous[13] eyes.

55.   There can they call for every kind of fruit in peace and security;

56.   Nor will they there taste Death, except the first death; and He
       will preserve them from the Chastisement of the Blazing Fire,

57.   As a Bounty from your Lord! that will be the supreme
       achievement!

58.   Verily, We have made this (Qur'an) easy, in your tongue, in
       order that they may give heed[14].

59.   So you wait and watch; for they (too) are waiting.

---

12.   Thick silk   13.   Shiny
14.   Bear in mind

SURAH—45
SURAH AL-JATHIYA
(INTRODUCTION)

This is the sixth Surah of Ha-Mim series: for their general theme and chronology, see the Introduction to S.40.

SURAH AL-JATHIYA (BOWING THE KNEE)

In the name of Allah, Most Gracious, Most Merciful.

1. Ha-Mim.

2. The revelation of the Book is from Allah, the Exalted in Power, full of Wisdom.

3. Verily in the heavens and the earth, are Signs for those who believe.

4. And in the creation of your-selves and the fact that animals are scattered (through the earth), are Signs for those of assured Faith.

5. And in the alternation[1] of Night and Day, and the fact that Allah sends down Sustenance from the sky, and revives[2] there with the earth after its death, and in the change of the winds,- are Signs for those that are wise.

6. These are the Signs of Allah, which We rehearse[3] to you in Truth; then in what exposition[4] will they believe after (rejecting) Allah and His Signs?

7. Woe to each sinful dealer in Falsehoods:

8. He hears the Signs of Allah rehearsed to him, yet is obstinate[5] and lofty[6], as if he had not heard them: then announce to him a Chastisement Grievous!

9. And when he learns something of Our Signs, he takes them in jest: for such there will be a humiliating Penalty.

10. In front of them is Hell: and of no profit to them is anything they may have earned, nor any protectors they may have taken to themselves besides Allah: for them is a tremendous[7]

1.	Succession	2.	Gives life
3.	Recount, repeat	4.	Explanation, discourse
5.	Stubborn	6.	Arrogant, proud
7.	Great, dreadful		

Chastisement.

11.	This is (true) Guidance and for those who reject the Signs of their Lord, is a grievous Chastisement of abomination.

12.	It is Allah Who has subjected[8] the sea to you, that ships may sail through it by His command, that you may seek of His Bounty, and that you may be grateful.

13.	And He has subjected to you, as from Him, all that is in the heavens and on earth: behold, in that are Signs indeed for those who reflect[9].

14.	Tell those who believe, to forgive those who do not look forward to the Days of Allah: It is for Him to recompense[10] (for good or ill) each People according to what they have earned.

15.	If any one does a righteous deed, it ensures[11] to the benefit of his own soul; if he does evil, it works against (his own soul). In the end will you (all) be brought back to your Lord.

16.	We did aforetime grant to the Children of Israel the Book, the Power of Command, and Prophethood; We gave them, for Sustenance, things good and pure; and We favoured them above the nations.

17.	And We granted them Clear Signs in affairs (of Religion): it was only after knowledge had been granted to them that they fell into schisms[12], through insolent envy[13] among themselves. Verily your Lord will judge between them on the Day of Judgment as to those matters in which they set up differences.

18.	Then We put you on the (right) Way of Religion: so you follow that (Way), and do not follow the desires of those who do not know .

19.	They will be of no use to you in the sight of Allah: it is only Wrong-doers (that stand as) protectors, one to another: but Allah is the Protector of the Righteous.

20.	These are clear evidences[14] to men and a Guidance and Mercy

---

8.	Pressed into your service

9.	Think, ponder

10.	Reward

11.	Takes, ponder

12.	Became divided into mutually hostile parties.

13.	Rivalry

14.	Proofs, eye-opening evidence

to those of assured Faith.

21. What! do those who seek after evil ways think that We shall hold them equal with those who believe and do righteous deeds,- that equal will be their life and their death? Ill is the judgment that they make.

22. Allah created the heavens and the earth for just ends, and in order that each soul may find the recompense of what it has earned, and none of them be wronged.

23. Do you see such a one as takes as his god his own vain desire? Allah has, knowing (him as such), left him astray, and sealed his hearing and his heart (and understanding), and put a cover on his sight. Who, then, will guide him after Allah (has withdrawn Guidance)? Will you not then receive admonition[15]?

24. And they say: "What is there but our life in this world? We shall die and we live, and nothing but Time can destroy us." But of that they have no knowledge: they merely conjecture[16]:

25. And when Our Clear Signs are rehearsed[17] to them, their argument is nothing but this: they say, "Bring (back) our forefathers, if what you say is true!"

26. Say: "It is Allah Who gives you life, then gives you death; then He will gather you together for the Day of Judgment about which there is no doubt": But most men do not understand.

27. To Allah belongs the dominion of the heavens and the earth, and the Day that the Hour of Judgment is established,- that Day will the dealers in False-hood perish!

28. And you will see every nation bowing the knee: every nation will be called to its Record: "This Day you shall be recompensed[18] for all that you did!

29. "This Our Record speaks about you with truth: for We were wont[19] to put on Record all that you did."

30. Then, as to those who believed and did righteous deeds, their Lord will admit them to His Mercy, that will be the achievement

---

15. Warning, advice   16. Guess, surmise, assume
17. Recited   18. Rewarded
19. Accustomed to

for all to see.

31.   But as to those who rejected Allah, (to them will be said): "Were not Our Signs rehearsed to you? But you were arrogant, and were a people given to sin!

32.   "And when it was said that the promise of Allah was true, and that the Hour- there was no doubt about its (coming), you used to say, 'We do not know what is the Hour: we only think it is an idea, and we have no firm assurance.'"

33.   Then will appear to them the evil (fruits) of what they did, and they will be completely encircled by that which they used to mock[20] at!

34.   It will also be said: "This Day We will forget you as you forgot the meeting of this Day of yours! and your abode[21] is the Fire, and you do not have any helpers!

35.   "This, because you used to take the Signs of Allah in jest, and the life of the world deceived you:" (from) that Day, therefore, they shall not be taken out thence, nor shall they be received into Grace.

36.   Then Praise be to Allah, Lord of the heavens and Lord of the earth,- Lord and Cherisher of all the Worlds!

37.   To Him belongs Greatness throughout the heavens and the earth: and He is Exalted in Power, full of Wisdom!

---

20.   Laugh at, make fun of   21.   Home

SURAH—46
SURAH AL-AHQAF
(INTRODUCTION)

This is the seventh and last Surah of the *Ha-Mim* series. For the general theme and chronological place of these Surahs see the. Introduction to S. 40.

The *Ahqaf* (mentioned in verse 21) are the long and winding crooked tracts of sand-hills, characteristic of the country of the 'Ad people, adjoining Hadhramaut and Yaman: See 7:65. These people had, at that time, probably a fertile irrigated country, but their sins brought on the calamity, mentioned in 46: 24-25. The lesson of this Surah is that if the Truth is challenged, the challenge will be duly answered, and Truth vindicated.

SURAH AL-AHQAF (WINDING SAND-TRACTS)
In the name of Allah, Most Gracious, Most Merciful.

1. Ha-Mim.

2. The Revelation of the Book is from Allah, the Exalted in Power, full of Wisdom.

3. We did not create the heavens and the earth and all between them but for just ends[1], and for a term appointed[2]. But those who reject Faith turn away from that whereof[3] they are warned.

4. Say: "Do you see what it is you invoke besides Allah? Show me what it is they have created on earth, or have they a share in the heavens, bring me a book (revealed) before this, or any remnant[4] of knowledge (you may have), if you are telling the truth!

5. And who is more astray than one who invokes besides Allah, such as will not answer him to the Day of Judgment, and who (in fact) are unconscious of their call (to them)?

6. And when mankind are gathered together (at the Resur-rection), they will be hostile to them and reject their worship (altogether)!

7. When Our Clear Signs are rehearsed to them, the Unbelie-vers say, of the Truth when it comes to them: "This is evident

---

1. Purpose
3. About or against which
2. Fixed period of time
4. Surving trace of

sorcery!"

8. Or do they say, "He has forged it"? Say: "Had I forged it, then you will not at all be able to save me from the wrath of Allah. He knows best of that whereof you talk (so glibly[5])! Enough is He for a witness between me and you! And He is Oft-Forgiving, Most Merciful."

9. Say: "I am no bringer of newfangled[6] doctrine[7] among the Apostles, nor do I know what will be done with me or with you. I follow but that which is revealed to me by inspiration; I am but a Warner open and clear."

10. Say: "Do you see? If (this teaching) be from Allah, and you reject it, and a witness from among the Children of Israel testifies to its similarity (with earlier scripture[8]), and has believed while you are arrogant, (how unjust you are!) truly, Allah does not guide a people unjust."

11. The Unbelievers say of those who believe: "If (this Mes-sage) were a good thing, (such men) would not have gone to it first, before us!" And seeing that they do not guide themselves thereby, they will say, "this is an old falsehood!"

12. And before this, was the Book of Moses as a guide and a mercy: and this Book confirms (it) in the Arabic tongue; to admonish the unjust, and as glad tidings[9] to those who do right.

13. Verily those who say, "Our Lord is Allah," and remain firm (on that Path),- on them shall be no fear, nor shall they grieve.

14. Such shall be Companions of the Garden, dwelling therein (for ever): a recompense for their (good) deeds.

15. We have enjoined[10] on man kindness to his parents: In pain did his mother bear him, and in pain did she give him birth. The carrying of the (child) to his weaning[11] is (a period of) thirty months. At length, when he reaches the age of full strength and attains forty years, he says, "O my Lord! Grant me that I may

---

5.	Readily, carelessly	6.	Different from the old
7.	Faith, religion, creed	8.	Revealed Book
9	Happy news	10.	Commanded, prescribed
11.	To accustom an infant to food other than breast milk		

be grateful for Your favour which You have bestowed upon me, and upon both my parents, and that I may work righteous-ness such as You may approve; and be gracious to me in my issue[12]. Truly have I turned to You and truly do I bow (to You) in Islam."

16. Such are they from whom We shall accept the best of their deeds and pass by their ill deeds: (they shall be) among the Companions of the Garden: a promise of truth, which was made to them (in this life).

17. But (there is one) who says to his parents, "Fie[13] on you! Do you hold out the promise to me that I shall be raised up, even though generations have passed before me (without rising again)?" And they two seek Allah's aid, (and rebuke[14] the son): "Woe to you! Have Faith! for the promise of Allah is true." But he says, "This is nothing but tales of the ancients!"

18. Such are they against whom is proved the sentence among the previous generations of Jinns and men, that have passed away; for they will be (utterly)[15] lost.

19. And to all are (assigned)[16] degrees according to the deeds which they (have done), and in order that (Allah) may recom-pense their deeds, and no injustice be done to them.

20. And on the Day that the Unbelievers will be placed before the Fire, (It will be said to them): "You received your good things in the life of the world, and you took your pleasure out of them: but today you shall be recompensed with a Chastise-ment of humiliation: for that you were arrogant on earth without just cause, and that you (ever) transgressed."

21. Mention (Hud) one of 'Ad's (own) brethren: behold, he warned his people about the winding Sandtracts: and there have been indeed warners before him and after him: "You worship none other than Allah: truly I fear for you the Chastisement of a Mighty Day."

22. They said: "Have you come in order to turn us aside[17] from our

---

12. Offspring	13. An expression of disgust
14. Admonish, reprimand	15. Completely
16. Allotted	17. Away from

gods? Then bring upon us the (calamity) with which you threaten us, if you are telling the truth?"

23.   He said: "The Knowledge (of when it will come) is only with Allah: I proclaim to you the mission on which I have been sent: but I see that you are a people in ignorance!"

24.   Then, when they saw a cloud advancing towards their valleys, they said, "This cloud will give us rain!" "Nay, it is the (calamity) you were asking to be hastened, a wind wherein is a grievous hastisement.

25.   "It will destroy everything by the command of its Lord!" Then by the morning they became such that nothing was to be seen but (the ruins of) their houses! Thus do We re-compense those given to sin!

26.   And We had firmly established them in a (prosperity and) power which We have not given to you (you Quraish!) and We had endowed them with (facul-ties of) hearing, sight, heart and intellect: but of no profit to them were their (faculties of) hearing, sight, and heart and intellect, when they went on rejecting the Signs of Allah; and they were (completely) encircled by that which they used to mock at!

27.   We destroyed (aforetime) populations round about you; and We have shown the Signs in various ways, that they may turn (to Us).

28.   Why then was no help forthcoming to them from those whom they worshipped as gods, besides Allah, as a means of access (to Allah)? Nay, they left them in the lurch[18]: but that was their falsehood and their invention[19].

29.   Behold, We turned towards you a company of Jinns (quietly) listening to the Qur'an: when they stood in the presence thereof, they said, "Listen in silence!" When the (reading) was finished, they returned to their people, to warn (them of their sins).

30.   They said, "O our people! We have heard a Book revealed after Moses, confirming what came before it: it guides (men) to the Truth and to a Straight Path.

---

18.   Most difficult time or turn   19.   Fabrication

31. "O our people, hearken[20] to the one who invites (you) to Allah, and believe in him: He will forgive you your faults, and deliver you from a Chastise-ment Grievous.

32. "If any does not hearken to the one who invites (us) to Allah, he cannot frustrate[21] (Allah's Plan) on earth, and no protectors can he have besides Allah: such men (wander) in manifest error."

33. Don't they see that Allah, Who created the heavens and the earth, and never wearied[22] with their creation, is able to give life to the dead? Yes, verily He has power over all things.

34. And on the Day that the Unbelievers will be placed before the Fire, (they will be asked,) "Is this not the Truth?" they will say, "Yes, by our Lord!" (One will say:) "Then you taste the Chas-tisement, for that you were wont[23] to deny (Truth)!"

35. Therefore patiently persevere[24], as did (all) Apostles of inflexible[25] purpose; and be in no haste about the (Unbelievers). On the Day that they see the (Punishment) promised them, (it will be) as if they had not tarried[26] more than an hour in a single day. (Yours but) to proclaim the Message: but shall any be destroyed except those who transgress?

---

20. Listen
21. Thwart, defeat
22. Exhausted
23. Used to, were accustomed to
24. Be steadfast, constant
25. Strong
26. Stayed
27. Violate the bound of law and decency

SURAH—47
SURAH MUHAMMAD
(INTRODUCTION)

We have examined and followed the current arrangement of the Surahs according to .subject-matter and independently of Chronology, and we have found that a logical thread runs through them. We have now finished more that five-sixths of the Quran. The remaining sixth consists of short Surahs, but these are again grouped according to subject-matter.

We begin the first of such groups with a group of three Surahs (47 to 49), which deal with the organisation of the Muslim *Ummah* or community both for external defence and in internal relations. The present Surah deals with the necessity of defence against external foes by courage and strenuous fighting, and dates from about the first of the Hijra, when the Muslims were under threat of extinction by invasion from Makkah.

SURAH MUHAMMAD (THE PROPHET)

In the name of Allah, Most Gracious, Most Merciful.

1.   Those who reject Allah and hinder (men) from the Path of Allah,- Allah will render their deeds astray (from their mark).

2.   But those who believe and work deeds of righteousness, and believe in the (Revelation) sent down to Muhammad - for it is the Truth from their Lord,- He will remove from them their ills and improve their condition.

3.   This is because those who reject Allah, follow falsehood[1], while those who believe follow the Truth from their Lord: thus Allah sets forth for men their lessons by similitudes.[2]

4.   Therefore, when you meet the Unbelievers (in fight), smite[3] at their necks; at length, when you have thoroughly subdued[4] them, bind a bond[5] firmly (on them): thereafter (is the time for) either generosity or ransom[6]: until the war lays down its burdens[7].

---

1.   Baseless things or ideas   2.   Parables   3.   Strike
4.   Defeated, brought them under control
5.   Tie, i.e., bind them and make the prisoners
6.   Payment in return for their freedom.
7.   That is, until the war comes to an end.

Thus (are you commanded): but if it had been Allah's Will, He could certainly have exacted retribution[8] from them (Himself); but (He lets you fight) in order to test you, some with others. But those who are slain[9] in the Way of Allah,- He will never let their deeds be lost.

5. Soon He will guide them and improve their condition,

6. And admit them to the Garden which He has announ-ced for them.

7. O you who believe! If you will aid (the cause of) Allah, He will aid you, and plant your feet firmly.

8. But those who reject (Allah),- for them is destruction, and (Allah) will render their deeds worthless[10].

9. That is because they hate the Revelation of Allah; so He has made their deeds fruitless.

10. Do they not travel through the earth, and see what was the End of those before them (who did evil)? Allah brought utter[11] destruction on them, and similar (fates await) those who reject Allah.

11. That is because Allah is the Protector of those who believe, but those who reject Allah have no protector.

12. Verily Allah will admit those who believe and do righteous deeds, to Gardens beneath which rivers flow; while those who reject Allah will enjoy (this world) and eat as cattle eat; and the Fire will be their abode.

13. And how many cities, with more power than your city which has driven you out, have We destroyed (for their sins)? and there was none to aid them.

14. Is then one who is on a clear (Path) from his Lord, like the one to whom the evil of his conduct seems pleasing, and such as follow their own lusts[12]?

15. (Here is) a parable of the Garden which the righteous are promised: in it are rivers of water unstaling[13]; rivers of milk of

---

8. Punishment   9.   Killed
10. Their works will produce no results   11. Complete
12. Desires   13. That which does not change or become bad.

which the taste never changes; rivers of wine, a joy to those who drink; and rivers of honey pure and clear. In it there are for them all kinds of fruits; and Grace[14] from their Lord. (Can those in such Bliss[15]) be compared to such as shall dwell for ever in the Fire, and be given, to drink, boiling water, so that it cuts up their bowels (to pieces)?

16. And among them are men who listen to you, but in the end, when they go out from you, they say to those who have received Knowledge, "What is it he said just then?" Such are men whose hearts Allah has sealed, and who follow their own lusts.

17. But to those who receive Guidance, He increases the (light of) Guidance, and bestows on them their piety and restraint[16] (from evil).

18. Do they then only wait for the Hour,- that it should come on them of a sudden? But already some tokens[17] thereof have come, and when it (actually) is on them, how can they benefit then by their admonition?[18]

19. Know, therefore, that there is no god but Allah, and ask forgiveness for your fault, and for the men and women who believe: for Allah knows how you move about and how you dwell in your homes.

20. Those who believe say, "Why is not a *surah* sent down (for us)?" But when a *surah* of basic or categorical[19] meaning is revealed, and fighting is mentioned therein, you will see those in whose hearts is a disease looking at you with a look of one in swoon[20] at the approach of death. But more fitting for them-

21. Were it to obey and say what is just, and when a matter is resolved[21] on, it were best for them if they were true to Allah.

22. Then, is it to be expected of you, if you were put in authority, that you will do mischief in the land, and break your ties of kith and kin?[22]

14.	Mercy	15.	Happiness and contentment
16.	The strength to keep away from	17.	Signs
18.	Advice, reminder	19.	Decisive
20.	Fainting	21.	Settled, decided
22.	Blood relations		

23. Such are the men whom Allah has cursed for He has made them deaf and blinded their sight.

24. Do they not then earnestly[23] seek to understand the Qur'an, or are their hearts locked up by them?

25. Those who turn back as apostates[24] after Guidance was clearly shown to them,- the Evil One has instigated[25] them and buoyed[26] them up with false hopes.

26. This is, because they said to those who hate what Allah has revealed, "We will obey you in part of (this) matter"; but Allah knows their (inner) secrets.

27. But how (will it be) when the angels take their souls at death, and smite their faces and their backs?

28. This is because they fol-lowed that which called forth the Wrath of Allah, and they hated Allah's good pleasure; so He made their deeds of no effect.

29. Or do those in whose hearts is a disease, think that Allah will not bring to light all their rancour?[27]

30. If We had so willed, We could have shown them up to you, and you should have known them by their marks: but surely you will know them by the tone of their speech! And Allah knows all that you do.

31. And We shall try you until We test those among you who strive their utmost and persevere[28] in patience; and We shall try your reported (mettle[29]).

32. Those who reject Allah, hinder (men) from the Path of Allah, and resist the Apostle, after Guidance has been clearly shown to them, will not injure Allah in the least, but He will make their deeds of no effect.

33. O you who believe! Obey Allah, and obey the Apostle, and make not vain[30] your deeds!

---

23. Seriously
24. Abandoning Faith, turning back after accepting guidance.
25. Urged on, incited   26. Encouraged, kept afloat
27. Malice, animosity, spite   28. Are constant
29. Courage and constancy, fortitude   30. Worthless

34. Those who reject Allah, and hinder (men) from the Path of Allah, then die rejecting Allah,- Allah will not forgive them.

35. Be not weary and faint-hearted, crying for peace, when you should be uppermost: for Allah is with you, and will never put you in loss for your (good) deeds.

36. The life of this world is but play and amusement: and if you believe and guard against Evil, He will grant you your recompense, and will not ask you (to give up) your possessions[31].

37. If He were to ask you for all of them, and press you, you would covetously[32] withhold, and He would bring out all your ill-feeling.

38. Behold, you are those invited to spend (of your substance[33]) in the Way of Allah: but among you are some that are niggardly[34]. But any who are niggardly are so at the expense of their own souls. But Allah is free of all wants, and it is you that are needy. If you turn back (from the Path), He will substitute[35] in your stead[36] another people; then they would not be like you!

---

31. Wealth, property
33. Wealth
35. Replace with

32. Eagerly
34. Miserly, stingy
36. In your place

SURAH—48

SURAH AL-FATH

(INTRODUCTION)

1. This is the second of the group of three Madinah Surahs described in the Introduction to S. 47. Its date is fixed by the mention of the Treaty of Hudaibiya, Zul-qa'd A.M. 6=Feb. 628.

2. Hudaibiya is a plain, a short day's march to the north of Makkah, a little to the west of the Madinah-Makkah road, as used in the Prophet's time. Six years had passed since the Prophet had left his beloved City, and it had been in the hands of the Pagan autocracy. But Islam had grown during these six years. Its Qibla was towards the *K'aba.* The Pagans had tried to attack Islam at various times and had been foiled. By Arab custom every Arab was entitled to visit the Sacred Enclosure unarmed, and fighting of any kind was prohibited during the Sacred Months which included the month of Zul-Qa'd. In Zul-qa'd A.H. 6, therefore, the Prophet desired to perform the 'Umra or lesser Pilgrimage, unarmed but accompanied with his followers. A large following joined him, to the number of fourteen to fifteen hundred.

3. This was not to the liking of the Pagan autocracy at Makkah, which took alarm, and in breach of all Arab tradition and usage, prepared to prevent me peaceful party from performing the rites of Pilgrimage. They marched out to fight the unarmed party. The Prophet turned a little to the west of the road, and encamped at Hudaibiya, where negotiations took place. ON the one hand the Prophet was unwilling to give the Quraish any pretended excuse for violence in the Sacred Territory; on the other, the Quraish had learnt, by six years' bitter experience, that their power was crumbling on all sides, and Islam was growing with its moral and spiritual forces, which were also reflected in its power of organisation and resistance. The enthusiasm with which the Covenant of Fealty was entered into under a tree in Hudaibiya (48: 18) by that great multitude united in devotion to

their great leader, was evidence of the great power which he commanded even in a worldly sense if the Quraish had chosen to try conclusions with him.

4. A peaceful Treaty was therefore concluded, known as the Treaty of Hudaibiya. It stipulated: (1) that there was to be peace between the parties for ten years; (2) that any tribe or person was free to join either party or make an alliance with it; (3) that if a Quraish person from Makkah, under guardianship, should join the Prophet without the guardian's permission, he (or she) should be sent back to the guardian, but in the contrary case, they

should not be sent back; and (4) that the Prophet and his party were not to enter Makkah that year, but that they could enter unarmed the following year.

5. Item (3), not being reciprocal was objected to in the Muslim camp, but it really was of little importance. Muslims under guardianship, sent back to Makkah, were not likely to renounce the blessings of Islam: on the other hand, Muslims going to Makkah would be centers of influence for Islam, and it was more important that they should be allowed to remain there than that they should be sent back to Madinah. It was impossible to think that there would be apostates or renegades to Paganism! "Look on this picture, and on that!"

6. The Muslims faithfully observed the terms of the Treaty. The following year (A.H. 7) they performed the lesser Pilgrimage in great state for three days. It is true that the Makkans later on broke the Peace in the attack which one of their allied tribes (the Banu Bakr) made on the Muslim Banu Khuza'a (who were in alliance with the Prophet), but this led to the conquest of Makkah and the sweeping away of the autocracy. Meanwhile Hudaibiya was a great victory, moral and social, as well as political, and its lessons are expounded in this Surah, as the lessons of Badr were expounded in 8: 42-48, and of Uhud in 3: 121-129, 149-180.

SURAH FATH (VICTORY)

In the name of Allah, Most Gracious, Most Merciful.

1. Verily We have granted you a manifest[1] Victory:

2. That Allah may forgive you your faults of the past and those to follow; fulfil His favour to you; and guide you on the Straight Way;

3. And that Allah may help you with powerful help.

4. It is He Who sent down tranquillity[2] into the hearts of the Believers, that they may add faith to their faith;- for to Allah belong the Forces of the heavens and the earth; and Allah is full of Knowledge and Wisdom;-

5. That He may admit the men and women who believe, to Gardens beneath[3] which rivers flow, to dwell therein for ever, and remove

---

1.   Clear, obvious   2.   Calm, serenity
3.   Under

their ills from them;- and that is, in the sight of Allah, the highest achievement (for man),-

6. And that He may punish the Hypocrites[4], men and women, and the Polytheists[5], men and women, who imagine an evil opinion of Allah. On them is a round of Evil: the Wrath of Allah is on them: He has cursed them and got Hell ready for them: and evil is it for a destination.

7. For to Allah belong the Forces of the heavens and the earth; and Allah is Exalted in Power, full of Wisdom.

8. We have truly sent you as a witness, as a bringer of Glad Tidings[6], and as a Warner:

9. In order that you (O men) may believe in Allah and His Apostle, that you may assist and honour Him, and celebrate His praises morning and evening.

10. Surely those who plight[7] their fealty[8] to you do in fact plight their fealty to Allah: the Hand of Allah is over their hands: then any one who violates His oath, does so to the harm of His own soul, and any one who fulfils what he has covenanted[9] with Allah,- Allah will soon grant him a great Reward.

11. The desert Arabs who lagged behind will say to you: "We were engaged in (looking after) our flocks and herds, and our families: you then ask forgiveness for us." They say with their tongues what is not in their hearts. Say: "Who then has any power at all (to intervene)[10] on your behalf with Allah, if His Will is to give you some loss or to give you some profit? But Allah is well acquainted with all that you do.

12. "Nay, you thought that the Apostle and the Believers would never return to their families; this seemed pleasing in your hearts, and you conceived an evil thought, for you are a people lost (in wickedness)."

---

4. Those who pretend they are Muslims, but in reality are not.
5. Those who worship false gods or idols besides One True Allah.
6. Happy news
7. Pledge their Faith, promise
8. Allegiance, loyalty, devotion
9. Solemnly promised
10. Intercede

13.   And if any do not believe in Allah and His Apostle, We have prepared, for those who reject Allah, a Blazing Fire!

14.   To Allah belongs the dominion[11] of the heavens and the earth: He forgives whom He wills, and He punishes whom He wills: but Allah is Oft-Forgiving, Most Merciful.

15.   Those who lagged behind (will say), when you (are free to) march and take booty[12] (in war): "Permit us to follow you." They wish to change Allah's decree[13]: say: "Not thus will you follow us: Allah has already declared (this) beforehand": then they will say, "But you are jealous of us." Nay, but little do they understand (such things).

16.   Say to the desert Arabs who lagged behind: "You shall be summoned (to fight) against a people given to vehement[14] war: then you shall fight, or they shall submit. Then if you show obedience, Allah will grant you a goodly reward, but if you turn back as you did before, He will punish you with a grievous Chastisement."

17.   No blame is there on the blind, nor is there blame on the lame, nor on one ill (if he does not join the war): but he that obeys Allah and His Apostle,- (Allah) will admit him to Gardens beneath which rivers flow; and he who turns back, (Allah) will punish him with a grievous Chastisement.

18.   Allah's Good Pleasure was on the Believers when they swore allegiance to you under the Tree: He knew what was in their hearts, and He sent down Tranquillity to them; and He rewarded them with a speedy Victory;

19.   And many gains will they acquire (besides): and Allah is Exalted in Power, full of Wisdom.

20.   Allah has promised you many gains that you shall acquire, and He has given you these beforehand; and He has restrained the hands of men from you; that it may be a Sign for the Believers, and that He may guide you to a Straight Path;

---

21. And other (gains there are), which are not within your power, but which Allah has composed[15] and Allah has power over all things.

22. If the Unbelievers should fight you, they would certainly turn their backs; then would they find neither protector nor helper.

23. (Such has been) the practice (approved) of Allah already in the past: no change will you find in the practice (approved) of Allah.

24. And it is He Who has restrained their hands from you and your hands from them in the midst of Makka, after that He gave you the victory over them. And Allah sees well all that you do.

25. They are the ones who denied Revelation and hindered you from the Sacred Mosque and the sacrificial animals, detained from reaching their place of sacrifice. Had there not been believing men and believing women whom you did not know that you were trampling[16] down and on whose account a crime would have accrued[17] to you without (your) knowledge, (Allah would have allowed you to force your way, but He held back your hands) that Allah may admit to His Mercy whom He will. If they had been apart[18], We should certainly have punished the Unbelievers among them with a grievous Punishment.

26. While the Unbelievers got up in their hearts heat and cant[19] - the heat and cant of ignorance,-Allah sent down His Tranquillity to His Apostle and to the Believers, and made them stick close to the command of self-restraint; and well were they entitled[20] to it and worthy of it. And Allah has full knowledge of all things.

27. Truly did Allah fulfil the vision for His Apostle: you shall enter the Sacred Mosque, if Allah wills, with minds secure, heads shaved, hair cut short, and without fear. For He knew what you did not know, and He granted, besides this, a speedy victory.

---

15. Has them within His knowledge and power.
16. Tread underfoot, press down or crush
17. Collected (against you), will have afflicted
18. Separate from others
19. Hypocrisy, insincere use of words implying piety.
20. Qualified for it.

28.   It is He Who has sent His Apostle with Guidance and the
      Religion of Truth, to proclaim it over all religion: and enough
      is Allah for a Witness.

29.   Muhammad is the Apostle of Allah; and those who are with
      him are strong against Unbelievers, (but) compassionate
      amongst each other. You will see them bow and prostrate
      themselves (in prayer), seeking Grace from Allah and (His) Good
      Pleasure. On their faces are their marks, (being) the traces of
      their prostration. This is their similitude in the Taurat; and their
      similitude in the Gospel is: like a seed which sends forth its
      blade, then makes it strong; it then becomes thick, and it stands
      on its own stem, (filling) the sowers with wonder and delight.
      As a result, it fills the Unbelievers with rage at them. Allah has
      promised those among them who believe and do righteous deeds
      forgiveness, and a great Reward.

---

21.   A flat spear-shaped leaf of grass and cereals.

SURAH—49

SURAH AL-HUJURAT

(INTRODUCTION)

This is the third of the group of three Madinah Surahs, which began with S. 47. See the Introduction to that Surah.

Its subject-matter is the manners to be observed by the members of the rapidly-growing Muslim community, among themselves and towards its Leader. The keyword *"Hujurat"* (Inner Apartments) occurs in verse 4.

Its date is referred to the Year of Deputations, A.M. 9, when a large number of deputations of all kinds visited Madinah to offer their allegiance to Islam.

SURAH AL-HUJURAT (THE INNER APARTMENTS)

In the name of Allah, Most Gracious, Most Merciful.

1. O you who believe! Do not put yourselves forward before Allah and His Apostle; but fear Allah: for Allah is He Who hears and knows all things.

2. O you who believe! Do not raise your voices above the voice of the Prophet, nor speak aloud to him in talk, as you may speak aloud to one another, lest your deeds become vain and you do not perceive.

3. Those that lower their voices in the presence of Allah's Apostle,- their hearts Allah has tested for piety: for them is Forgiveness and a great Reward.

4. Those who shout out to you from without the inner Apartments - most of them lack understanding.

5. If only they had patience until you could come out to them, it would be best for them: but Allah is Oft-Forgiving, Most Merciful.

6. O you who believe! If a wicked person comes to you with any news, ascertain the truth, lest you harm people unwittingly[1], and afterwards become full of repentance for what you have done.

---

1. Unknowingly

7.   And know that among you is Allah's Apostle: were he, in many matters, to follow your (wishes), you would certainly fall into misfortune: but Allah has endeared the Faith to you, and has made it beautiful in your hearts, and He has made hateful to you Unbelief, wickedness, and rebellion: such indeed are those who walk in righteousness;-

8.   A Grace and Favour from Allah; and Allah is full of Knowledge and Wisdom.

9.   If two parties among the Believers fall into a quarrel, you make peace between them: but if one of them transgresses beyond bounds against the other, then you (all) fight against the one that transgresses until it complies with the command of Allah; but if it complies, then make peace between them with justice, and be fair: for Allah loves those who are fair (and just).

10.   The Believers are but a single Brotherhood: so make peace and reconciliation between your two (contending[2]) brothers; and fear Allah, that you may receive Mercy.

11.   O you who believe! Let not some men among you laugh at others: It may be that the (latter) are better than the (former): nor let some women laugh at others: It may be that the (latter) are better than the (former): nor defame[3] nor be sarcastic[4] to each other, nor call each other by (offensive[5]) nicknames[6]: Ill-seeming is a name connoting[7] wickedness, (to be used of one) after he has believed: and those who do not desist[8] are (indeed) doing wrong.

12.   O you who believe! Avoid suspicion as much (as possible): for suspicion in some cases is a sin: and spy not on each other, nor speak ill of each other behind their backs. Would any of you like to eat the flesh of his dead brother? Nay, you would abhor[9] it...But fear Allah: For Allah is Oft-Returning, Most Merciful.

2.	Disputing, at odds	3.	Slander
4.	Scornful	5.	Insulting
6.	A name jokingly or admiringly or contemptuously added to or used in place of a person's proper name.	7.	Suggesting or indicating
8.	Refrain	9.	Hate, despise

13. O mankind! We created you from a single (pair) of a male and a female, and made you into nations and tribes, that you may know each other (not that you may despise[10] each other). Verily the most honoured of you in the sight of Allah is (he who is) the most righteous of you. And Allah has full knowledge and is well acquainted (with all things).

14. The desert Arabs say, "We believe." Say, "You have no faith; but you (only) say, 'We have submitted our wills to Allah,' for Faith has not yet entered your hearts. But if you obey Allah and His Apostle, He will not belittle[11] anything of your deeds: for Allah is Oft-Forgiving, Most Merciful."

15. Only those are Believers who have believed in Allah and His Apostle, and have never since doubted, but have striven with their belongings and their persons in the Cause of Allah: such are the sincere ones.

16. Say: "What! Will you instruct Allah about your religion? But Allah knows all that is in the heavens and on earth: He has full knowledge of all things.

17. They impress on you as a favour that they have embraced Islam. Say, "Do not count your Islam as a favour upon me: nay, Allah has conferred[12] a favour upon you that He has guided you to the Faith, if you be true and sincere.

18. "Verily Allah knows the secrets of the heavens and the earth: and Allah sees well all that you do."

---

10. Hate
11. Decrease, diminish
12. Bestowed

SURAH—50

SURAH QAF

(INTRODUCTION)

We now come to a group of seven Makkan Surahs (50-56) dealing with Allah's revelation through nature, through history, and through the mouths of the prophets, and pointing to the Hereafter. We saw that the last group of three (47-49) dealt -with the external and internal relations of the *Ummah* when formed. In the present group our attention is more particularly directed to aspects eschatological,—the Future before us when this life is done.

This particular Surah belongs to the early Makkan period. After an appeal to nature and to the fate of wicked peoples in history, it removes, as it were, the evil (verse 22) form the Future after death.

SURAH QAF

In the name of Allah, Most Gracious, Most Merciful.

1. Qaf: By the Glorious Qur'an (You are Allah's Apostle).

2. But they wonder that there has come to them a Warner from among themselves. So the Unbelievers say: "This is a wonderful thing

3. "What! When we die and become dust, (shall we live again?) That is a (sort of) return far (from our understanding)."

4. We already know how much of them the earth takes away: with Us is a record guarding (the full account).

5. But they deny the Truth when it comes to them: so they are in a confused state.

6. Do they not look at the sky above them?- How We have made it and adorned[1] it, and there are no flaws[2] in it?

7. And the earth- We have spread it out, and set thereon mountains standing firm, and produced therein every kind of beautiful growth (in pairs[3]).—

8. To be observed and commemorated by every devotee[4] turning (to Allah).

---

1. Beautiful	2. Defects
3. Remembered, celebrated	4. Devoted worshipper or servant

9.   And We send down from the sky rain charted[5] with blessing, and We produce therewith gardens and grain for harvests;

10.   And tall (and stately[6]) palmtrees, with shoots[7] of fruit-stalks[8], piled one over another;-

11.   As sustenance for (Allah's) servants;- and We give (new) life therewith to land that is dead: thus will be the Resurrection.

12.   Before them was denied (the Hereafter) by the People of Noah[9], the Companions of the Rass[10], the Thamud,

13.   The 'Ad, Pharaoh, the Brethren of Lut,

14.   The Companions of the Wood, and the People of Tubba[11]'; each one (of them) rejected the Apostles, and My warning was duly fulfilled (in them).

15.   Were We then weary with the first Creation, that they should be in confused doubt about a new Creation?

16.   It was We Who created man, and We know what dark suggestions his soul makes to him: for We are nearer to him than (his) jugular[12] vein.

17.   Behold, two (watchful angels) appointed to record (his doings) one sitting on the right and one on the left.

18.   Not a word does he utter but there is a sentinel[13] by him, ready (to note it).

19.   And the stupor[14] of death will bring Truth (before his eyes): "This was the thing which you were trying to escape!"

20.   And the Trumpet shall be blown: that will be the Day whereof Warning (had been given).

21.   And there will come forth every soul: with each will be an (angel) to drive, and an (angel) to bear witness.

22.   (It will be said:) "You were heedless of this; now have We removed your veil, and sharp is your sight this Day!"

---

5.   Full of, saturated with   6.   Grand, imposing

7.   Buds, blossom, sprout   8.   Offshoot, small branch

9.   See Qur'an 11:25—48, 71:28

10.   See Qur'an 25:38. According to some they were the people of Madian to whom Prophet Shuaib was sent to warn.   11.   See also Qur'an 44:37

12.   Life vein   13.   A watcher

14.   Helpless amazement, dazed state

23.   And his Companion will say: "Here is (his Record) ready with me!"

24.   (The sentence will be:) "Throw, both of you into Hell every contumacious[15] rejecter (of Allah)!-

25.   "Who forbade what was good, transgressed all bounds, cast doubts and suspicions;

26.   "Who set up another god beside Allah: throw him into a severe Chastisement."

27.   His Companion will say: "Our Lord! I did not make him transgress, but he was (himself) far astray."

28.   He will say: "Do not dispute with each other in My Presence: I had already in advance sent you Warning.

29.   "The Word does not change before Me, and I do not do the least injustice to My servants."

30.   That Day We will ask Hell, "Are you filled to the full?" It will say, "Are there any more (to come)?"

31.   And the Garden will be brought near to the Righteous,- no more a thing distant.

32.   (A voice will say:) "This is what was promised for you,- for every one who turned (to Allah) in sincere repentance, Who kept (His Law),

33.   "Who feared (Allah) Most Gracious Unseen, and brought a heart turned in devotion (to Him):

34.   "You enter therein in Peace and Security; this is a Day of Eternal Life!"

35.   There will be for them therein all that they wish,- and more besides in Our Presence.

36.   But how many generations before them did We destroy (for their sins),- stronger in power than they? Then did they wander through the land: was there any place of escape (for them)?

37.   Verily in this is a Message for any that has a heart and under-standing or who gives ear and earnestly[16] witnesses (the truth).

38.   We created the heavens and the earth and all between them in

---

15.   Stubbornly or willfully disobedient, rebellious
16.   Seriously

Six Days, nor did any sense of weariness touch Us.

39. Bear, then, with patience, all that they say, and celebrate the praises of your Lord, before the rising of the sun and before (its) setting.

40. And during part of the night, (also,) celebrate His praises, and (so likewise) after the postures of adoration.[17]

41. And listen for the Day when the Caller will call out from a place quiet near,-

42. The Day when they will hear a (mighty) Blast[18] in (very) truth: that will be the Day of Resurrection.

43. Verily it is We Who give Life and Death; and to Us is the Final Goal-

44. The Day when the Earth will be rent asunder, from (men) hurrying out: that will be a gathering together,- quite easy for Us.

45. We know best what they say; and you are not one to overawe[19] them by force. So admonish[20] with the Qur'an such as fear My Warning!

---

17. That is, after the reuglar prayer   18.   Loud sound
19. Compel by force, daunt by arousing fear or reverence
20. Warn

SURAH—51
SURAH AZ-ZARIYAT
(INTRODUCTION)

This is an early Makkan Surah, with a highly mystic meaning. It is the second of the seven Surahs forming a group dealing with Revelation and the Hereafter. See Introduction to S. 50. This Surah deals with the varying ways in which Truth prevails irresistibly even against all human probabilities.

SURAH AZ-ZARIYAT
(THE WINDS THAT SCATTER)

In the name of Allah, Most Gracious, Most Merciful.

1.   By the (winds) that scatter broadcast[1];

2.   And those that lift and bear away heavy weights;

3.   And those that flow with ease and gentleness;

4.   And those that distribute and apportion[2] by Command;

5.   Verily that which you are promised is true;

6.   And verily Judgment and Justice must indeed come to pass.

7.   By the Sky with (its) numerous Paths,

8.   Truly you are in a doctrine[3] discordant[4],

9.   Through which are deluded[5] (away from the Truth) such as would be deluded.

10.   Woe to the falsehood-mongers,-

11.   Those who (flounder[6]) heedless in a flood of confusion:

12.   They ask, "When will be the Day of Judgment and Justice?"

13.   (It will be) a Day when they will be tried (and tested) over the Fire!

14.   "You taste your trial! This is what you used to ask to be hastened!"

15.   As to the Righteous, they will be in the midst of Gardens and

---

1.   Scatter or spread freely   2.   Give as due share
3.   Not in harmony, disagreeing, conflicting
4.   Creed, beliefs   5.   Deceived
6.   Struggle and plunge (as) in mud or when wading, manage badly or with difficulty.

Springs,

16. Taking joy in the things which their Lord gives them, because, before then, they lived a good life.

17. They were in the habit of sleeping but little by night,

18. And in the hours of early dawn, they (were found) praying for Forgiveness;

19. And in their wealth the beggar and the outcast had due share.

20. On the earth are Signs for those of assured Faith,

21. As also in your own selves: will you not then see?

22. And in heaven is your Sustenance, as (also) that which you are promised.

23. Then, by the Lord of heaven and earth, this is the very Truth, as much as the fact that you can speak intelligently to each other.

24. Has the story reached you, of the honoured guests of Abraham?

25. Behold, they entered his presence, and said: "Peace!" He said, "Peace!" (and thought, "These seem) unusual people.

26. Then he turned quickly to his household, brought out a fatted calf,

27. And placed it before them.. he said, "Will you not eat?"

28. (When they did not eat), He conceived a fear of them. They said, "Fear not," and they gave him glad tidings of a son endowed with knowledge.

29. But his wife came forward (laughing) aloud: she smote her face and said: "A barren old woman!"

30. They said, "Even so your Lord has spoken: and He is full of Wisdom and Knowledge."

31. (Abraham) said: "And what, O you Messengers, is your errand[7] (now)?"

32. They said, "We have been sent to a people (deep) in sin;-

33. "To bring on, on them, (a shower of) stones of clay (brimstone[8]),

34. "Marked as from your Lord for those who trespass[9] beyond bounds."

35. Then We evacuated[10] those of the Believers who were there,

---

7. Purpose or mission 8. Sulphur
9. Transgress, violate or infringe upon 10. Vacated

36. But We did not find there any just (Muslim) persons except in one house:

37. And We left there a Sign for such as fear the Grievous Chastisement.

38. And in Moses (was another Sign): behold, We sent him to Pharaoh, with authority manifest[11].

39. But (Pharaoh) turned back with his Chiefs, and said, "A sorcerer, or one possessed!"

40. So We took him and his forces, and threw them into the sea; and his was the blame.

41. And in the 'Ad (people) (was another Sign): behold, We sent against them the devastating[12] Wind:

42. It left nothing whatever that it came up against, but reduced it to ruin and rottenness.

43. And in the Thamud (was another Sign): behold, they were told, "Enjoy (your brief day) for a little while!"

44. But they insolently[13] defied[14] the Command of their Lord: so the stunning[15] noise (of an earthquake) seized them, even while they were looking on.

45. Then they could not even stand (on their feet), nor could they help themselves.

46. So were the People of Noah before them for they wickedly transgressed.

47. With power and skill We constructed the Firmament[16]: for it is We Who create the vastness of space.

48. And We have spread out the (spacious) earth: how excel-lently We do spread out!

49. And of every thing We have created pairs: that you may receive instruction.

---

11. Clear, obvious
12. Disastrous
13. Rudely, arrogantly
14. Resisted, spurned
15. Shocking
16. Vault of Heaven with its cloud and stars

50. Then you hasten (at once) to Allah: I am from Him a Warner to you, clear and open!

51. And make not another an object of worship with Allah: I am from Him a Warner to you, clear and open!

52. Similarly, no Apostle came to the Peoples before them, but they said (of him) in like manner, "A sorcerer, or one possessed"!

53. Is this the legacy[17] they have transmitted, one to another? Nay, they are themselves a people transgressing beyond bounds!

54. So turn away from them: not blame on you.

55. But teach (your Message) for teaching benefits the Be-lievers.

56. And I have not created Jinns and men, except that they may serve (worship) Me.

57. No Sustenance do I require of them, nor do I require that they should feed Me.

58. For Allah is He Who gives (all) Sustenance,- Lord of Power,- Steadfast (for ever).

59. For the Wrong-doers, their portion is like unto the portion of their fellows (of earlier genera-tions): then let them not ask Me to hasten (that portion)!

60. Woe, then, to the Unbelievers, on account of that Day of theirs which they have been promised!

---

17. Heritage, tradition

SURAH—52
SURAH AT-TUR
(INTRODUCTION)

This is the third of the group of seven Makkan Surahs described in the Introduction to S. 50.

It is, like its predecessor, an early Makkan Surah. The points here emphasised are: that Revelation is in accord with all Allah's Signs, including previous Revelations, and that the Hereafter is inevitable, and we must prepare for it.

SURAH AT-TUR (THE MOUNT)

In the name of Allah, Most Gracious, Most Merciful.

1. By the Mount (of Reve-lation);
2. By a Decree inscribed[1];
3. In a Scroll[2] unfolded;
4. And by the much-frequented Fane[3];
5. And by the Canopy raised High;
6. And by the Ocean filled with Swell[4];-
7. Verily, the Doom[5] of your Lord will indeed come to pass;-
8. There is none can avert it;-
9. On the Day when the firmament will be in dreadful commotion[6].
10. And the mountains will fly hither and thither.
11. Then woe that Day to those that treat (Truth) as Falsehood;-
12. That play (and paddle) in shallow trifles.
13. That Day they shall be thrust down to the Fire of Hell, irresistibly.
14. "This:, it will be said, "Is the Fire,- which you were wont to deny!
15. "Is this then a fake, or is it you that do not see?
16. "You burn therein: the same is it to you whether you bear it with patience, or not: you but receive the recompense of your (own) deeds."
17. As to the Righteous, they will be in Gardens, and in Happiness,-

---

1. Recorded, written
2. A roll of paper or parchment
3. Temple, house of worship
4. A series of long unbroken waves
5. (Arch) Sentence, decision, condemnation
6. Disturbance

18. Enjoying the (Bliss) which their Lord has bestowed on them, and their Lord shall deliver them from the Chastisement of the Fire.

19. (To them will be said:) "You eat and drink with good pleasure, because of your (good) deeds."

20. They will recline (with ease) on Thrones (of dignity) arranged in ranks; and We shall join them to Companions, with beautiful, big and lustrous eyes.

21. And those who believe and whose families follow them in Faith,- to them We shall join their families: nor shall We deprive them (of the fruit) of anything of their works: (yet) each indi-vidual is in pledge for his deeds.

22. And We shall bestow on them, of fruit and meat, anything they shall desire.

23. They shall exchange there one with another, a (loving) cup free of frivolity[7], free of all taint[8] of ill.

24. Round about them will serve, (devoted) to them, youths (handsome) as Pearls well-guarded.

25. They will advance to each other, engaging in mutual enquiry.

26. They will say: "Surely, aforetime, we were not without fear for the sake of our people.

27. "But Allah has been gracious to us, and has delivered us from the Penalty of the Scorching Wind.

28. "Truly, we called Him from of old: truly it is He, the Beneficent, the Merciful!"

29. Therefore you proclaim the praises (of your Lord): for by the Grace of your Lord, you are no (vulgar[9]) soothsayer[10], nor you are one possessed.

30. Or do they say:- "A Poet! for him we await some calamity (hatched[11]) by Time!"

31. You say: "You await!- I too will wait along with you!"

32. Is it that their faculties of understanding urge them to this, or are they but a people transgressing beyond bounds?

---

7. Silliness, nonsense
8. Stain
9. Common, coarse
10. Foreteller, diviner
11. Produced, brought about by

33.   Or do they say, "He fabricated the (Message)"? Nay, they have
       no faith!

34.   Let them then produce a recital[12] like it,- If (it be) they speak
       the truth!

35.   Were they created of nothing, or were they themselves the creators?

36.   Or did they create the heavens and the earth? Nay, they have no
       firm belief.

37.   Or are the Treasures of your Lord with them, or are they the
       managers (of affairs)?

38.   Or have they a ladder, by which they can (climb up to heaven
       and) listen (to its sec-rets)? Then let (such a) listener of theirs
       produce a manifest proof.

39.   Or has He only daughters and you have sons?

40.   Or is it that you do ask for a reward, so that they are burdened
       with a load of debt?-

41.   Or that the Unseen is in their hands, and they write it down?

42.   Or do they intend a plot (against you)? But those who defy
       Allah are themselves involved in a Plot!

43.   Or have they a god other than Allah? Exalted is Allah far above
       the things they associate with Him!

44.   Were they to see a piece of the sky falling (on them), they would
       (only) say: "Clouds gathered in heaps!"

45.   So leave them alone until they encounter that Day of theirs,
       wherein they shall (perforce)[13] swoon[14] (with terror),-

46.   The Day when their plotting will avail them nothing and no
       help shall be given them.

47.   And verily, for those who do wrong, there is another punishment
       besides this: but most of them do not understand.

48.   Now await in patience the command of your Lord: for verily
       you are in Our eyes: and celebrate the praises of your Lord the
       while you stand forth,

49.   And for part of the night also you praise Him,- and at the retreat
       of the stars!

---

12.   A book, a narration   13.   Necessarily, unavoidable

14.   Pass out, faint

SURAH—53

SURAH AN-NAJM
(INTRODUCTION)

This is an early Makkan Surah, and is the fourth of the series of seven which were described in the Introduction to S. 50.

The particular theme of this Surah is that Revelation is not an illusion: the illusion is in the minds of those who doubt and have false ideas of Allah: Allah is the source and goal of all things.

In some Surahs the consecutive arrangement is shown or suggested by a cue-word. Here the cue-word is "star," corresponding to "stars" in the last verse of the last Surah. So in 46: 1, the words: "Exalted in Power, Full of Wisdom": are carried forward from the last verse of S. 45, and indeed the same words occur in the first verse of S. 45. So, again the words: "Most Merciful, Oft-Forgiving": in 34: 2, refer back to the words: "Oft-Forgiving, Most Merciful" in the last line of S. 33. In S. 54: 1, the nearness of Judgment recalls the same idea at the end of the previous Surah (53: 57). Other examples will also be found.

SURAH NAJM (THE STAR)
In the name of Allah, Most Gracious, Most Merciful.

1. By the Star when it goes down,-
2. Your Companion is neither astray nor being misled.
3. Nor does he say (anything) of (his own) Desire.
4. It is no less than inspiration sent down to him:
5. He was taught by one Mighty in Power,
6. Endued with Wisdom: for he appeared (in stately form);
7. While he was in the highest part of the horizon:
8. Then he approached and came closer,
9. And was at a distance of but two bow-lengths or (even) nearer;
10. So did (Allah) convey the inspiration to His Servant (conveyed) what He (meant) to convey.
11. The (Prophet's) (mind and) heart in no way falsified that which he saw.
12. Will you then dispute with him concerning what he saw?
13. For indeed he saw him at a second descent,
14. Near the Lote-tree beyond which none may pass:

15.   Near it is the Garden of Abode.

16.   Behold, the Lote-tree was shrouded (in mystery unspeak-able!)

17.   (His) sight never swerved, nor did it go wrong!

18.   For truly he saw of the Signs of his Lord, the Greatest!

19.   Have you seen Lat and 'Uzza,

20.   And another, the third (goddess), Manat?

21.   What! for you the male sex, and for Him, the female?

22.   Behold, such would be indeed a division most unfair!

23.   These are nothing but names which you have devised,- you and your fathers,- for which Allah has sent down no authority (whatever). They follow nothing but conjecture and what their own souls desire!- Even though there has already come to them Guidance from their Lord!

24.   Nay, shall man have (just) anything he hankers after?

25.   But it is to Allah that the End and the Beginning (of all things) belong.

26.   How many-so-ever be the angels in the heavens, their intercession will avail nothing except after Allah has given leave for whom He pleases and that he is acceptable to Him.

27.   Those who do not believe in the Hereafter, name the angels with female names.

28.   But they have no knowled-ge therein. They follow nothing but conjecture; and conjecture avails nothing against Truth.

29.   Therefore shun those who turn away from Our Message and desire nothing but the life of this world.

30.   That is as far as knowledge will reach them. Verily your Lord knows best those who stray from His Path, and He knows best those who receive guidance.

31.   Yes, to Allah belongs all that is in the heavens and on earth: so that He rewards those who do evil, according to their deeds, and He rewards those who do good, with what is best.

32.   Those who avoid great sins and shameful deeds, only (falling into) small faults,- verily your Lord is ample in forgiveness. He knows you well when He brings you out of the earth, and when

---

1.   Guesswork   2. Crave or long for   3. Avoid

you are hidden in your mothers' wombs. Therefore, do not justify your-selves: He knows best who it is that guards against evil.

33. Do you see one who turns back,

34. Gives a little, then hardens (his heart)?

35. What! Has he knowledge of the Unseen so that he can see?

36. Nay, is he not acquainted with what is in the books of Moses.

37. And of Abraham who fulfilled his engagements?-

38. Namely, that no bearer of burdens can bear the burden of another;

39. That man can have nothing but what he strives for;

40. That (the fruit of) his striving will soon come in sight:

41. Then will he be rewarded with a reward complete;

42. That to your Lord is the final Goal;

43. That it is He Who grants Laughter and Tears;

44. That it is He Who grants Death and Life;

45. That He created in pairs,- male and female,

46. From a seed when lodged (in its place);

47. That He has promised a Second Creation (raising of the Dead);

48. That it is He Who gives wealth and satisfaction;

49. That He is the Lord of Sirius (the Mighty Star);

50. And that it is He Who destroyed the former (tribe of) 'Aad,

51. And the Thamud, nor gave them a lease of perpetual life.

52. And before them, the people of Noah, for that they were (all) most unjust and most insolent transgressors,

53. And He destroyed the Overthrown Cities (of Sodom and Gomorrah),

54. So that (ruins unknown) have covered them up.

55. Then which of the gifts of your Lord, (O man,) will you dispute about?

56. This is a Warner, of the (series of) Warners of old!

57. The (Judgment) ever approaching draws near:

58. No (soul) but Allah can lay it bare.

59. Do you then wonder at this recital?

60. And will you laugh and not weep,-

61. Wasting your time in vanities?

62. But you fall down in pros-tration to Allah, and adore (Him)

4.   Contact   5. Eternal, endless   6. Useless things

SURAH—54

SURAH AL-QAMAR

(INTRODUCTION)

This is an early Makkan Surah, the fifth in the series dealing with Judgment, and the truth of Revelation, as explained in the Introduction to S. 50.

The theme of the Surah is explained by the refrain: "Is there any that will receive admonition?" which occurs six times, at the end of each reference to a past story of sin and rejection of warnings and in the appeal to the simplicity of the Quran (verses 15, 17, 22, 32, 40, and 51). There is an invitation to listen to the Message and turn to truth and Righteousness.

SURAH QAMAR (THE MOON)

In the name of Allah, Most Gracious, Most Merciful.

1.   The Hour (of judgement) is nigh,[1] and the moon is cleft asunder[2].

2.   But if they see a Sign, they turn away, and say, "This is (but) transient[3] magic."

3.   They reject (the warning) and follow their (own) lusts but every matter has its appointed time.

4.   There have already come to them such tidings[4] as contain a deterrent–

5.   Mature wisdom; but (the preaching of) Warners does not profit them.

6.   Therefore, (O Prophet,) turn away from them. The Day that the Caller will call (them) to a terrible affair,

7.   They will come forth,- their eyes humbled - from (their) graves, (torpid[5]) like locusts scattered abroad,

8.   Hastening, with eyes transfixed[6], towards the Caller!- "Hard is this Day!", the Unbelievers will say.

9.   Before them the People of Noah rejected (their Apostle): they

---

1.   Near   2.   Split
3.   Momentary, of a short duration, quickly passing away
4.   A detailed account of a number of connected incidents, a narrtive.
5.   Sluggish, sleepy, listless
6.   Rooh (a person) to the spot (because of horror), paralyse faculties of.

rejected Our servant, and said, "Here is one possessed!", and he was driven out.

10. Then he called on his Lord: "I am one overcome: do You then help (me)!"

11. So We opened the gates of heaven, with water pouring forth.

12. And We caused the earth to gush forth with springs, so the waters met (and rose) to the extent decreed.

13. But We bore him on an (Ark) made of broad planks[7] and caulked[8] with palm-fiber:,

14. She floats under our eyes (and care): a recompense to one who had been rejected (with scorn)!

15. And We have left this as a Sign (for all time): then is there any that will receive admonition?[9]

16. But how (terrible) was My Chastisement and My Warning?

17. And We have indeed made the Qur'an easy to understand and remember: then is there any that will receive admonition?

18. The 'Ad (people) (too) rejected (Truth): then how terrible was My Chastisement and My Warning?

19. For We sent against them a furious wind, on a Day of violent Disaster,

20. Plucking out men as if they were roots of palm-trees torn up (from the ground).

21. Yes, how (terrible) was My Chastisement and My Warning!

22. But We have indeed made the Qur'an easy to understand and remember: then is there any that will receive admonition?

23. The Thamud (also) rejected (their) Warners.

24. For they said: "What! a man! a solitary one from among ourselves! shall we follow such a one? Truly we should then be straying in mind, and mad!

25. "Is it that the Message is sent to him, of all people amongst us? Nay, he is a liar, an insolent one!"

26. Ah! they will know on the morrow, which is the liar, the insolent

---

7. Long wide piece of timber
8. Stop up seams of ship with waterproofing material, etc.,
9. Warning, counsel

one!

27.   For We will send the she-camel by way of trial for them. So watch them, (O Salih), and possess yourself in patience!

28.   And inform them that the water is to be shared between them. each one's right to drink being brought forward (by suitable turns).

29.   But they called to their companion, and he took a sword in hand, and hamstrung[10] (her).

30.   Ah! how (terrible) was My Chastisement and My Warning!

31.   For We sent against them a single Mighty Blast, and they became like the dry stubble[11] used by one who pens[12] cattle.

32.   And We have indeed made the Qur'an easy to understand and remember: then is there any that will receive admonition?

33.   The people of Lut rejected (his) warning.

34.   We sent against them a violent tornado[13] with showers of stones, (which destroyed them), except Lut's household: We delivered them by early Dawn,-

35.   As a Grace from Us: thus do We reward those who give thanks.

36.   And (Lut) warned them of Our Punishment, but they disputed about the Warning.

37.   And they even sought to snatch away his guests from him, but We blinded their eyes. (They heard:) "Now you taste My Wrath and My Warning."

38.   Early on the morrow an abiding Punishment seized them:

39.   "So you taste My Wrath and My Warning."

40.   And We have indeed made the Qur'an easy to understand and remember: then is there any that will receive admonition?

41.   To the People of Pharaoh, too, aforetime[14], came Warners (from Allah).

42.   The (people) rejected all Our Signs; but We seized them with such Chastisement (as comes) from One Exalted in Power, able

10.   Crippled
11.   Cut stalks of cereal plants left sticking up after harvest
12.   Enclose, shut in (cattle etc.) in pen or a small enclosure
13.   A voilent storm of whirling winds
14.   Previously

to carry out His Will.

43. Are you Unbelievers, (O Quraish), better than they? Or do you have an immunity[15] in the Sacred Books?

44. Or do they say: "We acting together can defend ourselves"?

45. Soon will their multitude be put to flight, and they will show their backs.

46. Nay, the Hour (of Judgment) is the time promised them (for their full recompense): and that Hour will be most grievous and most bitter.

47. Truly those in sin are the ones straying in mind, and mad.

48. The Day they will be dragged through the Fire on their faces, (they will hear:) "you taste the touch of Hell!"

49. Verily! We have created every thing by measure.

50. And Our Command is but a single (Act),- like the twinkling of an eye.

51. And (oft) in the past, We have destroyed gangs like you: then is there any that will receive admonition?

52. All that they do is noted in (their) Books (of Deeds):

53. Every matter, small and great, is on record.

54. As to the Righteous, they will be in the midst of Gardens and Rivers,

55. In an Assembly of Truth, in the Presence of a Sovereign Omnipotent[16].

---

15. Exemption

16. All-Powerful, supreme

SURAH—55

SURAH AR-RAHMAN

(INTRODUCTION)

The majority of Commentators consider this an early Makkan Surah, though some consider at least a part of it as dating from Madinah. The greater part of it is undoubtedly early Makkan.

It is highly poetical and mystical, and the refrain "Then which of the favours of your Lord wilL ye deny?" is interspersed 31 times among its 78 verses.

It is the sixth of the series of seven dealing with Revelation, the favours of Allah, and the Hereafter: see Introduction to S. 50.

Here the special theme is indicated by the refrain. The rhyme in most cases is in the Dual grammatical form and the Argument implies that though things are created in pairs, there is an underlying Unity, through the Creator, in the favours which He bestows, and in the goal to which they are marching.

SURAH RAHMAN (ALLAH, MOST GRACIOUS)

In the name of Allah, Most Gracious, Most Merciful.

1.   (Allah) Most Gracious!

2.   It is He Who has taught the Qur'an.

3.   He has created man:

4.   He has taught him speech (and given him intelligence).

5.   The sun and the moon follow courses (exactly) computed[1];

6.   And the stars and the trees —both (alike) bow in adoration.

7.   And He has uplifted the sky and He has set up the balance.

8.   In order that you may not transgress (due) balance.

9.   So establish weight with justice and do not fall short in the balance.

10. It is He Who has spread out the earth for (His) creatures:

11. Therein is fruit and date-palms, producing spathes[2] (enclosing dates);

12. Also corn, with (its) leaves and stalk for fodder, and sweet-smelling plants.

13. Then which of the favours of your Lord will you deny?

---

1.   Reckoned, calculated
2.   Large bract or painr of bracts enveloping flower-cluster

14.   He created man from sounding clay like unto pottery,

15.   And He created Jinns from fire free of smoke:

16.   Then which of the favours of your Lord will you deny?

17.   (He is) Lord of the two Easts and Lord of the two Wests:

18.   Then which of the favours of your Lord will you deny?

19.   He has let free the two seas meeting together.

20.   Between them is a Barrier which they do not transgress:

21.   Then which of the favours of your Lord will you deny?

22.   Out of them come Pearls and Coral:[3]

23.   Then which of the favours of your Lord will you deny?

24.   And His are the Ships sailing smoothly through the seas, lofty as mountains:

25.   Then which of the favours of your Lord will you deny?

26.   All that is on earth will perish:

27.   But will abide[4] (for ever) the Face of your Lord,- full of Majesty[5], Bounty[6] and Honour.

28.   Then which of the favours of your Lord will you deny?

29.   Of Him seeks (its need) every creature in the heavens and on earth: every day He (shines) in (new) Splendour!

30.   Then which of the favours of your Lord will you deny?

31.   Soon We shall settle your affairs, O both you worlds.

32.   Then which of the favours of your Lord will you deny?

33.   O you assembly of Jinns and men! If it be you can pass beyond the zones of the heavens and the earth, you pass! not without authority shall you be able to pass!

34.   Then which of the favours of your Lord will you deny?

35.   On you will be sent (O you evil ones twain[7]) a flame of fire (to burn) and a smoke (to choke): no defence will you have:

36.   Then which of the favours of your Lord will you deny?

37.   When the sky is rent asunder, and it becomes red like ointment:

38.   Then which of the favours of your Lord will you deny?

---

3.   A substance composed of calcium carbonate (red, pink, white etc.) secreted by marine polyps for support and habitation.

4.   Endure   5.   Magnifience, Glory

6.   Munificence, benevolence   7.   Two (persons or things)

39. On that Day no question will be asked of man or Jinn as to his sin.

40. Then which of the favours of your Lord will you deny?

41. (For) the sinners will be known by their marks: and they will be seized by their forelocks and their feet.

42. Then which of the favours of your Lord will you deny?

43. This is the Hell which the Sinners deny:

44. In its midst and in the midst of boiling hot water will they wander round!

45. Then which of the favours of your Lord will you deny?

46. But for him who fear the standing before his Lord there will be two gardens.

47. Then which of the favours of your Lord will you deny?-

48. Containing all kinds (of trees and delights);-

49. Then which of the favours of your Lord will you deny?-

50. In them (each) will be two springs flowing (free);

51. Then which of the favours of your Lord will you deny?-

52. In them will be Fruits of every kind, two and two.

53. Then which of the favours of your Lord will you deny?

54. They will recline on carpets, whose inner linings will be of rich brocade[8]: the Fruit of the Gardens will be near (and easy of reach).

55. Then which of the favours of your Lord will you deny?

56. In them will be (Maidens), chaste, restraining their glances, whom no man or Jinn before them has touched;-

57. Then which of the favours of your Lord will you deny?-

58. Like unto rubies and coral.

59. Then which of the favours of your Lord will you deny?

60. Is there any Reward for Good - other than Good?

61. Then which of the favours of your Lord will you deny?

62. And besides these two, there are two other Gardens,-

63. Then which of the favours of your Lord will you deny?-

64. Dark-green in colour (from plentiful watering).

---

8. Fabric woven with raised patterns (of added metal threads)

65. Then which of the favours of your Lord will you deny?

66. In them (each) will be two springs pouring forth water in continuous abundance.

67. Then which of the favours of your Lord will you deny?

68. In them will be Fruits, and dates and pomegranates:

69. Then which of the favours of your Lord will you deny?

70. In them will be fair (Companions), good, beautiful;-

71. Then which of the favours of your Lord will you deny?-

72. Maidens restrained (as to their glances), in (goodly) pavilions[9].

73. Then which of the favours of your Lord will you deny?-

74. Whom no man or Jinn before them has touched;-

75. Then which of the favours of your Lord will you deny?-

76. Reclining on green cushi-ons and rich carpets of beauty.

77. Then which of the favours of your Lord will you deny?

78. Blessed be the name of your Lord, full of Majesty, Bounty and Honour.

---

9. Large peaked tents

SURAH—56

SURAH AL-WAQI'A

(INTRODUCTION)

This is the seventh and last Surah of the series devoted to Revelation and the Hereafter, as explained in the Introduction to S. 50.

It belongs to the early Makkan period, with the possible exception of one or two verses.

The theme is the certainty of the Day of Judgment and its adjustment of true Values (56: 1-56); Allah's Power, Goodness and Glory (56: 57-74): and the truth of Revelation (56: 75-96).

SURAH WAQI'A (THE INEVITABLE EVENT)

In the name of Allah, Most Gracious, Most Merciful.

1.   When the inevitable event comes to pass,
2.   Then will no (soul) deny its coming.
3.   (Many) will it bring low; (many) will it exalt[1];
4.   When the earth shall be shaken to its depths,
5.   And the mountains shall be crumbled to atoms,
6.   Becoming dust scattered abroad,
7.   And you shall be sorted out into three classes.
8.   Then (there will be) the Companions of the Right Hand;– What will be the Companions of the Right Hand?
9.   And the Companions of the Left Hand,–what will be the Companions of the Left Hand?
10. And those Foremost (in Faith) will be Foremost (in the Hereafter)
11. These will be those Nearest to Allah:
12. In Gardens of Bliss:
13. A number of people from those of old,
14. And a few from those of later times.
15. (They will be) on couches encrusted[2] (with gold and precious stones),

---

1.   Raise high, elevate
2.   Overlaid with ornamental layer (or crust) of precious material.

16. Reclining on them, facing each other.

17. Round about them will (serve) youths of perpetual (freshness),

18. With goblets[3], (shining) beakers[4], and cups (filled) out of clear-flowing fountains:

19. No after-ache[5] will they receive therefrom, nor will they suffer intoxication[6]:

20. And with fruits, any that they may select:

21. And the flesh of fowls, any that they may desire.

22. And (there will be) Companions with beautiful, big, and lustrous eyes,—

23. Like unto Pearls well-guarded.

24. A Reward for the deeds of their past (life).

25. No frivolity[7] will they hear therein, nor any taint[8] of ill,-

26. Only the saying, "Peace! Peace".

27. The Companions of the Right Hand,- what will be the Companions of the Right Hand?

28. (They will be) among lote-trees without thorns,

29. Among Talh[9] trees with flowers (or fruits) piled one above another,—

30. In shade long-extended,

31. By water flowing constantly.

32. And fruit in abundance.

33. Whose season is not limited, nor (supply) forbidden,

34. And on Thrones (of Dignity), raised high.

35. We have created them a (new) creation.

36. And made them virgin–pure (and undefiled[10]), —

37. Beloved (by nature), equal in age-

38. For the Companions of the Right Hand.

39. A (goodly) number from those of old,

---

3. Drinking cups   4. Large drinking cup
5. Hangover, unpleasant after-effects of something
6. Drunkeneess   7. Silliness
8. Stain
9. Banana tree, or a special kind of acacia tree, which flowers profusely, the flowers appearing in tiers one above another
10. Clean and pure

40. And a (goodly) number from those of later times.

41. The Companions of the Left Hand,- what will be the Companions of the Left Hand?

42. In scorching wind and scalding water.

43. And in the shades of Black Smoke:

44. Nothing (will there be) to refresh, nor to please:

45. For that they were wont[11] to be indulged[12], before that, in wealth and luxury,

46. And persisted obstinately in supreme wickedness!

47. And they used to say, "What! when we die and become dust and bones, shall we then indeed be raised up again?-

48. "(We) and our fathers of old?"

49. Say: "Yes, those of old and those of later times,

50. "All will certainly be gathered together for the meeting appointed for a Day well-known.

51. "Then will you truly,– O you that go wrong, and deny (the Truth)

52. "You will surely taste of the Tree of Zaqqum.

53. "Then will you fill your insides therewith,

54. "And drink Boiling Water on top of it:

55. "Indeed you shall drink like diseased camels raging[13] with thirst!".

56. This will be their welcome on the Day of Requital[14].

57. It is We Who have created you: why will you not admit the Truth?

58. Do you then see? the (human seed) that you throw out,–

59. Is it you who create it, or are We the Creators?

60. We have decreed Death to be your common lot, and We are not to be frustrated[15]

61. from changing your Forms and creating you (again) in (forms) that you do not know.

62. And you certainly know already the first form of creation: why

---

11. Accustomed to, used to   12. All their desires were granted
13. Seething, roaming, violent   14. Reward of punishment
15. Thwart, prevent, or baffle

then do you not celebrate His praises?

63. Do you see the seed that you sow in the ground?

64. Is it you that cause it to grow, or are We the Cause?

65. Were it Our Will, We could make it broken orts. And you would be left in wonderment,

66. (Saying), "We are indeed left with debts (for nothing):

67. "Indeed are we shut out (of the fruits of our labour)"

68. Do you see the water which you drink?

69. Do you bring it down (in rain) from the cloud or do We?

70. Were it Our Will, We could make it salt (and unpalatable[16]): then why do you not give thanks?

71. Do you see the Fire which you kindle?

72. Is it you who grow the tree which feeds the fire, or do We grow it?

73. We have made it a memorial (of Our handiwork), and an article of comfort and convenience for the denizens[17] of deserts.

74. Then celebrate with praises the name of your Lord, the Supreme!

75. Furthermore I call to witness the setting of the Stars,-

76. And! that is indeed a mighty adjuration[18], if you but knew–

77. That this is indeed a Qur'an Most Honourable,

78. In a Book well-guarded,

79. Which none shall touch but those who are clean:

80. A Revelation from the Lord of the Worlds.

81. Is it such a Message that you would hold in light esteem?

82. And have you made it your livelihood that you should declare it false?

83. Then why do you not (intervene) when (the soul of the dying man) reaches the throat,—

84. And you the while (sit) looking on,-

85. But We are nearer to him than you, and yet do not see ,-

86. Then why do you not,—if you are exempt from (future)

---

16. Unpleasant to the taste
17. Dwellers, residents
18. Oath

account,—

87. Call back the soul, if you are true (in your claim of Independence)?

88. Thus, then, if he be of those Nearest to Allah,

89. (There is for him) Rest and Satisfaction, and a Garden of Delights. .

90. And if he be of the Companions of the Right Hand,

91. (For him is the salutation), "Peace be unto you", from the Companions of the Right Hand.

92. And if he be of those who treat (Truth) as Falsehood, who go wrong,

93. For him is Entertainment with Boiling Water.

94. And burning in Hell-Fire.

95. Verily, this is the very Truth of assured certainty.

96. So celebrate with praises the name of your Lord, the Supreme.

SURAH—57

SURAH AL-HADID
(INTRODUCTION)

We have now studied the contents of nearly nine-tenths of the Qur'an. We have found that the arrangement of the Surahs in the present Text is not haphazard, but that they follow a distinct logical order more helpful for study than the chronological order. The comprehensive scheme of building up the new *Umrnah* or Brotherhood and its spiritual implications is now complete. The remaining tenth of the Quran may be roughly considered in two parts. The first contains ten Surahs (S. 57 to 66), all revealed in Madinah, and each dealing with some special point which needs emphasis in the social life of the *Ummah*. The second (S. 67 to S. 114) contains short Makkan lyrics, each dealing with some aspect of spiritual life, expressed in language of great mystic beauty.

The present Madinah Surah is chiefly concerned with spiritual humility and the avoidance of arrogance, and a warning that retirement from the world may not be the best way of seeking the good pleasure of Allah. Its probable date is after the conquest of Makkah A.H. 8.

SURAH HADID (IRON)

In the name of Allah, Most Gracious, Most Merciful.

1. Whatever is in the heavens and on the earth glorifies Allah; and He is the Mighty, the Wise.

2. To Him belongs the dominion[1] of the heavens and the earth: it is He Who gives Life and Death; and He has Power over all things.

3. He is the First and the Last, the Evident and the Hidden[2]: and He has full knowledge of all things.

4. He it is Who created the heavens and the earth in Six Days, and is moreover firmly established on the Throne (of Authority). He knows what enters within the earth and what comes forth out of it, what comes down from heaven and what mounts up to it. And He is with you wheresoever you may be. And Allah sees

---

1. Sovereignty, power
2. Indwelling, inherent (in), permanently pervading the universe

well all that you do.

5.   To Him belongs the dominion of the heavens and the earth: and all affairs are referred back to Allah.

6.   He merges Night into Day, and He merges Day into Night; and He has full knowledge of the secrets of (all) hearts.

7.   Believe in Allah and His Apostle, and spend (in charity) out of the (substance[3]) whereof He has made you heirs. For, those of you who believe and spend (in charity),- for them is a great Reward.

8.   What cause do you have why you should not believe in Allah?- and the Apostle invites you to believe in your Lord, and has indeed taken your Covenant, if you are men of Faith.

9.   He is the One Who sends to His Servant Manifest Signs, that He may lead you from the depths of Darkness into the Light and verily Allah is to you most kind and Merciful.

10.   And what cause do you have why you should not spend in the cause of Allah? For to Allah belongs the heritage of the heavens and the earth. Not equal among you are those who spent (freely) and fought, before the Victory, (with those who did so later). Those are higher in rank than those who spent (freely) and fought afterwards. But to all has Allah promised a goodly (reward). And Allah is well acquainted with all that you do.

11.   Who is he that will loan to Allah a beautiful loan? for (Allah) will increase it manifold to his credit, and he will have (besides) a liberal reward.

12.   One Day you will see the believing men and the believing women- how their Light runs forward before them and by their right hands: (their greeting will be): "Good News for you this Day! Gardens beneath which flow rivers to dwell therein for ever! This is indeed the highest Achievement!"

13.   One Day will the Hypocri-tes- men and women - say to the Believers: "Wait for us! Let us borrow (a light) from your Light!" It will be said: "You turn back to your rear[4]! then seek a Light

---

3.   Riches   4.   Back part (of a thing)

(where you can)!" So a wall will be put up between them, with a gate therein. Within it will be Mercy throughout, and without it, all alongside, will be (Wrath and) Punishment!

14. (Those without) will call out, "Were we not with you?" (The others) will reply, "True! but you led yourselves into temptation[5]; you looked forward (to our ruin); you doubted (Allah's Promise); and (your false) desires deceived you; until there issued the Command of Allah. And the Deceiver deceived you in respect of Allah.

15. "This Day shall no ransom be accepted of you, nor of those who rejected Allah." Your abode is the Fire: that is the proper place to claim you: and an evil refuge it is!"

16. Has not the time arrived for the Believers that their hearts in all humility should engage in the remembrance of Allah and of the Truth which has been revealed (to them), and that they should not become like those to whom was given Revelation aforetime, but long ages passed over them and their hearts grew hard? For many among them are rebellious transgressors.

17. You (all) know that Allah gives life to the earth after its death! already have We shown the Signs plainly to you, that you may learn wisdom.

18. For those who give in charity, men and women, and loan to Allah a beautiful loan, it shall be increased manifold (to their credit), and they shall have (besides) a liberal reward.

19. And those who believe in Allah and His Apostles- they are the Sincere (lovers of Truth), and the witnesses (who testify), in the eyes of their Lord: they shall have their Reward and their Light. But those who reject Allah and deny Our Signs,- they are the Companions of Hell-Fire.

20. You (all) know that the life of this world is but play and amusement, pomp and mutual boasting and multiplying, (in rivalry) among yourselves, riches and children. Here is a similitude[6]: how rain and the growth which it brings forth, delight (the hearts of) the tillers; soon it withers; you will see it

---

5. (Incitement to) sin   6. Likeness, parable

grow yellow; then it becomes dry and crumbles away. But in the Hereafter is a Chastisement severe (for the devotees of wrong). And Forgiveness from Allah and (His) Good Pleasure (for the devotees of Allah). And what is the life of this world, but goods and chattels[7] of deception?

21.   You be foremost (in seeking) Forgiveness from your Lord, and a Garden (of Bliss), the width whereof is as the width of heaven and earth, prepared for those who believe in Allah and His Apostles: that is the Grace of Allah, which He bestows on whom He pleases: and Allah is the Lord of Grace abounding[8].

22.   No misfortune can happen on earth or in your souls but is recorded in a decree before We bring it into existence: that is truly easy for Allah:

23.   In order that you may not despair over matters that pass you by, nor exult[9] over favours bestowed upon you. For Allah does not love any vainglorious[10] boaster,-

24.   Such persons as are covetous[11] and commend covetous-ness to men. And if any turn back (from Allah's Way), verily Allah is Free of all needs, Worthy of all Praise.

25.   We sent aforetime Our Apostles with Clear Signs and sent down with them the Book and the Balance (of Right and Wrong), that men may stand forth in justice; and We sent down Iron, in which is (material for) mighty war, as well as many benefits for mankind, that Allah may test who it is that will help, unseen, Him and His Apostles: for Allah is Full of Strength, Exalted in Might (and able to enforce His Will).

26.   And We sent Noah and Abraham, and established in their line Prophethood and Revelation: and some of them were on right guidance. But many of them became rebellious transgressors.

27.   Then, in their wake, We followed them up with (others of) Our Apostles: We sent after them Jesus the son of Mary, and bestowed on him the Gospel; and We ordained in the hearts of

---

7.   Movable possessions   8.   Plentiful, abundant
9.   Feel proud, happy   10.   Boastful, extremely vain
11.   Miserly

those who followed him compassion and mercy. But the Monasticism which they invented for themselves, We did not prescribe for them: (We commanded) only the seeking for the Good Pleasure of Allah; but that they did not foster[12] as they should have done. Yet We bestowed, on those among them who believed, their (due) rewa rd, but many of them are rebel-lious transgressors.

28. O you that believe! Fear Allah, and believe in His Apostle, and He will bestow on you a double portion of His Mercy: He will provide for you a Light by which you shall walk (straight in your path), and He will forgive you (your past): for Allah is Oft- Forgiving, Most Merciful.

29. That the People of the Book may know that they have no power whatever over the Grace of Allah, that (His) Grace is (entirely) in His Hand, to bestow it on whomsoever He wills. For Allah is the Lord of Grace abounding.

---

12. Promote, cherish

SURAH—58
SURAH AL-MUJADILA
(INTRODUCTION)

This is the second of the ten Madinah Surahs referred to in the Introduction to the last Surah. Its subject-matter is the acceptance of a women's Plea on behalf of herself and her children and a condemnation of all secret counsels and intrigues in the Muslim Brotherhood.

The date is somewhat close to that of S. 33, say between A.H. 5. and A.H. 7.

SURAH MUJADALA (THE WOMAN WHO PLEADS)

In the name of Allah, Most Gracious, Most Merciful.

1.   Allah has indeed heard (and accepted) the statement of the woman who pleads with you concerning her husband and carries her complaint (in prayer) to Allah: and Allah (always) hears the arguments between both sides among you: for Allah hears and sees (all things).

2.   If any men among you divorce their wives by Zihar (calling them mothers), they cannot be their mothers: none can be their mothers except those who gave them birth. And in fact they use words (both) iniquitous[1] and false: but truly Allah is One that blots out (sins), and forgives (again and again).

3.   But those who divorce their wives by Zihar, then wish to go back on the words they uttered,- (It is ordained that such a one) should free a slave before they touch each other: this you are admonished to perform: and Allah is well-acquainted with (all) that you do.

4.   And if any has not (the wherewithal[2]), he should fast for two months consecutively[3] before they touch each other. But if any is unable to do so, he should feed sixty indigent[4] ones, this, that you may show your faith in Allah and His Apostle. Those are limits (set by) Allah. For those who reject (Him), there is a

---

1. Grossly unjust, evil	2. Means of money
3. Continuously, one after the other	4. Needy

grievous Chastisement.

5.   Those who resist Allah and His Apostle will be humbled to dust, as were those before them: for We have already sent down Clear Signs. And the Unbelie-vers (will have) a humiliating Chastisement,-

6.   On the Day that Allah will raise them all up (again) and show them the Truth (and meaning) of their conduct. Allah has reckoned its (value), though they may have forgotten it, for Allah is Witness to all things.

7.   Don't you see that Allah knows (all) that is in the heavens and on earth? There is not a secret consultation between three, but He makes the fourth among them, - Nor between five but He makes the sixth,- nor between fewer nor more, but He is in their midst, wheresoever they be: in the end He will tell them the truth of their conduct, on the Day of Judgment. For Allah has full knowledge of all things.

8.   Don't you turn your sight towards those who were for-bidden secret counsels yet revert to that which they were forbidden (to do)? And they hold secret counsels among themselves for iniquity[5] and hostility, and disobedience to the Apostle. And when they come to you, they salute you, not as Allah salutes you, (but in crooked ways): and they say to themselves, "Why does not Allah punish us for our words?" Enough for them is Hell: in it they will burn, and evil is that destination!

9.   O you who believe! When you hold secret counsel, do not do it for iniquity and hostility, and disobedience to the Prophet; but do it for righteousness and self- restraint; and fear Allah, to Whom you shall be brought back.

10. Secret counsels are only (inspired) by the Evil One, in order that he may cause grief to the Believers; but he cannot harm them in the least, except as Allah permits; and on Allah let the Believers put their trust.

11. O you who believe! When you are told to make room in the assemblies, (spread out and) make room: (ample) room will

_____

5.   Injustice, wrongdoing

Allah provide for you. And when you are told to rise up, rise up, Allah will raise up, to (suitable) ranks (and degrees) those of you who believe and who have been granted (mystic) Knowledge. And Allah is well- acquainted with all you do.

12. O you who believe! When you consult the Apostle in private, spend something in charity before your private consultation. That will be best for you, and most conducive[6] to purity (of conduct). But if you do not find (the wherewithal), Allah is Oft- Forgiving, Most Merciful.

13. Is it that you are afraid of spending sums in charity before your private consultation (with him)? If, then, you do not so, and Allah forgives you, then (at least) establish regular prayer; practise regular charity; and obey Allah and His Apostle. And Allah is well-acquainted with all that you do.

14. Don't you turn your attention to those who turn (in friendship) to such as have the Wrath of Allah upon them? They are neither of you nor of them, and they swear to falsehood knowingly.

15. Allah has prepared for them a severe Chastisement: evil indeed are their deeds.

16. They have made their oaths a screen (for their misdeeds): thus they obstruct (men) from the Path of Allah: therefore they shall have a humiliating Chastisement.

17. Of no profit whatever to them, against Allah, will be their riches nor their sons: they will be Companions of the Fire, to dwell therein (for ever)!

18. One day Allah will raise them all up (for Judgment): then will they swear to Him as they swear to you: and they think that they have something (to stand upon). No, indeed! they are but liars!

19. The Evil One has got the better of them: so he has made them lose the remembrance of Allah. They are the Party of the Evil One. Truly, it is the Party of the Evil One that will perish!

20. Those who resist Allah and His Apostle will be among those most humiliated.

---

6.   Helpful

21. Allah has decreed: "It is I and My Apostles who must prevail": for Allah is One full of strength, able to enforce His Will.

22. You will not find any people who believe in Allah and the Last Day, loving those who resist Allah and His Apostle, even though they were their fathers or their sons, or their brothers, or their kindred[7]. For such He has written Faith in their hearts, and strengthened them with a spirit from Himself. And He will admit them to Gardens beneath which Rivers flow, to dwell therein (for ever). Allah will be well pleased with them, and they with Him. They are the Party of Allah. Truly it is the Party of Allah that will achieve felicity[8].

---

7. Relatives   8. Bliss, happiness

SURAH—59

SURAH AL-HASHR

(INTRODUCTION)

This is the third often short Madinah Surahs, dealing each with a special point in the life of the *Ummah* see Introduction to S. 57. The special theme here is how treachery to the *Ummah* on the part of its enemies recoils on the enemies themselves, while it strengthens the bond between the different sections of the *Ummah* itself, and this is illustrated by the story of the expulsion of the Jewish tribe of the Banu Nadhir in Rabi I A.H. 4.

This fixes the date of the Surah.

SURAH HASHR (THE GATHERING)

In the name of Allah, Most Gracious, Most Merciful.

1. Whatever is in the heavens and on earth, let it declare the Praises and Glory of Allah: for He is the Exalted in Might, the Wise.

2. It is He Who got out the Unbelievers among the People of the Book from their homes at the first gathering (of the forces). Little did you think that they would get out: and they thought that their fortresses would defend them from Allah! But the (Wrath of) Allah came to them from quarters from which they little expected (it), and cast terror into their hearts, so that they destroyed their dwellings by their own hands and the hands of the Believers. Take warning, then, O you with eyes (to see)!

3. And had it not been that Allah had decreed banishment for them, He would certainly have punished them in this world: and in the Hereafter they shall (certainly) have the Punishment of the Fire.

4. That is because they resisted Allah and His Apostle: and if any one resists Allah, verily Allah is severe in Punishment.

5. Whether you cut down (O you Muslims) the tender palm-trees, or you left them standing on their roots, it was by leave of Allah, and in order that He might cover with shame the rebellious transgressors.

6. What Allah has bestowed on His Apostle (and taken away) from them - for this you made no expedition with either cavalry or

camelry: but Allah gives power to His Apostles over any He pleases: and Allah has power over all things.

7. WhatAllah has bestowed on HisApostle (and taken away) from the people of the townships,- belongs to Allah,- to His Apostle and to kindred[1] and orphans, the needy and the wayfarer[2]; In order that it may not (merely) make a circuit[3] between the wealthy among you. So take what the Apostle assigns to you, and deny yourselves that which he withholds[4] from you. And fear Allah; for Allah is strict in Punishment.

8. (Some part is due) to the indigent[5] Muhajirs, those who were expelled from their homes and their property, while seeking Grace from Allah and (His) Good Pleasure, and aiding Allah and His Apostle: such are indeed the sincere ones:-

9. But those who before them, had homes (in Medina) and had adopted the Faith,- show their affection to such as came to them for refuge, and entertain no desire in their hearts for things given to the (latter), but give them prefe-rence over themselves, even though poverty was their (own lot). And those saved from the covetousness of their own souls,- they are the ones that achieve prosperity.

10. And those who came after them say: "Our Lord! Forgive us, and our brethren who came before us into the Faith, and leave not, in our hearts, rancour[6] (or sense of injury) against those who have believed. Our Lord! You are indeed Full of Kind-ness, Most Merciful."

11. Have you not observed the Hypocrites say to their mis-believing brethren among the People of the Book? - "If you are expelled, we too will go out with you, and we will never hearken[7] to any one in your affair; and if you are attacked (in fight) we will help you". But Allah is Witness that they are indeed liars.

12. If they are expelled, never will they go out with them; and if

---

1.	Relatives	2.	Traveller
3.	Circulation	4.	Restrains
5.	Needy, poor	6.	Hostility, malice
7.	Listen to, obey		

they are attacked (in fight), they will never help them; and if they do help them, they will turn their backs; so they will receive no help.

13. Of a truth you are stronger (than they) because of the terror in their hearts, (sent) by Allah. This is because they are men devoid of understanding.

14. They will not fight you (even) together, except in fortified townships, or from behind walls. Strong is their fighting (spirit) amongst them-selves: you would think they were united, but their hearts are divided: that is because they are a people devoid of wisdom.

15. Like those who lately preceded them, they have tasted the evil result of their conduct; and (in the Hereafter there is) for them a grievous Chastisement;-

16. (Their allies deceived them), like the Evil One, when he says to man, "Deny Allah": but when (man) denies Allah, (the Evil One) says, "I am free of you: I do fear Allah, the Lord of the Worlds!"

17. The end of both will be that they will go into the Fire, dwelling therein for ever. Such is the reward of the wrong-doers.

18. O you who believe! Fear Allah, and let every soul look to what (provision) he has sent forth for the morrow[8]. Yes, fear Allah: for Allah is well-acquainted with (all) that you do.

19. And you be not like those who forgot Allah; and He made them forget their own souls! Such are the rebellious trans-gressors!

20. Not equal are the Compa-nions of the Fire and the Com-panions of the Garden: it is the Companions of the Garden that will achieve felicity[9].

21. Had We sent down this Qur'an on a mountain, verily, you would have seen it humble itself and cleave asunder for fear of Allah. Such are the similitudes which We propound[10] to men, that they may reflect[11].

22. Allah is He, than Whom there is no other god;- Who knows (all

---

8. Tomorrow, i.e., for the life to come
9. Bliss, happiness
10. Offer for consideration, propose
11. Ponder

things) both secret and open; He, Most Gracious, Most Merciful.

23. Allah is He, than Whom there is no other god;- the Sovereign, the Holy One, the Source of Peace (and Perfection), the Guardian of Faith, the Preser-ver of Safety, the Exalted in Might, the Irresistible, the Sup-reme: Glory to Allah! (High is He) above the partners they attri-bute to Him.

24. He is Allah, the Creator, the Evolver, the Bestower of Forms (or Colours). To Him belong the Most Beautiful Names: whatever is in the heavens and on earth, declares His Praises and Glory: and He is the Exalted in Might, the Wise.

SURAH—60

SURAH AL-MUMTAHINA

(INTRODUCTION)

This is the fourth of the ten Madinah Surahs, each dealing with a special point in the life of the *Ummah*.

Here the point is: what social relations are possible with the Unbelievers? A distinction is made between those who persecute you for your Faith and want to destroy you and your Faith, and those who have shown no such rancour. For the latter there is hope of mercy and forgiveness. The question of women and cross-marriages is equitably dealt with.

The date is after the Pagans had broken the treaty of Hudaibiya, for which see Introduction to S. 47 — say about A.H. 8, not long before the conquest of Makkah.

SURAH MUMTAHINA

(THE WOMAN TO BE EXAMINED)

In the name of Allah, Most Gracious, Most Merciful.

1.   O you who believe! Take not my enemies and yours as friends (or protectors),- offering them (your) love, even though they have rejected the Truth that has come to you, and have (on the contrary) driven out the Prophet and yourselves (from your homes), (simply) because you believe in Allah your Lord! If you have come out to strive in My Way and to seek My Good Pleasure, (take them not as friends), holding secret conclave[1] of love (and friendship) with them: for I know full well all that you conceal and all that you reveal. And any of you that does this has strayed from the Straight Path.

2.   If they were to get the better of you, they would behave to you as enemies, and stretch forth their hands and their tongues against you for evil: and they desire that you should reject the Truth.

3.   Of no profit to you will be your relatives and your children on the Day of Judgment: He will judge between you: for Allah sees well all that you do.

---

1.   Meeting

4.   There is for you an excellent example (to follow) in Abraham and those with him, when they said to their people: "We are clear of you and of whatever you worship besides Allah: we have rejected you, and there has arisen, between us and you, enmity and hatred for ever,- unless you believe in Allah and Him alone": But not when Abraham said to his father: "I will pray for forgive-ness for you, though I have no power (to get) anything on your behalf from Allah." (They prayed): "Our Lord! in You do we trust, and to You do we turn in repentance: to You is (our) Final Goal.

5.   "Our Lord! Make us not a (test and) trial for the Unbelie-vers, but forgive us, our Lord! for You are the Exalted in Might, the Wise."

6.   There was indeed in them an excellent example for you to follow,-for those whose hope is in Allah and in the Last Day. But if any turn away, truly Allah is Free of all Wants, Worthy of all Praise.

7.   It may be that Allah will grant love (and friendship) between you and those whom you (now) hold as enemies. For Allah has power (over all things); and Allah is Oft-Forgiving, Most Merciful.

8.   Allah does not forbid you, with regard to those who do not fight you for (your) Faith nor drive you out of your homes, from dealing kindly and justly with them: for Allah loves those who are just.

9.   Allah only forbids you, with regard to those who fight you for (your) Faith, and drive you out of your homes, and support (others) in driving you out, from turning to them (for friendship and protection). It is such as turn to them (in these circumstances), that do wrong.

10.   O you who believe! When there come to you believing women refugees, examine (and test) them: Allah knows best as to their Faith: if you ascertain that they are Believers, then do not send them back to the Unbelievers. They are not lawful (wives) for the Unbelievers, nor are the (Unbelievers) lawful (husbands)

for them. But pay the Unbelievers what they have spent (on their dower), and there will be no blame on you if you marry them on payment of their dower to them. But do not hold to the guardianship of unbelieving women: ask for what you have spent on their dowers, and let the (Unbelievers) ask for what they have spent (on the dowers of women who come over to you). Such is the command of Allah: He judges (with justice) between you. And Allah is Full of Know-ledge and Wisdom.

11.   And if any of your wives deserts you to the Unbelievers, and you have an accession (by the coming over of a woman from the other side), then pay to those whose wives have deserted the equivalent of what they had spent (on their dower). And fear Allah, in Whom you believe.

12.   O Prophet! When belie-ving women come to you to take the oath of fealty[2] to you, that they will not associate in wor-ship any other thing whatever with Allah, that they will not steal, that they will not commit adultery (or fornication), that they will not kill their children, that they will not utter slander, intentionally forging falsehood, and that they will not disobey you in any just matter,- then you receive their fealty, and pray to Allah for the forgiveness (of their sins): for Allah is Oft-Forgiving, Most Merciful.

13.   O you who believe! Do not turn (for friendship) to people on whom is the Wrath of Allah. Of the Hereafter they are already in despair, just as the Unbelievers are in despair about those (buried) in graves.

---

2.   Allegiance, fidelity

SURAH—61

SURAH AS-SAFF
(INTRODUCTION)

This is the fifth Surah of the series of short Madinah Surahs beginning with S. 57. Its subject-matter is the need for discipline, practical work, and self-sacrifice in the cause of the *Ummah*. Its date is uncertain, but it was probably shortly after the battle of Uhud, which was fought in Shawwal, A.H. 3.

SURAH SAFF (BATTLE ARRAY)
In the name of Allah, Most Gracious, Most Merciful.

1.   Whatever is in the heavens and on earth, let it declare the Praises and Glory of Allah: for He is the Exalted in Might, the Wise.

2.   O you who believe, why do you say that which you do not?

3.   Grievously odious[1] is it in the sight of Allah that you say that which you do not.

4.   Truly Allah loves those who fight in His Cause in battle array, as if they were a solid cemented structure.

5.   And remember, Moses said to his people: "O my people! why do you vex[2] and insult me, though you know that I am the Apostle of Allah (sent) to you?" Then when they went wrong, Allah let their hearts go wrong. For Allah does not guide those who are rebellious transgressors.

6.   And remember, Jesus, the son of Mary, said: "O Children of Israel! I am the Apostle of Allah (sent) to you, confirming the Law (which came) before me, and giving Glad Tidings of an Apostle to come after me, whose name shall be Ahmad." But when he came to them with Clear Signs, they said, "this is evident sorcery!"

7.   Who does greater wrong than one who invents falsehood against Allah, even as he is being invited to Islam? And Allah does not guide those who do wrong.

8.   Their intention is to extinguish Allah's Light (by blowing) with

---

1.   Disgusting, abhorent, loathsome   2.   Annoy

their mouths: but Allah will complete (the reve-lation of) His Light, even though the Unbelievers may detest (it).

9.   It is He Who has sent His Apostle with Guidance and the Religion of Truth, that he may proclaim it over all religion, even though the Pagans may detest (it).

10. O you who believe! Shall I lead you to a bargain that will save you from a grievous Chastisement?-

11. That you believe in Allah and His Apostle, and that you strive (your utmost) in the Cause of Allah, with your property and your persons: that will be best for you, if you but knew!

12. He will forgive you your sins, and admit you to Gardens beneath which Rivers flow, and to beautiful mansions[3] in Gardens of Eternity: that is indeed the Supreme Achievement.

13. And another (favour will He bestow,) which you do love,- help from Allah and a speedy victory. So give the Glad Tidings to the Believers.

14. O you who believe! You be helpers of Allah: as said Jesus the son of Mary to the Disciples, "Who will be my helpers to (the work of) Allah?" Said the Disciples, "We are Allah's helpers!" then a portion of the Children of Israel believed, and a portion disbelieved: but We gave power to those who believed, against their enemies, and they became the ones that prevailed.

---

3.   Large residences

SURAH—62

SURAH AL-JUMU'A

(INTRODUCTION)

This is the sixth Surah in the Madinah series of short Surahs which began with S. 57.

The special theme here is the need for mutual contact in the Community for worship and understanding: for the spirit of the Message is for all, ignorant and learned, in order that they may be purified and may learn wisdom.

The date has no special significance: it may be placed in the early Madinah period, say between A.H. 2 and 5.

SURAH JUMU'A (THE ASSEMBLY - FRIDAY PRAYER)

In the name of Allah, Most Gracious, Most Merciful.

1. Whatever is in the heavens and on earth, declares the Praises and Glory of Allah,- the Sovereign, the Holy One, the Exalted in Might, the Wise.

2. It is He Who has sent amongst the Unlettered an Apostle from among themselves, to rehearse[1] to them His Signs, to purify[2] them, and to instruct them in Scripture and Wisdom,- although they had been, before, in manifest error;-

3. As well as (to confer all these benefits upon) others of them, who have not already joined them: and He is Exalted in Might, Wise.

4. Such is the Bounty of Allah, which He bestows on whom He will: and Allah is the Lord of the highest bounty.

5. The similitude of those who were charged with the (obligations of the) Mosaic Law, but who subsequently failed in those (obligations), is that of a donkey which carries huge tomes[3] (but does not understand them). Evil is the similitude of people who falsify the Signs of Allah: and Allah does not guide people who do wrong.

---

1. Recite
2. Books, volumes (of book), esp large heavy ones.
3. Trade

6.   Say: "O you that stand on Judaism! If you think that you are friends to Allah, to the exclusion of (other) men, then express your desire for Death, if you are truthful!"

7.   But never will they express their desire (for Death), because of the (deeds) their hands have sent on before them! and Allah knows well those that do wrong!

8.   Say: "The Death from which you flee will truly overtake you: then you will be sent back to the Knower of things secret and open: and He will tell you (the truth of) the things that you did!"

9.   O you who believe! When the call is proclaimed to prayer on Friday (the Day of Assemb-ly), hasten earnestly to the Remembrance of Allah, and leave off business (and traffic): That is best for you if you but knew!

10.   And when the Prayer is finished, then you may disperse through the land, and seek of the Bounty of Allah: and celebrate the Praises of Allah often (and without stint): that you may prosper.

11.   But when they see some bargain or some amusement, they disperse headlong to it, and leave you standing. Say: "The (blessing) from the Presence of Allah is better than any amusement or bargain! and Allah is the Best to provide (for all needs)."

SURAH—63
SURAH AL-MUNAFIQUN
(INTRODUCTION)

This is the seventh of the ten short Madinah Surahs dealing with a special feature in the social life of the Brotherhood.

The special feature here dealt with is the wiles and mischief of the Hypocrite element in any community, and the need of guarding against it and against the temptation it throws in the way of the Believers.

The battle of Uhud (Shawwal A.H. 3) unmasked the Hypocrites in. Madinah: see 3: 167. This Surah may be referred to sometimes after that event, say about 4 A.H. or possibly 5 A.H. If the words reported in verse 8 were uttered in the expedition against the Banu Mustaliq, A.H. 5.

SURAH MUNAFIQUN (THE HYPOCRITES)
In the name of Allah, Most Gracious, Most Merciful.

1. When the Hypocrites come to you, they say, "We bear witness that you are indeed the Apostle of Allah." Yes, Allah knows that you are indeed His Apostle, and Allah bears witness that the Hypocrites are indeed liars.

2. They have made their oaths a screen[1] (for their misdeeds): thus they obstruct (men) from the Path of Allah: truly evil are their deeds.

3. That is because they belie-ved, then they rejected Faith: so a seal was set on their hearts: therefore they do not understand.

4. When you look at them, their exteriors please you; and when they speak, you listen to their words. They are as (worthless as hollow) pieces of timber propped up, (unable to stand on their own). They think that every cry is against them. They are the enemies; so beware of them. The curse of Allah be on them! How are they deluded (away from the Truth)!

5. And when it is said to them, "Come, the Apostle of Allah will pray for your forgiveness", they turn aside their heads, and you would see them turning away their faces in arrogance.

---

1. Cover, mask

6.   It is equal to them whether you pray for their forgiveness or not. Allah will not forgive them. Truly Allah does not guide rebellious transgressors.

7.   They are the ones who say, "Spend nothing on those who are with Allah's Apostle, to the end that they may disperse (and quit Medina)." But to Allah belong the treasures of the heavens and the earth; but the Hypocrites do not understand.

8.   They say, "If we return to Medina, surely the more honourable (element) will expel therefrom the meaner." But honour belongs to Allah and His Apostle, and to the Believers; but the Hypocrites do not know.

9.   O you who believe! Let not your riches or your children divert you from the remembrance of Allah. If any act thus, the loss is their own.

10. And spend something (in charity) out of the substance which We have bestowed on you, before Death should come to any of you and he should say, "O my Lord! why did You not give me respite[2] for a little while? I should then have given (largely) in charity, and I should have been one of the doers of good".

11. But to no soul will Allah grant respite when the time appointed (for it) has come; and Allah is well acquainted with (all) that you do.

---

2.   Delay

SURAH—64

SURAH AT-TAGHABUN

(INTRODUCTION)

This is the eighth of the ten short Madinah Surahs, each dealing with a special aspect of the life of the Community.

The special aspect spoken of here is the mutual gain and loss of Good and Evil, contrasted in this life and in the Hereafter.

It is an early Madinah Surah, of the year 1 of the Hijra or possibly even of the Makkan period just before the *Hijrat.*

SURAH TAGHABUN (MUTUAL LOSS AND GAIN)

In the name of Allah, Most Gracious, Most Merciful.

1.   Whatever is in the heavens and on earth, declares the Praises and Glory of Allah: to Him belongs dominion, and to Him belongs praise: and He has power over all things.

2.   It is He Who has created you; and of you are some that are Unbelievers, and some that are Believers: and Allah sees well all that you do.

3.   He has created the heavens and the earth in just proportions, and has given you shape, and made your shapes beautiful: and to Him is the final Goal.

4.   He knows what is in the heavens and on earth; and He knows what you conceal and what you reveal: yes, Allah knows well the (secrets) of (all) hearts.

5.   Has not the story reached you, of those who rejected Faith aforetime? So they tasted the evil result of their conduct; and they had a grievous Chastisement.

6.   That was because there came to them Apostles with Clear Signs, but they said: "Shall (mere) human beings direct us?" So they rejected (the Message) and turned away. But Allah can do without (them): and Allah is free of all needs, worthy of all praise.

7.   The Unbelievers think that they will not be raised up (for Judgment). Say: "Yes, by my Lord, you shall surely be raised up: then you shall be told (the truth) of all that you did. And that is easy for Allah."

8.   Believe, therefore, in Allah and His Apostle, and in the Light which We have sent down. And Allah is well acquainted with all that you do.

9.   The Day that He assem-bles you (all) for a Day of Assembly,- that will be a Day of mutual loss and gain (among you), and those who believe in Allah and work righteousness,- He will remove from them their ills, and He will admit them to Gardens beneath which Rivers flow, to dwell therein for ever: that will be the Supreme Achievement.

10.   But those who reject Faith and treat Our Signs as false-hoods, they will be Companions of the Fire, to dwell therein for ever: and evil is that Goal.

11.   No kind of calamity can occur, except by the leave of Allah: and if any one believes in Allah, (Allah) guides his heart (aright): for Allah knows all things.

12.   So obey Allah, and obey His Apostle: but if you turn back, the duty of Our Apostle is but to proclaim (the Message) clearly and openly.

13.   Allah! There is no god but He: and on Allah, therefore, let the Believers put their trust.

14.   O you who believe! Truly, among your wives and your children are (some that are) enemies to yourselves: so beware of them! But if you forgive and overlook, and cover up (their faults), verily Allah is Oft-Forgiving, Most Merciful.

15.   Your riches and your children may be but a trial: but in the Presence of Allah, is the highest Reward.

16.   So fear Allah as much as you can; listen and obey and spend in charity for the benefit of your own souls. And those saved from the covetousness of their own souls,- they are the ones that achieve prosperity.

17.   If you loan to Allah a beautiful loan, He will double it to your (credit), and He will grant you Forgiveness: for Allah is most ready to appreciate (service), Most Forbearing,-

18.   Knower of what is hidden and what is open, Exalted in Might, Full of Wisdom.

SURAH—65

SURAH AT-TALAQ

(INTRODUCTION)

This is the ninth of the ten short Madinah Surahs dealing with the social life of the Community. The aspect dealt with here is Divorce and the necessity of precautions to guard against its abuse. The relations of the sexes are an important factor in the social life of the Community, and this and the following Surah deal with certain aspects of it. "Of all things permitted by law," said the Prophet, "divorce is the most hateful in the sight of Allah" *(Abu Da-ud, Sunan,* 13:3) While the sanctity of marriage is the essential basis of family life, the incompatibility of individuals and the weaknesses of human nature require certain outlets and safeguards if that sanctity is not to be made into a fetish at the expense of human life. That is why the question of Divorce is in the Surah linked with the question of insolent impiety and its punishment.

The date is somewhere about A.H. 6, but the chronology has no significance.

SURAH TALAQ (DIVORCE)

In the name of Allah, Most Gracious, Most Merciful.

1. O Prophet! When you do divorce women, divorce them at their prescribed periods, and count (accurately), their prescribed periods: and fear Allah your Lord: and do not turn them out of their houses, nor shall they (themselves) leave, except in case they are guilty of some open lewdness[1], those are limits set by Allah: and any who transgresses the limits of Allah, does verily wrong his (own) soul: you do not know if perchance[2] Allah will bring about thereafter some new situation.

2. Thus when they fulfil their term appointed, either take them back on equitable[3] terms or part with them on equitable terms; and take for witness two persons from among you, endued with justice, and establish the evidence (as) before Allah. Such is the admonition given to him who believes in Allah and the Last Day. And for those who fear Allah, He (ever) prepares a way out,

---

1. Indecency, obsenity
2. (Arch.) By chance, may be
3. Just

3.   And He provides for him from (sources) he never could imagine. And if any one puts his trust in Allah, sufficient is (Allah) for him. For Allah will surely accomplish His purpose: verily, for all things has Allah appointed a due proportion.

4.   Such of your women as have passed the age of monthly courses, for them the prescribed period, if you have any doubts, is three months, and for those who have no courses (it is the same): for those who carry (life within their wombs), their period is until they deliver their burdens: and for those who fear Allah, He will make their path easy.

5.   That is the Command of Allah, which He has sent down to you: and if any one fears Allah, He will remove his ills from him, and will enlarge his reward.

6.   Let the women live (in 'iddat) in the same style as you live, according to your means: do not annoy them, so as to restrict them. And if they carry (life in their wombs), then spend (your substance) on them until they deliver their burden: and if they suckle your (offspring), give them their recompense: and take mutual counsel together, according to what is just and reasonable. And if you find yourselves in difficulties, let another woman suckle (the child) on the (father's) behalf.

7.   Let the man of means spend according to his means: and the man whose resources are restricted, let him spend according to what Allah has given him. Allah puts no burden on any person beyond what He has given him. After a difficulty, Allah will soon grant relief.

8.   How many populations that insolently opposed the Command of their Lord and of His Apostles, did We not then call to account,- to severe account?- and We imposed on them an exemplary Punishment.

9.   Then they tasted the evil result of their conduct, and the End of their conduct was Perdition.[4]

10.   Allah has prepared for them a severe Punishment (in the Hereafter). Therefore fear Allah, O you men of understanding -

---

4.   Ruin

who have believed!- for Allah has indeed sent down to you a Message,-

11. An Apostle, who rehearses to you the Signs of Allah containing clear explanations, that he may lead forth those who believe and do righteous deeds from the depths of Darkness into Light. And those who believe in Allah and work righteousness, He will admit to Gardens beneath which Rivers flow, to dwell therein for ever: Allah has indeed granted for them a most excellent Provision.

12. Allah is He Who created seven Firmaments and of the earth a similar number. Through the midst of them (all) descends His Command: that you may know that Allah has power over all things, and that Allah comp-rehends all things in (His) Knowledge.

SURAH—66
SURAH AT-TAHRIM
(INTRODUCTION)

This is the tenth and last of the series of ten short Madinah Surahs which began with S. 57: see Introduction to that Surah. The point dealt with here is: how far the turning away from sex or the opposition of one sex against another or a want of harmony between the sexes may injure the higher interests of society.

The date may be taken to be somewhere about A.H. 7.

SURAH TAHRIM
(HOLDING -SOMETHING- TO BE FORBIDDEN)
In the name of Allah, Most Gracious, Most Merciful.

1. O Prophet! Why do you hold to be forbidden that which Allah has made lawful to you? You seek to please your consorts[1]. But Allah is Oft-Forgiving, Most Merciful.

2. Allah has already ordained for you, (O men), the absolution[2] of your oaths (in some cases): and Allah is your Protector, and He is Full of Knowledge and Wisdom.

3. When the Prophet di-closed a matter in confidence to one of his consorts, and she then divulged[3] it (to another), and Allah made it known to him, he confirmed part thereof and repudiated a part. Then when he told her thereof, she said, "Who told you this? "He said, "He told me Who knows and is well-acquainted (with all things)."

4. If you two turn in repentance to Him, your hearts are indeed so inclined; but if you back up each other against him, truly Allah is His Protector, and Gabriel, and (every) righteous one among those who believe,- and furthermore, the angels - will back (him) up.

5. It may be, if he divorced you (all), that Allah will give him in exchange consorts better than you,- who submit (their wills),

---

1. Wives
3. Disclosed
2. Undoing or getting out of

who believe, who are devout, who turn to Allah in repentance, who worship (in humility), who travel (for Faith) and fast, - previously married or virgins.

6. O you who believe! save yourselves and your families from a Fire whose fuel is Men and Stones, over which are (appointed) angels stern (and) severe, who do not flinch[4] (from executing) the Commands they receive from Allah, but do (precisely) what they are commanded.

7. (They will say), "O you Unbelievers! Make no excuses this Day! You are being but requited for all that you did!"

8. O you who believe! Turn to Allah with sincere repen-tance: in the hope that your Lord will remove from you your ills and admit you to Gardens beneath which Rivers flow,- the Day that Allah will not permit to be humiliated the Prophet and those who believe with him. Their Light will run forward before them and by their right hands, while they say, "Our Lord! Perfect our Light for us, and grant us Forgiveness: for You have power over all things."

9. O Prophet! Strive hard against the Unbelievers and the Hypocrites, and be firm against them. Their abode is Hell,- an evil refuge (indeed).

10. Allah sets forth, for an example to the Unbelievers, the wife of Noah and the wife of Lut: they were (respectively) under two of our righteous servants, but they were false to their (husbands), and they profited nothing before Allah on their account, but were told: "You enter the Fire along with (others) that enter!"

11. And Allah sets forth, as an example to those who believe, the wife of Pharaoh: behold she said: "O my Lord! build for me, in nearness to You, a mansion in the Garden, and save me from Pharaoh and his doings, and save me from those that do wrong"

12. And Mary the daughter of 'Imran, who guarded her chastity; and We breathed into (her body) of Our spirit; and she testified to the truth of the words of her Lord and of His Reve-lations, and was one of the devout (servants).

---

4. Draw back (from duty)

SURAH—67
SURAH AL-MULK
(INTRODUCTION)

We have now done fourteen-fifteenths of the Quran-an, and have followed step by step the development of its argument establishing the *(Ummah* or Brotherhood of Islam.

There is a logical break here. The remaining fifteenth consists of short spiritual Lyrics, mostly of the Makkan period, dealing mainly with the inner life of man, and in its individual aspects. They may be compared to Hymns or Psalms in other religious literature. But these short Quranic Surahs have a grandeur, a beauty, a mystic meaning, and a force of earnestness under persecution, all their own. With their sources in the sublimes regions of the Empyrean, their light penetrates into the darkest recesses of Life, into the concrete facts which are often mistaken for the whole of Reality, though they are but an insignificant portion and on the surface and fleeting. There is much symbolism in language and thought, in describing the spiritual in terms of the things we see and understand.

It is the contrast between the shadows of Reality here and the eternal Reality, between the surface world and the profound inner World, that is urged on our attention here.

This Surah of 30 verses belongs to the middle Makkan period, just before S. 69 and S. 70. Allah is mentioned here by the name *Rahman* (Most Gracious), as He is mentioned by the names of *Rabb* (Lord and Cherishes) and *Rahman* (Most Gracious) in S. 19.

SURAH MULK (DOMINION)

In the name of Allah, Most Gracious, Most Merciful.

1. Blessed be He in Whose hands is Dominion; and He over all things has Power;-

2. He Who created Death and Life, that He may try which of you is best in deed: and He is the Exalted in Might, Oft-Forgiving;-

3. He Who created the seven heavens one above another: no want of proportion will you see in the Creation of (Allah) Most Gracious. So turn your vision again: do you see any flaw?

4. Again turn your vision a second time: (your) vision will come back to you dull and discomfited[1], in a state worn out.

---

1. Baffled, confused, (arch) defeated

5. And We have, (from of old), adorned the lowest heaven with Lamps, and We have made such (Lamps) (as) missiles[2] to drive away the Evil Ones, and have prepared for them the Chastisement of the Blazing Fire.

6. For those who reject their Lord (and Cherisher) is the Penalty of Hell: and evil is (such), destination.

7. When they are cast therein, they will hear the (terrible) drawing in of its breath even as it blazes forth,

8. Almost bursting with fury: every time a Group is cast therein, its Keepers will ask, "Did no Warner come to you?"

9. They will say: "Yes indeed; a Warner did come to us, but we rejected him and said, 'Allah never sent down any (Message): you are in nothing but an egregious[3] delusion!'"

10. They will further say: "had we but listened or used our intelligence, we should not (now) be among the Companions of the Blazing Fire!"

11. They will then confess their sins: but far will be (Forgiveness) from the Compa-nions of the Blazing Fire!

12. As for those who fear their Lord unseen, for them is Forgiveness and a great Reward.

13. And whether you hide your word or publish it, He certainly has (full) knowledge, of the secrets of (all) hearts.

14. Should He not know,- He that created? and He is the One that understands the finest mysteries (and) is well-acquainted (with them).

15. It is He Who has made the earth manageable for you, so you traverse[4] through its tracts and enjoy of the Sustenance which He furnishes: but unto Him is the Resurrection.

16. Do you feel secure that He Who is in Heaven will not cause you to be swallowed up by the earth even it shakes (as in an earthquake)?

17. Or do you feel secure that He Who is in Heaven will not send against you a violent tornado (with showers of stones), so that

---

2. (Object or weapon) for throwing at a target
3. Deplorable, outrageous   4. Travel

you shall know how (terrible) was My warning?

18. But indeed men before them rejected (My warning): then how (terrible) was My rejection (of them)?

19. Do they not observe the birds above them, spreading their wings and folding them in? None can uphold them except (Allah) Most Gracious: truly it is He that watches over all things.

20. Nay, who is there that can help you, (even as) an army, besides (Allah) Most Merciful? In nothing but delusion are the Unbelievers.

21. Or who is there that can provide you with Sustenance if He were to withhold[5] His provision? Nay, they obstinately persist in insolent impiety and flight (from the Truth).

22. Is then one who walks headlong, with his face grovelling[6], better guided,- or one who walks evenly on a Straight Way?

23. Say: "It is He Who has created you (and made you grow), and made for you the faculties of hearing, seeing, feeling and understanding: little thanks it is you give.

24. Say: "It is He Who has multiplied you through the earth, and to Him shall you be gathered together."

25. They ask: When will this promise be (fulfilled)? - If you are telling the truth.

26. Say: "As to the knowledge of the time, it is with Allah alone: I am (sent) only to warn plainly in public."

27. At length, when they see it close at hand, grieved will be the faces of the Unbelievers, and it will be said (to them): "This is (the promise fulfilled), which you were calling for!"

28. Say: "You see?- If Allah were to destroy me, and those with me, or if He bestows His Mercy on us,- yet who can deliver the Unbelievers from a grievous Chastisement?"

29. Say: "He is (Allah) Most Gracious: we have believed in Him, and on Him have we put our trust: so, soon will you know which (of us) it is that is in manifest error."

30. Say: "You see?- If your stream be some morning lost (in the underground earth), who then can supply you with clear-flowing water?"

---

5.   Hold back   6.   Prone, with face downwards

SURAH 68
SURAH AL-QALAM
(INTRODUCTION)

This is a very early Makkan revelation. The general Muslim opinion is that a great part of it was second in order of revelation, the first being S. 96. *(Iqraa),* verses 1-5: see *Itqan,* Chapter 7.

The last Surah having defined the true Reality in contrast with the false standards set up by men, this illustrates the theme by an actual historical example. Our Holy Prophet was the sanest and wisest of men: those who could not understand him called him mad or possessed. So, in every age, it is the habit of the world to call Truth Falsehood and Wisdom Madness, and, on the other hand, to exalt Selfishness as Planning, and Arrogance as Power. The contrast is shown up between the two kinds of men and their inner worth.

SURAH QALAM (THE PEN, OR NUN)

In the name of Allah, Most Gracious, Most Merciful.

1. Nun. By the Pen and by the (Record) which (men) write,-
2. You are not, by the Grace of your Lord, mad or possessed.
3. Nay, verily for you is a Reward unfailing:
4. And you (stand) on an exalted standard of character.
5. Soon will you see, and they will see,
6. Which of you is afflicted with madness.
7. Verily it is your Lord that knows best, which (among men) have strayed from His Path: and He knows best those who receive (true) Guidance.
8. So hearken not to those who deny (the Truth).
9. Their desire is that you should be pliant[1]: so would they be pliant.
10. Do not obey every mean swearer;
11. A slanderer, going about with calumnies[2],
12. (Habitually) hindering (all) good, transgressing beyond bounds, deep in sin,

---

1. Bending easily, yielding, compliant
2. Slanderous reports, malicious misrepresentations, false charges

13.   Violent (and cruel),- with all that, base-born,-

14.   Because he possesses wealth and (numerous) sons.

15.   When to him are rehearsed Our Signs, he cries "Tales of the ancients", !

16.   Soon shall We brand[3] (the beast) on the snout[4]!

17.   Verily We have tried them as We tried the People of the Garden, when they resolved to gather the fruits of the (garden) in the morning.

18.   But made no reservation, ("If it be Allah's Will").

19.   Then there came on the (garden) a visitation from your Lord, (which swept away) all around, while they were asleep.

20.   So the (garden) became, by the morning, like a dark and desolate[5] spot, (whose fruit had been gathered) .

21.   As the morning broke, they called out, one to another,-

22.   "You go to your tilth (betimes) in the morning, if you would gather the fruits."

23.   So they departed, conver-sing in secret low tones, (saying)-

24.   "Let not a single indigent person break in upon you into the (garden) this day."

25.   And they opened the morning, strong in an (unjust) resolve.

26.   But when they saw the (garden), they said: "We have surely lost our way:

27.   "Indeed we are shut out (of the fruits of our labour)!"

28.   Said one of them, more just (than the rest): "Did I not say to you, "Why not glorify (Allah)?'"

29.   They said: "Glory to our Lord! Verily we have been doing wrong!"

30.   Then they turned, one against another, in reproach.

31.   They said: "Alas for us! We have indeed transgressed!

32.   "It may be that our Lord will give us in exchange a better (garden) than this: for we do turn to Him (in repentance)!"

33.   Such is the Punishment (in this life); but greater is the Punishment in the Hereafter,- if only they knew!

---

3.   Burn with hot iron to apply mark (of ownership)

4.   Projecting nose of an animal, (derogatory) human nose

5.   Deserted

34. Verily, for the Righteous, are Gardens of Delight, in the Presence of their Lord.

35. Shall We then treat the People of Faith like the People of Sin?

36. What is the matter with you? How judge you?

37. Or do you have a book through which you learn-

38. That you shall have, through it whatever you choose?

39. Or do you have Covenants with Us on oath, reaching to the Day of Judgment, (providing) that you shall have whatever you shall demand?

40. You ask them, which of them will stand surety for that!

41. Or have they some "Part-ners" (in Godhead)? Then let them produce their "partners", if they are truthful!

42. The Day that the shin[6] shall be laid bare, and they shall be summoned to bow in adoration, but they shall not be able,-

43. Their eyes will be cast down,- ignominy[7] will cover them; seeing that they had been summoned aforetime to bow in adoration[8], while they were hale and healthy, (and had refused).

44. Then leave Me alone with such as reject this Message: by degrees shall We punish them from directions they do not perceive.

45. A (long) respite will I grant them: truly powerful is My Plan.

46. Or is it that you does ask them for a reward, so that they are burdened with a load of debt?-

47. Or that the Unseen is in their hands, so that they can write it down?

48. So wait with patience for the Command of your Lord, and be not like the Companion of the Fish,- when he cried out in agony.

49. Had not Grace from his Lord reached him, he would indeed have been cast off on the naked shore, in disgrace.

50. Thus did his Lord choose him and make him of the Company of the Righteous.

51. And the Unbelievers would almost trip[9] you up with their eyes when they hear the Message; and they say: "Surely he is possessed!"

52. But it is nothing less than a Message to all the worlds.

---

6. Front of leg below knee
7. Disgrace
8. Worship
9. Stumble, slip

SURAH—69
SURAH AL-HAQQA
(INTRODUCTION)

This Surah belongs to the early middle period of Makkan Revelation. The eschatological argument is pressed home: "the absolute Truth cannot fail; it must prevail; therefore, be not lured by false appearances in this life; it is Revelation that points to the sure and certain Reality."

SURAH HAQQA (THE SURE REALITY)

In the name of Allah, Most Gracious, Most Merciful.

1. The Sure Reality!

2. What is the Sure Reality?

3. And what will make you realize what the Sure Reality is?

4. The Thamûd and the 'Ad People (branded) as false the Stunning Calamity!

5. As for Thamûd, they were destroyed by a terrible Storm of thunder and lightning!

6. And the 'Ad, they were destroyed by a furious Wind, exceedingly violent;

7. He made it rage against them seven nights and eight days in succession: so that you could see the (whole) people lying prostrate in its (path), as if they had been roots of hollow palm-trees tumbled down!

8. Then do you see any of them left surviving?

9. And Pharaoh, and those before him, and the Cities Over-thrown, committed habitual Sin.

10. And disobeyed (each) the Apostle of their Lord; so He punished them with an abundant Chastisement.

11. We, when the water (of Noah's Flood) overflowed beyond its limits, carried you (mankind), in the floating (Ark),

12. That We might make it a Message unto you, and that ears (that should hear the tale and) retain its memory should bear its (lessons) in remembrance.

13. Then, when one blast is sounded on the Trumpet,

14. And the earth is moved, and its mountains, and they are crushed to powder at one stroke,-

15. On that Day shall the (Great) Event come to pass.

16. And the sky will be rent asunder, for it will that Day be flimsy[1],

17. And the angels will be on its sides, and eight will, that Day, bear the Throne of your Lord above them.

18. On that day you shall be exposed; not a secret of you will be hidden.

19. Then he that will be given his Record in his right hand will say: "Ah here! You read my Record!

20. "I did really understand that my Account would (One Day) reach me!"

21. And he will be in a life of Bliss,

22. In a Garden on high,

23. The Fruits whereof (will hang in bunches) low and near.

24. "You eat and you drink, with full satisfaction; because of the (good) that you sent before you, in the days that are gone!"

25. And he that will be given his Record in his left hand, will say: "Ah! Would that my Record had not been given to me!

26. "And that I had never reali-sed how my account (stood)!

27. "Ah! Would that (Death) had made an end of me!

28. "Of no profit to me has been my wealth!

29. "My power has perished from me!"...

30. (The stern command will say): "You seize him, and you bind him,

31. "And you burn him in the Blazing Fire.

32. "Further, make him march in a chain, whereof the length is seventy cubits[2]!

33. "This was he that would not believe in Allah Most High.

34. "And would not encourage the feeding of the indigent!

35. "So no friend he has here this Day.

36. "Nor he has any food except the corruption from the washing of wounds,

---

1. Weak
2. Ancient measures of length, approximately equal to length of forearm.

37.   "Which none do eat but those in sin."

38.   So I do call to witness what you see,

39.   And what you do not see,

40.   That this is verily the word of an honoured Apostle;

41.   It is not the word of a poet: little it is you believe!

42.   Nor is it the word of a soothsayer[3]: little admonition it is you receive.

43.   (This is) a Message sent down from the Lord of the Worlds.

44.   And if the Apostle were to invent any sayings in Our name,

45.   We should certainly seize him by his right hand,

46.   An We should certainly then cut off the artery of his heart:

47.   Nor could any of you withhold him (from Our wrath).

48.   But verily this is a Message for the God-fearing.

49.   And We certainly know that there are amongst you those that reject (it).

50.   But truly (Revelation) is a cause of sorrow for the Unbelievers.

51.   But verily it is Truth of assured certainty.

52.   So glorify the name of your Lord Most High.

---

3.   Foreteller, diviner

SURAH—70
SURAH AL-MA'ARIJ
(INTRODUCTION)

This is another eschatological Surah closely connected in subject-matter with the last one. Patience and the mystery of Time will show the ways that climb to heaven. Sin and Goodness must each eventually come to its own.

Chronologically it belongs to the late early or early middle Makkan period, possibly soon after S. 69.

SURAH MA'ARIJ (THE WAYS OF ASCENT)

In the name of Allah, Most Gracious, Most Merciful.

1. A questioner asked about a Chastisement to befall-
2. The Unbelievers, the which there is none to ward off,-
3. (A Penalty) from Allah, Lord of the Ways of Ascent.
4. The angels and the spirit ascend unto Him in a Day the measure whereof is (as) fifty thousand years:
5. Therefore you hold patience,-a patience of beautiful (contentment).
6. They see the (Day) indeed as a far-off (event):
7. But We see it (quite) near.
8. The Day that the sky will be like molten brass,
9. And the mountains will be like wool,
10. And no friend will ask after a friend,
11. Though they will be put in sight of each other,-the sinner's desire will be: would that he could redeem himself from the Chastisement of that Day by (sacrificing) his children.
12. His wife and his brother,
13. His kindred who sheltered him,
14. And all, all that is on earth,- so it could deliver him:
15. By no means! for it would be the Fire of Hell!-
16. Plucking out (his being) right to the skull!-
17. Inviting (all) such as turn their backs and turn away their faces (from the Right),
18. And collect (wealth) and hide it (from use)!
19. Truly man was created very impatient;-

20. Fretful when evil touches him;

21. And niggardly when good reaches him;-

22. Not so those devoted to Prayer;-

23. Those who remain stead-fast to their prayer;

24. And those in whose wealth is a recognised right.

25. For the beggar and the destitute;

26. And those who hold to the truth of the Day of Judgment;

27. And those who fear the displeasure of their Lord,-

28. For their Lord's displeasure is the opposite of Peace and Tranquillity;-

29. And those who guard their chastity,

30. Except with their wives and the (captives) whom their right hands possess,- for (then) they are not to be blamed,

31. But those who trespass beyond this are transgressors;

32. And those who respect their trusts and covenants;

33. And those who stand firm in their testimonies;

34. And those who guard (the sacredness) of their worship;-

35. Such will be the honoured ones in the Gardens (of Bliss).

36. Now what is the matter with the Unbelievers that they rush madly before you–

37. From the right and from the left, in crowds?

38. Does every man of them long to enter the Garden of Bliss?

39. By no means! For We have created them out of the (base matter) they know about.

40. Now I do call to witness the Lord of all points in the East and the West that We can certainly-

41. Substitute for them better (men) than they; and We are not to be defeated (in Our Plan).

42. So leave them to plunge in vain talk and play about, until they encounter that Day of theirs which they have been promised!-

43. The Day whereon they will issue from their sepulchres[1] in sudden haste as if they were rushing to a goal-post (fixed for them),

44. Their eyes lowered in dejection,- ignominy covering them (all over)! such is the Day the which they are promised!

---

1. Tombs, burial vault or cave

SURAH—71
SURAH NUH
(INTRODUCTION)

This is another early Makkan Surah, of which the date has no significance. The theme is that while Good must uphold the standard of Truth and Righteousness, a stage is reached when it must definitely part company with Evil, lest Evil should spread its corruption abroad. This theme is embodied in the prayer of Noah just before the Flood. The story of Noah's agony is almost a Parable for the Holy Prophet's persecution in the Makkan period.

SURAH NUH (NOAH)

In the name of Allah, Most Gracious, Most Merciful.

1. We sent Noah to his People (with the Command): "Warn your People before there comes to them a grievous Chastisement."

2. He said: O my People! I am a plain warner unto you.

3. "That you should worship Allah, fear Him and obey me:

4. "So that He may forgive you your sins and give you respite for a stated Term: for when the Term given by Allah is accomplished, it cannot be put forward: if you only knew."

5. He said: "O my Lord! I have called to my People night and day:

6. "But my call only increases (their) flight (from the Right).

7. "And every time I have called to them, that You might forgive them, they have (only) thrust their fingers into their ears, covered themselves up with their garments, grown obstinate, and given themselves up to arrogance.

8. "So I have called to them aloud;

9. "Further I have spoken to them in public and secretly in private,

10. "Saying, 'Ask forgive-ness from your Lord; for He is Oft-Forgiving;

11. "'He will send rain to you in abundance;

12. "'Give you increase in wealth and sons; and bestow on you gardens and bestow on you rivers (of flowing water).

13. " 'What is the matter with you, that you are not conscious of Allah's Majesty,–

14.   " 'Seeing that it is He that has created you in diverse stages?

15.   'Don't you see how Allah has created the seven heavens one above another,

16.   "'And made the moon a light in their midst, and made the sun as a (Glorious) Lamp?

17.   "'And Allah has pro-duced you from the earth growing (gradually),

18.   "'And in the End He will return you into the (earth), and raise you forth (again at the Resurrection[1])?

19.   And Allah has made the earth for you as a carpet (spread out),.

20.   'That you may go about therein, in spacious roads.'

21.   Noah said: "O my Lord! They have disobeyed me, but they follow (men) whose wealth and children give them no increase but only loss.

22.   "And they have devised a tremendous[2] Plot.

23.   "And they have said (to each other), 'Do not abandon your gods: abandon neither Wadd nor Suwa', neither Yaguth nor Ya'uq, nor Nasr[3]';-

24.   "They have already mis-led many; and You grant no increase to the wrong-doers but in straying (from their mark)."

25.   Because of their sins they were drowned (in the flood), and were made to enter the Fire (of Punishment): and they found in lieu of Allah- none to help them.

26.   And Noah said: "O my Lord! Do not leave of the Unbelievers, a single one on earth!

27.   "For, if You leave (any of) them, they will but mislead Your devotees, and they willy breed none but wicked ungrateful ones.

28.   "O my Lord! Forgive me, my parents, all who enter my house in Faith, and (all) believing men and believing women: and to the wrong-doers You grant no increase but in perdition[4]!"

---

1.   Rising again of the dead on the Day of Judgement   2. Immense
3.   The names of their five false gods. Of these Wadd was depicted in the shape of a man (manly power), Suwa in that of a Woman (beauty), Yaghuth in that of a lion (brute strength), Ya'uq in that of a horse (swiftness), and Nasr in that of an eagle (sharp sight or insight).   4. Ruin

SURAH—72
SURAH AL-JINN
(INTRODUCTION)

This is a late Makkan Surah, of which we can be tolerably certain of the date. It was two years before the Hijrat, when the Prophet, despised and rejected in his native city of Makkah, went to evangelise the lordly men of Taif. They maltreated him and nearly killed him; what caused him even greater pain was the maltreatment of the humble and lowly men who went with him. "Tabari has handed down that memorable Prayer of faith and humility which he offered in the midst of his suffering. On his return journey to Makkah, a glorious vision was revealed to him, -hidden spiritual forces working for him, -people not known to him accepting his mission while his own people were still rejecting him. Within two months some strangers from Madinah had privately met him and laid the foundations of that Hijrat which was to change the fate of Arabia and the course of world history.

SURAH JINN (THE SPIRITS)
In the name of Allah, Most Gracious, Most Merciful.

1. Say: It has been revealed to me that a company of Jinns listened (to the Qur'an). They said, 'We have really heard a wonderful Recital!

2. 'It gives guidance to the Right, and we have believed therein: we shall not join (in wor-ship) any (gods) with our Lord.

3. 'And Exalted is the Majesty of our Lord: He has taken neither a wife nor a son.

4. 'There were some foolish ones among us, who used to utter extravagant[1] lies against Allah;

5. 'But we do think that no man or spirit should say anything that is untrue against Allah.

6. 'True, there were persons among mankind who took shelter with persons among the Jinns, but they increased them in folly.

7. 'And they (came to) think as you thought, that Allah would not raise up any one (to Judg-ment).

---

1.   Immoderate, extreme

8.   'And we pried[2] into the secrets of heaven; but we found it filled with stern guards and flaming fires.

9.   'We used, indeed, to sit there in (hidden) stations, to (steal) a hearing; but any who listens now will find a flaming fire watching him in ambush[3].

10.   And we understand not whether ill is intended to those on earth, or whether their Lord (really) intends to guide them to right conduct.

11.   'There are among us some that are righteous, and some the contrary: we follow divergent[4] paths.

12.   'But we think that we can by no means frustrate Allah throughout the earth, nor can we frustrate Him by flight.

13.   'And as for us, since we have listened to the Guidance, we have accepted it: and any who believes in his Lord has no fear, either of a short (account) or of any injustice.

14.   'Amongst us are some that submit their wills (to Allah), and some that swerve from justice. Now those who submit their wills - they have sought out (the path) of right conduct:

15.   'But those who swerve,- they are (but) fuel for Hell-fire'-

16.   (And Allah's Message is): "if they (the Pagans) had (only) remained on the (right) Way, We should certainly have bestowed on them Rain in abundance.

17.   "That We might try them by that (means). But if any turns away from the remembrance of his Lord, He will cause him to undergo a severe Chastisement.

18.   "And the places of wor-ship are for Allah (alone): so invoke not any one along with Allah;

19.   "Yet when the devotee[5] of Allah stands forth to invoke Him, they just make round him a dense crowd."

20.   Say: "I do no more than invoke my Lord, and I do not join with Him any (false god)."

---

2.   Look or peer inquisitively, inquire impertinently into (affairs, etc.)

3.   Hiding   4.   Separate, different

5.   Devoted servant

21. Say: "It is not in my power to cause you harm, or to bring you to right conduct."

22. Say: "No one can deliver me from Allah (If I were to disobey Him), nor should I find refuge except in Him,

23. "Unless I proclaim what I receive from Allah and His Messages: for any that disobey Allah and His Apostle,- for them is Hell: they shall dwell therein for ever."

24. At length, when they see (with their own eyes) that which they are promised,- then will they know who it is that is weakest in (his) helper and least important in point of numbers.

25. Say: "I do not know whether the (Punishment) which you are promised is near, or whether my Lord will appoint for it a distant term.

26. "He (alone) knows the Unseen, nor does He make any one acquainted with His mys-teries,-

27. "Except an Apostle whom He has chosen: and then He makes a band of watchers march before him and behind him,

28. "Except a messenger whom He has chosen: and then He makes a band of watchers march before him and behind him.

SURAH—73
SURAH AL-MUZZAMMIL
(INTRODUCTION)

H This is one of the earliest Surahs to have been revealed. The first was S. 96: 1-5 *(Iqraa),* in the fortieth year of the Prophet's life, say about 12 years before the Hijra. Then there was an interruption *(Fatra),* of which the duration cannot be exactly ascertained, as there was no external history connected with it. The usual estimate puts it at about six months, but it may have been a year or two years. The years were then counted by the lunisolar calendar: The second Surah in chronological order was probably a great portion of S. 68 *(Qalam),* which came after the *Fatra* was over. About the same time came this Surah (say third) and S. 74, which follows (say fourth), and the remainder of 96. We may roughly put the date of this Surah at about 1 to 10 ears before the Hijra.

The subject-matter is the significance of Prayer and Humility in spiritual life and the terrible fate of those who reject Faith and Revelation.

SURAH AL-MUZZAMMIL (FOLDED IN GARMENTS)

In the name of Allah, Most Gracious, Most Merciful.

1. O you folded in garments!
2. Stand (to prayer) by night, but not all night,-
3. Half of it,- or a little less,
4. Or a little more; and recite the Qur'an in slow, measured rhythmic tones.
5. Soon shall We send down to you a weighty Message.
6. Truly the rising by night is most potent[1] for governing (the soul), and most suitable for (framing) the words (of prayer and praise).
7. True, there is for you by day prolonged occupation with manifold duties.
8. But keep in remembrance the name of your Lord and devote yourself to Him whole-heartedly.
9. (He is) Lord of the East and the West: there is no god but He: take Him therefore for (your) Disposer of Affairs.
10. And have patience with what they say, and leave them with

---

1.   Powerful, effective

noble (dignity).

11.   And leave Me (alone to deal with) those in possession of the good things of life, who (yet) deny the Truth; and bear with them for a little while.

12.   With Us are Fetters (to bind them), and a Fire (to burn them).

13.   And a Food that chokes, and a Chastisement Grievous.

14.   On the Day when the earth and the mountains will be in violent commotion[2]. And the mountains will be as a heap of sand poured out and flowing down.

15.   We have sent to you, (O men!) an Apostle, to be a witness concerning you, even as We sent an Apostle to Pharaoh.

16.   But Pharaoh disobeyed the Apostle; so We seized him with a heavy Punishment.

17.   Then how shall you, if you deny (Allah), guard your-selves against a Day that will make children hoary-headed[3]?-

18.   Whereon the sky will be cleft asunder? His Promise needs must be accomplished.

19.   Verily this is an Admoni-tion: therefore, whoso will, let him take a (straight) path to his Lord!

20.   Your Lord knows that you stand forth (to prayer) nearly two-thirds of the night, or half the night, or a third of the night, and so does a party of those with you. But Allah appoints night and day in due measure. He knows that you are unable to keep count thereof. So He has turned to you (in mercy): you read, therefore, of the Qur'an as much as may be easy (for you) He knows that there may be (some) among you in ill-health; others travelling through the land, seeking of Allah's bounty ; yet others fighting in Allah's Cause, you read, therefore, as much of the Qur'an as may be easy (for you); and establish regular Prayer and give regular Charity; and loan to Allah a Beautiful Loan. And whatever good you send forth for your souls, you shall find it in Allah's Presence,- yes, better and greater, in Reward and you seek the forgiveness of Allah: for Allah is Oft-Forgiving, Most Merciful.

---

2.   Turmoil   3.   Gray-headed

SURAH—74

SURAH AL-MUDDASSIR

(INTRODUCTION)

This Surah dates from about the same time as the last one. Its subject-matter is also similar: Prayer, and Praise, and the need of patience in a period of great spiritual stress; the unjust who cause sorrow and suffering now will themselves experience agony in the Hereafter.

SURAH AL-MUDDASSIR

(THE ONE WRAPPED UP)

In the name of Allah, Most Gracious, Most Merciful.

1.   O you wrapped up (in the mantle)!
2.   Arise and deliver your warning!
3.   And your Lord do you magnify!
4.   And keep your garments free from stain!
5.   And shun all abomination[1]!
6.   Nor expect, in giving, any increase (for yourself)!
7.   But, for your Lord's (Ca-use), be patient and constant!
8.   Finally, when the trum-pet is sounded,
9.   That will be- that Day - a Day of Distress,-
10.   Far from easy for those without Faith.
11.   Leave Me alone (to deal) with the (creature) whom I created alone,
12.   To whom I granted resources in abundance,
13.   And sons to be by his side!-
14.   To whom I made (life) smooth and comfortable!
15.   Yet is he greedy-that I should add (yet more);-
16.   By no means! For to Our Signs he has been refractory![2]
17.   Soon will I visit him with a mount of calamities!
18.   For he thought and he plotted;-
19.   And woe to him! How he plotted!-
20.   Yes, woe to him; How he plotted!-
21.   Then he looked round;

---

1.   Loathsome evil   2.   Stubborn, rebellious

22. Then he frowned and he scowled;

23. Then he turned back and was haughty;

24. Then he said; "This is nothing but magic, derived from of old;

25. "This is nothing but the word of a mortal!"

26. Soon will I cast him into Hell-Fire!

27. And what will explain to you what Hell-Fire is?

28. Nothing does it permit to endure, and nothing does it leave alone!—

29. Darkening and changing the colour of man!

30. Over it are Nineteen.

31. And We have set none but angels as Guardians of the Fire; and We have fixed their number only as a trial for Unbelievers,- in order that the People of the Book may arrive at certainty, and the Believers may increase in Faith,- and that no doubts may be left for the People of the Book and the Believers, and that those in whose hearts is a disease and the Unbelievers may say, "What symbol does Allah intend by this ?" Thus Allah leaves to stray whom He pleases, and guide whom He pleases: and none can know the forces of your Lord, except He and this is no other than a warning to mankind.

32. Nay, verily: by the Moon,

33. And by the Night as it retreats,

34. And by the Dawn as it shines forth,-

35. This is but one of the mighty (portents),

36. A warning to mankind,-

37. To any of you that chooses to press forward, or to follow behind;-

38. Every soul will be (held) in pledge for its deeds.

39. Except the Companions of the Right Hand.

40. In Gardens they will ask one another,

41. And (ask) of the Sinners:

42. "What led you into Hell– Fire?"

43. They will say: "We were not of those who prayed;

44. "Nor were we of those who fed the indigent;

45. "But we used to talk vanities[3] with vain talkers;

---

3.   Gossip, idle talk

46. "And we used to deny the Day of Judgment,

47. "Until there came to us (the Hour) that is certain."

48. Then will no intercession[4] of (any) intercessors profit them.

49. Then what is the matter with them that they turn away from admonition?—,

50. As if they were affrighted[5] asses,

51. Fleeing from a lion!

52. Forsooth, each one of them wants to be given scrolls (of revelation) spread out!

53. By no means! But they do not fear the Hereafter,

54. Nay, this surely is an admonition:

55. Let any who will, keep it in remembrance!

56. But none will keep it in remembrance except as Allah wills: He is the Lord of Righteousness, and the Lord of Forgiveness.

---

4.   Mediation   5.   Frightened

SURAH—75

SURAH AL-QIYAMAT
(INTRODUCTION)

This Surah belongs of the early Makkan period, but comes chronologically a good deal later than the last two Surahs.

Its subject-matter is the Resurrection, viewed from the point of view of Man, especially unregenerate Man, as he is now, and as he will be then — his inner and psychological history.

SURAH AL-QIYAMAT (THE RESURRECTION)

In the name of Allah, Most Gracious, Most Merciful.

1. I do call to witness the Resurrection Day;
2. And I do swear by the self-reproaching soul[1];.
3. Does man think that We cannot assemble his bones?
4. Nay, We are able to put together in perfect order the very tips of his fingers.
5. But man wishes to do wrong (even) in the time in front of him.
6. He questions: "When is the Day of Resurrection?"
7. At length, when the sight is dazed,
8. And the moon is buried in darkness.
9. And the sun and moon are joined together,-
10. That Day Man will say: "Where is the refuge?"
11. By no means! No place of safety!
12. Before your Lord (alone), that Day will be the place of rest.
13. That Day Man will be told (all) that he put forward, and all that he put back.
14. Nay, man will be evidence against himself,
15. Even though he were to put up his excuses.
16. Do not move your tongue concerning the (Qur'an) to make haste therewith.
17. It is for Us to collect it and to promulgate it:
18. But when We have promulgated it, you follow its recital (as promulgated):

---

1.   Avoid

19.   Nay more, it is for Us to explain it (and make it clear):

20.   Nay, (you men!) but you love the fleeting[2] life,

21.   And leave alone the Hereafter.

22.   Some faces, that Day, will beam (in brightness and beauty);-

23.   Looking towards their Lord;

24.   And some faces, that Day, will be sad and dismal[3],

25.   In the thought that some back-breaking calamity was about to be inflicted on them;

26.   Yes, when (the soul) reaches to the collar-bone (in its exit).

27.   And there will be a cry, "Who is a magician (to restore him)?

28.   And he will conclude that it was (the Time) of Parting;

29.   And one leg will be joined with another:

30.   That Day the Drive will be (all) to your Lord!

31.   So he gave nothing in charity, nor did he pray!-

32.   But on the contrary, he rejected Truth and turned away!

33.   Then he stalk[4] to his family in full conceit[5]!

34.   Woe to you, (O man!), yes, woe!

35.   Again, woe to you, (O man!), yes, woe!

36.   Does man think that he will be left uncontrolled, (without purpose)?

37.   Was he not a drop of sperm emitted[6] (in lowly form)?

38.   Then he became a leach-like clot; then (Allah) made and fashioned (him) in due proportion.

39.   And of him He made two sexes, male and female.

40.   Has He not, (the same), the power to give life to the dead.

---

2.   Transitory, passing   3.   Gloomy
4.   Walk in stately or imposing manner, stride
5.   Vanity   6.   Discharged

SURAH—76
SURAH AL-INSAN (AD-DAHR)
(INTRODUCTION)

The revelation of this Surah was probably in the early Makkan period, with the possible exception of some verses, but its date has no significance.

Its theme is the contrast between the two classes of men, those who choose good and those who choose evil, with special reference to the former.

The title of the Surah recalls a Pagan Arab idea, which personified Time as existing spontaneously from eternity to enternity and responsible for the misery or the happiness of mankind. In 45:24 we read: "They say,...., 'nothing but Time can destroy us.' "This attitude is of course wrong, Time is a created thing: it has its mysteries, but it is no more eternal than matter. It is also relative to our conceptions and not absolute, as Einstein has proved. It is only Allah Who is Self Subsisting, Eternal from the beginning and Eternal to the end, the absolute Existence and Reality. We must not transfer His attributes to any figments of our imagination.

This deification of Time *(Dahr)* as against a living personal Allah has given rise to the term *dahriya,* as applied to an atheist or a materialist.

The whole of the Surah is full of the highest symbolism, as is generally the case with Makkan Surahs, and this should always by remembered in their interpretation.

SURAH AL-DAHR (TIME; OR INSAN, OR MAN)

In the name of Allah, Most Gracious, Most Merciful.

1. Has there not been over Man a long period of Time, when he was nothing - (not even) mentioned?

2. Verily We created Man from a drop of mingled sperm, in order to try him: so We gave him (the gifts), of Hearing and Sight.

3. We showed him the Way: whether he be grateful or ungrateful (rests on his will).

4. For the Rejecters We have prepared chains, yokes[1], and a blazing Fire.

5. As to the Righteous, they shall drink of a Cup mixed with *Kafur*[2],-

6. A Fountain where the Devotees of Allah do drink, making it

---

1. Wooden cross-piece fastened over necks of two oxen, etc.
2. Literally, camphor, it is a fountain in Paradise.

flow in unstinted[3] abundance.

7.   They perform (their) vows, and they fear a Day whose evil flies far and wide.

8.   And they feed, for the love of Allah, the indigent, the orphan, and the captive,-

9.   (Saying),"We feed you for the sake of Allah alone: no reward do we desire from you, nor thanks.

10.   "We only fear a Day of distressful Wrath from the side of our Lord."

11.   But Allah will deliver them from the evil of that Day, and will shed over them a Light of Beauty and a (blissful) Joy.

12.   And because they were patient and constant, He will reward them with a Garden and (garments of) silk.

13.   Reclining in the (Garden) on raised thrones, they will see there neither the sun's (excessive heat) nor excessive cold.

14.   And the shades of the (Garden) will come low over them, and the bunches (of fruit), there, will hang low in humility.

15.   And amongst them will be passed round vessels of silver and goblets of crystal,-

16.   Crystal-clear, made of silver: they will determine the measure thereof (according to their wishes).

17.   And they will be given to drink there of a Cup (of Wine) mixed with *Zanjabil*[4],-

18.   A fountain there, called *Salsabil*.[5]

19.   And round about them will (serve) youths of perpetual (freshness): If you see them, you would think them scattered Pearls.

20.   And when you look, it is there you will see a Bliss and a Realm Magnificent.

21.   Upon them will be green Garments of fine silk and heavy brocade, and they will be adorned with Bracelets of silver; and their Lord will give to them to drink a drink pure and holy.

22.   "Verily this is a Reward for you, and your Endeavour is accepted

---

3.   Unlimited   4.   Literally means ginger
5.   Literally means "Seek the way."

and recognised."

23. It is We Who have sent down the Qur'an to you by stages.

24. Therefore, be patient with constancy to the Command of your Lord, and do not obey the sinner or the ingrate[6] among them.

25. And celebrate the name of your Lord morning and evening,

26. And part of the night, prostrate yourself to Him; and glorify Him a long night through.

27. As to these, they love the fleeting life, and put away behind them a Day (that will be) hard.

28. It is We Who created them, and We have made their joints strong; but, when We will, We can substitute the like of them by a complete change.

29. This is an admonition: whosoever will, let him take a (straight) Path to his Lord.

30. But you will not, except as Allah wills; for Allah is full of Knowledge and Wisdom.

31. He will admit to His Mercy whom He will; but the wrong-doers,- for them He has prepared a grievous Chastisement.

---

6. Ungrateful

SURAH—77
SURAH AL-MURSALAT
(INTRODUCTION)

This Surah belongs to the early Makkan period, somewhere near to S. 75 *(Qiyamat)*. The theme is some what similar. It denounces the horrors of the Hereafter, for those who rejected Truth. The refrain, "Ah woe, that Day, to the Rejecters of Truth !" which occurs ten times in its fifty verses, or on an average, once in every five verses, indicates the *leitmotif*.

SURAH AL- MURSALAT (THOSE SENT FORTH)

In the name of Allah, Most Gracious, Most Merciful.

1.   By the (Winds) sent forth one after another (to man's profit);
2.   Which then blow violently in tempestuous[1] gusts[2],
3.   And scatter (things) far and wide;
4.   Then separate them, one from another,
5.   Then spread abroad a Message,
6.   Whether of Justification or of Warning;-
7.   Assuredly, what you are promised must come to pass.
8.   Then when the stars become dim;
9.   When the heaven is cleft asunder;
10. When the mountains are scattered (to the winds) as dust;
11. And when the time fixed for the gathering of all Apostles comes.
12. For what Day are these (portents[3]) deferred?
13. For the Day of Sorting out.
14. And what will explain to you what is the Day of Sorting out?
15. Ah woe, that Day, to the Rejecters of Truth!
16. Did We not destroy the men of old (for their evil)?
17. So shall We make later (generations) follow them.
18. Thus do We deal with men of sin.
19. Ah woe, that Day, to the Rejecters of Truth!
20. Have We not created you from a fluid (held) despicable[4]?
21. Which We placed in a place of rest, firmly fixed,

---

1.   Fierce, stormy   2.   Blasts
3.   Omen, Significant sign of something to come
4.   Abhorrent

22. For a period (of gestation[5]), determined (according to need)?

23. For We do determine (according to need); for We are the Best to determine (things).

24. Ah woe, that Day! to the Rejecters of Truth!

25. Have We not made the earth (as a place) to draw together.

26. The living and the dead,

27. And made therein mountains standing firm, lofty (in stature); and provided for you sweet (and wholesome) water?

28. Ah woe, that Day, to the Rejecters of Truth!

29. (It will be said:) "You depart to that which you used to reject as false!

30. You depart to a Shadow (of smoke ascending) in three columns.

31. "(Which yields) no shade of coolness, and is of no use against the fierce Blaze.

32. "Indeed it throws about sparks (huge) as Forts,

33. "As if there were (a string of) yellow camels (marching swiftly)."

34. Ah woe, that Day, to the Rejecters of Truth!

35. That will be a Day when they shall not be able to speak.

36. Nor will it be open to them to put forth pleas.

37. Ah woe, that Day, to the Rejecters of Truth!

38. That will be a Day of Sorting out! We shall gather you together and those before (you)!

39. Now, if you have a trick (or plot), use it against Me!

40. Ah woe, that Day, to the Rejecters of Truth!

41. As to the Righteous, they shall be amidst (cool) shades and springs (of water).

42. And (they shall have) fruits,- all they desire.

43. "You eat and you drink to your heart's content: for that you worked (Righteousness).

44. Thus do We certainly reward the Doers of Good.

45. Ah woe, that Day, to the Rejecters of Truth!

---

5. The period of carrying or being carried in the womb between conception and birth.

46.   (O you unjust!) You eat and enjoy yourselves (but) a little while, for that you are Sinners.

47.   Ah woe, that Day, to the Rejecters of Truth!

48.   And when it is said to them: bow down, they bow not down!

49.   Ah woe, that Day, to the Rejecters of Truth!

50.   Then what Message, after that, will they believe in?

SURAH—78
SURAH AN-NABAA
(INTRODUCTION)

This beautiful Makkan Surah is not quite so early as the last (S. 77), nor quite so late as S. 76, but nearer in time to the latter.

It sets forth Allah's loving care in a fine nature-passage, and deduces from it the Promise of the Future, when Evil will be destroyed and Good will come to its own; and invites all who have the will, to seek refuge with their Lord.

SURAH AN-NABAA (THE (GREAT) NEWS)
In the name of Allah, Most Gracious, Most Merciful.

1.   Concerning what are they disputing?
2.   Concerning the Great News,
3.   About which they cannot agree.
4.   Verily, they shall soon (come to) know!
5.   Verily, verily they shall soon (come to) know!
6.   Have We not made the earth as a wide expanse[1],
7.   And the mountains as pegs?
8.   And (have We not) created you in pairs,
9.   And made your sleep for rest,
10.   And made the night as a covering,
11.   And made the day as a means of subsistence?
12.   And (have We not) built over you the seven firmaments,
13.   And placed (therein) a Light of Splendour?
14.   And do We not send down from the clouds water in abundance,
15.   That We may produce therewith corn and vegetables,
16.   And gardens[2] of luxurious growth?
17.   Verily the Day of Sorting out is a thing appointed,
18.   The Day that the Trumpet shall be sounded, and you will come forth in crowds;
19.   And the heavens shall be opened as if there were doors,

---

1.   Wide aree or extent   2.   Lavish, rich

20. And the mountains shall vanish, as if they were a mirage[3].
21. Truly Hell is as a place of ambush,
22. For the transgressors a place of destination:
23. They will dwell therein for ages.
24. Nothing cool shall they taste therein, nor any drink,
25. Save a boiling fluid and a fluid, dark, murky[4], intensely cold,:
26. A fitting recompense (for them).
27. For that they used not to fear any account (for their deeds),
28. But they (impudently[5]) treated Our Signs as false.
29. And all things have We preserved on record.
30. "So you taste (the fruits of your deeds); for no increase shall We grant you, except in Chastisement.
31. Verily for the Righteous there will be an Achievement.
32. Gardens enclosed, and grapevines;
33. Companions of equal age;
34. And a cup full (to the brim[6]).
35. No vanity shall they hear therein, nor Untruth:-
36. Recompense from your Lord, a gift, (amply) sufficient,
37. (From) the Lord of the heavens and the earth, and all between,— the Most Gracious: none shall have power to argue with Him..
38. The Day that the Spirit and the angels will stand forth in ranks, none shall speak except any who is permitted by (Allah) Most Gracious, and He will say what is right.
39. That Day will be the sure Reality: therefore, whoso will, let him take a (straight) return to his Lord!
40. Verily, We have warned you of a Chastisement near, the Day when man will see (the deeds) which his hands have sent forth, and the Unbeliever will say, "Woe unto me! Would that I were (mere) dust!

---

3. Optical illusion caused by atmospheric conditions, esp. appearence of sheet of water in desert or hot road, illusory thing.
4. Muddy   5.   Arrogantly, insolently
6. Brink

SURAH—79
SURAH AN-NAZI'AT
(INTRODUCTION)

This is also an early Makkan Surah, of about the same date as the last, and deals with the mystic theme of Judgment from the point of view of Pride and its Fall. The parable of Pharaoh occupies a central place in the argument: for he said, "I am your Lord Most High," and perished with his followers.

SURAH AN-NAZI'AT (THOSE WHO TEAR OUT)

In the name of Allah, Most Gracious, Most Merciful.

1. By the (angels) who tear out (the souls of the wicked) with violence;
2. By those who gently draw out (the souls of the blessed);
3. And by those who glide along (on errands[1] of mercy),
4. Then press forward as in a race,
5. Then arrange to do (the Commands of their Lord),
6. The Day everything that can be in commotion[2], will be in violent commotion,
7. Followed by oft-repeated (commotions):
8. Hearts that Day will be in agitation;
9. Cast down will be (their owners') eyes.
10. They say (now): "What! shall we indeed be returned to (our) former state?
11. "What! - when we shall have become rotten bones?"
12. They say: "It would, in that case, be a return with loss!"
13. But verily, it will be but a single (compelling) Cry,
14. When, behold, they will be brought out to the open.
15. Has the story of Moses reached you?
16. Behold, your Lord called him in the sacred valley of Tuwa:-
17. "You go to Pharaoh, for he has indeed transgressed all bounds:
18. "And say to him, 'Would you (like) that you should be purified (from sin)?—
19. "'And that I guide you to your Lord, so you should fear Him?'"

---

1. Short journey to carry or deliver something
2. Turmoil, disturbance

20.   Then (Moses) showed him the Great Sign.

21.   But (Pharaoh) rejected it and disobeyed (guidance);

22.   Further, he turned his back, striving hard (against Allah).

23.   Then he collected (his men) and made a proclamation,

24.   Saying, "I am your Lord, Most High".

25.   But Allah seized him, with punishment (and made an) example of him,—in the Hereafter, as in this life.

26.   Verily in this is a lesson for whosoever fears (Allah).

27.   What! Are you the more difficult to create or the heaven (above)? (Allah) has constructed it:

28.   On high has He raised its canopy, and He has given it order and perfection.

29.   Its night does He endow with darkness, and its splendour does He bring out (with light).

30.   And the earth, moreover, He has extended (to a wide expanse);

31.   He draws out therefrom its moisture and its pasture;

32.   And the mountains He has firmly fixed;-

33.   A provision for you and your cattle.

34.   Therefore, when there comes the great, overwhelming (Event),—

35.   The Day when Man shall remember (all) that he strove for,

36.   And Hell-Fire shall be placed in full view for him who sees.—

37.   Then, for such as had transgressed all bounds,

38.   And had preferred the life of this world,

39.   The Abode will be Hell-Fire;

40.   And for such as had enter-tained the fear of standing before their Lord's (Tribunal[3]) and had restrained (their) soul from lower desires,

41.   Their abode will be the Garden.

42.   They ask you about the Hour,—'When will be its appointed time?'

43.   Wherein are you (concerned) with the declaration thereof?

44.   With your Lord is the time fixed therefor.

45.   You are but a Warner for such as fear it.

46.   The Day they see it, (it will be) as if they had tarried[4] but a single evening, or (at most till) the following morn!

---

3.   Judgement-seat   4.   Remained, lived

SURAH—80
SURAH 'ABASA
(INTRODUCTION)

This is an early Makkan Surah, and is Connected with an incident which reflects the highest honour on the Prophet's sincerity in the Revelations that were vouchsafed to him even if they seemed to reprove him for some natural and human zeal that led him to a false step in his mission according to his own high standards.

He was once deeply and earnestly engaged in trying to explain the Holy Quran to Pagan Quraish leaders, when he was interrupted by a blind man,' Abdullah Umrn Maktum, one who was also poor, so that no one took any notice of him. He wanted to learn the Quran. The Holy Prophet naturally disliked the interruption and showed impatience. Perhaps the poor man's feelings were hurt. But he whose gentle heart ever sympathised with the poor and the afflicted got new Light from above, and without the least hesitation published this revelation, which forms part of the sacred scripture of Islam, as described in verses 13-16. And the Prophet always afterwards held the man in high honour.

The incident was only a passing incident, but after explaining the eternal principles of revelation, the Surah recapitulates the Mercies of Allah to man, and the consequences of a good or a wicked life here, as seen in the spiritual world to come, in the Hereafter.

SURAH 'ABASA (HE FROWNED)

In the name of Allah, Most Gracious, Most Merciful.

1. He (The Prophet) frowned and turned away,
2. Because there came to him the blind man (interrupting).
3. But what could tell you but that perchance he might grow in purity?
4. Or that he might receive admonition, and the teaching might profit him?
5. As to one who regards himself as self-sufficient,
6. To him you do attend;
7. Though it is no blame to you if he grow not in purity.
8. But as to him who came to you striving earnestly,
9. And with fear (in his heart),
10. Of him you were unmind-ful.

11.   Nay, but verily it is an Admonishment,

12.   Therefore let whoso will, keep it in remembrance.

13.   (It is) in Books held (greatly) in honour,

14.   Exalted (in dignity), kept pure and holy,

15.   (Written) by the hands of scribes-

16.   Honourable and Pious and Just.

17.   Woe to man! What has made him reject Allah;

18.   From what stuff has He created him?

19.   From a sperm-drop: He has created him, and then moulded him in due Proportion;

20.   Then He makes his path smooth for him;

21.   Then He causes him to die, and puts him in his grave;

22.   Then, when it is His Will, He will raise him up (again).

23.   By no means he has fulfilled what Allah has commanded him.

24.   Then let man look at his food, (and how We provide it):

25.   For that We pour forth water in abundance,

26.   And We split the earth in fragments,

27.   And produce therein corn,

28.   And Grapes and nutri-tious plants,

29.   And Olives and Dates,

30.   And enclosed Gardens, dense with lofty trees,

31.   And fruits and fodder,-

32.   For use and convenience to you and your cattle.

33.   At length, when there comes the Deafening Noise,-

34.   That Day shall a man flee from his own brother,

35.   And from his mother and his father,

36.   And from his wife and his children.

37.   Each one of them, that Day, will have enough concern (of his own) to make him unmindful to the others.

38.   Some faces that Day will be beaming,

39.   Laughing, rejoicing.

40.   And other faces that Day will be dust-stained,

41.   Blackness will cover them:

42.   Such will be the Rejecters of Allah, the Doers of iniquity[1].

---

1.   Evil, gross injustice

SURAH 81

SURAH AT-TAKWIR

(INTRODUCTION)

This is quite an early Makkan Surah, perhaps the sixth or seventh in chronological order. It opens with a series of highly mystical metaphors suggesting the break-up of the world as we know it (verses 1-13) and the enforcement of complete personal responsibility for each soul (verse 14). Then there is a mystical passage showing how the Quranic Revelation was true, and revealed through the angel Gabriel, and not merely a rhapsody from one possessed. Revelation is given for man's spiritual guidance (verses 14-29).

Comparable with this Surah are the Surah 82 and 84 which may be read with this.

_____

SURAH AT-TAKWIR (THE FOLDING UP)

In the Name of Allah, Most Gracious, Most Merciful.

1. When the sun (with its spacious light) is folded up;
2. When the stars fall, losing their lustre[1];
3. When the mountains vanish (like a mirage);
4. When the she-camels, ten months with young, are left untended;
5. When the wild beasts are herded together (in the human habitations[2]),
6. When the oceans boil over with a swell;
7. When the souls are sorted out, (being joined, like with like);
8. When the female (infant), buried alive, is questioned -
9. For what crime she was killed;
10. When the scrolls are laid open;
11. When the sky is unveiled;
12. When the Blazing Fire is kindled to fierce heat;
13. And when the Garden is brought near;-
14. (Then) shall each soul know what it has put forward.
15. So verily I call to witness the planets - that recede,
16. Go straight, or hide;

---

1.   Brilliance, shining light   2.   Living places

17. And the Night as it dissipates[3];
18. And the Dawn as it breathes away the darkness;-
19. Verily this is the word of a most honourable Messenger,
20. Endued with Power, held in honour by the Lord of the Throne,
21. With authority there, (and) faithful to his trust.
22. And (O people!) your companion is not one possessed;
23. And without doubt he saw him in the clear horizon.
24. Neither does he withhold grudgingly a knowledge of the Unseen.
25. Nor is it the word of an evil spirit accursed.
26. When whither do you go?
27. Verily this is no less than a Message to (all) the Worlds:
28. (With profit) to whoever among you wills to go straight:
29. But you shall not will except as Allah wills,- the Cherisher of the Worlds.

---

3.   Disappear

SURAH—82
SURAH AL-INFITAR
(INTRODUCTION)

In subject-matter this Surah is cognate to the last, though the best authorities consider it a good deal later in chronology in the early Makkan period.

Its argument is subject to the threefold interpretation referring (1) to the final Day of Judgment, (2) to the Lesser Judgment, on an individual's death, and (3) to the awakening of the Inner Light in the soul at any time, that being considered as Death to the Falsities of this life and a Rebirth to the true spiritual Reality.

SURAH AL-INFITAR
(THE CLEAVING ASUNDER)

In the name of Allah, Most Gracious, Most Merciful.

1. When the Sky is cleft asunder;
2. When the Stars are scattered;
3. When the Oceans are suffered[1] to burst forth;
4. And when the Graves are turned upside down;-
5. (Then) shall each soul know what it has sent forward and (what it has) kept back..
6. O man! What has seduced[2] you from your Lord Most Beneficent?-
7. Him Who created you, fashioned you in due proportion, and gave you a just bias[3];
8. In whatever form He wills, He puts you together.
9. Nay, but you do reject Right and Judgment!
10. But verily over you (are appointed angels) to protect you,—
11. Kind and honourable,- writing down (your deeds):
12. They know (and understand) all that you do.
13. As for the Righteous, they will be in bliss;

---

1. Allowed
2. Lead astray, tempted to sin or crime
3. Leaning, disposition

14. And the Wicked - they will be in the Hell,
15. Which they will enter on the Day of Judgment,
16. And they will not be able to keep away therefrom.
17. And what will explain to you what the Day of Judgment is?
18.   Again, what will explain to you what the Day of Judgment is?
19. (It will be) the Day when no soul shall have power (to do) any-thing for another: for the com-mand, that Day, will be (wholly) with Allah.

_____

SURAH—83
SURAH AL-MUTAFFIFEEN
(INTRODUCTION)

This Surah is close in time to the last one and the next one.

It condemns all fraud—in daily dealings, as well as and especially in matters of Religion and the higher spiritual life.

SURAH AL-MUTAFFIFEEN
(THE DEALERS IN FRAUD)

In the name of Allah, Most Gracious, Most Merciful.

1. Woe to those that deal in fraud,-

2. Those who, when they have to receive by measure from men, exact full measure,

3. But when they have to give by measure or weight to men, give less than due.

4. Do they not think that they will be called to account?-

5. On a Mighty Day,

6. The day when (all) man-kind stand before the Lord of the Worlds?

7. Nay! Surely the record of the wicked is (preserved) in *Sijjîn*.[1]

8. And what will explain to you what Sijjin is?

9. (There is) a Register (fully) inscribed.[2]

10. Woe, that Day, to those that deny-

11. Those that deny the Day of Judgment.

12. And none can deny it but the transgressor beyond bounds, the sinner!

13. When Our Signs are rehearsed to him, he says, "Tales of the ancients!"

14. By no means! but on their hearts is the stain of the (ill) which they do!

15. Verily, from (the Light of) their Lord, that Day, will they be veiled.

---

1. From the root *sijn*, a prison, *sijjin* here mean a well-guarded place.
2. In which records are preserved, written down

16.   Further, they will enter the Fire of Hell.

17.   Further, it will be said to them: "This is the (reality) which you rejected as false!

18.   Nay, but the record of the righteous is in '*Illiyin*![3]—

19.   And what will explain to you what 'Illiyin is?

20.   (There is) a Register (fully) inscribed,

21.   To which bear witness those Nearest (to Allah).

22.   Truly the Righteous will be in Bliss:

23.   On raised couches will they command a sight (of all things):

24.   You will recognise in their faces the beaming brightness of Bliss.

25.   Their thirst will be slaked[4] with Pure Wine sealed:

26.   The seal thereof will be musk: and for this let those aspire, who have aspirations:

27.   With it will be (given) a mixture of *Tasnim*:

28.   A spring, from (the waters) whereof drink those Nearest to Allah.

29.   Those in sin used to laugh at those who believed,

30.   And whenever they passed by them, used to wink at each other (in mockery[6]);

31.   And when they returned to their own people, they returned jesting;

32.   And whenever they saw them, they would say, "Behold! These are the people truly astray!"

33.   But they had not been sent as keepers over them!

34.   But on this Day the Believers will laugh at the Unbelievers:

35.   On raised couches they will command (a sight) (of all things).

36.   Will not the Unbelievers have been paid back for what they did?

---

3.   *Illiyyun* or *illiyyin* literally, means "high places."
4.   Quenched, satisfied
5.   The name of a heavenly fountain, literally it indicates height, fulness, opulence.
6.   Jest

SURAH—84
SURAH AL-INSHIQAQ
(INTRODUCTION)

Chronologically this Surah is closely connected with the last one. In subject-matter it resembles more S. 82, and 81 with which it may be compared.

By a number of mystic metaphors it is shown that the present phenomenal order will not last, and Allah's full Judgment will certainly be established: man should therefore strive for that World of Eternity and True Values.

SURAH AL-INSHIQAQ (THE RENDING ASUNDER)

In the name of Allah, Most Gracious, Most Merciful.

1. When the Sky is rent asunder,
2. And hearkens to (the Command of) its Lord,—and it must needs (do so);—
3. And when the earth is flattened out,
4. And casts forth what is within it and becomes (clean) empty.
5. And hearkens to (the Command of) its Lord,—and it must needs (do so);—(then will come home the full Reality).
6. O you man! Verily you are ever toiling on towards your Lord-painfully toiling,- but you shall meet Him.
7. Then he who is given his Record in his right hand,
8. Soon will his account be taken by an easy reckoning,
9. And he will turn to his people, rejoicing!
10. But he who is given his Record behind his back,-
11. Soon will he cry for perdition[1],
12. And he will enter a Bla-zing Fire.
13. Truly, did he go about among his people, rejoicing!
14. Truly, did he think that he would not have to return (to Us)!
15. Nay, nay! for his Lord was (ever) watchful of him!
16. So I do call to witness the ruddy[2] glow of Sunset;
17. The Night and its Homing;
18. And the Moon in her fullness:

---

1. Eternal death
2. Reddish

19.   You shall surely travel from stage to stage.

20.   What then is the matter with them, that they do not believe?-

21.   And when the Qur'an is read to them, they do not fall prostrate,

22.   But on the contrary the Unbelievers reject (it).

23.   But Allah has full knowledge of what they secrete[3] (in their breasts).

24.   So announce to them a Chastisement Grievous,

25.   Except to those who believe and work righteous deeds: for them is a Reward that will never fail.

---

3.   Hide

SURAH—86
SURAH AT-TARIQ
(INTRODUCTION)

This Surah also belongs to the early Makkan period, perhaps not far removed from the last Surah.

Its subject-matter is the protection afforded to every soul in the darkest period of its spiritual history. The physical nature of man may be insignificant, but the soul given to him by Allah must win a glorious Future in the end.

SURAH AL-TARIQ (THE NIGHT-VISITANT)

In the name of Allah, Most Gracious, Most Merciful.

1. By the Sky and the Night-Visitant[1] (therein);-
2. And what will explain to you what the Night-Visitant is?
3. (It is) the Star of piercing brightness;-
4. There is no soul but has a protector over it.
5. Now let man but think from what he is created!
6. He is created from a drop emitted[2],
7. Proceeding from between the backbone and the ribs:
8. Surely (Allah) is able to bring him back (to life)!
9. The Day that (all) hidden things shall be made manifest.
10. (Man) will have no power, and no helper.
11. By the Firmament which gives the recurring rain,
12. And by the Earth which opens out (for the gushing of springs or the sprouting of vegetation),—
13. Lo! This (Qur'an) is a conclusive word,
14. It is not a thing for amusement.
15. As for them, they are but plotting a scheme,
16. And I am planning a scheme.
17. Therefore grant a delay to the Unbelievers: give respite to them gently (for awhile).

---

1. Visitant (archaic): visitor, esp. a super natural one.
2. Discharged

SURAH—87
SURAH AL-A'LA
(INTRODUCTION)

This is one of the earliest of the Makkan Surahs, being usually placed eighth in chronological order, and immediately after S. 81.

The argument is that Allah has made man capable of progress by ordered steps, and by His revelation will lead him still higher to purification and perfection.

SURAH AL-A'LA (THE MOST HIGH)
In the name of Allah, Most Gracious, Most Merciful.

1.   Glorify the name of your Guardian-Lord, Most High,
2.   Who has created, and further, given order and proportion;
3.   Who has ordained law, and granted guidance;
4.   And Who brings out the (green and luscious[1]) pasture,
5.   And then makes it (but) swarthy[2] stubble[3].
6.   By degrees shall We teach you to declare (the Message), so you shall not forget,
7.   Except as Allah wills: for He knows what is manifest and what is hidden.
8.   An We will make it easy for you (to follow) the simple (Path).
9.   Therefore give admo-nition in case the admonition profits (the hearer).
10. The admonition will be received by those who fear (Allah)
11. But it will be avoided by those most unfortunate ones,
12. Who will enter the Great Fire,
13. In which they will then neither die nor live.
14. But those will prosper who purify themselves,
15. And glorify the name of their Guardian - Lord, and pray.
16. Nay, (behold) you prefer the life of this world;
17. But the Hereafter is better and more enduring.
18. And this is in the Books of the earliest (Revelations),-
19. The Books of Abraham and Moses.

---

1.   Richly sweet in taste or smell   2.   Dark
3.   Cut stalks of cereal plants left sticking up after harvest

SURAH —88
SURAH AL-GHASHIYA
(INTRODUCTION)

This is a late Surah of the early Makkan period, perhaps close in date to S. 52. Its subject-matter is the contrast between the destinies of the Good and the Evil in the Hereafter,— on the Day when the true balance will be restored: the Signs of Allah even in this life should remind us of the Day of Account, for Allah is good and just, and His creation is for a just Purpose.

SURAH AL-GHASHIYA
(THE OVERWHELMING EVENT)

In the name of Allah, Most Gracious, Most Merciful.

1. Has the story reached you, of the Overwhelming[1] (Event)?
2. Some faces, that Day, will be humiliated,
3. Labouring (hard), weary,-
4. The while they enter the Blazing Fire,-
5. The while they are given, to drink, of a boiling hot spring,
6. There will be no food for them but a bitter Dhari'[2]
7. Which will neither nou-rish nor satisfy hunger.
8. (Other) faces that Day will be joyful,
9. Pleased with their striving,-
10. In a Garden on high,
11. Where they shall hear no (word) of vanity:
12. Therein will be a bub-bling spring:
13. Therein will be Thrones (of dignity), raised on high,
14. Goblets placed (ready),
15. And cushions set in rows,
16. And rich carpets (all) spread out.
17. Do they not look at the Camels, how they are made?-
18. And at the Sky, how it is raised high?-
19. And at the Mountains, how they are fixed firm?-
20. And at the Earth, how it is spread out?

---

1. Bringing to sudden ruin or destruction, over-powering
2. A plant, bitter and thorny, loathsome in smell and appearance.

21. Therefore you give admonition, for you are one to admonish.
22. You are not one to manage (men's) affairs.
23. But if any turn away and reject Allah,-
24. Allah will punish him with a mighty Punishment,
25. For to Us will be their return;
26. Then it will be for Us to call them to account.

SURAH —89
SURAH AL-FAJR
(INTRODUCTION)

This is one of the earliest of the Surahs to be revealed, probably within the first ten in chronological order.

Its mystic meaning is suggested by contrasts, — contrasts in nature and in man's long history. Thus does it enforce the lesson of Faith in the Hereafter to "those who understand". Man's history and legendary lore show that greatness does not last and the proudest are brought low. For enforcing moral and spiritual truths, the strictest history is no better than legend. Indeed all artistic history is legend, for it is written from a special point of view

Man is easily cowed by contrasts in his own fortunes, and yet he does not learn from them the lesson of forbearance and kindness to others, and the final elevation of goodness in the Hereafter. When all the things on which his mind and heart are set on this earth shall be crushed to nothingness, he will see the real glory and power, love and beauty, of Allah, for these are the light of the Garden of Paradise.

SURAH AL-FAJR (THE BREAK OF DAY)

In the name of Allah, Most Gracious, Most Merciful.

1. By the break of Day;
2. By the ten Nights.
3. By the even and odd (contrasted);
4. And by the Night when it passes away;-
5. Is there (not) in these an adjuration[1] (or evidence) for those who understand?.
6. Don't you see how your Lord dealt with the 'Ad (people),
7. Of the (city of) Iram, with lofty pillars,
8. The like of which were not produced in (all) the land?
9. And with the Thamud (people), who cut out (huge) rocks in the valley?-
10. And with Pharaoh, lord of stakes?
11. (All) these transgressed beyond bounds in the lands,

---

1.   Request earnestly, appeal

12. And heaped therein mischief (on mischief).

13. Therefore your Lord poured on them a scourge of diverse chastisements:

14. For your Lord is (as a Guardian) on a watch-tower.

15. Now, as for man, when his Lord tries him, giving him honour and gifts, then he says, (puffed up), "My Lord has honoured me."

16. But when He tries him, restricting his subsistence for him, then he says (in despair), "My Lord has humiliated me!"

17. Nay, nay! but you do not honour the orphans!

18. Nor do you encourage one another to feed the poor!-

19. And you devour inheri-tance - all with greed,

20. And you love wealth with inordinate love!

21. Nay! When the earth is pounded to powder,

22. And your Lord comes, and His angels rank upon rank,

23. And Hell,—that Day, is brought (face to face), on that Day man will remember, but how will that remembrance profit him?

24. He will say: "Ah! Would that I had sent forth (good deeds) for (this) my (Future) Life!"

25. For, that Day, His Chastisement will be such as none (else) can inflict,

26. And His bonds will be such as none (other) can bind.

27. (To the righteous soul will be said:) "O (you) soul, in (complete) rest and satisfaction!

28. You come back to your Lord,- well pleased (yourself), and well-pleasing unto Him!

29. "You enter, then, among My Devotees!

30. "Yes, you enter My Heaven!

---

2. Poles. See also 38:12
3. Whip for punishment.
4. Swollen (with pride)
5. Sustenance
6. Immoderate, exessive

SURAH —90
AL-BALAD
(INTRODUCTION)

This is an early Makkan revelation, and refers to the mystic relation (by divine sanction) of the Holy Prophet with the city of Makkah. He was born in that City, which had already been sacred for ages before. He was nurtured in that City and had (to use a modern phrase) the freedom of that City, belonging, as he did, to the noble family which held the government of its sacred precincts in its hands. But he was an orphan, and orphans in his day had a poor time. But his mind was turned to things divine. He protested against the prevailing idolatry and sin, and his parent City persecuted him and cast him out. He made another City, Yathrib, his own: it became the Madinat-un-Nabi, the City of the Prophet, and it has ever since been Madinah. We can speak of Madinah as the Prophet's child. But the Prophet ever cherished in his heart the love of his parent City of Makkah, and in the fullness of time was received in triumph there. He purified it from all idols and abominations, re-established the worship of the One True Allah, overthrew the purse-proud selfish autocracy, restored the sway of the righteous (people of the Right Hand), the liberty of the slave, and the rights of the poor and downtrodden. What a wonderful career centring round a City! It becomes a symbol of the world's spiritual history.

SURAH AL-BALAD (THE CITY)

In the name of Allah, Most Gracious, Most Merciful.

1. I do call to witness this City;-
2. And you are a freeman of this City;-
3. And (the mystic ties of) parent and child;-
4. Verily We have created Man into toil and struggle.
5. Does he think that none has power over him?
6. He may say (boastfully): "I have squandered[1] wealth in abundance!"
7. Does he think that none beholds him?
8. Have We not made for him a pair of eyes?-
9. And a tongue, and a pair of lips?-

---

1. Consumed, spent, misused

10.   And shown him the two highways?

11.   But he has made no haste on the path that is steep.

12.   And what will explain to you the path that is steep?-

13.   (It is:) freeing the bondman;

14.   Or the giving of food in a day of privation.

15.   To the orphan with claims of relationship,

16.   Or to the indigent[2] (down) in the dust.

17.   Then he will be of those who believe, and enjoin patience, (constancy, and self-restraint), and enjoin deeds of kindness and compassion.

18.   Such are the Companions of the Right Hand.

19.   But those who reject Our Signs, they are the (unhappy) Companions of the Left Hand.

20.   On them will be Fire vaulted[3] over (all round).

---

2.   Destitute, needy
3.   Closed in upon them in arched, vault-like, covering

SURAH —91
SURAH ASH-SHAMS
(INTRODUCTION)

This is one of the early Makkan revelations. Beginning with a fine nature passage, and leading up to man's need of realising his spiritual responsibility, it ends with a warning of the terrible consequences for those who fear not the Hereafter.

SURAH ASH-SHAMS (THE SUN)

In the name of Allah, Most Gracious, Most Merciful.

1. By the Sun and his (glorious) splendour;
2. By the Moon as she follows him;
3. By the Day as it shows up (the Sun's) glory;
4. By the Night as it con-ceals it;
5. By the Firmament and its (wonderful) structure;
6. By the Earth and its (wide) expanse:
7. By the Soul, and the proportion and order given to it.
8. And its enlightenment as to its wrong and its right;-
9. Truly he succeeds that purifies it,
10. And he fails that corrupts it!
11. The Thamud (people) rejected (their prophet) through their inordinate wrong-doing,
12. Behold, the most wicked man among them was deputed (for impiety),
13. But the Apostle of Allah said to them: "It is a She-camel of Allah! And (do not bar[1] her from) having her drink!"
14. Then they rejected him (as a false prophet), and they hamstrung[2] her. So their Lord, on account of their crime, obliterated[3] their traces and made them equal (in destruction, high and low)!
15. And for Him is no fear of its consequences.

---

1. Prevent
2. Crippled
3. Wiped out

SURAH—92
SURAH AL-LAIL
(INTRODUCTION)

This was one of the first Surahs to be revealed, within the first ten; and may be placed in date close to S. 89 and S. 93. Note that in all these Surahs the mystery and the contrast as between Night and Day are appealed to for the consolation of man in his spiritual yearning. Here we are told to strive our utmost towards Allah, and He will give us every help and satisfaction.

SURAH AL-LAIL (THE NIGHT)

In the name of Allah, Most Gracious, Most Merciful.

1. By the Night as it conceals (the light);
2. By the Day as it appears in glory;
3. By (the mystery of) the creation of male and female;-
4. Verily, (the ends) you strive for are diverse.
5. So he who gives (in charity) and fears (Allah),
6. And (in all sincerity) testifies to the best,-
7. We will indeed make smooth for him the path to Bliss.
8. But he who is a greedy miser and thinks himself self-sufficient,
9. And gives the lie to the best,-
10. We will indeed make smooth for him the path to Misery;
11. Nor will his wealth profit him when he falls headlong (into the Pit).
12. Verily We take upon Ourselves to guide,
13. And verily to Us (belong) the End and the Beginning.
14. Therefore do I warn you of a Fire blazing fiercely,
15. None shall reach it but those most unfortunate ones.
16. Who give the lie to Truth and turn their backs.
17. But those most devoted to Allah shall be removed far from it,-
18. Those who spend their wealth for increase in self-purification,
19. And have in their minds no favour from anyone for which a reward is expected in return,
20. But only the desire to seek for the Countenance of their Lord Most High;
21. And soon will they attain (complete) satisfaction.

SURAH AZ-ZUHA
(INTRODUCTION)

This Surah is close in date to Surahs 89 and 92, and the imagery drawn from the contrast of Night and Day is common to all three. In this Surah the vicissitudes of human life are referred to, and a massage of hope and consolation is given to man's soul from Allah's past mercies, and he is bidden to pursue the path of goodness and proclaim the bounties of Allah. This is the general meaning. In particular, the Surah seems to have been revealed in a dark period in the outer life of the Holy Prophet, when a man of less resolute will might have been discouraged. But the Prophet is told to hold the present of less account than the glorious Hereafter which awaited him like the glorious morning after a night of stillness and gloom. The Hereafter was, not only in the Future Life, but in his later life on this earth, full of victory and satisfaction.

SURAH AD-DHUHA
(THE GLORIOUS MORNING LIGHT)
In the name of Allah, Most Gracious, Most Merciful.

1. By the Glorious Morning Light,
2. And by the Night when it is still,-
3. Your Guardian-Lord has not for-saken you, nor is He displeased.
4. And verily the Hereafter will be better for you than the present.
5. And soon will your Guardian-Lord give you (that wherewith) you shall be well-pleased.
6. Did He not find you an orphan and give you shelter (and care)?
7. And He found you wande-ring, and He gave you guidance.
8. And He found you in need, and made you independent.
9. Therefore, do not treat the orphan with harshness,
10. Nor repulse the petitioner (unheard);
11. But the bounty of your Lord - rehearse and proclaim!

SURAH—94
SURAH AL-INSHIRAH
(INTRODUCTION)

This short Surah gives a message of hope and encouragement in a time of darkness and difficulty. It was revealed to the Holy Prophet soon after the last Surah *(Zuha)*, whose argument it supplements.

SURAH INSHIRAH (THE EXPANSION)

In the name of Allah, Most Gracious, Most Merciful.

1.   Have We not expanded you your breast?-
2.   And removed from you your burden
3.   Which did gall[1] your back?—
4.   And raised high the es-teem (in which) you (are held)?
5.   So, verily, with every difficulty, there is relief:
6.   Verily, with every diffi-culty there is relief.
7.   Therefore, when you are free (from your immediate task), still labour hard,
8.   And to your Lord turn (all) your attention.

---

1.   Rub sore, injure by rubbing, mental soreness

SURAH—95
SURAH AT-TIN
(INTRODUCTION)

This is also a very early Surah. It appeals to the most sacred symbols to show that Allah created man in the best of moulds, but that man is capable of the utmost degradation unless he has Faith and leads a good life. In subject-matter this Surah closely resembles S. 103.

SURAH AT-TIN (THE FIG)

In the name of Allah, Most Gracious, Most Merciful.

1. By the Fig and the Olive,
2. And the Mount of Sinai,
3. And this City of security,-
4. We have indeed created man in the best of moulds,
5. Then do We abase him (to be) the lowest of the low,-
6. Except such as believe and do righteous deeds: for they shall have a reward unfailing.
7. Then what can, after this, contradict you, as to the judgment (to come)?
8. Is not Allah the Greatest of judges?

SURAH—96
SURAH AL-'ALAQ
(INTRODUCTION)

Verses 1 -5 of this Surah were the first direct Revelation to the Holy Prophet.

After that there was an interval or break *(Fatra),* extending over some months or perhaps over a year. S. 68 is usually considered to have been the next revelation in point of time. But the remainder of the Surah (96: 6-1 9) came soon after the *Fatra,* and that portion is joined on to the first five verses containing the command to preach, because it explains the chief obstacle to the delivery of the message to man, viz. man's own obstinacy, vanity, and insolence.

SURAH IQRAA
(READ! OR PROCLAIM! OR AL-'ALAQ,
OR THE LEECH-LIKE CLOT)

In the name of Allah, Most Gracious, Most Merciful.

1.   Read! (or proclaim!) in the name of your Lord and Cheri-sher, Who created-

2.   Created man, out of a (mere) clot of congealed[1] blood:

3.   Proclaim! And your Lord is Most Bountiful[2],-

4.   He Who taught (the use of) the Pen,-

5.   Taught man that which he did not know.

6.   Nay, but man transgresses all bounds,

7.   In that he looks upon himself as self-sufficient.

8.   Verily, to your Lord is the return (of all).

9 .   Do you see one who forbids-

10.   A votary[3] when he (turns) to pray?

11.   Do you see if he is on (the road of) Guidance?-

12.   Or enjoins Righteousness?

13.   Do you see if he denies (Truth) and turns away?

14.   Does not he know that Allah sees?

---

1.   Thick, solidified   2.   Generous
3.   One devoted to service of Allah.

15. Let him beware! If he does not desist We will drag him by the forelock,-

16. A lying, sinful forelock!

17. Then, let him call (for help) to his council (of comrades):

18. We will call on the angels of punishment (to deal with him)!

19. Nay, do not obey him but bow down in adoration, and bring yourself the closer (to Allah)!

———————

SURAH—97
SURAH AL-QADR
(INTRODUCTION)

The chronology of this Surah has no significance. It is probably Makkan, though some hold that it was revealed in Madinah.

The subject-matter as the mystic Night of Power (or Honour), in which Revelation comes down to a benighted world, — it may be to the wonderful Cosmos of an individual and transforms the conflict of wrong-doing into Peace and Harmony-through the agency of the angelic host, representing the spiritual powers of the Mercy of Allah.

SURAH AL-QADR
(THE NIGHT OF POWER OR HONOR)

In the name of Allah, Most Gracious, Most Merciful.

1.   We have indeed revealed this (Message) in the Night of Power:

2.   And what will explain to you what the Night of Power is?

3.   The Night of Power is better than a thousand months.

4.   Therein come down the angels and the Spirit by Allah's permission, on every errand:

5.   Peace!...This until the rise of Morn!

SURAH—98

SURAH AL-BAIYYINAH

(INTRODUCTION)

This Surah was probably an early Madinah Surah, or possibly a late Makkan Surah.

In subject-matter it carries forward the argument of the last Surah. The mystic night of revelation is indeed blessed: but those who reject Truth are impervious to Allah's Message, however clear may be the evidence in support of it.

SURAH AL-BAYYINAH

(THE CLEAR EVIDENCE)

In the name of Allah, Most Gracious, Most Merciful.

1. Those who reject (Truth), among the People of the Book and among the Polytheists[1], were not going to depart (from their ways) until there should come to them Clear Evidence,-

2. An Apostle from Allah, rehearsing scriptures kept pure and holy:

3. Wherein are laws (or decrees) right and straight.

4. Nor did the People of the Book make schisms[2], until after there came to them Clear Evidence.

5. And they have been commanded no more than this: to worship Allah, offering Him sincere devotion, being true (in faith); to establish regular prayer; and to practise regular charity; and that is the Religion Right and Straight.

6. Those who reject (Truth), among the People of the Book and among the Polytheists, will be in Hell-Fire, to dwell therein (for ever). They are the worst of creatures.

7. Those who have faith and do righteous deeds,- they are the best of creatures.

8. Their reward is with their Lord: Gardens of Eternity[3], beneath which rivers flow; they will dwell therein for ever; Allah well pleased with them, and they with Him: all this for such as fear their Lord and Cherisher.

---

1. Idolators, those who associate false gods with One True Allah
2. Division into mutual opposing parties.
3. Eternal, perpetuity

SURAH—99
SURAH AL-ZALZALAH
(INTRODUCTION)

This Surah is close in date to the last: it is generally referred to the early Madinah period, though it may possibly be of the late Makkan period.

It refers to the tremendous convulsion and uprooting which will take place when the present order of the world is dissolved and the new spiritual world of Justice and Truth takes its place. The symbol used is that of an earthquake which will shake our present material and phenomenal world to its very foundations. The mystic words in which the earthquake is described are remarkable for both power and graphic aptness. With that shaking all hidden mysteries will be brought to light.

SURAH AZ-ZILZAL
(THE CONVULSION)

In the name of Allah, Most Gracious, Most Merciful.

1. When the earth is shaken to her (utmost) convulsion[1],
2. And the earth throws up her burdens (from within),
3. And man cries (distressed): 'What is the matter with her?'-
4. On that Day she will declare her tidings:
5. For that your Lord will have given her inspiration.
6. On that Day men will pro-ceed in companies sorted out, to be shown the deeds that they (had done).
7. Then anyone who has done an atom's weight of good, shall see it!
8. And anyone who has done an atom's weight of evil, shall see it.

---

1.   Violent irregular movement due to involuntary contraction.

SURAH—100
SURAH AL-ADIYAT
(INTRODUCTION)

This is one of the earlier Makkan Surahs. In the depth of its mystery and the rhythm and sublimity of its language and symbolism, it may be compared with S. 79. Its subject-matter is the irresistible nature of spiritual power and knowledge, contrasted with unregenerate man's ingratitude, pettiness, helplessness, and ignorance.

SURAH AL-'ADIYAT (THOSE THAT RUN)

In the name of Allah, Most Gracious, Most Merciful.

1. By the (steeds[1]) that run, with panting (breath),
2. And strike sparks of fire,
3. And push home the charge in the morning,
4. And raise the dust in clouds the while,
5. And penetrate forthwith into the midst (of the foe) en masse[2];-
6. Truly man is, to his Lord, ungrateful;
7. And to that (fact) he bears witness (by his deeds);
8. And he is violent in his love of wealth.
9. Does he not know,- when that which is in the graves is scattered abroad.
10. And that which is (locked up) in (human) breasts is made manifest-
11. That their Lord had been well-acquainted with them, (even to) that Day.?

---

1. War horses
2. All together

SURAH—101
SURAH AL-QARI'A
(INTRODUCTION)

This Makkan Surah describes the Judgment Day as the Day of Clamour, when men will be distracted and the landMarks of this world will be lost, but every deed will be weighed in a just balance, and find its real value and setting.

SURAH AL-QARI'AH
(THE DAY OF NOISE AND CLAMOR)

In the name of Allah, Most Gracious, Most Merciful.

1. The (Day) of Noise and Clamour[1]:
2. What is the (Day) of Noise and Clamor?
3. And what will explain to you what the (Day) of Noise and Clamour is?
4. (It is) a Day whereon men will be like moths[2] scattered about,
5. And the mountains will be like carded[3] wool.
6. Then, he whose balance (of good deeds) will be (found) heavy,
7. Will be in a life of good pleasure and satisfaction.
8. But he whose balance (of good deeds) will be (found) light,-
9. Will have his home in a (bottomless) Pit.
10. And what will explain to you what this is?
11. (It is) a Fire blazing fiercely!

---

1. Shouting, confused noise, loud appeal
2. Small night insects.
3. Cleansed, combed fibres of wool.

SURAH—102
SURAH AT-TAKASUR
(INTRODUCTION)

This probably early Makkan Surah gives a warning against acquisitiveness, i.e., the passion for piling up quantities or numbers, whether in the good things of this world, or in man-power or in other forms of megalomania, which leave no time or opportunity for pursuing the higher things of life.

SURAH AL-TAKATHUR (THE PILING UP)

In the name of Allah, Most Gracious, Most Merciful.

1. The mutual rivalry for piling up (the good things of this world) diver-ts you (from the more serious things),
2. Until you visit the graves.
3. But nay, you soon shall know (the reality).
4. Again, you soon shall know!
5. Nay, were you to know with certainty of mind, (you would beware!)
6. You shall certainly see Hell-fire!
7. Again, you shall see it with certainty of sight!
8. Then, you shall be questioned that Day about the joy (you indulged in!).

SURAH—103
SURAH AL-'ASR
(INTRODUCTION)

This early Makkan Surah refers to the testimony of Time through the Ages. All history shows that Evil came to an evil end. But Time is always in favour of those who have Faith, live clean and pure lives, and know how to wait, in patience and constancy. Cf. the theme of S. 95.

SURAH AL-'ASR
(TIME THROUGH THE AGES)

In the name of Allah, Most Gracious, Most Merciful.

1. By (the Token of) Time (through the ages),
2. Verily Man is in loss,
3. Except such as have Faith, and do righteous deeds, and (join together) in the mutual teaching of Truth, and of Patience and Constancy.

SURAH—104
SURAH AL-HUMAZA
(INTRODUCTION)

This Makkan Surah condemns all sorts of scandal, backbiting, and selfish hoarding of wealth, as destroying the hearts and affection of men.

SURAH AL-HUMAZA
(THE SCANDAL-MONGER)

In the name of Allah, Most Gracious, Most Merciful.

1. Woe to every (kind of) scandal-monger and backbiter,
2. Who piles up wealth and lays it by counting (penny by penny).
3. Thinking that his wealth would make him last for ever!
4. By no means! He will be sure to be thrown into that which breaks to pieces.
5. And what will explain to you that which breaks to pieces?
6. (It is) the Fire of (the Wrath of) Allah kindled (to a blaze),
7. That which mounts (right) up to the Hearts:
8. It shall be made into a vault[1] over them,
9. In columns outstretched.

---

1. An arched roof

SURAH—105
SURAH AL-FIL
(INTRODUCTION)

This early Makkan Surah refers to an event that happened in the year of the birth of our Holy Prophet, say, about 570 A.D. Yaman was then under the rule of the Abyssinian (Christians), who had driven out the Jewish Himyar rulers. Abraha Ashram was the Abyssinian governor or viceroy. Intoxicated with power and fired by religious fanaticism, he led a big expedition against Makkah, intending to destroy the *K'aba*. He had an elephant or elephants in his train. But his sacrilegious intentions were defeated by a miracle. No defence was offered by the custodians of the *K'aba* as the army was too strong for them, but it was believed that a shower of stones, thrown by flocks of birds, destroyed the invading army almost to a man. The stones produced sores and pustules on the skin, which spread like a pestilence.

SURAH AL-FIL (THE ELEPHANT)
In the name of Allah, Most Gracious, Most Merciful.

1. Don't you see how your Lord dealt with the Companions of the Elephant?
2. Did He not make their treacherous plan go astray?
3. And He sent against them flights of Birds,
4. Striking them with stones of baked clay.
5. Then He made them like an empty field of stalks[1] and straw, (of which the corn) has been eaten up.

---

1.   Stems

SURAH—106

SURAH QURAISH

(INTRODUCTION)

This Makkan Surah may well be considered as a pendant to the last. If the Quraish were fond of Makkah and proud of it, if they profited by its central position and its guaranteed security, from their caravans of trade and commerce, let them be grateful, adore the One True Allah, and accept His Message.

SURAH QURAISH

(THE TRIBE OF QURAISH)

In the name of Allah, Most Gracious, Most Merciful.

1. For the covenants (of security and safeguard enjoyed) by the Quraish,
2. Their covenants (covering safe) journeys by winter and summer,-
3. Let them adore the Lord of this House,
4. Who provides them with food against hunger, and with security against fear (of danger).

SURAH—107
SURAH AL-MA'UN
(INTRODUCTION)

This Surah at least the first half of it — belongs to the early Makkan period. The subject-matter is the meaning of true worship, which requires Faith, the practical and helpful love of those in need, and sincerity rather than show in devotion and charity.

SURAH AL-MA'UN
(THE NEIGHBORLY NEEDS)

In the name of Allah, Most Gracious, Most Merciful.

1.   Do you see one who denies the Judgment (to come)?
2.   Then such is the (man) who repulses the orphan (with harshness),
3.   And does not encourage the feeding of the indigent.
4.   So woe to the worshippers,
5.   Who are neglectful of their prayers,
6.   Those who (want but) to be seen (of men),
7.   But refuse (to supply) (even) neighbourly needs.

---

1.   Drive back, repel

SURAH—108

SURAH AL-KAUSAR

(INTRODUCTION)

This very brief early Makkan Surah sums up in the single mystic word Kausar (Abundance) the doctrine of spiritual Riches through devotion and sacrifice. The converse also follows: indulgence in hatred means the cutting off of all hope of this life and the Hereafter.

———————

SURAH AL-KAUTHAR (THE ABUNDANCE)

In the name of Allah, Most Gracious, Most Merciful.

1. To you We have granted the Fount[1] (of Abundance).
2. Therefore, to your Lord turn in Prayer and Sacrifice.
3. For he who hates you, he will be cut off (from Future Hope)

———————

---

1. Fountain

SURAH—109
SURAH AL-KAFIRUN
(INTRODUCTION)

This is another early Makkan Surah. It defines the right attitude to those who reject Faith: in matters of Truth we can make no compromise, but there is no need to persecute or abuse anyone for his faith or belief.

SURAH AL-KAFIRUN
(THOSE WHO REJECT FAITH)

In the name of Allah, Most Gracious, Most Merciful.

1.   Say : O you that reject Faith!
2.   I do not worship that which you worship,
3.   Nor will you worship that which I worship.
4.   And I will not worship that which you have been wont[1] to worship,
5.   Nor will you worship that which I worship.
6.   To you be your Way, and to me mine.

---

1.   Accustomed to

SURAH—110
SURAH AN-NASR
(INTRODUCTION)

This beautiful Surah was the last of the Surahs to be revealed as a whole, though the portion of the verse 5:3, "This day have I perfected your religion for you:' etc., contains probably the last words of the Quran to be revealed.

The date of this Surah was only a few months before the passing away of the Holy Prophet from this world, Rabi'I,

A.H. 11. The place was either the precincts of Makkah at the Farewell Pilgrimage, Zulhijja, A.H. 10, or Madinah after his return from the Farewell Pilgrimage.

Victory is the crown of service, not an occasion for exultation. All victory comes from the help of Allah.

SURAH AN-NASR (THE HELP)

In the name of Allah, Most Gracious, Most Merciful.

1. When comes the Help of Allah, and Victory,
2. And you see the people enter Allah's Religion in crowds,
3. Celebrate the praises of your Lord, and pray for His For-giveness: for He is Oft-Retur-ning (in Grace and Mercy).

SURAH—111
SURAH AL-MASAD (AL-LAHAB)
(INTRODUCTION)

This very early Makkan Surah, though it referred in the first instance to a particular incident in a cruel and relentless persecution, carries the general lesson that cruelty ultimately ruins itself. The man who rages against holy things is burnt up in his own rage. His hands, which are the instruments of his action, perish, and he perishes him self. No boasted wealth or position will save him. The women, who are made for nobler emotions, may, if they go wrong, feed unholy rage with fiercer fuel — to their own loss. For they may twist the torturing rope round their own neck. It is a common experience that people perish by the very means by which they seek to destroy others.

SURAH AL-LAHAB [(THE FATHER OF) FLAME]

In the name of Allah, Most Gracious, Most Merciful.

1.   Perish the hands of the Father of Flame! Perish he!
2.   No benefit to him from all his wealth, and all his gain!
3.   He will be burnt soon in a Fire of Blazing Flame!
4.   And his wife, the carrier of the (crackling) wood - as fuel!-
5.   A twisted rope of palm-leaf fibre round her (own) neck!

SURAH—112
SURAH AL-IKHLAS
(INTRODUCTION)

This early Makkan Surah sums up in a few terse words the Unity of the Godhead — often professed, but frequently mixed up in the popular mind with debasing superstitions.

SURAH AL-IKHLAS [PURITY (OF FAITH)]
In the name of Allah, Most Gracious, Most Merciful.

1. Say: He is Allah, the One and Only;
2. Allah, the Eternal, Absolute;
3. He begets not, nor is He begotten;
4. And there is none like unto Him.

SURAH AL-FALAQ

(INTRODUCTION)

This early Makkan Surah provides the antidote to superstition and fear by teaching us to seek refuge in Allah from every kind of ill arising from outer nature and from dark and evil plottings and envy on the part of others.

SURAH AL-FALAQ (THE DAWN)

In the name of Allah, Most Gracious, Most Merciful.

1.   Say: I seek refuge with the Lord of the Dawn.
2.   From the mischief of created things;
3.   From the mischief of Darkness as it overspreads;
4.   From the mischief of those who blow on knots;
5.   And from the mischief of the envious one as he practises envy.

SURAH 114
SURAH AN-NAS
(INTRODUCTION)

This early Makkan Surah is a pendant to the last Surah, and concludes the Holy Quran with an appeal to us to trust in Allah, rather than man, as our sure shield and protection. It warns us specially against the secret whispers of evil within our own hearts.

———————

SURAH AN-NAS (MANKIND)

In the name of Allah, Most Gracious, Most Merciful.

1. Say: I seek refuge with the Lord (and Cherisher) of Mankind,
2. The King (or Ruler) of Mankind,
3. The God (Allah) (or Judge) of Mankind,-
4. From the mischief of the whisperer (of Evil), who with-draws (after his whisper),-
5. (The same) who whispers into the hearts of Mankind,-
6. Among Jinns and among Men.

———————

Index